A Cross Section of Nursing Research

Journal Articles for Discussion and Evaluation

Fourth Edition

Roberta J. Peteva

Editor

 Pyrczak Publishing
P.O. Box 250430 • Glendale, CA 91225

"Pyrczak Publishing" is an imprint of Fred Pyrczak, Publisher, A California Corporation.

Although the author and publisher have made every effort to ensure the accuracy and completeness of information contained in this book, we assume no responsibility for errors, inaccuracies, omissions, or any inconsistency herein. Any slights of people, places, or organizations are unintentional.

Project Director: Monica Lopez.

Editorial assistance provided by Cheryl Alcorn, Randall R. Bruce, Brenda Koplin, Jack Petit, Erica Simmons, and Sharon Young.

Cover design by Robert Kibler and Larry Nichols.

Printed in the United States of America by Malloy, Inc.

ISBN 1-884585-77-9

Contents

Continued →

---

*New to the Fourth Edition.

---

* New to the Fourth Edition.

Combined Qualitative and Quantitative Research

Test Reliability and Validity Research

Meta-Analysis

---

*New to the Fourth Edition.

Notes:

Introduction

This book is designed for students who are learning how to evaluate published nursing research. The 42 research articles in this collection provide the stimulus material for such a course.

Selection of the Articles

Several criteria were used in the selection of the articles. The first was that the articles be comprehensible to students taking their first research methods course. Thus, it was necessary that the articles have straightforward research designs and employ only basic statistics.

Second, the articles were to illustrate a wide variety of approaches to research. You will notice in the Contents that the articles represent nine types of research such as True Experimental Research, Program Evaluation/Process Evaluation, Qualitative Research, and so on.

Finally, the articles were to be drawn from a large number of different journals. Because each journal has its own genre as well as criteria for the selection of submissions for publication, students can get a sense of the wide variations in approaches to nursing research only by reading articles from a wide variety of journals.

How to Use This Book

This collection of research articles can be used for instruction in several ways. Most common is to assign one or two articles for homework at each class meeting. At the next class meeting, the article(s) can be discussed with the instructor leading the discussion of the answers to the questions at the end of each article. Another common use is to make each student responsible for leading the discussion of one or two of the articles after all members of the class have read them for homework.

About the Questions at the End of Each Article

There are three types of questions at the end of each article. First, there are *Factual Questions*. The answers for these are explicitly stated in the articles. In addition to writing down the answers, students should record the line numbers where they found the answers. The line numbers will facilitate discussions if there are disagreements on what constitutes a correct answer to a question.

Second, there are *Questions for Discussion*. Because these are designed to stimulate classroom discussions, most of the questions ask for students' opinions on various decisions made by the researchers in conducting and writing up their research. In field tests, these questions led to lively classroom discussions. Since professional researchers often debate such issues with each other, students should not be surprised by such debates taking place in their own classrooms.

Third, students are asked to make *Quality Ratings* for each article. This is done by applying thirteen fundamental criteria for evaluating research, which are repeated at the end of each article.

Reading the Statistics in This Book

Students who have taken a statistics class as a prerequisite to their research methods class should feel quite comfortable with the overwhelming majority of statistics found in this collection because articles that contained large numbers of obscure or highly advanced statistics were excluded from this book.

Students who are learning about statistics for the first time in the course in which they are using this book may need some additional help from their instructors. Keep in mind that it is not realistic to expect instructors of a methods class to also teach a full-fledged course in statistical methods. Thus, there may be times when an instructor asks students to concentrate on the researcher's *interpretation* of statistics without getting bogged down in discussions of the theory underlying specific statistics. It is possible to focus on the interpretation instead of specific statistics because almost all researchers describe their results in words as well as numbers.

The Classification of the Articles

If you examine a number of research methods textbooks, you will probably find that they differ to some extent in their system for classifying various types of research. While some labels such as "true experiment" and "qualitative research" are common to almost all textbooks, others that you find in some textbooks may be more idiosyncratic. In addition, some categories of research overlap. An interesting classroom discussion topic is whether a given article can be classified as more than one type of research.

About the Fourth Edition

The Fourth Edition contains most of the articles that were in the Third Edition. The Fourth Edition also contains 18 additional articles (i.e., article numbers 3, 4, 6, 7, 8, 10, 16, 17, 18, 19, 21, 22, 24, 25, 27, 28, 34, and 41), which provide more variety and keep this volume up-to-date.

Acknowledgments

I am grateful to Mildred L. Patten, who is the author of a similar collection titled *Educational and Psychological Research: A Cross Section of* *Journal Articles for Analysis and Evaluation*. Her popular book emphasizes broad issues of interest to both psychologists and educators, while this book emphasizes topics of interest to students preparing for careers as nursing professionals. Some structural elements of Patten's book were employed in this one, such as the inclusion of three types of questions at the end of each article.

I am indebted to the publishers who hold the copyrights to the articles in this book. Without their cooperation, it would not be possible to amass a collection such as you find here.

Roberta J. Peteva

Article 1

Reasons Registered Nurses Leave
or Change Employment Status

Ellen Strachota, PhD, RN, **Pamela Normandin**, MSN, RN, CCRC, **Nancy O'Brien**, AMLS,
Mary Clary, RN, CCRC, **Belva Krukow**, MSN, RN[*]

ABSTRACT. High turnover of nurses compromises patient care and adds to the cost of healthcare. To determine why nurses changed positions or left a Midwestern health system, the authors surveyed registered nurses who voluntarily terminated or changed their employment status to as-needed (PRN) within a 9-month period. They discuss the most frequent reasons given for these changes and suggest solutions for retention.

From *Journal of Nursing Administration, 33,* 111–117. Copyright

A typical turnover rate for hospital nurses is 15% per year.[1] At a Midwestern health system, there was concern when 183 registered nurses (6.8%) voluntarily changed their employment status over a 9-month period. Although this number is less than the national trend, the financial burden and loss of skilled workforce was substantial.

The health system consists of three separate hospitals: a 578-bed tertiary care center, a 465-bed community hospital, and a 96-bed pediatric hospital. The nurses surveyed represent a wide variety of clinical specialties, ranging from critical care to outpatient surgery. The results indicate that the specialty areas, especially intensive care, had the highest nurse turnover rate (26%).

High nurse turnover rates add to the escalating costs of healthcare. The estimated cost of replacing a medical–surgical nurse is $42,000 and a specialty nurse is $64,000.[1] These figures include the cost of recruitment, orientation, precepting, and lost productivity. The cost of lost productivity alone is nearly 80% of the total turnover cost.

Another consequence of nurse turnover is the negative effect it has on patient care. When nurses leave, the quality of nursing care may decline due to the loss of expertise.[2] Novice nurses may not have the commitment to the organization or the ability, intuition, and confidence of an expert nurse.

Patient care also suffers when employees are unhappy with their work situation. The literature shows that nurse retention is directly related to job satisfaction. Results from a Press, Ganey study found that hospitals with the lowest employee satisfaction had the lowest patient satisfaction, and hospitals with the highest employee satisfaction had the highest patient satisfaction.[3] Dissatisfied patients may choose competitive alternatives for their future healthcare needs. In addition, if the quality of patient care is an issue, physicians and third-party payers may seek other healthcare venues.

Retention of staff is better than "quick fixes" when addressing the turnover crisis. Often, hospitals attempt to solve the problem by increasing their recruitment efforts. An immediate solution may be to offer creative perks and incentives, but this answer does not address the problem. It is far less expensive and disruptive to retain nurses than to replace them. Once the causes of nurse turnover have been clearly identified, effective strategies can be implemented to better orient, educate, satisfy, motivate, and retain quality nursing staff.

Purpose of the Study

The nursing shortage adversely affects the mission of hospitals. Hospitals are faced with both high staff turnover and limited applicants. The purpose of this study was to uncover reasons that registered nurses (RNs) voluntarily left their nursing positions or changed their employment status to PRN at a Midwestern health system.

Review of Literature

The literature reports multifaceted and complex reasons that an employee leaves his or her job. Reasons for discontentment fall into four major categories: job satisfaction, supervision, work environment, and personal factors.

Job Satisfaction

Job satisfaction plays an integral role in voluntary turnover among nurses in long-term psychiatric settings. Carrying heavy patient loads while lacking suffi-

[*]*Ellen Strachota*, Department of Nursing, Grand View College, Des Moines, Iowa. *Pamela Normandin, Nancy O'Brien, Mary Clary*, and *Belva Krukow*, Iowa Methodist/Iowa Lutheran/Blank Children's Hospital, Des Moines, Iowa.

cient autonomy to implement procedures and make decisions is frustrating for nurses. Higher workloads increase both mental and physical demands on the workers.[4]

Kangas et al. found no correlation between job satisfaction and the nursing care delivery model used.[5] If RNs perceive themselves as valued employees who are vital to the institution and to their patients' well being, then structural changes in the work environment are handled with ease. If the opposite is true, and the RN feels devalued with little contribution to patient care, then differences in nursing care delivery models have no effect on job satisfaction. A supportive culture contributes to the development and enhancement of self-esteem, affiliation, achievement, and nurse autonomy.[3]

Dissatisfaction and rapid turnover of RNs challenge nurse administrators. In a longitudinal study, staff nurses perceived autonomy to be the most important determinant of their job satisfaction and decision to stay or leave the hospital.[6] Nurses higher on the clinical ladder are more satisfied with their jobs. Job satisfaction increases relative to pay, task requirements, and nursing administration. Variables of work content and environment appear to have stronger relationships with satisfaction than economic or demographic variables such as age, background, sex, and economic status.[7]

In a large multinational study, Aiken et al. found that low morale among hospital nurses was not unique to the United States.[8] More than 40% of nurses in Pennsylvania report being dissatisfied with their jobs. This compares to 32.9% in Canada, 36.1% in England, 37.7% in Scotland, and only 17.4% in Germany. They also found that 3 in 10 nurses in England and Scotland and more than 2 in 10 in the United States plan to leave their jobs within a year.

Supervision

Managers' leadership styles contribute to the retention of professional nurses.[9] Fisher et al. found a significant relationship between first-line and middle managers' supervisory environment and intent to stay. Nurses tended to stay on the job longer when managers used a participative model and encouraged staff input into decision-making.

Supervisor/employee relations, confidence in management, communication, and administrative effectiveness are all related to morale.[10–12] A positive supervisor/employee relationship leads to increased morale and the retention of nurses. Effective managers actively encourage two-way communication. In addition to financial and job security, they demonstrate a commitment to career development for their nurses.[13]

Work Environment

Employee friendliness and cooperation are the most favorable reasons why nurses stay with their jobs.[5, 10, 11] Satisfaction with co-workers is important to the delivery of quality nursing care and in the retention of nurses. Other key factors include new employee orientation and perceived staff competence.

Nurses' perception of staffing adequacy also relates to their level of satisfaction. Understaffing and heavy workloads are intense stressors. Aiken et al. found that 60% to 70% of nurses thought unit staffing levels were poor and did not give them enough time to provide quality patient care.[8] Many nurses also believe they are taking on more management and personnel responsibilities, which in turn limits the time they have to spend with patients.

Leveck and Jones found that when healthcare organizations restructure, downsize, or merge, stress levels increase in the practice environment. Stress comes packaged with change and cannot be ignored for the sake of cost containment and efficiency.[11] Registered nurses may change jobs for better working conditions even when they are somewhat satisfied with their current situation. Healthcare institutions need to be aware of how economic and noneconomic factors influence nurse turnover.

Personal Factors

In addition to aspects of the work environment, personal factors play a key role in nurse retention. One personal factor influencing retention is age. Alexander et al.[4] and Blegen[12] found that nurses in the older age bracket would stay until retirement because they have so much invested in the position. In contrast, younger nurses want a variety of experiences and may decide to leave the institution or the profession.

Education is another personal factor contributing to nursing turnover. MacRobert et al. found the higher the education, the more motivated the nurse.[10] They studied why RNs stayed in their positions in community health, and concluded that nurses with more education are able to actualize their professional roles and have more autonomy at work.

Turnover rates are highest in the first year of employment.[14] Nurses new to the profession often convey higher levels of stress and job dissatisfaction than experienced nurses.[15] Borda and Norman found that kinship responsibility also influenced absence.[16] Absence may be related to and predict turnover.

Methods

Design

A survey design was used to investigate the reasons why nurses changed their employment status. The authors developed a questionnaire and conducted telephone interviews. They asked probing and clarifying questions to verify responses.

Sample

The sample consisted of all nurses who had voluntarily terminated or changed their employment status within a 9-month period at a major Midwestern health system. The human resources department identified eligible nurses and mailed postcards to announce the project. Nurses had the option to notify the human resources department and request that they not be called. Postcards were sent to 183 nurses; two nurses declined to be a part of the study.

Using phone numbers supplied by human resources, the authors called all participants multiple times. Fifty-four nurses had disconnected phones with no forwarding number, and 43 did not answer the phone. The authors interviewed 84 nurses over 4 months of data collection, resulting in a 46% rate of return.

Questionnaire

The questionnaire consisted of open-ended questions asking the reasons why the nurse changed employment status (Figure 1). A script was used to begin the conversation. Opening statements identified the authors and reinforced that the data would be confidential and anonymous. Verbal consent for participation was obtained. Every nurse was given the chance to proceed or to end the survey at any time. If the call came at a bad time, a recall was arranged. The authors found that nurses wanted to tell their story and were repeatedly thanked for their call.

---

1. Please explain the reason you left.
2. What did you like about your job?
3. What factors did you dislike about your job?
   Did that influence your decision to leave?
4. To what extent were you able to deliver quality patient care? Was quality of care the reason you left?
5. Tell me about your relationship with:
   Your co-workers
   Physicians
   Other departments
6. How did you perceive the supervision you received? Was this a factor in your leaving?
7. Describe the adequacy of the resources available to you. *Specifically*, tell me about:
   Staffing
   Equipment
   Reference material
   Education
   Salary
   Benefits
   Vacation
   Health
   Dental
   Retirement
8. Was there opportunity for you to meet your career goals? Did you make use of the advancement process?
9. Were there additional personal reasons why you left or changed your position?
10. What are you doing now?
11. What is your base education?
    Do you have further formal education/certification?
12. How many years have you been employed as a nurse?
    Full-time
    Part-time

Figure 1. Questionnaire.

The tool was evaluated and deemed valid by a researcher from a major university who is an expert in job restructuring and retention. Reliability of the tool was established through alternate forms of questions. The tool was revised following a pilot interview with eight nurses.

Procedure

To establish protocol for the study, the authors, as a group, conducted a pilot interview on a speakerphone. In pairs, the authors interviewed 38 nurses to guarantee consistency in recording responses. The remaining calls were made alone. The nurses were categorized by full-time, part-time, or PRN employment and by department. The response sheets were coded using numbers; nurses' names were not used. Eighty-four RNs were surveyed. The phone interviews averaged 25 minutes in length with some exceeding 1 hour.

The authors independently analyzed the results, finding common themes and categories. All identified themes were listed and then collapsed into major ones. A frequency distribution of responses was created for each question. To ensure inter-rater reliability, the surveys were redistributed to another author, who independently assessed all the responses and developed a separate frequency distribution for each question. The frequency distributions were compared and matched with a 54% to 99% agreement; most questions had an agreement rate greater than 75%.

Results

The nurses interviewed were selected from all three hospitals. They represent both the novice as well as the experienced nurse, and are voices from a variety of nursing units. As is demonstrated in the literature, the authors found that nurses new to the profession left more often than their experienced colleagues. However, 52% of the sample who left had practiced nursing for more than 10 years. The loss of these experienced, competent nurses who mentor the new graduates and provide expertise in patient care is significant. Nurses in specialty areas, such as critical care, also had the highest turnover rate (Table 1).

Nurses often gave more than one reason why they changed their position (Table 2). The most common reason, provided by half the respondents, was hours worked. Working long shifts, overtime, weekends, nights, and holidays prompted nurses to look for another job. One nurse said scheduling was a major problem. She worked three main holidays, was on call for the others, and worked every other weekend.

Of the nurses surveyed, 70% shared a passion for nursing. They liked giving good patient care and enjoyed being nurses. One nurse said she loved her job and being there for families in crisis. Nurses also liked their co-workers (62%), the job challenge (20%), and the flexibility of their hours (6%).

Nurses surveyed were unhappy with staffing levels (37%), management support (37%), and the variety of

250 hours they were required to work (37%). The authors were overwhelmed with comments about the workload being too heavy with no relief in sight; units were disorganized and short of full-time staff, and were forced to use agency help. Nurses mentioned several reasons for their discontent, but stress was noted by 18%.

Table 1
Turnover Rates

	Sample (n = 84)	
	%	n
Years of service		
< 4	30	25
5–9	19	16
10–14	14	12
15–19	14	12
20–24	11	9
> 25	12	10
Units worked		
Critical care	26	22
Labor and delivery	11	9
Emergency	7	6
Oncology	5	4
Education		
AND	43	36
AD	30	25
BSN	27	23
BA (nursing)	9	8
BA (non-nursing)	9	8
MSN	2	2
National certification	14	12
Current status		
Other nursing jobs	80	67
Stay at home	12	10
Return to school	8	7

255 Forty-six percent of the nurses were frustrated with the quality of care they could deliver because of low staffing and increased demands. Many relayed incidents of unsafe patient care practices and commented that they didn't become a nurse to give substandard 260 care. Others voiced concerns about medication errors and maintaining their licensure.

Overall, the nurses surveyed had positive relationships with co-workers, physicians, and other departments. Only 9% indicated problems with physicians or 265 co-workers, and 19% reported some troubles with other departments.

Fifty-two percent of the nurses shared concerns about hospital or nursing unit management. Responses varied by manager, director, or supervisor, and were 270 coded negative or not supportive if at any time the nurse perceived substandard supervision. This correlates with the literature findings; nurses prefer a supportive work environment and to be recognized for their work.

275 Among resources, the major complaint was manpower. Seventy-six percent complained about staffing levels. Salary was the second most mentioned resource

problem (55%). Other resources were unproblematic. Many found equipment to be adequate (64%); refer- 280 ence materials were accessible (66%); in-service educational opportunities were available (71%); and benefits were competitive (78%).

Table 2
Reasons for Changing Positions

Percentage[*]	Please explain the reason you left the institution (n = 84)
50	Work hours/every other weekend/still working majority of holidays/working nights with no possibility of days/no flexibility
31	Better job opportunity for more money and better hours
19	Family reasons—stay at home with children or elderly parents
15	Pay and benefits were unsatisfactory
15	Staffing was poor and unable to deliver quality patient care
15	Management was not supportive, expected the staff to go the extra mile but management did not
14	Work environment was unacceptable, the people unhappy
12	Stress of working with too little staff/heavy load of sick patients
8	No opportunity for advancement
8	Returned to school
7	Personal health problems
5	Moved

[*]Percentages do not total 100 because nurses gave more than one reason for leaving.

Seventy percent of the nurses felt they were able to meet their career goals. Many shared that their goals 285 were to deliver quality patient care. What they liked best about being a nurse was helping people and feeling good at the end of the day if they had given quality care.

Forty percent offered additional personal reasons 290 for leaving. These reasons included caring for young children or older parents, spouse's job responsibilities, returning to school, and physical and emotional illness. With sicker patients and less staff, nurses may feel overwhelmed at the end of the day, returning home 295 remembering the many promises to patients they couldn't keep.[17]

A positive finding of this study is that nurses, even though they are leaving hospital-based nursing, are not leaving the profession. Eighty percent of the nurses are 300 still employed in nursing. Some have chosen to stay home with family responsibilities or return to school, but not one of the 84 pursued employment opportunities outside nursing.

Limitations and Future Research

Limitations to the study were few, but include the

305 following: the sample size in this study ($n = 84$) is relatively small in proportion to the magnitude of the nursing turnover problem. Ideally, researchers would have been able to contact all eligible participants. This is a convenience sample. Although the numbers were small
310 and limited to registered nurses in one Midwestern health system, common themes readily emerged from the data collected.

All data were collected by telephone interviews, and answers were recorded by hand. The authors
315 knowingly chose not to tape-record interviews; bias may therefore be reflected in the answers recorded, as they were not transcribed verbatim.

Future studies might investigate the reasons that nurses choose to stay at the health system and what
320 motivates them to do so. Another study might focus on why nurses remain at the institution, but transfer to other units. Although findings in this study are comparable to those of other turnover studies, comparative research by geographic regions may cast a new light on
325 important issues.

Solutions

The current nursing shortage is very different from those of the past because it is both a supply and demand shortage. It is more complex, and therefore more difficult to remedy. There is a continuing aging of the
330 workforce. Sixty percent of the actively licensed nurses in Iowa will be over 50 years of age and may be retired by 2009. To compound the problem, there is a declining interest in nursing as a career. Nurses' salaries have been flat since 1992, affecting incentives to enter nurs-
335 ing.[18] In Iowa, between 1993 and 1999, admissions to RN education programs declined 40% and graduations declined 27%.[19]

There is an increasing need for highly educated, experienced nurses to care for more acutely ill patients.
340 Nurses are caring for sicker patients in the hospital for shorter periods of time. New technologies in patient care add to the demands and frustrations of the nurse. This shortage is most evident in critical care, emergency services, and perioperative care.[20]
345 To address these issues and the results of this study, health system leadership undertook several key initiatives. Concurrently with the time of the study, there was a change in the nurse executive officer position. Top administrators supported nurses by promoting a
350 nurse leader who demonstrated a voice for nursing, a nurse's nurse. She has created a management team that has a vision and can move the health system forward.

Because staffing, scheduling, and the ability to provide quality patient care were major concerns identified
355 in this study, one of the first steps taken by the management team was to enhance the existing weekend package and create a flex staff position. Nurses choosing the weekend package work 24 hours, 3 out of 4 weekends per month. They are paid time and a half.
360 This allows the full-time nurses to work fewer week-

ends. Nurses employed as flex staff set their own schedule. They work only as needed and receive no benefits, but are paid at a higher rate. Fifty-five nurses have already been hired for this position, addressing
365 the need for additional staff. This will ultimately reduce the need for agency staff, increase the number of nurses per patient, and improve the quality of patient care.

This study also stimulated a renewed interest in ex-
370 amining scheduling options on individual units. For example, one unit with a high turnover rate designated several straight day shifts for senior staff nurses. Managers gained a heightened awareness of the unique needs of their units and were empowered to actualize
375 innovative solutions.

The professional nurse practice model has been in place for several years and was affirmed based on results of this study. Staff nurses are encouraged to participate in nursing committees, assume leadership
380 roles, and be decision makers. A peer-reviewed, clinical advancement award was also created to recognize clinical excellence in nursing. At the unit level, obstetrical nurses are piloting implementation of the practice model.
385 Recognition for nurses has also become more noticeable at the organizational level. A newly established President's Award is presented quarterly to a unit to celebrate service excellence and patient satisfaction. Selections are made based on stories and direct
390 communications from patients. Service awards for employment anniversaries are published in the health system newsletter, and nurses selected to be preceptors are compensated for their role.

To attract individuals to the nursing profession,
395 nursing administrators are collaborating with local nurse educators. Endeavors include marketing nursing as an exciting career, providing scholarships, and sharing physical resources. Managers are hiring nursing students and providing flexible scheduling options
400 while they attend classes.

Because many of the nurses who leave the health system may be willing to return, a 1-year reinstatement policy has been implemented. This replaces a 30-day policy. Within 90 days after their resignation, letters
405 are sent to all eligible nurses thanking them for their contributions to the organization and asking if they are interested in returning to the health system.

Retention of nurses is vital to managing the nursing shortage. The health system has a commitment to im-
410 prove the work environment as part of its strategic plan. One goal is to regain magnet hospital status. This recognition for nurses and the institution would help recruit and retain nursing staff. Meanwhile, nurse managers are addressing issues and barriers on the unit
415 level that prevent nurses from achieving their goals; they are creating dynamic teams. Leadership training is offered on a regular basis and tools are available to enhance nurse autonomy and accountability.

Conclusion

420 Findings in this and other studies agree that factors related to the workplace are predictors of intent to leave. Many of these variables can be monitored and controlled by the institution. As the nursing shortage persists and fewer students are pursuing nursing as a career, institutions need to address several basic issues 425 in order to keep competent, motivated, and happy nurses. Management needs to increase job stability and flexibility and provide predictable work schedules. Through focus groups, units could voice their concerns and individual needs; what works well for one unit may 430 not be the best solution for another. If health systems want to retain high-quality nursing staff, management must listen to concerns of nurses and provide flexible scheduling, adequate staffing levels, and appropriate rewards and recognition. In light of the cost of hiring 435 and training new nurses, a few steps taken toward retention will heighten job satisfaction and result in higher levels of quality care for patients.

References

1. The Advisory Board Company. Reversing the flight of talent. *Executive Briefing*. Vol 1. Washington, DC: Nursing Executive Center: 2000.
2. Persson L, Hallberg IR, Athlin E. Nurse turnover with special reference to factors relating to nursing itself. *Scand J Caring Sci*. 1993;7(1):29–36.
3. Kaldenberg DO. Do satisfied patients depend on satisfied employees? Or, do satisfied employees depend on satisfied patients? *The Satisfaction Report*. Vol 3. South Bend, Ind: Press, Ganey Associates, Inc.: 1999.
4. Alexander JA, Lichtenstein R, Oh HJ, Ullman E. A causal model of voluntary turnover among nursing personnel in long-term psychiatric settings. *Res Nurs Health*. 1998;21(5):415–427.
5. Kangas S, Kee CC, McKee-Waddle R. Organizational factors, nurses' job satisfaction, and patient satisfaction with nursing care. *J Nurs Admin*. 1999;29(1):32–42.
6. Pierce LL, Hazel CM, Mion LC. Effect of a professional practice model on autonomy, job satisfaction and turnover. *Nurs Manage*. 1996;27(2 Contin Care Ed):48M, 48P, 48R–T.
7. Irvine DM, Evans MG. Job satisfaction and turnover among nurses: integrating research findings across studies. *Nurs Res*. 1995;44(4):246–253.
8. Aiken LH, Clarke SP, Sloane DM, et al. Nurses' reports on hospital care in five countries. *Health Aff (Millwood)*. 2001;20(1):43–52.
9. Fisher ML, Hinson N, Deets C. Selected predictors of registered nurses' intent to stay. *J Adv Nurs*. 1994;20(5):950–957.
10. MacRobert M, Schmele JA, Henson R. An analysis of job morale factors of community health nurses who report low turnover rate. *J Nurs Admin*. 1993;23(6):22–28.
11. Leveck ML, Jones CB. The nursing practice environment, staff retention and quality care. *Res Nurs Health*. 1996;19(4):331–343.
12. Blegen MA. Nurses' job satisfaction: a meta-analysis of related variables. *Nurs Res*. 1993;42(1):36–41.
13. Hutchinson M, Mattice S. Attract and retain RNs. *Modern Healthcare*. 2000;30(5):22.
14. Prior MM, Cottington EM, Kolski BJ, Shogan JO. Nurse turnover as a function of employment, experience and unit. *Nurs Manage*. 1990;21(7):27–28.
15. Shader K, Broome ME, Broome CD, West ME, Nash M. Factors influencing satisfaction and anticipated turnover for nurses in an academic medical center. *J Nurs Admin*. 2001;31(4):210–216.
16. Borda RG, Norman IJ. Factors influencing turnover and absence of nurses: a research review. *Int J Nurs Stud*. 1997;34(6):385–394.
17. Huff C. Job satisfaction: why your job isn't a bowl of cherries. *Nurseweek*. Available at: http://www.nurseweek.com/features/97–10/jobsatis.html. Accessed March 5, 2002.
18. Kendig S. Addressing the nursing shortage. *AWHONN Lifelines*. 2002;5(3):22–23.
19. Iowa Nurses Association. *Nursing Shortage Fact Sheet*. Available at: http://www.iowanurses.org/nsfacts.htm. Accessed March 7, 2002.
20. Odom J. Nursing shortage: impending doom or challenging opportunity. *J Perianesth Nurs*. 2000;15(5):348–349.

Acknowledgment: The authors thank Daniel W. Russell, PhD, Professor, Department of Psychology, Iowa State University, Ames, Iowa, for his advice and consultation on the questionnaire.

Address correspondence to: Ellen Strachota, PhD, RN, Department of Nursing, Grand View College, 120 Grandview Ave., Des Moines, IA 50316-1599. E-mail: Estrachota@gvc.edu

Exercise for Article 1

Factual Questions

1. Did the results from a previous study find a relationship between employee satisfaction and patient satisfaction? Explain.

2. According to the literature review, what are the four major categories for discontentment?

3. According to the literature review, turnover rates are highest in which year of employment?

4. Nurses often gave more than one reason why they changed their position. What was the most common reason?

5. Why do the percentages in Table 2 not sum to 100%?

6. The researchers discuss the limitations of their study. What is the first limitation that they mention?

Questions for Discussion

7. Of the 183 nurses who were identified as potential participants in this study, 84 were interviewed for a 46% participation rate. In your opinion, could the failure of 54% to participte have an effect on the outcomes of this study? Explain. (See lines 170–182.)

8. If you were asked to participate in a study of this type, how important would it be to you to know that data would be confidential and anonymous? (See lines 186–188.)

9. The tool (i.e., questionnaire) was revised following a pilot interview with eight nurses. If you had planned this study, would you have included a pilot test of the questionnaire in your plans? Explain. (See lines 198–199.)

10. In your opinion, was the inter-rater reliability (i.e., rate of agreement) sufficiently high? (See lines 210–220.)

11. Answers were recorded by hand. The authors knowingly chose not to tape-record interviews. If you had conducted this study, would you have chosen to tape-record the interviews? Explain. (See lines 313–317.)

12. In your opinion, do the results of this study have important practical implications? Explain.

Quality Ratings

Directions: Indicate your level of agreement with each of the following statements by circling a number from 5 for strongly agree (SA) to 1 for strongly disagree (SD). If you believe an item is not applicable to this research article, leave it blank. Be prepared to explain your ratings. When responding to criteria A and B below, keep in mind that brief titles and abstracts are conventional in published research.

A. The title of the article is appropriate.

    SA   5   4   3   2   1   SD

B. The abstract provides an effective overview of the research article.

    SA   5   4   3   2   1   SD

C. The introduction establishes the importance of the study.

    SA   5   4   3   2   1   SD

D. The literature review establishes the context for the study.

    SA   5   4   3   2   1   SD

E. The research purpose, question, or hypothesis is clearly stated.

    SA   5   4   3   2   1   SD

F. The method of sampling is sound.

    SA   5   4   3   2   1   SD

G. Relevant demographics (for example, age, gender, and ethnicity) are described.

    SA   5   4   3   2   1   SD

H. Measurement procedures are adequate.

    SA   5   4   3   2   1   SD

I. All procedures have been described in sufficient detail to permit a replication of the study.

    SA   5   4   3   2   1   SD

J. The participants have been adequately protected from potential harm.

    SA   5   4   3   2   1   SD

K. The results are clearly described.

    SA   5   4   3   2   1   SD

L. The discussion/conclusion is appropriate.

    SA   5   4   3   2   1   SD

M. Despite any flaws, the report is worthy of publication.

    SA   5   4   3   2   1   SD

Article 2

Post-Anesthesia Care Unit Nurses' Knowledge of Pulse Oximetry

John P. Harper, MSN, RN, BC[*]

ABSTRACT. The purpose of this study was to assess post-anesthesia care unit (PACU) nurses' knowledge of pulse oximetry. A convenience sample of 19 nurses completed a 32-item questionnaire that included a 20-item true–false test on pulse oximetry. Overall, nurses demonstrated a knowledge deficit in pulse oximetry. Competency in the use of pulse oximetry is vital to ensure a positive clinical outcome. Nurse educators are responsible for identifying knowledge deficits among staff and implementing strategies to correct these deficits. It is incumbent on nurse educators to provide research-based education on pulse oximetry and opportunities to participate in continuing education.

From *Journal for Nurses in Staff Development*, 20, 177–180. Copyright © 2004 by Lippincott Williams & Wilkins, Inc. Reprinted with permission.

Pulse oximetry (SpO_2), a measurement of arterial oxygen saturation, has been used for years in the post-anesthesia care unit (PACU) to detect hypoxemia in patients emerging from anesthesia. Consequently,
5 competency in the use of pulse oximetry is vital to ensure a positive clinical outcome. Severinghaus and Astrup (1986) described pulse oximetry as one of the most significant technological advances made in monitoring the well-being and safety of patients during an-
10 esthesia, recovery, and critical care. Today, pulse oximetry is used throughout the entire continuum of patient care. The purpose of this study was to assess PACU nurses' knowledge of pulse oximetry.

Literature Review

Stoneham, Saville, and Wilson (1994) reported on a
15 study that assessed knowledge of pulse oximetry among medical and nursing staff. This study sample consisted of 30 senior house officers and 30 staff nurses employed at a general hospital in the United Kingdom. Questions were asked about the theory be-
20 hind pulse oximetry, factors affecting readings, "normal" values in various patients, values in hypothetical clinical situations, and what education participants had received. Ninety-seven percent of physicians and nurses did not understand how a pulse oximeter

25 worked and were confused about factors influencing readings. Respondents gave a wide range of acceptable saturation values (e.g., 90–l00% for a fit adult). In addition, there were serious errors made in evaluating saturation readings in hypothetical clinical situations.
30 Kruger and Longden (1997) surveyed physicians, nurses, and anesthesia technicians ($N = 203$) at an Australian Base Hospital to assess their knowledge of the principles of pulse oximetry. Less than 50% of participants believed they had adequate education in the use
35 of pulse oximetry. Only 68.5% of the participants correctly stated what the pulse oximeter measures. Answers to questions regarding the principles of pulse oximetry, potential errors, normal ranges, and the physiology of oxygen hemoglobin dissociation varied
40 but generally reflected limited understanding.

Howell (2002) reported on 50 staff members, consisting of both physicians and nurses, within a large general hospital in the United Kingdom. Participants' responses to a questionnaire and to six clinical scenar-
45 ios on pulse oximetry were analyzed. Overall, there was a deficit in participants' knowledge of pulse oximetry.

There were no studies in the literature that assessed PACU nurses' knowledge of pulse oximetry. An ex-
50 tremely beneficial monitoring tool, pulse oximetry can detect hypoxemia before it is clinically evident. PACU nurses routinely monitor arterial oxygen saturation, using pulse oximetry technology on all patients emerging from anesthesia. Based on the results of previous
55 studies, it is important to assess PACU nurses' understanding of pulse oximetry to ensure continued competence during this critical phase of anesthesia care.

Research Question

The following research question was addressed: What is the knowledge of PACU nurses regarding the
60 basic concepts and physiology of pulse oximetry?

Method

Research Design

A descriptive correlational design was used. This design permitted description of the phenomena of in-

---

[*]*John P. Harper* is quality monitoring-improvement reviewer and per diem clinical educator, Taylor Hospital, Ridley Park, Pennsylvania.

terest and the relationships among selected variables and knowledge of pulse oximetry.

Sample and Setting

The target population was PACU nurses working in a four-hospital healthcare system in the Mid-Atlantic region. Nineteen nurses constituted the convenience sample for the study.

Instrument

The data collection instrument was a 32-item investigator-developed questionnaire. Twelve items elicited demographic information; a 20-item true–false test was designed to assess knowledge of pulse oximetry. Content validity was established by having a panel of three critical care and PACU nurse educators review the questionnaire. Minor changes were incorporated in the final version. The questionnaire was pilot tested by two PACU nurses and additional revisions were made to improve clarity.

Data Collection

The study was approved by the Institutional Review Boards at the four hospitals. Data were collected over a 4-week period in June and July 2003. Packets containing a cover letter explaining the study, the questionnaire, and test were distributed to PACU nurses working on the day of data collection. Completion of the questionnaire and test was considered as consent to participate. The respondents were asked not to use any reference materials or discuss test items with their colleagues. Upon completion of the questionnaire and test, the respondents sealed the completed questionnaire and test in a manila envelope and returned it to the investigator.

Data Analysis

Descriptive statistics, including frequencies, were used to describe the sample. Pearson's correlation was used to identify relationships among selected variables and knowledge of pulse oximetry. The true–false test was used to assess knowledge of pulse oximetry and scored electronically.

Results

A total of 19 questionnaires were returned. Of the 19 respondents who completed the survey, 88% were female and 12% were male. The age of the respondents ranged from 30 to 55 years, with a mean of 47 ± 6.9 years. The highest level of nursing education for 44% of the respondents was a baccalaureate; 28% had an associate's degree; and 17% had a diploma. Eleven percent had a master's degree. The nurses' experience in the PACU ranged from 1.5 to 27 years, with a mean of 9.5 ± 7.8 years. Their experience with pulse oximetry ranged from 4 to 28 years, with a mean of 13 ± 6.2 years (see Table 1). All regularly worked during the day shift.

Respondents first learned about pulse oximetry from a colleague (39%), nursing school (33%), in-service education (22%), or through a journal article/reference book (6%). Fifty-nine percent indicated that the initial learning session was adequate. Thirty-five percent of respondents reported that they had participated in continuing education on pulse oximetry since their initial learning session.

Table 1
Demographic Profile of Survey Respondents (N = 19)

Variable	Frequency	Percent
Gender		
Female	15	88
Male	2	12
Highest level of education		
Baccalaureate	8	44.4
Associate's degree	5	27.8
Diploma	3	16.7
Master's	2	11.1
Hours worked per week		
36–40	12	66.7
20–35	4	22.1
> 40	1	5.6
< 20	1	5.6

Test scores ranged from 40 to 75, with a mean of 62 ± 9.09 on a scale of 0 to 100. Thirty-two percent of the respondents thought the pulse oximeter measured the absorption of electrical waves by hemoglob' The pulse oximeter measures the absorption of light moglobin (Grap, 2002).

Twenty-one percent of the respondents tho SpO_2 value was the same as the partial pressure rial oxygen (paO_2) value on the arterial b' (ABG). SpO_2 is an estimation of arterial oxyge tion (SaO_2) (Grap, 2002).

Eighty-nine percent of respondents thoug the SpO_2, 95% of the data fell within $\pm 1\%$ of arterial oxygen saturation. Actually, the data $\pm 4\%$ of the actual saturation, within a 95% level (Grap, 2002). For example, in a patie SpO_2 of 90%, 95% of the time the SaO_2 value, as measured by the ABG, would be between 86% and 94%.

Eighty-nine percent of respondents thought the normal SpO_2 in adults ranged between 93% and 100%, and 84% thought the normal SpO_2 in children ranged between 97% and 100%. The normal SpO_2 for both adults and children is 95–100% (Grap, 2002).

Forty-two percent of respondents thought that SpO_2 is a reliable indicator of ventilation status. SpO_2 is an indicator of oxygenation, the amount of hemoglobin that is saturated with oxygen. It does not directly measure ventilation (Grap, 2002).

Only 63% of respondents thought that performance of a probe placed on a finger is generally better than performance of a probe placed at other sites. In addition, only 58% of respondents thought the finger probe might damage skin integrity. Overall, performance of finger probes is generally found to be better than performance of probes at other sites. Digital injury induced by the oximeter probe has been reported (Grap, 2002).

Thirty-seven percent of respondents thought the finger probe could be used on the same extremity as an arterial line and blood pressure cuff. The probe should be placed on the extremity opposite an arterial line and blood pressure cuff so that pulsatile flow is not interrupted (Grap, 2002).

Forty-two percent of respondents thought a falsely low SpO_2 value may occur in smokers. Actually, a falsely high SpO_2 value may be obtained from smokers because of the presence of carbon monoxide. The carbon monoxide turns hemoglobin bright red and the pulse oximeter is unable to determine the difference between hemoglobin molecules saturated with oxygen and those carrying carbon monoxide (Howell, 2002).

Only 79% of respondents thought a patient with hypovolemia may have an altered SpO_2 value. Oximeter readings are altered in low perfusion states (Howell, 2002).

All respondents thought the SpO_2 would decrease in cardiac arrest. The oximeter requires a pulsatile signal and an alarm will sound when the pulse is lost. As a result, there will be no reading displayed (Howell, 2002).

Fifty-three percent of respondents thought obtaining ABGs was the first priority for a sudden fall or sustained trend of falling SpO_2 values. With a change in SpO_2 values, assessment of the airway and breathing is the first priority (Howell, 2002).

Pearson's correlation was used to identify relationships among selected variables and knowledge of pulse oximetry. There was a positive correlation between level of education and test scores ($r = .25$) and between length of experience with pulse oximetry and test scores ($r = .14$).

Discussion and Implications

Although measurement of arterial oxygen saturation by pulse oximetry is a standard of care in the PACU (American Society of Perianesthesia Nurses, 2002), it may be taken for granted and considered a simple monitoring technique. Overall, nurses demonstrated a knowledge deficit in pulse oximetry that is comparable to previous studies (Howell, 2002; Kruger & Longden, 1997; Stoneham et al., 1994).

While respondents first learned about pulse oximetry from a colleague (39%), nursing school (33%), in-service education (22%), or through a journal article/reference book (6%), only 59% indicated that the initial learning session was adequate. Thirty-five percent of respondents reported that they had participated in continuing education on pulse oximetry since their initial learning session. Learning about pulse oximetry came from several sources and may reflect different information. The majority of nurses had not participated in continuing education on pulse oximetry and therefore may lack current knowledge in pulse oximetry. To increase staff awareness of the need for such knowledge, the results of the study were published in the hospitals' *Nursing Research Newsletter* and distributed to all staff throughout the healthcare system.

Nurse educators are responsible for identifying knowledge deficits among staff and implementing strategies to correct these deficits. It is incumbent on nurse educators to provide research-based education on pulse oximetry and opportunities to participate in continuing education. Since nurses initially learn about pulse oximetry from a variety of sources, competency should be validated during orientation and on a regular basis. Competency in the use of pulse oximetry on patients emerging from anesthesia is vital to ensure a positive clinical outcome.

References

American Society of Perianesthesia Nurses. (2002). *2002 Standards of perianesthesia nursing practice.* Cherry Hill, NJ: American Society of Perianesthesia Nurses.

Grap, M. (2002). Protocols for practice: Pulse oximetry. *Critical Care Nurse, 22*, 69–76.

Howell, M. (2002). Pulse oximetry: An audit of nursing and medical staff understanding. *British Journal of Nursing, 11*, 191–197.

Kruger, P., & Longden, P. (1997). A study of a hospital staff's knowledge of pulse oximetry. *Anesthesia and Intensive Care, 25*, 38–41.

Severinghaus, J., & Astrup, P. (1986). History of blood gas analysis, VI: Oximetry. *Journal of Clinical Monitoring, 2*, 270–288.

Stoneham, M., Saville, G., & Wilson, I. (1994). Knowledge about pulse oximetry among medical and nursing staff. *Lancet, 344*, 1339–1342.

Acknowledgment: The author acknowledges the assistance and support of Elizabeth W. Bayley, PhD, RN.

Address correspondence to: John P. Harper, 408 Essington Avenue, Essington, PA 19029-1237. E-mail: HarpJP2@aol.com

Exercise for Article 2

Factual Questions

1. According to the literature review, were there previous studies in the literature that assessed PACU nurses' knowledge of pulse oximetry?

2. Of the 32 items in the data collection instrument, how many were designed to assess knowledge of pulse oximetry?

3. How was content validity established?

4. What was the mean test score?

5. What does a pulse oximeter measure?

6. What was the value of the Pearson correlation coefficient for the relationship between level of education and test scores?

Questions for Discussion

7. The researcher refers to the sample in this study as a "convenience sample." What is your understanding of the meaning of this term? (See lines 67–68.)

8. The researcher states that the questionnaire was pilot tested by two PACU nurses and additional revisions were made to improve clarity. In your opinion, was this step in the research important? Explain. (See lines 76–78.)

9. The respondents were asked not to use any reference materials or discuss test items with their colleagues. In your opinion, is it likely that all the respondents followed these instructions? Explain. (See lines 86–88.)

10. Although the researcher states that a total of 19 questionnaires were returned, he does not indicate how many questionnaires were distributed. Would this be useful information to know? Explain. (See line 98.)

11. The correlation coefficient for the relationship between length of experience with pulse oximetry and test scores is reported as .14. In your opinion, is this a strong relationship? Explain. (See lines 187–190.)

12. If you were conducting a study on the same topic, what changes in the research methodology, if any, would you make?

Quality Ratings

Directions: Indicate your level of agreement with each of the following statements by circling a number from 5 for strongly agree (SA) to 1 for strongly disagree (SD). If you believe an item is not applicable to this research article, leave it blank. Be prepared to explain your ratings. When responding to criteria A and B below, keep in mind that brief titles and abstracts are conventional in published research.

A. The title of the article is appropriate.

   SA   5   4   3   2   1   SD

B. The abstract provides an effective overview of the research article.

   SA   5   4   3   2   1   SD

C. The introduction establishes the importance of the study.

   SA   5   4   3   2   1   SD

D. The literature review establishes the context for the study.

   SA   5   4   3   2   1   SD

E. The research purpose, question, or hypothesis is clearly stated.

   SA   5   4   3   2   1   SD

F. The method of sampling is sound.

   SA   5   4   3   2   1   SD

G. Relevant demographics (for example, age, gender, and ethnicity) are described.

   SA   5   4   3   2   1   SD

H. Measurement procedures are adequate.

   SA   5   4   3   2   1   SD

I. All procedures have been described in sufficient detail to permit a replication of the study.

   SA   5   4   3   2   1   SD

J. The participants have been adequately protected from potential harm.

   SA   5   4   3   2   1   SD

K. The results are clearly described.

   SA   5   4   3   2   1   SD

L. The discussion/conclusion is appropriate.

   SA   5   4   3   2   1   SD

M. Despite any flaws, the report is worthy of publication.

   SA   5   4   3   2   1   SD

Article 3

Ethical Issues Faced by Nursing Editors

Margaret Comerford Freda, EdD, RN, CHES, FAAN, **Margaret H. Kearney**, PhD, RN, FAAN[*]

ABSTRACT. This study reports on ethical issues faced by editors of nursing journals, a topic which has not appeared in the nursing literature. A survey of nursing editors (n = 88) was conducted via e-mail; this article is the content analysis of survey questions about ethics. Eight categories of ethical issues emerged: problems with society/association/publisher; decisions about inflammatory submissions; informed consent or IRB issues; conflicts of interest; advertising pressures; duplicate publications and/or plagiarism; difficult interactions with authors; and authorship. Some issues were similar to those published about medical editors; however, others were unique. This study can assist authors to better understand some of the ethical issues in publishing, can help editors to view their issues in the context of what others experience, and can assist societies and publishers to work toward avoiding these ethical issues in the future. Professional discussions about ethics in nursing publications should be the subject of ongoing research and scientific inquiry.

From *Western Journal of Nursing Research,* 2005, *27,* 487–499.

Nursing editors are powerful gatekeepers for the nursing literature. Their practice, however, has received little attention in the literature. The findings reported here are from an international survey of nurs-
5 ing editors that was aimed at discovering elements of nursing editors' practice; this article presents the results about ethical issues faced by nursing editors.

Ethical Issues in Professional Publishing

The Committee on Publication Ethics (COPE), an international organization founded to be a "sounding
10 board for editors...struggling with possible breaches in research and publication ethics" (COPE, 2003, para. 1) has published guidelines on good publication practice. Their guidelines cover ethical issues of (a) study design and ethical approval, (b) data analysis, (c) authorship,
15 (d) conflicts of interest, (e) peer review, (f) redundant publication, (g) plagiarism, (h) duties of editors, (i) media relations, and (j) advertising. The guidelines also suggest methods of dealing with ethical misconduct that is serious or less serious and conclude that editors

20 have an ethical responsibility to take all suspicions of misconduct seriously, and publish notices in the journal when true ethical misconduct has been discovered.

Common Ethical Issues

The subject of ethical issues in editorial practice has been addressed frequently in the literature about editors of professional biomedical journals. Kempers
25 (2001) described several common ethical issues in publishing: duplicative or redundant publication (defined as using the same data more than once, and sometimes the same article being published in multiple journals);
30 authorship (multiple authorship, misconduct among authors, guest authorship, order of authorship, credit for undeserving authors); research misconduct (lack of informed consent or Institutional Review Board [IRB] approval), and conflict of interest (financial considera-
35 tions influencing the author, reviewer, or editor).

Redundant Publication

Redundant or duplicative publications was studied by Yank and Barnes (2003), who found agreement between 99 editors and 99 authors that duplicate publication in professional journals was unacceptable but
40 did not find agreement between editors and authors about the acceptability of publishing duplicate material in non-peer-reviewed publications, or for different audiences. Two-thirds of authors felt that repeat use of data in alternative publications was acceptable practice,
45 while editors disagreed (Yank & Barnes, 2003). In this study (Yank & Barnes, 2003), authors and editors suggested that redundant publication occurs because authors are pressured to publish frequently, and because journals do not sufficiently punish cases of redundant
50 or duplicate publication.

Authorship and Ethical Behavior of Authors

Authorship and ethical behavior of authors has also been examined. Some of these behaviors include ghost writing by pharmaceutical company writers (Bevan, 2002), so-called gift authorship (defined as authorship
55 which is not earned) (Asai & Shingu, 1999; Bhopal et al., 1997; King, McGuire, Longman, & Carroll-Johnson, 1997), the order in which authors' names appear (Kempers, 2001), and management of author ap-

[*] *Margaret Comerford Freda* is professor, Department of Obstetrics and Gynecology and Women's Health, Albert Einstein College of Medicine, Montefiore Medical Center. *Margaret H. Kearney* is associate editor of the *Journal of Obstetric, Gynecologic, and Neonatal Nursing,* and professor, School of Nursing, University of Rochester.

peals by an editorial office (Callaham, 2003). Some
journals have instituted strict guidelines for avoiding
gift authorship and authorship that is not truly earned
by participation in the research. Some journals suggest
methods for how authors' names should be listed;
however, this is not universal.

IRB Approval

Amdur and Biddle (1997) explored whether all
published research has IRB approval. They found in a
study of 102 journals that only 47% required a statement of IRB approval when human participants were
the sample.

Conflict of Interest

Conflict of interest has been addressed frequently in
the literature. This is clearly an ethical issue for all
participants in publishing: authors, editors, reviewers,
and societies or associations that own journals. Editorial independence at medical journals owned by professional associations can become an ethical dilemma for
many reasons: Associations might have relationships
with advertisers who want certain material published in
the journal, or boards of directors might wish to influence the content of professional journals. In their study,
Davis and Mullner (2002) found that of 33 medical
editors surveyed, 23 said they had complete control of
editorial content, while the rest felt they were pressured
by the association about editorial content. They suggested that editors and associations need specific
guidelines concerning control of journal content. Conflict of interest can also be manifested when authors are
consultants for companies that fund research submitted
to journals. One study found that only 10% of journals
required that authors disclose such conflict of interest
(Asai & Shingu, 1999). Krimsky and Rothenberg
(2001) found that 66% of 1,396 highly ranked medical
journals contained no information at all about financial
considerations of authors and their research; they concluded that this could mean there was no financial conflict of interest, or it could also mean that authors had
not complied with journal disclosure rules. Pitkin
(1998) wrote about the commercialization of medicine,
the common practice of commercial sponsorship of
research, and the consequent risk to the credibility of
medical research and publications.

Ethical Treatment of Authors by Editors

One final ethical difficulty was discussed by Horton
(1998), who wrote that editors themselves could be
unethical in their treatment of authors through long
delays in dealing with manuscripts, being discourteous
to authors, failure to follow standardized procedures,
and lack of ethical standards for the journal.

Purpose

The purpose of this secondary analysis was to describe the kinds of ethically difficult situations nursing
editors faced in their work.

Design

The larger study was a cross-sectional descriptive
study using an instrument developed by the authors and
distributed and returned by e-mail. The component
reported here was a qualitative content analysis of textual data provided by survey respondents.

Sample

Nurse editors and associate editors who had decision-making responsibilities for journal content and
policy were the target population. The authors identified 177 possible nursing editors through a search of
international publishing Web sites, lists of American
Academy of Nursing conference attendees, lists of International Academy of Nursing Editors conference
attendees, World Wide Web searches, and referrals
from the editors contacted. E-mail addresses could not
be verified for 13 of the 177 possible editors, resulting
in a possible sample of 164 editors. One hundred
thirty-seven editors expressed a willingness to participate. Eighty-eight editors ultimately completed the
survey (66% response rate) and described practices for
90 journals. As reported elsewhere (Freda & Kearney,
2005), 71 of the journals were published in the United
States and 19 outside the United States, including 10
from England, 4 from Australia, 2 from Canada, 1 from
South Africa, and 2 that were based in more than one
country. Of the 78 journals described by their editor as
scholarly journals, 52 (66%) were official journals of
professional associations. Ninety-seven percent of the
U.S. editors were women; this number was 63% for
international editors. Editors' average age was 53
(range ages 34 to 69 years), and they had a mean of 36
years in nursing (range 14 to 50) and 9 as an editor
(range 0.9 to 32). The most commonly reported nursing
specialties were administration and education (each
reported by 24%); however, a wide range of other specialties and subspecialties also was represented.

Methods

The survey was developed by the authors to collect
data from nurse editors about their concerns, and to
collect evidence of differences in editorial practices.
Items in the survey were included based on reading the
medical literature about editorial practice, discussion
with nurse editors, and the experience of the authors
themselves as editors of nursing journals. Eleven editors reviewed the draft tool, contributed new questions,
and modified others. The final survey was 108 descriptive questions, multiple choice and open ended, and
included questions concerning context of the editor
role; editors' personal and professional background;
manuscript sources and author compensation; manuscript predecision processing; editorial staff; peer review policies and practices; the size, selection, and
preparation of the review panel and the editorial board;
use and role of associate editors; editorial decision
processes; manuscript tracking and handling in the
publishing process; and editors' experiences, beliefs,

and opinions about being an editor. For this secondary
165 analysis of the data, textual responses to three questions that concerned ethical issues were analyzed. The
relevant questions were:

- Do you feel that you have editorial control over
  the content of your journal, or is the content of cer-
170 tain areas of your journal dictated by others, such
  as the publisher, or the society or association?
  Please explain.
- If your journal accepts advertising, are there ever
  times when you feel pressured to either accept ar-
175 ticles on certain topics, or reject articles on certain
  topics due to pressure about advertising from publishers, societies or associations, or advertisers
  themselves? Please explain.
- Since becoming an editor, have you had difficult
180 ethical decisions to make? Please list the most important ones.

In late 2002, after obtaining IRB approval for the
study from Albert Einstein College of Medicine,
Bronx, New York, e-mail was sent to 164 editors ask-
185 ing them to verify their status as editors and interest in
participating in the study. The survey was sent by e-
mail attachment in early 2003 to the 137 who responded positively, giving their consent for participation. Separate responses were requested about each
190 journal from those who edited more than one journal.
After two reminders (at 45 days and 60 days), 90 completed surveys from 88 editors had been returned. Identification of respondents was deleted, and surveys were
saved as numbered documents. Textual responses to
195 open-ended questions and commentary added by respondents were copied from the original surveys and
pasted into tables by item number, with responses labeled by respondent ID number.

Analysis

Text was analyzed using content analysis tech-
200 niques, and the results represented by frequency within
the data as well as by the content of the text (Morgan,
1993). The authors decided on individual sentences as
the unit of analysis. The authors independently reviewed and coded the responses; interrater reliability
205 was 89%. Exhaustive categories were developed. An
initial 10 categories were reduced to 8 as the analysis
proceeded. A total of 96 responses from 56 editors
were sorted into these categories. The content of the
responses within each category was summarized and
210 represented in brief textual labels.

Findings

Some type of ethical dilemma was reported by 56
editors (64% of the 88 editors who participated in the
survey). The eight categories of ethical issues faced by
nursing editors are presented in Table 1 in order of
215 frequency, from most often listed to least.

Table 1
*Categories of Ethical Issues, and Number of Affirmative
Responses*[a]

Category	# Responses	%
Problems with association/society/publisher	26	46
Advertising pressure	24	42
Duplicate publication and plagiarism	14	25
Difficult interactions with authors	14	25
Informed consent or Institutional Review Board issues	6	11
Conflict of interest	5	9
Decisions about inflammatory submissions	4	7
Authorship of articles	3	5

[a] 96 responses from 56 editors.

Problems with Society, Association, or Publisher

While most of the editors queried stated they had
"total control" over the content of their journal, there
were 26 responses complaining that they had experienced problems with their society or publisher in this
220 regard. This was the most commonly perceived ethical
complaint from editors. For the editors of society or
association journals, the problems they encountered
were described as "publishing topics the founder of the
society was against," "resisting the dictates of society
225 members," "occasionally the society wants things published without peer review, but I refuse," "there is clear
tension between what the society wants and what I
want," "dismissing editorial board members," and "society director has a big input and makes decisions that
230 should be mine." Problems with publishers included
"occasional tension with the publisher if the content is
'too researchy,'" "I need to have control (over content)
in writing (as in a contract)," "I have a new publisher
now—we'll see what happens," "my publisher makes
235 some suggestions about content," and "editorial control
is very important but requires regular discussions."

Editors suggested that it was essential to work in
close partnership with societies or associations who
own journals to avoid conflicts over editorial control.
240 They said that the issue of who controls content in
journals should be in a contract, and that the best way
of controlling content is to be sure that some portion of
the journal be allotted to the society for its own purposes, with the understanding that this portion is the
245 only one they will control. They offered these solutions
as ones that had worked for them to reduce ethical issues with editorial control.

Advertising Pressures

Forty-two percent of the responses were related to
pressure of some sort concerning advertising in their
250 journals. This pressure manifested itself in several
ways: articles submitted that promoted products, being
asked to write copy for advertisers, asking for approval
of advertisements but being denied such approval, having to keep the editorial content of the journal sepa-
255 rated from the sales force, advertisers asking for feature
articles to be written to coincide with their product

advertisements, advertisers who want to make changes to accepted manuscripts, editors refusing to accept advertisements for certain products (one specifically
260 named was infant formula), being careful about pharmaceutical companies who sponsor authors, being asked by salespeople to see the yearly editorial calendar to improve advertising sales, publishing a research study that describes the failure of a particular product
265 when the society has a relationship with that company, being asked by a company to run a regular column, feeling that the journal "lives and dies by advertisements," and regular pressure by a society to run articles that endorse products.
270   Some editors who wrote that they did not feel pressured by advertisers volunteered that they had pre-approval rights for all advertisements in tide journals, they had a written policy in place that journal content is never to be influenced by advertisers: "I did [feel pres-
275 sured] at first, but now I won't give the sales staff an editorial calendar, nor will I give them copies of articles," "I feel some pressure, but I won't give in," "Occasionally there's a push for a certain topic, but I've never been forced," and "My publisher is great about
280 this—I get no pressure at all."

Duplicate Publication or Plagiarism

    Duplicate publication or plagiarism was the topic of 25% of the responses. These problems were not always known to the editor until after the publication occurred and the editor was notified by someone that a similar
285 (or the same) article appeared elsewhere. Occasionally the editor recognized that a submission was very similar to an article currently in the literature, and some editors recalled that peer reviewers had notified them that a similar manuscript was reviewed for another
290 publication. In some cases, the plagiarism occurs in one or more sections of the manuscript such as the literature review (which might be word-for-word exactly as appearing in another published article), or in the original article. Some editors described this as "aca-
295 demic dishonesty," "literary theft," "duplicate or redundant publication," "plagiarism," or "duplicated material."

Difficult Interactions with Authors

    Difficult interactions with authors were described in 25% of the responses. Some of these issues con-
300 cerned emotional responses to notifying authors of bad reviews: "I felt really bad because I knew this was a dissertation, and I knew the author got bad advice from faculty," worry that rejection of a certain author might lead to legal problems, receiving manuscripts from
305 well-known authors who write unacceptable manuscripts, "inheriting bad manuscripts from the previous editor and knowing you have to contact the author and now reject them," soliciting a manuscript that then comes in and is not acceptable, dealing with conflicts
310 between coauthors, "deciding to publish an article which is still not good enough, but the author cannot do

any better," rejecting an article from a close colleague or editorial board member, dealing with questionable data in a manuscript, and telling an author to delete
315 certain data before the manuscript can be accepted. These issues with authors were viewed as ethical issues, for the editors felt unsure where the ethical lines should be drawn.

Informed Consent or IRB Issues

    Eleven percent of the responses described ethical
320 issues they had faced with informed consent or IRB issues. They described refusing to publish an article when the author could not produce proof of IRB approval for a study, and authors being angry and saying their integrity was being questioned when asked about
325 IRB approval.

Conflict of Interest

    A few editors mentioned conflict of interest as a problematic ethical issue. These problems were manifested when the sponsor of the research had an interest in the results, when the editor was a member of a board
330 that could be influenced by a study result, and when financial interests of authors could not be determined. One editor was concerned about conflicts of interest with reviewers, and whether they should be required to sign conflict-of-interest statements before reviewing
335 submissions.

Decisions about Inflammatory Submissions

    Some editors had been faced with decisions about inflammatory submissions and felt that this represented an ethical dilemma. Should they publish articles with a political point of view, such as an antiwar submission?
340 Another stated that a submission that could alienate government agencies that ultimately fund health projects was a problem for her journal, and she feared its publication would have ethical implications for patient care. Another editor had received "vicious" letters, and
345 did not know whether publishing them was ethically correct in the name of honest discourse.

Authorship of Articles

    Only 5% of the responses mentioned authorship of articles as an ethical dilemma. Some of these issues included publishing an article submitted as if written
350 by a student nurse; however, the editor knew that the author was actually a faculty member, dealing with a faculty member who seemed to have claimed a student's work as her own, and concern about whether all of the listed authors had contributed to a particular
355 manuscript.

Discussion

    This information about the work being done by nursing editors has not been examined before and is important for all who participate in the professional publishing process to appreciate. Shining the light on
360 editorial practice can assist editors to understand where their practice lies on the continuum of editorial prac-

tice, and can help publishers, societies or associations, and authors better understand their role in ethical practices for publishing. Nurses who author nursing articles should be aware of the ethics involved in publishing to understand how to act ethically when submitting manuscripts; nurses who are readers of nursing journals can learn more about the publication process by reading this research. In the current survey, editors were asked to describe the ethical problem, but not how they solved the problem. Although some offered solutions spontaneously, additional information about how editors resolve their perceived ethical issues would be helpful in exploring this topic more fully.

The editors who participated in this survey described many of the same ethical problems faced by medical editors, as well as some not depicted in the biomedical literature (Davis & Mullner, 2002; Krimsky & Rothenberg, 2001; Yank & Barnes, 2003). Medical and nursing editors share ethical concerns about pressure from advertisers, problems with journals owned by societies or associations, duplicate publication and plagiarism, conflict of interest for authors and reviewers, and informed consent or IRB issues. There were also some topics that only nursing editors discussed: ethical problems with authors such as rejecting well-known authors, worrying that legal issues might be raised when a manuscript is rejected, concern for an unacceptable student manuscript which the editor views as the result of poor faculty advice, dealing with inflammatory submissions, and conflicts between authors.

One possible explanation for these additional ethical concerns is that nursing editors, socialized in the caring, ethical nature of nursing, might be more highly attuned to interpersonal conflict resolution than their medical colleagues. The nursing editors surveyed had been practicing nurses for an average of 36 years and thus had a professional lifetime to assimilate nursing's core values of caring and ethics as represented by the American Nurses Association *Code of Ethics* (ANA, 2001). The first provision of this Code states that "The nurse, in all professional relationships, practices with compassion and respect for the inherent dignity, worth and uniqueness of every individual, unrestricted by considerations of social or economic status, personal attributes, or the nature of health problems" (ANA, 2001, Provision 1, Respect for Human Dignity). This focus on compassion and respect could set nursing editors apart from their editor colleagues in other disciplines in their perceptions of ethical issues and dilemmas.

One of the major ethical concerns of the nursing editors in the current study was control of journal content by owners of the journal, be they societies, associations, or publishers. Forty-six percent of the responses focused on this problem. As with their counterparts in medical journals, these nursing editors faced ethical issues when the society or publisher asked them to publish an article or column for purposes other than scholarly ones (Davis & Mullner, 2002). Some of the pressures they faced were due to advertisers requesting that articles be written to accompany paid advertising materials, pressure from society board members to publish specific articles without peer review, and pressure from societies to suppress articles that report negative results about companies that advertise in the journal.

Difficulties with IRBs and conflict of interest for researchers was not a major focus of these editors' responses, perhaps reflecting the fact that not all nursing journals publish research, and that nursing publications might deal less often than medical journals with the testing of proprietary products such as drugs and devices. Duplicate publication and plagiarism, however, was a major response. The editors were not asked to offer their suggestions for how to deal with this problem, and most just stated that it was a problem. The medical literature suggests that editors must take an active role in punishing instances of duplicate publication, although clear definitions of duplicate publication are lacking (for instance, is the use of the same so-called methods section in two publications reporting different data from the same study considered duplicate publication?) (Mason, 2004). We currently have no literature that describes whether nursing editors are aware of the guidelines for ethical publication practice from COPE (2003), what nursing editors have done when they have discovered redundant publication in the past, or what they do currently.

Limitations

The current survey was aimed at descriptions of editors' practices. It was a convenience sample but was recruited vigorously. The use of a convenience sample, however, does carry the risk that editors who participated were different from editors who chose not to participate. Another limitation was the nature of the survey, which asked for descriptive information about ethical issues, but only as a part of a larger survey.

References

Amdur, R. J., & Biddle, C. (1997). Institutional review board approval and publication of human research results. *Journal of the American Medical Association, 271,* 909–914.

American Nurses Association. (2001). *Code of ethics.* Retrieved December 15, 2004, from www.nursingworld.org/ethics/code/ethicscode150.htm#1.1

Asai, T., & Shingu, K. (1999). Ethical considerations in anaesthesia journals. *Anaesthesia, 54,* 108–109.

Bevan, J. C. (2002). Ethical behaviour of authors in biomedical journalism. *Annals of the Royal College of Physicians and Surgeons of Canada, 35,* 81–85.

Bhopal, R., Rankin, J., McColl, E., Rhomas, L., Kaner, E., Stacy, R., et al. (1997). The vexed question of authorship: Views of researchers in a British medical faculty. *British Medical Journal, 324,* 1009–1012.

Callaham, M. L. (2003). Journal policy on ethics in scientific publications. *Annals of Emergency Medicine, 41,* 82–89.

Committee on Publication Ethics. (2003). Guidelines on good publication practice. *The COPE report.* Retrieved December 15, 2004, from www.publicationethics.org.uk/about/

Davis, R., & Mullner, M. (2002). Editorial independence at medical journals owned by professional associations: A survey of editors. *Science and Engineering Ethics, 8,* 513–528.

Freda, M. C., & Kearney, M. H. (2005). An international survey of nurse editors' roles and practices. *Journal of Nursing Scholarship, 37*(1).

Horton, R. (1998). The journal ombudsperson: A step toward scientific press oversight. *Journal of the American Medical Association, 280,* 298–299.

Kempers, R. D. (2001). Ethical issues in biomedical publications. *Human Fertility, 4,* 261–266.

King, C., McGuire, D., Longman, A., & Carroll-Johnson, R. (1997). Peer review, authorship, ethics, and conflict of interest. *Journal of Nursing Scholarship, 29,* 163–167.

Krimsky, S., & Rothenberg, L. (2001). Conflict of interest policies in science and medical journals: Editorial practices and author disclosures. *Science and Engineering Ethics, 7,* 205–218.

Mason, D. (2004, August). *Hot topics in publishing.* Paper presented at a meeting of the International Academy of Nursing Editors, Nassau, The Bahamas.

Morgan, D. L. (1993). Qualitative content analysis: A guide to paths not taken. *Qualitative Health Research, 3,* 112–121.

Pitkin, R. (1998). Ethical and quasi-ethical issues in medical editing and publishing. *Croatian Medical Journal, 39,* 95–101.

Yank, V., & Barnes, D. (2003). Consensus and contention regarding redundant publications in clinical research: Cross sectional survey of editors and authors. *Journal of Medical Ethics, 29,* 109–114.

Acknowledgment: This research was supported in part by a grant from Lippincott Williams & Wilkins, Inc., Philadelphia, PA.

Note: Both authors participated in developing the survey, collecting the data, analyzing the data, and writing the article for this study.

Exercise for Article 3

Factual Questions

1. E-mail addresses could not be verified for how many of the 177 possible editors?

2. The 88 editors who completed the survey represented how many journals?

3. What was the response rate?

4. The results of this study are based on editors' responses to how many questions?

5. What percentage of the responses cited advertising pressure as a concern?

Questions for Discussion

6. Is the literature review in lines 23–106 helpful even though it deals with biomedical journals? Explain.

7. In your opinion, is the demographic information on the editors important? Explain. (See lines 136–144.)

8. Was it a good idea to delete identification of respondents? Explain. (See lines 192–194.)

9. How important is it to have information on inter-rater reliability? Explain. (See lines 203–205.)

10. In your opinion, how important are the limitations described in lines 451–458? Explain.

11. If you were to conduct a follow-up study on the same topic, what changes, if any, would you make in the research methodology?

Quality Ratings

Directions: Indicate your level of agreement with each of the following statements by circling a number from 5 for strongly agree (SA) to 1 for strongly disagree (SD). If you believe an item is not applicable to this research article, leave it blank. Be prepared to explain your ratings. When responding to criteria A and B below, keep in mind that brief titles and abstracts are conventional in published research.

A. The title of the article is appropriate.
   SA   5   4   3   2   1   SD

B. The abstract provides an effective overview of the research article.
   SA   5   4   3   2   1   SD

C. The introduction establishes the importance of the study.
   SA   5   4   3   2   1   SD

D. The literature review establishes the context for the study.
   SA   5   4   3   2   1   SD

E. The research purpose, question, or hypothesis is clearly stated.
   SA   5   4   3   2   1   SD

F. The method of sampling is sound.
   SA   5   4   3   2   1   SD

G. Relevant demographics (for example, age, gender, and ethnicity) are described.
   SA   5   4   3   2   1   SD

H. Measurement procedures are adequate.
   SA   5   4   3   2   1   SD

I. All procedures have been described in sufficient detail to permit a replication of the study.
   SA   5   4   3   2   1   SD

J. The participants have been adequately protected from potential harm.
   SA   5   4   3   2   1   SD

K. The results are clearly described.
   SA   5   4   3   2   1   SD

L. The discussion/conclusion is appropriate.
   SA   5   4   3   2   1   SD

M. Despite any flaws, the report is worthy of publication.
   SA   5   4   3   2   1   SD

Article 4

Physical Activity Barriers and Program Preferences Among Indigent Internal Medicine Patients with Arthritis

Hammad A. Bajwa, MD, **Laura Q. Rogers**, MD, MPH[*]

ABSTRACT. The study purpose was to determine, among indigent arthritis patients, physical activity barriers, program preference frequencies and demographic associations. A structured interview of 223 indigent, internal medicine clinic patients with self-reported arthritis was administered in a cross-sectional study design. The two most frequently reported barriers included bad health (52%) and pain (51%). The majority preferred to exercise alone (54%), close to home (76%), and in the early morning/evening (83%). The preferred method of receiving exercise information was by video or audio tape. Frequency of reported barriers was significantly associated with age, ethnicity, and gender; specific program preferences were significantly associated with age and gender only. Exercise programs for indigent patients with arthritis should be home-based with flexible scheduling. Educational material should include both video and audio tape formats. Future interventions should consider barriers related to poor health and pain while remaining responsive to age, gender, and ethnic differences. Nurses can play a pivotal role in such interventions.

From *Rehabilitation Nursing, 32*, 31–34. Copyright © 2007 by the Association of Rehabilitation Nurses. Reprinted with permission.

Exercise reduces pain (Ettinger et al., 1997; Fransen, McConnell, & Bell, 2003; Kovar et al., 1992; O'Reilly, Muir, & Doherty, 1999; Petrella, 2000; Rejeski, Ettinger, Martin, & Morgan, 1998; Smidt et al., 2005) and disability (Ettinger et al.; Rejeski et al.; O'Reilly et al.; Penninx et al., 2001; Roddy, Zhang, & Doherty, 2005) among patients with arthritis, which is the major cause of disability in the United States (Centers for Disease Control and Prevention, 2001, 2006). Patients with arthritis are less active (Hirata et al., 2006; Hootman, Marcera, Ham, Helmick, & Sniezek, 2003; Shih, Hootman, Kruger, & Helmick, 2006) and enhancing physical activity requires providers to understand the barriers and program preferences reported by this population. Only two studies have evaluated such barriers, and none has evaluated program preferences (Fontaine & Haaz, 2006; Neuberger, Kasal, Smith, Hassanein, & Deviney, 1994). Such information is needed to facilitate the efforts of rehabilitation health professionals to enhance the activity level of patients with arthritis. The study aims were to determine (1) physical activity barriers and program preferences among indigent internal medicine clinic patients with arthritis and (2) the influence of gender, age, and ethnicity on barriers and program preferences.

Materials and Methods

Adult patients in an academic internal medicine clinic participated in a cross-sectional study. Non-English speaking, acutely ill, demented, or psychotic patients were excluded. Overall response rate was 393 out of 444 (88.5%). Of these, 223 had a self-reported diagnosis of arthritis; results from these 223 patients are reported.

A pilot-tested structured interview was administered by trained research staff. The study was approved by the local institutional review board and informed consent was obtained prior to data collection. Patients were asked how often 18 barriers interfered with exercise (5-point Likert-type scale, 1 = *never* to 5 = *very often*). Program preferences measurement utilized yes/no and multiple choice questions. Body mass index (BMI) was calculated from self-reported height and weight.

Chi-square and Fisher's exact test were used to test gender and ethnicity differences for barriers and program preferences; age differences were examined with independent t tests and ANOVA. Spearman's correlation was used to test the association between age and each barrier. Likert-scale items were dichotomized (*infrequent* = 1, 2, 3; *frequent* = 4, 5) for descriptive analyses. All Likert-scale categories were used for Spearman's correlations.

Results

A majority of patients were Caucasian women with fewer than 12 years of education and annual income of

---

[*] *Hammad A. Bajwa* is a rheumatology fellow at the University of Minnesota. *Laura Q. Rogers* is associate professor of medicine at SIU Department of Medicine.

under $20,000 (see Table 1). Patients were older (mean = 53 ± 9.1) and obese (mean BMI = 32 ± 7.7); the majority (78%) perceived their health as fair or poor. Payer status information was available on 125 (56%) of participants. Seventy-five (60%) were self-pay, with 46 (37%) being Medicaid/Medicare and 4 (3%) being other.

Table 1
Demographic Characteristics of Respondents

Characteristic	n (%)
Gender	
Men	55 (25)
Women	168 (75)
Ethnic group	
Caucasian	146 (65)
African American	77 (35)
Level of education	
Less than 12 years	148 (66)
12 years	56 (25)
13 or more years	19 (9)
Yearly income level	
Under $5,000	42 (19)
$5,000–$9,999	97 (44)
$10,000–$14,999	40 (18)
$15,000–$19,999	22 (10)
Over $20,000	10 (4)
Missing	12 (5)
Patient perception of health	
Excellent	4 (2)
Very good	12 (5)
Good	33 (15)
Fair	79 (35)
Poor	95 (43)

Note. Mean age = 53 (Range = 24–73, Standard deviation = 9.1)
Mean body mass index = 32 (Range = 16–55, Standard deviation = 7.7)

The most frequently reported barriers included bad health, pain, discouragement, fear of injury, lack of discipline, lack of interest, lack of equipment, and lack of time (Figure 1). Barriers that interfered with exercise in fewer than 10% of respondents included cost, lack of enjoyment, weather, knowledge, lack of company, lack of facilities, lack of transportation, embarrassment, lack of skill, and lack of family support.

Discouragement interfered with exercise more in women than men (19% versus 7%, $p = .039$). When compared with African American patients, Caucasians more frequently reported lack of discipline (32% versus 9%, $p < .001$), time (16% versus 7%, $p = .036$), and fear of injury (17% versus 7%, $p = .027$). Age was negatively correlated with embarrassment ($r = -0.24$, $p < .001$), lack of time ($r = -0.16$, $p = .015$), discouragement ($r = -0.20$, $p = .004$), lack of equipment ($r = -0.15$, $p = .022$), transportation ($r = -0.19$, $p = .004$), pain ($r = -0.18$, $p = .009$), and fear of injury ($r = -0.18$, $p = .007$).

Exercising alone was preferred (54%) and 29% wished to exercise with a family member (Table 2). Only 24% preferred to exercise away from home, and 83% preferred to exercise in the early morning/evening. Almost half of respondents (43%) preferred to receive exercise information via videotape or audiotape, with 29% preferring written materials or information from another source (class or friend). The four most popular group exercise components included good music, fun exercises, convenient scheduling, and an enthusiastic leader.

Table 2
Exercise Program Preferences Among Indigent Arthritis Patients

Program aspects	n (%)
Where would you like to exercise?	
Outdoors in neighborhood	84 (38)
Inside apartment or home	82 (37)
Away from home (e.g., community center, work, health spa, YMCA)	53 (24)
When would you like to exercise?	
Early morning	101 (48)
During the day	36 (17)
Early evening	73 (35)
With whom would you like to exercise?	
By myself	121 (54)
Family member	65 (29)
Another person (e.g., co-worker, friend, exercise class)	37 (17)
How would you like to receive information on how to exercise?	
Written (e.g., mail, brochure, book)	62 (28)
Video or audiotape	96 (43)
Other (e.g., class or lecture at recreation center, friend)	64 (29)
Elements that a group exercise program needed to make you want to attend?*	
Good music	156 (85)
Fun exercises	190 (85)
Classes at convenient time	187 (84)
Enthusiastic leader	184 (83)
Mats or carpets on the floor	170 (76)
Neighborhood leader	96 (43)
Information on diet or weight control	166 (74)
Videotaped leader	91 (41)
Hard exercise	69 (31)

*Participants were asked to check "all that apply"; therefore, some percentages add up to greater than 100%.

More women than men preferred good music (75% versus 57%, $p = 0.01$), fun exercises (89% versus 76%, $p = .012$), mats/carpets (82% versus 62%, $p = .004$), and videotaped leader (45% versus 28%, $p = .029$). No ethnic differences existed in program preferences. Patients preferring exercise in early morning were older than those preferring early evening (mean age 55 versus 50, $p = .001$). Older patients also preferred exercising outdoors near their home (mean age = 55) compared with those preferring their home or another site (mean age = 51; $p = .017$ and 0.047, respectively). Younger patients preferred fun exercises and convenient scheduling (mean age 52 versus 57 for both; $p = .003$ and .005, respectively).

Discussion

Bad health and pain were major barriers to exercise among indigent internal medicine patients with arthritis. The majority preferred to exercise alone or with a

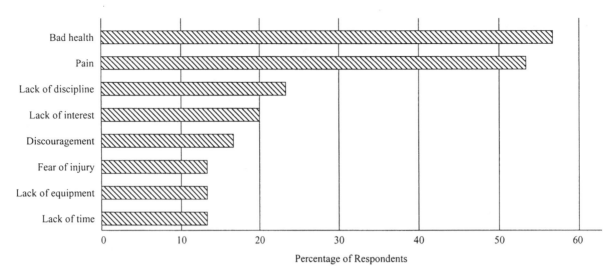

Figure 1. Most frequent reported barriers to physical activity among arthritis patients.

family member, close to home, and in the early morning/evening. The preferred method for information dissemination was video or audio tape. Preferred group exercise components included good music, fun exercises, convenient scheduling, and an enthusiastic leader. Several barriers were significantly associated with age, ethnicity, and gender; and specific program preferences were associated with age and gender only.

Neuberger et al. (1994) studied 100 primarily Caucasian adult outpatients (nonindigent, mean age = 53) with rheumatoid or osteoarthritis, able to undergo bicycle ergometer testing. Major barriers included "exercise was tiring" (57%), "exercise was hard work" (40%), lack of time (33%), inaccessibility to exercise facilities (27%), inconvenient facility schedules (25%), and lack of encouragement by family/friends (25%). Unlike our study, pain and age did not influence barriers, possibly because Neuberger et al. studied a healthier subject population. Consistent with our results, Fontaine and Haaz (2006) reported that joint pain and poor health were associated with reduced levels of physical activity. Ethnicity and gender differences were not examined in either study, and no prior study has evaluated program preferences in patients with arthritis.

Ethnicity influences studied by Masse and Anderson (2003) found that African American women in the lower income group perceived more barriers to physical activity than African American women in the higher income group. A similar difference was not seen for Hispanic women. Differences in specific barriers were not examined. Dergance and colleagues (2003) surveyed elderly Mexican American and European Americans with or without arthritis about physical activity barriers. Mexican Americans reported lack of time as a barrier, and, similar to our findings, European Americans reported lack of discipline. Unlike our results, no ethnic differences existed in fear of injury. Prevalent barriers were similar to those reported by our participants with the exception of pain, which may be

due to differences in the study population (i.e., community dwelling rather than clinic based).

Although the use of self-reported diagnosis of arthritis (as opposed to physician and/or radiographic diagnosis) is a possible study limitation, the measure is most likely to have identified patients with clinically symptomatic arthritis (and, hence, clinically significant disease). Sampling for our study was clinic based (not population based), possibly reducing the generalizability of our study results and explaining the frequent reporting of bad health as a barrier. Study strengths include an adequate sample size for evaluating age, gender, and ethnic differences. Also, our study is unique in its focus on an indigent population with minority representation and its examination of specific physical activity barriers and program preferences among arthritis patients.

Future exercise interventions for indigent patients with arthritis should be home based (especially for older patients) with flexible scheduling (allowing differences in age preferences). Educational materials should include video and audio tape formats. Traditional behavior modification techniques should be included to address barriers such as lack of discipline and discouragement. Furthermore, interventions should consider barriers related to poor health and pain while remaining responsive to age, gender, and ethnic differences in physical activity barriers and program preferences.

Conclusions

Patients with arthritis are aware of the importance of exercise but lack the necessary information for initiating and maintaining an exercise program (Rosemann et al., 2006). Much-needed exercise interventions in the clinical setting for chronic disease patients such as those with arthritis could be optimized by collaboration between physicians and rehabilitation nurses. Lack of time is the most prevalent physical activity counseling barrier reported by physicians (Walsh, Swangard,

David, & McPhee, 1999). Although it is important for the physician to write a prescription for exercise type, intensity, and duration based on the presence of arthritis and other co-existing and limiting chronic diseases, 190 nurses can play a critical role in assisting the patients with implementing these prescriptions. Nursing professionals can design or adapt available patient educational materials related to exercise, apply basic behavioral modification techniques, and use a self-195 management approach to helping patients exercise regularly (Blixen, Branstedt, Hammel, & Tilley, 2004; Kinion, Christie, & Villella, 1993; Tulloch, Fortier, & Hogg, in press). They can provide the majority of education and behavior reinforcement through initial and 200 follow-up counseling sessions. They can address barriers to physical activity, discuss relapse prevention, and collaborate with the physician to provide optimal exercise counseling with minimal physician time commitment. Nursing interventions reduce time demands on 205 physicians, yet provide individualized care necessary for physical activity maintenance.

With increasing evidence supporting the benefit of exercise for patients with arthritis, nursing professionals can take a lead role in exercise counseling in an 210 effort to improve quality of healthcare delivery for patients with arthritis. Because of the pivotal role that nurses play in patient care and their clinical knowledge and experience, they are particularly well-suited for helping patients address the health-related barriers reported in our study. The complementary nature of the 215 nurse and physician clinical roles could be used as an opportunity to help patients with arthritis become more active and, in so doing, potentially improve their quality of life.

References

Blixen, C. E., Branstedt, K. A., Hammel, J. P., & Tilley, B. C. (2004). A pilot study of health education via a nurse-run telephone self-management programme for elderly people with osteoarthritis. *Journal of Telemedicine and Telecare, 10,* 44–49.

Centers for Disease Control and Prevention. (2001). Prevalence of disabilities and associated health conditions among adults: United States, 1999. *Morbidity and Mortality Weekly Report, 50,* 120–125.

Centers for Disease Control and Prevention. (2006). State prevalence of self-reported doctor-diagnosed arthritis and arthritis-attributable activity limitation—United States, 2003. *Morbidity and Mortality Weekly Report, 55,* 477–481.

Dergance, J. M., Calmbach, W. L., Dhanda, R., Miles, T. P., Hazuda, H. P., & Mouton, C. P. (2003). Barriers to and benefits of leisure time physical activity in the elderly: Differences across cultures. *Journal of the American Geriatric Society, 51,* 863–868.

Ettinger, W. H. Jr., Bums, R., Messier, S. P., Applegate, W., Rejeski, W. J., Morgan, T. et al. (1997). A randomized trial comparing aerobic exercise and resistance exercise with a health education program in older adults with knee osteoarthritis. *Journal of the American Medical Association, 277,* 25–31.

Fontaine, K. R., & Haaz, S. (2006). Risk factors for lack of recent exercise in adults with self-reported, professionally diagnosed arthritis. *Journal of Clinical Rheumatology, 12,* 66–69.

Fransen, M., McConnell, S., & Bell, M. (2003). Exercise for osteoarthritis of the hip or knee. *Cochrane Database Systems Review, 3,* CD004286.

Hirata, S., Ono, R., Yamada, M. Takikawa, S., Nishiyama, T., Hasuda, K. et al. (2006). Ambulatory physical activity, disease severity, and employment status in adult women with osteoarthritis of the hip. *Journal of Rheumatology, 33,* 939–945.

Hootman, J. M., Marcera, C. A., Ham, S. A., Helmick, C. G., & Sniezek, J. E. (2003). Physical activity levels among the general US adult population and in adults with and without arthritis. *Arthritis Care and Research, 49,* 129–135.

Kinion, E. S., Christie, N., & Villella, A M. (1993). Promoting activity in the elderly through interdisciplinary linkages. *Nursing Connections, 6,* 19–26.

Kovar, P., Allegrante, J., Mackenzie, C., Peterson, M. G., Gutin, B., & Charlson, M.E. (1992). Supervised fitness walking in patients with osteoarthritis of the knee—a randomized, controlled trial. *Annals of Internal Medicine, 116,* 529–534.

Masse, L. C., & Anderson, C. B. (2003). Ethnic differences among correlates of physical activity in women. *American Journal of Health Promotion, 17,* 357–360.

Neuberger, G. B., Kasal, S., Smith, K. V., Hassanein, R., & Deviney, S. (1994). Determinants of exercise and aerobic fitness in outpatients with arthritis. *Nursing Research, 43,* 11–17.

O'Reilly, S., Muir, K., & Doherty, M. (1999). Effectiveness of home exercise on pain and disability from osteoarthritis of the knee: A randomized controlled trial. *Annals of Rheumatic Diseases, 58,* 15–19.

Penninx, B. W., Messier, S. P., Rejeski, J., Williamson, J. D., DiBari, M., Cavazzini, C., et al. (2001). Physical exercise and the prevention of disability in activities of daily living in older persons with osteoarthritis. *Archives of Internal Medicine, 161,* 2309–2316.

Petrella, R. J. (2000). Is exercise effective treatment for osteoarthritis of the knee? *British Journal of Sports Medicine, 34,* 326–331.

Rejeski, W. J., Ettinger, W. H. Jr., Martin, K., & Morgan, T. (1998). Treating disability in knee osteoarthritis with exercise therapy: A central role for self-efficacy and pain. *Arthritis Care and Research, 11,* 94–101.

Roddy, E., Zhang, W., & Doherty, M. (2005). Aerobic walking or strengthening exercise for osteoarthritis of the knee? A systematic review. *Annals of Rheumatic Disease, 64,* 544–548.

Shih, M., Hootman, J. M., Kruger, J., & Helmick, C. G. (2006). Physical activity in men and women with arthritis, National Health Interview Survey, 2002. *American Journal of Preventive Medicine, 30,* 385–393.

Smidt, N., de Vet, H. C., Bouter, L. M., Dekker, J., Arendzen, J. H., De Bie, R. A., et al. (2005). Effectiveness of exercise therapy: A best-evidence summary of systematic reviews. *Australian Journal of Physiotherapy, 51,* 195.

Tulloch, H., Fortier, M., & Hogg, W. (in press). Physical activity counseling in primary care: Who has and who should be counseling? *Patient Education and Counseling.*

Walsh, J. M., Swangard, D. M., David, T., & McPhee, S. J. (1999). Exercise counseling by primary care physicians in the era of managed care. *American Journal of Preventive Medicine, 16,* 307–313.

Acknowledgment: This work was supported by Georgia Affiliate American Heart Association Grant-in-aid.

Address correspondence to: Laura Q. Rogers, SIU School of Medicine, Department of Medicine, P.O. Box 19636, Springfield, IL 62794-9636.

Exercise for Article 4

Factual Questions

1. What four types of patients were excluded from this study?

2. What percentage of the participants were women?

3. "Cost" was cited as a barrier to exercise by what percentage of the participants?

4. What is the value of the correlation coefficient for the relationship between age and embarrassment?

5. Did "women" *or* "men" prefer good music? What probability is associated with this difference?

6. The researchers mention two "study strengths." What is the first one they mention?

Questions for Discussion

7. Is the response rate adequate? Explain. (See lines 29–30.)

8. Is it important to know that informed consent was obtained? Explain. (See lines 34–36.)

9. If you had conducted this study, would you have used self-reported height and weight? Explain. (See lines 40–42.)

10. All the correlation coefficients in lines 74–80 have negative signs. What is your understanding of the meaning of a negative correlation?

11. Do you agree with the researchers that the use of self-reported diagnosis of arthritis is a possible study limitation? Explain. (See lines 150–155.)

12. Do you think that this study has important implications for nursing professionals? (See lines 191–215.)

Quality Ratings

Directions: Indicate your level of agreement with each of the following statements by circling a number from 5 for strongly agree (SA) to 1 for strongly disagree (SD). If you believe an item is not applicable to this research article, leave it blank. Be prepared to explain your ratings. When responding to criteria A and B below, keep in mind that brief titles and abstracts are conventional in published research.

A. The title of the article is appropriate.

SA   5   4   3   2   1   SD

B. The abstract provides an effective overview of the research article.

SA   5   4   3   2   1   SD

C. The introduction establishes the importance of the study.

SA   5   4   3   2   1   SD

D. The literature review establishes the context for the study.

SA   5   4   3   2   1   SD

E. The research purpose, question, or hypothesis is clearly stated.

SA   5   4   3   2   1   SD

F. The method of sampling is sound.

SA   5   4   3   2   1   SD

G. Relevant demographics (for example, age, gender, and ethnicity) are described.

SA   5   4   3   2   1   SD

H. Measurement procedures are adequate.

SA   5   4   3   2   1   SD

I. All procedures have been described in sufficient detail to permit a replication of the study.

SA   5   4   3   2   1   SD

J. The participants have been adequately protected from potential harm.

SA   5   4   3   2   1   SD

K. The results are clearly described.

SA   5   4   3   2   1   SD

L. The discussion/conclusion is appropriate.

SA   5   4   3   2   1   SD

M. Despite any flaws, the report is worthy of publication.

SA   5   4   3   2   1   SD

Article 5

Ethics Content in Community Health Nursing Textbooks

Susan J. Zahner, MPH, RN[*]

ABSTRACT. Nurses learn ethics content and ethical decision-making strategies through textbooks, basic curricula, continuing education, and professional experience. The author describes an ethics content analysis of community health nursing textbooks, offers suggestions for the improvement of ethics content for textbooks, and raises awareness of the need for more emphasis on public health ethics in nursing and public health professional education.

From *Nurse Educator*, 25, 186–194. Copyright © 2000 by Lippincott Williams & Wilkins, Inc. Reprinted with permission.

Recent calls for public health ethics educational improvements[1-3] have tended to be directed primarily toward graduate-level public health educational programs (Masters of Public Health from Schools of Public Health) and often are specifically directed toward epidemiology training programs. Many professionals working in the field of public health, however, are not in either of these categories yet have needs for ethics education and skills in ethical decision making. This article examines public health ethics education for public health nurses, the single largest professional group working in public health, accounting for 23% of the nation's public health work force.[4]

Public health nursing is defined as "the practice of promoting and protecting the health of populations using knowledge from nursing, social, and public health sciences."[5] Services provided by public health nurses are conducted in collaboration with communities, employers, families, and individuals and include ongoing health assessment, coordinated interventions, and care management.[5] Public health nurses can be found in all levels of the official public health system, as well as in nongovernmental community health organizations. The term *community health nursing* is also used to refer to nursing specialties in public health and other community health settings. The terms are used synonymously in this article.

Ethical conduct for all nurses is guided by a professional code of ethics first adopted by the American Nurses Association (ANA) in 1950 and updated periodically since that time, with the most recent version published in 1985.[6] The code offers universal moral principles that prescribe and justify nursing actions that include respect for persons, autonomy, beneficence, nonmaleficence, veracity, confidentiality, fidelity, and justice.[6] The ANA Code for Nurses, while offering a traditional biomedical ethics perspective relevant to nurses in positions of providing health care to individuals, is limited in its guidance for nurses concerned with population-based services. Fowler, in a recent call for revision of the Code, criticizes the current version for giving "too little attention to the social conditions that foster disease, injury, and illness, nationally and worldwide."[7] Increased attention to these issues would be helpful in moving toward inclusion of needed guidance in addressing ethical issues arising in the provision of services to aggregates.

The ANA has adopted a position statement on human rights that describes the relationship between ethics and human rights.[8] This document defines three responsibilities for nurses: 1) delivery of nursing care that meets the needs of the individual and is consistent with their goals; 2) social action and reform to increase the availability of nursing care and to facilitate access to needed health care for all; and 3) patient education and advocacy to ensure that individuals are aware of all options and their consequences and can make informed choices about health care.[8] A second, logical source for ethics guidance for public health nurses would be the American Public Health Association. However, this association of public health professionals has not adopted a code of ethics for public health workers.

Public health nurses learn about ethics in nursing school curricula, through nursing textbooks, in advanced or continuing education in public health or social sciences, and through professional and personal experience. The adequacy of these methods in providing the information and decision-making skills that are needed by nurses working in public health settings can be questioned. As noted, the biomedical perspective alone is inadequate for addressing ethical issues in public health, yet this is clearly the dominant perspective reflected in the Code for Nurses.

---

[*]*Susan J. Zahner is a doctoral candidate at the School of Public Health, University of California, Berkeley.*

Table 1
Inclusion and Exclusion Criteria

"Public Health Nursing" and "Community Health Nursing" in title	Not specialty-specific (such as maternity or home health)
	Not a "reader" type of text
	Not supervision or management focused
	Not history focused
	Not focused solely on technical procedures

Two research studies have been conducted on this issue. Aroskar[9] reported that community health nurses turn to colleagues, supervisors, administrators, friends, and family as helpers in dealing with ethical problems, with none identifying formal ethics courses as being a helpful guide. Folmar et al.[10] reported that nurses working in public health settings indicated confidence in their ability to identify ethical problems but less confidence in their ability to resolve ethical conflicts or dilemmas. Formal instruction in ethics was reported by greater than 50% of the nurses surveyed by Aroskar and only 38% of those studied by Folmar et al.[9,10] These data indicate that public health nurses have not uniformly received education in ethics, nor have they found formal education helpful in resolving ethical issues in practice. Clearly, ethics education must be improved to facilitate the resolution of ethical problems facing nurses working in communities.

How can ethics education for public health nurses be improved in the future? To answer this question, it is helpful to reflect on what has constituted ethics education in the past. A thorough review of all ethics-related curricula in nursing education and continuing education programs was beyond the scope of this article. A critical examination of the ethics content of one venue of education for public health nurses, the public health nursing textbook, is presented here. Four research questions were posed:

1. What content on ethics is included in public health nursing textbooks?
2. What ethical theories have formed the basis for ethics education for public health nurses through public health nursing textbooks?
3. Has the ethics content or theoretical base changed over time?
4. How could the ethics content of textbooks be changed to improve public health ethics education for public health nurses?

A priori, it was expected that a biomedical perspective would dominate the ethics content of the texts and that the more recent texts would be more likely to include a wider range of perspectives useful in addressing public health challenges.

Study Methods

A systematic search for relevant textbooks was conducted using a computerized academic library system at a large, western United States university. The search terms *public health nursing* and *community health nursing* were used to identify texts specific to the nursing specialty area. The search was limited to books published in the English language. The initial search yielded 529 citations. This list was narrowed to 93 citations through the application of inclusion and exclusion criteria listed in Table 1 and through the elimination of duplicate citations. A two-stage sampling procedure was used to narrow the list of texts. First, a convenience sample based on location at two nearby university libraries or in the author's personal collection was used. Next, a random sample of the texts within each twentieth century decade was used to achieve a sample that included 50% of the texts identified in each decade. This procedure resulted in the final sample of 48 textbooks reviewed for this analysis. On examination of the 48 texts, four were found to not meet the inclusion/exclusion criteria. In summary, 44 community health and public health nursing textbooks were included in this analysis (Table 2).

A data extraction form was designed and systematically used in reviewing each text. First, the text index was checked to identify listings for ethics-related content. Terms including "ethics," "values," "morals," and "philosophy" were noted. Next, the table of contents was examined for chapters with any of the above terms in the title. The content thus identified was then examined for evidence of underlying ethical theory (utilitarian, deontology, human rights, and distributive justice) and for general content and approach. Evidence of the underlying theoretical framework was judged by explicit discussion of the theory and, more often, through content that implied the underlying theoretical base.

A utilitarian base was identified when content reflected concepts of maximizing good outcomes for the whole population over the individual. A deontology base was identified when text content reflected duty to alleviate suffering of individuals, duty to respect individual values, and issues of informed consent. Human rights as a theoretical base was noted when the content included reference to inviolable rights of humans and the right to health. A distributive justice framework was identified when content addressed the distribution of resources and equity in access to health care. These four theoretical approaches are most useful in understanding and resolving ethical problems in public health[1] and should be addressed in any adequate discussion of ethics and public health.

---

[1] Lecture by Dr. Jodi Halpern, UC Berkeley, Public Health Ethics: Research and Practice course, January 27, 1999.

Table 2
Ethics Content of Public Health Nursing and Community Health Nursing Textbooks

Author	Year	Index	Chapter	Theoretical Bases				Primary Focus/Content
				Utilitarian	Duty	Human Rights	Distributive Justice	
Gardner (11)	1916				✓		✓	Noninterference with religious views Observance of professional etiquette Service for those unable to pay
Gardner (12)	1924				✓		✓	Same as above
Bryan (13)	1935	✓	✓	✓	✓	✓		Individual subservient to universal good Respect for privacy, individual values Sacred value of human life
Gardner (33)	1936				✓	✓	✓	Observe professional ethics Provide service without distinction for race, creed, or color Service available without regard for ability to pay
NOPHN (34)	1939	✓			✓			Duty to physician
Gilbert (35)	1940							No ethics content
Grant (36)	1942							No ethics content
Rue (14)	1944	✓			✓	✓		Duty to physician Worth of human beings and interest in welfare of mankind
Waterman (37)	1944							No ethics content
Freeman (38)	1950				✓		✓	Respect right to self-determination Make basic services available to all
Freeman (39)	1957							No ethics content
Freeman (40)	1963							No ethics content
Kallins (41)	1967							No ethics content
Freeman (42)	1970					✓		Subordination of professional desires to human needs of group being served Maximum self-determination for recipients of care
Tinkham and Voorhies (43)	1972				✓			Respect for individual values
Lesser et al. (44)	1975							No ethics content
Benson and McDevitt (45)	1976							No ethics content
Leahy et al. (46)	1977				✓			Worth and dignity of individual
Archer and Fleshman (15)	1979				✓			Informed consent in research settings Respect for patient values
Fromer (16)	1979	✓	✓		✓			Informed consent Respect for individual values Content on biomedical ethics theories and dilemmas Discussed Code for Nurses (1977) Patient's Bill of Rights
Clemen et al. (47)	1981				✓			Working with families with different values
Freeman and Heinrich (48)	1981					✓		Alludes to human rights movement and importance for the future of health services
Helvie (17)	1981	✓	✓		✓			Code for Nurses Respect for client values Informed consent in decision making
Jarvis (49)	1981							No ethics content
Spradley (50)	1981							No ethics content

Continued

Table 2
Ethics Content of Public Health Nursing and Community Health Nursing Textbooks

Author	Year	Index	Chapter	Theoretical Bases				Primary Focus/Content
				Utilitarian	Duty	Human Rights	Distributive Justice	
Leahy et al. (51)	1982	✓			✓			Code for Nurses Informed consent
Fromer (18)	1983	✓	✓		✓	✓		Biomedical ethics perspective Informed consent in research settings History of Nuremberg Code Raises many questions about ethical issues (e.g., euthanasia, genetic cloning, organ transplants)
Burgess and Ragland (19)	1983	✓	✓	✓	✓		✓	Describes utilitarian and justice (Rawls) theory Steps in ethical decision making Case examples
Stanhope and Lancaster (20)	1984	✓	✓	✓	✓	✓	✓	Conflict between individual and aggregate focus of community health Code for Nurses, duty of veracity, confidentiality Right to health as a natural human good Discussed theories of justice
Jarvis (52)	1985							No ethics content
Spradley (21)	1985	✓	✓		✓		✓	Values, values clarification, value systems Equity in access to health care Values clarification exercises
Clemen-Stone et al. (53)	1987	✓			✓	✓	✓	Code for Nurses, role of ethics committees Decisions on use of resources as ethical issues
Turner and Chavigny (54)	1988							No ethics content (epidemiology-focused text)
McMurray (29)	1990							No ethics content (Note: Australian text)
Bullough and Bullough (55)	1990	✓						Brief mention of ethics in relation to women's right to work and occupation health hazards
Clemen-Stone et al. (56)	1991	✓			✓			Ethical approaches in decision making Role of ethics committees Code for Nurses
Cookfair (22)	1991	✓	✓	✓	✓	✓		Discusses ethical theories (utilitarian, deontology) Discusses human rights as claims recognized by law Code for Nurses Model for ethical analysis
Helvie (24)	1991	✓			✓			Code for Nurses Values clarification Ethical decision-making framework
Clark (23)	1992	✓	✓	✓	✓		✓	Discusses ethical theories (utilitarian, deontology, libertarianism) Codes of ethics Egalitarian perspectives on distribution of resources Ethical decision-making framework

Continued

Table 2
Ethics Content of Public Health Nursing and Community Health Nursing Textbooks

| Author | Year | Index | Chapter | Theoretical Bases | | | | Primary Focus/Content |
				Utilitarian	Duty	Human Rights	Distributive Justice	
Stanhope and Lancaster (26)	1992		✓	✓	✓	✓	✓	Discusses ethical theories, principles, rules Professional codes of ethics Resolving ethical problems framework Right to health as a basic human right
Anderson and MacFarlane (27)	1996	✓	✓		✓			Ethics of advocacy and formation of partnerships with community Respect for client freedom of choice
Spradley and Allender (25)	1996	✓	✓		✓		✓	Fundamental ethical principles Basic human values Access to health care according to benefit or needs Ethical decision-making framework
Hertenstein-McKinnon (57)	1997	✓	✓		✓			Addresses autonomy, respect, self-determination Professional accountability Case studies with study questions
Clemen-Stone et al. (28)	1998	✓			✓			Ethical principles Professional ethical responsibilities

Study Results

The findings of the review are summarized in Table 2 by decade of publication. The table includes notation of the presence of a reference to ethics in the text index, the presence of a chapter devoted to ethics, reference to one of four major ethical theoretical bases, and comments reflecting the content. The text publication dates in this sample ranged from 1916 to 1998, with 24 (55%) of the texts published since 1980. Ethics was noted in the indices of 20 (45%) texts overall and 16 (67%) of the texts published since 1980. Separate chapters on ethics were found in 13 (30%) of the texts and in 11 (46%) texts published since 1980.

The ethics content of each text was assessed with regard to explicit or implicit reference to any or all of four common ethical theories: utilitarianism, deontology or duty based, human rights, and distributive justice. The dominant theoretical framework identified in this sample of textbooks was deontologic and was apparent in 28 texts (64%). Although common in public health literature, a utilitarian perspective was relatively rare in these textbooks ($n = 6$, 14%). Human rights and distributive justice theories were noted in 10 (23%) and 11 (25%) of the texts, respectively. The ethics content of the texts changed over time. More recent texts were more likely to include chapters on ethics and also addressed more theoretical perspectives. However, the texts published in the 1930s included a broader range of theoretical perspectives on average than any other decade. Only two texts, both by the same authors, Stanhope and Lancaster (1984,[11] 1992[12]), included all four theoretical perspectives.

Table 2 includes short comments on the content found in each text. Early texts touched on ethics with regard to "professional etiquette" or the obligation to respect the physician. For example, Gardner (1916)[13] stated that public health nurses "...should never criticise, by word or unspoken action, any member of the medical profession."[13] Respect for individual values was also emphasized in one of Gardner's nine principles for public health nurses, which stated "...that there should be no interference with the religious views of the patient."[14] A strong emphasis on the responsibility of the nurse to provide services regardless of the ability to pay was also identified in these texts.

The first text to include a full chapter on ethics was Edith Bryan's "The Art of Public Health Nursing," published in 1935.[15] This chapter reflects for the first time a utilitarian perspective, explaining that the nurse "...always looks on her work with a thought of evaluation from the standpoint of the greatest good to the greatest number, for the future as well as the present."[15] Respect for privacy, for individual values, and for the importance of doing no harm were strongly emphasized. A human rights perspective was noted in discussion of the "sacred value of human life" and "persons may be deprived of their freedom for the sake of preserving the life or well-being of their fellows."[15] Also of interest in this text was discussion of concepts supportive of eugenics, reflecting the popular movement of the time. Bryan wrote, "Not only must life be preserved, but it must be saved and protected on the high level of efficiency and well-being, and more recently comes the concept that it should not be created without the promise of a certain perfection. We have gone be-

235 yond the idea of a bare life to a fuller concept of the possibility of life with full development and fruition, unhindered by physical or mental handicaps."[15]

The eight texts in this sample published in the next three decades included little content on ethics. References to ethical concepts were identified in just two of these texts, predominantly reflecting a duty-based theo-

240 retical perspective. A human rights approach also might be implied in Rue's words: "Values in public health nursing are incomplete and shallow unless the nurse has a sincere feeling for the worth of the human being and an honest and far-reaching interest in the

245 welfare of mankind."[16]

With the exception of Margot Joan Fromer's 1979 text,[17] the ethics content of textbooks written in the decade of the 1970s was sparse. Of interest was the first mention of the concept of informed consent, in a

250 research setting in Archer and Fleshman (1979),[18] and in a lengthy discussion using Katz criteria in Fromer (1979).[17,18] The Fromer (1979) text was the first to include significant content on the range of ethical problems that face professionals working in health care

255 (genetic counseling, euthanasia, organ transplantation, fetal research, etc.), perhaps reflecting the tremendous growth in technology occurring at the time. This text was the first to describe the Tuskegee experiment and discuss the ethical issues it raised. The Code for

260 Nurses, the official code of ethics for professional nurses created by the ANA and discussed previously, was also first discussed in this text, despite having been initially published in 1950.[19]

The textbooks from the 1980s varied considerably

265 in their ethics content, with equal numbers of texts ($n = 4$) including no ethics-related content and including a full chapter on ethics. Duty-based theory and biomedical ethics approaches dominated the content in most of these texts. Case scenarios as a teaching tool were first

270 used by Helvie (1981).[19] The second edition text by Fromer (1983)[20] noted distinctions between professional codes of behavior and ethics by writing, "Although most codes make a concerted effort to include only behavior that is ethical, one must never accept

275 these codes at face value. They are not *necessarily* ethically correct. Ethics is a process of search and discovery rather than a behavioral indoctrination."[20] The first text to describe an ethical decision-making process was Burgess and Ragland (1983).[21] Four steps were

280 described for an ethical inquiry: 1) clarification of facts; 2) discussion of decision-making options; 3) implementation of options selected; and 4) acceptance of the consequences of action and case examples are used to educate readers on the use of the inquiry process.[21]

285 Stanhope and Lancaster (1984),[11] in a chapter written by Sara T. Fry, a nurse and philosopher, were the first authors to include a thorough discussion of ethical theory (utilitarian, deontology, natural law), ethical principles (autonomy, beneficence, justice), and ethical

290 rules (informed consent, veracity, protect privacy) and to apply them to community health nursing examples.[11] This text was the first to include information about the Universal Declaration of Human Rights of the United Nations Assembly as a strong statement of the positive

295 right to health as well as the negative right to be protected from harm.[11] The tension for public health nurses between the utilitarian "public health ethic" perspective ("net benefit to population groups over possible health harms") and the duty-based protection

300 from harm was described in this way: "This emphasis does not align with the highly individualistic emphasis of the Code for Nurses."[11] The Spradley (1985)[22] text includes a chapter, also written by Sara T. Fry, focused on values and values clarification.[22] Values and ethics

305 are connected: "Ethics necessarily involves making evaluative judgments. Moving from the judgment that we *can* do something to the judgment that we ought to do something involves incorporating a set of norms—of judgments of value, right, duties, and responsibili-

310 ties."[22]

The texts of the 1990s show continued growth of the nursing profession and increasing sophistication about the importance and impact of ethics in public health nursing practice. Over half of the texts sampled

315 included separate chapters on ethics ($N = 6$, 55%), and only one text included no ethics content. A number of the texts included models or frameworks for use in ethical decision making. Cookfair (1991)[23] described a six-step model for ethical analysis from the work of

320 Curtin and Flaherty (1982) and used case studies to illustrate the use of the framework.[23] Clark (1992)[24] also described a six-step model that included diagnosis of the ethical dilemma, diagnosis of underlying value conflicts, assessment of priority of values, selection of

325 a course of action, implementation, and evaluation of the action.[24] Two texts used a framework by Thompson and Thompson (1981) to identify and clarify values as part of ethical decision making.[25,26] Stanhope and Lancaster (1992)[12] presented a framework from philoso-

330 pher Andy Jameton for resolving ethics problems. As with the earlier edition of this text, Stanhope and Lancaster (1992) also offered the most thorough presentation of ethics theory, principles, and rules of any of the most recent texts reviewed. Anderson and McFarlane

335 (1996)[27] added a different dimension to the discussion of ethics and community health nursing with their advocacy perspective: "An ethic of advocacy calls for the formation of partnerships between professionals and community members in order to enhance community

340 self-determination."[27] The most recently published text in the sample, Clemen-Stone et al. (1998),[28] offered little ethics content but offered a new term—"care-based ethics"—that seemed to describe the traditional deontologic approach and was focused on the nurse-

345 client relationship and the moral obligations of professionals to promote well-being of clients.[28]

28

Discussion

Although this sample of texts included almost half of the relevant texts available in the academic library system used, it may not be fully representative of all community health/public health nursing textbooks. It included only texts written in English and, with one exception, published in the United States.[29] Ethics content of nursing textbooks is a limited way of examining ethics education available to public health nurses. Nursing ethics texts, course curricula, continuing education courses, and journal articles are additional means for nurses to receive education about ethics and public health. It is also possible that important ethics-related content was missed during data extraction.

Despite the limitations of the approach, answers to the research questions established a priori were possible. This sample of community health and public health nursing textbooks included ethics content, described above, from all four major theoretical frameworks important in public health and biomedical ethics traditions, but, as expected, focused most heavily on content reflective of the duty-based, health-care provider tradition. The ethics content in the texts changed over time in three ways: 1) the amount of ethics information presented increased; 2) a broader scope of perspectives was presented; and 3) the focus on methods or frameworks for ethical decision-making processes increased. Overall, the lack of ethics content in many of the texts was disappointing. Of all the texts in the sample, the 1992 Stanhope and Lancaster[12] text offered the most thorough and useful discussion of ethics and community health nursing. No text provided a good discussion of public health ethics as an issue distinct from biomedical and professional ethics.

Recommendations for Improvement

Community or public health nursing textbooks educate nursing students on the processes and procedures of nursing in community and public health settings. These texts also serve as references for nurses already practicing in these specialty fields. A number of recommendations related to the ethics content of public health nursing textbooks can be made that would improve the usefulness of the texts to both undergraduate nursing students and for continuing education in the field. First, emphasis should be given to ethical theory and perspectives useful for understanding and resolving ethical problems that arise in public health settings regarding the protection of welfare of the aggregate as well as protection of the welfare of the individual. Both traditional biomedical ethics and public health ethics should be described and the differences between them made clear. Public health nurses face conflicting issues of individual and population welfare with other public health professionals as members of collaborative teams in communities as well as in their daily practice as individual public health nurses and as individual members of society. At a minimum, the ethical theories and

perspectives that should be addressed in such a discussion include utilitarianism, deontology, human rights, and distributive justice. The origins and history of these perspectives as well as how they inform current ethical debates in nursing and in public health should be addressed.

Second, a systematic ethical decision-making process should be described and used in discussion of examples of "real life" ethical problems that include both individual and aggregate welfare issues. The process used should be a step-by-step approach that is easy to remember and to follow in an individual decision-making situation as well as with a group of decision-makers. A number of case studies should be included that illustrate the use of the ethical decision-making process by individual community health nurses as well as by teams of public health professionals.

Third, an ideal text would include a number of case studies with discussion questions that could be used by individual students in thinking through ethical problems or by groups of students in classroom discussions. Discussion and interaction between students and with professionals in the field would facilitate learning conceptual ethical content and decision-making skills.

Fourth, community health and public health nursing textbooks should include information about ANA's Code for Nursing, because this professional code provides a set of guidelines applicable to all nurses. An ideal text would also interpret these guidelines with reference to issues faced in public health and community-based settings.

Fifth, because most community health nursing faculty are not highly educated in ethics and philosophy, a text that included a rich "more references" section or a "teacher's guide" would be helpful. Such sections would include more detailed information on the ethical theories and suggestions on ways to present the information to facilitate active learning.

Sixth, public health nursing texts should include information relevant to the ethical conduct of public health and nursing research. This is important from at least two perspectives: First, nurses working in community settings are often in positions to observe the impact of research on individuals and populations being studied and have responsibilities for protection of such vulnerable populations from unethical research practices. Second, nurses will have increasing opportunities for participation and collaboration in research projects as more research is planned and conducted in community settings.

Seventh, future texts should include discussion of ethical issues arising in emergent technologies such as genetic testing and computerized data banks as well as in evolving organizational approaches such as managed care and welfare reform. Students should be able to take away from these texts new knowledge of ethical approaches and decision-making processes as well as a sense of confidence regarding how to approach the

460 resolution of the many future ethical dilemmas that will inevitably arise.

Finally, community health and public health nursing textbooks in the future should include more emphasis on our ethical responsibilities to advocate policies
465 that promote human rights and social justice. Kathleen Chafey calls for "...a community-based practice ethic that can address the just allocation of scarce resources, universal access to health care, and benevolent public policy governing the distribution of social goods."[30]
470 Chafey also recommends an ethic that is socially just and benevolent that promotes healthy communities, described by the World Health Organization as communities with clean and safe physical environments, that have sustainable ecosystems, satisfy basic human
475 needs, optimal levels of accessible, quality public health and illness care, lifelong educational opportunities, and diversified, vital economies.[30] Educating public health nurses in the ethics of social justice will help in societal efforts to achieve optimal population health.

Conclusion

480 This article examined and made recommendations for improvements in only one, limited route for ethics education, the public health nursing textbook. An assessment of ethics curricula in nursing schools as well as the availability of continuing education opportuni-
485 ties in public health ethics would be needed to make more complete recommendations for the improvement of ethics education for public health nurses. Such a survey of ethics education in schools of public health (an avenue for graduate education for many public
490 health nurses) indicated limited required courses and elective offerings in public health ethics.[31] Ethics education in the past for public health nurses has generally been limited in scope and based on the individually focused, traditional biomedical/deontologic approach.
495 This analysis leads one to suspect that nurses educated before 1980 were unlikely to receive education on ethics. It also seems possible from this analysis that even nurses educated in the 1990s may have been exposed to textbooks lacking in ethics content in general and al-
500 most certainly lacking content specific to public health ethics.

The future of ethics education for public health nurses seems more promising with recent calls for revisions of the professional code of ethics, more emphasis
505 on human rights by the professional nursing association, a general trend toward more thorough discussions of ethics included in more recent textbooks, and recently published recommendations for education in public health ethics for public health professionals.
510 However, a lack of awareness of the importance of public health ethics education continues, as evidenced by the lack of mention of ethics in a recently proposed core curriculum for public health workers.[32] Improvements in public health ethics education for all public
515 health professionals are urgently needed to assure that

the knowledge and tools are readily available to address the ever more challenging ethical issues of the future.

References

1. Coughlin SS. Model curricula in public health ethics. *Am J Prev Med.* 1996;12:247–251.
2. Rossignol A, Goodmonson S. Are ethical topics in epidemiology included in the graduate epidemiology curricula? *Am J Epidemiol.* 1995;142:1265–1268.
3. Coughlin S, Etheredge G. On the need for ethics curricula in epidemiology. *Epidemiology.* 1995;6:566–567.
4. Stevens R. A study of public health nursing directors in state health departments. *Public Health Nursing.* 1995;12:432–435.
5. APHA Public Health Nursing Section. *The Definition and Role of Public Health Nursing—A Statement of the APHA Public Health Nursing Section.* Washington, D.C.: American Public Health Association, Public Health Nursing Section; 1996.
6. ANA. Code for Nurses with Interpretive Statements. Washington, D.C.: American Nurses Publishing; 1985.
7. Fowler M. Ethics: Relic or Resource? The Code for Nurses. *Am J Nurs.* 1999;99(3):56–57.
8. ANA. *Ethics and Human Rights.* Kansas City, MO: American Nurses Association; 1991.
9. Aroskar MA. Community health nurses—their most significant ethical decision-making problems. *Nurs Clin North Am.* 1989;24:967–975.
10. Folmar J, Coughlin SS, Bessinger R, Sacknoff D. Ethics in public health practice: a survey of public health nurses in southern Louisiana. *Public Health Nurs.* 1997;14:156–160.
11. Stanhope M, Lancaster J. *Community Health Nursing Process and Practice for Promoting Health.* St. Louis: CV Mosby Company; 1984.
12. Stanhope M, Lancaster J. *Community Health Nursing Process and Practice for Promoting Health.* 3rd ed. St. Louis: Mosby Year Book; 1992.
13. Gardner MS. *Public Health Nursing.* New York: The MacMillan Company; 1916.
14. Gardner MS. *Public Health Nursing.* 2nd ed. New York: The MacMillan Company; 1924.
15. Bryan ES. *The Art of Public Health Nursing.* Philadelphia: WB Saunders Company; 1935.
16. Rue CB. *The Public Health Nurse in the Community.* Philadelphia: WB Saunders Company; 1944.
17. Fromer M. *Community Health Care and the Nursing Process.* St. Louis: The CV Mosby Company; 1979.
18. Archer S, Fleshman R. *Community Health Nursing: Patterns and Practice.* North Scituate, MA: Duxbury Press; 1979.
19. Helvie C. *Community Health Nursing Theory and Process.* Philadelphia: Harper and Row, Publishers; 1981.
20. Fromer M. *Community Health Care and the Nursing Process.* 2nd ed. St. Louis: CV Mosby Company; 1983.
21. Burgess W., Ragland E. *Community Health Nursing: Philosophy, Process, Practice.* 1983.
22. Spradley B. *Community Health Nursing: Concepts and Practice.* Boston: Little, Brown, and Company; 1985.
23. Cookfair J. *Nursing Process and Practice in the Community.* St. Louis: Mosby Year Book; 1991.
24. Clark M. *Nursing in the Community.* Norwalk, CT: Appleton and Lange; 1992.
25. Helvie C. *Community Health Nursing Theory and Practice.* New York: Springer Publishing Company; 1991.
26. Spradley B., Allender J. *Community Health Nursing: Concepts and Practice.* Philadelphia: Lippincott; 1996.
27. Anderson E., McFarlane J. *Community as Partner: Theory and Practice in Nursing.* 2nd ed. Philadelphia: Lippincott; 1996.
28. Clemen-Stone S., McGuire S., Eigsti D. *Comprehensive Community Health Nursing: Family, Aggregate, and Community Practice.* St. Louis: Mosby; 1998.
29. McMurray A. *Community Health Nursing: Primary Care in Practice.* Melbourne: Churchill Livingston; 1990.
30. Chafey K. Caring is not enough: ethical paradigms for community-based care. In: Spradley B., Allender J., eds. *Readings in Community Health Nursing.* 5th ed. Philadelphia: Lippincott; 1997:211–220.
31. Coughlin SS, Katz WH, Mattison DR. Ethics instruction at schools of public health in the United States. *Am J Public Health.* 1999;89:768–770.
32. Gebbie KM. The Public Health Workforce: Key to Public Health Infrastructure. *Am J Public Health.* 1999;89:660–661.
33. Gardner M. *Public Health Nursing.* New York: The MacMillan Company; 1936.
34. Nursing NOPHN. *Manual of Public Health Nursing.* 3rd ed. New York: The MacMillan Company; 1939.
35. Gilbert R. *The Public Health Nurse and Her Patient.* New York: The Commonwealth Fund; 1940.

36. Grant A. *Nursing: A Community Health Service.* Philadelphia: WB Saunders; 1942.
37. Waterman T. *Nursing for Community Health.* Philadelphia: FA Davis Company; 1944.
38. Freeman R. *Public Health Nursing Practice.* Philadelphia: WB Saunders Company; 1950.
39. Freeman R. *Public Health Nursing Practice.* Philadelphia: WB Saunders Company; 1957.
40. Freeman R. *Public Health Nursing Practice.* 3rd ed. Philadelphia: WB Saunders Company; 1963.
41. Kallins E. *Textbook of Public Health Nursing.* St. Louis: CV Mosby Company; 1967.
42. Freeman R. *Community Health Nursing Practice.* Philadelphia: WB Saunders Company; 1970.
43. Tinkham C, Voorhies E. *Community Health Nursing: Evolution and Process.* New York: Appleton Century Crofts; 1972.
44. Leeser I, Tuchalski C, Carotenuto R. *Community Health Nursing.* Flushing, NY: Medical Examination Publishing Company; 1975.
45. Benson E, McDevitt J. *Community Health and Nursing Practice.* Englewood Cliffs, NJ: Prentice-Hall Inc.; 1976.
46. Leahy K, Cobb M, Jones M. *Community Health Nursing.* 3rd ed. New York: McGraw-Hill Book Company; 1977.
47. Clemen-Stone, Eigsti D, McGuire S. *Comprehensive Family and Community Health Nursing.* New York: McGraw-Hill Book Company; 1981.
48. Freeman R, Heinrich J. *Community Health Nursing Practice.* 2nd ed. Philadelphia: WB Saunders Company; 1981.
49. Jarvis L. *Community Health Nursing: Keeping the Public Healthy.* Philadelphia: FA Davis Company; 1981.
50. Spradley B. *Community Health Nursing Concepts and Practice.* Boston: Little Brown and Company; 1981.
51. Leahy K, Cobb M, Jones M. *Community Health Nursing.* 4th ed. New York: McGraw-Hill Book Company; 1982.
52. Jarvis L. *Community Health Nursing: Keeping the Public Healthy.* 2nd ed. Philadelphia: FA Davis Company; 1985.
53. Clemen-Stone S, Eigsti D, McGuire S. *Comprehensive Family and Community Health.* New York: McGraw-Hill Book Company; 1987.
54. Turner J, Chavigny K. *Community Health Nursing: An Epidemiologic Perspective Through the Nursing Process.* Philadelphia: JB Lippincott Company; 1988.
55. Bullough B, Bullough V. *Nursing in the Community.* St. Louis: CV Mosby Company; 1990.
56. Clemen-Stone S, Eigsti D, McGuire S. *Comprehensive Family and Community Health Nursing.* 3rd ed. St. Louis: CV Mosby Year Book; 1991.
57. Hertenstein-McKinnon T. *Community Health Nursing: A Case Study Approach.* Philadelphia: Lippincott; 1997.

Acknowledgments: This article was originally prepared for "Public Health Ethics: Research and Practice," a graduate course at the University of California, Berkeley, School of Public Health. The author thanks Dr. Patricia Buffler, Dr. Jodi Halpern, and Dr. Thomasine Kushner for the class content and their support and encouragement in this analysis.

Exercise for Article 5

Factual Questions

1. According to the researcher, what is the dominant perspective in the Code for Nurses?

2. What search terms were used to identify texts specific in the nursing specialty area of interest to the researcher?

3. When examining a text, what did the researcher check first to identify ethics-related content?

4. The researcher states that a utilitarian perspective was relatively rare in the textbooks that were studied. According to the researcher, is this perspective uncommon in public health literature?

5. The researcher reports that only two texts, both by the same authors, included all four theoretical perspectives. What are the authors' names?

6. How many of the texts of the 1990s included separate chapters on ethics?

7. According to the researcher, an "ideal text" would include what?

Questions for Discussion

8. The researcher mentions a two-stage sampling procedure. The first stage used a "convenience sample." What is your understanding of the meaning of this term? (See lines 130–132.)

9. An important concern in evaluating research reports is whether the researcher has described her or his research methods in sufficient detail to permit a replication of the study. Do you think that the methods used in this study are described in sufficient detail? Do you think that a replication by another researcher would be useful? Explain.

10. Do you think that the historical perspective obtained by analyzing textbooks published as early as 1916 is useful in helping you understand the issues examined and the results of this study? (See, for example, the first entry in Table 2.) Explain.

11. An inherent weakness of content analysis of written material is that the results describe only what selected authors (in this case, textbook authors) say and, presumably, believe. It cannot tell us what practicing public health nurses know and believe. Despite this weakness, do you think the content analysis presented in this article provides useful information? In general, do you think that content analysis is a useful research approach for examining important issues in nursing? Explain.

12. The researcher makes eight recommendations for improvement in the section of her report called "Recommendations for Improvement." Do you agree with all the recommendations? Do you think that some are more important than others? Explain.

Quality Ratings

Directions: Indicate your level of agreement with each of the following statements by circling a number from 5 for strongly agree (SA) to 1 for strongly disagree (SD). If you believe an item is not applicable to this research article, leave it blank. Be prepared to explain your ratings. When responding to criteria A and B below, keep in mind that brief titles and abstracts are conventional in published research.

A.   The title of the article is appropriate.

SA   5   4   3   2   1   SD

B.   The abstract provides an effective overview of the research article.

SA   5   4   3   2   1   SD

C.   The introduction establishes the importance of the study.

SA   5   4   3   2   1   SD

D.   The literature review establishes the context for the study.

SA   5   4   3   2   1   SD

E.   The research purpose, question, or hypothesis is clearly stated.

SA   5   4   3   2   1   SD

F.   The method of sampling is sound.

SA   5   4   3   2   1   SD

G.   Relevant demographics (for example, age, gender, and ethnicity) are described.

SA   5   4   3   2   1   SD

H.   Measurement procedures are adequate.

SA   5   4   3   2   1   SD

I.   All procedures have been described in sufficient detail to permit a replication of the study.

SA   5   4   3   2   1   SD

J.   The participants have been adequately protected from potential harm.

SA   5   4   3   2   1   SD

K.   The results are clearly described.

SA   5   4   3   2   1   SD

L.   The discussion/conclusion is appropriate.

SA   5   4   3   2   1   SD

M.   Despite any flaws, the report is worthy of publication.

SA   5   4   3   2   1   SD

Article 6

Buried Alive: The Presence of Nursing on Hospital Web Sites

Alice R. Boyington, RN, PhD, **Cheryl B. Jones**, RN, PhD, FAAN, **Dianna L. Wilson**, RN, MSN[*]

ABSTRACT

Background: Increasingly, hospitals are using sites on the World Wide Web (Web) to market their services and products and to advertise employment opportunities. These Web sites are a potential resource for information on the hospitals' nursing care and nurses' impact on patient outcomes.

Objective: The aim of this study was to explore the presence of nursing—accessible and visible data on nurses, nursing practice, or nursing care—on hospital Web sites.

Methods: A random sample of 50 hospital Web sites from the *U.S. News and World Report's* 2003 list of America's best hospitals was examined. A tool developed to capture the characteristics that denote a presence of nursing was used to examine hospital Web sites.

Results: All 50 sites had at least two occurrences of visible data in the form of pictures, graphics, or text that related to nurses, nursing care, or nursing practice. However, nurse-related content on these hospital Web sites was minimally to somewhat present and was frequently located on pages deep within the site.

Discussion: The presence of nursing on hospital Web sites could represent the importance of nursing, nursing practice, or nursing care for patients entering hospital systems. Instead, nursing content on hospital Web sites primarily focuses on nursing employment.

The portrayal of nurses in traditional forms of media has been well-documented. Historically, the importance of nurses and their contributions have been underplayed in the entertainment media (Kalisch &
5 Kalisch, 1982, 1986). References to nurses and their roles in healthcare delivery have been virtually omitted in the print media (Sigma Theta Tau International, 1997). Following the healthcare quality initiative launched in 1996 by the Institute of Medicine, the nurs-
10 ing shortage and the impact on the quality of care have been emphasized through the mass communications media; consumers have been reminded that decreased levels of nurse staffing can have a negative impact on the quality of care and patient safety (Aiken, Clarke,
15 Cheung, Sloane, & Silber, 2003; Kovner, Jones, Zhan, Gergen, & Basu, 2002; Needleman, Buerhaus, Mattke, Stewart, & Zelevinsky, 2002; Page, 2004). Although the public has been informed through the media about the problems or failures of the nursing profession, of-
20 ten, the many accomplishments of nurses are not shown (Gordon, 2005).

A newer type of communications media, the World Wide Web (Web) on the Internet, is popular in the United States and is used throughout the healthcare
25 industry. For instance, Johnson & Johnson developed a Web site (www.discovernursing.com) as part of its advertising program, "The Campaign for Nursing's Future." The site contains in-depth information on nursing education and careers and targets the recruit-
30 ment of potential candidates into the profession. Countless Web sites offer health and medical information, and healthcare consumers increasingly visit those sites (Fox & Fallows, 2003).

The popularity of the Web among healthcare con-
35 sumers has not gone unnoticed by hospital marketing professionals. More and more hospitals are using the Web as a marketing tool to promote their healthcare products, services, and employment opportunities (Fell & Shepherd, 2001; Sanchez, 2000; Sanchez & Maier-
40 Donati, 1999). Hospital Web sites have been analyzed with respect to content and purpose. For example, Sanchez and Maier-Donati (1999) derived descriptive categories of hospital Web site characteristics from reviews of the literature and Web sites to guide site
45 evaluation and recommendations for site content. Zingmond, Lim, Etter, and Carlisle (2001) reported that hospitals were using the Web for marketing care that emphasized wellness, health information, and quality of services and that promoted their affiliated
50 physicians. Other researchers included indicators of quality of care in their evaluation of Web sites (Kind, Wheeler, Robinson, & Cabana, 2004). Fell and Shepherd (2001) reported on specific online marketing ac-

[*]*Alice R. Boyington* is associate professor, School of Nursing, University of North Carolina at Chapel Hill. *Cheryl B. Jones* is associate professor, School of Nursing, University of North Carolina at Chapel Hill. *Dianna L. Wilson* is staff nurse, Alamance Regional Medical Center, Burlington, North Carolina.

tivities such as employee recruitment. Although it is
unknown whether a nursing product was marketed on
any of the hospital Web sites in the above studies, the
published reports have not mentioned nurses or nursing
care.

The lack of nurse-related findings in the above reports support the observations of Gordon (2005) and
Carty, Coughlin, Kasoff, and Sullivan (2000) that
nurses (but not physicians) are invisible on hospital
Web sites. Medicine is the focus of advertising that
highlights descriptions of physician accomplishments
and pictures of physicians providing care to patients. A
lack of a presence of nursing on hospital Web sites
may be one of the standard industry practices that un-
dervalue nurses' knowledge and skills and that underestimate contributions by nurses to hospitals and to
patient care (Weinberg, 2003).

Although the low visibility of nurses and nursing
care on hospital Web sites is apparent from casual observation, quantitative data to document this invisibility
and promote changes in the current focus on medical
care and physicians are not found. The absence of messages about the contributions, qualifications, and accomplishments of nurses on hospital Web sites may
subtly but negatively influence the public's perception
of care that they can expect to receive in hospitals.
Omission of positive messages about nurses and their
work on hospital Web sites also hinders efforts to attract people available and qualified to work in hospitals
and individuals who might want to enter the nursing
profession. The most damaging effect of this omission
is the subliminal message that misleads the public by
failing to recognize nurses as important members of the
healthcare team who are responsible for overseeing
most of the care patients will receive.

The purpose of the study was to determine (a)
whether there is a presence of nursing, (b) the accessibility (based on site depth of the nurse-related content)
of the presence of nursing, and (c) the characteristics of
the presence of nursing on U.S. hospital Web sites.
Literature from healthcare marketing (Fell & Shepherd,
2001; Sanchez, 2000; Sanchez & Maier-Donati, 1999),
information science (Atzeni, Merialdo, & Sindoni,
2002; Morkes & Nielsen, 1997; Pirouz, 1997), and
nursing science (Kalisch & Kalisch, 1982, 1986; Sigma
Theta Tau International, 1997) were used to guide the
study.

Methods

Sample

A descriptive design was used to explore Web sites
for hospitals and medical centers[1] ranked in 2003 by
the *U.S. News and World Report*. This ranking of
"America's Best Hospitals" is reported annually in
their print and Web media so that hospitals can use that

ranking to market services. This ranking is more likely
to be used by healthcare consumers than, for example,
the lesser known "HCIA-Sachs Institute 100 Top Hospitals" or "Solucient's 100 Top Hospitals."

The 2003 online publication of the rankings (*U.S.
News and World Report*, 2003) included Web site addresses for all 203 of the ranked hospitals in 17 specialties. Seventeen of the 203 hospitals appeared on an
"Honor Roll" that denoted leadership and high-quality
care in six or more medical specialties. The sample (*N*
= 50) for this study included all 17 hospitals on the
"Honor Roll" and an additional 33 selected from the
remaining 186 hospitals using an electronic random
number generator. A statistician was consulted to verify the number of hospitals needed and the selection
process; the sample represented 25% of the total population of hospitals on the list and was deemed sufficient
for the study. Each of the hospital Web sites in the
sample was accessed via the link provided on the *U.S.
News and World Report* Web site.

Development and Use of the Study Checklist

The development of the Presence of Nursing: Hospital Web Site Checklist included in-depth preliminary
work to identify and categorize nurse-related content
on hospital Web sites. Forty hospitals ranked on the
U.S. News and World Report Web site in 2002 were
reviewed, and a list of characteristics relevant to the
nursing profession was compiled. The research team,
composed of members with expertise in current nursing
practice, healthcare systems, healthcare informatics,
and the communications media, reviewed this initial
list of characteristics.

As a pilot test, the research team used the checklist
to examine four hospital Web sites selected from hospitals in the 2002 list. Items to capture the geographical
location and type of each hospital were added to the
checklist because of this pilot session. The final list of
75 characteristics was organized into five major categories (Table 1), facilitating the flow of the review of
hospital Web sites: (a) hospital Web site home page
(13 characteristics); (b) nursing organization (17 characteristics); (c) nursing employment, recruitment, and
retention (19 characteristics); (d) nursing education and
research (18 characteristics); and (e) nursing news (8
characteristics). Each category included an *other* item
to capture nurse-related characteristics not on the
checklist. This categorical list was formatted in tabular
form for purposes of data collection; one column was
designated for placement of a checkmark to indicate
that the characteristic was present on the Web site.

During the checklist development phase of the
study, the research team created a scale to rate the total
number of characteristics (range = 0–75) found on hospital Web sites: (a) absent = *no characteristics*, (b)
minimally present = *1–15 characteristics*, (c) somewhat present = *16–37 characteristics*, (d) moderately

---

[1] The term "hospitals" will denote both hospitals and medical centers.

present = *38–59 characteristics*, and (e) very present = *60–75 characteristics.*

Table 1
Categories and Examples of Characteristics from Presence of Nursing Hospital Web Site Checklist

Category	Characteristic
Hospital Web site home page	Direct link to nursing Web site on home page
	Nursing link under health professions
	Recognition of nursing care on hospital Web site
Nursing organization	Identification of nursing leaders or administrators
	Mission or vision of nursing department
	Nurse-to-patient ratios or nurse-staffing
Nursing employment, recruitment, and retention	List of positions
	Job descriptions
	Programs for new graduate nurses (preceptorship, nurse internship, or residency)
Nursing education and research	Descriptions of continuing education programs
	Nursing research center or department or program
	Emphasis on importance of nursing research
Nursing news	Online nursing newsletter
	Professional awards or recognition
	Educational achievements

Note. For more information about the checklist, please contact the authors.

A second scale was developed to measure the accessibility of the presence of nursing on the hospital Web sites. Accessibility was defined according to the site depth of the nurse-related content and was based on the number of pages the user had to click through to get to that content (Pirouz, 1997). Because Web content placed deep within a site is considered to be invisible (Gil, n.d.), this definition of accessibility was used to determine the visibility of nurse-related content on hospital Web sites. The categories to denote accessibility and visibility of nurse-related content were the following: (a) absent = *having to click through six or more pages*, (b) minimally accessible = *having to click through five pages*, (c) somewhat accessible = *having to click through four pages*, (d) moderately accessible = *having to click through three pages*, and (e) very accessible = *having to click through one or two pages.*

Items in the investigator-developed checklist were selected based on the review of literature in healthcare marketing, information science, and nursing science. An iterative process was used in the development and pilot testing of the checklist to categorize nurse-related content on hospital Web sites. Although no reliability and validity tests were conducted, the varied expertise of the research team members was used to verify the face validity of the checklist.

Data Collection

Three members of the research team used the study checklist to evaluate the first five Web sites in the selected sample ($N = 50$), and findings were compared to promote a consistent evaluation of sites. All discrepancies in data collection were discussed to reach 100% consensus and to establish a plan for consistently reviewing the study Web sites. The remaining 45 hospital Web sites were accessed and evaluated. The time period for the data collection was kept to a minimum to decrease the influence of any site changes and updates. The checklist data were entered into a Microsoft Excel database.

Analysis

Data were analyzed using descriptive statistics to determine whether there was a presence of nursing on the hospital Web sites. Frequencies and other descriptive statistics were used to describe the demographic characteristics of the hospitals, the proportion of hospital Web sites with a presence of nursing, the accessibility of nursing information on the hospital Web sites, and the distribution of the individual characteristics reflecting the presence of nursing.

Findings

All hospital Web sites in the sample ($N = 50$) were available using the links on the Web version of the "America's Best Hospitals 2003" (*U.S. News and World Report*, 2003). The hospitals with these Web sites were located throughout the United States: 12 hospitals (24%) were in the North Atlantic region, 6 (12%) were in the South Atlantic region, 14 (28%) were in the North Central region, 7 (14%) were in the South Central region, and 11 (22%) were in the Pacific and Mountain region. Of 50 hospitals, 47 (94%) were academic institutions, 2 (4%) were nonacademic, and 1 was unidentifiable.

All 50 Web sites had at least two occurrences of visible data in the form of pictures, graphics, or text that related to nurses, nursing care, or nursing practice. From the possible 75 characteristics on the checklist, the number identified for the 50 sites ranged from 2 to 42 ($M = 18.2$; $SD = 10.56$). Twenty-three (46%) sites had minimal nursing presence (1–15 characteristics), 23 (46%) had somewhat of a presence (16–37 characteristics), 4 (8%) had a moderate presence (38–59 characteristics), and no site achieved a rating of very present (60–75 characteristics).

The rating of accessibility of the presence of nursing reflected the number of pages that the reviewer had to click through to get to a characteristic of the presence of nursing (Table 2). The presence of nursing on 11 (22%) sites was rated as invisible, and only 1 (2%) site displayed a presence that was very accessible.

Descriptive information for the categories of characteristics assessed on the 50 hospital Web sites is presented in Table 3. All but one hospital Web site had some nursing information in the nursing employment,

245 recruitment, and retention category. The category with the fewest nurse-related characteristics present on hospital Web sites was nursing news, invisible on most (68%) sites. No themes or additions to the checklist were revealed in the items listed as *other*. Details of the characteristics within the five categories follow.

Table 2
Accessibility of the Presence of Nursing on Hospital Web Sites (n = 50)

Accessibility of nursing presence	n	%
Absent (≥6 clicks)	11	22
Minimally accessible (5 clicks)	16	32
Somewhat accessible (4 clicks)	11	22
Moderately accessible (3 clicks)	11	22
Very accessible (1–2 clicks)	1	2

Note. The accessibility of the presence of nursing on these hospital Web sites was measured by the number of pages the user had to click through to find the nurse-related content.

Table 3
Descriptive Information on Nursing Presence on 50 Hospital Web Sites

Number of characteristics per category	Hospital Web sites n (%)	Characteristics observed per category M (SD)
Hospital Web site home page		3.34 (2.18)
0	4 (8)	
1–3	26 (52)	
4–6	15 (30)	
7–9	5 (10)	
10–12	0	
13	0	
Nursing organization		2.24 (2.44)
0	17 (34)	
1–3	17 (34)	
4–6	14 (28)	
7–9	2 (4)	
10–12	0	
13–15	0	
16–17	0	
Nursing employment, recruitment, and retention		8.22 (3.35)
0	1 (2)	
1–3	4 (8)	
4–6	10 (20)	
7–9	18 (36)	
10–12	12 (24)	
13–15	5 (10)	
16–18	0	
19	0	
Nursing education and research		3.08 (3.37)
0	14 (28)	
1–3	18 (36)	
4–6	9 (18)	
7–9	5 (10)	
10–12	4 (8)	
13–15	0	
16–18	0	
Nursing news		1.22 (2.34)
0	34 (68)	
1–3	9 (18)	
4–6	2 (4)	
7–8	5 (10)	

Hospital Web Site Home Page

250 A hospital home page was considered to be the Web page that served as an entry to the remaining pages on the site. Most Web sites (*n* = 44, 88%) had an internal search engine on the hospital home page. The search engine allowed a site visitor to look for specific information on pages throughout the site. Using *nurse* 255 and *nursing* as key search words disclosed nurse-related content on 24 (48%) sites, but on many sites, several links had to be followed to locate nurse-related content. Magnet status, the highest level of recognition awarded by the American Nurses Credentialing Center 260 to nursing services in the United States and international healthcare communities, was acknowledged with a Magnet symbol on only five (10%) home pages, although 15 of the 50 (30%) hospitals had been granted this prestigious award, as was noted on pages deeper in 265 the site. Six hospital Web site home pages (12%) included testimonials from patients regarding the quality of nursing care as they perceived it. On five (10%) of the home pages, quality nursing care was identified as an important aspect of services provided.

Nursing Organization

270 Nurse leaders or administrators in the organization were identified on 10 (20%) hospital Web sites. A nursing philosophy was stated on 11 (22%) hospital Web sites, information on the missions or visions of their nursing departments was provided on 9 (18%), 275 and a nursing slogan or phrase was displayed on 7 (14%). Although nursing departments are typically organized by specialty areas, and job vacancies may be organized and advertised accordingly, a description of specialty areas was shown on only 15 (30%) sites. At 280 least one message from a staff nurse describing nursing practice within the organization was found on 19 (38%) sites.

Nursing Employment, Recruitment, and Retention

Information on how to apply for vacant positions in nursing was given on 44 (88%) sites, job vacancies 285 with a direct link to employment opportunities for nurses were listed on 43 (86%), and a prospective nurse could complete an online employment application on 40 (80%). Employee benefits were listed on 42 (84%) sites. Innovative scheduling options other than 290 the traditional 8- and 12-hr shifts were described on 11 (22%) sites. Recognition of clinical expertise, such as a clinical ladders program, was present on 11 (22%) sites, and some form of nurse retention program was identified on 6 (12%) sites.

295 Information on a summer internship/externship program for nursing students who are about to enter their senior year of study was given on 23 (46%) sites. Details on the programs indicated that nursing students worked under the supervision of a nurse within the 300 organization, practiced skills learned in their nursing program, learned about the real world of nursing in

practice, and began an acculturation into the organization.

A flexible work schedule that allowed nursing students to attend classes and work at the hospital was described on one Web site.

Nursing Education and Research

A link to a college or school of nursing affiliated with the organization was present on 17 (34%) sites, although a collaboration between nursing services and a college or school of nursing on projects or research that might indicate endeavors to study and improve nursing practice was identified on only 4 (8%). Nursing research endeavors had very little visibility; a nursing research center or department was listed on 10 (20%) sites, but none described research programs or initiatives.

Nursing News

A way to communicate information on the achievements of nurses, such as an online nursing newsletter or a list of current nurse-related events, was present on only six (12%) of the sites. Professional awards were published on 12 (24%) sites, and educational achievements were noted on 6 (12%) sites.

Limitations

One limitation is that hospital Web sites not on the list of "America's Best Hospitals 2003" (*U.S. News and World Report*, 2003) or not in the sample used from this list could produce different results. A potential bias in sample selection exists because 94% of the hospitals were academic health centers. The instrument to evaluate the presence of nursing on the hospital Web sites was developed specifically for this project and may not contain an exhaustive list of characteristics. The data also were collected and analyzed primarily by a single investigator and are thus subject to bias. However, attempts were made to overcome this limitation by defining the characteristics clearly, using specific criteria for evaluation and comparing the reviews of three researchers on five randomly selected sites. As with any research, potential bias exists when subjective data are interpreted.

Discussion

In this study, hospital Web sites varied greatly in content and appearance, as did the presence of nursing on those sites. Although all Web sites studied had at least two characteristics denoting a presence of nursing, the nurse-related content was not located easily. This result is consistent with the Woodhull study (Sigma Theta Tau International, 1997) that reported minimal nurse-related content in print publications. Although perhaps unintentional, the unstated message revealed by findings in this study of hospital Web sites is that the nursing profession is not important, nurses do not play an important role in the delivery of services, and in turn, the nursing profession does not warrant space on hospital Web sites.

Further data analysis of this sample of hospital Web sites revealed that the presence of nursing, often located several pages deep within the site, is somewhat difficult to access and may be invisible to site visitors. Content located deep within a Web site is deemed invisible (Gil, n.d.) and is not indexed in the major external search engines (Spink, Jansen, Wolfram, & Saracevic, 2002). Thus, Web users who desire specific information on nursing services in hospitals may have minimal search yields and have little patience with searching the Web further.

Visitors to hospital Web site home pages, both prospective patients and potential nurse applicants, may have difficulty locating the information they seek. Users of the Web are known to scan pages, pick out individual words, or conduct a keyword search (Morkes & Nielsen, 1997) to fulfill their information need. Users move on to another site if they do not retrieve what they want efficiently. Thus, the empty search results on the terms *nurse* or *nursing* that were evident on more than half of the hospital Web sites in this sample could be a barrier to locating relevant information.

The primary reason patients are admitted to healthcare facilities is to receive care that they cannot receive elsewhere. Given that nurses are generally the largest group of healthcare professionals within most hospitals and they provide hands-on care to patients during most hospital admissions (Jones & Lusk, 2002), it follows that prospective patients may seek specific information on nursing care to better inform decisions on care delivery. The small number of hospital Web sites in the current study that described characteristics of the nursing organization reveals that prospective patients cannot obtain information on nurse leaders, areas with specialty nurses, nurse-to-patient ratios, staff skill mix, or advanced practice nurses. This lack of information perpetuates the view of Gordon (2005) that the public has a poor understanding of the complexity of nursing care and its influence on patient outcomes and further supports that information that would enlighten the public on the crucial service it receives from nurses is basically absent from information on hospital Web sites (Gordon).

Interestingly, today's healthcare consumers are becoming more selective in choosing a hospital and are seeking information on the quality of agencies and care providers. Yet only one-third of the 15 hospitals in this sample that had achieved the Magnet status for excellence in nursing elected to place the Magnet symbol on the hospital home page. If information such as Magnet status is buried within a Web site, site visitors may not be aware of this recognition of nursing excellence.

All sites had some nurse recruitment content, and by far, the one category where hospitals excelled was by providing information on nurse employment opportunities. Surprisingly, only 27 (54%) sites provided job descriptions with information on requirements for education, experience, and skills, which may communicate that nurses are interchangeable at the agency. Less information was provided on innovative retention strategies. The omission of detailed employment information is a missed opportunity for hospitals to display information that would attract nurses to the agency and perhaps attract individuals into the profession.

Exploration of characteristics of nursing education and research revealed that very few hospital Web sites contained any information on collaborative activities between nursing services in the agencies and schools or colleges of nursing. Such relationships may attract nurses who wish to advance their formal education.

Also, very few sites showcased the organization's nurses. For example, in very few instances were nurses recognized for professional awards or educational achievements. Inclusion of this information would inform nurses about the successes of others, make them feel valuable when their achievements are acknowledged publicly, and communicate to others outside the organization that nurses are supported and valued.

The overall finding that hospital Web sites lack a strong presence of nursing is consistent with the literature (Gordon, 2005; Sigma Theta Tau International, 1997). Hospital marketers have not focused on nurses or nursing care on Web sites but have focused on medicine and employee recruitment (Fell & Shepherd, 2001; Sanchez, 2000; Zingmond et al., 2001). Hospital marketers could collaborate with nurses to ensure the presence of nursing on the Web sites.

Thus, implications for practice center on the involvement of nurses on hospital committees charged with Web site development. Similarly, nurse leaders should collaborate with hospital marketers and Web site developers to ensure that sites promote the nursing profession. Examples of information on nursing on hospital Web sites that should be included are the role of nurses in quality improvement initiatives, specialty areas of care and nurse-patient ratios in these areas, achievements of nursing staff, results of nursing research, and collaborations between nurses and professionals from other disciplines as team members in care delivery. Putting this information on the Web will communicate the important role that nurses play in care delivery, that nurses are valued, and that they are essential members of the healthcare team.

Although nurse-related characteristics were used to denote the presence of nursing in this study, the characteristics that are appropriate and beneficial on hospital Web sites are largely unknown. Further study is needed to determine the important characteristics that should be present on hospital Web sites, including those that are relevant to nursing. This might involve an examination of the checklist developed for this study to verify validity, ensuring that all relevant characteristics and information are captured. In addition, research could show whether the five categories of characteristics and individual characteristics of presence should be weighted in terms of the importance or quality. Finally, studies with larger and more current samples would contribute to advancing our knowledge of the evolving presence of nursing found in this newer form of communication medium by U.S. hospitals.

In keeping with previous research, the lack of visible data in the form of pictures, graphics, or text related to nurses, nursing care, or nursing practice in all communications media must be recognized as a serious concern (Sigma Theta Tau International, 1997). The professional standards upon which nurses base their practice, instead of being advertised, remain unstated, which contributes to the public's lack of comprehension of nurses. This omission sends a message to the public that nurses are not valued as critical members of the healthcare team or as major contributors to hospital services. Hospital Web sites can be used to inform the public of the important role that nurses play in patient outcomes and the role that their collaboration with other disciplines plays to make comprehensive care possible. Because of publicizing the roles and contributions of nurses on hospital Web sites, the nursing profession could attain a visible presence.

References

Aiken, L. H., Clarke, S. P., Cheung, R. B., Sloane, D. M., & Silber, J. H. (2003). Educational levels of hospital nurses and surgical patient mortality. *Journal of the American Medical Association, 290*, 1617–1623.

Atzeni, P., Merialdo, P., & Sindoni, G. (2002). Web site evaluation: Methodology and case study [Electronic version]. *Lecture Notes in Computer Science, 2465*, 253–263.

Carty, B., Coughlin, C., Kasoff, J., & Sullivan, B. (2000). Where is the nursing presence on the medical center's Web site? *The Journal of Nursing Administration, 30*, 569–570.

Fell, D., & Shepherd, C. D. (2001). Hospitals and the Web: A maturing relationship [Electronic version]. *Marketing Health Services, 21*, 36–38.

Fox, S., & Fallows, D. (2003). *Internet health resources.* Retrieved February 15, 2005, from http://www.pewinternet.org/pdfs/PIP_Health_Report_July_2003.pdf

Gil, P. (n.d.). 2 Layers of visibility, 4 layers of specialization. In *Tutorial: The layers of the World Wide Web.* Retrieved February, 19, 2005, from http://netforbeginners.about.com/cs/invisibleweb/a/web_four_layers.htm

Gordon, S. (2005). *Nursing against the odds: How health care cost cutting, media stereotypes, and medical hubris undermine nurses and patient care.* Ithaca, NY: Cornell University Press.

Jones, C. B., & Lusk, S. L. (2002). Incorporating health services research into nursing doctoral programs. *Nursing Outlook, 50*, 225–231.

Kalisch, P. A., & Kalisch, B. J. (1982). Nurses on prime-time television. [Electronic version]. *The American Journal of Nursing, 82*, 264–270.

Kalisch, P. A., & Kalisch, B. J. (1986). A comparative analysis of nurse and physician characters in the entertainment media. [Electronic version]. *Journal of Advanced Nursing, 11*, 179–195.

Kind, T., Wheeler, K. L., Robinson, B., & Cabana, M. D. (2004). Do the leading children's hospitals have quality Web sites? A description of children's hospital Web sites [Electronic version]. *Journal of Medical Internet Research, 6*, e20.

Kovner, C., Jones, C., Zhan, C., Gergen, P. J., & Basu, J. (2002). Nurse staffing and postsurgical adverse events: An analysis of administrative data from a sample of U.S. hospitals, 1990–1996. *Health Services Research, 37*, 611–629.

Morkes, J., & Nielsen, J. (1997). *Concise, SCANNABLE, and objective: How to write for the Web.* Retrieved February 19, 2005, from http://www.useit.com/papers/webwriting/writing.html

Needleman, J., Buerhaus, P., Mattke, S., Stewart, M., & Zelevinsky, K. (2002). Nurse-staffing levels and the quality of care in hospitals. *The New England Journal of Medicine, 346*, 1715–1722.

Page, A. (2004). *Keeping patients safe: Transforming the work environment of nurses.* Committee on the Work Environment for Nurses and Patient Safety. Washington, DC: National Academy Press.

Pirouz, R. (1997). *Click Here. Web Communication Design.* Indianapolis, IN: New Riders.

Sanchez, P. M. (2000). The potential of hospital Web site marketing. *Health Marketing Quarterly, 18*, 45–57.

Sanchez, P. M., & Maier-Donati, P. (1999). Hospital Web site marketing: Analysis, issues, and trends. *Journal of Hospital Marketing, 13*, 87–103.

Sigma Theta Tau International (1997). *The Woodhull study on nursing and the future: Health care's invisible partner (final report)*. Indianapolis, IN: Center Nursing Press Sigma Theta Tau International.

Spink, A., Jansen, B. J., Wolfram, D., & Saracevic, T. (2002). From e-sex to e-commerce: Web search changes. *IEEE Computer, 35*, 107–109.

U.S. News and World Report (2003). America's best hospitals 2003. Retrieved December 15, 2003, from http://www.usnews.com/usnrew/nycu/health/hosptl/directory/hosp_alph.htm

Weinberg, D. B. (2003). *Code green: Money-driven hospitals and the dismantling of nursing*. Ithaca, NY: Cornell University Press.

Zingmond, D. S., Lim, Y. W., Ettner, S. L., & Carlisle, D. M. (2001). Information superhighway or billboards by the roadside? An analysis of hospital Web sites [Electronic version]. *The Western Journal of Medicine, 175*, 385–391.

Address correspondence to: Alice R. Boyington, RN, PhD, School of Nursing, CB 7460, University of North Carolina at Chapel Hill, Chapel Hill, NC 27599-7460. E-mail: ddboying@email.unc.edu

Exercise for Article 6

Factual Questions

1. The sample of hospitals for this study represented what percentage of the total population of hospitals?

2. A pilot test was conducted using how many hospital Web sites?

3. How did the researchers define "accessibility"?

4. All 50 sites had at least two occurrences of "visible data." This type of data was in what form?

5. According to the researchers, in what one category did the hospital Web sites "excel"?

6. The researchers explicitly state what implication?

Questions for Discussion

7. Is it important to know that the additional 17 hospitals were selected at random? Explain. (See lines 115–119.)

8. A sample of the 75 characteristics is shown in Table 1. Is the sample sufficient? Would it help to see all 75? (See lines 141–149 and Table 1.)

9. In your opinion, how important is "accessibility"? (See lines 163–179.)

10. The researchers mention "face validity." What is your understanding of the meaning of this term? (See lines 186–188.)

11. Overall, how helpful are Tables 2 and 3 in giving you an overview of the results of this study? Would the results be as clear without the tables? Explain.

12. In your opinion, how important is the limitation described in lines 323–328?

Quality Ratings

Directions: Indicate your level of agreement with each of the following statements by circling a number from 5 for strongly agree (SA) to 1 for strongly disagree (SD). If you believe an item is not applicable to this research article, leave it blank. Be prepared to explain your ratings. When responding to criteria A and B below, keep in mind that brief titles and abstracts are conventional in published research.

A. The title of the article is appropriate.

    SA   5   4   3   2   1   SD

B. The abstract provides an effective overview of the research article.

    SA   5   4   3   2   1   SD

C. The introduction establishes the importance of the study.

    SA   5   4   3   2   1   SD

D. The literature review establishes the context for the study.

    SA   5   4   3   2   1   SD

E. The research purpose, question, or hypothesis is clearly stated.

    SA   5   4   3   2   1   SD

F. The method of sampling is sound.

    SA   5   4   3   2   1   SD

G. Relevant demographics (for example, age, gender, and ethnicity) are described.

    SA   5   4   3   2   1   SD

H. Measurement procedures are adequate.

    SA   5   4   3   2   1   SD

I. All procedures have been described in sufficient detail to permit a replication of the study.

    SA   5   4   3   2   1   SD

J. The participants have been adequately protected from potential harm.

    SA   5   4   3   2   1   SD

K. The results are clearly described.

    SA   5   4   3   2   1   SD

L.   The discussion/conclusion is appropriate.

SA   5   4   3   2   1   SD

M.   Despite any flaws, the report is worthy of publication.

SA   5   4   3   2   1   SD

Article 7

Relationships of Assertiveness, Depression, and Social Support Among Older Nursing Home Residents

Daniel L. Segal, PhD[*]

ABSTRACT. This study assessed the relationships of assertiveness, depression, and social support among nursing home residents. The sample included 50 older nursing home residents (mean age = 75 years; 75% female; 92% Caucasian). There was a significant correlation between assertiveness and depression ($r = -.33$), but the correlations between social support and depression ($r = -.15$) and between social support and assertiveness ($r = -.03$) were small and nonsignificant. The correlation between overall physical health (a subjective self-rating) and depression was strong and negative ($r = -.50$), with lower levels of health associated with higher depression. An implication of this study is that an intervention for depression among nursing home residents that is targeted at increasing assertiveness and bolstering health status may be more effective than the one that solely targets social support.

From *Behavior Modification*, 29, 689–695. Copyright © 2005 by Sage Publications, Inc. Reprinted with permission.

Most older adults prefer and are successful at "aging in place"—that is, maintaining their independence in their own home. For the frailest and most debilitated older adults, however, nursing home placement is of-
5 tentimes necessary. About 5% of older adults live in a nursing home at any point in time, a figure that has remained stable since the early 1970s (National Center for Health Statistics, 2002). Depression is one of the most prevalent and serious psychological problems
10 among nursing home residents. About 15% to 50% of residents suffer from diagnosable depression (see review by Streim & Katz, 1996).

Social support is also an important factor in mental health among nursing home residents, and psychosocial
15 interventions often seek to bolster the resident's level of supportive relationships.

Assertiveness training plays an important role in traditional behavioral therapy with adults, and it has been recommended as a treatment component among
20 older adults with diverse psychological problems as well (Gambrill, 1986). Assertiveness may be def[ined as] the ability to express one's thoughts, feelings, [and] and rights in an open, honest, and appropriate [way. A] key component of assertiveness is that the comm[unica-]
25 tion does not violate the rights of others, as is [true] in aggressive communications. It is logical that [nursing] home residents with good assertiveness skill[s would] more often get what they want and need. Havi[ng one's] needs met is a natural goal of all people, and [failure to]
30 do so could lead to depression or other psyc[hological] problems. Personal control has long been not[ed to im-]prove mental health among nursing home residents (see Langer & Rodin, 1976), and assertiveness training would likely help residents express more clearly their
35 desires and needs.

Two studies have examined links between assertiveness, depression, and social support among older adult groups. Among 69 community-dwelling older adults, Kogan, Van Hasselt, Hersen, and Kabacoff
40 (1995) found that those who are less assertive and have less social support are at increased risk for depression. Among 100 visually impaired older adults, Hersen et al. (1995) reported that higher levels of social support and assertiveness were associated with lower levels of
45 depression. Assertiveness may rightly be an important skill among nursing home residents because workers at the institutional setting may not be as attuned to the emotional needs of a passive resident and the workers may respond poorly to the aggressive and acting-out
50 resident. However, little is known about the nature and impact of assertiveness in long-term care settings. The purpose of this study, therefore, was to assess relationships of assertiveness, social support, and depression among nursing home residents, thus extending the lit-
55 erature to a unique population.

Method

Participants were recruited at several local nursing homes. Staff identified potential volunteers who were ostensibly free of cognitive impairment. Participants

[*]Daniel L. Segal received his PhD in clinical psychology from the University of Miami in 1992. He is an associate professor in the Department of Psychology at the University of Colorado at Colorado Springs. His research interests include diagnostic and assessment issues in geropsychology, suicide prevention and aging, bereavement, and personality disorders across the lifespan.

41

completed anonymously the following self-report
measures: Wolpe-Lazarus Assertiveness Scale
(WLAS) (Wolpe & Lazarus, 1966), Geriatric Depression Scale (GDS) (Yesavage et al., 1983), and the Social Support List of Interactions (SSL12-I) (Kempen &
van Eijk, 1995). The WLAS consists of 30 yes/no
items and measures levels of assertive behavior. Scores
can range from 0 to 30, with higher scores reflecting
higher levels of assertiveness. The GDS includes 30
yes/no items and evaluates depressive symptoms specifically among older adults. Scores can range from 0
to 30, with higher scores indicating higher levels of
depression. The SSL12-I is a 12-item measure of received social support that has good psychometric properties among community-dwelling older adults. Respondents indicate on a 4-point scale the extent to
which they received a specific type of support from a
member of their primary social network (1 = seldom or
never, 2 = now and then, 3 = regularly, 4 = very often).
Scores can range from 12 to 48 with higher scores corresponding to higher levels of support. The sample
included 50 older adult residents (mean age = 74.9
years, SD = 11.9, age range = 50–96 years; 75% female; 92% Caucasian).

Results and Discussion

The mean WLAS was 18.1 (SD = 4.1), the mean
GDS was 9.0 (SD = 5.5), and the mean SSL12-I was
29.2 (SD = 7.3). The correlation between the WLAS
and GDS was moderate and negative ($r = -.33$, $p <
.05$), with lower levels of assertiveness associated with
higher depression. The correlation between the SSL12-
I and GDS was small and nonsignificant ($r = -.15$, ns),
indicating a slight negative relationship between overall support and depression. Similarly, the correlation
between the SSL12-I and WLAS was small and nonsignificant ($r = -.03$, ns), indicating almost no relationship between overall support and assertiveness. Next,
correlations between a subjective self-rating of overall
physical health status (0–100 scale, higher scores indicating better health) and the WLAS, GDS, and SSL12-
I were calculated. As expected, the correlation between
physical health and GDS was strong and negative
($r = -.50$, $p < .01$), with poorer health associated with
higher depression. The correlation between health and
WLAS was positive in direction but small and nonsignificant ($r = .17$, ns), indicating little relationship between health and assertiveness. Similarly, the correlation between health and SSL12-I was also small and
nonsignificant ($r = -.02$, ns), indicating no relationship
between health and overall support. The slight relationship between health and assertiveness is an encouraging sign because it suggests that assertiveness (which is
primarily achieved through effective verbalizations) is
not limited to only the least physically impaired nursing home residents. Finally, gender differences on all
dependent measures were examined (independent t

tests) and no significant differences were found (all ps
> .05).

Notably, the mean assertion and depression scores
among nursing home residents are consistent with
means on identical measures in community-dwelling
older adults (assertion M = 19.1; depression M = 7.9;
Kogan et al., 1995) and visually impaired older adults
(assertion M = 18.3; depression M = 10.4; Hersen et
al., 1995), suggesting that the higher functioning group
of nursing home residents are no more depressed and
no less assertive than other samples of older persons.
Regarding social support, our nursing home sample
appeared to show somewhat higher levels of overall
support than community older adults in the normative
sample (N = 5,279, M = 25.5) in the SSL12-I validation study (Kempen & van Eijk, 1995). This may possibly be due to the nature of institutional living and the
large numbers of support staff and health care personnel.

The correlational results regarding the moderate
negative association between assertion and depression
are consistent with data from community-dwelling
older adults ($r = -.36$; Kogan et al., 1995) and visually
impaired older adults ($r = -.29$; Hersen et al., 1995),
suggesting a pervasive relationship among the variables in diverse older adult samples and extending the
findings to nursing home residents. Contrary to the
literature, the relationship between social support and
depression among nursing home residents was weaker
than the one reported in community-dwelling older
adults ($r = -.50$; Kogan et al., 1995) and visually impaired older adults ($r = -.48$; Hersen et al., 1995). The
relationship between assertiveness and overall support
in this study was almost nonexistent, also contrary to
earlier reports in which the relationship was moderate
and positive in direction. Our results are consistent
with prior research showing no gender differences
among older adults in assertiveness, depression, and
social support using similar assessment tools (Hersen et
al., 1995; Kogan et al., 1995). This study also suggests
a strong negative relationship between health status and
depression among nursing home residents. An implication of this study is that an intervention for depression
among nursing home residents that is targeted at increasing assertiveness and bolstering health status may
be more effective than the one that solely targets social
support.

Several limitations are offered concerning this
study. First, the sample size was modest and the sample
was almost exclusively Caucasian. Future studies with
more diverse nursing home residents would add to the
knowledge base in this area. All measures were self-
report, and future studies with structured interviews
and behavioral assessments would be stronger. We are
also concerned somewhat about the extent to which the
WLAS is content-valid for older adults. Notably, a
measure of assertive behavior competence has been
developed specifically for use with community-

dwelling older adults (Northrop & Edelstein, 1998), and this measure appears to be a good choice for future research in the area. A final limitation was that partici-
175 pants were likely the highest functioning of residents because they were required to be able to complete the measures independently and were selected out if there was any overt cognitive impairment (although no formal screening for cognitive impairment was done),
180 thus limiting generalizability to more frail nursing home residents. Cognitive screening should be done in future studies. Nonetheless, results of this study suggest a potentially important relationship between assertiveness and depression among nursing home residents.
185 Finally, it is imperative to highlight that there are many types of interventions to combat depression among nursing home residents: behavioral interventions to increase exercise, participation in social activities, and other pleasurable activities; cognitive inter-
190 ventions to reduce depressogenic thoughts; and pharmacotherapy, to name a few. (The interested reader is referred to Molinari, 2000, for a comprehensive description of psychological issues and interventions unique to long-term care settings.) The present data
195 suggest that training in assertiveness may be yet one additional option for psychosocial intervention in nursing homes. A controlled outcome study is warranted in which intensive assertiveness training is compared to a control group of nursing home residents who do not
200 receive such training. Only with such a study can cause-and-effect statements be made about the role that assertiveness skills training may play in the reduction of depressive symptoms among nursing home residents.

References

Gambrill, E. B. (1986). Social skills training with the elderly. In C. R. Hollin & P. Trower (Eds.), *Handbook of social skills training: Applications across the lifespan* (pp. 211–238). New York: Pergamon.

Hersen, M., Kabacoff, R. L., Van Hasselt, V. B., Null, J. A., Ryan, C. F., Melton, M. A., et al. (1995). Assertiveness, depression, and social support in older visually impaired adults. *Journal of Visual Impairment and Blindness, 7,* 524–530.

Kempen, G. I. J. M., & van Eijk, L. M. (1995). The psychometric properties of the SSL12-I, a short scale for measuring social support in the elderly. *Social Indicators Research, 35,* 303–312.

Kogan, S. E., Van Hasselt, B. V., Hersen, M., & Kabacoff, I. R. (1995). Relationship of depression, assertiveness, and social support in community-dwelling older adults. *Journal of Clinical Geropsychology, 1,* 157–163.

Langer, E. J., & Rodin, J. (1976). The effects of choice and enhanced personal responsibility for the aged: A field experiment in an institutional setting. *Journal of Personality and Social Psychology, 34,* 191–198.

Molinari, V. (Ed.). (2000). *Professional psychology in long-term care: A comprehensive guide.* New York: Hatherleigh.

National Center for Health Statistics. (2002). *Health, United States, 2002.* Hyattsville, MD: Author.

Northrop, L. M. E., & Edelstein, B. A. (1998). An assertive-behavior competence inventory for older adults. *Journal of Clinical Geropsychology, 4,* 315–331.

Streim, J. E., & Katz, I. R. (1996). Clinical psychiatry in the nursing home. In E. W. Busse & D. G. Blazer (Eds.), *Textbook of geriatric psychiatry* (2nd ed., pp. 413–432). Washington, DC: American Psychiatric Press.

Wolpe, J., & Lazarus, A. A. (1966). *Behavior therapy techniques.* New York: Pergamon.

Yesavage, J. A., Brink, T. L., Rose, T. L., Lum, O., Huang, V., Adey, M., et al. (1983). Development and validation of a geriatric depression screening scale: A preliminary report. *Journal of Psychiatric Research, 17,* 314–317.

Acknowledgment: The author thanks Jessica Corcoran, MA, for assistance with data collection and data entry.

Exercise for Article 7

Factual Questions

1. Were the participants cognitively impaired?

2. Was the mean score for the participants on the GDS near the highest possible score on this instrument? Explain.

3. What is the value of the correlation coefficient for the relationship between the WLAS and the GDS?

4. Was the relationship between SSL12-I and GDS strong?

5. Was the correlation coefficient for the relationship between SSL12-I and GDS statistically significant?

6. Was the relationship between physical health and GDS a direct relationship *or* an inverse relationship?

Questions for Discussion

7. The researcher obtained participants from "several" nursing homes. Is this better than obtaining them from a single nursing home? Explain. (See lines 56–57.)

8. The researcher characterizes the *r* of −.33 in line 86 as "moderate." Do you agree with this characterization? Explain.

9. In lines 85–107, the researcher reports the values of six correlation coefficients. Which one of these indicates the strongest relationship? Explain the basis for your choice.

10. In lines 85–107, the researcher reports the values of six correlation coefficients. Which one of these indicates the weakest relationship? Explain the basis for your choice.

11. For the *r* of −.50 in line 100, the researcher indicates that "*p* < .01." What is your understanding of the meaning of the symbol "*p*"? What is your understanding of ".01"?

12. Do you agree with the researcher that a different type of study is needed in order to determine the role of assertiveness skills training in the reduction of depressive symptoms? Explain. (See lines 197–204.)

Quality Ratings

Directions: Indicate your level of agreement with each of the following statements by circling a number from 5 for strongly agree (SA) to 1 for strongly disagree (SD). If you believe an item is not applicable to this research article, leave it blank. Be prepared to explain your ratings. When responding to criteria A and B below, keep in mind that brief titles and abstracts are conventional in published research.

A.   The title of the article is appropriate.

SA   5   4   3   2   1   SD

B.   The abstract provides an effective overview of the research article.

SA   5   4   3   2   1   SD

C.   The introduction establishes the importance of the study.

SA   5   4   3   2   1   SD

D.   The literature review establishes the context for the study.

SA   5   4   3   2   1   SD

E.   The research purpose, question, or hypothesis is clearly stated.

SA   5   4   3   2   1   SD

F.   The method of sampling is sound.

SA   5   4   3   2   1   SD

G.   Relevant demographics (for example, age, gender, and ethnicity) are described.

SA   5   4   3   2   1   SD

H.   Measurement procedures are adequate.

SA   5   4   3   2   1   SD

I.   All procedures have been described in sufficient detail to permit a replication of the study.

SA   5   4   3   2   1   SD

J.   The participants have been adequately protected from potential harm.

SA   5   4   3   2   1   SD

K.   The results are clearly described.

SA   5   4   3   2   1   SD

L.   The discussion/conclusion is appropriate.

SA   5   4   3   2   1   SD

M.   Despite any flaws, the report is worthy of publication.

SA   5   4   3   2   1   SD

Article 8

Extending Work Environment Research into Home Health Settings

Linda Flynn, PhD, RN[*]

ABSTRACT. Organizational attributes in work environments that support nursing practice are theoretically associated with superior nurse and patient outcomes, and lower frequencies of adverse events. This study explored associations between organizational support for nursing practice in home health care agencies and (a) the frequency of nurse-reported adverse events, (b) nurse-assessed quality of care, (c) nurse job satisfaction, and (d) nurses' intentions to leave their employing agency. Data were collected from a sample of 137 registered nurses employed as home health staff nurses in the United States and analyzed using descriptive techniques and bivariate correlation. As anticipated, organizational support for nursing was negatively associated with nurse-reported adverse patient events and intent to leave, and positively associated with nurse-assessed quality of care and job satisfaction. These findings may be helpful to nursing administrators who seek to create work environments in home health agencies that maximize patient outcomes and nurse satisfaction.

From *Western Journal of Nursing Research*, *29*, 200–212. Copyright © 2007 by Sage Publications, Inc. Reprinted with permission.

A large body of literature indicates that the presence of a set of organizational attributes of the nursing work environment, highly valued by hospital-based staff nurses as important to the support of their profes-
5 sional practice, are associated with positive inpatient outcomes and lower rates of adverse events, including mortality (Aiken, Havens, & Sloane, 2000). Although recent studies have demonstrated that this same set of supportive work environment attributes is similarly
10 valued by staff nurses who practice in the rapidly expanding arena of home health care, few studies have investigated the associations between these supportive attributes and home care outcomes. Using survey methodology, the current study is among the first to
15 explore associations between organizational attributes that support nursing practice, as indicative of a supportive work environment, and nurse-reported adverse patient events in home health care.

According to sociological theories of organizations
20 and professions, organizational attributes in health care settings that support clinical practice—such as decentralization of authority, managerial support, interdisciplinary collaboration, continuity of care, effective communication channels, and adequate resources—are
25 essential to the ability of clinicians, such as nurses, to identify and respond to fluctuating patient conditions. Thus, by supporting clinical surveillance and response, these organizational attributes contribute to high-quality patient care. Theorists further propose that
30 health care organizations that exhibit these supportive attributes will experience higher rates of positive patient outcomes, fewer adverse patient events, and higher levels of job satisfaction and retention among clinical staff (Flood & Scott, 1987; Freidson, 1970;
35 Peters & McKeon, 1998; Shortell & Kaluzny, 1988; Strauss, 1975).

During the past two decades, a large body of literature has been amassed providing empirical support for these propositions. Measured by the Nursing Work
40 Index–Revised (NWI-R; Aiken & Patrician, 2000), attributes of the nursing work environment that support professional practice have been linked to higher levels of job satisfaction, lower rates of burnout, lower rates of needlestick injuries, and lower rates of injury-related
45 disability among hospital-based staff nurses (Aiken, Clarke, & Sloane, 2002; Aiken & Sloane, 1997; Clarke, Sloane, & Aiken, 2002; Laschinger, Almost, & Tuer-Hodes, 2003; O'Brien-Pallas et al., 2004; Tigert & Laschinger, 2004). The presence of these supportive
50 work environment attributes has also been associated with a higher level of quality inpatient care, fewer adverse events, lower mortality, and higher levels of satisfaction with care among hospitalized patients (Aiken, Sloane, & Lake, 1997; Aiken, Sloane, Lake, Sochalski,
55 & Weber, 1999; Aiken, Smith, & Lake, 1994; Boyle, 2004; Estabrooks, Midodzi, Cummings, Ricker, & Giovannetti, 2005; Flynn & Aiken, 2002; Vahey, Aiken, Sloane, Clarke, & Vargas, 2004).

From these theoretical and empirical foundations, a
60 conceptual model of nursing organization and outcomes was developed (Aiken, Lake, Sochalski, & Sloane, 1997) and later refined (Aiken, Clarke, &

[*]*Linda Flynn* is an assistant professor at The New Jersey Collaborating Center for Nursing, College of Nursing, Rutgers, State University of New Jersey, at Newark.

Sloane, 2002). The model conceptualizes *organizational support* for nursing practice and nurse staffing levels, indicated by nurse-to-patient ratios, as related but distinct variables (Figure 1). *Organizational support for nursing practice*, defined as a set of core attributes of a supportive work environment that are modifiable through managerial decisions, includes those organizational attributes pertaining to (a) resource adequacy, (b) nurse autonomy, (c) nurse control of practice environment, and (d) facilitation of collegial nurse–physician relationships. According to the conceptual model, nurses provide clinical surveillance and early detection of adverse patient events and attempt to modify processes of care based on these assessments. The model further indicates that higher organizational support for nursing practice directly influences and enhances the processes and quality of care, promoting superior nurse and patient outcomes (Aiken, Clarke, & Sloane, 2002).

The research regarding supportive organizational attributes and outcomes has been conducted predominantly in hospitals. Although the empirical literature regarding supportive organizational attributes has guided efforts of hospital nursing administrators to create work environments that promote positive outcomes and prevent adverse events, administrators in the rapidly growing practice area of home health care have had little evidence to guide similar endeavors. This is unfortunate, as nursing leaders in home health care increasingly recognize the need to implement evidence-based initiatives within their agencies that support nursing practice, enhance nurse retention, promote quality patient care, and maximize positive patient outcomes (Ellenbecker & Cushman, 2001; Shaughnessy et al., 2002; Smith-Stoner, 2004). Prompted by recent federal initiatives that monitor the degree to which several selected patient outcomes are achieved, home care administrators are particularly interested in promoting patients' safe self-administration of medications, the effective management of acute and chronic pain, the prevention of unplanned hospitalizations, and the ability of patients to be maintained safely in the community on discharge from home health care services (Centers for Medicare and Medicaid Services [CMS], 2005; Shaughnessy et al., 2002).

Although recent studies (Flynn, Carryer, & Budge, 2005; Flynn & Deatrick, 2003) indicate that home care staff nurses similarly value the same set of supportive work environment attributes that are valued by hospital-based staff nurses, relationships between supportive work environments and positive staff and patient outcomes as proposed by sociological theories of organizations and professions (Flood & Scott, 1987; Freidson, 1970; Shortell & Kaluzny, 1988; Strauss, 1975), and as depicted by the nursing organization and outcomes model (Aiken, Clarke, & Sloane, 2002), have rarely been tested in home health care.

Purpose of the Study

The purpose of the current study was to preliminarily explore a subset of relationships depicted by the nursing organization and outcomes model. Associations between organizational support for nursing practice, as an indicator of a supportive work environment, in home health care agencies and (a) nurse-assessed quality of care; (b) adverse patient outcomes, such as nurse-reported frequencies of patient-administered medication errors, uncontrolled acute or chronic pain, unplanned hospitalization, and lack of preparation of patient or family member to manage care at time of discharge; (c) nurse job satisfaction; and (d) nurses' intentions to leave were investigated.

Operational Definitions

Consistent with the model of nursing organization and outcomes, *a supportive nursing work environment* was operationally defined as a score on the Organizational Support for Nursing subscale of the Nursing Work Index–Revised (Aiken, Clarke, & Sloane, 2002); higher scores indicate a more supportive work environment. A score on a 4-point rating scale operationally defined *job satisfaction* and *nurses' assessment of the quality of care* provided by their home care agency. The frequencies of (a) patient-administered medication errors, (b) uncontrolled acute or chronic pain, (c) unplanned hospitalization while receiving home health services, and (d) patient and/or family's lack of preparation to manage care at the time of discharge from home health care services were also operationally defined as scores on 4-point rating scales. The intent to leave an employing home health agency was operationally defined by a response to an item that elicited the respondents' intentions to resign from their current home health care agency within the next 12 months.

Design

The current study utilized a descriptive, correlational design. A modified Dillman (2000) survey method was used for data collection.

Sample

To obtain a sample of registered nurses (RNs) currently employed in home health staff nurse positions, 645 names were randomly selected to receive a mailed research packet from a list of subscribers to a prominent journal for home health care nurses. All 645 of the randomly selected subscribers resided in the United States. A total of 25 surveys were returned by the post office as undeliverable. Of the 620 delivered surveys, a response rate of 52.4% produced surveys from 325 nurse respondents. Among these respondents, 68 indicated that they no longer practiced in home health care, and an additional 120 indicated that although they worked in home health care, they were not employed in staff RN positions. Thus, the sample for the current study consisted of 137 RNs, employed as home health staff nurses, from 38 states. A total of 59% of respon-

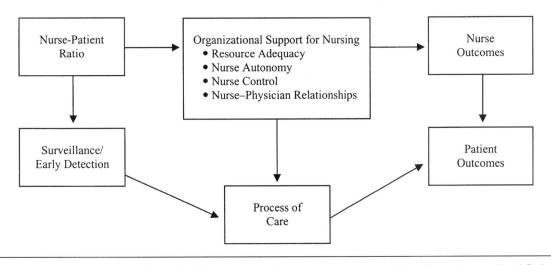

Figure 1. Aiken, Clarke, and Sloane (2002). Hospital staffing, organization, and quality of care: Cross-national findings. International Journal for Quality in Health Care, 14(1), 5 and 13. By permission of Oxford University Press.

dents worked full-time, 25% worked part-time, and 16% worked on a per-diem basis. Other demographic characteristics are presented in Table 1.

Table 1
Sample Characteristics (N = 137)

Variable	M	SD
Age	50.35	9.29
Years at employing agency	9.92	7.67

	n	%
Gender		
Female	134	97.8
Male	3	2.2
Race		
White	121	88.3
African American	6	4.4
Hispanic	2	1.5
Asian/Pacific Islander	4	2.9
Native American	2	1.5
Not reported	2	1.5
Nursing education		
Diploma	17	12.4
Associate degree	44	32.1
BSN	53	38.7
MSN or higher	22	16.1
Not reported	1	0.7

Note. BSN = bachelor of science in nursing; MSN = master of science in nursing.

Method

175   A key methodological feature of previous hospital-based work environment research has been the use of nurse surveys as a source of data regarding organizational attributes (Aiken, Clarke, & Sloane, 2002; Aiken, Clarke, Sloane, Sochalski, & Silber, 2002) and
180 nurse-reported patient outcomes (Sochalski, 2001, 2004). Staff RNs have been identified as reliable informants regarding organizational attributes and patient outcomes because of their close proximity to patients and their familiarity with the organizational features
185 present in their work environment. Therefore, extending work environment research into home health care,

the current study surveyed staff RNs using the same survey items and measures that have been demonstrated reliable and valid in previous hospital-based
190 research (Aiken, Clarke, Sloane, & Sochalski, 2001; Aiken, Clarke, Sloane, Sochalski, Busse et al., 2001; Sochalski, 2001, 2004).

To ensure that rights of participants were protected, the study protocol was reviewed and approved by the
195 university's Institutional Review Board prior to data collection. Selected subscribers to a home health care nursing journal received a research packet, mailed to their home, which contained a cover letter and survey. In accordance with a modified Dillman (2000) survey
200 method, a reminder postcard was mailed 1 week after the packet was sent, a repeat survey was sent to nonrespondents 2 weeks after the initial survey mailing, and a final reminder postcard was sent to the remaining nonrespondents 4 weeks after the initial survey mail-
205 ing.

Measures

The Organizational Support for Nursing subscale, a 9-item subset of the NWI-R, was used to measure the organization's support for nursing practice, defined as a set of core attributes of a supportive work environ-
210 ment that are modifiable through managerial decision making (Aiken, Clarke, & Sloane, 2002). The Organizational Support for Nursing subscale contains items measuring the presence of modifiable organizational features, influenced by administrative decisions, in-
215 cluding (a) resource adequacy, (b) nurse autonomy, (c) nurse control over the practice environment, and (d) nurse–physician relationships. Nurses were asked to rate the degree to which each item on the subscale is present in their current home health care agency; they
220 were not requested to identify their employing home health agency by name or location. Using a summative rating scale ranging from 1 (*strongly disagree* the attribute is present) to 4 (*strongly agree* the attribute is

Table 2
Descriptive Statistics and Correlation Coefficients of Organization Support and Study Variables (N = 137)

Variable	Minimum	Maximum	M	SD	Pearson Correlation
Job satisfaction	1	4	2.87	.96	.31***
Care quality	1	4	3.37	.65	.49***
Medication errors	1	4	2.36	.76	−.22**
Uncontrolled pain	1	4	2.41	.84	−.30***
Unprepared at discharge	1	4	2.28	.95	−.35***
Hospitalization	1	4	2.90	.68	−.13

**p < .01, ***p < .001 (2-tailed).

present), possible scores range from 9 to 36. Higher scores indicate a higher organizational support for nursing practice. The validity of the subscale was demonstrated in samples of hospital-based nurses (Aiken & Patrician, 2000), and in samples of U.S. home care and district nurses in New Zealand (Flynn, 2003; Flynn, Carryer, & Budge, 2005; Flynn & Deatrick, 2003). An internal consistency reliability of .91 was observed in a sample of 10,319 hospital-based nurses. In the current study, the internal consistency reliability coefficient was .84 in the sample of home care RNs.

The survey also included items, found to be reliable in previous research, that elicit nurses' responses regarding the frequency of adverse patient events (Aiken, Clarke, Sloane, & Sochalski, 2001; Sochalski, 2001, 2004). For the current study, some of these items underwent minor changes in wording to reflect home care practice. The adverse events selected for the current study are prevalent among care patients sensitive to organizational support, and their reduction has been identified by the Centers for Medicare and Medicaid (CMS) as important quality indicators in home health care practice (CMS, 2005; Shaughnessy et al., 2002). Home care staff nurses were instructed to rate on a 4-point scale, from 1 (*never*) to 4 (*frequently*), how often these events occurred to patients in their caseload during the past year.

As a measure of job satisfaction, a single item asked nurses to rate the level of satisfaction with their job on a 4-point scale ranging from 1 (*very dissatisfied*) to 4 (*very satisfied*). Similarly, a single item with a 4-point rating scale ranging from 1 (*poor*) to 4 (*excellent*) measured nurses' assessment of the quality of care delivered by their home health care agency. Nurses' intent to leave was measured by an item asking respondents to indicate if they do or do not have plans to leave their home health agency within the next 12 months. These global items, which in the current study substituted the word *home health care agency* for *hospital*, have been repeatedly used as measures among hospital-based nurses and have consistently correlated with theoretically relevant variables (Aiken, Clarke, & Sloane, 2002; Aiken, Clarke, Sloane, Sochalski, Busse et al., 2001; Sochalski, 2001, 2004).

Analysis of Data

Correlation coefficients were determined between

organizational support and (a) quality of care, (b) reported frequency of each adverse event, and (c) nurse job satisfaction. A logistic regression model estimated the effects of organizational support and job satisfaction on nurses' intent to leave. The demographic variables of level of nursing education and age have been identified in theoretical models as key individual nurse characteristics that may influence intent to leave (Ellenbecker, 2004; Lake, 1998). To control for these individual characteristics, the demographic variables of age and nursing education were included in the regression model.

Findings

Descriptive information for study variables and bivariate correlation coefficients between organizational support and study variables are presented in Table 2. The mean organizational support score and standard deviation for this sample, M = 25.94 (SD = 4.98), were slightly higher than those published for hospitals on the same measure, which ranged from M = 21.6 (SD = 1.8) to M = 23.0 (SD = .9), across 303 international hospitals (Aiken, Clarke, & Sloane, 2002). As anticipated, organizational support for nursing, as an indicator of a supportive work environment, was positively correlated with job satisfaction and nurse-assessed quality of care, and negatively correlated with reported frequencies of patient-administered medication errors, uncontrolled acute or chronic pain, and the inability of patients and/or family members to manage care on discharge from home health care services. Results indicated no significant correlation between organizational support and the frequency of unplanned hospitalization.

Regarding nurses' intentions to leave their agency, logistic regression was used to estimate the effects of organizational support and job satisfaction on nurses' intentions to leave, controlling for the demographic variables of age and nursing education. Among the two demographic variables, only nurses' *level of education*, defined as the highest nursing degree obtained, was significantly associated with intent to leave, in that nurses with a baccalaureate degree were significantly less likely to indicate an intent to leave than nurses with a master's degree or higher, odds ratio (OR) = .086 (.008, .963), p = .047. Although job satisfaction had no significant effect on intent to leave, organizational support was a significant predictor of nurses' intentions to leave their agency, OR = .792 (.692, .907), p = .001. The odds of intent to leave decreased as the score on the Organizational Support for Nursing subscale increased, indicating that higher organizational support for nursing was associated with lower odds on nurses' intentions to leave their employing agency. To interpret this association within a context of nurse retention, for every 1-point increase on the Organizational Support for Nursing subscale, the odds of nurses not planning to leave their agency increased by 26%, OR = 1.26 (1.10, 1.44), p = .001.

Discussion

Hospital-based work environment research has made significant contributions to the health services and nursing literatures regarding the impact of organizational attributes on nurses and patients. The current study is among the first to extend this line of inquiry into the home health care practice setting. Findings from the current study are consistent with the nursing organization and outcomes model (Aiken, Clarke, & Sloane, 2002) and indicate that the presence of attributes in nurses' work environments that reflect organizational support for nursing practice is associated with higher levels of nurse-reported quality of care, fewer nurse-reported adverse patient events, higher nurse job satisfaction, and lower odds of nurses' intentions to leave their employer.

Home health care administrators should carefully consider such findings. Throughout recent years, efforts to control costs have resulted in widespread organizational changes among some home health care agencies, including reductions in support services, disruptions in continuity of patient assignments, limitations in nurses' influence over practice decisions, and reductions in the number of middle-management positions that consequently limit nurses' managerial support (Narayan, 1999; Smith, Maloy, & Hawkins, 2000; Smith-Stoner, 2004). It is ironic to note that many of these managerial-induced changes adversely affect those organizational attributes that provide support for nursing practice, and that were associated in the current study with fewer adverse events.

Study results also indicate that the presence of agency attributes reflecting organizational support for nursing are associated with higher levels of nurse job satisfaction, and reduced odds on nurses' intentions to leave their employing home health agency. These findings may prove helpful to nursing administrators in home health care agencies that are becoming increasingly challenged by a shortfall of nursing staff. Estimates indicate that by 2020, the demand for home care nurses will reach a peak in that the number of RNs needed for home care practice will be twice the number needed in 2000. Unfortunately, this peak demand for home care nurses will occur at a time when the United States will have an estimated shortfall of one million nurses across practice sectors. Many home care agencies are already experiencing difficulty recruiting and retaining nurses, as evidenced by rising attrition and vacancy rates nationwide (Humphrey, 2005; U.S. General Accounting Office, 2001). Results from the current study indicate the implementation and maintenance of agency attributes that support nursing practice may increase nurse retention. Consequently, administrative initiatives undertaken in home health agencies to ensure adequate support services for clinical staff, access to competent and supportive managers, continuity of patient assignments, and facilitation of interdisciplinary collaboration appear to be worth the investment in light of the potential benefits.

No relationship was found in the current study between organizational support and nurse-reported frequencies of unplanned hospitalizations. This relationship can be further explored in subsequent larger studies linking work environment attributes with patient-level data.

Some limitations of the current study should be noted. Although nurses are considered reliable informants regarding their patients' experiences and conditions, individual nurses' reports regarding the frequency of adverse events may be inaccurate or biased. A second limitation is that the relatively small sample size limits analytic power. Third, because the study was not designed to obtain responses from multiple nurses employed in identifiable agencies, aggregation of measures to the organizational level was not possible. To prevent these limitations, subsequent larger and more comprehensive studies can be designed that sample large numbers of nurses from each agency, aggregate responses to the organizational level, and link organizational-level estimates of study variables with risk adjusted, patient-level outcome data.

Despite the limitations, the current study provides preliminary evidence for the relationships between attributes of the nursing work environment that reflect organizational support for nursing and nurses' reports regarding the frequencies of adverse patient events in home health care. By creating work environments that support nursing practice, the home health care sector may make significant strides toward achieving two important aims—retaining a nursing workforce sufficient in size to meet the growing demand, and reducing adverse events among the vulnerable recipients of home health care services.

References

Aiken, L. H., Clarke, S. P., & Sloane, D. M. (2002). Hospital staffing, organization, and quality of care: Cross-national findings. *International Journal for Quality in Health Care, 4*, 5–13.

Aiken, L. H., Clarke, S. P., Sloane, D. M., & Sochalski, J. A. (2001). An international perspective on hospital nurses' work environments: The case for reform. *Policy, Politics, & Nursing Practice, 2*, 255–263.

Aiken, L. H., Clarke, S. P., Sloane, D. M., Sochalski, J. A., Busse, R., Clarke, H., et al. (2001). Nurses' reports on hospital care in five countries. *Health Affairs, 20*, 43–53.

Aiken, L. H., Clarke, S. P., Sloane, D. M., Sochalski, J., & Silber, J. H. (2002). Hospital nurse staffing and patient mortality, nurse burnout, and job dissatisfaction. *Journal of the American Medical Association, 288*, 1987–1993.

Aiken, L. H., Havens, D. S., & Sloane, D. M. (2000). The Magnet Nursing Services Recognition Program: A comparison of two groups of Magnet hospitals. *American Journal of Nursing, 100*, 26–36.

Aiken, L. H., Lake, E. T., Sochalski, J., & Sloane, D. M. (1997). Design of an outcomes study of the organization of hospital AIDS care. *Research in the Sociology of Health Care, 14*, 3–26.

Aiken, L. H., & Patrician, P. (2000). Measuring organizational attributes of hospitals: The revised Nursing Work Index. *Nursing Research, 49*, 146–153.

Aiken, L. H., & Sloane, D. M. (1997). Effects of organizational innovations in AIDS care on burnout among urban hospital nurses. *Work and Occupations, 24*, 453–477.

Aiken, L. H., Sloane, D. M., & Lake, E. T. (1997). Satisfaction with inpatient acquired immunodeficiency syndrome care. *Medical Care, 35*, 948–962.

Aiken, L. H., Sloane, D. M., & Lake, E. T., Sochalski, J. A., & Weber, A. L. (1999). Organization and outcomes of inpatient AIDS care. *Medical Care, 37*, 760–772.

Aiken, L. H., Smith, H. L., & Lake, E. T. (1994). Lower Medicare mortality among a set of hospitals known for good nursing care. *Medical Care, 32*, 771–787.

Boyle, S. M. (2004). Nursing unit characteristics and patient outcomes. *Nursing Economics, 22*, 111–123.

Centers for Medicare and Medicaid Services. (2005). Home health compare. Retrieved October 14, 2005, from www.cms.hhs.gov/quality/hhqi/september2005Revisons.pdf

Clarke, S. P., Sloane, D. M., & Aiken, L. H. (2002). Effects of hospital staffing and organizational climate on needlestick injuries to nurses. *American Journal of Public Health, 92*, 1115–1119.

Dillman, D. A. (2000). *Mail and Internet surveys: The tailored design method.* New York: John Wiley.

Ellenbecker, C. H. (2004). A theoretical model of job retention for home health care nurses. *Journal of Advanced Nursing, 47*, 303–310.

Ellenbecker, C., & Cushman, M. J. (2001, July). The nursing shortage: A home care agency perspective. *Caring, 20*, 28–32.

Estabrooks, C. A., Midodzi, W. K., Cummings, G. G., Ricker, K. L., & Giovannetti, P. (2005). The impact of hospital nursing characteristics on 30-day mortality. *Nursing Research, 54*, 74–84.

Flood, A. B., & Scott, W. R. (1987). *Hospital structure and performance.* Baltimore: Johns Hopkins University Press.

Flynn, L. (2003). Agency characteristics most valued by home care nurses: Findings of a nationwide survey. *Home Healthcare Nurse, 21*, 812–817.

Flynn, L., & Aiken, L. H. (2002). Does international nurse recruitment influence practice values in U.S. hospitals? *Journal of Nursing Scholarship, 34*, 67–73.

Flynn, L., Carryer, J., & Budge, C. (2005). Organizational attributes valued by hospital, home care, and district nurses in the United States and New Zealand. *Journal of Nursing Scholarship, 37*, 67–72.

Flynn, L., & Deatrick, J. A. (2003). Home care nurses' descriptions of important agency attributes. *Journal of Nursing Scholarship, 35*, 385–390.

Freidson, E. (1970). *Profession of medicine.* New York: Dodd, Mead.

Humphrey, C. (2005). Exciting new research on recruitment and retention. *Home Healthcare Nurse, 23*, 347.

Lake, E. T. (1998). Advances in understanding and predicting nurse turnover. *Research in the Sociology of Health Care, 15*, 147–171.

Laschinger, H. K., Almost, J., & Ther-Hodes, D. (2003). Workplace empowerment and magnet hospital characteristics: Making the link. *Journal of Nursing Administration, 33*, 410–422.

Narayan, M. C. (1999). Survey highlights the concerns of home healthcare nurses. *Home Healthcare Nurse, 17*, 57.

O'Brien-Pallas, L., Shamian, J., Thomson, D., Alksnis, C., Koehoorn, M., Kerr, M., et al. (2004). Work related disability in Canadian nurses. *Journal of Nursing Scholarship, 36*, 352–357.

Peters, D. A., & McKeon, T. (1998). *Transforming home care: Quality, cost, and data management.* Gaithersburg, MD: Aspen.

Shaughnessy, P. W., Hittle, D. F., Crisler, K. S., Powell, M. C., Richard, A. A., Kramer, A. M., et al. (2002). Improving patient outcomes of home health care: Findings from two demonstration trials of outcome-based quality improvement. *Journal of the American Geriatrics Society, 50*, 1354–1364.

Shortell, S. M., & Kaluzny, A. D. (Eds.). (1988). *Health care management: A text in organizational theory and behavior.* New York: John Wiley.

Smith, B. M., Maloy, K. A., & Hawkins, D. J. (2000). An examination of Medicare home health services. *Care Management Journals, 2*, 238–247.

Smith-Stoner, M. (2004). Home care nurses' perceptions of agency and supervisory characteristics: Working in the rain. *Home Healthcare Nurse, 22*, 536–546.

Sochalski, J. A. (2001). Quality of care, nurse staffing, and patient outcomes. *Policy, Politics, and Nursing Practice, 2*, 9–18.

Sochalski, J. A. (2004). Is more better? The relationship between nurse staffing and the quality of nursing care in hospitals. *Medical Care, 42*(2 Supp), 1167–1172.

Strauss, A. (1975). *Professions, work and careers.* New Brunswick, NJ: Transaction Books.

Tigert, J. A., & Laschinger, H. K. S. (2004). Critical care nurses' perceptions of workplace empowerment, magnet hospital attributes, and mental health. *Dynamics, 15*, 19–23.

U.S. General Accounting Office. (2001, July). *Nursing workforce: Emerging nursing shortages due to multiple factors* (GAO-01-944). Retrieved October 17, 2005, from www.gao.gov/new.items/d011944.pdf

Vahey, D. C., Aiken, L. H., Sloane, D. M., Clarke, S. P., & Vargas, D. (2004). Nurse burnout and patient satisfaction. *Medical Care, 42*(2, Suppl. II), 57–66.

Acknowledgment: This study was funded by a research grant from Rutgers College of Nursing.

Exercise for Article 8

Factual Questions

1. How was "a supportive nursing work environment" operationally defined by the researcher?

2. The samples from this study were from how many states?

3. When was the repeat survey sent to nonrespondents?

4. What is the value of the Pearson correlation coefficient for the relationship between job satisfaction and organizational support? Is it statistically significant?

5. Which one of the study variables had the strongest relationship with organizational support as indicated by the Pearson correlation coefficients?

6. Was there a significant correlation between organizational support and frequency of unplanned hospitalization?

Questions for Discussion

7. Is it important to know that the names were drawn at random? Explain. (See lines 156–160.)

8. In your opinion, is the response rate of 52.4% a sufficiently high rate? Explain. (See lines 163–165.)

9. Are you surprised that the researcher conducted four mailings (a survey, a postcard, a repeat survey, and a final postcard)? Explain. (See lines 199–205.)

10. Would you characterize the Pearson correlation coefficient of −.22 in Table 2 as representing a very strong relationship? Explain.

11. Table 2 contains both positive and negative values of Pearson correlation coefficients. What is your understanding of the difference in meaning between positive and negative values?

12. In your opinion, does this study show that organizational support *causes* job satisfaction? Explain.

Quality Ratings

Directions: Indicate your level of agreement with each of the following statements by circling a number from 5 for strongly agree (SA) to 1 for strongly disagree (SD). If you believe an item is not applicable to this research article, leave it blank. Be prepared to explain your ratings. When responding to criteria A and B below, keep in mind that brief titles and abstracts are conventional in published research.

A. The title of the article is appropriate.

   SA   5   4   3   2   1   SD

B. The abstract provides an effective overview of the research article.

   SA   5   4   3   2   1   SD

C. The introduction establishes the importance of the study.

   SA   5   4   3   2   1   SD

D. The literature review establishes the context for the study.

   SA   5   4   3   2   1   SD

E. The research purpose, question, or hypothesis is clearly stated.

   SA   5   4   3   2   1   SD

F. The method of sampling is sound.

   SA   5   4   3   2   1   SD

G. Relevant demographics (for example, age, gender, and ethnicity) are described.

   SA   5   4   3   2   1   SD

H. Measurement procedures are adequate.

   SA   5   4   3   2   1   SD

I. All procedures have been described in sufficient detail to permit a replication of the study.

   SA   5   4   3   2   1   SD

J. The participants have been adequately protected from potential harm.

   SA   5   4   3   2   1   SD

K. The results are clearly described.

   SA   5   4   3   2   1   SD

L. The discussion/conclusion is appropriate.

   SA   5   4   3   2   1   SD

M. Despite any flaws, the report is worthy of publication.

   SA   5   4   3   2   1   SD

Article 9

Parent Behavior and Child Distress During Urethral Catheterization

Charmaine Kleiber, PhD(C), RN, CPNP, **Ann Marie McCarthy**, PhD, RN, PNP[*]

ABSTRACT

Issues and Purpose. Researchers need a clear understanding of the natural behaviors parents use to help their children cope. This study describes the relationships between naturally occurring parent behaviors and child distress behaviors during urethral catheterization.

Design and Methods. In this descriptive study, researchers videotaped the behaviors of parent–child interactions during urethral catheterization.

Results. Parents used distraction to maintain calm behavior during the first part of the procedure and used more reassurance when the children started to become distressed. Seven of the nine children displayed calm behavior at least half the time following distraction. Parental reassurance did not decrease distress behavior in most children.

Practice Implications. Early implementation of developmentally appropriate nursing interventions to decrease child distress is imperative. Parents may need specific instruction and practice to continue the use of distraction throughout procedures, even when the child is upset.

From *JSPN: Journal of the Society of Pediatric Nurses*, 4, 95–104. Copyright © 1999 by Nursecom, Inc. and the Society of Pediatric Nurses. Reprinted with permission.

Parents are frequently with their children during painful medical procedures, but many of them state they do not know what to say or do to help their children cope with the pain (Bauchner, Vinci, & Waring, 1989; Merritt, Sargent, & Osborn, 1990; Schepp, 1991). Although there is a great deal of interest in teaching parents and children to use cognitive–behavioral techniques (distraction, imagery, deep breathing, relaxation) to modify behavioral distress, few researchers have examined the relationships between specific naturally occurring parental behaviors and children's responses. Before interventions are implemented to modify parental behavior, researchers should have a clear understanding of the natural behaviors that parents use during painful procedures and the effects of those behaviors on children. Without that information, development of sound interventions cannot proceed in a scientific manner.

A few research groups have examined the relationships between naturally occurring parent behaviors and child distress and coping behaviors during procedures, but differences in the categories of behavior chosen for study and differences in analytic methods make it difficult to synthesize the results. Another issue is that most researchers have chosen children with cancer as the sample population. It may not be appropriate to generalize the behaviors of parents of children with cancer to parents of children with different health problems. It can be argued that parents of children with cancer are under greater emotional stress—the potential death of the child. The threat of death may influence how parents behave around their children during stressful situations. In investigating the effects of parental behavior on child behavior, it is important to include groups of children that do not have life-threatening illnesses.

A unique aspect of this study was that the children were undergoing urethral catheterization. Children undergoing this procedure were chosen for this study because these children typically do not have life-threatening conditions, yet they must undergo procedures that are frightening, uncomfortable, and take more than a minute or two to complete. There is evidence that catheterization of the bladder, a common medical procedure, is uncomfortable for children. In a study of children between the ages of 3 to 5 years who had the procedure, Merritt, Ornstein, and Spicker (1994) reported the mean observed distress score was 2.38 on the 5-point Observed Scale of Behavioral Distress (OSBD), and the mean pain rating was 64.78 on the 100-point Oucher pain scale. This indicates that children experience a moderate amount of distress and pain during the procedure. Indeed, for many years recommended practice for urethral catheterization has included the instillation of an anesthetic lubricant into the urethra to decrease discomfort (Chrispin, 1968; Gray, 1996).

---

[*]*Charmaine Kleiber* is an advanced practice nurse, University of Iowa Hospitals and Clinics. *Ann Marie McCarthy* is associate professor, College of Nursing, University of Iowa, Iowa City, Iowa.

The purpose of this pilot study was to investigate the relationships between naturally occurring parent behaviors and child distress behavior during urethral catheterization. This work adds to the developing research base on the relationships between the naturally occurring behaviors of parents and children during painful procedures. This information is crucial to the development of interventions to assist children and their parents in coping with painful procedures.

Background

Some parental behaviors that might be viewed intuitively as helping the child cope with a painful procedure, such as giving reassurance or information, have been found to be linked with increased child distress (Blount et al., 1989; Dahlquist, Power, Cox, & Fernbach, 1994; Manne et al., 1992). More needs to be learned about the effects of naturally occurring parental behaviors on children in stressful situations. Because the focus of this study is the relationship between parental behaviors and child distress, the literature review is limited to studies in that area.

Three groups of researchers have investigated the relationships between specific naturally occurring parental and child behaviors during painful procedures. Blount et al. (1989) audiotaped 23 children, ages 5 to 13 years, with cancer who were having a bone marrow aspiration and/or lumbar puncture. Verbalizations made by parents and children during the procedure were coded using the Child–Adult Medical Procedure Interaction Scale (CAMPIS), which consists of 12 adult-to-child vocal behaviors and 15 child vocal behaviors. Sackett's lag analysis was used to investigate the impact of particular vocalized behaviors on other behaviors. Thus, the impact of child behavior on adult behaviors was analyzed as well as the impact of adult behavior on child behavior. Conditional probabilities and behavioral chains, with each discrete behavior as the criterion starting the chain, were constructed. Major findings were that reassuring comments, apology, empathy, criticism, or giving control to the child by adults occurred before child distress behaviors ($p < .0001$ for each finding).

The timing of adult behaviors was the focus of a second analysis by Blount, Sturges, and Powers (1990). The relationship between adult and child behaviors was separated into phases of pre-, during, and postprocedure. The major findings were that child distress increased from preprocedure to during procedure, and remained high postprocedure. Adults used more distraction in the preprocedural phase and more commands to relax during the procedure. One limitation of these studies is that the temporal relationship—how much time elapsed—between adult and child behaviors is unknown. Another limitation is that the CAMPIS tool relies only on vocalizations audible on a tape recorder as indicators of distress in children.

Jacobsen et al. (1990) described the relationship between observed parental behavior and child distress during venipuncture in 3- to 10-year-old children ($N = 70$) with cancer using a tool developed by the researchers (Procedure Behavior Rating Scale–Venipuncture Version [PBRS–VV]). Analysis of variance revealed that children were more distressed if their parents used the behaviors of bargaining ($p = .001$), explaining ($p = .002$), or distracting ($p = .04$). Because the level of analysis did not allow for a temporal relationship, it was not possible to determine whether one behavior followed another.

To determine temporal relationships between behaviors, Manne et al. (1992) conducted a follow-up study, assessing the behaviors of 43 parent/child dyads. The children were cancer patients, ages 3 to 9 years, undergoing venipuncture. The researchers used an observational scale adapted from the CAMPIS and PBRS–VV that consisted of three child behavior categories and six adult behavior categories. An important difference between the behavioral observation tool used in this study and the CAMPIS tool used in the Blount study is that behaviors were defined using both visually observed and auditory categories. Another difference is that for parent behavior, the category "explanation" was added to the tool, and "reassurance" was deleted. The researchers used sequential analysis to assess the temporal relationships between parent and child behaviors. Behaviors had to occur within 5 seconds of each other to be counted as a sequence. Probable expectancies were calculated for all possible pairs of child and adult behavior categories. The results were that children used more coping behaviors when adults used distraction, and children exhibited fewer coping behaviors when adults used explanation, commands to use coping, praise, criticism, or giving control to the child. The only adult behavior that had beneficial results on both child coping and distress was distraction. All other adult behaviors decreased the likelihood that children would engage in coping behaviors.

Dahlquist et al. (1994) observed 66 children with cancer between the ages of 2 and 17 years during bone marrow aspiration. Child behavioral distress was measured with the Observed Scale of Behavioral Distress (OSBD) (Jay, Ozolins, Elliott, & Caldwell, 1983), which consists of 11 verbal, vocal, and motor distress behaviors that are assigned intensity weights. Parent–child interactions were recorded using the Dyadic Pre-Stressor Interaction Scale (DPIS) (Bush, Melamed, Sheras, & Greenbaum, 1986). Parent behaviors in this scale are informing, distracting, reassuring, ignoring, restraining, and agitation; child behaviors are attachment, distress, exploration, and prosocial behaviors. Pearson product–moment correlations were computed between parent and child DPIS behaviors and OSBD scores. For younger children (ages 2 to 7 years), "preprocedural" OSBD distress scores were positively correlated with parental reassurance ($r = .48$), and "dur-

170 ing-procedure" distress was positively related to parental restraining of the child ($r = .50$). For the older children, ages 8 to 17 years, none of the adult behaviors
significantly correlated with distress scores in the "preprocedural" phase, but "during-procedure" OSBD dis-
175 tress scores were positively correlated with parental
reassurance ($r = .40$) and parental information giving ($r
= .34$). Although this study found age- and phase-
specific relationships between the parental behaviors
"reassuring" and "informing" and child distress, the
180 use of correlation to describe relationships between
adult and child behaviors does not establish a temporal
link (e.g., information about the timing of the behaviors).

In summary, the relationships between child dis-
185 tress behavior and parent behaviors are unclear. Although several researchers have taught parents to use
behavioral strategies successfully, such as distraction,
to decrease their children's distress during painful procedures (Blount et al., 1992; Broome, Lillis, McGahee,
190 & Bates, 1992; Jay & Elliott, 1990; Manne et al., 1990;
Vessey, Carlson, & McGill, 1994), it is imperative that
such interventions be based on a clear understanding of
the interaction between parent and child behaviors.

The purpose of this study was to continue to inves-
195 tigate the relationship between naturally occurring parental behavior and child distress behaviors during a
specific medical procedure: urethral catheterization.
The specific research questions addressed in this study
were:

200 1. What behaviors do parents display during the urethral catheterization of their children?
2. To what extent do children display distress behaviors during urethral catheterization?
3. What are the relationships between parent behav-
205 ior and child distress behavior during urethral
catheterization? Specifically:
(a) What is the child's behavioral response to
parent behaviors?
(b) What is the parent's behavioral response to
210 child distress behavior?

Methods

Behavioral analysis of videotaped procedures was
used in this descriptive study of naturally occurring
parent–child interactions during urethral catheterization.

Setting

215 The setting was the urology clinic at a large terti-
ary-care Midwestern hospital. There was no program
of cognitive–behavioral therapy to assist families with
stress or pain during procedures in this clinic. Parents
were given the option to be with their children during
220 the procedure, but parents were not coached in what to
say or do to help their children.

Subjects

Subjects were children undergoing urethral cathe-

terization for diagnostic tests and the parents who were
present during the procedure. Inclusion criteria were
225 that the parents and children understood English and
the children were between the ages of 3 and 7 years.
The age of the children in this study was thus limited
because it has been shown that young children are most
likely to display distress behavior during medical pro-
230 cedures. The children were developmentally normal
and had no known abnormality in perineal sensation.

Twelve children and their parents were approached
to participate in this study. Two children declined. Ten
children (eight girls, two boys) and their parents were
235 recruited. The mean age was 4.6 years (range 3.2–6.9
years), and the average number of previous urinary
catheterizations the children had experienced was 5.8
(range 3–10). All the children were under follow-up for
recurrent urinary tract infections. Seven of the children
240 were accompanied by a mother, two were accompanied
by a father, and one child had both parents present
through the procedure.

Data Collection

Demographic and historical data were collected
from each family, including information on the child's
245 age, sex, and history of previous catheterizations or
other painful or uncomfortable procedures.

Behaviors recorded on the videotapes were coded
using a behavior coding scheme (Table 1) developed
by the investigators based on behavioral descriptors in
250 the Child Adult Medical Procedure Scale–Revised
(CAMPIS–R) (Blount et al., 1990) and the Observed
Scale of Behavioral Distress–Revised (OSBD) (Jay et
al., 1983). Concurrent validity of the CAMPIS–R has
been reported with significant correlations between
255 CAMPIS–R parent behavioral categories and child
behavioral distress as measured by the OSBD and the
Behavioral Approach–Avoidance and Distress Scale.
Parental behaviors comprised only verbalizations, including distraction, reassurance, information giving,
260 praise, and command to use a coping strategy. Verbalizations that did not fall into those categories were labeled "other." Child distress behaviors included vocalizations ranging from whimper to scream, and the motor
behaviors of physical fighting including kicking or
265 hitting. These behaviors were chosen because they indicate a higher level of distress than a frown or holding
the body rigidly. Coding for child behavior was simply
the presence or absence of any behavioral distress.

Procedure

Approval for the study was obtained from the Insti-
270 tutional Review Board. Families in the urology clinic
waiting room were approached by the principal investigator prior to their clinic visit to discuss the study and
obtain informed consent from the parent and verbal
assent from the child. If families agreed to participate,
275 demographic data were collected and the investigator
escorted the family to the procedure room.

Table 1
Definitions of Parent and Child Behaviors

Parent behaviors

Distraction
Non-procedure-related talk to child. Talk about the child's pets, school, activity, questions unrelated to the child's illness. Jokes or humorous statements made to the child.

Information
Procedure-related talk, including giving explanation, information. Any statement denoting what is about to occur, including washing, insertion of medical instrument. "This is going to feel cold." "You'll feel a little pressure."

Reassurance
Comments directed to the child with the intent to reassure or ease tension. "It's OK." "I'm almost through." "We're hurrying." "It's almost over."

Command to use coping strategy
Commands that required the child to participate in some coping behavior, such as, "Take a deep breath." "Relax." "Squeeze my hand." "Breathe in and out."

Praise
Statements referring to the child's past, present, or future behavior that is positive and shows approval. "You are doing great." "That's right." "Good job," and "Good girl."

Other
Talk directed to adults in the room; commands to the child to engage in some procedure-related activity (e.g., "Bring your legs up like a frog.").

Child behaviors

Distress behavior
Crying, screaming, whimpering, fighting, verbal noncompliance or verbal resistance, verbal pain, or verbal fear.

The sterile catheterization was performed by the urology clinic nurses using standard care procedures. The child was placed on the exam table with the parent positioned at the head. The child's perineal area was washed with a soap solution, rinsed, and then a small amount of sterile lidocaine anesthetic lubricant was instilled into the urethra with a prefilled smooth-tipped syringe (see Gray, 1996, p. 308, for a description of lidocaine lubricant use with urinary catheterization). After waiting a few minutes for the anesthetic to take effect, more of the lubricant was instilled. After waiting again for a few minutes, a Foley catheter (6 or 8 Fr.) was inserted.

The nurses informed the children about the sensations they would be feeling as each step of the procedure progressed. The investigator focused the video camera on the faces of the child and parent throughout the procedure. Videotaping started when the child was placed on the exam table in the treatment room and continued until the clinic nurse indicated that the catheter was in place and secured with tape.

Data Analysis

The audio portion of each videotape was transcribed to allow written, auditory, and visual data to be used for coding the behaviors. Prior to analysis, two practice tapes were used to train the investigators in the coding system and to establish interrater agreement.

First, all parent behaviors were coded. A parent behavior began with a parent's verbalization and ended when the parent paused, allowing for the child to respond. Then, each child behavior following every parent behavior was coded as either indicative of distress or not. Table 2 gives an example of a sequence of parent and child behaviors. In this example, there are four parent behaviors immediately following four child behaviors (1–2, 3–4, 5–6, 7–8). The mother used reassurance once, which was followed by child distress (1–2), and distraction three times, once followed by child distress (3–4) and twice followed by no distress (5–6, 7–8). Analyzing this passage for the parent's behavioral response to child distress, one needs to look at the child behaviors first. There are three child behaviors immediately followed by parent behavior (2–3, 4–5, 6–7). The child was distressed twice (2–3, 4–5) and calm once (6–7). The parent used distraction after each of the child's behaviors.

Table 2
Example of a Sequence of Parent and Child Behaviors

1. Mother (*softly*): "Shh. Hush now, it's OK." (**Reassurance**)
2. Child (*crying*). (**Distress**)
3. Mother: "Can you tell me where we are going to lunch today?" (**Distraction**)
4. Child (*whimpering*). (**Distress**)
5. Mother: "Tell me what your favorite pizza place is." (**Distraction**)
6. Child (*frowning but quiet*). (**No distress**)
7. Mother: "Should we have pizza with pepperoni or sausage on it?" (**Distraction**)
8. Child: "No sausage. Just cheese pizza." (**No distress**)

The videotapes were coded to 100% agreement by the two investigators. Disagreements were resolved by discussing the likely intent of parent behaviors. Sometimes the parent's tone of voice and the pattern of parent–child interaction had to be taken into consideration in categorizing verbalizations. For example, the "shhh" sound was used by parents to communicate different things. Some parents used it as a soft, soothing reassurance, but others appeared to use it as a command to be quiet. Each verbalization made by the parents was classified as distraction, reassurance, information giving, command to use coping strategy, praise, or "other." Nonverbal parent behaviors, such as stroking the child's head, were not coded. The presence or absence of child distress just prior to and immediately following each parent behavior was documented.

Because of the small sample size, the binomial sign test was chosen to determine the relationship between child distress and parent behaviors. The unit of analysis was "subject" rather than "behavior across subjects" in order to meet the assumption of independence. Two sets of analyses were conducted: how parents respond to children and how children respond to parents. Frequencies of parent behavior and child behavior just prior to and immediately following each parent behavior were tallied and percentages calculated for each parent/child dyad. For each parent/child dyad, the relationship between child distress and parent behavior was

350 given a positive sign if distress occurred more than
50% of the time, and a negative sign if distress occurred less than 50% of the time. For example, referring to the behavioral sequence in Table 2, the
mother's distraction behavior was preceded by child
355 distress two of three times. Because the child was distressed more than half of the time prior to distraction,
the dyad would receive a positive sign for "child distress present prior to parent distraction." The mother's
distraction was followed by child distress one out of
360 three times. Because the child displayed distress less
than 50% of the time immediately following the parent's distraction, the dyad would receive a negative
score for "child distress present following parent distraction."

Results

365   Data were collected on 10 parent/child dyads. One
videotape was not usable because the parent did not say
anything and stood still during the entire procedure.
For the remaining nine videotapes, the catheterization
procedures lasted an average of eight minutes from the
370 time the child was placed on the exam table to the time
the catheter was taped in place.

*Research Question 1: What behaviors do parents
display during the urinary catheterization of their
children?*

     Totals of 684 parent behaviors were coded and are
described in Table 3. The most commonly used behaviors were distraction (33%) and reassurance (23%);
375 however, there was a wide range in usage among the
nine parents in this sample. Distraction was used from
8 to 89 times (mean = 25), and reassurance was used
from 1 to 41 times (mean = 17.3) during the catheterization procedures. Information giving, praise, and
380 commands to use coping strategies were used infrequently on average (means = 6.6, 5.4, and 5.4, respectively).

Table 3
Description of 684 Parent Behaviors (N = 9)

Behavior	Frequency for total sample	Percentage of total behaviors	Mean frequency	Range of frequency
Distraction	225	33%	25.0	8–89
Reassurance	156	23%	7.3	1–41
Information	60	9%	6.6	1–19
Praise	49	7%	5.4	0–11
Command to cope	49	7%	5.4	0–26
Other	145	21%	16.0	5–26

*Research Question 2: To what extent do children
display distress behaviors during urinary
catheterization?*

     On average, the children displayed distress behav-
ior following 41% of all coded parent behaviors. The
385 range of distress behavior, however, was striking. One
child did not display any distress behavior; another
child displayed only one mild distress behavior. Four

children were more calm than distressed following
parent behavior. Two children displayed more distress
390 behavior than calm behavior, and one child screamed
and cried throughout the entire procedure regardless of
her parent's efforts to calm her.

     In this descriptive study, analysis of distress behav-
ior was done for the whole procedure rather than by
395 "phase" of procedure. In analyzing the tapes, several
"invasive" aspects to this procedure appeared: the
washing of the perineum, the instillation of anesthetic
jelly, and the insertion of the catheter. The beginning of
each aspect of the procedure was surmised from the
400 nurse verbalizations on the videotape. A trend was evident in that seven children showed signs of discomfort
(crying out; whining; saying, "It stings.") during the
washing part of the procedure, and eight of the nine
children screamed suddenly and loudly during the time
405 that the catheter was passed through the urethra. It appeared that most children were uncomfortable during
washing and anesthetic application, and experienced
sudden pain during the catheter insertion.

*Research Question 3: What is the child's behavioral
response to parent behaviors? What is the parent's
behavioral response to child distress behavior?*

     Table 4 shows the number of children who were
410 distressed immediately before and immediately after
the parent behaviors of distraction, information giving,
and reassurance. These parent behaviors were chosen
for analysis because they were used by all the parents
in the study and were the most frequently used parent
415 behaviors.

Table 4
*Time-Sensitive Relationships Between Parent Behaviors and
Child Distress Behavior*

	Child distress behavior	
	BEFORE the parent behavior	**AFTER** the parent behavior
	# of children showing distress (Sign Test)	# of children showing distress (Sign Test)
Distraction	3 of 9 ($p = .5$)	2 of 8[a] ($p = .28$)
Reassurance	6 of 9 ($p = .5$)	5 of 9 ($p = 1.0$)
Information giving	4 of 9 ($p = 1.0$)	6 of 9 ($p = .5$)

[a]One child displayed equal numbers of distress and nondistress behaviors
following parent distraction.

     None of the relationships between parent and child
behavior reached statistical significance, which is not
surprising considering the small sample size. However,
trends in the data are evident. Parents tended to use
420 distraction to maintain calm behavior in the child. Six
of the nine parents initiated distraction during calm
behavior. Seven of the nine children displayed calm
behavior at least half the time following distraction.

     Six of the nine children displayed distress before
425 the parents used reassurance, and five children continued to show distress following reassurance. Parents

tended to use reassurance later in the procedure, when the child was distressed. Six parents followed the pattern of using distraction first (when the child was calm during the beginning of the procedure), reassurance when the child started to become upset, and returned to using distraction when the child calmed down again.

Information was offered infrequently by the parents and often was meant to reinforce information given by the nurse, such as "The soap will feel cold." The children's behavior was mixed prior to and after receiving information.

Praise generally was offered at the end of the procedure. Eight parents told their children they did a good job during the procedure. Five parents gave praise when the children were calm, whereas two praised their children most frequently when they were still upset but winding down. One parent gave praise once when the child was upset and once when the child was calm.

Commands to cope were made by six parents. Although commands were used infrequently, it appeared that general instructions such as "just relax" had no noticeable effect on these young children. The children seemed more able to follow directive commands such as "take a deep breath" and "squeeze my hand."

Discussion

Parents tended to use distraction during times when the children were not distressed. When the children were presented with distraction by their parents, six of the nine children continued to remain calm, while two children tended to display distress, and one child displayed an equal number of calm and distress behaviors. The results of this study support the findings of Blount et al. (1990) that parents tend to use more distraction during the early part of the procedure, and the findings of Manne et al. (1992) that children tend not to show distress behavior following parent use of distraction.

Parents tended to use reassurance when the children became distressed, typically later in the procedure. This finding supports observations reported by two other research groups (Blount et al., 1990; Dahlquist et al., 1994) that child distress and reassurance are related. However, where other researchers have speculated that reassurance might evoke distress in the child, we suggest a different explanation: Child distress may evoke parent reassurance. This was evident in the pattern seen with parents using distraction initially, using reassurance when children start to show distress, and then going back to using distraction when the children were less distressed. Perhaps parents feel the need to acknowledge their children's discomfort by using reassuring comments like "it's OK" or "I know." Five of the nine children continued to be distressed after parental reassurance, but the children's level of distress did not escalate (e.g., from whining to crying) following reassurance. Although reassurance did not decrease distress behavior in most children, it did not seem to be a distress-promoting behavior.

Information was offered infrequently by parents in this study and often was used to reinforce sensory preparation by the nurse. The children's behavior prior to and following information was mixed. This does not support the conclusions of other researchers (Jacobsen et al., 1990; Manne et al., 1992) that information or explanation is linked with increased child distress.

The major limitation of this study is its small sample size. Although trends in patterns of behavior are evident, larger studies are needed to validate these findings. Another limitation is possible differences between male and female catheterizations. This study included two boys and eight girls, so comparisons of gender differences were not possible.

In summary, the pattern of parent behavior that emerged in this study was that parents used distraction to maintain calm behavior during the first part of the procedure when nothing painful was happening. When children had a marked behavior change indicative of more intense discomfort, however, some parents abandoned distraction and started using reassurance. This finding, in conjunction with previous research, has implications for researchers and clinicians. In a meta-analysis of 16 studies representing a total sample of 491 young children, Kleiber and Harper (1999) found that distraction had a positive effect on children's distress behavior during medical procedures. Additionally, there is evidence that child distress is influenced by distraction during both the anticipatory and the invasive phases of medical procedures. Blount et al. (1990) reported that directing the child to use coping strategies was associated with decreased child distress during the painful part of bone marrow aspiration. Manne et al. (1992) found that parent use of distraction had a significantly positive effect on child coping during the preparation, insertion, and completion phases of venipuncture. The results of the current study suggest that parents may need specific instruction and practice to continue the use of distraction or imagery throughout procedures.

Many children with urinary problems undergo repeated catheterizations. Future research should investigate children's behavioral responses during their first catheterization experience. In this study, children already had experienced between 3 and 10 urinary catheterizations. Other studies have found that the child's previous negative experience with procedures is a potent predictor of future distress (Dahlquist et al., 1986; Pate, Blount, Cohen, & Smith, 1996). Thus, for pediatric urology patients, early implementation of developmentally appropriate nursing interventions to decrease child distress is imperative. These interventions may include strategies for the child, the adults involved in the procedure, or both.

Conclusions

There is a broad variability in parents' behaviors and in children's distress behavior during urinary

catheterization. As a group, children showed distress
behavior after 41% of parent behaviors during the procedure. A pattern of parent behavior emerged in this
study: Parents used distraction to maintain calm behavior during the first part of the procedure and used more
reassurance when the children started to become distressed.

How Do I Apply These Findings to Nursing Practice?

To develop scientifically sound interventions, researchers and clinicians should have a clear understanding of the natural behaviors that parents use during medical procedures and the effects of those behaviors on children. This study suggests that parents tend
to use distraction early in the procedure to maintain
calm behavior and reassurance when the child becomes
distressed. Because previous research indicates that
distraction can decrease child distress behaviors during
both the preparatory and invasive phases of medical
procedures, parents may need assistance in using distraction throughout the procedure, even when the child
is upset.

Other researchers have identified a relationship between parent use of reassurance and child behavioral
distress. This study suggests that child distress behavior triggers parent use of reassurance. Although reassuring comments such as "it's OK" and "almost
through, just a little longer" did not seem to decrease
children's distress behavior, reassurance might have an
unrecognized psychological effect on children. Perhaps
reassurance lets children know their parents have not
abandoned them, and that their "upset" is acknowledged. Further research is needed to clarify how parents' use of distraction and reassurance influences children during medical procedures.

References

Bauchner, H., Vinci, R., & Waring, C. (1989). Pediatric procedures: Do parents want to watch? *Pediatrics, 84,* 907–909.

Blount, R.L., Bachanas, P.J., Powers, S.W., Cotter, M.C., Franklin, A., Chap- lin, W., Mayfield, J., Henderson, M., & Blount, S.D. (1992). Training chil- dren to cope and parents to coach them during routine immunizations: Ef- fects on child, parent, and staff behaviors. *Behavior Therapy, 23,* 689–705.

Blount, R.L., Corbin, S.M., Sturges, J.W., Wolfe, V.V., Prater, J.M., & James, L.D. (1989). The relationship between adult's behavior and child coping and distress during BMA/LP procedures: A sequential analysis. *Behavior Ther- apy, 20,* 585–601.

Blount, R.L., Sturges, J.W., & Powers, S.W. (1990). Analysis of child and adult behavioral variations by phase of medical procedure. *Behavior Ther- apy, 21,* 33–48.

Broome, M.E., Lillis, P., McGahee, T.W., & Bates, T. (1992). The use of distraction and imagery with children during painful procedures. *Oncology Nursing Forum, 19,* 499–502.

Bush, J.P., Melamed, B.G., Sheras, P.L., & Greenbaum, P.L. (1986). Mother– child patterns of coping with anticipatory medical distress. *Health Psychol- ogy, 5,* 137–157.

Chrispin, A. (1968). Radiological investigations. In D.I. Williams (Ed.), *Pae- diatric urology* (pp. 531–543). New York: Appleton-Century-Crofts.

Dahlquist, L.M., Gil, K.M., Armstrong, F.D., DeLawyer, D.D., Greene P., & Wuori, D. (1986). Preparing children for medical examinations: The impor- tance of previous medical experience. *Health Psychology, 5,* 249–259.

Dahlquist, L.M., Power, T.G., Cox, C.N., & Fernbach, D.J. (1994). Parenting and children distress during cancer procedures: A multi-dimensional as- sessment. *Children's Health Care, 23,* 149–166.

Gray, M. (1996). Atraumatic urethral catheterization of children. *Pediatric Nursing, 22,* 306–310.

Jacobsen, P.B., Manne, S.L., Gorfinkle, K., Schorr, O., Rapkin, B., & Redd, W. (1990). Analysis of child and parent behavior during painful medical procedures. *Health Psychology, 9,* 559–576.

Jay, S.M., & Elliott, C.H. (1990). A stress inoculation program for parents whose children are undergoing painful medical procedures. *Journal of Con- sulting and Clinical Psychology, 58,* 799–804.

Jay, S.M., Ozolins, M., Elliott, C. H., & Caldwell, S. (1983). Assessment of children's distress during painful medical procedures. *Health Psychology, 2,* 133–147.

Kleiber, C., & Harper, D. (1999). Effects of distraction on children's pain and distress during medical procedures: A meta-analysis. *Nursing Research, 48,* 44–49.

Manne, S.L., Bakeman, R., Jacobsen, P.B., Gorfinkle, K., Bernstein, D., & Redd, W. (1992). Adult–child interaction during invasive medical proce- dures. *Health Psychology, 11,* 241–249.

Manne, S.L., Redd, W.H., Jacobsen, P.B., Gorfinkle, K., Schorr, O., & Rapkin, B. (1990). Behavioral intervention to reduce child and parent distress during venipuncture. *Journal of Consulting and Clinical Psychology, 58,* 565–572.

Merritt, K.A., Ornstein, P.A., & Spicker, B. (1994). Children's memory for a salient medical procedure: Implications for testimony. *Pediatrics, 94,* 17–23.

Merritt, K.A., Sargent, J.R., & Osborn, L.M. (1990). Attitudes regarding paren- tal presence during medical procedures. *American Journal of Diseases in Children, 144,* 270–271.

Pate, J.T., Blount, R.L., Cohen, L.L., & Smith, A.J. (1996). Childhood medical experience and temperament as predictors of adult functioning in medical situations. *Children's Health Care, 25,* 281–298.

Schepp, K.G. (1991). Factors influencing the coping effort of mothers of hospitalized children. *Nursing Research, 40,* 42–46.

Vessey, J.A., Carlson, K.L., & McGill, J. (1994). Use of distraction with chil- dren during an acute pain experience. *Nursing Research, 43,* 369–372.

Acknowledgments: The authors wish to thank Bonnie Wagner, RN; Lisa Gerard, RN; and the staff of the UIHC Urology Clinic for their support of this research. This study was funded by a grant from the Society of Pediatric Nurses.

Address correspondence to: charmaine.kleiber@uiowa.edu, with a copy to the editor: roxie.foster@uchsc.edu

Exercise for Article 9

Factual Questions

1. Why were children undergoing urethral catheteri- zation chosen for this study?

2. Why was this study limited to children between the ages of 3 and 7 years?

3. On what did the investigator focus the video cam- era?

4. When coding the videotapes, what percentage of agreement was reached by the two investigators?

5. On average, the catheterization procedures lasted how many minutes?

6. Were any of the relationships between parent and child behavior statistically significant?

7. The researchers note that one limitation of the study is the small sample size. What is the other limitation that is explicitly mentioned?

Questions for Discussion

8. The researchers refer to their study as a "pilot study." Do you agree with this classification? Why? Why not? (See line 57.)

9. What is your opinion on the researchers' decision to exclude the children's nonverbal behaviors such as frowning or holding the body rigidly? (See lines 265–267.)

10. What is your opinion on the researchers' decision to exclude parents' nonverbal behaviors such as stroking the children's heads? (See lines 334–335.)

11. The children in this study had already experienced between 3 and 10 urinary catheterizations. Is this a limitation of the study? Explain. (See lines 235–238.)

12. If you were to conduct another study on the same topic, what changes in the research methodology, if any, would you make?

Quality Ratings

Directions: Indicate your level of agreement with each of the following statements by circling a number from 5 for strongly agree (SA) to 1 for strongly disagree (SD). If you believe an item is not applicable to this research article, leave it blank. Be prepared to explain your ratings. When responding to criteria A and B below, keep in mind that brief titles and abstracts are conventional in published research.

A. The title of the article is appropriate.

SA   5   4   3   2   1   SD

B. The abstract provides an effective overview of the research article.

SA   5   4   3   2   1   SD

C. The introduction establishes the importance of the study.

SA   5   4   3   2   1   SD

D. The literature review establishes the context for the study.

SA   5   4   3   2   1   SD

E. The research purpose, question, or hypothesis is clearly stated.

SA   5   4   3   2   1   SD

F. The method of sampling is sound.

SA   5   4   3   2   1   SD

G. Relevant demographics (for example, age, gender, and ethnicity) are described.

SA   5   4   3   2   1   SD

H. Measurement procedures are adequate.

SA   5   4   3   2   1   SD

I. All procedures have been described in sufficient detail to permit a replication of the study.

SA   5   4   3   2   1   SD

J. The participants have been adequately protected from potential harm.

SA   5   4   3   2   1   SD

K. The results are clearly described.

SA   5   4   3   2   1   SD

L. The discussion/conclusion is appropriate.

SA   5   4   3   2   1   SD

M. Despite any flaws, the report is worthy of publication.

SA   5   4   3   2   1   SD

Article 10

Survey Return Rates As a Function of Priority versus First Class Mailing

Christiane Brems, PhD, ABPP, **Mark E. Johnson**, PhD, **Teddy D. Warner**, PhD,
Laura Weiss Roberts, MD[*]

ABSTRACT. Prior research indicates survey procedures that signal significance and individualized mailings have higher response rates. Thus, it was hypothesized that surveys delivered via Priority mail would result in higher return rates than surveys delivered via First Class. Two-hundred and sixty surveys were sent to individuals randomly selected from lists of licensed physical and behavioral health care providers in Alaska and New Mexico. Half of the selected individuals were assigned randomly to receive mailings using Priority mail; the other half received First Class mailings. Return rate was 39% for First Class and 35% for Priority. Z tests of proportion indicated no statistically significant differences between methods. Given increased costs with no resultant increase in response rate, sending surveys to potential participants via Priority mail does not appear warranted.

From *Psychological Reports*, *99*, 496–501. Copyright © 2006 by Psychological Reports. Reprinted with permission.

With response rates to surveys having declined for at least two decades (Tourangeau, 2004), it is imperative that researchers use whatever cost-effective strategies are available to increase their response rates. One strategy empirically investigated for its effect on response rates has been type of mailing. One consistent finding is that using Certified mail has been shown to result in substantially higher response rates (Rimm, Stampfer, Colditz, Giovannuci, & Willet, 1990; Del Valle, Morgenstern, Rogstad, Albright, & Vickrey, 1997). The only mailing approach reported to yield higher rates has been the use of a private mail service (i.e., FedEx; Kasprzyk, Montano, St. Lawrence, & Phillips, 2001).

Less is known about the influence of Priority mail on response rates. One study (Gibson, Koepsell, Diehr, & Hale, 1999), comparing Priority mail and Certified mail, found the latter yielded a higher rate. In the current study, as part of a larger survey that examined differences between urban and rural health care providers, the effect of using Priority mail service versus regular First Class mail for survey mailings was investigated. It was hypothesized that Priority-delivered surveys would engender a higher return rate from potential participants given the higher cost of mailing and implied importance of the mailing. Given the nature of the larger study, it was also possible to examine whether mailing type differentially affected response rates from urban versus rural communities; however, no a priori hypotheses were established for this aspect of the study.

Method

Participants

To identify potential participants, lists of licensees were obtained from licensing boards in Alaska and New Mexico for physicians, nurse practitioners, registered nurses, licensed mental healthcare providers, social workers, physician assistants, and psychologists (New Mexico only). Each licensee list was stratified into urban and rural addresses, and participants were randomly selected by choosing each nth licensee (determined based on number in a given stratified list). For each of these seven groups, 10 licensees in urban communities and 10 licensees in rural communities were invited to participate. Thus, 40 physicians, 40 nurse practitioners, 40 registered nurses, 40 licensed mental health care providers, 40 social workers, 40 physician assistants, and 20 psychologists were selected. This resulted in a total of 120 individuals (60 urban, 60 rural) solicited in Alaska and a total of 140 (70 urban, 70 rural) in New Mexico. Of these participants, 174 (66.9%) were women and 86 (33.1%) were men. Primary cultural heritage reported by the individuals was 24 (9.4%) Hispanic American, 3 (1.2%) Asian American, 13 (4.9%) Alaska Native/Native American, 3 (1.2%) African American, 209 (80.3%) white (Anglo or Anglo-American), 5 (1.8%) other, and 3 (1.2%) did not respond. Their mean age was 48.9 yr. (SD = 9.5). These individuals were targeted for a survey about health care practices.

[*]*Christiane Brems* and *Mark E. Johnson*, Behavioral Health Research and Services, University of Alaska Anchorage. *Teddy D. Warner*, Family & Community Medicine, University of New Mexico School of Medicine. *Laura Weiss Roberts*, Department of Psychiatry and Behavioral Medicine, Medical College of Wisconsin.

Survey

As part of a larger study funded by the National Institute on Drug Abuse, a 21-page survey was developed to obtain health care providers' perspectives on a broad range of treatment and ethical issues. Based on extensive qualitative work and the extant literature, this survey included the following sections: ethical challenges, perceptions of illness stigma, training and resource needs, experiences in providing health care, barriers faced in providing care, adaptations to barriers, treatment issues related to providing care to minority groups, and providers' practice characteristics. Individual items were rated on an 11-point rating scale, anchored by 0: Not at all or never and 10: Very much or always. The survey required approximately 60 to 90 minutes to complete.

Procedures

Survey procedures recommended by Dillman (2000) were used for all aspects of the survey, which took place between March 1 and April 19, 2004. The only deviation from Dillman's recommendations was that additional time (i.e., two weeks instead of one week) was permitted between mailings to accommodate slower mail service to rural communities. A preletter was mailed two weeks prior to the mailing of the survey, outlining the survey's significance and other features. The survey mailing was followed up with a postcard mailing two weeks later to thank respondents and urge nonrespondents to complete the survey if they had not. Two weeks after the postcard, a second copy of the survey was mailed to nonrespondents. Responses to the second wave (i.e., the replacement survey) were not included in this study. Participants were compensated $50 for time spent in completing the survey.

During the first wave of the actual survey mailing (i.e., at the second contact with potential participants), the samples were randomly divided to receive their survey solicitation either via regular First Class mail or Priority mail. The randomization procedure involved stratifying the sample by Alaska versus New Mexico and by urban versus rural addresses. Then, within each of these four groups, every other name was assigned to receive Priority mail and the alternating name to receive First Class mail. This sampling procedure resulted in 30 rural and 30 urban dwellers in Alaska receiving Priority mailings and 30 rural and 30 urban dwellers in Alaska receiving surveys via First Class mail. In New Mexico, mailings went to 35 individuals per group. Thus, a total of 130 individuals received Priority mailings and 130 received First Class mailings, with half of each group urban and half rural dwellers. First Class mail was delivered in standard 9×11 envelopes; Priority mail was delivered in Priority-labeled envelopes provided by the United States Postal Service (USPS). Cost for the Priority mail was $2.85 and for the First Class mail was $1.10.

If surveys were returned by USPS with [...] warding addresses, the packet was remailed to [...] address exactly in the same format as the [...] packet. If surveys were returned by the USP[...] inability to deliver (i.e., wrong addresses or inc[...] who moved without forwarding addresses), a [...] ment addressee was chosen, and a new pac[...] mailed in the same format as that for the orig[...] dressee. This procedure assured that the usabl[...] size remained 120 in Alaska and 140 in New M[...]

Returned Rate Calculations

Surveys returned for undeliverable addresses were mailed to a replacement addressee, and the original addressee was not counted. Thus, the sample size remained constant at 120 in Alaska and 140 in New Mexico. Based on the lack of differential response rates between Priority and First Class mail during the first mailing, it was decided that it was cost prohibitive to use Priority mail during subsequent mailings. Thus, calculation of return rates was based on the total number of completed surveys received from the first survey mailing.

Results

Table 1 provides return rates separated by state and by community size, as well as for all data combined. An overall comparison of response rates across the eight groups (Alaska/New Mexico, urban/rural, Priority/First Class) yielded no significant differences ($\chi_7^2(N = 130) = 1.82, p = .97$). Given no overall differences, all responses were pooled across groups to test only Priority versus First Class mail. The return rate was 39.2% for First Class mail and 35.4% for Priority mail. The estimated difference between the proportions for Priority and First Class mail was 3.8% and the 95% confidence interval for this estimate runs from –8.1 % to 15.8%. A Z test of binomial proportions indicated no significant effect for method of mailing, $p = .52$.

Discussion

Based on this single survey mailing, response rates for First Class mail and Priority mail did not differ significantly. Thus, in terms of enhancing response rates, the additional expense of sending surveys to potential participants via Priority mail does not appear warranted. This information complements prior research indicating First Class mail is superior to other forms of mail for mail-out surveys, with the exception of Certified mail (Dillman, 2000).

When considering these findings, three limitations must be kept in mind. First, the small sample and resultant low power highlights the exploratory nature of this study and calls for replication. With samples of 130 in each of the two groups, there was only a 13% chance (power) of detecting a real increase from 50% to 55% at 5% significance or a 37% chance (power) of detecting an increase from 50% to 60%. Indeed, as a result of the limited power, the study data are still compatible

Table 1
Return Rates and 95% Confidence Intervals (CI) by Type of Mailing, State, and Community Size

	First Class mailing			Priority mailing			Response rate		
	Mailed	Returned	Return Rate %	Mailed	Returned	Return Rate %	Difference	95% CI	p
Alaska									
Rural	30	13	43.3	30	11	36.7	6.7	−18.8 to 32.1	.60
Urban	30	11	36.7	30	12	40.0	3.3	−20.9 to 27.6	.80
Total	60	24	40.0	60	23	38.3	1.7	−15.9 to 19.3	.85
New Mexico									
Rural	35	12	34.3	35	11	31.4	2.9	−19.4 to 25.1	.80
Urban	35	15	42.9	35	12	34.3	8.6	−15.0 to 32.2	.46
Total	70	27	38.6	70	23	32.9	5.7	−10.5 to 21.9	.48
Overall									
Rural	65	25	38.5	65	22	33.8	4.6	−12.2 to 21.4	.58
Urban	65	26	40.0	65	24	36.9	3.1	−13.9 to 20.0	.72
Total	130	51	39.2	130	46	35.4	3.8	−8.1 to 15.8	.52

with an approximate 8% increase in response rate using Priority mail as well as a 16% decrease in response rate using Priority mail. Second, the sample used in this study was that of professional health care providers (170) with likely multiple demands on their time. Other samples, such as the general population, could yield different results. Third, given that no data are available to compare respondents and nonrespondents on demographics data or any variables, some unmeasured factor (175) could have served as a mediator or moderator in the response to type of mailing.

References

Del Valle, M. L., Morgenstern, H., Rogstad, T. L., Albright, C., & Vickrey, B. G. (1997). A randomized trial of the impact of certified mail on response rate to a physician survey, and a cost-effectiveness study. *Evaluation & the Health Professions, 20,* 389–406.

Dillman, D. A. (2000). *Mail and Internet surveys: The tailored design method.* New York: Wiley.

Gibson, P. J., Koepsell, T. D., Diehr, P., & Hale, C. (1999). Increasing response rates for mailed surveys of Medicaid clients and other low-income populations. *American Journal of Epidemiology, 149,* 1057–1062.

Kasprzyk, D., Montano, D. E., St. Lawrence, J. S., & Phillips, W. R. (2001). The effects of variations in mode of delivery and monetary incentive on physicians' responses to a mailed survey assessing STD practice patterns. *Evaluation & the Health Professions, 24,* 3–17.

Rimm, E. B., Stampfer, M. J., Colditz, G. A., Giovannuci, E., & Willet, W. C. (1990). Effect of various mailing strategies among nonrespondents in a prospective cohort study. *American Journal of Epidemiology, 131,* 1068–1071.

Tourangeau, R. (2004). Survey research and societal change. *Annual Review of Psychology, 55,* 775–801.

Acknowledgments: This research was supported by Grant 1RO1DA13139 from the National Institute on Drug Abuse. Dr. Roberts also acknowledges the support of a Career Development Award (1KO2MH01918) from the National Institute of Mental Health. We gratefully acknowledge the contributions of Marcine Mullen in Alaska and of Dr. Pamela Monaghan and Audrey Solimon in New Mexico.

Address correspondence to: Christiane Brems, PhD, ABPP, Behavioral Health Research and Services, University of Alaska Anchorage, 3211 Providence Drive, Anchorage, AK 99508. E-mail: cbrems@uaa.alaska.edu

Exercise for Article 10

Factual Questions

1. How many registered nurses were selected to participate in this study?

2. Were the participants compensated for their participation? If yes, how much?

3. If a survey was returned by the USPS as undeliverable, what was done?

4. What was the total return rate for Priority mail?

5. How many First Class mailings were made to rural New Mexico?

6. What was the value of *p* for the significance of the difference between the two total return rates?

Questions for Discussion

7. The survey in this study was 21 pages and required 60 to 90 minutes to complete. Do you think that a shorter survey might have return rates that are different from those reported in this study? Explain. (See lines 59–73.)

8. Do you think it was a good idea to mail a preletter? Explain. (See lines 80–83.)

9. Is the use of randomization important? Explain. (See lines 92–101.)

10. Do you agree with the second limitation mentioned by the researchers? (See lines 169–173.)

11. This research is classified as "True Experimental Research" in the table of contents of this book. Do you agree with the classification? Explain.

12. If you were to conduct a follow-up study on the same topic, what changes, if any, would you make in the research methodology?

Quality Ratings

Directions: Indicate your level of agreement with each of the following statements by circling a number from 5 for strongly agree (SA) to 1 for strongly disagree (SD). If you believe an item is not applicable to this research article, leave it blank. Be prepared to explain your ratings. When responding to criteria A and B below, keep in mind that brief titles and abstracts are conventional in published research.

A. The title of the article is appropriate.

SA   5   4   3   2   1   SD

B. The abstract provides an effective overview of the research article.

SA   5   4   3   2   1   SD

C. The introduction establishes the importance of the study.

SA   5   4   3   2   1   SD

D. The literature review establishes the context for the study.

SA   5   4   3   2   1   SD

E. The research purpose, question, or hypothesis is clearly stated.

SA   5   4   3   2   1   SD

F. The method of sampling is sound.

SA   5   4   3   2   1   SD

G. Relevant demographics (for example, age, gender, and ethnicity) are described.

SA   5   4   3   2   1   SD

H. Measurement procedures are adequate.

SA   5   4   3   2   1   SD

I. All procedures have been described in sufficient detail to permit a replication of the study.

SA   5   4   3   2   1   SD

J. The participants have been adequately protected from potential harm.

SA   5   4   3   2   1   SD

K. The results are clearly described.

SA   5   4   3   2   1   SD

L. The discussion/conclusion is appropriate.

SA   5   4   3   2   1   SD

M. Despite any flaws, the report is worthy of publication.

SA   5   4   3   2   1   SD

Article 11

Life Review Therapy As an Intervention to Manage Depression and Enhance Life Satisfaction in Individuals with Right Hemisphere Cerebral Vascular Accidents

Marsha Courville Davis, PhD, RN, CRRN, LPC, NCC[*]

ABSTRACT. This pilot study sought to determine if the use of Life Review Therapy would result in lower levels of depression and higher degrees of life satisfaction in individuals with right hemisphere cerebral vascular accidents (CVAs). Fourteen subjects in a southern rehabilitation center were randomly assigned to either an experimental or control group. The experimental group received three one-hour sessions of Life Review Therapy and the control group viewed three one-hour sessions of neutral video with a follow-up discussion. Following the third session of each group, subjects were administered the Zung Scale for Depression and the Life Satisfaction Index–Form Z. A one-way ANOVA revealed a significantly lower level of depression ($p < .01$) and a significantly higher degree of life satisfaction ($p < .01$) in the Life Review Therapy group.

From *Issues in Mental Health Nursing*, 25, 503–515. Copyright © 2004 by Taylor and Francis, Inc. Reprinted with permission.

Cerebral Vascular Accident (CVA) is a leading cause of adult disability affecting approximately 750,000 people per year in the United States (Williams, Jaing, Matchar, & Samsa, 1999). Depression is the
5 most commonly reported psychiatric diagnosis in individuals who have experienced a CVA. Rates of post-stroke depression have ranged from 25% to 60% (Andersen, Vestergaard, Ingemann-Nielsen, & Lauritzen, 1995; Astrom, Adolfsson, & Asplund, 1993; Hermann,
10 Black, Lawrence, Szekely, & Szalai, 1998; Paolucci, Antonucci, Pratesi, Traballesi, Grasso, & Lubich, 1999).

Life review therapy is a treatment strategy defined as "the process of facilitation of the life review experi-
15 ence or mental process of reviewing one's life" (Butler, 1963, p. 66). Butler postulated that the life review is a natural process experienced by the elderly, by younger persons for whom death is imminent, and by those experiencing a crisis or a transition. It is a process of re-
20 membering and mentally reviewing life histories and addressing unsettled conflicts. Life review therapy may be one alternative nonpharmacological strategy to improve the quality of life in the CVA patient population.

No known existing studies of using life review
25 therapy for a crisis such as a CVA were found in the review of the literature. Additionally, the empirical studies on life review therapy are limited and show inconsistent results. Because of the limited nature of the empirical studies and the lack of research on life
30 review therapy with patients in crisis and the high incidence of CVA in the United States, this research study sought to add to the body of knowledge of life review therapy as well as that of psychological adjustment to CVA. The purpose of the study, therefore, was to de-
35 termine if life review therapy could produce lower levels of depression and higher levels of life satisfaction among individuals with CVA.

Rationale
The adjustment process is individual for each person. Difficulties with adjustment have, therefore, his-
40 torically been treated as they arise. If it could be determined that life review therapy could produce lower levels of depression and higher levels of life satisfaction in the CVA population, thereby facilitating adjustment, the life review process could be initiated with
45 this population in crisis and allow the patient an opportunity to be more quickly involved in the business of learning to proceed with his or her life.

Review of the Literature
Theoretical Framework
Butler's (1963) Life Review was the framework for this study. According to Butler, life review helps the
50 patient to maintain self-esteem, reaffirm a sense of identity, reduce feelings of loss and isolation, and emphasize the positive aspects of one's life. The theorist points out that life review is not merely reminiscence—the art or process of recalling the past—but it is a pur-
55 posive process leading to personality reintegration. The

---

[*] *Marsha Courville Davis* is former associate professor of nursing at Southeastern Louisiana University.

function of the life review is to allow for an opening of the personality so that it is free to evolve and change in response to the experiences of life.

Life Review Process

Haight (1991) published a 30-year literature search on the subject of life review/reminiscence. Haight concluded that there was a rapidly growing interest in the subject and called for more well-designed research. Merriam (1993) argued that the life review process may not be a universal one, experienced by all people as they enter old age, as Butler (1963) had postulated. Kropf and Greene (1993) concluded that undergoing the life review process helped parents who care for developmentally disabled family members gain a stronger sense of control over their lives. Waters (1990) reported on methods of facilitation of the life review by mental health counselors. O'Connor (1994) identified salient themes in the life review of frail elderly men and women in London. Peachey (1992) offered a set of life review questions. Muntz and White (1989) concluded that there was no evidence that the life satisfaction, psychological well-being, or depression scores of high-risk mentally competent older adults were affected significantly by the life review. Froehlich and Nelson (1986) explored affective meanings of life review through activities and discussions in groups. They perceived life review as "powerful" (p. 32) and encouraged the use of activities to facilitate the life review. Sherman (1987) conducted a study to determine whether social support and a sense of well-being among the elderly could be developed using reminiscence groups. Both experimental groups in his study increased in life satisfaction and self-concept.

Giltinan (1990) explored the effect of life review and discussion on the self-actualization process in elderly women. A self-actualization measure was administered prior to six life review sessions for the experimental group and to a comparison group that received no treatment. No significant differences between groups were shown in self-actualization at posttest. Haight (1992) studied the long-term effects of the structured life review process in a group of 52 homebound elderly clients. Subjects tested one year posttreatment revealed little change on (a) life satisfaction, (b) psychological well-being, (c) depression, or (d) activities of daily living. Stevens-Ratchford (1993) investigated the effects of life review and reminiscence on self-esteem and depression in older adults. Results showed no significant effects on self-esteem and depression scores using a life review reminiscence treatment. Molinari, Cully, Kendjelic, and Kunik (2001) studied reminiscence in older psychiatric patients as it related to attachment and personality in an effort to explain the apparent efficacy of life review treatment. The findings revealed higher scores on the teach/inform reminiscence function for securely attached patients. Extroversion and conversation reminiscence were found to be related, as was the personality factor of openness with identity and problem solving.

Adjustment to CVA

Paolucci, Antonucci, Pratesi, Traballesi, Grasso, and Lubich (1999) studied post-stroke depression and its role in rehabilitation. Results revealed depression occurring in 27% of the population of 470 patients, with female patients showing more depression than males. The authors recommended that antidepressant therapy be initiated as soon as possible preferring serotonergic drugs over the tricyclics because of side effects and safety factors.

The meaning of stroke in elderly women was investigated by Hilton (2002). Themes of transformation and transition were identified. The elderly women revealed they were unable to "become themselves again as they had known themselves to be" (Hilton, 2002, p. 23). In adjusting to transformation, the women were able to identify new roles and coping strategies as well as accept the realities of their new limitations. With regard to identification of themes of meaning of stroke, the elderly women identified changes as a result of the stroke, developed new strategies to overcome obstacles, mourned losses, and were able to resolve issues that arose. The women experienced uncertainty and regret, reduction of autonomy, and despair, isolation, and frustration.

Self-care self-efficacy as it related to quality of life after stroke was explored by Robinson-Smith (2002). The research revealed that patients with higher self-care self-efficacy reported fewer depression symptoms. Motivation of patients to develop strategies to enhance their quality of life, especially as it related to independence, was recommended.

Rochette and Desrosiers (2002) investigated coping strategies post-stroke. Coping strategies were not found to change over time, and women were found to use more coping strategies than men, despite the fact that in this study the women were not more depressed than the men. The researchers argued that the level of actualization of those experiencing a stroke may affect the type of coping strategies used, with more positive coping strategies chosen by those with a higher level of self-actualization. Employing more positive coping strategies may facilitate adaptation according to the authors.

Psychological well-being three years after severe stroke was studied by Lofgren, Gustafson, and Nyberg (1998). Results revealed that 64% of the study participants show high or middlerange scores for psychological well-being. A strong association between psychological well-being and depression also was found, with lower levels of depression in those subjects with high psychological well-being.

Method

Research Design

A posttest-only control-group design was used in the study. This design was chosen due to the short period of time that generally existed between attempting pretest and posttest. The researcher sought to guard
170 against effects of a pretest (Polit, Beck, & Hungler, 2001). Using a table of computer-generated random numbers, the researcher randomly assigned subjects to the experimental or alternative treatment. At the end of the last session for the subjects assigned to each treat-
175 ment, posttest measures of the dependent variables were administered by the researcher.

Sample

Participants were recruited through referral from their physician or designated staff members at the rehabilitation center where the study was conducted. Criteria
180 for inclusion in the study included: (a) no previous history of CVA, (b) onset of CVA within 6 months at the time of the study, (c) no other acute medical or psychiatric/psychological complications since the occurrence of the CVA, and (d) ability to verbally com-
185 municate.

Setting

The sessions were conducted by the researcher in a physical rehabilitation center in the USA in the evening after the completion of the evening meal. The same room was used to administer the Life Review treatment
190 and alternative treatment.

Procedure

A consent form was developed and approved by the Institutional Review Board (IRB) of the rehabilitation center. The proposal for the study was reviewed by the IRB and permission for the study to begin was given.
195 In order to identify a sample for this study, the researcher distributed the list of criteria for inclusion in the study to designated staff members who were responsible for generating referrals, insofar as the researcher was not an employee and had no access to
200 medical records. The staff members were to screen all new CVA admissions and then refer possible participants to the researcher. The researcher made contact with at least one staff member responsible for screening the new admissions on a weekly basis, even if no
205 referrals were received, to encourage continued interest in the study. As referrals were received and consent given, the researcher randomly assigned the participants to either the experimental or the control treatment using a computer-generated table of random numbers.
210 The researcher flipped a coin and determined that the elements designated as "1" would be the experimental group, leaving the element designated as "0" for the control group. There was no restriction in the random assignment such as blocking or stratification. Be-
215 cause the lengths of stays in rehabilitation centers at the time of this study were shorter than they had been pre-

viously, and the possibility of early discharge existed, the sessions began the following weekday of the referral and were conducted on consecutive days as often as
220 possible.

Materials utilized in the study were Haight's Life Review and Experiencing Form (Haight, 1982), as well as three video recordings on the subjects of food safety, fire safety, and telephone courtesy. The video re-
225 cordings were chosen due to their neutral but informative content and entertaining nature, as well as for their appropriate length of approximately 35 minutes for each video. Questions to stimulate discussion following each video also were developed.

230 Each of the participants in the experimental treatment received three individually administered one-hour sessions of life review therapy using Haight's (1982) Life Review and Experiencing Form. This instrument is composed of 68 items that cover childhood adoles-
235 cence, family and home, adulthood, and a summary. During the first session, childhood items were reviewed (through the fifth adolescence question). The childhood items included such questions as earliest memory of life and memories of brothers or sisters.
240 The first five adolescence questions reviewed items such as earliest teenage memories and school activity. Session two presented the remainder of adolescence questions as well as family and home questions and concluded with adulthood question number five. Ex-
245 amples of the last adolescence items included questions about hardships and first love.

The family and home section reviewed such memories as relationships and atmosphere of the home. The first five adult items included memories such as impor-
250 tance of religion and work experience. In session three, adulthood and summary questions were reviewed. The final adulthood questions involved memories about significant relationships, marriage, and difficulties of adult years. The summary questions elicited such
255 thoughts as what the person would change or leave unchanged and main satisfactions of the person's life.

For the control treatment, each participant spent the same amount of time individually with the researcher in an alternative activity. Each participant viewed three
260 videos, one each during three one-hour sessions. Following each of the videos, the researcher asked the participant a number of predetermined questions regarding the content of the video, and engaged in a discussion of the video with the participant. There was no
265 therapeutic intent in this activity.

Following the third session of each participant in both treatments, the researcher administered the Zung Scale for Depression (ZSD; Zung, 1967) and the Life Satisfaction Index–Form Z (LSI–Z; Wood, Wylie, &
270 Schaeffer, 1969). Due to vision problems associated with CVAs, the researcher read the inventories to each participant.

Instruments

Two instruments were used in this study—the Zung Scale for Depression (ZSD) and the Life Satisfaction Index–Form Z (LSI–Z). Following review of other possible instruments and a pilot study, these were chosen due to their simplicity and the ten-minute length of time for administration, considering the fatigue factor of the participants.

The ZSD is a Likert scale instrument composed of 20 items, each coded one, two, three, or four for none or little of the time, some of the time, good part of the time, or most or all of the time. If a participant chooses most or all of the time for the item, "I feel down-hearted, blue and sad," he or she would score four points on that item, for instance. The total points are then computed for each participant, yielding the depression score.

There are only minimal data available concerning the reliability of the ZSD, either internal or temporal. No reliability correlations could be found. However, validity of the instrument is well documented. Numerous studies have demonstrated the ZSD to reliably distinguish between normal and clinically depressed individuals. Scores on the ZSD, according to Keyser and Sweetland (1985), correlated highly with scores on the Hamilton Rating Scale, Beck Depression Inventory (.79), Costello-Comrey Depression Scale (.74), and Depression Scale of the Multiple Affect Adjective Check List (.57).

The Life Satisfaction Index was designed to measure life satisfaction and is composed of 13 agree or disagree statements. Each of the statements is coded either two or zero for agree, or two or zero for disagree. The items coded as two are those indicative of high life satisfaction. The participant marks either one of the choices, and the total score is then computed. A high life satisfaction is based upon a high score, with the highest score possible of 26. Wood et al. (1969) reported a split-half reliability coefficient of .79. Wood et al. (1969) also report a correlation of .57 between the LSI–Z and the clinically based Life Satisfaction Ratings Instrument. The correlation is considered weak evidence, however, for the convergent validity of the LSI–Z. Baiyewu and Jegede (1992) reported an internal consistency value of zero following administration of the LSI–Z to 945 Nigerians, age 60 and over. Factor composition analysis revealed that LSI–Z scores correlated significantly with items on self-assessed health, loneliness, and sex. Items that measured social contact did not correlate at a significant level.

Null Hypotheses

Hypothesis 1: There will be no statistically significant difference in the mean scores of the Zung Scale for Depression (Zung, 1967) between the individuals who were administered life review therapy and the individuals who viewed the videos.

Hypothesis 2: There will be no statistically significant difference in the mean scores of the Life Satisfaction Index–Form Z (Wood, Wylie, & Schaefer, 1969) between the individuals who were administered life review therapy and the individuals who viewed the videos.

Data Analysis

The hypotheses were tested using a one-way analysis of variance (ANOVA). The scores on each of the instruments were compared from experimental group to control group to determine if there was a significant difference. An alpha level of .05 was set for statistical significance.

Results and Discussion

Results

The first hypothesis was tested using the scores from the ZSD from the experimental and control groups in a one-way ANOVA. The ANOVA revealed a significant difference between groups $F(1,12) = 22.46$ $p < .01$. The mean of the experimental group posttest score ($M = 31.9$, $SD = 3.24$) was lower than that of the control group ($M = 44.6$, $SD = 5.68$). Therefore, the first null hypothesis was rejected.

The second hypothesis was tested using the scores from the LSI–Z from the experimental and control groups in a one-way ANOVA. The ANOVA revealed a significant difference between groups $F(2,12) = 14.98$, $p < .01$. The mean scores of the experimental group ($M = 24.3$, $SD = 3.24$) were found to be significantly higher than the control group ($M = 20.3$, $SD = 5.68$). The second null hypothesis was rejected.

Eighteen individuals had originally agreed to participate in the study. Two participants who had been assigned to the control treatment withdrew from the study during the data collection phase. Additionally, the researcher eliminated data from two other individuals, one from the experimental group and one from the control group. The latter participants were withdrawn from the study because it was determined that they subsequently did not meet the criteria for inclusion. The participant from the control group expressed to the researcher that she had given inaccurate answers on the posttest because for religious reasons she did not want to give negative answers. The participant in the experimental group began to cry during the last session, sharing that he had recently been diagnosed with prostate cancer and that his wife of 46 years had died within the last month.

The remaining 14 individuals ranged in age from 45 to 87, with a mean age of 68. There were three females and four males in the experimental group as well as in the control group. The mean age of the control group was 67.5; 68.5 was the mean age of the experimental group. All participants were Caucasian, although two of the original 18 were African American. Eleven were married, one was divorced, and two were widows.

Discussion

This exploratory pilot study is the first to examine Life Review as a treatment to manage depression and increase life satisfaction in individuals who have ex-
385 perienced CVAs. The study involved a small sample (*n* = 14) due to the restrictive nature of the criteria for admission to the study. Three years were required to obtain the small sample, possibly due to the restrictive inclusion criteria. The researcher was receiving refer-
390 rals on an extremely irregular basis and decided after three years to accept the sample size of 14.

Experiencing a CVA is considered to be a major life crisis, changing an individual's and his or her family's life. Butler (1963) postulated that the life review
395 process occurs at times of crisis; this process can be facilitated psychodynamically, either individually or in groups. In this study, facilitation of the life review demonstrated at < .01 level of significance a difference between experimental and control groups with regard
400 to higher degree of life satisfaction and lower levels of depression.

Lower levels of depression and higher degrees of life satisfaction with the life review process with individuals who have experienced a CVA could also mean
405 that life review therapy could be beneficial in assisting the participants in the adjustment process related to their CVA, thereby helping them to overcome the life crisis of a CVA.

Previous data-based and theoretical studies on the
410 life review process have yielded conflicting results. Muntz and White (1989) and Stevens-Ratchford (1993) revealed no significant effects using the life review. The longitudinal study of Haight (1992) is most consistent with the present study, demonstrating no increases
415 in depression nor decreases in self-esteem one-year post-life review treatment and significant gains in life satisfaction and psychological well-being eight weeks post-life review treatment.

Limitations

There were several limitations of the study.

420   1. The sample size was only 14. The high acuity level of admitted patients at the time of the study may have been a significant factor as well as the restrictive inclusion criteria.

   2. The researcher administered the treatment and al-
425   ternative treatments to individuals in the experimental and control group as well as administering the instruments. Experimenter bias may have occurred.

   3. The participants had interaction with other health-
430   care providers and family members, which could have influenced responses on the posttest.

   4. Family dynamics that may have influenced depression and life satisfaction could have been present unbeknownst to the researcher.

435   5. The cultural composition of the sample was Caucasian. African Americans and Asian Americans,

however, were considered for the study but did not meet inclusion criteria. This final sample may pose a problem with generalizability.

440   Even though there were limitations, the results of this pilot study add to the growing body of literature supporting the need for nonpharmacological interventions for this population. As one subject stated, "Now I don't feel like I'm just a person with a left arm and leg
445   that don't work. I realize that I am still a valuable person with a lot to offer people around me."

Implications

Current research utilizing life review therapy is inconsistent with regard to therapeutic efficacy but does lead one to assume that there may be value to the inter-
450   vention. This intervention could be implemented by nurses in rehabilitation settings as well as in home health settings with CVA patients. When working with patients having depressive or other mental disorders, it is recommended that a qualified practitioner be avail-
455   able in the event that follow-up counseling is needed to address sensitive issues.

The researcher cautiously interprets the results due to the small sample size. However, the results of this study have theoretical implications in that this study
460   addressed the issue of the process of the life review occurring during time of crisis. The findings of the study support the psychodynamic theory of life review and crisis. Because this study demonstrated significantly lower levels of depression and a higher degree
465   of life satisfaction, the researcher very cautiously concludes that the participants in the experimental group may possibly be better able to meet the crisis of a right hemisphere CVA. Further research with a larger sample size is recommended.

References

Anderson, G., Vestergaard, K., Ingemann-Nielsen, M., & Lauritzen, L. (1995). Risk factors for post-stroke depression. *Acta Psychiatrica Scandinavica, 92,* 193–198.

Astrom, M., Adolfsson, R., & Asplund, K. (1993). Major depression in stroke patients: A three-year longitudinal study. *Stroke, 24,* 976–982.

Baiyewu, O., & Jegede, O. (1992). Life satisfaction in elderly Nigerians: Reliability and factor composition of the Life Satisfaction Index–Z. *Age and Aging, 21,* 256.

Butler, R. (1963). The life review: An interpretation of reminiscence in the aged. *Psychiatry, 26,* 65–76.

Froehlich, J., & Nelson, D. (1986). Affective meanings of life review through activities and discussion. *American Journal of Occupational Therapy, 40,* 27–33.

Giltinan, J. (1990). Using life review to facilitate self-actualization in elderly women. *Gerontology and Geriatrics Education, 10,* 75–83.

Haight, B. (1982). *Haight's life review and experiencing form.* Unpublished instrument. Medical University of South Carolina, Charleston, SC.

Haight, B. (1991). Reminiscing: The state of the art as a basis for practice. *International Journal of Aging and Human Development, 33,* 1–32.

Haight, B. (1992). Long-term effects of a structured life review process. *Journal of Gerontology, 47,* 312–315.

Hermann, N., Black, S. E., Lawrence, J., Szekely, C., & Szalai, J. P. (1998). The Sunnybrook stroke study of depressive symptoms and functional outcome. *Stroke, 29,* 618–624.

Hilton, E. (2002). The meaning of stroke in elderly women. *Journal of Gerontological Nursing, 28,* 19–26.

Keyser, D. J., & Sweetland, R. C. (Eds.). (1985). *Test critiques* (vol. 3). Kansas City, MO: Westport.

Kropf, N., & Greene, R. (1993). Life review with families who care for developmentally disabled members: A model. *Journal of Gerontological Social Work, 2,* 25–39.

Lofgren, B., Gustafson, Y., & Nyberg, L. (1998). Psychological well-being three years after severe stroke. *Stroke, 30,* 567–572.

Merriam, S. (1993). Butler's life review: How universal is it? *International Journal of Aging and Human Development, 37,* 163–175.

Molinari, Y., Cully, J., Kendjelic, E., & Kunik, M. (2001). Reminiscence and its relationship to attachment and personality in gero-psychiatric patients. *International Journal of Aging and Human Development, 52,* 173–184.

Muntz, M., & White, J. (1989). The use of a structured life review process as a therapeutic nursing intervention with institutionalized older adults. Unpublished manuscript.

O'Connor, P. (1994). Salient themes in the life review of a sample of frail elderly respondents in London. *Gerontologist, 24,* 224–230.

Paolucci, S., Antonucci, G., Pratesi, L., Traballesi, M., Grasso, M., & Lubich, S. (1999). Post stroke depression and its role in rehabilitation patients. *Archives of Physical Medicine and Rehabilitation, 80,* 985–990.

Peachey, N. (1992). Helping the elderly person resolve integrity versus despair. *Perspectives in Psychiatric Care, 28,* 29–30.

Polit, D. P., Beck, C. T., & Hungler. B. P. (2001). *Essentials of Nursing Research.* Philadelphia: Lippincott.

Robinson-Smith, G. (2002). Self-efficacy and quality of life after stroke. *Journal of Neuroscience Nursing, 34,* 91–98.

Rochette, A., & Desrosiers, J. (2002). Coping with the consequences of a stroke. *International Journal of Rehabilitation Research, 25,* 17–24.

Sherman, E. (1987). Reminiscence groups for community elderly. *Gerontologist, 7,* 569–572.

Stevens-Ratchford, R. (1993). The effect of life review reminiscence activities on depression and self-esteem in older adults. *American Journal of Occupational Therapy, 47,* 413–430.

Waters, E. (1990). The life review: Strategies for working with individual and groups. *Journal of Mental Health Counseling, 12,* 270–278.

Williams, G. R., Jaing, J. G., Matchar, D. B., & Samsa, G. P. (1999). Incidence and occurrence of total (first-ever and recurrent) stroke. *Stroke, 30,* 2523–2528.

Wood, V., Wylie, M. L., & Schaefer, B. (1969). An analysis of a short self-report measure of life satisfaction: Correlation with rater judgments. *Journal of Gerontology, 24,* 465–469.

Zung, W. (1967). A self-rating depression scale. *Archives of General Psychiatry, 12,* 63–70.

Address correspondence to: Marsha Courville Davis, 801 Harmony Lane, Mandeville, LA 70471. E-mail: litlnurs@bellsouth.net

Exercise for Article 11

Factual Questions

1. What is the explicitly stated purpose of the study?

2. What method was used to assign subjects to the experimental or alternative treatments?

3. Participants were recruited through referral from whom?

4. Each of the participants in the experimental treatment received three individually administered sessions of life review therapy. How long did each session last?

5. Did members of the control group engage in activities with the researcher?

6. Of the original eighteen individuals who had originally agreed to participate in the study, how many completed the study?

7. Were both null hypotheses rejected?

Questions for Discussion

8. How important is the "Theoretical Framework" presented in lines 48–58 in helping you understand the study?

9. The researcher did not administer pretests. In your opinion, is this a flaw in the research methodology? Explain. (See lines 166–169.)

10. In lines 191–194, the researcher states that "A consent form was developed and approved by the Institutional Review Board (IRB) of the rehabilitation center. The proposal for the study was reviewed by the IRB and permission for the study to begin was given." In your opinion, is it important for researchers to make such statements in their research reports? Explain.

11. The Life Review Therapy administered to participants in the experimental group is described in lines 230–256. In your opinion, is it described in sufficient detail? Explain. While answering this question, keep in mind that the researcher has provided references where a consumer of research can obtain additional information on this type of therapy.

12. Is it important to know that scores on the ZSD correlated highly with scores on other measures of depression such as the Beck Depression Inventory? Explain. (See lines 295–300.)

13. Do you agree with the researcher that this study is an "exploratory pilot study"? Why? Why not? (See lines 382–385.)

14. This research article is classified as an example of "True Experimental Research" in the table of contents for this book. Do you agree with this classification? Explain.

Quality Ratings

Directions: Indicate your level of agreement with each of the following statements by circling a number from 5 for strongly agree (SA) to 1 for strongly disagree (SD). If you believe an item is not applicable to this research article, leave it blank. Be prepared to explain your ratings. When responding to criteria A and B below, keep in mind that brief titles and abstracts are conventional in published research.

A.   The title of the article is appropriate.

SA   5   4   3   2   1   SD

B. The abstract provides an effective overview of the research article.

    SA   5   4   3   2   1   SD

C. The introduction establishes the importance of the study.

    SA   5   4   3   2   1   SD

D. The literature review establishes the context for the study.

    SA   5   4   3   2   1   SD

E. The research purpose, question, or hypothesis is clearly stated.

    SA   5   4   3   2   1   SD

F. The method of sampling is sound.

    SA   5   4   3   2   1   SD

G. Relevant demographics (for example, age, gender, and ethnicity) are described.

    SA   5   4   3   2   1   SD

H. Measurement procedures are adequate.

    SA   5   4   3   2   1   SD

I. All procedures have been described in sufficient detail to permit a replication of the study.

    SA   5   4   3   2   1   SD

J. The participants have been adequately protected from potential harm.

    SA   5   4   3   2   1   SD

K. The results are clearly described.

    SA   5   4   3   2   1   SD

L. The discussion/conclusion is appropriate.

    SA   5   4   3   2   1   SD

M. Despite any flaws, the report is worthy of publication.

    SA   5   4   3   2   1   SD

Article 12

Preop Fluid Bolus Reduces Risk of Postop Nausea and Vomiting: A Pilot Study

S. Monti, CRNA, MS, **M. E. Pokorny**, PhD, RN[*]

ABSTRACT. Postoperative nausea and vomiting (PONV) are distressing and common occurrences after operative procedures requiring general anesthesia. The purpose of this study was to determine the effect of a preoperative 1-liter fluid bolus of normal saline on a patient's postoperative nausea and vomiting. This pilot study compared the incidence of nausea and vomiting between an experimental group that received a 1-liter fluid bolus preoperatively and a control group that was given the standard fluid requirements. Subjects consisted of 90 females who underwent gynecological laparoscopic surgery. The two groups were evenly divided, with 45 in each group. There was no difference in the mean age of the two groups. The average age in the control and the study groups was 33. The weight of the control group was significantly higher, 80 kg vs. 69 kg, in the experimental group ($p = .018$). Thirty percent of the control group had nausea, and 5% experienced vomiting. The experimental group had a 12% nausea rate and no vomiting. When episodes of nausea and vomiting were combined, there was a significant difference between the groups ($p = .001$). Fifty-one percent of the control group had an episode of nausea/vomiting while only 17% of the experimental group experienced nausea or vomiting. Our findings suggest that administering a liter of saline fluid bolus decreases the incidence of nausea and vomiting in this population. Further studies need to examine the use of hydration without the use of antiemetics and control for other factors that might affect nausea and vomiting.

From *The Internet Journal of Advanced Nursing Practice, 4.*
Copyright © 2000 by Internet Scientific Publications. Reprinted with permission.

Introduction

Postoperative nausea and vomiting (PONV) are distressing and common occurrences after operative procedures requiring general anesthesia. PONV may prolong recovery time, increase postoperative morbidity,
5 delay patient discharge, and increase hospital costs.[1] Many factors have been associated with PONV, including anesthetic techniques, anesthetic agents, narcotics, pain, types of surgical procedures, anxiety, sex, obesity, and prior history of PONV or motion sick-
10 ness.[2,3,4,5] The general view is that modern anesthetic drugs and techniques have reduced the incidence of PONV, but the data indicate that the incidence has changed little in the past 30 years and is still unacceptably high, ranging from 5–30%.[6,7,8,9,10] Although
15 some rank nausea and vomiting as a "minor" complication, in a survey of dissatisfied ambulatory surgery patients, PONV was cited by 71% as the reason for their poor rating of the postoperative experience. Many patients were more willing to accept pain than to suffer
20 from nausea and vomiting.[5]

Much has been written on the etiology, prevention, and treatment of this complication. Several studies have examined nontraditional methods of preventing or treating nausea and vomiting, including the use of can-
25 nabinoids, propofol, and acupressure/acupuncture.[11,12]

Recent research suggests that dehydration may be a precipitating factor in the occurrence of PONV.[13] Studies have shown that the functional extracellular fluid volume is reduced in both minor and major surgery.
30 Preop fasting can leave a large fluid deficit in the surgical patient. For example, eight hours of fasting in a 70 kg patient can cause at least a 1-liter fluid deficit. The risk of dehydration is greater in patients who receive preop bowel preps, the elderly, children, patients
35 with acities, burns, trauma, bowel obstruction, or peritonitis and those who undergo surgery later in the day. During a surgical procedure, there are many avenues of fluid loss. Unhumidified anesthetic gasses, perspiration, evaporation, blood loss, urine, and loss of other
40 body fluids (acities, GI contents) are among the most common causes of loss. All of these contribute to dehydration.[14]

In 1995, Yogendran and Asokremoar investigated the impact of preoperative fluid status on clinical out-
45 comes. Two hundred ASA Grade 1–3 ambulatory surgical patients were randomized into two groups to receive high (20 cc/kg) or low (2 cc/kg) infusion of isotonic electrolytes preoperatively. Outcomes were assessed at 30 and 60 minutes after surgery, at discharge,
50 and on the first preop day. The incidences of thirst, drowsiness, and dizziness were significantly lower in

[*]*S. Monti* is employed by the Ft. Sanders Anesthesia Group and works at Ft. Sanders Regional Medical Center, Knoxville, Tennessee. *M. E. Pokorny* is a professor, Adult Health, School of Nursing, East Carolina University, Greenville, North Carolina.

the high infusion group. However, the study was too small to allow broad generalizations.[6]

In 1997, Elhakim et al. reported the effect of intra-operative fluid load on postoperative nausea and vomiting over three days after day-case termination of pregnancy. In a randomized study, 100 patients were allocated into one of two groups receiving 1000 cc of compound sodium lactate solution during surgery or no intraoperative fluid. The scores of nausea were significantly lower in the fluid groups compared with the control group.[15]

Berry (1991), outlining the causes and treatment of postoperative nausea and vomiting, advocates delaying oral administration of fluids from 6 to 8 hours postop. Berry suggests hydrating children up to age 3 the first hour with 25 cc/kg, with subsequent administration of 15 cc/kg per hr. For older children, he recommends 15 cc/kg for the first hour, then 10 cc/kg thereafter. He notes that incidence of nausea in this group is very low.[1]

In a recent survey conducted in the Post Anesthesia Recovery Room (PACU) at a large teaching hospital, the nausea and vomiting rate for the general surgical population was 8%. For patients undergoing GYN laparoscopic procedures, the rate increased to 11%.[16] The PACU nurses noticed a decrease in the nausea and vomiting rate in those patients who had received an extra amount of IV fluid. This study was undertaken in order to further explore the relationship between the degrees of hydration preoperatively and nausea and vomiting following surgery.

Methodology

This pilot study compared the incidence of nausea and vomiting with an experimental group that received a 1-liter fluid bolus preoperatively and a control group that was given the standard fluid requirements. After review and approval from the Institutional Review Board, the study was conducted in the Operating Room, Post Anesthesia Care Unit and the Ambulatory Surgical Unit (ASU) at a large teaching hospital in the Southeast. Subjects consisted of 90 females who underwent gynecological laparoscopic surgery. Criteria used for inclusion in the study were age 18–55, nonemergent, nonpregnant, ambulatory admission status, no prior history of nausea or vomiting, and ASA Class 1 or 2. Class 1 patients have no organic, physiologic, biochemical, or psychiatric disturbance. The pathologic process for which the operation is to be performed is localized and does not entail a systemic disturbance. Class 2 patients have mild to moderate system disturbances caused either by the condition to be treated or by other pathophysiologic processes.[15]

The OR schedule was reviewed the day before surgery to identify potential subjects. After obtaining informed consent, subjects were randomly assigned to either the control or the experimental group, using a random distribution table. All patients underwent the usual preoperative anesthesia assessment. Those in the experimental group received 1000 cc of normal saline as a preop fluid bolus. Those in the control group received the usual IV fluid of Lactated Ringers in an amount decided by the anesthetist. The amount of fluid received was recorded. The anesthetics, drugs used, and anesthesia techniques were decided by the attending anesthesiologist/anesthetist. Surgery proceeded as usual. During the stay in the PACU, patients were evaluated by the nurse for the presence or absence of nausea or vomiting. Nausea was defined as awareness of the tendency to vomit. Vomiting was the forceful expelling of gastric contents through the mouth. The PACU nurses were instructed not to make suggestions to the patients about the feeling of nausea. All episodes of nausea and vomiting were recorded on a data flow sheet. After discharge to the ASU, the subjects continued to be observed for any late signs of nausea and vomiting, and episodes were recorded on the flow sheet.

Demographic information was analyzed using descriptive statistics. Analysis of variance was conducted to test for differences between the mean frequencies of nausea and vomiting of the two groups. An alpha level of .05 was used to determine significance.

Results

The two groups were evenly divided, with 45 in each group. There was no difference in the mean age of the two groups. The average age in the control and the study groups was 33. However, the weight of the control group was significantly higher. The control group was 80 kg vs. 69 kg in the experimental group ($p = .018$). Thirty percent of the subjects in the control group had nausea and 5% experienced vomiting. The experimental group had a 12% nausea rate and no vomiting. When episodes of nausea and vomiting were combined, there was a significant difference between the groups ($p = .001$). Fifty-one percent of the subjects in the control group had an episode of nausea/vomiting while only 17% of the experimental group experienced nausea or vomiting.

The use of antiemetics was recorded to see if their usage might have affected the incidence of nausea and vomiting. The antiemetics used were ondansetron, metoclopamide and droperidol. There was no significant difference between the groups in the use of antiemetics. Thirty-seven percent of the subjects in the control group received antiemetics and 33% of the study group received antiemetics. This fact is interesting in that despite the prophylactic use of antiemetics in both groups, the rate of nausea and vomiting was still high.

The volumes of fluid received by the two groups were also compared. The control group received a mean amount of 1803 cc while the experimental group received 1212 cc. There was a significant difference in this amount ($p < .05$).

Discussion

This study found a difference in the rate of nausea
and vomiting between patients who were administered
165 a fluid bolus preoperatively and those who were not.
This difference existed regardless of the use of antiemetics. This finding is consistent with Yogendran et al.
(1995) and Elhakim et al. (1998), who concluded that
patients who received higher amounts of fluid preop-
170 eratively tended to have less postoperative nausea and
vomiting.[6,13] The correlation between weight and vomiting and nausea was not studied. The control group
was heavier and also had more nausea and vomiting,
which is similar to Watcha and White (1992) and
175 Mannino (1990), who found that there is a positive
correlation between weight and nausea and vomiting.[5,17] It would be interesting to separate obese patients in both groups to examine their rate of nau-
sea/vomiting.

180   Our findings suggest that administering a liter of
saline fluid bolus decreases the incidence of nausea and
vomiting in this population. However, the study was
limited by its small sample and by the fact that only
patients who were ASA Class 1 and 2 were included.
185 Further, there was no control for the timing of surgery.
Some cases started as the first case of the day, while
others did not start until the afternoon, increasing the
chances of dehydration in those subjects. A standard
regime for fluid replacement was not followed. Instead,
190 fluid replacement was left to the discretion of the anesthetist. What needs to be clarified in future studies is
the timing of the fluid bolus and inclusion of a standardized fluid replacement formula. Further research is
needed to identify how the different antiemetics af-
195 fected nausea and vomiting in each group. Future studies need to examine the use of hydration without the
use of antiemetics and control for other factors that
might affect nausea and vomiting.

References

1. Berry FA. Post-op vomiting, causes and treatment. Current Review Nurse Anesthesia 1991;13(22):175.
2. Paxton LD, McKay AC, Mirakhur RK. Prevention of nausea and vomiting after a day case gynecological laparoscopy. Anesthesia 1995;50:403–406.
3. Wetchler BV. Postoperative nausea and vomiting in day case surgery. British Journal of Anesthesia 1992;69:13s–39s.
4. White PF, White LD. Cost containment in the operating room: Who is responsible? J. Clinical Anesthesia 1994;6:351–356.
5. Watcha MF, White PF. Postoperative nausea and vomiting. Its etiology, treatment, and prevention. Anesthesiology 1992;77:162–184.
6. Yogendran S, Asokremoar B. A prospective double-blinded study of the effect of IV fluid therapy on averse outcomes on outpatient surgery. Anesth Analg 1995;80(682–686):682.
7. Quinn AC, Brown JH. Studies in post-op sequelae. Nausea and vomiting—still a problem. Anesthesia 1994;49(62–68):62.
8. Haigh CA, Chaplain LA, Durham IM, Dupeyron MH, Kenny, GNC. Nausea and vomiting after gynecological surgery: A meta-analysis of factors affecting their incidence. British Journal of Anesthesia 1993;71:517–522.
9. Cohen MM, Duncan PG, DeBoer DP, Tweed WA. The postoperative interview: Assessing risk factors for nausea and vomiting. Anesth Analg 1994;78:716.
10. Cohen MM, Rose KD, Yee DA. Changing anesthesiologist's practice patterns, Can it be done? Anesthesiology 1996;85:260–269.
11. Dundee JW, Ghaly, RG, McKinney MS. P6 acupuncture antiemesis comparison of invasive and noninvasive techniques (Abstracts). Anesthesiology 1990;73:A36.
12. Gonzalez-Rosales F, Walsh D. Intractable nausea and vomiting due to gastrointestinal mucosal metastases relieved by tetrahydrocannabinol (dronabinol). Journal of Pain & Symptom Management 1997;14(5):311–314.
13. Suntheralingham Y, Buvanendran A, Davy CHC, Frances C. A prospective randomized double-blinded study of the effect of intravenous fluid therapy on adverse outcomes on outpatient surgery. Anesth Analg 1995;80:682–686.
14. Lewis SM, Heitkemper, MM, Dirksen, SR. Medical-surgical nursing: Assessment and management of clinical problems. 5th ed. St. Louis (MO): CV Mosby; 2000.
15. Barash PG, Cullen BF, Stoelting RK. Clinical Anesthesia. Philadelphia (PA): Lippincott Williams & Wilkins; 2000.
16. Pitt County Memorial Hospital. Quality assurance data. Greenville, NC: Pitt County Memorial Hospital; 1996–97.
17. Mannino, MI. Nausea and vomiting in ambulatory surgery. CRNA: The Clinical Forum for Nurse Anesthetists, I, 1990;32–35.

Exercise for Article 12

Factual Questions

1. PONV was cited in a previous survey as the reason for their poor rating of the postoperative experience by what percentage of the participants in that survey?

2. The researchers indicate that the 1995 study by Yogendran and Asokremoar was too small to allow what?

3. What treatment was given to the experimental group that was not given to the control group?

4. What was the total number of subjects (i.e., participants) in this study?

5. The subjects were assigned at random to the two groups. Did the random assignment produce two groups that were, on average, equal in age? Were they, on average, equal in weight?

6. When episodes of nausea and vomiting were combined, was there a significant difference between the two groups? If yes, at what probability level was it significant?

7. The researchers suggest that further research is needed to identify how the different antiemetics affect what?

Questions for Discussion

8. The researchers refer to their study as a "pilot study." (See line 83.) What is your understanding of the meaning of this term? Do you agree that their study is a pilot study? Explain.

9. The subjects were "randomly assigned" to either the control or experimental group. How important is it to know that random assignment was used? Explain. (See lines 104–107.)

10. When the PACU nurses were collecting the data, they were instructed not to make suggestions to the patients about the feeling of nausea. Speculate on why the nurses were given this instruction. (See lines 120–122.)

11. Do you agree with the researchers that it would be interesting to study obese patients separately from those who are not obese? Explain. (See lines 171–179.)

12. Suppose another researcher submitted a proposal for funding of another, more definitive study on the same general topic. Further, suppose that you are a member of the committee and that the committee has access to adequate funds to sponsor research. Would you be in favor of funding additional research on this topic? In light of this study, are there any particular suggestions or recommendations you would make to the researcher? Explain.

Quality Ratings

Directions: Indicate your level of agreement with each of the following statements by circling a number from 5 for strongly agree (SA) to 1 for strongly disagree (SD). If you believe an item is not applicable to this research article, leave it blank. Be prepared to explain your ratings. When responding to criteria A and B below, keep in mind that brief titles and abstracts are conventional in published research.

A. The title of the article is appropriate.

SA   5   4   3   2   1   SD

B. The abstract provides an effective overview of the research article.

SA   5   4   3   2   1   SD

C. The introduction establishes the importance of the study.

SA   5   4   3   2   1   SD

D. The literature review establishes the context for the study.

SA   5   4   3   2   1   SD

E. The research purpose, question, or hypothesis is clearly stated.

SA   5   4   3   2   1   SD

F. The method of sampling is sound.

SA   5   4   3   2   1   SD

G. Relevant demographics (for example, age, gender, and ethnicity) are described.

SA   5   4   3   2   1   SD

H. Measurement procedures are adequate.

SA   5   4   3   2   1   SD

I. All procedures have been described in sufficient detail to permit a replication of the study.

SA   5   4   3   2   1   SD

J. The participants have been adequately protected from potential harm.

SA   5   4   3   2   1   SD

K. The results are clearly described.

SA   5   4   3   2   1   SD

L. The discussion/conclusion is appropriate.

SA   5   4   3   2   1   SD

M. Despite any flaws, the report is worthy of publication.

SA   5   4   3   2   1   SD

Article 13

An Intervention Study to Enhance Medication Compliance in Community-Dwelling Elderly Individuals

Terry T. Fulmer, PhD, RN, FAAN, Penny Hollander Feldman, PhD, Tae Sook Kim, RN, MSN, Barbara Carty, EdD, RN, Mark Beers, MD, Maria Molina, MD, Margaret Putnam, BA[*]

ABSTRACT

Objective: To determine whether daily videotelephone or regular telephone reminders would increase the proportion of prescribed cardiac medications taken in a sample of elderly individuals who have congestive heart failure (CHF).

Methods: The authors recruited community-dwelling individuals age 65 and older who had the primary or secondary diagnosis of CHF into a randomized controlled trial of reminder calls designed to enhance medication compliance. There were three arms: a control group that received usual care; a group that received regular daily telephone call reminders; and a group that received daily videotelephone call reminders. Compliance was defined as the percent of therapeutic coverage as recorded by Medication Event Monitoring System (MEMS) caps. Subjects were recruited from two sources: a large urban home health care agency and a large urban ambulatory clinic of a major teaching hospital. Baseline and post-intervention MOS 36-Item Short-Form Health Survey (SF-36) scores and Minnesota Living with Heart Failure (MLHF) scores were obtained.

Results: There was a significant time effect during the course of the study from baseline to post-intervention ($F[2,34] = 4.08$, $p < .05$). Over time the elderly individuals who were called, either by telephone or videotelephone, showed enhanced medication compliance relative to the control group. There was a trend, but no significant difference between the two intervention groups. Both SF-36 and MLHF scores improved from baseline to post-intervention for all groups. There was no significant change in the SF-36 scores for the sample, but there was a significant change for the MLHF scores ($p < .001$). The control group had a significant falloff in the medication compliance rate during the course of the study, dropping from 81% to 57%.

Conclusions: Telephone interventions are effective in enhancing medication compliance and may prove more cost effective than clinic visits or preparation of pre-poured pill boxes in the home. Technologic advances which enable clinicians to monitor and enhance patient medication compliance may reduce costly and distressing hospitalization for elderly individuals with CHF.

From *Journal of Gerontological Nursing*, 25, 6–14. Copyright © 1999 by SLACK Incorporated. Reprinted with permission.

Medication compliance is a critical element in the successful management of treatable diseases and symptoms. Noncompliance poses a serious health risk to those who are unable or unwilling to take their medica-
5   tions as prescribed, and certain populations may be at increased risk for the complications resulting from poor adherence to a medication regimen. Elderly individuals who live at home are such a population. It has been well documented that the compliance rate, in general,
10   for elderly individuals taking medications is problematic (Cargill, 1992; Kruse et al., 1992; Salzman, 1995).

Estimates of noncompliance in the geriatric population vary from study to study, depending in part on the definition used and the method of measurement. Kruse
15   et al. (1992) used the microprocessor-based Medication Event Monitoring System (MEMS) (Cramer, Mattson, Prevey, Scheyer, & Ouellette, 1989; Kruse & Weber, 1990) to measure compliance, which was defined as the percentage of prescribed doses taken. The reliabil-
20   ity and validity of the MEMS for measuring compliance has been addressed (DeGeest, Dunbar-Jacob, & Vanhaeckel, 1998) in a hypertension study where interviews were conducted to compare patient reports of compliance versus the MEMS data, and superior speci-
25   ficity and reliability were documented. Based on a sample of 18 independently living elderly patients discharged from the hospital, they reported patient-specific noncompliance rates ranging from 0% to 76%, with a mean of 31% in the third week after discharge
30   (DeGeest et al., 1998). Fineman and DeFelice (1992) measured compliance by administering a 20-question survey instrument to elderly individuals attending senior citizen centers. Using this self-report method, they found 15% of their sample to be noncompliant with a
35   prescribed medication regimen (Fineman & DeFelice, 1992).

---

[*]*Terry T. Fulmer* is professor, Division of Nursing, New York University, New York, New York. *Tae Sook Kim* is research doctoral fellow, Division of Nursing, New York University, New York, New York. *Barbara Carty* is clinical associate professor, Division of Nursing, New York University, New York, New York. *Penny Hollander Feldman* is director, Center for Home Care Policy and Research of the Visiting Nurse Service, New York, New York. *Margaret Putnam* is project coordinator, Center for Home Care Policy and Research of the Visiting Nurse Service, New York, New York. *Mark Beers* is associate editor, *Merck Manuals* and Senior Director Geriatrics, Merck and Company, West Point, Pennsylvania. *Maria Molina* is intern, Elmhurst General Hospital, Elmhurst, New York.

Regardless of the exact range or percentage of coverage one accepts as the true reflection of medication noncompliance, practitioners agree that the health risks associated with poor adherence warrant serious experimentation with strategies designed to improve compliance rates. This article reports one such experiment: a randomized trial aimed at testing two interventions for enhancing medication compliance among elderly patients with congestive heart failure (CHF). The purpose of the study was to determine whether daily videotelephone or regular telephone reminders would increase the proportion of prescribed cardiac medications taken by these patients. The authors anticipated that the modest commitment of time required for a daily call to each elderly individual would yield a significant improvement in compliance.

Factors Affecting Medication Compliance

Researchers have studied a variety of factors posited to affect medication compliance among elderly individuals. Patient-related factors include: knowledge and understanding of the medication regimen and its purpose (Fineman & DeFelice, 1992; Fitten, Coleman, Siembieda, Yu, & Ganzell, 1995; Klein, German, McPhee, Smith, & Levine, 1982; Wolfe & Schirm, 1992); cognitive functioning (Isaac & Tamblyn, 1993); age; and depressive symptomatology (Spiers & Kutzik, 1995). Overall, researchers have not found a significant relationship between knowledge and compliance behaviors in elderly individuals. In contrast, elderly individuals, ages, cognitive abilities, and levels of depression have been found to be significant predictors of compliance (Isaac & Tamblyn, 1993; Spiers & Kutzik, 1995).

Other factors posited to affect medication compliance are associated with the medication regimen per se. These include the number of medications, the number of pills, the complexity of the drug regimen, and the packaging of the prescribed medication. Evidence on these factors is mixed. Isaac and Tamblyn (1993) found no relationship between medication compliance and the number of medications, number of pills, or complexity of the regimen. On the other hand, in a randomized study of medication dosing and packaging alternatives, Murray, Birt, Manatunga, and Darnell (1993) found evidence to suggest that simplifying complex drug regimens to twice-daily administration with unit-of-use packages may improve medication compliance rates.

Strategies for Enhancing Compliance

Strategies for improving compliance can be categorized into three groups: enabling, consequence, and stimulant (McKinney, Munroe, & Wright, 1992). Enabling strategies are intended to equip patients to be compliant. Such strategies include counseling patients, providing patient education, simplifying the medication regimen, increasing access to medical care and prescription sources, and prescribing less costly therapies. Consequence strategies are aimed at reinforcing compliant behavior. Instructing patients to maintain records of pill-taking and rewarding them for acceptable compliance levels is an example of this approach. Stimulant strategies are intended to prompt pill taking. Examples of tested approaches include tailoring doses to daily rituals, placing reminder cards in prominent places in patients' homes, visiting the patients' homes to reinforce compliance, having spouses or friends remind patients to take their medications, and using special drug packaging to organize and prompt dose-taking.

The results of studies using enabling strategies are mixed, suggesting that neither patient education nor increased knowledge of medications per se necessarily leads to improved compliance. Wolfe and Schirm (1992) investigated the effect of medication counseling by a nurse on elderly individuals' medication knowledge and compliance behaviors and found no significant compliance differences between patients who received medication counseling and those who did not. Cargill (1992) tested the relative impact of a 20-minute teaching session, including a review of medication times, compared to a similar 20-minute teaching session followed by a 1-week to 2-week follow-up telephone call in which a nurse reviewed the medication regimen with the patients. Those patients who received a telephone call in addition to the teaching session showed a significantly greater improvement in medication-taking behavior ($F = .31, p < .01$). The patients in the teaching group who did not receive a telephone call demonstrated only a weak and insignificant increase in pill percentage compliance. The findings of the Cargill (1992) study suggest that a stimulant intervention (e.g., a follow-up telephone call) added to an enabling strategy may enhance home medication-taking behaviors.

Because of advanced technology, several electronic aids currently are available to support stimulant strategies designed to increase medication compliance. Examples are computer-generated reminder charts (Raynor, Booth, & Blenkinsopp, 1993); electronic medication compliance aids (McKinney et al., 1992); and MEMS (Lee et al., 1996; Matsuyama, Mason, & Jue, 1993). The latter have been described extensively in the literature, with excellent validity and with multiple methods of understanding the adherence based on the method of calculation (Rohay, Dunbar-Jacobs, Sereika, Kwoh, & Burke, 1998). McKinney et al. (1992) investigated the impact of an electronic medication compliance aid on long-term blood pressure control in ambulant patients residing in a retirement community or attending a primary care center. Patients were assigned randomly to one of two groups: an experimental group that received antihypertensive medication in vials fit with an electronic timepiece cap; and a control group that received antihypertensive medication in vials fit with standard caps. Patients in the experimental group received one timepiece cap for each drug prescribed. Blood pressure was recorded at the outset of the study and monitored periodically during

150 the subsequent 12 weeks. Subjects using the timepiece cap showed an average compliance rate of 95.1%, an average decrease in systolic pressure of 7.6 mm Hg ($p < .01$), and an average decrease in diastolic pressure of 8.8 mm Hg ($p < .01$). Subjects in the control group had
155 an average compliance rate of only 78% and a decrease of only 2.8 mm Hg and .2 mm Hg in systolic and diastolic pressures, respectively.

Raynor et al. (1993) studied the effect of computer-generated reminder charts on patients' compliance with
160 drug regimens after discharge from the hospital. Patients were assigned randomly to four groups: Group A received brief counseling from a nurse (usual care); Group B received the counseling from a nurse, plus a reminder chart; Group C received structured counsel-
165 ing from a pharmacist; Group D received structured counseling from a pharmacist, plus a reminder chart. Of those patients who received the reminder chart, 83% correctly described their dose regimen, compared with 47% of those without the chart ($p < .001$). Raynor et al.
170 (1993) concluded that an automatically generated individualized reminder chart could be a practical and cost-effective aid to compliance.

The study described in this article also used advanced technology to support a stimulant strategy. It
175 was designed to test the effectiveness of videotelephone reminders—compared to regular telephone calls or usual care—in improving medication compliance among a home-based elderly population with a chronic illness. Medication Event Monitoring System (MEMS)
180 caps (Aprex Corporation, Fremont, California)—computerized medication caps placed on a participant's medication bottles—were employed as the means for measuring compliance. Based on the stimulant strategy literature (McKinney et al., 1992), both auditory and
185 visual stimulation were selected as prompts to determine any differences. The Medical Outcome Survey 36-Item Short-Form Health Survey (SF-36) (Ware & Sherbourne, 1992) was selected to determine if quality-of-life scores would be affected by adherence. The
190 Minnesota Living with Heart Failure (MLHF) Questionnaire (Rector, Kubo, & Cohn, 1987) was used to understand specific symptoms of the disease related to medication compliance. It was hypothesized that improved medication compliance would improve both
195 SF-36 and MLHF scores.

Methods

The authors recruited community-dwelling individuals age 65 and older who had the primary or secondary diagnosis of CHF to participate in a randomized controlled study of reminder calls designed to enhance
200 medication compliance. The study consisted of three arms: a control group receiving usual care ($n = 18$); a group that received daily telephone calls ($n = 15$); and a group that received daily videotelephone calls ($n = 17$). The rationale for varying the prompt mode (video-
205 telephone versus telephone) came from a clinical belief that elderly individuals would do better and improve medication-taking behavior with a video (i.e., face-to-face simulation) rather than through a telephone intervention alone. Compliance was defined as the percent
210 of therapeutic coverage (proportion of prescribed medication doses taken) as recorded by the MEMS caps.

Subject Recruitment

Subjects were referred from two sources: a large urban home health care agency and a large urban am-
215 bulatory care clinic of a major teaching hospital. Institutional review board (IRB) approval was obtained for each site. Inclusion criteria were:

- Current patient of the Visiting Nurse Service (VNS) of New York or Columbia Presbyterian Medical
220 Center (CPMC).
- Primary or secondary diagnosis of CHF, age 65 or older.
- Resident of Manhattan.
- No pre-pour medications order (i.e., medications
225 were not dispensed via unit of use packages such as daily or weekly dosing dispensers).
- Use of an angiotensin-converting enzyme (ACE) inhibitor, calcium channel blocker, or beta-blocker.
- Fluency in English or Spanish.
230 - Mini Mental-Status Examination (MMSE) (Folstein, Folstein, & McHugh, 1975) score of 20 or better.
- Experience in using a telephone.
- Home equipped with a telephone and a modular
235 telephone jack.
- Home not in a high-crime building requiring a security guard to accompany research interviewer.

At VNS, eligible subjects were identified through an automated flag implemented via the agency's man-
240 agement information system. At CPMC, eligible subjects were identified by the use of a medical logic module in the CPMC informatics network. Both methods had IRB approval. After referral, subjects were either asked in person by the nurse or asked by tele-
245 phone by a research assistant to participate. All subjects were offered $20 to participate. Approximately 600 eligible patients were referred; of these, 60 agreed to participate. The major reason for refusal to participate was the patient's or their family's perception that
250 the patient was too ill to comply with the study protocol. In fact, the target group for the study was a very frail group with repeated hospitalizations. Randomization occurred using a table of random numbers after the elderly individuals agreed to participate and finished an
255 in-person baseline data-collection interview. Subsequent to randomization, four patients died, two sets of caps were lost, and four people withdrew before completing the study. These 10 subjects were excluded from the analysis.

Data Collection Procedures

260   After consent was obtained, a research assistant went to the subjects' homes to complete the mental status screen (Folstein et al., 1975) and collect the baseline battery data, which included the SF-36 (Ware & Sherbourne, 1992) and the MLHF (Rector et al., 265 1987).

    The MMSE was selected for its clinical brevity and widespread use in the field. It is a 30-item inventory divided into two sections which gives a gross measure of cognition (Folstein et al., 1975). A score of 20 or 270 less greatly increases the chance of cognitive impairment; therefore, the authors selected a cut score of 20 to exclude individuals who may be very impaired, and yet enroll the maximum number of subjects into the study (Siu, Reuben, & Moore, 1994). The SF-36 con-275 tains eight scales that measure both physical and mental dimensions of health status: physical functioning, role limitations secondary to physical functioning, bodily pain, general health perception, vitality, social functioning, role limitations because of emotional prob-280 lems, and mental health. Each scale is scored separately, resulting in a profile of eight scores for each respondent. Items are answered in a Likert-response format. This measure was selected to obtain a baseline of physical and mental function to compare the groups. 285 Similarly, the MLHF questionnaire (Rector et al., 1987), a 21-item survey based on a range of ranking from 0 to 5, was administered at baseline and at the end of the study to determine the degree of symptom management difficulty across groups. All of the aforemen-290 tioned instruments have extensive psychometric testing (Folstein et al., 1975; Rector et al., 1987; Ware & Sherbourne, 1992). After the questionnaires were completed, MEMS caps were placed on a maximum of four medication bottles for each enrolled elderly patient. 295 The number four was selected to provide an average across medications and control for variance. The cost of the caps precluded capping all pill bottles. Medications selected for capping were: ACE inhibitors, calcium channel blockers, beta-blockers, and thereafter, 300 cardiac-related medications such as digoxin, diuretics, and vasodilators. Some elderly patients were taking fewer than four medications and, therefore, had fewer caps. The protocol included a 2-week period of baseline compliance monitoring, a 6-week intervention 305 phase with daily telephone or videotelephone calls, and a 2-week post-intervention compliance monitoring period. Caps were picked up by the research assistant at the end of the 2-week post-intervention period. At that time, a post-interview was conducted, consisting of 310 the SF-36, MLHF, and a set of questions regarding the patient's experience with the study.

The Intervention

    After the 2-week baseline compliance monitoring period had ended, patients were randomized to one of the three study arms. The research assistant went to the

315 home of those in the videotelephone group, installed the videotelephone apparatus, and taught the patients how to use it. At that point, the research assistant also determined a convenient time for the patient to receive daily medication reminder calls. Patients in the stan-320 dard telephone group provided this information via the telephone. Thereafter, during the 6-week intervention period, a telephone or a videotelephone call was made daily (Monday through Friday) during the time window agreed on by the patient and the research assistant. 325 Whether by telephone or videotelephone, the research assistant's reminder call consisted of a brief greeting, and the patients then were asked whether they had taken their medications the previous day. No effort was made to conduct directly observed therapy, and this 330 was not a goal of the study. Calls usually lasted from 3 to 5 minutes, with longer calls occurring when the patient had questions. If there was no answer, the call was placed at regular intervals for the remainder of the day until contact was made. When no contact was made, a 335 notation was made on the study protocol records, and calls were resumed the next day. The only difference between the videotelephone and regular telephone reminder was that the videotelephone group could see the image of the research assistant on the videotelephone 340 screen and vice versa. The videotelephone images are limited by a 2-second frame delay, which can make motion choppy for the individual on the other end of the phone but allows the two individuals to see each other as they speak.

Data Analysis

345   Using the Statistical Package for the Social Sciences-Personal Computer (SPSS-PC) and MANOVA, the three groups were compared to determine any differences in medication compliance as recorded by the MEMS caps. The cap printouts were reviewed, and a 350 percent compliance rate was calculated for each of three time periods: T1 (average of 2-week baseline percent compliance), T2 (average of 6-week intervention compliance), and T3 (average of 2-week postintervention compliance). Compliance was calculated 355 using the approach described by Kruse et al. (1992), and expanded by Rohay et al. (1998). Using the daily events adherence method of calculation, which is based on the number of events that occur each day and then averaged over the interval, the method is stated to be 360 comparable to the average of daily pill counts. An average compliance measure was calculated for each of the three time periods using repeated measures ANOVA. The compliance rates were compared in a three-by-three design (i.e., control, telephone, and 365 videotelephone at T1, T2, and T3). Pre-intervention and post-intervention scores were calculated for the MLHF and SF-36.

Results

Baseline Equivalence

    Table 1 reports selected demographic data for the

study sample. The mean age was 74.2 ($SD = 6.8$), with a median age of 72. The mean number of years of education was 9.3 ($SD = 4.9$; median, 10.5). More than 70% of subjects were either widowed or divorced. Only two individuals were working for pay outside of the home on a part-time basis. The group was 14% White, 30% Black, 54% other, and 2% "missing," reflecting the diversity of New York and the limitations of racial labels. Half of the interviews were conducted in Spanish to accommodate the language of preference. There were no statistically significant demographic differences between the experimental and control groups.

Table 1
*Selected Demographics**

Variable	Control	Telephone	Video-telephone
Number	18	15	17
Race			
White	0	3	4
Black	6	5	4
Other	11	7	9
Marital Status			
Married	1	4	3
Widowed	7	6	8
Divorced or separated	8	2	5
Never married	0	3	1
Years of Education	mean = 7.8 (SD = 5.7)	mean = 11.5 (SD = 3.8)	mean = 9 (SD = 4.7)
Age	mean = 73.7 (SD = 5.3)	mean = 76.2 (SD = 8.8)	mean = 73.1 (SD = 6.5)

* Not significant across groups.

Intervention Effects

During the 2-week baseline compliance monitoring period, there were no statistically significant differences in the compliance rates of the intervention and control groups. The average compliance rates across the three groups were: 81% for the controls, 76% for the telephone group, and 82% for the videotelephone group. During the subsequent two time periods (6 weeks intervention and 2 weeks post-intervention), the compliance rate of the control group dropped significantly (from 81% at T1 to 57% at T3, $p < .04$), while the compliance rates of the two intervention groups remained steady (Figure 1, Table 2). Thus, there was a statistically significant time effect during the course of the study from baseline to post-intervention ($F[2, 34] = 4.08, p < .05$). Over time, the elderly patients who were called either by telephone or videotelephone showed enhanced medication compliance relative to the control group, demonstrating an effect from the calling interventions. However, there was no significant difference in compliance rates between the two intervention groups. The enhanced technology offered by the video-

telephone images apparently did not offer a relative advantage over regular telephone reminders regarding the elderly patients' compliance behavior. Multiple regression analysis did not yield any demographic predictors for better compliance.

Both the SF-36 scores and the MLHF scores improved from baseline to post-intervention for all groups. There was no significant change in the SF-36 scores for the sample, but there was improvement in the MLHF scores ($p < .001$), indicating improved self-reported clinical status. Group membership did not make a difference for either score (Table 3).

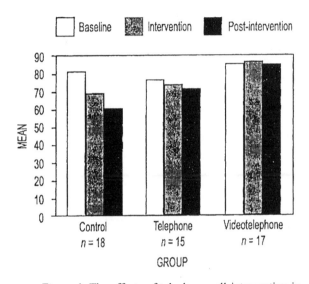

Figure 1. The effects of telephone call intervention in medication compliance for three experimental groups of community-dwelling elderly individuals during 2-week baseline, 6-week intervention, and 2-week post-intervention.

Table 2
Intervention Effects on Medication Compliance of Community-Dwelling Elderly Individuals

Time	Control	Telephone	Videotele-phone
Time 1	81%	76%	82%
Time 3	57%	74%	84%

Note: The Time 1 to Time 3 difference for the control group was significant at $p < .04$.

Discussion and Nursing Implications

The most striking finding of this study is the significant falloff in the control group's medication compliance rate over time, compared to the rates of the two intervention groups. Between T1 and T3, compliance in the control group fell 24 percentage points, while compliance in the two reminder groups fluctuated by no more than 2 percentage points. By the end of the 10-week period during which compliance rates were measured, the control group was taking on average only 57% of prescribed medication doses, while the

Table 3
Intervention Effects

	Measure							
	SF-36 Scores				MLHF Scores			
	Pre-Intervention		Post-Intervention		Pre-Intervention		Post-Intervention	
Group	Mean	SD	Mean	SD	Mean	SD	Mean	SD
Control ($n = 14$)	87.3	24.3	91.7	22.7	46.6	27.7	32.9	22.9
Telephone ($n = 13$)	81.0	15.2	90.1	20.6	54.4	21.1	32.9	25.2
Videotelephone ($n = 15$)	86.1	17.0	85.9	18.9	43.1	20.8	36.7	19.9

other two groups—exposed to daily medication reminders—were taking between 74% to 84%. With the advent of managed care and cuts in home care reimbursement, the ability to enhance medication compliance by such simple means as a telephone call is important. The usual practice of pre-pouring medications for the week, often performed by home care nurses at the cost of a visit, may be replaced by telephone calls by the home care nurse, saving travel time, increasing the number of contacts, and obtaining better compliance. In large part, these are patients who are quite ill, and the daily reminder to take medications could have a positive effect on overall symptom management and well-being, which should be investigated in the future.

One may ask why the baseline compliance rates across the three groups were so high, ranging from 76% to 82%, and why the pattern of compliance observed in the study involved differential falloff from a relatively high percentage of doses completed rather than a differential improvement from a relatively low level of initial compliance. One plausible explanation is that the compliance rates observed during the 2-week baseline monitoring period may have been an artifact of the study's measurement technology. One could argue that the action of placing MEMS caps on patients' pill bottles—an action necessary for measuring compliance throughout the study—was itself an intervention and could have produced a Hawthorne effect that raised compliance beyond its natural level in the study population. Because the protocol of placing caps on bottles was identical across the three groups, this effect was observed more or less uniformly across the control and intervention groups at baseline. As the presence of the electronic bottle caps became routine, its effect could be expected to wear off, leaving compliance rates to fall to what was presumably their prior level. In the absence of any other intervention, this is apparently what happened in the control group. In contrast, the introduction of the telephone and videotelephone reminders in the two intervention groups evidently worked to sustain the relatively high levels of compliance that were observed at baseline. Why these levels were sustained during the 2 weeks postintervention (after daily reminders were no longer received) and for how long the apparent benefit associated with the reminders will endure are questions for future study.

The second substantive finding of this study is the absence of a significant difference between the two intervention groups. The opportunity afforded by the videotelephone for the patient and the individual providing the medication reminder to see each other was presumed to establish greater rapport through visual contact and was expected to yield a stronger compliance effect relative to regular telephone communication. However, no significant advantage could be detected, although the trend for a greater effect was there. This may be partly because of the small sample participating in the study because the trend toward a stronger effect with the videotelephone is evident. It may also be partly because of perceived limitations of the videotelephone technology. The videotelephones are somewhat more awkward to use than regular phones and the images are neither vivid nor in real time. In any case, the small magnitude of the discernable difference between the two types of reminders suggests that either technology could be used to positive effect. Since this study, technology has improved and the "CU-SeeMe" (Cornell University, Ithaca, NY) systems along with Internet television hold promise as creative venues for personal contact. Finally, the change in the MLHF scores cannot be interpreted meaningfully in this study because of sample size but warrant further consideration in a larger trial. Further, in a next phase, the investigators hope to explore the question of "dose." That is, how frequently must calls be made to get the desired enhanced compliance effect.

This study has at least two important limitations. First is the extremely low participation rate (approximately 10%), which reflects national trends in heart failure studies (Goodyer, Miskelly, & Milligan, 1996). The refusal-to-participate rate is a concern. Focus groups using potential subjects to help understand their hesitation to participate would be of value. Selecting younger, healthier subjects is always an option but would result in a different study. Given the large numbers of very frail community-dwelling elderly individuals in the United States, it makes more sense to focus on their participation. The modest stipend for enrollees ($20) did not provide a strong incentive for

515 participation, although elderly individuals were not asked specifically if more money would change their minds. Furthermore, the severity of illness of the patients referred to the study was clearly a deterrent to participation. Sicker individuals were more likely to 520 decline to participate, and sensory impairments such as hearing and vision deficits further reduced participation.

The second limitation of the study was the exclusion of individuals who routinely relied on pre-poured 525 medications, such as daily or weekly pillboxes and dosing dispensers. Because the MEMS compliance measurement methodology requires that computerized medication caps be placed on the patients' medication bottles, individuals who did not routinely take their 530 pills from the bottle, but rather from a special pillbox, could not be included. It should be stressed that this exclusion was a requirement of the research measurement methodology and not the reminder strategy per se. There is inherently no obvious reason why such 535 individuals could not benefit from daily medication reminders. However, any research study designed to include this group would have to rely on some other method of measuring compliance.

Given the mixed results of patient education inter-540 ventions designed to increase medication compliance among frail elderly individuals, increasing attention has focused on stimulant strategies designed to augment medication information and to prompt pill-taking behavior. Despite its small sample, this study demon-545 strated that daily telephone calls or electronic home visits could improve medication compliance significantly in a sample of elderly individuals with CHF who took, on average, 3 to 15 doses of medication every day. In addition, monitoring with computerized medi-550 cation caps provided an accurate and consistent method of electronic observation. Patients who have been hospitalized for CHF have a high rate of rehospitalization, which may be attributable in part to poor medication compliance and to resultant illness. This pilot study 555 demonstrated a simple, inexpensive approach with promising results. These results suggest the importance of conducting the intervention on a larger scale.

References

Cargill, J.M. (1992). Medication compliance in elderly people: Influencing variables and interventions. *Journal of Advanced Nursing, 17,* 422–426.

Cramer, J.A., Mattson, R.H., Prevey, M.L., Scheyer, R.D., & Ouellette, V.L. (1989). How often is medication taken as prescribed? A novel assessment technique. *Journal of the American Medical Association, 261,* 3273–3277.

DeGeest, S., Dunbar-Jacob, J., & Vanhaeckel, J. (1998). *Diagnostic value of structured interviews in assessing non-compliance with immunosuppressive therapy in heart transplant patients.* Manuscript submitted for publication.

Fineman, B., & DeFelice, C. (1992). A study of medication compliance. *Home Healthcare Nurse, 10*(5), 26–29.

Fitten, L.J., Coleman, L., Siembieda, D.W., Yu, M., & Ganzell, S. (1995). Assessment of capacity to comply with medication regimens in older patients. *Journal of the American Geriatrics Society, 43,* 361–367.

Folstein, M.F., Folstein, S.E., & McHugh, P.R. (1975). Mini-Mental State: A practical guide for grading the cognitive state of patients for the clinician. *Journal of Psychiatric Research, 12,* 189–198.

Goodyer, L.I., Miskelly, F., & Milligan, P. (1996). Does encouraging good compliance improve patients' clinical condition in heart failure? *British Journal of Clinical Pharmacology, 49,* 173–176.

Isaac, L.M., & Tamblyn, R.M. (1993). Compliance and cognitive function: A methodological approach to measuring unintentional errors in medication compliance in the elderly. *The Gerontologist, 33,* 772–781.

Klein, L.E., German, P.S., McPhee, S.J., Smith, C.R., & Levine, D.M. (1982). Aging and its relationship to health knowledge and medication compliance. *The Gerontologist, 22,* 384–387.

Kruse, W., Koch-Gwinner, P., Nikolaus, T., Oster, P., Schlierf, G., & Weber, E. (1992). Measurement of drug compliance by continuous electronic monitoring: A pilot study in elderly patients discharged from hospital. *Journal of the American Geriatrics Society, 40,* 1151–1155.

Kruse, W., & Weber, E. (1990). Dynamics of drug regimen compliance—Its assessment by microprocessor-based monitoring. *European Journal of Clinical Pharmacology, 38,* 561–565.

Lee, J.Y., Kusek, J.W., Greene, P.G., Bernhard, S., Norris, K., Smith, D., Wilkening, B., & Wright, J.T. (1996). Assessing medication adherence by pill count and electronic monitoring in the African American Study of Kidney Disease (AASK) pilot study. *The American Journal of Hypertension, 9,* 719–725.

Matsuyama, J.R., Mason, B.J., & Jue, S.G. (1993). Pharmacists' interventions using an electronic medication-event monitoring device's adherence data versus pill counts. *Annals of Pharmacotherapy, 27,* 851–855.

McKinney, J.M., Munroe, W.P., & Wright, J.T. (1992). Impact of an electronic medication compliance aid on long-term blood pressure control. *Journal of Clinical Pharmacology, 32,* 277–283.

Murray, M.D., Birt, J.A., Manatunga, A.K., & Darnell, J.C. (1993). Medication compliance in elderly outpatients using twice-daily dosing and unit-of-use packaging. *Annals of Pharmacotherapy, 27,* 616–621.

Raynor, D.K., Booth, T.G., & Blenkinsopp, A. (1993). Effects of computer generated reminder charts on patients' compliance with drug regimens. *British Medical Journal, 306,* 1158–1161.

Rector, T.S., Kubo, S.H., & Cohn, J.N. (1987). Patients' self-assessment of their congestive heart failure: Part 2: Content, reliability and validity of a new measure, the Minnesota Living with Heart Failure Questionnaire. *Heart Failure, 124,* 198–209.

Rohay, J.M., Dunbar-Jacob, J., Sereika, S., Kwoh, K., & Burke, L.E. (1998). *The impact of method of calculation of electronically monitored adherence data controlled clinical trials.* Manuscript submitted for publication.

Salzman, C. (1995). Medication compliance in the elderly. *Journal of Clinical Psychiatry, 56*(Suppl. 1), 18–22.

Siu, A.L., Reuben, D.B., & Moore, A.A. (1994). Comprehensive geriatric assessment. In W.R. Hazzard, E.L. Bierman, J.P. Blass, W.H. Ettinger, & J.B. Halter (Eds.), *Principles of geriatric medicine and gerontology* (pp. 203–211). New York: McGraw-Hill.

Spiers, M.V., & Kutzik, D.M. (1995). Self-reported memory of medication use by the elderly. *American Journal of Health-System Pharmacy, 52,* 985–990.

Ware, J.E., & Sherbourne, C.D. (1992). The MOS 36-item short-form health survey (SF-36), I: Conceptual framework and item selection. *Medical Care, 30,* 473–483.

Wolfe, S.C., & Schirm, V. (1992). Medication counseling for the elderly: Effects on knowledge and compliance after hospital discharge. *Geriatric Nursing, 13*(3), 134–138.

Note: This project was funded by The Merck Company Foundation, Merck-Medco Managed Care LLC, West Point, Pennsylvania, and the Frederick and Amelia Schimper Foundation, New York, New York.

Address correspondence to: Terry T. Fulmer, PhD, RN, FAAN, Professor, New York University, Division of Nursing, 429 Shimkin Hall, 50 West 4th Street, New York, NY 10012.

Exercise for Article 13

Factual Questions

1. Which one of the three types of strategies for enhancing compliance is intended to *prompt* pill taking?

2. Subjects were referred from what two sources?

3. How many of the original subjects in this study withdrew before completing it?

4. What precluded capping all pill bottles?

5. Which one of the three groups had the highest average years of education?

6. Was the drop in the control group's compliance rate from Time 1 to Time 3 statistically significant?

7. According to the researchers, what is the "second substantive finding" of the study?

Questions for Discussion

8. Speculate on what the researchers mean by "Likert-response format." (See lines 282–283.)

9. The footnote to Table 1 indicates that the differences in demographics across groups were not significant. Is this important information? Explain.

10. In the paragraph beginning on line 439, the researchers speculate on why the initial (baseline) compliance rates were so high. Does their speculation make sense? Why? Why not?

11. In the paragraph beginning on line 502, the researchers identify the low participation rate as an "important limitation." Do you agree that it is important? Explain.

12. If you were to conduct another study on the same topic, what changes in the research methodology, if any, would you make?

Quality Ratings

Directions: Indicate your level of agreement with each of the following statements by circling a number from 5 for strongly agree (SA) to 1 for strongly disagree (SD). If you believe an item is not applicable to this research article, leave it blank. Be prepared to explain your ratings. When responding to criteria A and B below, keep in mind that brief titles and abstracts are conventional in published research.

A. The title of the article is appropriate.

SA   5   4   3   2   1   SD

B. The abstract provides an effective overview of the research article.

SA   5   4   3   2   1   SD

C. The introduction establishes the importance of the study.

SA   5   4   3   2   1   SD

D. The literature review establishes the context for the study.

SA   5   4   3   2   1   SD

E. The research purpose, question, or hypothesis is clearly stated.

SA   5   4   3   2   1   SD

F. The method of sampling is sound.

SA   5   4   3   2   1   SD

G. Relevant demographics (for example, age, gender, and ethnicity) are described.

SA   5   4   3   2   1   SD

H. Measurement procedures are adequate.

SA   5   4   3   2   1   SD

I. All procedures have been described in sufficient detail to permit a replication of the study.

SA   5   4   3   2   1   SD

J. The participants have been adequately protected from potential harm.

SA   5   4   3   2   1   SD

K. The results are clearly described.

SA   5   4   3   2   1   SD

L.. The discussion/conclusion is appropriate.

SA   5   4   3   2   1   SD

M. Despite any flaws, the report is worthy of publication.

SA   5   4   3   2   1   SD

Article 14

The Impact of an HIV/AIDS Training Course for Baccalaureate Nursing Students

Jamie S. Carney, PhD, **James L. Werth, Jr.**, PhD, **Jane S. Martin**, PhD, RN[*]

ABSTRACT. This study focuses on the impact of a specialized course to train baccalaureate nursing students to work with individuals with HIV disease. The overall goals of the course were to increase general and specific knowledge while improving beliefs regarding individuals with HIV disease. The course outline included components to increase knowledge in the areas of epidemiology, medical considerations, treatment, ethical and legal issues, and psychosocial issues. Pretests and posttests were given to participants and to a comparison group which had not received educational training. Results indicated the training significantly increased HIV/AIDS knowledge, and participants reported more positive beliefs about individuals with HIV disease.

From *Journal of Nursing Education*, 38, 39–41. Copyright © 1999 by SLACK Incorporated. Reprinted with permission.

Human immunodeficiency virus disease has presented the medical community with tremendous challenges. Early in the epidemic, when etiology was unknown and those infected and affected appeared to be
5 constrained to marginalized groups, research demonstrated that, similar to the general public, medical professionals held negative stereotypes and beliefs about individuals with HIV disease (Douglas, Kalman, & Kalman, 1985; Kelly, St. Lawrence, Hood, Smith, &
10 Cook, 1988a, 1988b; van Servellen, Lewis, & Leake, 1988). This included nurses and nursing students (Lester & Beard, 1988; Royse & Birge, 1987). More recently, there has been a shift, with several studies indicating that attitudes among these professionals toward
15 individuals with HIV disease may be improving (Bowman, Brown, & Eason, 1994; Brown, Calder, & Rae, 1990; Goldenberg & Laschinger, 1991; Gross & Passannante, 1993; Jemmott, Jemmott, & Cruz-Collins, 1992; Strasser & Damrosch, 1992).
20 This change in part may be because of increased attention to HIV disease in nursing curricula and continuing education programs (Duffy, 1993; Grimes, 1992; Gross & Passannante, 1993; Sowell & Spicer, 1992). However, there is limited research on the actual

25 impact of such educational training methods on attitudes and knowledge development. The intent of this study was to examine the impact of a specialized course for baccalaureate nursing students. The goals of the course included educational components in the ar-
30 eas of:

- Disease progression.
- Testing.
- Epidemiological considerations.
- Immunologic concerns.
35 - Issues related to medical treatment.
- Consideration of psychosocial issues.
- Legal and ethical concerns.

In addition to these didactic components, the course also included discussions on treatment issues and so-
40 cietal stigma; activities to increase self-awareness stigma; and case presentations, with the overall goal of improving attitudes toward and concerning working with individuals with HIV disease.

Method

Participants

The sample consisted of 60 baccalaureate nursing
45 students. The majority of participants were women (n = 38), one-third were men (n = 20), and there were two missing cases. Participants were classified into four age groups: 19 to 22 (n = 31), 23 to 26 (n = 20), 27 to 30 (n = 4), and upper age categories were collapsed into one
50 group of age 30 and older (n = 3). Of those reporting self-identified race, the majority were White (n = 49), 7 were Black, and 2 were other racial identifications. Of the total sample, 29 participants were enrolled in the specialized training course. The control group (n = 31)
55 were enrolled in another course required in the nursing curriculum. This latter course did not address issues related to HIV/AIDS training.

Instruments

Demographic Questionnaire. Participants were asked about their age, gender, race, and whether they
60 had previous training related to HIV/AIDS.

[*]*Dr. Carney* is associate professor, Counseling and Counseling Psychology, Auburn University, Auburn, Alabama. *Dr. Werth* is post-doctoral research associate, Law/Psychology Program, University of Nebraska at Lincoln, Lincoln, Nebraska. *Dr. Martin* is assistant professor, Samford University, Birmingham, Alabama.

HIV/AIDS Knowledge Inventory. This instrument (Carney, Werth, & Emanuelson, 1994) measures general knowledge about HIV/AIDS. This 25-item, true or false instrument reflects content in the areas of etiology, transmission, prevalence, and symptomatology. The authors report Cronbach's alpha coefficients ranging from .48 to .71. Higher scores indicate higher levels of HIV/AIDS knowledge.

AIDS Attitude Scale (AAS). The AAS (Shrum, Turner, & Bruce, 1989) measures attitudes toward AIDS and individuals with AIDS. The instrument consists of 54 statements to which participants respond using a 5-point Likert scale (1 = strongly disagree to 5 = strongly agree). The authors report a coefficient alpha reliability of .96. Higher scores on this instrument reflect more positive attitudes.

Procedure

Participants in this quasi-experimental study were not randomly assigned to either group. Participants in both classes, representing the treatment (i.e., enrolled in the HIV/AIDS course) and the control group (i.e., another course within the curriculum), were provided a pretest packet. This packet was dispensed on the first day of course enrollment. Included in the packet was an informed consent form and the pretests. The informed consent clarified that participation in the study was voluntary, and participants could refuse to participate by simply returning a noncompleted form in the envelope provided. After 10 weeks, one week following completion of the HIV/AIDS course, a posttest was administered to participants in both groups.

Results

A preliminary analysis was performed to determine the impact of prior training regarding HIV/AIDS issues on participants' knowledge about HIV/AIDS and beliefs about individuals with the disease. The proportion of individuals who received prior training was similar for each group, treatment ($n = 22$) and control ($n = 20$) ($\chi^2 = .095$, $p > .05$). Analysis revealed this prior training regarding HIV/AIDS issues had no impact on either knowledge ($t = 1.10$, $p > .05$) or beliefs ($t = -.09$, $p > .05$).

The reliability (internal consistencies) of the belief and knowledge measures were estimated using Cronbach's alpha. These estimates consistently were higher for the belief measure. Specifically, pretest and posttest scores on the belief instrument yielded reliability estimates of .88 and .82. The corresponding estimates for the pretest and posttest knowledge measure were .58 and .52, respectively.

The results from the mixed model analysis of variance indicated there was an interaction effect for both knowledge ($F[1,58] = 30.23$, $p < .001$) and beliefs ($F[1,58] = 56.31$, $p < .001$). While participants experienced increases for both knowledge and beliefs, only those in the treatment group reported a significant increase. Specifically, the average knowledge score for the treatment group increased from 17.77 to 21.83. The improvement for the control group was only slight; scores increased from 17.26 to 17.94.

A similar group interaction effect was demonstrated on belief scores. The treatment group's scores on the belief measure increased from 64.9 to 75.45, while the control group's scores essentially stayed consistent. The control group's average score on the pretest was 65.67, and on the posttest their average score only increased to 65.68.

Discussion

The present study investigated the use of a specialized HIV/AIDS training course for baccalaureate level nursing students. The course provided a broad overview of issues related to the progression, transmission, prevalence, psychosocial issues, and treatment of HIV disease. A special emphasis of the course was the exploration of personal attitudes or beliefs related to working with individuals with HIV disease. The overall goals were to increase knowledge and improve attitudes toward working with this population. The results indicated the course was successful in accomplishing these goals. Specifically, knowledge levels increased, and more positive attitudes were demonstrated by those who participated in the course.

The results of this study have significant implications for nurse educators. There are indications that such a course can accomplish the goals of improving both general and specific treatment knowledge. More important, this type of training also may improve attitudes toward and potential interactions with individuals with HIV disease. However, future research is needed to determine the long-term implications of these types of educational modalities. It also is essential that nurse educators begin to examine how training influences the actual treatment of individuals with HIV disease by nursing professionals. It is clear that nurses' role in the treatment and care of individuals with this disease will only increase in the next decade. An essential aspect of that role will be informed and competent care.

References

Bowman, J.M., Brown, S.T., & Eason, F.R. (1994). Attitudes of baccalaureate nursing students in one school toward acquired immune deficiency syndrome. *AIDS Education and Prevention, 6,* 535–541.

Brown, Y., Calder, B., & Rae, D. (1990). The effect of knowledge on nursing students' attitudes toward individuals with AIDS. *Journal of Nursing Education, 29,* 367–372.

Carney, J., Werth, J.L., Jr., & Emanuelson, G. (1994). The relationship between attitudes toward persons who are gay and persons with AIDS, and HIV and AIDS knowledge. *Journal of Counseling and Development, 72,* 646–650.

Douglas, C.J., Kalman, C.M., & Kalman, T.P. (1985). Homophobia among physicians and nurses: An empirical study. *Hospital and Community Psychiatry, 36,* 1309–1311.

Duffy, P.R. (1993). A model for the integration of HIV/AIDS content into baccalaureate nursing curricula. *Journal of Nursing Education, 32,* 347–351.

Goldenberg, D., & Laschinger, H. (1991). Attitudes and normative beliefs of nursing students as predictors of intended care behaviors with AIDS patients: A test of the Ajzen-Fishbein theory of reasoned action. *Journal of Nursing Education, 30,* 119–126.

Grimes, R.M. (1992). Meeting the AIDS/HIV educational needs of the nurse. *Imprint, 39*(4), 76–78.

Gross, E.J., & Passannante, M. (1993). Educating school nurses to care for HIV-infected children in school. *Journal of School Health, 63,* 307–311.

Jemmott, L.S., Jemmott, J.B., III, & Cruz-Collins, M. (1992). Predicting AIDS patient care intentions among nursing students. *Nursing Research, 41*, 172–177.

Kelly, J.A., St. Lawrence, J.S., Hood, H.V., Smith, S., & Cook D.J. (1988a). Nurses' attitudes toward AIDS. *The Journal of Continuing Education in Nursing, 19*, 78–83.

Kelly, J.A., St. Lawrence, J.S., Hood, H.V., Smith, S., & Cook, D.J. (1988b). Stigmatization of AIDS patients by physicians. *American Journal of Public Health, 77*, 789–791.

Lester, L.B., & Beard, B.J. (1988). Nursing students' attitudes toward AIDS. *Journal of Nursing Education, 27*, 399–404.

Royse, D., & Birge, B. (1987). Homophobia and attitudes toward AIDS patients among medical, nursing, and paramedical students. *Psychological Reports, 61*, 867–870.

Shrum, I.C., Turner, N.H., & Bruce, K.E.M. (1989). Development of an instrument to measure attitudes toward acquired immune deficiency syndrome. *AIDS Education and Prevention, 1*, 222–230.

Sowell, R.L., & Spicer, T. (1992). Nursing education and HIV disease: A call for action. *Nurse Educator, 17*, 23–26.

Strasser, J.A., & Damrosch, S. (1992). Graduate nursing students' attitudes toward gay and hemophiliac men with AIDS. *Evaluation and the Health Professions, 15*, 115–127.

van Servellen, G.M., Lewis, C.E., & Leake, B. (1988). Nurses' responses to the AIDS crisis: Implications for coding education programs. *The Journal of Continuing Education in Nursing, 19*, 4–8.

Address reprint requests to: Jamie S. Carney, PhD, associate professor, Counseling and Counseling Psychology, 2084 Haley Center, Auburn University, Auburn, AL 36849-5222.

Exercise for Article 14

Factual Questions

1. How many of the students were in the 23 to 26 age group?

2. What content areas were reflected on the HIV/AIDS Knowledge Inventory?

3. What is the value of the coefficient alpha reliability reported by the authors of the AAS?

4. Participants could refuse to participate by doing what?

5. Was the difference between the proportions of the two groups that received prior training statistically significant?

6. The average knowledge score for the treatment group increased from 17.77 to what value?

7. The average belief score for the control group increased from 65.67 to what value?

Questions for Discussion

8. On line 77, the researchers refer to this study as "quasi-experimental." Is this a strength or weakness of this study? Explain.

9. Is the information in lines 91–100 important in interpreting the validity of this study? Explain.

10. Are you surprised by the results of this study? Why? Why not?

11. If you were conducting a study on the same topic, what changes in the research methodology, if any, would you make?

Quality Ratings

Directions: Indicate your level of agreement with each of the following statements by circling a number from 5 for strongly agree (SA) to 1 for strongly disagree (SD). If you believe an item is not applicable to this research article, leave it blank. Be prepared to explain your ratings. When responding to criteria A and B below, keep in mind that brief titles and abstracts are conventional in published research.

A. The title of the article is appropriate.

SA   5   4   3   2   1   SD

B. The abstract provides an effective overview of the research article.

SA   5   4   3   2   1   SD

C. The introduction establishes the importance of the study.

SA   5   4   3   2   1   SD

D. The literature review establishes the context for the study.

SA   5   4   3   2   1   SD

E. The research purpose, question, or hypothesis is clearly stated.

SA   5   4   3   2   1   SD

F. The method of sampling is sound.

SA   5   4   3   2   1   SD

G. Relevant demographics (for example, age, gender, and ethnicity) are described.

SA   5   4   3   2   1   SD

H. Measurement procedures are adequate.

SA   5   4   3   2   1   SD

I. All procedures have been described in sufficient detail to permit a replication of the study.

SA   5   4   3   2   1   SD

J. The participants have been adequately protected from potential harm.

SA   5   4   3   2   1   SD

K. The results are clearly described.

SA   5   4   3   2   1   SD

L.   The discussion/conclusion is appropriate.

      SA   5   4   3   2   1   SD

M.   Despite any flaws, the report is worthy of publication.

      SA   5   4   3   2   1   SD

Article 15

Effects of Two Educational Methods on the Knowledge, Attitude, and Practice of Women High School Teachers in Prevention of Cervical Cancer

Mahin Baradaran Rezaei, MSc, **Simin Seydi**, MSc, **Sakineh Mohammad Alizadeh**, MSc[*]

ABSTRACT. Because of the increased emphasis on prevention and early detection of cervical cancer, we studied the effects of 2 educational methods on the knowledge, attitude, and practice, regarding prevention of cervical cancer, of women high school teachers in Tabriz. This study was a semiexperimental research. Samples were 129 female teachers divided into 3 groups: experimental 1 (educated by pamphlets), experimental 2 (educated by a lecture and flash cards), and control group (not manipulated). After doing pretest in the 3 groups, investigators used 2 educational methods for experimental groups. Data regarding the knowledge and attitude of 3 groups were gathered after 14 days and data regarding practice were gathered after 2 months. Chi-square and 1-way ANOVA were used for data analysis. Before education, knowledge, attitude, and practice of the 3 groups were the same, but after education there were significant differences in mean scores of knowledge and attitude of 2 experimental groups as compared with the control group and also between the 2 experimental groups ($p < .001$). Education by lecture and flash cards was more effective than by pamphlets. In regard to Pap smear practice, there was a significant difference between the 2 experimental groups as compared with the control group ($p = .001$), but there was no significant difference between the 2 experimental groups. Therefore, educational methods were effective on knowledge, attitude, and practice of teachers regarding prevention of cervical cancer and education by lecture and flash cards was more effective than by pamphlets in increasing knowledge and inducing a positive attitude, but the 2 educational methods had the same effect on practice of teachers.

From *Cancer Nursing*, *27*, 364–369. Copyright © 2004 by Lippincott Williams & Wilkins, Inc. Reprinted with permission.

The report of the WHO (World Health Organization) in 1998 categorized cervical cancer as the fourth widespread cancer among women.[1] Seventy percent of the cases of genital cancer among women are of cervi-
5 cal cancer.[2] The report of the cytology unit of the Iranian Ministry of Health, Treatment, and Medical Education in 1999 indicated that 0.2% of the microscopic slides received from women between the ages of 20 and 45, who had been referred to the health centers,
10 contained some degree of displasia and cervical cancer. This rate in the East Azerbaijan Province was 0.2%. (It should be noted that women experiencing menopause and other women at risk were not included in the statistics.)[3]

15 Pap smear is an effective test for cervical cancer screening, and women can get 3 Pap smears done in 1 year; if the test is repeated once in 3 years, up to 90% mortality from cancer can be prevented.[4,5] Although the efficiency of regular cytology tests such as Pap smear
20 has already proved to reduce the rate of mortality from cervical cancer, its application in the developing countries is less than that in the developed countries. This is because of the low knowledge of this important factor among women.[2]

25 The lack of knowledge concerning cervical cancer, the possibility of its diagnosis, the possibility of its full treatment in case of an early detection, and the lack of awareness of the existence of Pap smear as a means of diagnosis are all obstacles for Pap smear. Several stud-
30 ies indicate that the practice of getting Pap smears done in women is dependent on the degree of their sensitivity to the disease, their attitudes toward cancer, their beliefs, and also their awareness of the advantages of early detection.[6] To achieve a permanent change in
35 behavior and to bring about changes in personal practices, one finds that it is necessary to give people proper knowledge and to establish logical attitudes through health education programs.[7] One of the effective policies concerning the best use of cervical cancer
40 screening by women is the accessibility of cervical cancer screening programs for the community and instructing people about cervical cancer, and a change in the attitude of the community toward this cancer.[8]

[*]*Mahin Baradaran Rezaei* is an instructor of basic sciences, Nursing & Midwifery, Tabriz University of Medical Sciences, Tabriz, Iran. *Sakineh Mohammad Alizadeh* is the deputy dean of Research, Nursing & Midwifery, Tabriz University of Medical Sciences, Tabriz, Iran.

Table 1
Teachers' Demographics

Characteristics	%		
	Experimental group 1	Experimental group 2	Control group
Age			
≤ 34	39.6	39.6	37.2
35–39	34.9	32.6	18.6
40–44	14.0	7.0	27.9
≥ 45	11.6	21.0	16.3
First marriage, age			
< 20	14.0	9.3	4.7
20–24	44.0	39.5	46.5
25–29	34.9	34.9	25.6
≥ 30	7.0	16.3	23.3
Number of pregnancies			
None	2.3	11.6	7.0
1–2	81.4	11.6	81.4
≥ 3	16.3	20.9	11.6
Main source for information			
Intermedia	55.8	46.5	65.1
Health workers	14.0	9.3	27.9
Friends	23.3	9.3	0.0
Others	11.6	16.3	20.9

Groups: Experimental group 1 was educated by pamphlets, experimental group 2 was educated by a lecture and flash cards, and the control group was not manipulated (number of participants in each group was 43).

Through the application of these programs, the use of Pap smear has increased 3 times in the developed countries.[2]

In the developing countries where people are not sufficiently informed of the screening tests, especially Pap smear, the basic role of public health education and awareness of community should be emphasized.[9]

The variety of the methods of education is not only very effective in the process of teaching and learning, but it is also necessary to produce an interest and attract the cooperation of the addressee.[10,11]

Several studies that determined the knowledge, attitude, and practice of women regarding the prevention of cervical cancer were not appropriate.[12] The urgency of the problem caused the present researchers to study the effects of 2 educational methods on the knowledge, attitude, and practice of women high school teachers in Tabriz in prevention of cervical cancer.

Teachers are believed to be a group of women who play a fundamental role in the education of young girls in this region of the country and they should necessarily be conscious of the ways to prevent cervical cancer[13] so that they can teach the ways of its prevention to the members of their own society.

Researchers hope that the findings of this study will lead the authorities of the Education Department, and those in charge of education in the Departments of Health, Treatment, and Medical Education, to include effective cervical cancer screening programs in their schedules. It is also hoped that the minds will be oriented to the methods of prevention in order to lengthen, as much as possible, the lives of human beings, the invaluable treasures walking on Earth.

Literature Review

Researchers had frequently realized that women's knowledge, attitude, and practice in terms of the prevention of cervical cancer and undergoing Pap smear are not satisfactory.

Findings of Kottke et al., titled "Cancer screening behaviors and attitudes of women in southeastern Minnesota," showed that in women aged 18 years and older, 60% reported having had a Pap smear within the preceding year. More than 90% of the respondents expressed a willingness to have this test if their physicians were to advise them that the tests were needed.[14]

Another study was performed in China, titled "The knowledge and attitude of cancer prevention among junior high school teachers," by National Yang-Ming Medical College. The results showed that the cognizance rate of cervical cancer as the leading cancer (by that time) and the most curable for women in Taiwan was 69.3% and 37.5%, respectively. Pap smear was known to 96.8% of the teachers.[15]

Seyami and her colleagues studied the "knowledge and behavior (Pap smear) of women who referred to Tehran Health Centers." Findings showed that the knowledge of the majority of the participants (75.7%) was low and the knowledge of 18.29% of the participants was moderate.[16]

The study done by Baradaran and Alizadeh in Tabriz, Iran, on the topic "Nurses' and teachers' knowledge, attitude, and practice regarding prevention

Table 2
Teachers' Knowledge by Groups* at Preeducation and Posteducation

Knowledge	Preeducation[†]			Posteducation[‡]		
	Experimental group 1	Experimental group 2	Control group	Experimental group 1	Experimental group 2	Control group
Knowledge level, %						
Low (0–8)	32.6	23.3	37.2	0.0	0.0	49.5
Moderate (9–16)	65.1	72.1	62.8	27.9	9.3	60.5
High (17–24)	2.3	4.7	0.0	72.1	90.7	0.0
Knowledge score						
Mean	10.49	10.19	8.65	18.76	19.93	9.28
SD	4.27	4.51	5.0	2.83	1.91	4.38

*Groups: Experimental group 1 was educated by pamphlets, experimental group 2 was educated by a lecture and flash cards, and the control group was not manipulated (number of participants in each group was 43).
[†]Difference between groups is statistically not significant ($p > .05$).
[‡]Difference between groups is statistically significant ($p = .0001$).

105 of cervical cancer" enhances the subject in this respect. They indicated that 73.9% of nurses and 33.3% of teachers had appropriate knowledge and 17.4% of nurses and 20% of teachers had a positive attitude in this regard. Regarding regular performing of Pap
110 smear, 95.6% of nurses and 90% of teachers had poor practice.[12]

Dignan et al. performed a survey on the topic "Effectiveness of health education to increase screening for cervical cancer among Eastern-band Cherokee In-
115 dian women in North Carolina." The results showed that women who received the educational programs exhibited a greater knowledge about cervical cancer prevention and were more likely to have reported having had a Pap smear within the past year than did
120 women who did not receive the educational programs.[17]

Mcavoy and her colleagues showed that health education interventions increased the uptake of cervical cytology among Asian women in Leicester who had
125 never been tested. Personal visits were most effective, irrespective of the health education materials used, but there was some evidence that home videos may be particularly effective in one of the most hard to reach groups.[18]

Method

130 This study is a quasi-experimental research. To do this, 129 teachers were chosen as the sample, all from among women high school teachers teaching in Tabriz.

The sample was randomly divided into 3 groups, each group comprising 43 teachers. Thus, 43 teachers
135 were included in the control group, 43 teachers in experimental group 1, being educated by pamphlets, and 43 teachers in experimental group 2, being educated by a lecture and flash cards.

Cluster sampling was used for data gathering.
140 Three high schools from each of the 5 education districts in Tabriz were chosen and overall 15 high schools were randomly selected. From the 3 high schools in each district, randomly one was assumed as control group, the second as experimental group 1, and

145 the third as experimental group 2. Regarding the number of teachers in each district, the samples were chosen via stratification sampling from each high school.

The self-structured questionnaire was evaluated by 10 experts in nursing and midwifery science, and on-
150 cology practitioners and its format were also considered by a statistics expert. Another factor that contributed to content validity was the theoretical concepts that were operationalized on the basis of previous studies. Reliability was measured by test–retest. The Pear-
155 son correlation coefficient for knowledge items was $r = 0.87$ and for attitude items was $r = 0.85$.

The questionnaire contained 4 parts: there were 7 questions on demographic characteristics, 24 relating to knowledge, 16 on attitude, and 11 questions on prac-
160 tice. The questionnaires were completed by the teachers. After reviewing them, the researchers identified the educational requirements of the teachers. Based on the information collected and following the opinions of experts, books, and various articles, pamphlets and the
165 texts of lectures together with 10 flash cards that included basic points related to Pap smear were provided. Pamphlets were then distributed among the teachers in group 1, and the teachers in group 2 were educated, in a session of 30 minutes, through a lecture and flash
170 cards. The control group did not receive any education. The part of the questionnaire related to knowledge and attitude was again completed after 2 weeks and the part related to practice was completed after 2 months for the 3 groups.

175 Only married teachers (who have sexual activity) were included in the study as Iranian culture and religious norms permit women to have sexual activity only after marriage.

To analyze the data, descriptive statistics such as
180 mean and standard deviation and analytical statistics such as test and 1-way ANOVA were used.

Table 3
Teachers' Attitude by Groups* at Preeducation and Posteducation

Attitude	Preeducation[†]			Posteducation[‡]		
	Experimental group 1	Experimental group 2	Control group	Experimental group 1	Experimental group 2	Control group
Attitude, %						
Negative (16–48)	34.9	39.5	44.2	20.9	0.0	39.5
Positive (49–80)	65.1	60.5	55.8	79.1	100	60.5
Attitude score						
Mean	51.16	49.84	49.35	54.19	58.21	50.28
SD	5.17	5.81	5.87	5.02	5.84	7.25

*Groups: Experimental group 1 was educated by pamphlets, experimental group 2 was educated by a lecture and flash cards, and the control group was not manipulated (number of participants in each group was 43).
[†]Difference between groups is statistically not significant ($p > .05$).
[‡]Difference between groups is statistically significant ($p = .0001$).

Results

The average age of the teachers in group 1 was 36.28 years, 36.17 in group 2, and 37.74 in the control group. The average age at the first marriage was 23.93 in group 1, 24.79 in group 2, and 25.16 in the control group. The average number of pregnancies was 1.84 in group 1, 1.81 in group 2, and 1.79 in the control group.

No significant difference was observed among the groups in age, the age at the first marriage, and the numbers of pregnancies through a 1-way variance analysis. All the teachers had bachelor's degrees and all had married only once (Table 1).

Before education, the majority of the teachers had a moderate knowledge related to cervical cancer; very few had high knowledge. There was not a significant difference among the groups in the mean of knowledge scores. No person in groups 1 and 2 had a low knowledge after education; however, 49.5% of the control group had low knowledge. A significant difference was observed between the control and the experimental groups in knowledge ($p = .0001$). In a one-to-one comparison, there was a significant difference between groups 1 and 2 and the control group ($p < .0001$) and between group 1 and group 2 ($p < .05$) (Table 2).

Concerning the attitude toward the prevention of cervical cancer, approximately one-third of the samples had negative attitudes. There was no significant difference between the groups in terms of the degree of their attitudes before education; however, there was a significant difference between the groups after education ($p = .0001$). In a one-to-one comparison, a meaningful difference was observed between groups 1 and 2 and the control group ($p < .0001$) and between group 1 and group 2 ($p < 0.05$) (Table 3).

In terms of the practice of Pap smear, approximately 46% of the teachers had no practical experience of Pap smear, and there seemed to be no significant difference among the groups. However, 74.4% of the experimental groups 1 and 2 had gotten Pap smear done after education, while only 46.5% of the control group had gotten Pap smear done only once. There was a significant difference between the groups ($p = .0001$); and in a one-to-one comparison, there was a significant difference between experimental groups 1 and 2 and the control group ($p = .0001$). There was no significant difference between group 1 and group 2 (Table 4).

Discussion

Regarding the results of the research, both methods managed to increase the knowledge of the teachers about the prevention of cervical cancer. Nevertheless, education through flash cards and giving lectures had been more effective than using the pamphlets.

The study done by Gremiel and colleagues in England is indicative of the positive effect of 4 different education methods on the degree of women's knowledge in this respect; however, the degree of knowledge of women educated through lectures and educational figures was more than that of women educated through other methods. In terms of the degree of effectiveness, education through lectures alone was the second best, and education through the use of video films was the third, over education through written materials.[19] Gremiel et al.'s research enhances the results gained in the present research concerning the priority of education through lectures and flash cards over education through giving written texts. Because of the face-to-face encounter between the educator and the receiver of education in the process of education through lectures and flash cards, the communication is reciprocal and the flash cards impart more objectivity to the issue under consideration, letting the samples use both sight and hearing senses. The result is an increase in learning.

The research proved that both of the educational methods managed to induce positive attitudes toward the prevention of cervical cancer, education through lectures and flash cards being more effective than education through the use of pamphlets.

The study of Heydarnia and his colleagues showed that education with a synthetic method (including face-to-face meeting, the use of posters and pamphlets) had caused a positive change in the attitudes of the participants.[20]

Table 4

Teachers' Practice in Relation to Doing Pap Smear by Groups* at Preeducation and Posteducation

Behavior (Pap smear)	Preeducation[†]			Posteducation[‡]		
	Experimental group 1	Experimental group 2	Control group	Experimental group 1	Experimental group 2	Control group
Yes	62.1	51.2	46.5	74.4	74.4	46.5
No	34.9	48.8	53.5	7.0	2.3	44.2
Intended to get a Pap smear during the next time[§]	—	—	—	18.6	23.3	9.3

*Groups: Experimental group 1 was educated by pamphlets, experimental group 2 was educated by a lecture and flash cards, and the control group was not manipulated (number of participants in each group was 43).

[†]Difference between groups is statistically not significant ($p > .05$).

[‡]Difference between groups is statistically significant ($p = .0001$).

[§]This has not been considered in pre-education practice.

It would seem that the effectiveness of the education through lectures and flash cards on attitude is because of the face-to-face encounter of the educator and the receiver of education, the lecturer's emphasis on the significance of early diagnosis and treatment of the disease, and the confidence gained by the teachers in believing that the treatments are not aggressive in case of early diagnosis and that this cancer can be completely cured. The lectures highlight the texts and the flash cards prove and substantiate what is taught, although these issues are written in the pamphlets. The present study showed that both methods had equal impact on the practice of Pap smear. A study by Mcavoy and colleagues indicated that 47% of the women educated through video films together with face-to-face meetings and 37% of women educated by flash cards and face-to-face meetings underwent Pap smear. The rate of getting Pap smear done in the group that had received pamphlets was only 11%, while only 5% of the control group had gotten Pap smear done.[21] The lack of difference between the effects of the 2 methods in the present study may be due to the insufficiency of a 2-month period for practice (because of the limit on the time of the research) and also of the insufficiency of the number of samples.

Considering the results of this research, the health personnel should employ appropriate methods for every occasion and encourage people to receive the Pap smear. The lecture and flash cards method may be very appropriate for illiterate people (especially in rural communities), because it is very objective. The use of pamphlets can be useful in urban areas with educated people, because the pamphlets are cheap, the education is done very fast, and it covers a vast group of people.

The value and importance of screening are not well known in the developing countries. The people often do not visit the doctor unless they are ill.[18] Therefore, to encourage women to do Pap smear regularly, the authorities should pay due attention to the practice of Pap smear in their educational programs. The belief should be internalized in the women that they should primarily visit a doctor to prevent the disease by getting a Pap smear done. This will be very effective in the prevention of cancer, and it will also decrease the mortality rate.

Suggestions

Regarding the unpleasant physical and mental outcomes in people suffering from malignant diseases, educating people through various effective methods to visit the doctors for early detection of the probable cancer can be one of the basic attempts to increase the public knowledge, attitude, and practice, and it can solve a fatal problem.

To achieve the objectives of the WHO and to conduct practically the motto "Health for All" up to 2000, teachers should receive proper health education, because they are impressive persons in the society and they encounter a large group of prospective mothers and women. Thus, a suitable and effective education for teachers can lead to the promotion of screening programs and their success.

It is hoped that the Department of Education and those in charge of the school textbooks will consider the teaching of this aspect of health to the very important half of the population.

Moreover, the managers and the authorities of the local health centers should provide necessary pamphlets and flash cards with high quality and distribute them among women.

They should also prepare suitable booklets and pamphlets for the health personnel in order to use them to increase the information of the women.

References

1. *The World Health Organization (WHO) Report*. 1998.
2. Baheiraei Azam. *Methods of Cervical Cancer Prevention*. 1st ed. Tehran: Boshra Co; 1996:6–24.
3. Iranian Ministry of Health Cytology Unit. *Treatment and Medical Education: Family Health Word*. Iranian Ministry of Health Cytology Unit; 2000.
4. Ryan KJ, Robert W. *Kistner's Gynecology and Women's Health*. 7th ed. St Louis, Mo: Mosby; 1999:93–118.
5. Recommendations of frequency of Pap test screening. *Int J Gynecol Obstet*. March 1995;152:210–211.
6. Lobeal M, Bay C. Barriers to cancer screening in Mexican American women. *Mayo Clin Proc*. 1998;73(4):307–308.
7. Darmalingum T, Ramachandran L. *Health Education*. Fourogh S, trans. Tehran: Tehran University Press; 1992:20–23.
8. Miller AB. Cervical cancer screening, International Agency for Research on Cancer, Lyon, France. In: XV Asia Pacific Cancer Conference; December 12–15, 1999; Madras, India.

9. Mehdeezadeh KH, Mohammadalizadeh S, Forudnia F. Effect of education of girls' primary school teachers on their knowledge about the importance and practice of Pap smear test. *J Kerman Univ Med Sci.* 1996; 3(1):28–34.

10. Helmserresht P, Delpishe E. *Health Education and Healthy Preferences for Education.* Tehran: Chahr Co; 1996:119–162.

11. Ewles L, Simnet I. *Health Education: A Practical Guide for Health Professionals.* Shidfar MA, trans. Tehran: Cyaroosh Co; 1993:28–50.

12. Baradaran M, Mohammad Alizadeh S. Study of knowledge, attitude, and practice regarding prevention of cervical cancer in female nurses and teachers. In: Seminar on Cancer: From Prevention to Rehabilitation. 1997; Tabriz.

13. Julaei S, Amin M. Effect of education on knowledge and practice regarding breast self-examination and Pap smear test in teachers. *J Hyat.* 1998;5(9):19–27.

14. Kottke TE, Trapp MA, Fores MM, et al. Cancer screening behaviors and attitudes of women in Southeastern Minnesota. *JAMA.* 1995;273(74):1099–1105.

15. Cheng Ch, Choupp G. The knowledge and attitude of cancer prevention among junior high school teachers. *Chung Hua I Hsueh Isa Chin Taipie.* 1994;53(6, suppl):1–8 (abstract for Med).

16. Seyami SH, Shafiey F. The knowledge & behavior (Pap smear) of women about cervical cancer who referred to Tehran health centers. *Med J Shahid Beheshty Univ.* 12:25–32.

17. Dignan M, Michelutee R, Bliason K. Effectiveness of health education to increase screening for cervical cancer among Eastern-band Cherokee Indian women in North Carolina. *J Natl Cancer Inst.* 1996;88(22):70–73.

18. Mcavoy BR, Raza R. Can health education increase uprate of cervical smear testing among Asian women? *BMJ.* 1991;302(6):833–836.

19. Gremiel ER, Gappmayer-Locker E, Girardi FL, et al. Increasing women's knowledge and satisfaction with cervical cancer screening. *J Psychosom Obstet Gynecol.* 1997;18(4):273–279.

20. Heydarnia A, Faghih-Zadeh S, Asgari H. The investigation about health education effectiveness on knowledge, attitude and practices of mothers who have children under age of five in rural areas of Central Province. *J Shahed Univ.* 1998;5(20):9–12.

21. Kelly AW, Wollan PC, Trapp MA. A program to increase breast and cervical cancer screening for Cambodian women in a midwestern community. *Mayo Clin Proc.* 1996;72:437–444.

Acknowledgments: It is a desirable duty to thank the high school officials in Tabriz and also to thank all the teachers who took part in this research.

Exercise for Article 15

Factual Questions

1. How many questions on the questionnaire related to knowledge?

2. How was experimental group 2 educated?

3. What was the mean knowledge score for experimental group 1 on the pretest (i.e., preeducation) and on the posttest (i.e., posteducation)?

4. Did the mean attitude score for experimental group 2 go up from pretest (i.e., preeducation) to posttest (i.e., posteducation)? Explain.

5. At the preeducation stage of this study, which group had a majority who had not had a Pap smear test?

6. Was a significant difference observed between the control and the experimental groups in knowledge? If yes, at what probability level was it significant?

Questions for Discussion

7. The researchers refer to this study as "quasi-experimental." What is your understanding of the meaning of this term? (See line 130.)

8. In your opinion, is the design of the study clearly described in lines 130–147?

9. The researchers discuss the content validity of the questionnaire in lines 148–154. In your opinion, is this discussed in sufficient detail?

10. The researchers state that reliability was measured by the test–retest method and that the Pearson correlation coefficient for knowledge items was $r = 0.87$ and for attitude items was $r = 0.85$. Based on what you know about reliability, are the coefficients at an acceptable level? (See lines 154–156.)

11. Do you believe that this study has important practical implications? Explain.

12. If you were conducting a study on the same topic, what changes, if any, would you make in the research methodology?

Quality Ratings

Directions: Indicate your level of agreement with each of the following statements by circling a number from 5 for strongly agree (SA) to 1 for strongly disagree (SD). If you believe an item is not applicable to this research article, leave it blank. Be prepared to explain your ratings. When responding to criteria A and B below, keep in mind that brief titles and abstracts are conventional in published research.

A. The title of the article is appropriate.
SA   5   4   3   2   1   SD

B. The abstract provides an effective overview of the research article.
SA   5   4   3   2   1   SD

C. The introduction establishes the importance of the study.
SA   5   4   3   2   1   SD

D. The literature review establishes the context for the study.
SA   5   4   3   2   1   SD

E. The research purpose, question, or hypothesis is clearly stated.
SA   5   4   3   2   1   SD

F. The method of sampling is sound.
SA   5   4   3   2   1   SD

G. Relevant demographics (for example, age, gender, and ethnicity) are described.

SA   5   4   3   2   1   SD

H. Measurement procedures are adequate.

SA   5   4   3   2   1   SD

I. All procedures have been described in sufficient detail to permit a replication of the study.

SA   5   4   3   2   1   SD

J. The participants have been adequately protected from potential harm.

SA   5   4   3   2   1   SD

K. The results are clearly described.

SA   5   4   3   2   1   SD

L. The discussion/conclusion is appropriate.

SA   5   4   3   2   1   SD

M. Despite any flaws, the report is worthy of publication.

SA   5   4   3   2   1   SD

Article 16

Physical Restraint Reduction in the Acute Rehabilitation Setting: A Quality Improvement Study

Shelly Amato, MSN, RN, CNS, CRRN, **Judy P. Salter**, MSN, RN, CNS, CRRN, **Lorraine C. Mion**, PhD, RN, FAAN[*]

ABSTRACT. A prospective, continuous quality improvement study was implemented at a hospital on two rehabilitation units: stroke and brain injury. The purpose of the study was to decrease restraint use by 25% and to maintain fall rates no greater than 10% over baseline. A multicomponent restraint reduction program was implemented that focused on administrative support, education, consultation, and feedback. Monthly restraint rates and fall rates were monitored and compared to the previous year's rates. Both units reduced restraint use. Importantly, this reduction was accomplished at the same time as a decline in fall rates.

From *Rehabilitation Nursing*, *31*, 235–241. Copyright © 2006 by the Association of Rehabilitation Nurses. Reprinted with permission.

Nurses have utilized physical restraints as part of patient care for many years in a variety of settings. For example, acute care nurses use physical restraints to prevent delirious or agitated patients from prematurely
5 disrupting therapy devices (Minnick, Mion, Leipzig, Lamb, & Palmer, 1998). Nurses in acute rehabilitation settings physically restrain patients to prevent falls, to manage agitation, and to manage impulsive behavior (Mion, Frengley, Jakovcic, & Marino, 1989; Schleen-
10 baker, McDowell, Moore, Costich, & Prater, 1994). Many patients in acute rehabilitation suffer from neurological conditions, such as brain injury or stroke, that increase their risk for falls and agitated behavior.

Although they are considered beneficial, physical
15 restraints do not necessarily prevent patient falls. Indeed, up to 34% of rehabilitation patients who fall do so while in physical restraint (Arbesman & Wright, 1999; Mion et al., 1989; Schleenbaker et al., 1994). In addition, physical restraints can have adverse effects
20 and may even cause death (Bromberg & Vogel, 1996; Miles & Irvine, 1992). Given the questionable risk–benefit ratio of physical restraints, federal regulation and accreditation standards have restricted the use of physical restraint in all patient settings (Health Care
25 Financing Administration [HCFA], 1999; Joint Commission on Accreditation of Healthcare Organizations [JCAHO], 2005). As a result, many healthcare organizations have actively pursued reducing their use of physical restraints.

30 Studies have shown that restraint reduction programs in both acute care and long-term care settings have been effective in reducing restraint use while maintaining patient safety (Evans et al., 1997; Mion et al., 2001; Neufeld, Libow, Foley, & White, 1995). A
35 review of the literature yielded a descriptive report (Weeks, 1997) but found that no studies have systematically examined physical restraint reduction in the rehabilitation setting.

To establish the feasibility and effectiveness of
40 nonrestraint strategies in an acute rehabilitation setting, a continuous quality improvement (CQI) study was implemented on two acute rehabilitation units, brain injury, and stroke. The study's purpose was to determine whether a multi-component intervention strategy,
45 adapted from strategies used in long-term care and acute care settings, could safely reduce the use of physical restraints in acute rehabilitation units.

Methods

Setting

The Restraint Reduction Program (RRP) was implemented from March 2004 through March 2005 on
50 two acute rehabilitation units at a 732-bed county teaching hospital in the Midwest. The two units involved were the stroke rehabilitation unit (a 16-bed unit) and the brain injury rehabilitation unit (an 18-bed unit.)

Restraint Reduction Program (RRP)

55 Interventions in the RRP were adapted from programs successfully implemented in acute and long-term care settings (Evans et al., 1997; Mion et al., 2001). The planning committee for the program con-

---

[*]*Shelly Amato* is clinical nurse specialist for the Brain Injury and Stroke Rehabilitation Units at MetroHealth Medical Center. *Judy P. Salter* is clinical instructor, Lorain County Community College. *Lorraine C. Mion* is director of research at MetroHealth Medical Center.

sisted of clinical nurse specialists, unit nurse managers,
60 nurse–patient care coordinators, physical therapists,
occupational therapists, and staff nurses.

The program consisted of four components: administration, education, consultation, and feedback. The administrative component involved gaining the
65 active support of the director of nursing, nurse managers, patient care coordinators, physician leaders, and therapists prior to implementation of the program. The clinical nurse specialists met with the leadership group to discuss the high use of restraints on both rehabilita-
70 tion units, the significance of the restraint use issue, and the proposed Restraint Reduction Program. Updates given during regularly scheduled meetings included progress reports on the program, barriers to implementation, and suggestions for facilitating staff
75 adoption of the program.

The education component consisted of both formal and informal information sessions for all levels of nursing staff. These sessions focused on the restraint and seclusion policy as well as the hospital's philosophy
80 regarding restraint use. A local vendor demonstrated restraint alternatives available for purchase. Staff members chose the devices that they felt would be most effective for their patient population, then tested the devices on a trial basis for effectiveness, after
85 which the selected devices were purchased for the program. The staff received training on proper use of the devices. Staff also received formal education on falls: risk factors, universal precautions, and targeted interventions using the selected physical restraint alterna-
90 tives. Content for those sessions was drawn from best evidence and practice guidelines (American Geriatrics Society, 2001; Leipzig, Cumming, & Tinetti, 1999a; Leipzig, Cumming & Tinetti, 1999b) and from the hospital's own Fall Prevention Protocol.
95 For the consultation component of the program, the clinical nurse specialists went on rounds with staff nurses, initially biweekly and then weekly after the RRP was firmly established. Rounds focused on patients who were restrained, patients who had fallen, or
100 patients judged to be at risk for falling. For example, the clinical nurse specialist and the nurse caring for a restrained patient might discuss issues for that particular patient such as impulsivity, steadiness of gait, and cognition. When a nurse identified that a patient was
105 starting to use the call light appropriately, or if a patient's gait was improving, a wheelchair and/or bed alarm respectively, would be recommended. The nurse caring for the patient would then make the final decision to remove the restraint based on the nurse's as-
110 sessment of the patient. During the next consultation session, the clinical nurse specialist would evaluate whether recommendations had been carried out. For any patient who had experienced a fall, the clinical nurse specialist would explore circumstances leading to
115 the fall and discuss any interventions nurses may have put in place following the fall. Fall-prevention strate-

gies found to be most effective in reducing restraint use included using alarms (for the bed or wheelchair), increased surveillance techniques (such as 15-minute
120 checks or moving patients closer to the nurses' station), and changing patient routines to facilitate surveillance and staff contact.

The feedback component was twofold. First, the nurses' adherence to the plan of care was monitored
125 and reviewed during the ongoing consultation rounds, at which time individual nurse-to-nurse feedback was provided. Second, the quality management department provided aggregate data in the form of monthly run charts for fall rates and physical restraint use on each
130 unit (see Figure 1).

The institutional review board (IRB) approved the study in late 2003. The administrative and education components began on both units in early 2004, with the consultation component starting in March 2004 and the
135 feedback component in April of that year.

Outcome Variables

The outcome variables for this study were the rates of physical restraint use and patient falls. Physical restraint was defined as "any device, material, or equipment attached or adjacent to the patient's body that the
140 patient cannot remove easily, that restricts freedom of movement, and that is not intended as part of the standard practice of care" (HCFA, 1999). Restraints included mitt(s), wrist restraints, waist restraints, pelvic restraints, and full side rails. Monthly restraint rates
145 were calculated as the total number of restraint hours per 100 patient days. Patient falls were defined as any witnessed or unwitnessed event in which the patient was found on the ground secondary to an unplanned event. Fall rates were calculated as the number of pa-
150 tient falls per 1,000 patient days.

Data Collection Procedures

Physical restraint data were collected from nursing documentation. Unit secretaries input the information into a computer database. At this hospital, quality management department personnel conduct ongoing audits
155 to ensure data collection consistency; any noted deviations are addressed at the time of the audit. Falls data were collected using the incident reports that nurses completed following any patient fall.

Analysis

Monthly prevalence rates for both restraint use and
160 falls were calculated for the year prior to implementation of the study (baseline: March 2003 through February 2004) and compared with the rates observed during the RRP (post: March 2004 through February 2005). Physical restraint benchmarks were established for
165 both units using a 25% reduction rate from baseline. Relative reduction rates were calculated using the mean yearly rates with the following equation: [(baseline-post)/baseline] × 100. An upper safety limit for fall rates was established as a 10% relative increase over

---

What Is Quality Improvement (QI)?

- Also called performance improvement (PI), quality management (QM) and continuous quality improvement (CQI), QI is a disciplined approach to continuously improve outcomes using management techniques, existing improvement efforts, and technical tools.

QI in Nursing

- Florence Nightingale was the first healthcare professional that used and encouraged systematic inquiry into practices that might explain variation in outcomes.
- National organizations, such as the Joint Commission on Accreditation of Healthcare Organizations and the American Nurses Credentialing Center for Magnet Hospital designation, determine whether QI processes are a part of the nursing department's activities.

What Outcomes Are Important to Nursing?

- A number of patient outcomes have been shown to be affected by either nursing structure and resources or by nursing practices. These nurse-sensitive outcomes include patient falls, physical restraints, nosocomial infections, pressure ulcers and medication errors.

How Does One Determine Whether Outcomes Need to Be Improved or if Processes Have Improved Chosen Outcomes?

- Many outcomes have national benchmarks established by which to compare your organization's rates to those considered to be "best practice." Most outcomes are reported as a prevalence rate per patient-days (either per 100 patient-days or 1000 patient-days) rather than as an incidence rate (percentage of patients developing an outcome). This is done in order to maintain an "apple-to-apple" comparison since hospitals and units vary in size and characteristics. Outcomes can be expressed as a duration (e.g., number of hours/patient-days), or as an event (e.g., number of falls/patient-days).
- If an organization's outcome is worse than the national benchmark (the baseline value), then a team is assembled and possible sources or reasons for the problem are identified.
- The team brainstorms on possible solutions for improving the outcome and implements these actions.
- Outcome results are monitored continuously, typically in monthly reports.

  Run or Trend Charts (see figures in this article) display the data points over time. A target or benchmark value can be added to the chart as a horizontal line. Healthcare providers monitor whether their practices or processes bring the outcome rates close to or better than the targeted benchmark value. If outcome rates continue to be worse than benchmark for more than a predetermined amount of time (e.g., three months, five months, etc.), then the process improvement activities are re-evaluated and modified.

  Statistical control charts also display the points over time. Month-to-month fluctuations in the outcome rate are normal. To determine if there are times when the fluctuation is greater or lesser than expected, two additional horizontal lines are added. These horizontal lines are typically three standard deviations above and below the mean, and are referred to as upper and lower control limits. If a monthly outcome rate occurs that is abnormally high or low (greater than three standard deviations), then the team immediately examines potential causes to explain the excessive variation (root cause analysis) and institutes changes in processes as needed.

From Claflin, N., DaMert, L., Hughes, J.D., Spath, P., Stephan, M., & Guthmann, I. (1998). NAHQ Guide to Quality Management, 8th Edition. Glenview, IL: National Association for Healthcare Quality; Langley, G.J., Nolan, K., Nolan, T.W., Norman, C.L., & Provost, L. P. (1996). The Improvement Guide: A Practical Approach to Enhancing Organizational Performance. San Francisco, CA: Jossey-Bass.

Figure 1. Understanding and utilizing quality improvement techniques.

---

170 baseline. The quality management office aggregated the data and reported it to the units.

Results

Both the stroke rehabilitation unit and the brain injury rehabilitation unit reduced their overall restraint rates (Figures 2 and 3). The stroke rehabilitation unit
175 reduced restraint use from 216.6 hours per 100 patient days to 153.3 hours per 100 patient days, representing a 29.2% relative reduction in overall restraint use. The brain injury unit reduced restraint use from 1054.3 hours per 100 patient days to 883.3 hours per 100 pa-
180 tient days—a 16.2% relative reduction.

Fall rates also decreased on both units (Figures 4 and 5). Stroke rehabilitation patients' fall rates declined from 11.4 to 6.1 falls per 1,000 patient days, a 45.5% relative reduction. Fall rates on the brain injury reha-
185 bilitation unit declined from 9.1 to 3.3 falls per 1,000 patient days, a 64.2% relative reduction.

Discussion

Federal regulations mandate the restriction of physical restraints in all patient settings, including rehabilitation (HCFA, 1999). Thus, rehabilitation nurses
190 must examine other ways to prevent falls among these high-risk patients. A restraint reduction program, fo-cusing on fall risk and impulsive or agitated behavior in stroke and brain injury rehabilitation patients, proved safe as well as effective. Our aim was to reduce
195 restraints while maintaining fall rates within 10% of baseline. Our achievement of both objectives demonstrates the feasibility and effectiveness of this systematic approach.

We found that the RRP program was more success-
200 ful on the stroke unit than on the brain injury unit. Several factors may account for this. First, the units are shaped differently. The stroke unit is circular, while the brain injury unit is a rectangular space with only a few beds visible from the nurses' station. Indeed, the two
205 most common strategies on the brain injury unit involved surveillance: moving a patient to a room closer to the nurses' station and/or instituting 15-minute surveillance checks. Another published report of a restraint reduction program also emphasized surveillance
210 strategies (Weeks, 1997). The nature of patients' medical conditions may also explain the differences in reduction rates. Although stroke patients may have cognitive deficits, such as poor judgment or lack of insight, brain injury patients tend to have greater impulsivity
215 and agitation.

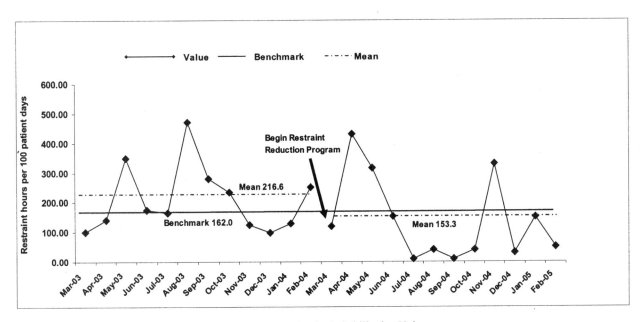

Figure 2. Changes in physical restraint rates—Stroke Rehabilitation Unit.

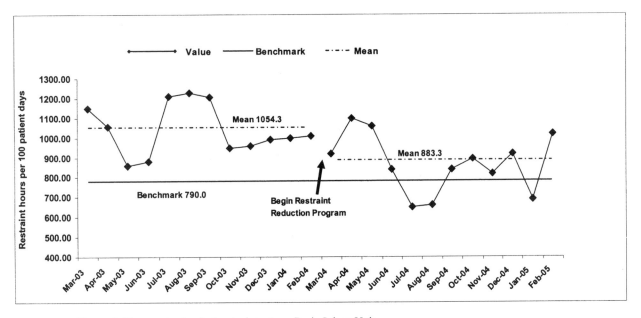

Figure 3. Changes in physical restraint rates—Brain Injury Unit.

Of note, both units had spikes in restraint use upon the initiation of the RRP as well as at later points in the program. These occasional increases were not associated with falls, and the rates were within the upper control limits of the mean (see Figure 1 for explanation). The initial spikes may reflect staff resistance toward implementing a new program, but the initial and later occasional spikes may simply reflect normal variations in restraint use over time. Given the successful results in restraint reduction, future plans for the stroke unit are to continue monitoring restraint use and fall rates and to ensure that restraint reduction strategies continue to be implemented in a safe manner.

Although restraint reduction was also successful on the brain injury unit, the outcome difference was not as great as that seen on the stroke unit. The brain injury unit staff will implement a unit-based restraint committee, which will be led by the clinical nurse specialist and will meet monthly. Membership will include all nursing staff as well as the nurse manager. The committee will focus on restraint reduction, examination of the causes of falls, and restraint documentation. In response to the challenge of reducing restraints while maintaining safety in the high-risk brain injury population, a "day room" has been designated and is under current remodeling on the brain injury unit. The room,

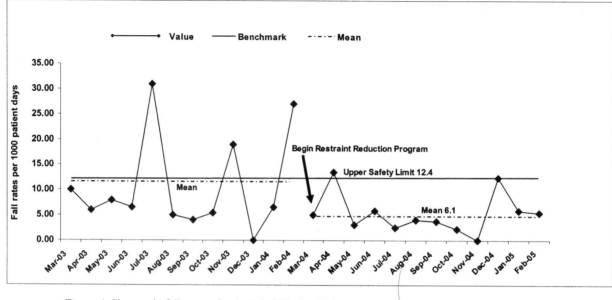

Figure 4. Changes in fall rates—Stroke Rehabilitation Unit.

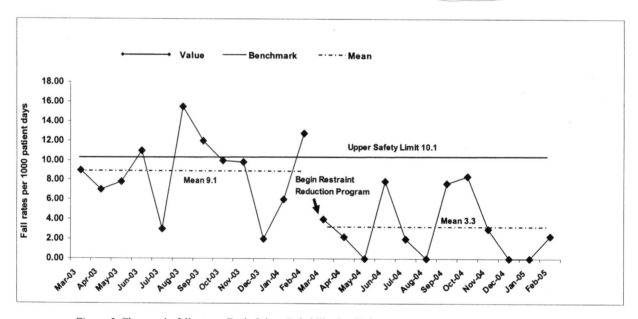

Figure 5. Changes in fall rates—Brain Injury Rehabilitation Unit.

which is to be staffed by a patient care provider, will provide a place where high-risk patients can be monitored closely during the daytime hours that they are not 245 in therapy.

In summary, in an acute rehabilitation setting, a restraint reduction program that emphasizes restraint alternatives can provide safe care that is effective in preventing falls while preserving patients' rights and 250 dignity.

References

American Geriatrics Society, British Geriatrics Society, and American Academy of Orthopaedic Surgeons Panel on Falls Prevention. (2001). Guideline for the prevention of falls in older persons. *Journal of the American Geriatrics Society, 49,* 664–672.

Arbesman, M. C., & Wright, C. (1999). Mechanical restraints, rehabilitation therapies, and staffing adequacy as risk factors for falls in an elderly hospitalized population. *Rehabilitation Nursing, 24,* 122–128.

Bromberg, M. B., & Vogel, C. M. (1996). Vest restraint palsy. *Archives of Physical Medicine and Rehabilitation, 77,* 1316–1319.

Evans, L. K., Strumpf, N. E., Allen-Taylor, S. L., Capezuti, E., Maislin, G., & Jacobsen, B. (1997). A clinical trial to reduce restraints in nursing homes. *Journal of the American Geriatrics Society, 45,* 675–681.

Health Care Financing Administration. (1999). *Medicare and Medicaid Programs. Hospital Conditions of Participation: Patients' Rights; Interim Final Rule.* 42 CFR Part 482. *Federal Register* (64:127).

Joint Commission on Accreditation of Healthcare Organizations. (2005). *2006 Comprehensive Accreditation Manual for Hospitals: The Official Handbook.* Oakbrook Terrace, IL: Author.

Leipzig, R. M., Cumming, R. G., & Tinetti, M. E. (1999a). Drugs and falls in older people: A systematic review and meta-analysis: I. Psychotropic Drugs. *Journal of the American Geriatrics Society, 47*, 30–39.

Leipzig, R. M., Cumming, R. G., & Tinetti, M. E. (1999b). Drugs and falls in older people: A systematic review and meta-analysis: II. Cardiac and analgesic drugs. *Journal of the American Geriatrics Society, 47*, 40–50.

Miles, S. H., & Irvine, P. (1992). Deaths caused by physical restraints. *Gerontologist, 32*, 762–766.

Minnick, A. F., Mion, L. C., Leipzig, R., Lamb, K., & Palmer, R. M. (1998). Prevalence and patterns of physical restraint use in the acute care setting. *Journal of Nursing Administration, 28*, 19–24.

Mion, L. C., Fogel, J., Sandhu, S., Palmer, R. M., Minnick, A. F., & Cranston, T. (2001). Outcomes following physical restraint reduction programs in two acute care hospitals. *The Joint Commission Journal on Quality Improvement, 27*, 605–618.

Mion, L. C., Frengley, J. D., Jakovcic, C. A., & Marino, J. A. (1989). A further exploration of the use of physical restraints in hospitalized patients. *Journal of the American Geriatrics Society, 37*, 949–956.

Mion, L. C., Gregor, S., Buettner, M., Chwirchak, D., Lee, O., & Paras, W. (1989). Falls in the rehabilitation setting: Incidence and characteristics. *Rehabilitation Nursing, 14*, 17–22.

Neufeld, R. R., Libow, L. S., Foley, W. J., & White, H. (1995). Can physically restrained nursing-home residents be untied safely? Intervention and evaluation design. *Journal of the American Geriatrics Society, 43*, 1264–1268.

Schleenbaker, R. E., McDowell, S. M., Moore, R. W., Costich, J. F., & Prater, G. (1994). Restraint use in inpatient rehabilitation: Incidence, predictors, and implications. *Archives of Physical Medicine and Rehabilitation, 75*, 427–30.

Weeks, S. K. (1997). RAP: A Restraint Alternative Protocol that works. *Rehabilitation Nursing, 22*, 154–156.

Acknowledgments: The authors wish to acknowledge the staff nurses on the stroke and brain injury rehabilitation units for implementing the Restraint Reduction Program, Kathleen McCarthy for the data analysis portion of this study, and the MetroHealth Foundation (grant no. 57-2003) for the funding to purchase restraint alternatives for this study.

Address correspondence to: Shelly Amato, MetroHealth Medical Center, 2500 MetroHealth Drive, Cleveland, OH 44109. E-mail: samato@metrohealth.org

Exercise for Article 16

Factual Questions

1. The brain injury rehabilitation unit had how many beds?

2. How was "patient falls" defined?

3. How long did the baseline last?

4. As a percentage, what was the relative reduction in overall restraint use?

5. Fall rates on the brain injury rehabilitation unit had what percentage relative reduction?

Questions for Discussion

6. Is the intervention described in sufficient detail? (See lines 55–135.)

7. How important was Figure 1 in helping you understand the background for this study? Would the report be as effective without the figure? Explain.

8. How important were Figures 2 through 5 in helping you understand the results of this study? Would the report be as effective without the figures? Explain.

9. To what extent has this study convinced you of the effectiveness of the intervention? Explain.

10. If you were planning a follow-up study on this topic, would you include a control group? Explain.

Quality Ratings

Directions: Indicate your level of agreement with each of the following statements by circling a number from 5 for strongly agree (SA) to 1 for strongly disagree (SD). If you believe an item is not applicable to this research article, leave it blank. Be prepared to explain your ratings. When responding to criteria A and B below, keep in mind that brief titles and abstracts are conventional in published research.

A. The title of the article is appropriate.

   SA   5   4   3   2   1   SD

B. The abstract provides an effective overview of the research article.

   SA   5   4   3   2   1   SD

C. The introduction establishes the importance of the study.

   SA   5   4   3   2   1   SD

D. The literature review establishes the context for the study.

   SA   5   4   3   2   1   SD

E. The research purpose, question, or hypothesis is clearly stated.

   SA   5   4   3   2   1   SD

F. The method of sampling is sound.

   SA   5   4   3   2   1   SD

G. Relevant demographics (for example, age, gender, and ethnicity) are described.

   SA   5   4   3   2   1   SD

H. Measurement procedures are adequate.

   SA   5   4   3   2   1   SD

I. All procedures have been described in sufficient detail to permit a replication of the study.

   SA   5   4   3   2   1   SD

J. The participants have been adequately protected from potential harm.

   SA   5   4   3   2   1   SD

K. The results are clearly described.

   SA   5   4   3   2   1   SD

L.   The discussion/conclusion is appropriate.

        SA   5   4   3   2   1   SD

M.   Despite any flaws, the report is worthy of publication.

        SA   5   4   3   2   1   SD

Article 17

An Intervention to Enhance Nursing Staff Teamwork and Engagement

Beatrice J. Kalisch, PhD, RN, FAAN, **Millie Curley**, MS, RN, **Susan Stefanov**, BSN, RN[*]

ABSTRACT. Numerous studies have concluded that work group teamwork leads to higher staff job satisfaction, increased patient safety, improved quality of care, and greater patient satisfaction. Although there have been studies on the impact of multidisciplinary teamwork in healthcare, the teamwork among nursing staff on a patient care unit has received very little attention from researchers. In this study, an intervention to enhance teamwork and staff engagement was tested on a medical unit in an acute care hospital. The results showed that the intervention resulted in a significantly lower patient fall rate, staff ratings of improved teamwork on the unit, and lower staff turnover and vacancy rates. Patient satisfaction ratings approached, but did not reach, statistical significance.

From *The Journal of Nursing Administration*, 37, 77–84. Copyright © 2007 by Lippincott Williams & Wilkins, Inc. Reprinted with permission.

The importance of quality teamwork in healthcare has been the subject of a number of studies in healthcare. Teamwork has been associated with a higher level of job staff satisfaction,[1–6] a higher quality of care,[4,7–13] an increase in patient safety,[5,14–19] greater patient satisfaction with their care,[11,20] more productivity,[21] and a decreased stress level.[22,23] Highly functioning teams have also been shown to offer a wider range of support to inexperienced staff.[22]

Outside healthcare, there have been a plethora of studies highlighting the value of teamwork. For example, one investigation of flight crews demonstrated the link between teamwork and safety. These researchers evaluated the impact of fatigue on error rate and found that staff who had flown together for several days made fewer errors than teams who were rested and had not worked together for very long. The fatigued team actually made more errors, but because the team had worked together, they were able to compensate and catch one another's near misses. This is due to less stress, knowledge of the vulnerabilities and strengths of other team members, and the practice of monitoring performance and giving feedback to one another.[22]

Many studies have tested interventions to improve teamwork. Approaches which have been found to enhance teamwork include cross training,[24,25] teamwork skills training,[26] Crew Resource Training,[14,27–31] role playing,[32] simulation,[33,34] automation,[35] posttraining feedback,[36] team-building activities,[37,38] and a combination of training and action groups.[39]

Specifically within healthcare, there has been a growing awareness of the need to improve teamwork. The Joint Commission on Accreditation of Healthcare Organizations (JCAHO) in July 2004 released a Sentinel Event Alert on the prevention of infant deaths. Its database showed that nearly three-quarters of hospitals cited communication breakdown and teamwork problems as a major reason for these deaths. The JCAHO recommended that hospitals conduct formal team training to the obstetrical/perinatal team.[40] In a study conducted by Dynamics Research Corporation, weaknesses and error patterns in emergency department teamwork were assessed, and a prospective evaluation of a formal teamwork training intervention was conducted. Improvements were obtained in five key teamwork measures, and most important, clinical errors were significantly reduced.[41] Hope et al.[42] found that a team-building initiative for health profession students resulted in an improved interdisciplinary understanding, team atmosphere, and teamwork skills. In another study, teamwork training of emergency department physicians and nurses significantly increased the quality of team behaviors, attitudes toward teamwork, and decreased clinical errors.[16]

Only a few studies have tested methods of increasing nursing teamwork. Amos et al.[43] found that the introduction of team-building activities resulted in greater staff communication, stronger interpersonal relationships, and greater job satisfaction. Britton[44] reported that a team development program conducted for hospital nurse managers led to greater understanding and clarity of work roles and improved cohesion and teamwork at the management level. In another study, a team-building intervention showed an im-

[*]*Beatrice J. Kalisch*, director, Nursing Business and Health Systems and Titus distinguished professor of nursing, School of Nursing, University of Michigan, Ann Arbor, MI. *Millie Curley*, vice president nursing, and *Susan Stefanov*, nursing project manager, Parrish Medical Center, Titusville, FL.

65 provement in group cohesion, nurse satisfaction, and turnover rates.[45]

This article reports the results of a study that will add to the body of knowledge about nursing teamwork. It evaluates the impact of an intervention designed to
70 enhance teamwork and promote staff engagement. The staff engagement component was considered an essential element of the intervention in that teamwork could not be achieved without the involvement and commitment of the staff. The aim of this project was to deter-
75 mine the impact of an intervention designed to enhance teamwork and staff engagement on the rate of patient falls, patient satisfaction, the staff's assessment of level of teamwork on their unit, and vacancy and turnover rates.

Project Method

Study Subjects

80 The study was conducted on a 41-bed medical–oncology unit in a community hospital in 2004/2005. There were 55 staff members on the unit—32 registered nurses (RNs), 2 licensed practical nurses, 15 certified nurse assistants (CNAs), and 6 unit secretaries.

Measures

85 Measures for this project were patient fall rates, patient satisfaction scores, staff assessment of level of teamwork, staff vacancy, and turnover rates.

Patient falls per 1,000 patient days were collected before (January 2000–August 2004) and after (Sep-
90 tember 2004–June 2005) the teamwork and engagement intervention.

Patient satisfaction was measured with the Professional Research Consultants Patient Satisfaction Survey Tool, which has been utilized in hospitals through-
95 out the United States for 20 years.[46] Scoring is based on a point scale with weighting factors: Excellent (100), Very Good (80), Good (60), Fair (40), and Poor (20). In terms of validity of the instrument, Professional Research Consultants reports that they have per-
100 formed various tests of internal validity. The Cronbach α was .936 ($n = 824$) for the data from the medical unit utilized in this investigation. Professional Research Consultants also reports that they have conducted "side-by-side studies to compare various methodolo-
105 gies" and that by "utilizing norm data, they have demonstrated stability and consistency across various groups."[46]

Staff ratings of level of teamwork were completed 6 months after the intervention implementation. Confi-
110 dential interviews were conducted with 48 of 55 of the unit's staff by an external data collector who had no previous contact with the organization. The interviews were a combination of structured questions (e.g., "Has teamwork improved, stayed the same, or gotten
115 worse?") and semistructured, open-ended questions (e.g., "How do you assess the RN and CNA relationships at this time compared to before the project? Give specific examples").

Staff turnover, exclusive of relocation, return to
120 school, retirement, or death, was calculated by dividing the preventable turnover FTEs by the budgeted FTEs for full-time and part-time RNs, licensed practical nurses, and CNA employees minus the open positions for the period before (March–August 2004) and after
125 the intervention (March–August 2005). Staff *vacancy rates* were calculated by determining the average of the vacant positions each pay period divided by the budgeted positions. This was collected for the 6 months before and 6 months after the teamwork and engage-
130 ment project.

Description of the Intervention

The teamwork and engagement enhancement intervention tested in this study was based on principles of teamwork,[11,14,16,19,30] change in management,[47] training,[32–34,36,39,42] and staff engagement.[47] The steps in the
135 intervention can be seen in Figure 1.

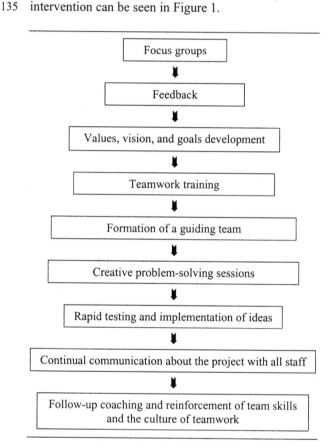

Figure 1. Staff teamwork and engagement enhancement intervention.

In the first step, 11 focus groups were conducted with RNs (5 groups), licensed practical nurses (1 group), CNAs (4 groups), and unit secretaries (2 groups) to determine their perceptions of the level of
140 teamwork on the unit and issues that inhibit and enhance teamwork. A total of 56 staff were interviewed, a participation rate of 97% of the unit staff. The purpose of the focus groups was to assess the level and nature

of teamwork on the unit as well as the staff educational
needs in the area of teamwork. Focus groups and interviews were also conducted with key stakeholders. Two
focus groups with former unit patients were selected
randomly from a list of discharged patients from the
unit for a month prior to the implementation of the intervention. In addition, individual interviews were conducted with the 6 physicians who admitted the most
patients to the unit. All of the focus groups and interviews were transcribed and analyzed using the N-Vivo
qualitative research software. Major themes were identified.

Feedback

These focus group data were compiled into a report
which was presented in several feedback sessions,
making it possible for each staff member on the unit to
attend. The purpose of this second step in the process
was not only to give the staff a report of the results of
the focus groups they participated in but also to create
a need for change. According to Kotter,[47] the first step
in any change process is to create a sense of urgency.
He notes that "we underestimate the enormity of the
task [of change], especially the first step, establishing a
sense of urgency."[47(p35)] It is not uncommon for teams
to deny that they have problems working together effectively even when they are obvious. Kotter[47(p36)]
points out: "People will find a thousand ingenious
ways to withhold cooperation from a process" they do
not buy into. Focus group data using quotations from
staff members themselves, their patients, and the physicians they work with were designed to be compelling
and mitigate tendencies of staff to discount reality.
These data were referred to repeatedly during the project.

After each presentation, staff members were asked
if they were interested in working on a project to improve teamwork. As noted above, it is crucial in a
change process to overcome complacency in order to
gain the cooperation of those involved. Each group of
staff indicated that they were committed to improving
teamwork and supporting a project designed to improve it.

Values, Vision, and Goals

The next step was to conduct values, vision, and
goals sessions, involving all unit staff in the process.
Values (enduring beliefs which determine behavior)
and vision (a compelling, inspirational, achievable, and
comprehensible picture of the unit at some point in the
future) gave direction to the unit staff and allowed the
team to share in the development of a common unified
direction.[48] Once the values and vision were finalized,
the entire staff engaged in a gap analysis. They looked
at where they were now and compared it to their vision
statement or where they wanted to be. They then identified the goals for the project or the first priorities they
felt they should work on to achieve their vision.

Training

Each staff member then attended a day-long team
training program. As mentioned above, the focus
groups served as the needs analysis for the teamwork–
training requirements of the staff and also as a source
of scenarios used in the role playing aspects of the
training program. This information was used to specify
the objectives, content, and posttraining evaluation of
the program. Major deficiencies in teamwork knowledge, skills, and abilities—namely, feedback, conflict
management, listening, and understanding of team information processing styles—were evident and formed
the focus for the teamwork training.

Guiding Teams

Two guiding teams (which were soon combined
into one due to confusion over overlapping efforts)
were created to address the specified project goals of
improving staff relationships (with an emphasis on the
relationship between nurses and CNAs) and redesign-
ing the work to facilitate teamwork and improve quality of care. Following Kotter's guidelines, guiding team
membership included managers (with position power),
representatives from the different job categories so that
all viewpoints would be represented, credible staff with
good reputations on the unit so that their ideas would
be taken seriously by other employees, and staff with
leadership capabilities.[47(p57)] In addition, staff with different information processing styles were selected to
balance the talents of the group.[49]

The guiding team initiated their work with several
intense day and half-day meetings, which focused on
creative idea generation and the classification of ideas
into a 4-cell diagram in which "easy- to hard-to-
implement" was on one axis and "high and low cost"
on the other axis.[50] The idea was to assist the staff in
selecting the easy-to-implement, low-cost ideas first so
that early successes, or what Kotter refers to as "short
term wins," could be achieved.[47] A major change like
this one takes a considerable amount of time. Yet unit
staff members look for convincing evidence that the
work of the guiding team is paying off. By addressing
the easy/low-cost items first, the guiding team met the
needs of the staff, thus making it easier for the guiding
team to take the time necessary to work on the more
complex issues.

Rapid Testing and Implementation

Rapid testing of ideas was the next step. For example, ideas, such as redesign of the patient change-of-
shift report, were tested on one of 3 of the unit's wings
before being adapted unit-wide. A similar approach
was used when the team decided to move all staff to
12-hour shifts from a mix of 8- and 12-hour shifts to
decrease the number of handoffs between staff members and the number of different people they worked
with.[51] Implementation of permanent changes occurred
when the testing of ideas proved successful. Mainte-

nance of the changes was monitored on an ongoing basis by the guiding team.

Communication

Communication was a vital component of the project. The guiding teams adopted the assumption that they needed to communicate their messages in at least 4 ways before they could expect that staff members actually would hear and understand the messages. Kotter[47(p94)] notes that "effective information transferal almost always relies on repetition." Each guiding team member was assigned to five to six of the unit staff members (constituents) who were not on the team, and was responsible for keeping these staff members informed of the work of the team and gaining feedback from them. At the end of each meeting, a decision was made about what would be reported to the constituent staff members about the meeting, as well as what areas of feedback from the staff were needed for the next meeting. This communication occurred within 24 hours of the end of each guiding team meeting. A second method of communication involved the development of a special bulletin board in the staff lounge devoted to keeping everyone informed about the work of the project. The third method was an e-mail sent by the nurse manager to all staff members at the end of each meeting, and the fourth communication tool was a report about the project in each monthly unit staff meeting.

Coaching

The ninth element of the project involved a systematic reinforcement by managers and guiding team members on the knowledge, skills, and attitude taught in the training programs. This step was considered essential because training is a learning process and not a one-time event. Like any skill, teamwork competencies will decay without periodic reinforcement and practice. Thus, the awareness training (which focused on knowledge and attitudes) was followed by skills practice and recurrent skills maintenance.[26]

Project Results

Patient Falls

As can be seen in Figure 2, the 2-sample t test showed that the patient fall rates dropped significantly from a mean of 7.73 per 1,000 patient days before the team intervention to 2.99 after the intervention ($t = 3.98, p < .001$).

Patient Satisfaction

Comparisons of the "excellent" scores on the Professional Research Consultants Patient Satisfaction Survey Tool for the study unit for quarters before and after the intervention approached but did not reach statistical significance. Patients' perceptions of nurses' promptness in responding to calls increased from 32.0% to 49.0%; nurses' communication with patients and family increased from 36.7% to 48.0%; and overall quality of nursing care increased from 46.0% to 52.0%.

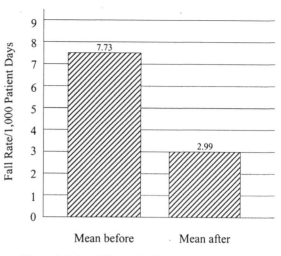

Figure 2. Mean fall rates before and after intervention. $t = 3.98, df = 64, p = .00.$

Staff Ratings of Level of Teamwork

The staff ratings of level of teamwork were completed in July 2005, and showed that staff felt that teamwork had improved ($\chi^2 = 36.065, p = .000$). Figure 3 contains a graphic distribution of the responses to the question "Has teamwork improved, stayed the same, or gotten worse since the teamwork intervention?" When analyzed by shift, 84% of the nurses and 80% of the CNAs on days and 35% of the nurses and 60% of the CNAs on nights reported that teamwork had improved on the unit. The discrepancy between shifts was reported to be due to the fact that the night shift felt that their level of teamwork was higher than the day shift before the project was initiated. Figure 4 shows more changes that staff felt had helped to improve teamwork.

Staff Turnover and Vacancy Rates

As can be seen in Figure 5, 2-sample t test showed that there was a significant drop in staff turnover rates after the intervention from 13.14 to 8.05 ($t = 2.18, p = .033$). Similarly, the vacancy rates declined significantly from before to after the teamwork enhancement project from 6.14 to 5.23 ($t = 4.55, p = .0000$).

Limitations

The major limitation of this study centered on the measurement of patient satisfaction. Not only was the number of patients surveyed small but the tool is proprietary and the data were collected by the company rather than by the researchers. In future studies, patient satisfaction should be measured directly by the researchers to ensure accuracy in data collection and analysis. This study needs to be replicated with other nursing teams and in other settings. Exploration of additional measures of teamwork and patient outcomes needs to be developed.

Discussion

This study tests a specific intervention for improving nursing staff teamwork and engagement on a hospi-

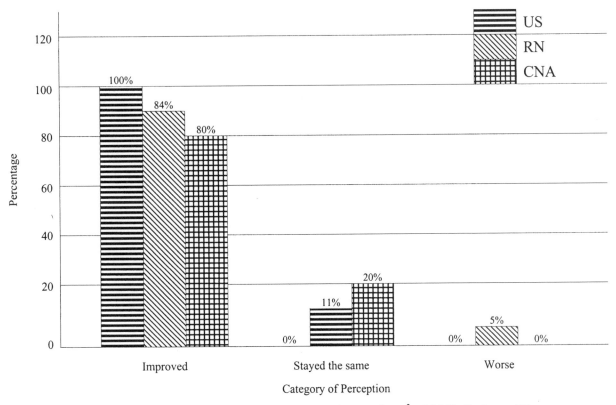

Figure 3. Staff Perception of changes in teamwork after the intervention. $\chi^2 = 36.065$, *df* = 2, *p* = .000.

Moving to an all 12-hour shift as opposed to the mix of 8- and 12-hour shifts (RN: The 12-hour shifts have helped significantly. There are only one CNA and RN working together. You can follow up easier. It helps with continuity of care and patient satisfaction increases.).

Greater team awareness of one another and more back-up behaviors (RN: We are working really well with each other. It is a mentality of "our patients" not just "my patients"; RN: We are more aware of each of their problems and issues, more open to helping each other than before; CNA: People are finding out more about each other. RN: The CNA/RN relationship is better; CNA: Nurses are helping out more with patient care. Nurses will help with things I cannot do on my own, like turning a patient or doing a bath. They didn't used to.).

Eliminating the different call light colors for the nurse and CNA (RN: Everyone is answering all of the call lights.).

Redistribution of certain tasks across both shifts and the development of a belief that the patients are "all of ours, no matter what shift we work" (CNA: The night shifts are doing the baths, and it takes some of the workload off the day shift.).

Clarification of roles of team members (RN: I feel like everyone is much clearer about our roles. There is much less of this feeling that the CNAs think we are goofing off when we are at the computer documenting.).

Improved ability to give feedback and deal with conflict (RN: We are much more likely to tell each other when there is a problem. We used to pass it to the manager.).

Figure 4. Staff perception of changes that improved teamwork. RN indicates registered nurse, CNA, certified nursing assistant.

tal medical unit. The intervention was based on established principles of change, training, teamwork, and empowerment. It involved extensive upfront efforts to establish a sense of urgency among a large proportion of the unit staff undergoing the change. The intervention included involvement of the entire unit staff in the development of values, vision, and goals to guide the project; a teamwork training needs assessment; training in teamwork knowledge, skills, and attitudes customized to the unit; the appointment of a guiding team made up of unit staff and managers who engaged in creative idea generation, testing, and implementation of ideas for change; a comprehensive communication strategy to keep the entire unit staff informed and involved in the project; and follow-up after training by managers and guiding team members to reinforce the new behaviors and ultimately change the culture of the unit to one that supports and expects teamwork.

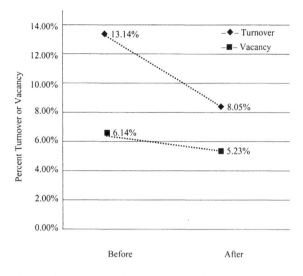

Figure 5. Turnover and vacancy rate before and after intervention. Turnover *t* = 2.18, *df* = 63, *p* = .033; vacancy *t* = 4.55, *df* = 58, *p* = .0000.

The team enhancement and engagement intervention followed a specific protocol developed before the initiation of the project but still allowed for flexibility
355 within it to meet the specific needs of the participants. For example, unit staff made the decisions as to what specific changes they wished to make on their unit to foster teamwork.

The outcomes of this study are promising in that
360 there was a significantly lower patient fall rate, lower turnover and vacancy rates, as well as staff self-reports of improved teamwork. Patient satisfaction improved but did not reach statistical significance, perhaps because the number surveyed was small.

365 Although this intervention was relatively extensive in scope, the potential to increase the quality of nursing care, avoid errors, decrease staff turnover, lower staff vacancy rates, and increase productivity makes the time and effort expended in this intervention worthy of
370 the effort. Potential cost savings, although not measured in this study, would appear to be substantial (e.g., decreased staff turnover, fewer errors, decreased length of stay, etc.).

The results of the staff interviews, as well as ongo-
375 ing observations of work behavior, demonstrate a continual need to work with staff in the areas of listening, feedback, and conflict management. The team is currently working on dividing themselves into smaller units in an effort to reduce the number of different in-
380 dividuals they are working with so that they can develop the culture necessary to function as a high performing team and to be able to monitor one another's performance, give feedback, conduct closed loop communication, put the team above the individual, and
385 provide the team leadership needed.

References

1. Rafferty AM, Ball J, Aiken LH. Are teamwork and professional autonomy compatible, and do they result in improved hospital care? *Qual Saf Health Care.* 2001;10(II): 32–37.
2. Gifford BD, Zammuto RF, Goodman EA. The relationship between hospital unit culture and nurses' quality of work life. *Health Care Manag.* 2002;47:13–26.
3. Collette JE. Retention of staff—a team-based approach. *Aust Health Rev.* 2004;28(3):349–356.
4. Horak BJ, Guarino JH, Knight CC, Kweder SL. Building a team on a medical floor. *Health Care Manage Rev.* 1991;16(2):65–71.
5. Leppa CJ. Nurse relationships and work group disruption. *J Nurs Adm.* 1996;26(10):23–27.
6. Cox KB. The effects of unit morale and interpersonal relations on conflict in the nursing unit. *J Adv Nurs.* 2001;35(1):17–25.
7. Knaus WA, Draper EA, Wagner DP, Zimmerman JE. An evaluation of outcomes from intensive care in major medical centers. *Ann Intern Med.* 1986;104(3):410–419.
8. Shortell SM, O'Brien JL, Carman JM. Assessing the impact of continuous quality improvement/total quality management: Concept versus implementation. *Health Serv Res.* 1995;30(2):377–401.
9. Shortell SM, Zimmerman JE, Rousseau DM, Gillies RR. The performance of intensive care units: Does good management make a difference? *Med Care.* 1994;32(5):508–525.
10. Young GJ, Charns MP, Desai KR, et al. Patterns of coordination and clinical outcomes: A study of surgical services. *Health Serv Res.* 1998;33(5):1211–1236.
11. Mickan S, Rodger S, Characteristics of effective teams: A literature review. *Aust Health Rev.* 2000;23(3):201–208.
12. Grumbach K, Bodenheimer T. Can health care teams improve primary care practice? *JAMA.* 2004;291(10):1246–1251.
13. Wheelan SA, Burchill CN, Tilin F. The link between teamwork and patients' outcomes in intensive care units. *Am J Crit Care.* 2003;12(6):527–534.
14. Baker DP, Gustafson S, Beaubien JM, Salas E, Barach P. Medical team training programs in healthcare. In: Henriksen K, Battles JB, Marks ES, Lewin DI, eds. *Advances in Patient Safety: From Research to Implementation. Volume 4: Programs, Tools and Products.* Rockville, MD: Agency for Healthcare Research and Quality; 2005:253–267.
15. Firth-Couzens J. Cultures for improving patient safety through learning: The role of teamwork. *Qual Health Care.* 2001;10(2):26–31.
16. Morey JC, Simon R, Jay GD, et al. Error reduction and performance improvement in the emergency department through formal teamwork training: Evaluation results of the MedTeams Project. *Health Serv Res.* 2002;37(6):1553–1581.
17. Silen-Lipponen M, Tossavainen K, Hannele T, Smith A. Potential errors and their prevention in operating room teamwork as experienced by Finnish, British and American nurses. *Int J Nurs Pract.* 2005;11(1):21–32.
18. Gristwood J. Seeing the benefits of teamwork on falls prevention programmes. *Nurs Times.* 2004;100(26):39.
19. Kaissi A, Johnson R, Kirschbaum MS. Measuring teamwork and patient safety attitudes of high-risk areas. *Nurs Econ.* 2003;21(5):211–219.
20. Meterko M, Mohr DC, Young GJ. Teamwork culture and patient satisfaction in hospitals. *Med Care.* 2004;42(5):492–498.
21. Rondeau KV, Wagar TH. Hospital chief executive officer perceptions of organizational culture and performance. *Hosp Top.* 1998;76:14–31.
22. Carter AJ, West MA. Sharing the burden: Teamwork in the healthcare setting. In: Firth-Cozens J, Payne RL, eds. *Stress in Health Professionals.* Chichester: Wiley; 1999:191–201.
23. Sonnetag S. Work group factors and individual well-being. In: West MA, ed. *Handbook of Work Group Psychology.* Chichester: Wiley; 1996.
24. Volpe CE, Cannon-Bowles JA, Salas E. The impact of cross training on team functioning: An empirical investigation. *Hum Factors.* 1996;38(1):87.
25. Cannon-Bowers JA, Salas E, Blickensderfer E, Bowers CA. The impact of cross-training and workload on team functioning: A replication and extension of initial findings. *Hum Factors.* 1998;40(1):92–101.
26. Beaubien JM, Baker DP. The use of simulation for training teamwork skills in healthcare: How low can you go? *Qual Saf Health Care.* 2004;13:51–56.
27. Salas E, Fowlkes JE, Stout RJ, Milanovich DM, Prince C. Does CRM training improve teamwork skills in the cockpit? Two evaluation studies. *Hum Factors.* 1999;41(2):326–343.
28. Salas E, Rhodenizer L, Bowers CA. The design and delivery of crew resource management training: Exploiting available resources. *Hum Factors.* 2000;42(3):490–511.
29. Salas E, Burke CS, Bowers CA, Wilson KA. Team training in the sky: Does crew resources management training work? *Hum Factors.* 2001;43:641–674.
30. Grogan EL, Stiles RA. The impact of aviation-based teamwork training on the attitudes of health-care professionals. *J Am Coll Surg.* 2004;199(6):843–848.

31. Blum RH, Raemer DB, Carroll JS, Sunder N, Feinstein DM, Copper JB. Crisis resource management training for an anesthesia faculty: A new approach to continuing education. *Med Educ.* 2004;38:45–55.

32. Beard RI, Salas E, Prince C. Enhancing transfer of training: Using role plays to foster teamwork in the cockpit. *Int J Aviat Psychol.* 1995;5(2):131–143.

33. Swezey RW, Owens JM, Bergondy ML, Salas E. Task and training requirements analysis methodology (TTRAM): An analytic methodology for identifying potential training uses of simulator networks in teamwork-intensive task environments. *Ergonomics.* 1998;41:1678–1697.

34. Shapiro MJ, Morey JC, Small SD, et al. Simulation-based teamwork training for emergency department staff: Does it improve clinical team performance when added to an existing didactic teamwork curriculum? *Qual Saf Health Care.* 2004;13:417–421.

35. Wright MC, Kaber DB. Effects of automation of information-processing functions on teamwork. *Hum Factors.* 2005;47(1):20–66.

36. Beaubien JM, Baker DP. Post-training feedback: The relative effectiveness of team- versus instructor-led debriefs. *Proceedings of the 47th Annual Meeting of the Human Factors and Ergonomics Society.* Santa Monica, CA: Human Factors and Ergonomics Society; 2003:2033–2036.

37. Stoller JK, Dolgan C, Hoogwerf BJ, Rose M, Lee R. Teambuilding and leadership training in an internal medicine residency training program. *J Gen Intern Med.* 2004;19(6):692–697.

38. Horak BJ, Kerns J, Pauig J, Keidan B. Patient safety: A case study in team building and interdisciplinary collaboration. *J Healthc Qual.* 2004;26(2):6–12.

39. Ellis APJ, Bell BS, Ployhart RE, Hollenbeck DR. An evaluation of generic teamwork skills training with action teams: Effects on cognitive and skill-based outcomes. *Pers Psychol.* 2005;58(3):641–672.

40. Joint Commission on Accreditation of Healthcare Organizations. Available at: http://www.jcaho.org/SentinelEvents. Accessed July 2004.

41. Barrett J, Gifford C, Morey J, Risser D, Salisbury M. Enhancing patient safety through teamwork training. *J Healthc Risk Manag.* 2001;21(4):57–65.

42. Hope JM, Lugassy D, Meyer R, et al. Bringing interdisciplinary and multicultural team building to health care education: The downstate team-building initiative. *Acad Med.* 2005;80(1):74–83.

43. Amos MA, Hu J, Herrick CA. The impact of team building on communication and job satisfaction of nursing staff. *J Nurses Staff Dev.* 2005;21(1):10–16.

44. Britton L. Use of behavioral science concepts and processes to facilitate change: A team building program for nursing supervisors. *Aust Health Rev.* 1984;7(3):162–179.

45. DiMeglio K, Padula C, Korber S, et al. Group cohesion and nurse satisfaction: Examination of a team-building approach. *JONA.* 2005;35(3):110–120.

46. Inguanzo JM. Professional Research Consulting. Reliability and validity of the patient satisfaction tool. Unpublished document; 2005.

47. Kotter J. *Leading Change.* Boston: Harvard Business School Press; 1996.

48. Ingersoll GI, Witzel PA, Smith TC. Using organizational mission, vision, and values to guide professional practice model development and measurement of nurse performance. *JONA.* 2005;35(2):86–93.

49. Kalisch B, Begeny S. The informational processing styles of nurses and nurse managers: Impact on change and innovation. Unpublished document; 2006.

50. Institute for Health Care Improvement. Transforming care at the bedside: Sparking innovation and excitement on the hospital unit. Available at: http://www.IHI.org. Accessed July 2006.

51. Kalisch B, Begeny S. Improving nursing unit team work. *JONA.* 2005;35(12):550–556.

Acknowledgments: The authors acknowledge the contributions of the study unit staff and managers and Suzanne Begeny, MS, RN, for conducting and analyzing the staff interviews.

Address correspondence to: Beatrice J. Kalisch, Nursing Business and Health Systems, School of Nursing, University of Michigan, 400 N. Ingalls Street, Ann Arbor, MI 48109. E-Mail: bkalisch@umich.edu

Exercise for Article 17

Factual Questions

1. How many of the participants were certified nurse assistants?

2. Was the difference in fall rates statistically significant? If yes, at what probability level?

3. Was the difference in turnover rates statistically significant? If yes, at what probability level?

4. According to the researchers, a major limitation centered on what?

5. Do the researchers call for replication of this study?

Questions for Discussion

6. In your opinion, is the Patient Satisfaction Survey Tool described in sufficient detail? Explain. (See lines 92–107.)

7. Do you think it was a good idea to have the interviews conducted by an external data collector who had no previous contact with the organization? Explain. (See lines 109–112.)

8. In your opinion, is the intervention described in sufficient detail? Explain. (See lines 131–286.)

9. This research is classified as "Pre-Experimental Research" in the Contents of this book. Do you agree with the classification? Explain.

10. Do you think that "potential cost savings" is an important issue to examine in future studies? Explain. (See lines 370–373.)

11. If you were to conduct a follow-up study on the same topic, what changes, if any, would you make in the research methodology?

Quality Ratings

Directions: Indicate your level of agreement with each of the following statements by circling a number from 5 for strongly agree (SA) to 1 for strongly disagree (SD). If you believe an item is not applicable to this research article, leave it blank. Be prepared to explain your ratings. When responding to criteria A and B below, keep in mind that brief titles and abstracts are conventional in published research.

A. The title of the article is appropriate.

    SA   5   4   3   2   1   SD

B. The abstract provides an effective overview of the research article.

    SA   5   4   3   2   1   SD

C. The introduction establishes the importance of the study.

   SA   5   4   3   2   1   SD

D. The literature review establishes the context for the study.

   SA   5   4   3   2   1   SD

E. The research purpose, question, or hypothesis is clearly stated.

   SA   5   4   3   2   1   SD

F. The method of sampling is sound.

   SA   5   4   3   2   1   SD

G. Relevant demographics (for example, age, gender, and ethnicity) are described.

   SA   5   4   3   2   1   SD

H. Measurement procedures are adequate.

   SA   5   4   3   2   1   SD

I. All procedures have been described in sufficient detail to permit a replication of the study.

   SA   5   4   3   2   1   SD

J. The participants have been adequately protected from potential harm.

   SA   5   4   3   2   1   SD

K. The results are clearly described.

   SA   5   4   3   2   1   SD

L. The discussion/conclusion is appropriate.

   SA   5   4   3   2   1   SD

M. Despite any flaws, the report is worthy of publication.

   SA   5   4   3   2   1   SD

Article 18

Vaccine Risk/Benefit Communication: Effect of an Educational Package for Public Health Nurses

Terry C. Davis, PhD, **Doren D. Fredrickson**, MD, PhD, FAAP, FACPM,
Estela M. Kennen, MA, **Sharon G. Humiston**, MD, MPH, **Connie L. Arnold**, PhD,
Mackey S. Quinlin, BS, **Joseph A. Bocchini Jr.**, MD[*]

ABSTRACT. The purpose of this study was to determine whether an in-service for public health nurses (PHNs) and accompanying educational materials could improve vaccine risk/benefit communication. The content and timing of vaccine communication were recorded during 246 pre- and 217 postintervention visits in two public health immunization clinics. Pre-/postintervention comparisons showed PHN communication of severe side effects (13% vs. 44%, $p < .0001$) and their management (29% vs. 60%, $p < .0001$) increased. There was no significant change in discussion of vaccine benefits (48% vs. 51%) or common side effects (91% vs. 92%), screening for contraindications (71% vs. 77%), or distribution of written information (89% vs. 92%). More parents initiated vaccine questions postintervention (27% vs. 39%, $p < .01$) and were more satisfied with vaccine-risk communication (8.1 vs. 8.9 on a 10-point scale, $p < .01$). Average vaccine communication time increased from 16 to 22 seconds ($p < .01$).

From *Health Education & Behavior*, 33, 787–801. Copyright © 2006 by SOPHE. Reprinted with permission.

Risk communication is receiving increased attention in public health and clinical medicine (Leask, 2002; National Vaccine Advisory Committee, 2003). Clear risk/benefit communication may be particularly important for childhood immunization. As the number of childhood immunizations increases and the incidence of vaccine-preventable diseases decreases, parental concern about vaccine risks is increasing (Gellin, Maibach, & Marcuse, 2000; Marshall & Gellin, 2001). Risk/benefit issues may be heightened because both health care professionals and parents have a diminishing level of experience with the diseases that vaccines prevent, and vaccine information widely available to parents may be inaccurate and/or misleading (National Vaccine Advisory Committee, 2003). A national telephone survey found that although 87% of parents believed that immunizations were extremely important, almost one-fourth had misconceptions about vaccines (Gellin et al., 2000).

Limited or inaccurate information could undermine parent confidence in vaccine safety and affect parents' immunization decision making. A recent survey of pediatricians and family physicians found that more than two-thirds reported a substantial increase in parental concern about vaccine safety in the past year (Freed, Clark, Hibbs, & Santoli, 2004). The National Childhood Vaccine Injury Act (U.S. Government, 1986) mandates that all immunization providers give parents the applicable Vaccine Information Statements (VIS) developed by the Centers for Disease Control and Prevention (CDC) with each vaccine dose and provide appropriate verbal explanation (American Academy of Pediatrics, 2000; Evans, 2000; Freed et al., 2004; Simpson, Suarez, & Smith, 1997). Printed VISs are written at a 10th-grade level in English and are available in 30 languages through the Immunization Action Coalition (http://www.immunize.org/vis/).

Vaccine risk/benefit information needs to be communicated as simply as possible. The Institute of Medicine (2004) reported that most health information is unnecessarily complex and that 90 million Americans have trouble understanding and using health information. The report recommended that both written and spoken information be given to patients in everyday language. Clear vaccine communication is important in all childhood immunization settings, but recent findings indicate that parents at public health clinics (PHCs) in particular may need plain language information about vaccine risks and benefits. A notable proportion of U.S. children are immunized in the public sector. Gellin et al. (2000) found that parents who were Black, were Hispanic, or had less than a high school

Terry C. Davis, Louisiana State University Health Sciences Center, Shreveport. *Doren D. Fredrickson*, University of Kansas School of Medicine, Wichita. *Estela M. Kennen*, Louisiana State University Health Sciences Center, Shreveport. *Sharon G. Humiston*, University of Rochester School of Medicine and Dentistry, New York. *Connie L. Arnold, Mackey S. Quinlin*, and *Joseph A. Bocchini Jr.*, Louisiana State University Health Sciences Center, Shreveport.

education—those more likely to attend PHCs—were more likely to be concerned about vaccine side effects. In a separate study, parents in Texas attending PHCs had more concerns about vaccine safety than those attending private offices (Simpson et al., 1997).

Much of the background of the present study has been previously reported research by this team. The sequence of those studies included the following.

• Focus groups: We elicited feedback on written and spoken vaccine risk/benefit communication from health care providers and demographically diverse groups of parents in six U.S. cities (T. C. Davis et al., 2001; Fredrickson, Davis, & Bocchini, 2001; Page, Eason, Humiston, & Baker, 2000). Parents noted that VISs often "disintegrated in the diaper bag" and remained unread. Parents wanted a sturdy, to-the-point reference booklet before the child's first immunization visit as well as verbal information. They were particularly interested in practical information such as which shots their child would receive, common side effects, and the vaccine schedule, but they also wanted brief information on severe side effects. As noted in other studies (Ball, Evans, & Bostrom, 1998; Gellin & Schaffner, 2001), we found that parents wanted concise vaccine risk/benefit information from their own trusted provider. In provider focus groups (T. C. Davis et al., 2001), physicians and nurses stated that they rarely discussed severe vaccine side effects. Physicians felt such discussions would "open a can of worms," which in turn would cause them to be "in the exam room all day," whereas nurses felt that they lacked sufficient knowledge to address severe side effects.

• National survey: We mailed questionnaires that we developed based on focus group findings to a random national sample of immunizing private practice physicians (pediatricians and family physicians) and their nurses and to a geographically stratified, random national sample of public health nurses (PHNs) (T. C. Davis et al., 2001). Results showed that although the majority of providers reported discussing common side effects, severe side effects, and vaccine benefits, PHNs reported higher rates of communication than did private providers. Although most pediatricians (54%) reported lacking time to discuss risks and benefits, only 37% of PHNs reported time constraints. Almost half of PHNs (48%) reported having no barrier to risk/benefit communication. Health care providers of all types expressed the need for practical materials to help improve vaccine communication.

• Private physician office-based intervention: An immunization education package was developed based on the aforementioned studies and a review of the literature on improving provider adherence to health guidelines (Cabana et al., 1999; Dugan & Cohen, 1998; D. A. Davis, Thomson, Oxman, & Haynes 1995; D. A. Davis et al., 1999). The package included a clinic-based in-service that reviewed current vaccine guidelines, provided feedback on the clinics' current vaccine communication performance, and introduced educational materials. The educational materials included a poster titled "7 Questions Parents Need to Ask About Baby Shots" aimed at both providers and parents, an accompanying answer sheet for providers, and a contraindication screening sheet for providers. We assessed the efficacy of this educational package among pediatricians and their nurses in two private pediatric offices. The pediatric office-based package significantly increased six aspects of vaccine communication (discussion of contraindications, common side effects, treatment of common side effects, severe side effects, management of severe side effects, and schedule of the next vaccination), with less than a minute increase in visit time (T. C. Davis, Fredrickson, et al., 2002).

The purpose of the present study was to determine whether an intervention similar to the private office-based intervention, but tailored to PHNs and with the addition of an immunization booklet designed for parents, could improve vaccine risk/benefit communication in a timely manner among PHNs.

Method

The Intervention

We designed an intervention that included five components: a clinic-based in-service tailored for PHNs and four educational materials (a poster for the clinic, a vaccine information handout for PHNs, a contraindication screening sheet for PHNs, and a baby shot booklet for parents). Each of the materials was reviewed and supported by a national advisory board representing 14 agencies.[1] Materials were available for use only after the in-service session.

Poster. The poster was developed using patient education and health literacy principles (Doak, Doak, & Root, 1996; McGee, 1999; Rudd & Comings, 1994). It contained a brief list of what parents and providers indicated needed to be included in vaccine communication (T. C. Davis et al., 2001; Fredrickson et al., 2001). Designed to trigger provider/parent vaccine communication, it was formatted as seven simple questions. The colorful poster included age-specific photographs of vaccine-eligible children. It used a conversational tone including specific wording suggested by parents and providers in the demographically diverse focus groups in six U.S. cities (T. C. Davis, Frederickson, et al., 2002). For example, the poster used the term "severe side effects" rather than "risks" and "baby shots" rather than "immunizations" because more parents understood those terms. The poster was written at a fourth-grade reading level and was scored 100 (*very easy*) on the Flesch Reading Ease Scale (0-100; Flesch, 1949). Based on health literacy guidelines (Doak et al., 1996; Institute of Medicine, 2004; McGee, 1999; Rudd & Comings, 1994), the poster was extensively pilot tested for clarity, comprehension, cultural appropriateness, and appeal.

Vaccine information handout. A vaccine information handout titled "Answers to the Seven Questions" was designed specifically for providers to help them answer the questions on the poster. The handout included a brief discussion of the information on the VIS.

Contraindication screening sheet. We modified a self-administered contraindication screening sheet originally developed by the Immunization Action Coalition (http:// www.immunize.org/catg.d/p4060scr.pdf) and tailored it to be easily administered by PHNs and to be included in the clinic record.

Educational session. The clinic in-service was based on adult learning principles and effective continuing education strategies (D. A. Davis et al., 1995; Dugan & Cohen, 1998). The interactive academic in-service was taught by a local opinion leader (an infectious-disease physician who was head of the local medical school Department of Pediatrics [Louisiana] or the medical director of the Public Health Clinic [Kansas]). The leader reviewed the requirements of the National Childhood Vaccine Injury Act, the national data concerning compliance with the mandates, and the local clinic results from the preintervention observation of vaccine communication.

The leaders then introduced each of the educational materials. PHNs were encouraged to tailor the vaccine communication to fit their practice style and time demands as well as the knowledge, previous childhood immunization experience, and communication needs of each parent. In-service leaders encouraged PHNs to elicit parent concerns and discuss poster questions. They recommended providing the simplest layer of information first and modifying communication based on parent questions or concerns.

The leader elicited questions and concerns throughout the in-service. For example, although PHNs felt very comfortable mentioning common side effects, they felt unskilled in discussing severe risks. PHNs were encouraged to provide simple, general information about risks, such as, "There's a very small possibility that the vaccine could cause seizures or death."

Baby Shot Booklet. The parent-centered booklet was also developed using patient education and health literacy principles (Doak et al., 1996; Institute of Medicine, 2004; McGee, 1999; Rudd & Comings, 1994). The focus groups revealed that parents wanted a single, colorful, and durable easy-to-read source for all childhood vaccine information, organized sequentially by the child's age (T. C. Davis et al., 2001; Fredrickson et al., 2001; Page et al., 2000). They also requested immunization information that would not disintegrate in the diaper bag. The *Baby Shot Booklet* was designed

as such. Written at a fourth-grade level, it simplified and reformatted age-specific information from the VISs, including shots for that visit, possible side effects, instructions for follow-up care, and how to reach both the National Vaccine Injury Compensation Program and the Vaccine Adverse Event Reporting System. Photos were used to illustrate ages at which each vaccine should be administered. The booklet was extensively pilot tested for clarity, comprehension, organization, and appeal.

Study Design and Setting

The study was a pre-post trial in two immunization-only clinics in urban PHCs, one in Louisiana and one in Kansas. The sites were chosen because they served racially mixed populations of working poor families typical of PHCs and were in two distinct geographic areas. The Louisiana public health unit employed 1 clerk and 12 PHNs, all registered nurses (RNs), who rotated through the immunization clinic. Depending on clinic volume, 1 to 3 RNs were assigned to the immunization clinic each day. The Kansas unit employed 1 administrative aide, 9 clerks, and 3 immunization nurses, all RNs. These nurses did not rotate through other sections of the PHC. In Louisiana, 3 of the 12 PHNs missed the training and were separately inserviced by the head nurse. In Kansas, all 3 immunization nurses attended the training.

The Louisiana clinic's immunization practices were determined by a state Public Health Immunization Policy, which requires that the appropriate VIS be distributed with each dose of vaccine and that PHNs tell parents which vaccines are to be administered that visit, their contraindications, and side effects; review recommended comfort measures; and give the date of the next visit. The Kansas clinic immunization practices were determined locally; nurses had been given CDC guidelines to follow.

From June 2000 through August 2001, research assistants (RAs) shadowed a convenience sample of 463 immunization visits of children younger than 5 years of age. RAs shadowed 246 preintervention and 217 postintervention visits. Clinic staff members were aware of the observer's presence and the general topic of the study (i.e., childhood immunizations) but not of the specific communication variables recorded.

After clinic check-in, RAs asked parents for consent to participate in a study about how nurses communicate with parents. Parents were asked whether they would be willing to answer a few questions and allow the RA to shadow the visit. Fewer than 5% of parents refused to participate. The most common reasons given were being too busy with the children and not wanting to complete the literacy assessment. Consenting parents signed a consent form before the RA collected demographic information and measured literacy. The RA then became a silent observer during the clinic visit. After the visit, RAs assessed the parent's satisfaction.

The Institutional Review Board at Louisiana State University Health Sciences Center–Shreveport (LSUHSC-S) and the Committees on the Rights of Human Subjects at University of Kansas School of Medicine–Wichita (UKSM–W) both approved the study design and instruments.

Outcome Variables and Data Collection Instruments

Variables were recorded using a 41-item checklist, which included parent demographics, immunizations given, information about VIS distribution, what risk/benefit communication took place, who initiated it, and how long it lasted. We chose specific aspects of vaccine risk/benefit communication to study based on previous studies (T. C. Davis et al., 2001; Page et al., 2000). The items included mention of rare severe risks, what to do if they occurred, common side effects, how to treat them, benefits, contraindication screening, the next immunization visit, and the long-term vaccination schedule. We used the term "side effect" to refer to common side effects of childhood vaccinations, such as fever of less than 105°, soreness, swelling, and fussiness. Rare severe side effects, such as seizures, fever higher than 105°, and brain damage were referred to as "severe risks." Visit length and vaccine communication were timed using silent stopwatches

Parent literacy was assessed using the Rapid Estimate of Adult Literacy in Medicine (REALM), a commonly used health word recognition test (T. C. Davis, Long, & Jackson 1993; T. C. Davis, Michielutte, Askov, Williams, & Weiss, 1998). The REALM is highly correlated with other standardized reading tests and the Test of Functional Health Literacy (T. C. Davis et al., 1993; Parker, Baker, & Williams 1995).

Parent satisfaction with three specific aspects of vaccine communication (benefits, common side effects, and severe risks), their confidence in handling possible side effects and risks, and their trust in the PHN were assessed with 10-point, Likert-type scales. Pilot testing had revealed that very specific questions were required for parents to discriminate their degree of satisfaction regarding vaccine communication. During the postintervention period, parent satisfaction with, and perceived helpfulness of, the poster and *Baby Shot Booklet* were assessed with open-ended questions and 10-point, Likert-type scales. The checklist and survey questions were pilot tested in the LSUHSC-S Pediatric Resident Continuity Clinic.

Procedures for Quality Assurance

RAs were trained and supervised by an author at each site. Conference calls between sites were conducted to ensure standardized data collection procedures.

Data Management and Analysis

Data recording and analysis were completed using Statistical Analysis Software SAS 9.1 (2002). Visit records were grouped as pre- or postintervention. Cate- gorical variables were compared across the intervention groups using chi-square. Normally distributed continuous variables were compared using unpaired *t* tests. Child and family demographics and immunizations given were compared across the two study sites and among the pre- and postintervention groups to determine whether potential selection bias was present.

Response to the intervention by the special subgroup of parents bringing their first child for first immunization were compared with those of more experienced parents without such characteristics using stratified analysis. Demographic independent variables were compared with outcome measures using chi-square for categorical and student *t* test for continuous variables to determine whether any association was present which might indicate potential confounding.

Poststudy PHN Site Visit

One year after the intervention, we revisited the sites and conducted interviews with the PHNs at each clinic. Scripted probes were used to discover PHNs' satisfaction with each of the intervention materials, whether parents asked more questions (particularly those on the poster), influence on vaccine communication and time demands, and suggestions for improvement.

Results

Parent demographic characteristics are shown in Table 1. The only significant difference between pre- and postintervention groups was that more parents were in the self-pay category during the postintervention period. On average, parents in both groups had completed 12.4 years of school, but approximately one-quarter of parents tested were reading below a ninth-grade level.

As expected, the study population demographics were somewhat different at the two study sites. Compared to Kansas, the Louisiana study participants were more likely to be Black and pay with Medicaid, whereas Kansas participants were more likely to be White and pay with cash. No differences in child age, number of vaccines, or other variables were detected. The demographics at each site remained stable between pre- and postintervention periods, so study data from the two sites were merged and described as one study population for outcomes evaluation.

Vaccines administered by PHNs during the study included diphtheria/tetanus/acellular pertussis (DTaP), hepatitis B (HBV), *Haemophilus influenzae* type b (Hib), measles/mumps/rubella (MMR), inactivated polio (IPV), and varicella. A mean of 3.5 vaccine doses were given per visit in both pre- and postintervention time periods. No vaccines were refused during the study.

Table 1
Parent Demographic Characteristics: Comparison of Parents in the Pre- and Postintervention Groups

	Pre-intervention ($n = 246$)	Post-intervention ($n = 217$)	Significance of Difference
Parent present			
Mother	86%	87%	*ns*
Father	17%	16%	*ns*
Parent race			
White	41%	46%	*ns*
Black	56%	50%	*ns*
Other	3%	3%	*ns*
Parent literacy			
Ninth grade and higher	70%	78%	*ns*
Seventh to eighth grade	22%	16%	*ns*
Sixth grade and lower	8%	6%	*ns*
Payment method			
Medicaid	53%	50%	*ns*
Self-pay	30%	42%	$p < .01$
Free	13%	6%	*ns*
Private insurance	4%	1%	*ns*
Parent's first baby	33%	33%	*ns*
Baby's first visit	13%	9%	*ns*
	M (SD)	*M (SD)*	
Parent age in years	26.8 (7.8)	27.5 (8.6)	*ns*
Parent education	12.4 (2.0)	12.4 (1.9)	*ns*
No. of children in family	2.3 (1.3)	2.5 (1.6)	*ns*

Note: ns = not significant.

During both pre- and postintervention periods, the VIS distribution (89% vs. 92%) as well as communication about side effects (91% vs. 92%) and treatment of side effects (91% vs. 93%) occurred frequently. Providers significantly improved discussion of severe side effects (13% vs. 44%, $p < .001$) and their management (29% vs. 60%, $p < .001$). The proportion of visits in which specific side effects and severe side effects were addressed is shown in Table 2. Mention of the Vaccine Injury Compensation Program (VICP) increased to 11% from a baseline of 0% ($p < .0001$).

Discussion of the schedule of the next visit dropped significantly (93% vs. 81%, $p < .001$), although it was commonly addressed in both periods. Screening for contraindications was moderately high throughout and did not change significantly (71% vs. 77%). In Louisiana, an electronic immunization registry was introduced during the study and, although the Louisiana nurses referred to the contraindication sheet, they did not incorporate the results into the electronic record. Communication about vaccine benefits occurred in about half of visits pre- and postintervention (48% vs. 51%); the most commonly mentioned benefit was protection against disease.

The amount of time spent discussing vaccines ranged from 0 to 120 seconds pre-intervention and from 0 to 240 seconds postintervention; mean vaccine communication time increased by 6 seconds from a mean of 16 seconds to 22 seconds ($p < .001$), median

time increased from 11 seconds to 15 seconds. This included time spent referring to the contraindication sheet in Louisiana and using it as a checklist in Kansas. In the 19 visits in which communication lasted more than 60 seconds (8 pre and 11 post), mothers tended to be younger (24 years vs. 29, $p < .05$). There was no difference by race, parent's education, or child's age.

Comparison of demographic variables (e.g., first or subsequent visit, first child, presence of father, maternal age, race, high vs. low maternal education, number of vaccines given, and child insurance status) with outcome variables showed no statistically significant confounders present.

Table 2
Proportion of All Visits in Which Specific Side Effects Were Discussed Pre- and Postintervention

	Pre-intervention ($n = 246$)	Post-intervention ($n = 217$)	Significance of Difference
Common side effects discussed:			
Fever	70%	73%	*ns*
Soreness	70%	65%	*ns*
Fussiness	36%	33%	*ns*
Mean number discussed	2.00	2.41	*ns*
Severe side effects discussed:			
Fever of 105 degrees or higher	10%	34%	$p < .0001$
Seizures/severe brain reactions	7%	25%	$p < .0001$
Severe allergic reaction	2%	10%	$p < .0001$
Permanent brain damage	0%	4%	$p < .01$
Pneumonia	0%	1%	*ns*
Other	6%	21%	$p < .0001$
No rare/severe side effect discussed	87%	56%	$p < .0001$
Mean number discussed	0.24	0.97	$p < .0001$

Note: ns = not significant.

Parent Questions and Parent Satisfaction

A higher proportion of parents asked questions postintervention (27% pre versus 39% post, $p < .005$). When stratified by literacy level, this increase was seen only in parents reading above the sixth-grade level (28% pre versus 41% post, $p < .01$). Forty percent of parents who asked a question wanted to know about the schedule, making it the most frequently asked type of question.

Table 3 shows the mean scores (highest score = 10) for parents' satisfaction, confidence, and trust. The only significant change was in the parents' satisfaction with discussion of rare severe side effects, in which the percentage of dissatisfied parents (those who rated their

113

satisfaction level below 6) dropped significantly from 17% to 9% ($p < .05$).

Table 3
Mean Scores for Parent Satisfaction, Confidence, and Trust Pre- and Postintervention

	Pre-intervention ($n = 246$)	Post-intervention ($n = 217$)	Significance of Difference
Parent satisfaction with discussion of:			
Severe side effects	8.1	8.9	$p < .01$
Common mild side effects	9.1	9.4	*ns*
Vaccine benefits	9.0	8.9	*ns*
Parent level of confidence with their own ability to handle:			
Mild side effects	9.6	9.6	*ns*
Severe side effects	9.3	9.4	*ns*
Parent level of trust in the PHN	9.4	9.3	ns

Note: PHN = public health nurse. For mean scores, low = 0, high = 10; *ns* = not significant.

At the conclusion of the immunization visit, parents were asked for their responses to the material. Seventy-four percent recalled seeing the poster. Of parents receiving both the *Baby Shot Booklet* and the VIS prior to the visit with the nurse administering the immunization, 36% were observed reading the VISs and 42% reading the *Baby Shot Booklet*. Parents who reported looking at the materials rated them highly. On a 10-point scale, mean usefulness scores were 8.9 for the poster, 9.3 for the VIS, and 9.4 for the *Baby Shot Booklet*.

In response to an open-ended question on the poster, parents reported liking the photographs and finding the poster helped them know both what questions to ask and when their child should return. Some parents felt that the poster had too many words or admitted not having read all the poster questions. In response to an open-ended question about the booklet, parents reported that they liked the size, color, and sturdiness of the book. Many mothers suggested that the *Baby Shot Booklet* should be given before the visit, ideally at birth, so they could read it more thoroughly and/or show it to their husband or mother.

Provider discussion of vaccine benefits; the number of questions parents asked; parent satisfaction with the providers' discussion of benefits, common side effects, and rare side effects; and parent confidence in their ability to manage common or severe side effects did not increase after the intervention among the 20 parents with a first baby with first immunization. Time spent discussing all topics increased from 16 seconds to 21 seconds (*ns*) among these parents and from 16 to 22 seconds ($p < .01$) among all other parents.

Postintervention Site Visits

A year after the study ended, the posters were still hanging in the waiting room and exam rooms in both PHCs. In individual interviews, PHNs noted that parents and children were attracted to the poster photographs. PHNs felt that the poster was particularly helpful in structuring the discussions of vaccines. The nurses indicated that the poster and in-service helped them fine-tune their vaccine discussion and include mention of severe risks. In addition, although the nurses reported an increase in the number of parent questions, they did not perceive this to slow them down or add to visit time. They said that they felt more prepared to answer the questions and believed that the content of the questions needed to be discussed.

The PHNs felt that all parents should receive the booklet (ideally when their child was born) and found both the content and physical aspects of the booklet practical and inviting. PHNs at both sites gave booklets to parents as long as supplies lasted and then requested more booklets. Nurses also reported that parents continued to bring booklets to future visits and that new parents requested the booklets after having seen other parents use them. PHNs appreciated the contraindication screening sheets and found them quick and easy to use. PHNs said that they shifted from dreading the process to feeling confident that they knew specific contraindication questions to ask. They felt they were doing a more thorough screening.

Discussion

Providers and public health policy makers agree that parents need clear language explanations of vaccine risks and benefits. Our study found that vaccine communication materials developed with input from parents and providers could easily be introduced into PHCs and would be well received by PHNs and parents. As a tool to improve specific aspects of vaccine communication, the intervention package was effective in some ways, ineffective in some, and had no impact in others.

There were several positive effects of this intervention, the main one being a threefold increase in PHNs' discussion of severe side effects and how to manage them and parents' corresponding increase in satisfaction with the discussion of severe side effects. In this study of pre-school visits to public health immunization clinics, the increase in provider communication of severe side effects did not lead to vaccine refusals. The frequency with which PHNs discussed the VICP also increased significantly but was still minimal (11%) postintervention. Another positive finding was that the poster may have served as both a reminder and encouragement for parents to ask questions; the proportion of parents who read above a sixth-grade level asking questions increased from 27% to 40%.

Provider discussion of the vaccine schedule decreased postintervention. This may have occurred because the PHNs focused on improving the risk/benefit message. The most common parent questions pre- and postintervention involved the vaccine schedule, which validates parent desire for practical information. Because information about the next visit and long-term schedule are important aspects of vaccine communication to parents, they need to be clearly emphasized during the in-services.

In our present study, PHNs discussed side effects and gave the VIS in approximately 9 of 10 immunization visits, both pre- and postintervention and screened for contraindications 75% of the time. This observational study corroborated our previous finding that PHNs self-reported that they consistently distributed VISs and discussed common side effects and that screening for contraindications was also frequent (T. C. Davis et al., 2001).

This study was conducted in public health immunization-only clinics. No parents refused a vaccine in the pre- or postintervention periods. This is consistent with results of a national survey of public health clinics showing that the median refusal rate at these clinics was 0.4 refusals per 1,000 children immunized a year (Fredrickson et al., 2004).

Comparisons with Previous Studies

In a previous study, a very similar intervention was tested in two private pediatric offices (T. C. Davis, Fredrickson, Bocchini, et al., 2002) and was found to dramatically increase the overall content of provider vaccine communication. The size of the gains, with relatively little extra time required, indicate that little additional staff time is needed for this to-the-point communication.

It is important to note that although the educational in-services for the private pediatric practices and PHCs contained similar content, each was tailored according to clinic characteristics (time demands and the needs of their patients) and provider-initiated communication.

Findings from this and other studies indicate that vaccine communication concerning rare severe side effects and vaccine benefits is not common (T. C. Davis et al., 2001; T. C. Davis, Fredrickson, Bocchini, et al., 2002; Gellin et al., 2000). Potential severe risks are included in the VISs and so, from a legal standpoint, should be discussed. From a parent's standpoint, this discussion is also important as a way for providers to express respect and build trust (T. C. Davis et al., 2001; Fredrickson et al., 2001). Health care providers may also overlook the discussion of vaccine benefits, believing that the serious morbidity and mortality of vaccine-preventable diseases is common knowledge (T. C. Davis et al., 2001; T. C. Davis, Fredrickson, Bocchini, et al., 2002). This may not be the case; most parents today have limited experience with vaccine-preventable diseases. They may be more motivated to immunize their child because of school and day care admission rules, rather than disease prevention (Gellin et al., 2000). A simple, affirming message about vaccine benefits needs to be a standard aspect of every immunization visit to help parents understand why routine immunizations are recommended for all children.

Previous research has found that parents—especially those with limited literacy—tend to want information that is relevant to them, that emphasizes what they need to do, and that explains why this action would benefit them or their child (Doak et al., 1996). Abstract facts and statistics are usually not useful to parents with limited health literacy. Concrete, practical information is preferred (T. C. Davis, Williams, Mafin, Parker, & Glass, 2002; Doak et al., 1996). These principles were corroborated in our study.

The Seven Question Poster

Previous research has indicated that individuals' ability to independently comprehend material is usually two or three grade levels lower than their reading recognition level, which is measured by tests such as the REALM. Individuals with low literacy tend to ask fewer questions, often because they feel that they do not have the right words (Doak et al., 1996). Based on this information, the poster was designed with three things in mind. First, it invited parents to ask common vaccine questions. Second, it was envisioned as a potentially effective, low-cost method of triggering and structuring vaccine communication for nurses and physicians. Third, because the poster offered general questions appropriate to all vaccines, it would not need to be replaced despite continuing changes in the vaccine schedule. The poster could become outdated, however, if immunizations are recommended for ages not indicated by the pictures on the poster.

Even though the poster used in this study was brief (100 words) and was written on a fourth-grade level according to the Flesch Kincaid scale, parents in public health clinics indicated that it had too many words (including the title) and it looked too busy. In response to this feedback, we have modified the poster: We decreased it to 60 words and increased the amount of white space to increase readability. The new poster has a second-grade reading level and a perfect score (100) on the Flesch Reading Ease scale. Ideally, these modifications would be tested in future trials. In addition, it would be of interest to test the poster and provider information sheet without the in-service and other materials to see whether similar results could be obtained at a lower cost.

Limitations

The generalizability of our findings is limited by the fact that the study was conducted in only two PHCs, both urban and both conducted only in English. Translation of materials and testing in a wider variety of public health clinics are needed. General limitations of this simple, low-cost study design were typical of observational pre-post comparison studies that do not control for temporal trends.

640   The PHNs' vaccine communication and time allotted may have been influenced by the presence of the observer in the immunization visit. However, PHNs were not aware of the objective of the study or that certain aspects of the visit would be timed. Because observers were present both before and after the in-
645   service, parent satisfaction ratings may have been inflated in both time periods, potentially blunting the demonstrated efficacy of the intervention.

The time spent on discussion of predetermined vaccination topics was measured by trained RAs using
650   silent stopwatches, but the beginning and ending of these conversations were subjective. More accurate measurements using audio- or videotapes were beyond the scope of this project. Interrater reliability between sites was not tested. There was, however, no difference
655   in the mean time increase reported at our two sites. In a future study, the interactions may be audiotaped to allow more comprehensive coding and to minimize observer bias.

Because the intervention included a set of five
660   components (the education session and four materials), we could not separate the effects of each component, which in future studies could be tested separately.

The small number of parents (6% to 8%) reading below a sixth-grade level may have limited our ability
665   to detect changes in this group's asking questions. However, patient education literature indicates that patients with limited literacy tend to ask fewer questions (Doak et al., 1996).

Implications for Practitioners

One of the health objectives for the nation in
670   Healthy People 2010 is improving health communication and health literacy (U.S. Department of Health and Human Services, 2000). Improved vaccine risk/benefit communication and subsequent parent understanding may be important components of immunization deliv-
675   ery and overlooked aspects of building parent confidence in vaccine safety. In the United States today, approximately 45% of young children receive at least one vaccine in a public health clinic (National Immunization Program, 2001). Parents at these clinics are
680   more likely to have limited literacy skills and may require repeated, plain-language, oral vaccine risk and benefit information in addition to the VISs. Simple, appealing patient education materials developed with input from providers and parents and organized from a
685   parent's perspective might augment provider vaccine communication and subsequent parent understanding by encouraging parents to ask questions.

Vaccine risk/benefit communication has been mandated since 1986, but content based on what parents
690   and providers request and how it is most effectively delivered has not been adequately addressed (Page et

al., 2000; Simpson et al., 1997). The National Vaccine Advisory Committee (2003) Standards for Child and Adolescent Immunization indicate that health care pro-
695   fessionals should allow sufficient time to discuss the vaccines, the diseases they prevent, known risks, the immunization schedule, the need to receive vaccines at the recommended ages, and the importance of bringing the child's vaccine record to each health care visit. Our
700   research suggests that an efficient and systematic approach to discussion of risks and benefits can be done by busy PHNs in public health settings at every visit in a short amount of time.

In this study, we found that PHNs were doing a
705   good job of distributing the VIS and discussing common mild side effects, as mandated by their clinics' guidelines, but needed improvement in communication of vaccine risks and benefits. Our intervention, which used an academic outreach visit that included feedback
710   on baseline performance and provided PHNs with easy-to-use educational materials and prompts, significantly increased communication of severe side effects and increased parent vaccine questions and parent satisfaction with little expenditure of additional time.

715   The implications of this study have broader applications. As the number of licensed vaccines expands to include those for more common illnesses (e.g., rotavirus diarrhea), sexually transmitted infections (e.g., human papilloma virus), and frightening potential ill-
720   nesses (e.g., pandemic influenza), communication with patients and their parents will require even greater skill and more carefully tailored and tested messages. The effective continuing education strategies used in this study and the educational materials, which were de-
725   signed to be provider- and patient-centered, can be used with a wide array of health professionals. One of the important aspects of this study is that it explored creative approaches to making continuing education more provider-centered and health communication
730   more parent-centered. This study shows that it is possible to engage parents and providers in health communication without increasing the time burden or responsibility of either party.

Note

[1]The 14 agencies are as follows: American Academy of Pedi-
735   atrics, Ambulatory Pediatric Association, American Academy of Family Physicians, Society of Teachers of Family Medicine, American College of Obstetricians and Gynecologists, American Nurses Association, National Association of Pediatric Nurses and Practitioners, Association of Faculties of
740   Pediatric Nurse Practitioner/Associate Programs, National Association of Community Health Centers Inc., Association of Teachers of Preventive Medicine, Health Resources and Service Administration, Centers for Disease Control and Prevention, Food and Drug Administration, and McKesson
745   Bioservice Corporation.

References

American Academy of Pediatrics. (2000). Informing patients and parents. In L. K. Pickering (Ed.), *Red book: Report of the Committee on Infectious Diseases* (25th ed., pp. 4–6). Elk Grove Village, IL: Author.

Ball, L., Evans, G., & Bostrom, A. (1998). Risky business: Challenges in vaccine risk benefit communication. *Pediatrics, 101*, 453–458.

Cabana, M. D., Rand, C. S., Powe, N. R., Wu, A. W., Wilson, M. H., Abboud, P. A. C., et al. (1999). Why don't physicians follow clinical practice guidelines? A framework for improvement. *Journal of the American Medical Association, 282*, 1458–1465.

Davis, D. A., O'Brien, M. A. T., Freemantle, N., Wolf, F. M., Mazmanian, P., & Taylor-Vaisey, A. (1999). Impact of formal continuing medical education: Do conferences, workshops, rounds, and other traditional continuing education activities change physician behavior or health care outcomes? *Journal of the American Medical Association, 282*, 867–874.

Davis, D. A., Thomson, M. A., Oxman, A. D., & Haynes, R. B. (1995). Changing physician performance: A systematic review of the effect of continuing medical education strategies. *Journal of the American Medical Association, 274*, 700–705.

Davis, T. C., Fredrickson, D. D., Arnold, C. L., Cross, J. T., Humiston, S. G., Green, K., et al. (2001). Childhood vaccine risk/benefit communication in private practice office settings: A national survey. *Pediatrics, 107*, E17.

Davis, T. C., Fredrickson, D. D., Bocchini, C., Arnold, C. L., Green, K., Humiston, S., et al. (2002). Improving vaccine risk/benefit communication with an immunization education package: A pilot study. *Ambulatory Pediatrics, 2*, 193–200.

Davis, T. C., Long, S., & Jackson, R. (1993). Rapid estimate of adult literacy in medicine: A shortened screening instrument. *Family Medicine, 25*, 391–395.

Davis, T. C., Michielutte, R., Askov, E. N., Williams, M. V., & Weiss, B. (1998). Practical assessment of adult literacy in health care. *Health Education & Behavior, 25*, 613–624.

Davis, T. C., Williams, M., Marin, E., Parker, R. M., & Glass, J. (2002). Health literacy and cancer communication. *CA: A Cancer Journal for Clinicians, 52*, 134–149.

Doak, C. C., Doak, L. G., & Root, J. H. (1996). *Teaching patients with low-literacy skills* (2nd ed.). Philadelphia: J. B. Lippincott.

Dugan, E., & Cohen, S. J. (1998). Improving physicians' implementation of clinical practice guidelines: Enhancing primary care practice. In S. A. Shumaker, J. K. Ockene, & W. L. McBee (Eds.), *The handbook of health behavior change* (2nd ed., pp. 238–304). New York: Springer.

Evans, G. (2000). Pediatricians must use official Vaccine Information Statements. *American Academy of Pediatrics News, 16*, 14.

Flesch, R. (1949). *The art of readable writing.* New York: Harper & Row.

Fredrickson, D. D., Davis, T. C., Arnold, C. L., Kennen, E., Humiston, S. G., Cross, J. T., et al. (2004). Childhood immunization refusal: Provider and parent perceptions. *Family Medicine, 36*, 431–439.

Fredrickson, D. D., Davis, T. C., & Bocchini, J. A. (2001). Explaining the risks and benefits of vaccines to parents. *Pediatric Annals, 30*, 400–406.

Freed, G. L., Clark, S. J., Hibbs, B. F., & Santoli, J. M. (2004). Parental vaccine safety concerns: The experiences of pediatricians and family physicians. *American Journal of Preventive Medicine, 26*, 11–14.

Gellin, B. G., Maibach, E. W., & Marcuse, E. K. (2000). Do parents understand immunizations? A national telephone survey. *Pediatrics, 106*, 1097–1102.

Gellin, B. G., & Schaffner, W. (2001). The risk of vaccination: The importance of "negative" studies. *New England Journal of Medicine, 344*, 372–373.

Institute of Medicine. (2004). *Health literacy: A prescription to end confusion* (L. Nielson-Bohlman, A. Panzer, & D. A. Kindig, Eds.). Washington, DC: National Academies Press.

Leask, J. L. (2002). Vaccination and risk communication: Summary of a workshop, Arlington, Virginia, USA, 5–6 October 2000. *Journal of Paediatrics and Child Health, 38*, 124–128.

Marshall, G. S., & Gellin, B. G. (2001). Challenges to vaccine safety. *Primary Care, 28*, 853–868.

McGee, J. (1999). *Writing and designing print materials for beneficiaries: A guide for state Medicaid agencies* (HFCA Publication No. 10145). Baltimore: U.S. Department of Health and Human Services, Health Care Financing Administration, Center for Medicaid and State Operations.

National Immunization Program. (2001). *National Immunization Survey, Q3/2000–Q2/2001.* Atlanta, GA: Centers for Disease Control.

National Vaccine Advisory Committee. (2003). Standards for child and adolescent immunization practices. *Pediatrics, 112*, 978–981.

Page, D., Eason, P., Humiston, S., & Barker, W. (2000). Notes from the Association of Teachers of Preventive Medicine: Vaccine risk/benefit communication project. *American Journal of Preventive Medicine, 18*, 176–177.

Parker, R. M., Baker, D., & Williams, M. V. (1995). The Test of Functional Health Literacy in Adults (TOFHLA): A new instrument for measuring patients' literacy skills. *Journal of General Internal Medicine, 10*, 537–545.

Rudd, R. E., & Comings, J. P. (1994, Fall). Learner developed materials: An empowering product. *Health Education Quarterly, 21*, 313–327.

Simpson, D. M., Suarez, L., & Smith, D. R. (1997). Immunization rates among young children in the public and private health care sectors. *American Journal of Preventive Medicine, 13*, 84–88.

Statistical Analysis Software. 9.1 ed. (2002). Cary, NC: SAS Institute.

U.S. Department of Health and Human Services. (2000). Health communication. In *Healthy People 2010: Understanding and Improving Health* (2nd ed.). Washington, DC: Government Printing Office.

U.S. Government. (1986). National Childhood Vaccine Injury Act of 1986 (Publication No. 99-660), *42*, USC Sect 300aa-26.

Acknowledgment: The authors wish to acknowledge the nurses, clinic staff, and patients who participated in this study. They also would like to thank their research assistants Vicky Specian, Catherine Davis, Amanda McConnell, Cathy Lott, Terri Jones, Cameron Fahrenholtz, and Kim Hooten for their hard work and colleague Linda Martin for her careful reading of the article. This project was partially funded by the Health Resources and Services Administration (HRSA) through Cooperative Agreement 6U76 AH 00001 to the Association of Teachers of Preventive Medicine (ATPM).

Address correspondence to: Terry C. Davis, Louisiana State University Health Sciences Center–Shreveport, Departments of Pediatrics and Internal Medicine, 1501 Kings Hwy., Shreveport, LA 71130. E-mail: tdavisl@lsuhsc.edu

Exercise for Article 18

Factual Questions

1. The Kansas unit had how many immunization nurses?

2. What percentage of the parents refused to participate?

3. What percentage of the postintervention parents had Medicaid?

4. Was the pre-to-post difference in discussing severe allergic reactions statistically significant? If yes, at what probability level?

5. At the conclusion of the immunization visits, what percentage of the parents recalled seeing the poster?

6. How was time spent on discussion of predetermined vaccination topics measured?

Questions for Discussion

7. Are the educational sessions described in sufficient detail? Explain. (See lines 181–210.)

8. Could the fact that the staff members were aware of the observer's presence have affected the results of this study? Explain. (See lines 262–265.)

9. Is the fact that the research was approved by a board and committee important? Explain. (See lines 278–283.)

10. Is it important to know that the pre- and postintervention groups were similar in demographic characteristics? Explain. (See lines 355–362 and Table 1.)

11. Do you think it would be worthwhile to conduct a future study on each of the five components separately? Explain. (See lines 659–662.)

12. Do you think it would be worthwhile to include a control group in a future study on this topic? Why? Why not?

Quality Ratings

Directions: Indicate your level of agreement with each of the following statements by circling a number from 5 for strongly agree (SA) to 1 for strongly disagree (SD). If you believe an item is not applicable to this research article, leave it blank. Be prepared to explain your ratings. When responding to criteria A and B below, keep in mind that brief titles and abstracts are conventional in published research.

A. The title of the article is appropriate.

SA 5 4 3 2 1 SD

B. The abstract provides an effective overview of the research article.

SA 5 4 3 2 1 SD

C. The introduction establishes the importance of the study.

SA 5 4 3 2 1 SD

D. The literature review establishes the context for the study.

SA 5 4 3 2 1 SD

E. The research purpose, question, or hypothesis is clearly stated.

SA 5 4 3 2 1 SD

F. The method of sampling is sound.

SA 5 4 3 2 1 SD

G. Relevant demographics (for example, age, gender, and ethnicity) are described.

SA 5 4 3 2 1 SD

H. Measurement procedures are adequate.

SA 5 4 3 2 1 SD

I. All procedures have been described in sufficient detail to permit a replication of the study.

SA 5 4 3 2 1 SD

J. The participants have been adequately protected from potential harm.

SA 5 4 3 2 1 SD

K. The results are clearly described.

SA 5 4 3 2 1 SD

L. The discussion/conclusion is appropriate.

SA 5 4 3 2 1 SD

M. Despite any flaws, the report is worthy of publication.

SA 5 4 3 2 1 SD

Article 19

The Pain Management Knowledge of Nurses Practicing in a Rural Midwest Retirement Community

Laura Hanssen Textor, MSN, APRN, RN-C, **Davina Porock**, PhD, RN[*]

ABSTRACT. Pain is a significant health issue, especially among hospitalized patients and elders. Nurses are the key to effective pain management; however, several studies over the past 20 years have demonstrated that nurses lack the knowledge necessary to manage pain effectively. Staff development educators have used a number of education methods to address this deficit. Additionally, educators in staff development have the task of providing education in an effective and cost-efficient manner. The purpose of this study was to assess the pain knowledge scores of a group of nurses practicing in a rural Midwest retirement community before and at two points after a pain education intervention to determine the effectiveness of Knowles' Adult Learning Theory in increasing and sustaining rural nurses' pain knowledge scores.

From *Journal for Nurses in Staff Development*, 22, 307–312.

Pain is the most common reason in the United States to seek medical care (Turk & Okifuji, 1998) and is the second most common reason for hospital admissions among all age groups (P. Arnstein, personal communication, February 22, 2003). Every year, millions of Americans develop acute pain from surgery or injury and 50 million suffer from chronic pain (American Pain Foundation, 2000). Up to 50% of elders living in a community setting and up to 80% of institutionalized elders suffer from significant pain (American Geriatric Society, 2002), making pain a significant health issue.

Of all health professionals, nurses spend the most time with patients and are the key to effective pain management. However, for over 20 years, studies have shown nurses lack pain knowledge (Dalton et al., 1998; McCaffery & Ferrell, 1997) in multiple areas, including addiction (McCaffery & Ferrell, 1997), opiate properties (Sloman, Ahern, Wright, & Brown, 2001), adjuvants (Kubecka, Simon, & Boettcher, 1996), ceiling dose of morphine (Glajchen, 2001), pain and elders (Sloman et al., 2001), properties of meperidir jchen, 2001), reliability of patient's self-report fery & Ferrell, 1997), equianalgesia (Ferrell & fery, 1997), and risk of respiratory depression 1996).

Nurse educators have used a variety of techniques to increase nurses' pain knowledge, including videotape with self-learning module (Erkes, Parker, Carr, & Mayo, 2001), mandatory workshops (Simpson, Kautzman, & Dodd, 2001), and formal classes (Dalton et al., 1998). Programs have varied in length from 2 hours (Wallace, Graham, Ventura, & Burke, 1997) to 8 hours (Howell, Butler, Vincent, Watt-Watson, & Stearns, 2000) to 48 hours (Dalton et al., 1998), and the problem still persists.

Purpose of the Study

The purpose of this study was to determine the pain management knowledge of a group of nurses practicing in a rural Midwest community and to determine if a one-time 4-hour pain education program designed to meet the needs of the adult learner would be effective in increasing and maintaining knowledge scores for 1 month.

Theoretical Framework

Knowles' (1970) Adult Learning Theory was the theoretical framework tested in this study. According to Knowles, adults learn best when they (1) know the reason they should learn something; (2) are self-directed; (3) can use what they have learned; (4) are motivated; (5) can draw from past experience; and (6) use a task, problem, or life-centered approach. The learning environment should be one of acceptance, respect, support, and mutual learning that permits personal autonomy. The educational technique used should emphasize the practical application of the information and actively engage the learners in the learning process. Figure 1 demonstrates the application of Knowles' Adult Learning Theory to the educational intervention used in this study.

[*]*Laura Hanssen Textor* is clinical nurse specialist, St. Luke's Hospital, Pain Management Service, Kansas City, Missouri. *Davina Porok* is professor, Nursing Science, University of Nottingham, United Kingdom.

119

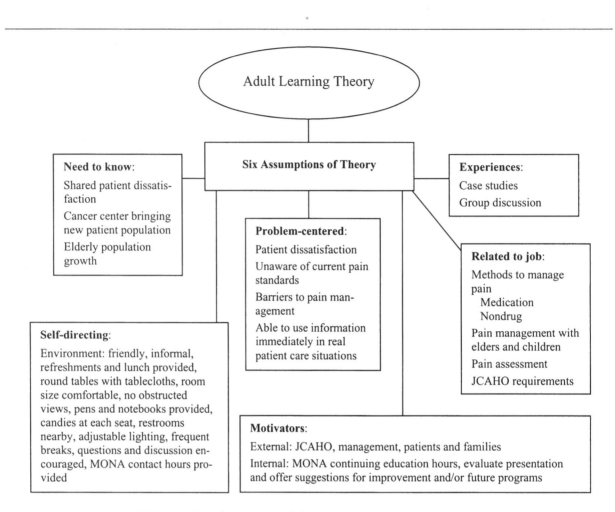

MONA: Missouri Nurses Association

JCAHO: Joint Commission on Accreditation of Healthcare Organizations

Figure 1. Application of Knowles' Adult Learning Theory.

Methods

Design

A one-group pretest and multiple posttest design
60 were used.

Sample and Setting

A convenience sample of registered nurses (RNs)
and licensed practical nurses (LPNs) working for the
study facility involved in direct patient care was used.
Of the 65 eligible nurses, 46 (71%) completed the Pre-
65 test and Posttest 1, and 35 (76%) also completed Posttest 2. The setting was a nonprofit health system located in a Midwest retirement community.

Instruments

Two instruments were used: The Nurses' Knowledge and Attitudes Survey Regarding Pain (NKASRP)
70 (Ferrell & McCaffery, 2002) and a sociodemographic
survey.

Procedure

Participants completed the NKASRP before, immediately after, and 4 weeks after a pain education
intervention.

Intervention

75   The intervention consisted of a one-time 4-hour
comprehensive overview of current pain management
practice designed and presented by a master's prepared
nurse with staff development and pain management
expertise. Teaching strategies included a PowerPoint
80 presentation, lecture, handouts, sharing of nursing experiences, question and answer, and discussion.

Results

The results of the data analysis present descriptive
statistics on the sociodemographics of the participants
(see Table 1). In the overall sample, 36 (78%) were
85 RNs and 10 (22%) were LPNs; 38 (83%) worked full-
time and 8 (17%) worked less than full-time; 26 (56%)
worked days and 20 (43%) worked nights; 16 (35%)

worked in a medical unit, 21 (46%) worked in a surgical unit, 4 (9%) worked in a skilled unit, and 5 (11%) worked in home health; 29 (66%) had not attended a pain education program in the past 2 years, 12 (27%) had attended one, 2 (5%) had attended two, and 1 (2%) had attended three; 5 (11%) had 3 years or less of nursing experience and 41 (89%) had more than 3 years.

Table 1
Sociodemographics Reported at Pretest (n = 46)

	Number of participants	Percentage
Education		
RN	36	78.3
LPN	10	21.7
Work Status		
Full-time	38	82.6
Less than full-time	8	17.4
Shift worked		
0700–1900	26	56.5
1900–0700	20	43.5
Unit worked		
Medical	16	34.8
Surgical	21	45.7
Skilled nursing	4	8.7
Home health	5	10.9
Pain education programs attended in past 2 years		
0	29	66.0
1	12	27.3
2	2	4.6
3	1	2.3
Years of experience		
3 or less	5	10.9
More than 3	41	89.1

Research Question 1

Research question 1 asked, "What is the pain management knowledge of nurses practicing in a rural Midwest retirement community?" The mean score for correct responses on the pretest was 70.8% (see Table 2). Responses to each question were reviewed to evaluate areas of greatest knowledge deficit (see Table 3).

Table 2
Knowledge Scores

	Number of participants	Mean score	Standard deviation	Range
Pretest	46	70.8	3.12	51.3–87.2
Posttest 1	46	87.3	2.49	69.2–100
Posttest 2	35	84.1	3.22	61.5–97.4

Research Question 2

Research question 2 asked, "Is a one-time four-hour education intervention sufficient to increase knowledge scores?" The mean score for correct responses on Posttest 1 was 87.3%, which was significantly higher than the pretest score ($p < .0001$).

Research Question 3

Research question 3 asked, "Is a one-time four-hour education intervention sufficient to sustain knowledge increases over one month?" The mean score for correct responses on Posttest 2 was 84%, which, although

lower than Posttest 1, was significantly higher than the pretest score ($p < .0001$).

Variables hypothesized to have an impact on knowledge scores were analyzed using *t* test and analysis of variance (see Table 4). There was no significant difference based on degree (Pretest [PT], $p = .06$; Posttest 1 [PT1], $p = 0.16$; Posttest 2 [PT2], $p = .73$), work status (PT, $p = .10$; PT1, $p = .31$; PT2, $p = .89$), shift worked (PT, $p = .68$; PT1, $p = .38$; PT2, $p = .91$), continuing education (PT, $p = .44$; PT1, $p = .76$; PT2, $p = .71$), and years of experience (PT, $p = .06$; PT1, $p = .80$; PT2, $p = .20$).

Analysis of variance was performed to determine if there was a significant Variable × Time interaction. There was no significant difference based on degree ($F = 0.93$, $p = .40$), work status ($F = 0.47$, $p = .10$), shift worked ($F = 0.78$, $p = .46$), and continuing education ($F = 0.64$, $p = .53$). There was a significant Experience × Time interaction ($F = 5.56$, $p = .007$); however, there were only five nurses with 3 years or less of nursing experience.

Implications

Nurses in staff development have the task of increasing the knowledge of nurses involved in patient care with the aim of improving patient care and outcomes in an effective and cost-efficient manner. This study demonstrates that Knowles' Adult Learning Theory, as a theoretical tool, is not only effective but also easy to apply when designing continuing education activities for nurses.

Limitations of the Study

Limitations of the study include small sample size ($n = 46$, $n = 35$), targeting only four of the facility's nursing areas and using participants from the same geographic area employed by one facility.

Conclusion

Nurses in this study demonstrated knowledge deficit in the areas of opiate pharmacology, meperidine, preferred route for opiate administration, cancer pain management, risk of addiction, ceiling dose of morphine, treating unrelieved pain, and risk of respiratory depression, which was similar to nurses in other studies (Closs, 1996; Dalton et al., 1998; Ferrell & McCaffery, 1997; Glajchen, 2001; Kubecka, Simon, & Boettcher, 1996; McCaffery & Ferrell, 1997; Sloman et al., 2001). Sociodemographic variables had no impact on knowledge scores, with the exception of years of experience. The effect of nursing experience was not constant over time; therefore, nursing experience had no true impact on knowledge scores. There were only five nurses in the study with 3 years or less of nursing experience. Results of this study demonstrate that application of Knowles' Adult Learning Theory when designing pain education for nurses is an effective and useful tool for staff development educators.

Table 3
Percentages of Correct Responses to Each Item on the Knowledge Tests

	PT	PT1	PT2
1. Vital sign changes must be relied on to verify pain.	95.6	97.8	97.1
2. Children under 2 years have decreased pain sensitivity and limited memory of painful events.	65.2*	100	94.3
3. Patients who can be distracted from pain usually do not have high pain intensity.	93.4	97.8	100
4. Patients may sleep in spite of severe pain.	89.1	97.8	100
5. Comparable stimuli produce the same pain intensity.	93.5	97.8	100
6. NSAIDs are not effective for bone pain from metastases.	50.0*	86.9	60.0*
7. Nondrug interventions are very effective for mild to moderate pain but rarely effective for severe pain.	47.8*	73.9	60.0*
8. Respiratory depression rarely occurs in patients taking opioids for several months.	41.3*	93.4	82.3
9. ASA 650 mg PO has the analgesic effect of meperidine 50 mg PO.	34.8*	89.1	74.3
10. The WHO ladder suggests single-agent analgesics rather than combining classes of drugs.	80.4	97.8	91.4
11. Usual duration of action of meperidine intramuscularly is 4–5 hours.	39.1*	71.1	65.7*
12. Research shows promethazine to be a reliable potentiator of opioids.	17.4*	80.4	68.6*
13. Patients with a history of substance abuse should not be given opioids for pain because they are at high risk for repeated addiction.	78.2	93.5	88.6
14. Beyond a certain dose, increasing morphine doses will not increase pain relief.	50.0*	82.6	52.9*
15. Elderly patients cannot tolerate opioids for pain relief.	91.3	97.8	91.4
16. Patients should endure as much pain as possible before resorting to pain relief measures.	100	100	100
17. Children younger than 11 years cannot reliably report pain; therefore, nurses should rely on the parents' report of pain intensity.	100	100	100
18. Religious beliefs may lead a patient to think pain and suffering are necessary.	97.8	97.8	100
19. After initial doses of opioids, subsequent doses are based on patient response.	91.3	97.8	100
20. Nondrug techniques should be used alone rather than in combination with pain medications.	95.6	97.8	100
21. Placebo is often useful in determining if pain is real.	89.1	93.5	94.2
22. To be effective, hot and cold should be applied only to the painful area.	71.7	30.0*	54.5*
23. Oral is the recommended route for opioid analgesics for prolonged cancer pain.	36.9*	65.2*	45.7*
24. IV is the recommended route for opioid analgesics for sudden severe pain.	91.3	91.3	97.1
25. Morphine is the opioid of choice for prolonged moderate to severe cancer pain.	63.0*	82.2	77.1
26. Morphine 10 mg IV q4h would be equivalent to morphine 30 mg PO q4h.	40.0*	41.3*	52.9*
27. Postoperative analgesics should initially be given round the clock on a fixed schedule.	80.4	100	97.1
28. Respiratory depression risk when increasing morphine doses for a patient taking morphine for 2 months is < 1 %.	28.2*	82.6	85.7
29. Analgesics for chronic cancer pain should be given on a fixed schedule around the clock.	91.3	100	100
30. Increased pain is the most likely explanation for why a patient would request an increase in pain medication.	91.3	95.6	97.1
31. Ibuprofen, hydromorphone, and amitriptyline are all useful drugs for treating cancer pain.	65.2*	91.3	88.6
32. The patient is the most accurate judge of pain intensity.	95.6	100	100
34. Percent of patients who overrate their pain is 0%.	13.0*	21.7*	11.4*
35. <1–5% of patients are likely to become addicted to opioids prescribed for pain.	64.4*	87.0	100
36. A smiling postoperative patient rates his pain at 8. Your assessment of his pain intensity is 8.	84.7	100	97.1
37. If a smiling postoperative patient reports pain of 6 to 8 after 2 mg of IV morphine, the next dose should be increased to 3 mg IV.	47.8*	91.3	82.9
38. A grimacing postoperative patient rates his pain at 8. Your assessment of his pain intensity is 8.	97.8	100	100
39. If a grimacing postoperative patient reports pain of 6 to 8 after 2 mg of IV morphine, the next dose should be increased to 3 mg IV.	71.7	89.1	88.6

PT indicates pretest, $n = 46$; PT1, Posttest 1, $n = 46$; PT2, Posttest 2, $n = 35$; PO, by mouth; NSAIDs, nonsteroidal antiinflammatory drugs.
*Denotes a very low score.

Table 4
Sociodemographic Variables

	Pretest score (p)	Posttest 1 (p)	Posttest 2 (p)	ANOVA (p)
RN vs. LPN	.06	.16	.73	.40
Work status	.10	.31	.89	.63
Shift worked	.68	.38	.91	.46
Pain education	.44	.76	.71	.53
Years of experience	.06	.80	.20	.007

References

American Geriatric Society (2002). The management of persistent pain in older persons. *Journal of American Geriatric Society Supplement, 50*, S205–S224.

American Pain Foundation. (2000). *Fast facts about pain.* Retrieved October 15, 2001, from http://www.painfoundation.org/whatsnew/summary030499.htm

Closs, S. (1996). Pain and elderly patients: A survey of nurses' knowledge and experiences. *Journal of Advanced Nursing, 23*, 237–242.

Dalton, J., Carlson, J., Mann, J., Blau, W., Bernard, S., & Youngblood, R. (1998). An examination of nursing attitudes and pain management practices. *Cancer Practice, 6*, 115–124.

Erkes, E., Parker, V., Carr, R., & Mayo, R. (2001). An examination of critical care nurses' knowledge and attitudes regarding pain management in hospitalized patients. *Pain Management Nursing, 2*, 47–53.

Ferrell, B., & McCaffery, M. (1997). Nurses' knowledge about equianalgesic and opioid dosing. *Cancer Nursing, 20*, 210–212.

Ferrell, B., & McCaffery, M. (2002). *Nurses' knowledge and attitudes survey regarding pain.* Retrieved May 17, 2002, from http://mayday.coh.org

Glajchen, M. (2001). Chronic pain: Treatment barriers and strategies for clinical practice. *Journal of American Board of Family Practice, 14*, 178–183.

Howell, D., Butler, L., Vincent, L., Watt-Watson, L., & Stearns, N. (2000). Influencing nurses' knowledge, attitudes, and practice in cancer pain management. *Cancer Nursing, 23*, 55–63.

Knowles, M. (1970). *The modern practice of adult education: Andragogy versus pedagogy.* New York: Associated Press.

Kubecka, K., Simon, J., & Boettcher, J. (1996). Pain management knowledge of hospital-based nurses in a rural Appalachian area. *Journal of Advanced Nursing, 23*, 861–867.

McCaffery, M., & Ferrell, B. (1997). Nurses' knowledge of pain assessment and management: How much progress have we made? *Journal of Pain and Symptom Management, 14*, 175–188.

Simpson, K., Kautzman, L., & Dodd, S. (2001). The effects of a pain management education program on the knowledge level and attitudes of clinical staff. *Pain Management Nursing, 3,* 87–93.

Sloman, R., Ahern, M., Wright, A., & Brown, L. (2001). Nurses' knowledge of pain in the elderly. *Journal of Pain and Symptom Management, 21,* 317–322.

Turk, D., & Okifuji, A. (1998). Treatment of chronic pain patients: Clinical outcomes, cost effectiveness, and cost-benefits of multidisciplinary pain centers. *Critical Reviews in Physical and Rehabilitation Medicine, 10,* 181–208.

Wallace, K., Graham, K., Ventura, M., & Burke, R. (1997). Lessons learned in implementing a staff education program in pain management in the acute care setting. *Journal of Nursing Staff Development, 13,* 24–31.

Address correspondence to: Laura Hanssen Textor, MSN, APRN, RN-C, Pain Service, St. Luke's Hospital, Kansas City, MO 64111. E-mail: ltextor@saint-lukes.org

Exercise for Article 19

Factual Questions

1. Did the researchers use a "convenience sample" *or* a "random sample"?

2. When was the second posttest (Posttest 2 with the NKASRP) administered?

3. Was the Posttest 1 mean knowledge score significantly higher than the pretest score? If yes, at what probability level?

4. How many of the participants had 3 years or less of nursing experience?

5. On the pretest, what percentage of the participants responded correctly to the statement "Patients may sleep in spite of severe pain"?

Questions for Discussion

6. In your opinion, how important is the information on the theoretical framework for understanding this study? Explain. (See lines 44–58 and Figure 1.)

7. While 46 nurses completed the pretest and first posttest, only 35 of them also completed the second posttest. Does this complicate the interpretation of the results? Explain. (See lines 64–66.)

8. Is the intervention described in sufficient detail? Explain. (See lines 75–81.)

9. How helpful is the demographic information in helping you get a mental image of the participants? Explain. (See lines 82–94 and Table 1.)

10. How important are the limitations described by the researchers in lines 139–142? Explain.

11. How helpful is it to see the list of items on the knowledge test? Would the report be as informative without the items? Explain. (See Table 3.)

12. This research is classified as "Pre-Experimental Research" in the Contents of this book. Do you agree with the classification? Explain.

Quality Ratings

Directions: Indicate your level of agreement with each of the following statements by circling a number from 5 for strongly agree (SA) to 1 for strongly disagree (SD). If you believe an item is not applicable to this research article, leave it blank. Be prepared to explain your ratings. When responding to criteria A and B below, keep in mind that brief titles and abstracts are conventional in published research.

A. The title of the article is appropriate.

　　　SA   5   4   3   2   1   SD

B. The abstract provides an effective overview of the research article.

　　　SA   5   4   3   2   1   SD

C. The introduction establishes the importance of the study.

　　　SA   5   4   3   2   1   SD

D. The literature review establishes the context for the study.

　　　SA   5   4   3   2   1   SD

E. The research purpose, question, or hypothesis is clearly stated.

　　　SA   5   4   3   2   1   SD

F. The method of sampling is sound.

　　　SA   5   4   3   2   1   SD

G. Relevant demographics (for example, age, gender, and ethnicity) are described.

　　　SA   5   4   3   2   1   SD

H. Measurement procedures are adequate.

　　　SA   5   4   3   2   1   SD

I. All procedures have been described in sufficient detail to permit a replication of the study.

　　　SA   5   4   3   2   1   SD

J. The participants have been adequately protected from potential harm.

　　　SA   5   4   3   2   1   SD

K. The results are clearly described.

　　　SA   5   4   3   2   1   SD

L. The discussion/conclusion is appropriate.

　　　SA   5   4   3   2   1   SD

M. Despite any flaws, the report is worthy of publica-
    tion.

          SA   5   4   3   2   1   SD

Article 20

A Comparison Pilot Study of Public Health Field Nursing Home Visitation Program Interventions for Pregnant Hispanic Adolescents

Jody Duong Nguyen, RN, MSN/MPH, Michael L. Carson, MS,
Kathleen M. Parris, RN, MSN, Patricia Place, BSN, BCRN, PHN[*]

ABSTRACT

Objective: Improve pregnancy outcomes in first-time Hispanic adolescent mothers and their infants.

Setting: Urban communities in Orange County, California.

Design and Methods: A comparison of the Nurse–Family Partnership pilot study home visitation program with traditional Public Health Field Nursing (PHFN) home visitation.

Participants: Two hundred twenty-five Hispanic adolescent mothers and their infants.

Interventions: Participants in the control group received the traditional PHFN services; the intervention group received interventions from advanced trained public health nurses. The control group received a minimum of three home visits: one initial client assessment and family profile, one antepartum visit, and one postpartum visit including newborn assessment. Participants in the intervention group received weekly home visits for the first 4 weeks, followed by visits every other week until delivery, weekly visits for the next 6 weeks, visits every other week until the child was 20 months, and monthly visits until the child was 24 months of age.

Results: Preliminary results indicate that home visitation by public health nurses (PHNs) positively affected the health of adolescent mothers and their infants. The incidence of premature births to adolescent mothers in the intervention group was lower than that found in the California population of adolescent mothers.

Conclusion: Preliminary results from this program showed that PHN home visitation (control and intervention groups) positively affects the birth outcomes of adolescent mothers and their infants.

From *Public Health Nursing*, 20, 412–418. Copyright © 2003 by Blackwell Publishing, Inc. Reprinted with permission.

Reduction of adolescent pregnancies has been identified as a public health priority. In 2000, President Clinton released a statement saying that he was encouraged by the new birth data released by the Centers for Disease Control and Prevention. The data showed that teen birth rates in the United States were at their lowest level since record keeping began 60 years before. Nevertheless, the president encouraged every sector of society to continue its efforts in reducing adolescent pregnancy. He called on Congress to enact his budget initiative to provide $25 million to support living arrangements for teen parents, help reduce repeat pregnancies, and improve the health of mothers and their children (U.S. Department of Health and Human Services [USDHHS], 2000). In addition, one of the Healthy People 2010 goals is to improve pregnancy planning, increase spacing between pregnancies, and prevent unintended pregnancy occurring within 24 months of a previous birth (USDHHS, 2000).

The primary focus of this article is not on prevention of adolescent pregnancy but rather on developing an intervention program that focuses on the health and well-being of pregnant adolescents and their children. This includes assisting teen mothers in preparing to deliver a healthy full-term baby, promoting healthy growth and development of the child, and identifying and accomplishing the mother's life goals. The federal government estimates that approximately $40 billion per year is spent on helping families that begin with a teenage birth. Studies show that providing early-intervention programs serving low-income mothers and their children can reduce federal government spending on adolescent pregnancy. The Nurse Home Visitation Program in Elmira, New York, based on the David Olds Home Visitation Model, shows a taxpayer savings of more than $18,000 per low-income first-time mother (Karoly, Greenwood, Everingham, Hoube, Kilburn, Rydell, Sanders, & Cheisa, 1998). Studies have demonstrated the effectiveness of the Olds Home Visitation Model in reducing the number of repeat pregnancies;

[*] *Jody Duong Nguyen* is supervising public health nurse, Orange County Health Care Agency, Santa Ana, CA. *Michael L. Carson* is senior epidemiologist, Orange County Health Care Agency, Santa Ana, CA. *Kathleen M. Parris* is public health nursing manager, Orange County Health Care Agency, Santa Ana, CA. *Patricia Place* is supervising public health nurse, Orange County Health Care Agency, Santa Ana, CA.

child abuse; and maternal behavioral problems due to use of alcohol and drugs, sexual partners, cigarettes smoked, and alcohol consumption in 15-year-old girls (Karoly et al., 1998). This article presents an overview of the Nurse–Family Partnership (NFP) Pilot Study in Orange County, California, and reviews early results of the pilot study. NFP is based on the Olds Home Visitation Model and is designed to improve adolescent pregnancy outcomes and early childhood health and development. NFP is a comprehensive program in which specially trained public health nurses visit women and families in their homes and link them with services they need during pregnancy and the first 2 years of their child's life.

Significance of the Problem

Despite the recent decline in the teen birth rate, adolescent pregnancy remains a significant problem in the United States. The U.S. teen birth rate is nearly double Great Britain's, at least four times that of France and Germany, and more than 10 times that of Japan (Singh & Darroch, 2000). Most teen pregnancies are unintended. Statistics show that four in 10 American teenage girls become pregnant at least once before they reach age 20, leading to almost 1 million pregnancies a year (National Campaign to Prevent Teen Pregnancy, 1997). Their babies are often low birthweight and have disproportionately high mortality rates. Approximately 80% of adolescent mothers who drop out of high school are likely to be poor. In contrast, just 8% of children born to married high school graduates aged 20 or older live in poverty (Maynard, 1997). Even though teen pregnancy is a problem affecting all populations, there are some subgroups that are more profoundly affected than others. Nationally, Hispanic adolescents now have the highest teen birth rates and are more likely to drop out of school and become pregnant than their non-Hispanic white and African-American counterparts (Manlove, 1998).

Repeat births account for 22% of adolescent pregnancies. The percentage of repeat births of all teen births within specific racial groups was 20% for whites, 28% for blacks, 22% for American Indians, and 21% for Asians. Of births to Hispanic adolescents of all races, 25% were repeat births (USDHHS, 2000). Teen multiparas have short pregnancy intervals, which could affect maternal and infant health. A study of 3,400 first-time teenage mothers who received public assistance in Chicago showed that 64% had at least one pregnancy during the follow-up period of approximately 29 months, and 21% had two or more pregnancies (Maynard & Rangarajan, 1994). Of the adolescent mothers who became pregnant again, 35% did so within one year of the birth of their first child, and 75% became pregnant again within 2 years. Three-quarters of the repeat pregnancies resulted in a live birth. In a study of almost 10,000 adolescents who had repeat live births between 1980 and 1988, 36% had pregnancy

intervals shorter than 7 months, and 26% were pregnant again between 7 and 12 months after the first birth (Hellerstedt & Perie, 1994). Adolescent mothers with the lowest education, skills, and economic circumstances are likely to have more repeat pregnancies during their adolescent years. Furthermore, studies have shown that adolescent mothers do not use an effective contraceptive method, which puts them at risk for rapid repeat pregnancies (Maynard & Rangarajan, 1994).

Consequences of Early Childbearing for Mothers

Adolescent mothers experience more pregnancy and delivery problems and have less healthy babies than adult mothers. These risks are associated with poverty and the environmental and social circumstances of young mothers. Adolescents experience a maternal death rate 2.5 times greater than that of mothers aged 20 to 24 years (Brown & Eisenberg, 1995). They may be disproportionately exposed to violence and have high rates of physical and sexual abuse histories (Bayatpour, Wells, & Holford, 1992). They are also at a higher risk for sexually transmitted diseases (STDs). At least 60% of all cases of STDs in the United States are in individuals who are 25 years old or younger. Furthermore, they are at a higher risk for substance abuse, stress, and depression (USDHHS, 2000). Common prenatal and obstetrical problems in adolescent mothers include inadequate prenatal care, poor weight gain and nutrition, hypertension, and anemia. Alternatively, excessive prenatal weight gain predisposes young mothers to adult obesity. Lactation may also adversely affect bone density in still-growing adolescents (National Campaign to Prevent Teen Pregnancy, 1997).

Consequences of Adolescent Childbearing for the Child

Children born to adolescent mothers have greater health and medical risks than children of adult mothers. They suffer from higher rates of low birthweight, intrauterine growth retardation, and preterm birth (Ventura, Martin, Curtin, & Mathews, 2001). Low birthweight increases the risk of infant mortality, blindness, deafness, chronic respiratory problems, mental retardation, mental illness, and cerebral palsy. Children of adolescent mothers receive less well-baby and preventive care and more medical treatment than children of adult mothers (Maynard, 1997). Furthermore, they are at risk of poor parenting skills, are often victims of abuse and neglect, and may suffer from poor school performance (National Campaign to Prevent Teen Pregnancy, 1997).

Target Population

As previously mentioned, adolescent pregnancy rates have decreased in the United States, but there are some racial/ethnic populations in which adolescent pregnancy rates remain the same and have not decreased when compared with other racial/ethnic groups. In the United States, three out of five Hispanic adolescent girls become pregnant at least once as a teen. Currently, California has more than 33 million residents, and the Hispanic population is the fastest-growing racial/ethnic group. Hispanic adolescents have the highest birth rates in California (Manlove, 1998). In Orange County, Hispanic teens (15 to 19 years old) have the highest birth rate compared with other racial/ethnic groups. In 1999, the Orange County Hispanic teen birth rate was 105.9 per 1,000 live births, followed by African American (36.6), American Indian (28.0), white (14.3), and Asian/Pacific Islander (11.3). The overall county birth rate for 15- to 19-year-olds in 1999 was 44.40 per 1,000 live births (Orange County Health Care Agency, 2001).

Setting

The setting is predominantly urban Orange County, California. The 2000 U.S. Census report showed the population to be more than 2.8 million, 24.4% of the population is aged 18 and under, and 30% is of Hispanic or Latino origin (U.S. Census Bureau, 2001). The Hispanic population is considered to be the largest racial/ethnic population in Orange County. In Santa Ana city, for example, Hispanics account for 71% of the overall population, compared with 17.1% non-Hispanic whites (Center for Demographic Research, 2000). In the next 20 years, the Hispanic adolescent population will grow much faster than the overall adolescent population in the United States. The projected 13- to 19-year-old Hispanic adolescent population growth in the United States for 2000–2020 is 60%, compared with 8% growth for all adolescents (Day, 1996).

Theoretical Framework

To affect the target population and to achieve program goals and objectives, the program must have a well-developed theoretical base to provide the foundation and context for program design, implementation, and evaluation. The theoretical framework for this program is based on the self-efficacy theory introduced by Albert Bandura (1977). The theory is grounded in his early work on social cognitive theory. The self-efficacy theory provides a useful framework for improving and promoting the adolescent's health behavior during pregnancy and childcare and her own personal growth and development.

Self-efficacy is defined as the individual's judgments of his or her capabilities to organize and execute courses of action required to successfully attain designated types of performances or behavior. Self-efficacy is the most influential authority in human nature and plays a powerful role in determining the choices people make, the effort they expend, how long they persist when confronted with obstacles, and the degree of anxiety or confidence they will bring to the task at hand. Self-efficacy helps explain why people's behavior differs widely even when they have similar knowledge and skills. What people do and how they behave is better predicted by their beliefs. Bandura (1977) identifies and distinguishes efficacy expectation from outcome expectations. A belief in one's own competence to execute a task is required to produce a desired outcome expectation. Self-efficacy expectations are derived from several sources of information: previous performance accomplishments, modeling, verbal persuasion, and emotional arousal (Bandura, 1977).

Successful accomplishment increases expectations of mastery, and repeated failures decrease it. Teenagers may recognize the outcome expectation that a subsequent pregnancy during the 12 months postpartum is damaging to their health. Modeling by a variety of personally significant individuals in adverse situations will encourage behavior changes.

The success of this program will depend on the public health nurses' reinforcement of the adolescents' behaviors that are consistent with the program's goal. Public health nurses hope to build the self-confidence of the adolescents and reinforce the positive behaviors and accomplishments. Verbal persuasion is employed to educate the adolescents about healthy practices, available health care services, and support resources. Public health nurses also serve as role models for adolescent mothers and provide reinforcement of previous accomplishments to increase the mothers' self-efficacy.

Design and Methods

Providers that serve pregnant adolescents in the community refer pregnant adolescents to the NFP. Providers include physicians, community clinics, schools, social services agencies, probation departments, pregnancy testing clinics, juvenile health services, and the supplemental food program for women, infants, and children (WIC). Participants for this pilot study were randomly assigned to the control or intervention group by the drawing of colored blocks. To participate in the study, participants needed to be on or eligible for Medi-Cal, at less than 28 weeks gestation, younger than 20 years old, and pregnant with their first child. Participants assigned to the control group received the traditional Public Health Field Nursing (PHFN) services, while the intervention group received services from advanced trained public health nurses (ATPHNs). Informed consent was obtained from all participants.

PHFN nurses are Bachelor of Science in Nursing (BSN)-prepared with maternal and child health experience and receive general field nursing orientation. In addition to general field orientation, ATPHNs receive 1 week of extensive training in Denver and two follow-up trainings; the follow-up trainings include a 3-day training on Partners in Parenting Education and a 2-day training on toddler protocols. The ATPHNs also receive training in home visitation protocols, clinical record keeping, the information management system, and the theoretical framework upon which the NFP is based.

Participants in the control group received a minimum of three PHFN home visits: one for initial assessment of the client and family profile, one antepartum visit (during which the PHN provides physical assessment, education, referral, and encourages compliance with prenatal care), and one postpartum and newborn visit. Participants in the intervention group received weekly ATPHN home visits for the first 4 weeks, followed by visits every other week until delivery, weekly for the next 6 weeks, every other week until the child was 21 months old, and monthly until the child was 24 months old. ATPHNs promote the self-efficacy of adolescents during the structured home visits by encouraging the adolescents to set personal goals. Adaptive behavior changes are encouraged to promote healthy outcomes of pregnancy, develop positive parenting skills, and optimize the developmental potential of the infant. The ATPHNs assist the adolescents in identifying and developing informal support systems of family and friends. In addition, they serve as a link for adolescents to community services for health care and welfare. Home visits usually last from 60 to 90 minutes and focus on personal health, environmental health, maternal role development, maternal life course development, child and family functioning, and knowledge and use of health and human service agencies.

Results

Preliminary results of the study from pregnancy through postpartum are discussed here. A total sample of 225 Hispanic adolescents was enrolled in the study: 121 in the control group and 104 in the intervention group. Initial demographic data for both groups are presented in Table 1. Significantly more control group adolescents than intervention group adolescents (74/121 vs. 45/103) were born outside the United States ($p = 0.007$). All 74 control group adolescents and 43 of the 45 (95.6%) intervention group adolescents born outside the United States were born in Mexico; the remaining two intervention group adolescents born outside the United States were born in Central/South America. Adolescents in both groups were more likely to be single, never married, enrolled in school, and planning to continue education postpartum. Median number of years of education completed was the same for adolescents in both groups: 10 years (range 2–14 years). Only 32 of 225 (14.2%) adolescents in the study were employed part-time or full-time at initial interview. Adolescents in both groups reported being "somewhat likely" or "very likely" to return to or find work within 6 months after giving birth. Sixty-eight percent and 69.3% of adolescents in the study reported receiving Medi-Cal and WIC, respectively. Only 5.3% of participants reported receiving food stamps. When asked to select their total household income from a predefined list, many participants declined or refused to answer. For the 97 control

(80.2%) and 81 intervention (77.9%) group adolescents answering the question, the median total household income range was $12,001 to $15,000.

Table 1
Initial Demographics

Variable	Control group	Intervention group	p value[*]
Place of birth ($n = 224$)			
United States	47	58	0.007
Other	74	45	
Marital status ($n = 225$)			
Single, never married	112	92	NS
Married	9	12	
Education ($n = 225$)			
Enrolled in school	61	63	NS
Not enrolled in school	60	41	
Educational plan ($n = 223$)			
Continue education	103	92	NS
No further education	17	11	
Employment ($n = 225$)			
Full- or part-time work	20	12	NS
Not working	101	92	
Likelihood of returning to or finding work within 6 months postpartum ($n = 224$)			
Not/not very likely	53	40	NS
Somewhat/very likely	68	63	
Receive Medi-Cal ($n = 225$)			
Yes	78	74	NS
No	43	30	
Receive aid from Women, Infants, and Children ($n = 225$)			
Yes	83	73	NS
No	38	31	
Receive food stamps ($n = 225$)			
Yes	8	4	NS
No	113	100	

[*]p values are based on chi-square tests of significance.
NS = not significant.

Of the 225 Hispanic adolescents enrolled in the study, information on infant birth outcome was available for 152 (67.6%): 82 (67.8%) in the control group and 70 (67.3%) in the intervention group. Twenty-seven of the mothers were still pregnant at the time of data analysis. Four mothers (3 in the control group and 1 in the intervention group) gave birth to twins; therefore, birth outcome information was available on 156 infants.

Of the 225 Hispanic adolescents, 49 were lost to follow-up. The most prevalent reasons for dropping out of the study during pregnancy included declined further participation, moved out of state/program area, and excessive missed appointments.

Adolescents in the control and intervention groups gave birth to more girls (55%) than boys. As shown in Table 2, adolescents in both groups had similar mean weight gain during pregnancy (40 pounds) and infant gestational age at birth (39 weeks), but a larger percentage of adolescents in the control group (8.2%) gave

Table 2
Birth Outcome Data

Outcome	n Mean (Range) SD	
	Control group	Intervention group
Maternal weight gain during pregnancy, pounds (*n* = 137)	69 40.35 (0–156) 73.89	68 39.87 (13–275) 35.00
Gestational age, weeks (*n* = 154)	85 38.92 (21–42) 2.70	69 38.88 (27–41) 2.23
Birth weight, grams (*n* = 156)	85 3130.06 (652.05–4422.60) 570.78	71 3294.32 (1077.30–5159.70) 567.56

birth to premature infants (< 37 weeks gestation) than did adolescents in the intervention group (Table 3).
340   Overall, the percentage of premature births in the study was 6.5%, which is a considerably smaller proportion than the 13.7% of California teens giving birth to premature infants (California Maternal and Child Health Branch, 1997).
345   Table 2 also shows that infants born to adolescents in the intervention group had a higher mean birthweight than infants born to adolescents in the control group (3294 g vs. 3130 g). As shown in Table 4, a larger percentage of infants born to mothers in the inter-
350   vention group had a birthweight of 3500 g or greater; two infants in each group weighed more than 4000 g, and one infant in the intervention group weighed more than 5000 g. A larger percentage of infants born to mothers in the control group had low birth weight (<
355   2500 g) (10.6% vs. 5.6%). Overall, the percentage of low birth weight infants in the study was 8.3%, which is higher than the 7.7% of California teens giving birth to infants weighing less than 2500 g (California Maternal and Child Health Branch, 1997).

Table 3
Gestational Age Group by Study Group

Gestational age group	n (%)		
	Control group	Intervention group	Total
< 37 weeks	7 (8.2)	3 (4.3)	10
37 weeks	78 (91.8)	66 (95.7)	144
Total	85	69	154

Table 4
Birthweight Group by Study Group

Birthweight group	n (%)		
	Control group	Intervention group	Total
< 2500 grams	9 (10.6)	4 (5.6)	13
2500–3499 grams	58 (68.2)	41 (57.8)	99
≥ 3500 grams	18 (21.2)	26 (36.6)	44
Total	85	71	156

360   Apgar scores were available for 24 control group infants and 44 experimental group infants. Mean 1-minute and 5-minute Apgar scores were similar for both groups (8.00 and 8.30 and 8.56 and 9.07, respectively); the range of 1-minute and 5-minute Apgar
365   scores was 2 to 10. No birth defects were reported in infants born to adolescents in either group, but birthing complications were reported in 19 (22.4%) control group deliveries and 16 (22.5%) intervention group deliveries. Birth complications identified included ce-
370   sarean section (due to failure to progress; slow heart rate or respiratory distress; or breech, transverse, or face-up position), abruptio placenta, sepsis, cord around the neck, 3+ meconium aspiration, pregnancy-induced hypertension, and maternal fever.

Implications

375   Previously published studies support the notion that home visitation by PHNs improves the health and well-being of adolescents and their infants and families (Olds, Henderson, Kitzman, Eckenrode, Cole, & Tatelbaum, 1999; Kitzman, Olds, Henderson, 1997; Kitz-
380   man, Olds, Sidora, Henderson, Hanks, Cole, Luckey, Bondy, Cole, & Glazner, 2000). Preliminary results from this program indicate that home visitation by PHNs positively affects the health of Hispanic adolescents and their infants. The prevalence of premature
385   birth is lower than in the general California teen population. Furthermore, both groups' results showed significant improved perinatal outcomes (e.g., initial birthweight, gestational age).

Public health nurses in the intervention group en-
390   countered many challenges during their home visits. Maintaining the schedule of home visits is sometimes difficult, especially the time of the visit. Before delivery, the clients are generally quite available; most attend school, and the home visit is planned around the
395   school schedule. Some of the adolescents work, which complicates the home visit dates and times. Many clients forget their scheduled visits. Program attrition of clients during pregnancy and during infancy is a concern and needs to be strengthened. The reasons mothers
400   dropped out during perinatal services were excessive

missed appointments, unable to locate client, and declined to participate. There are many reasons for the high rate of attrition. The main reason was that Orange County has a mobile population. Another reason was
405 that it is difficult to determine and control adolescent behavior.

A significant challenge was that some clients had not yet revealed their pregnancies to family members. Some wanted the PHN to tell the family for them. The
410 program also received more referrals than the available trained staff could accommodate. The PHNs reported it was sometimes difficult to explain to clients during the initial home visit that to participate in the program they would be randomly selected for the intervention or
415 control group and that the same nurse who visited them at the initial intake might not be their follow-up nurse. With this knowledge, many clients declined to participate.

Results from this program are preliminary. Addi-
420 tional study is needed to measure the effect of interventions at 12, 18, and 24 months postpartum. We hope to show statistically significant effects between the two groups at 12 months, 18 months, and 24 months follow-up. Two well-known studies on prenatal and in-
425 fancy home visitation by nurses conducted in Elmira, New York, and Memphis, Tennessee, showed effects at program termination as well as 3 to 4 and 15 years after (Olds, Henderson, Kitzman, Eckenrode, Cole, & Tatelbaum, 1999; Olds, Eckenrode, Henderson, Kitzman,
430 Powers, Cole, Sidora, Morris, Pettitt, & Luckey, 1997; Kitzman et al., 1997, 2000).

In conclusion, preliminary results from this program showed that PHN home visitation (both control and intervention groups) can positively affect the birth
435 outcomes of Hispanic adolescent mothers. Generalizability of these findings is limited to first-time pregnant adolescents in Orange County, California.

References

Bandura, A. (1977). *Social Learning Theory.* Englewood Cliffs, NJ: Prentice Hall.

Bayatpour, M., Wells, R. D., & Holford, S. (1992). Physical and sexual abuse as predictors of substance use and suicide among pregnant teenagers. *Journal of Adolescent Health, 13,* 128–132.

Brown, S., & Eisenberg, L. (Eds.). (1995). *The Best Intentions. Unintended Pregnancy and the Well-Being of Children and Families.* Washington, DC: National Academy Press.

California Maternal and Child Health Branch. (1997). The adolescent's family life program: Reporting of selected outcomes for clients active in AFLP as of November 30, 1997. Available on-line: http://www.dhs.ca.gov/pcfh/mchb/pdfs/AFLP_Report.pdf Accessed April 23, 2001.

Center for Demographic Research. (2000). *Orange County Progress Report.* California State University, Fullerton. Available on-line: http://www.fullerton.edu/cdr/ Accessed April 23, 2001.

Day, J. C. (1996). Population projections of the United States by Age, Sex, Race, and Hispanic Origin, 1995–2050. *Current Population Reports: P25-1130.*

Hellerstedt, W. L., & Perie, P. L. (1994). *The Association of Pregnancy Intervals and Infant Growth Among Infants Born to Adolescents.* American Public Health Association (annual meeting). Washington, DC, October 30–November 3, 1994.

Karoly, L. A., Greenwood, P. W., Everingham, S. S., Hoube, J., Kilburn, M. R., Rydell, C. P., Sanders, M., & Cheisa, J. (1998). *Investing in our children: What we know and don't know about the costs and benefits of early childhood interventions.* Washington, DC: RAND.

Kitzman, H., Olds, D. L., Henderson, C. R. Jr., Hanks, C., Cole, R., Tatebaum, R., McConnochie, K. M., Sidora, K., Luckey, D. W., Shaver, D., Engelhardt,
K., James, D., Barnard, K. (1997). Effect of prenatal and infancy home visitation by nurses on pregnancy outcomes, childhood injuries, and repeated childbearing: a randomized controlled trial. *Journal of the American Medical Association, 278,* 644–652.

Kitzman, H., Olds, D., Sidora, K., Henderson, C., Hanks, C., Cole, R., Luckey, D., Bondy, J., Cole, K., & Glazner, J. (2000). Enduring effects of nurse home visitation on maternal life course. *Journal of the American Medical Association, 283,* 1983–1989.

Manlove, J. (1998). The influence of high school dropout and school disengagement on the risk of school age pregnancy. *Journal of Research on Adolescence, 8,* 187–220.

Maynard, R. (Ed.). (1997). *Kids Having Kids: A Robin Hood Foundation Special Report on the Costs of Adolescent Childbearing.* New York: Robin Hood Foundation.

Maynard, R., & Rangarajan, A. (1994). Contraceptive use and repeat pregnancies among welfare-dependent teenage mothers. *Family Planning Perspectives, 26,* 198–205.

National Campaign to Prevent Teen Pregnancy. (1997). *Whatever happened to childhood? The problem of teen pregnancy in the United States.* Washington, DC: National Campaign to Prevent Teen Pregnancy.

Olds, D. L., Eckenrode, J., Henderson, C. R. Jr., Kitzman, H., Powers, J., Cole, R., Sidora, K., Morris, P., Pettitt, L. M., & Luckey, D. (1997). Long-term effects of home visitation on maternal life course and child abuse and neglect: 15-year follow-up of a randomized trial. *Journal of the American Medical Association, 278,* 637–643.

Olds, D. L., Henderson, C. R. Jr., Kitzman, H., Eckenrode, J., Cole, R., & Tatelbaum, R. (1999). Prenatal and infancy home visitation by nurses: recent findings. *Future of Children, 9,* 44–65.

Orange County Health Care Agency. (2001). Orange County, California, birth outcomes, 1999. Orange County Health Care Agency, Santa Ana, CA.

Singh, S., & Darroch, J. E. (2000). Adolescent pregnancy and childbearing: Levels and trends in developed countries. *Family Planning Perspectives, 32,* 14–23.

U.S. Census Bureau. (2001). *Population by sex, age, Hispanic origin, and race.* Washington, DC: Author. Available online: http://www.census.gov/population/socdemo/hispanic/p20-535/tab01–3.txt Accessed May 23, 2001.

U.S. Department of Health and Human Services. (2000). *Healthy People 2010: Understanding and Improving Health,* 2nd Ed. Washington, DC: U.S. Government Printing Office, Available on-line: http://www.health.gov/healthypeople Accessed May 23, 2001.

U.S. Department of Health and Human Services. (2000). *HHS fact sheet: Preventing teenage pregnancy.* Available on-line: http://www.hhs.gov/topics/teenpreg.html Accessed May 23, 2001.

Ventura, S. J., Martin, J. A., Curtin, S. C., & Mathews. T. J. (2001). Births: Final data for 1997. *National Vital Statistics Reports, 47(18).*

Address correspondence to: Jody Duong Nguyen, County of Orange Health Care Agency, 1725 W. 17th Street, Santa Ana, CA 92706. E-mail: jnguyen@hca.co.orange.ca.us

Exercise for Article 20

Factual Questions

1. According to the literature, which of the following experience more pregnancy and delivery problems and have less healthy babies than the other?
   A. Adolescent mothers
   B. Adult mothers

2. According to Bandura (1977), self-efficacy expectations are derived from what four sources of information?

3. How many participated in the control group, and how many participated in the intervention group?

4. Did the infants born to adolescents in the intervention group *or* the infants born to adolescents in the control group have a higher mean birthweight?

5. Of the 225 Hispanic adolescents, how many were unavailable for follow-up?

6. The researchers state that the generalizability of these findings is limited to what group?

Questions for Discussion

7. In your opinion, how important is the theoretical framework presented in lines 180–229 as a background for understanding this program evaluation?

8. An important characteristic of a report on a program evaluation is a clear explanation of the program components and how they work. In your opinion, are they sufficiently clear in this program evaluation? Consider the entire article when answering this question, especially lines 230–285.

9. In your opinion, was the random assignment to groups an important part of the research methodology in this evaluation? Explain. (See lines 236–238.)

10. Table 1 shows the initial demographics on nine variables. The two groups were significantly different on only one of them. Is it important to know that, to a large extent, the two groups were initially similar? Explain.

11. The researchers report that they asked participants to select their total household income from a predefined list; however, many declined or refused to answer? Does this surprise you? Explain. (See lines 312–314.)

12. The researchers state that the results from this program are preliminary, and additional study is needed. Do you agree? Explain. (See lines 419–424.)

Quality Ratings

Directions: Indicate your level of agreement with each of the following statements by circling a number from 5 for strongly agree (SA) to 1 for strongly disagree (SD). If you believe an item is not applicable to this research article, leave it blank. Be prepared to explain your ratings. When responding to criteria A and B below, keep in mind that brief titles and abstracts are conventional in published research.

A. The title of the article is appropriate.

SA   5   4   3   2   1   SD

B. The abstract provides an effective overview of the research article.

SA   5   4   3   2   1   SD

C. The introduction establishes the importance of the study.

SA   5   4   3   2   1   SD

D. The literature review establishes the context for the study.

SA   5   4   3   2   1   SD

E. The research purpose, question, or hypothesis is clearly stated.

SA   5   4   3   2   1   SD

F. The method of sampling is sound.

SA   5   4   3   2   1   SD

G. Relevant demographics (for example, age, gender, and ethnicity) are described.

SA   5   4   3   2   1   SD

H. Measurement procedures are adequate.

SA   5   4   3   2   1   SD

I. All procedures have been described in sufficient detail to permit a replication of the study.

SA   5   4   3   2   1   SD

J. The participants have been adequately protected from potential harm.

SA   5   4   3   2   1   SD

K. The results are clearly described.

SA   5   4   3   2   1   SD

L. The discussion/conclusion is appropriate.

SA   5   4   3   2   1   SD

M. Despite any flaws, the report is worthy of publication.

SA   5   4   3   2   1   SD

Article 21

Psychoeducation Program for Chinese Family Caregivers of Members with Schizophrenia

Lai-Yu Cheng, MN, RN, **Sally Chan**, RN, PhD[*]

ABSTRACT. The purpose of this study was to evaluate the effectiveness of a psychoeducation program for Chinese family caregivers of members with schizophrenia in Hong Kong. The participants consisted of 64 caregivers of clients with schizophrenia who were recruited from a local mental hospital and randomly assigned to the experimental and control arm (32 each). The experimental group received a psychoeducation program developed and implemented by mental health nurses based on Atkinson and Coia's framework. The control group received routine care. The outcome measures were family burden, self-efficacy, and perception of social support. The findings showed that the experimental group had more improvement on their perception of burden of care ($t = 5.25$, $p < .01$), self-efficacy ($t = -7.16$, $p < .01$), and social support ($t = -5.61$, $p < .01$). This study supports psychoeducation as an effective nursing intervention for Chinese family caregivers.

From *Western Journal of Nursing Research*, 2005, *27*, 583–599. Copyright © 2005 by Sage Publications, Inc. Reprinted with permission.

Schizophrenia is marked by significant disruptions in thought processes, behavior, and affect. In addition to positive and negative symptoms, many clients experience depression, suicidal thoughts, self-care defi-
5 cits, and social impairment (Gelder, Gath, Mayou, & Cowen, 1996). In Hong Kong, clients with a diagnosis of schizophrenia constitute 80% of the client population who are served by community mental health services (Chan, Mackenzie, Ng, & Leung, 2000). A large
10 proportion of clients with schizophrenia live with their family members after discharge from the hospitals. A review of the literature suggests, however, that there is inadequate help and support to the family caregivers of clients with serious mental illnesses. Many clients have
15 a long duration of illness, lack insight into their illness, and have frequent readmissions and relapse. Improving care outcomes for clients with schizophrenia is therefore a challenge to the mental health services in Hong Kong (Chan & Iu, 2004). Strategies have been imple-
20 mented to improve current care. Psychoeducation is considered a way to help family caregivers taking care

of mentally ill relatives in the community. This article reports a study on the evaluation of a psychoeducation program for family caregivers of members with schizo-
25 phrenia.

Psychoeducation As an Intervention for Family Caregivers

We have learned from history that in ancient China, clients with mental health problems were treated in a humanistic way. In traditional Chinese medicine, mental health problems are seen as related to the dysfunc-
30 tion of organs such as the heart, lung, liver, spleen, and kidney (Chung & Chau, 1997). Since the 18th century, however, the practice of medicine in Hong Kong has been progressively influenced by the Western medical model. Mental disorders are associated with stigma and
35 superstitions. Families often feel ashamed and hide the family member with a mental problem at home until such time as care becomes an impossible burden, resulting in treatment being seriously delayed (Chan & Cheng, 2001). Many clients have already suffered from
40 signs and symptoms for a long time before they have a chance to approach mental health services. This has a negative impact on their recovery.

In 1980, Hong Kong started the deinstitutionalization movement in the care of the mentally ill. As the
45 Chinese family structure is still relatively intact, with family members quite willing to look after their sick relatives, the majority of the clients with schizophrenia live with their family members after being discharged from the hospitals. Family members thus become the
50 most important caregivers (Chan & Iu, 2004). Marsh (1992) concurred that families now often serve as an extension of the mental health system. Meleis, Sawyer, Im, Hilfinger Messias, and Schumacher (2000) pointed out that various factors might influence the outcome of
55 the transition from hospital to home, such as the caregivers' preparation and knowledge and the availability of community resources. If caregivers do not have adequate knowledge and support, they might not be able to take up the responsibilities of taking care of the ill per-
60 sons, thus leading to relapse or readmission. Research has consistently indicated that the burden on family

---

[*]*Lai-Yu Cheng*, Kwai Chung Hospital. *Sally Chan* is professor, the Nethersole School of Nursing, The Chinese University of Hong Kong.

members caring for mentally ill clients is considerable and that the caregivers' well-being and mental health may become seriously impaired (Cuijpers & Stam, 2000). For example, a study by Chakrabarti and Kulhara (1999) in India found that more than 90% of families across different mentally ill client groups experienced moderate to severe burden. Mean scores of burden were the greatest among families of clients with schizophrenia.

Caring for a relative with mental illness could be burdensome in many ways. For example, family members may not be able to manage clients' problems, such as abusive behavior, poor personal hygiene, mood swings, or conflicts with neighbors. Anderson, Reiss, and Hogarty (1996) reported guilty feelings experienced by family members that were related to a lack of knowledge about the possible causes of this illness. Family members thought that they were the cause of the client's illness. Many family members also experienced a sense of sadness related to the loss of hope for the clients.

The Chinese family is dominated by Confucianist principles, with a strong emphasis on specific roles and proper relationships among family members, thus maintaining equilibrium. Occurrence of mental illness of a family member results in psychological and emotional disturbances of the whole family (Chien & Chan, 2004). A study in Hong Kong on the experiences of family caregivers of clients with schizophrenia found that caregivers expressed a need for information about their relatives' illness, the medication, services available, and the management of the problems associated with the illness. There was a serious gap, however, between the expectation and services provided (Ip & Mackenzie, 1998). Biegel, Song, and Milligan (1995) also reported similar complaints among family members in Cleveland, Ohio. Family members expected information, support, and guidance from the health care professionals but often these expectations were not met.

During the past decades, many psychosocial interventions for supporting family caregivers of mentally ill clients have been developed. A psychoeducation program is one of these psychosocial interventions. It is defined as a strategy of teaching patients and families about disorders, treatments, coping techniques, and resources. It was developed based on the observation that people can be better participants in their own care if knowledge deficits are removed (Mericle, 1999). By teaching skills such as problem solving and communication, caregivers' coping abilities would increase (Pekkala & Merinder, 2002). Solomon (1996) maintains that a psychoeducation program is directed at reducing clients' relapse rate and at supporting families.

Some effectiveness studies of a psychoeducation program had shown positive outcomes. For example, Pekkala and Merinder's (2002) systematic review on the effect of a psychoeducation program on clients with schizophrenia and their caregivers found a significant reduction of relapse or readmission rates when compared with standard care. The effect of a psychoeducation program on reducing stress and burden of family caregivers is less conclusive. Some studies demonstrated positive impacts of a psychoeducation program on families. For example, Abramowitz and Coursey (1989) reported that a psychoeducation program for caregivers was effective in increasing knowledge and reducing distress for families caring for relatives with schizophrenia. Mannion, Mueser, and Solomon (1994) reported improvement in coping strategies, personal distress, and negative attitudes toward the ill person in spouses of persons with serious mental illness after the psychoeducation program. Barbato and D'Avanzo (2000), however, reviewed 25 clinical trials on evaluating the effect of family intervention for caregivers of clients with schizophrenia and concluded that insufficient evidence exists on the positive effect of these interventions on family mental and social functioning.

There are various reasons for this inconclusive evidence. Berkowitz, Eberlein-Fries, Kuipers, and Leff (1984) maintained that caregivers of clients with schizophrenia had a tendency to retain their own individual beliefs about the etiology of mental illness. Education on its own might have a very limited impact on the relatives' belief systems. Barrowclough et al. (1987) pointed out that it was unlikely for relatives, particularly those of clients with a long history of illness, to change their views of the clients after a brief education component. Many studies of the psychoeducation program in clients with schizophrenia and caregivers reported a high attrition rate that would have a negative impact on the effectiveness of the psychoeducation program (Mannion et al., 1994). Cuijpers and Stam (2000) commented that the contents of the psychoeducation program varied greatly from one program to another. The success of the psychoeducation program depends very much on the focus of the program.

Nurses play an important role in the psychoeducation program. Because nurses have frequent contact with the caregivers, they should be able to have an indepth understanding of their needs. The increasing involvement of mental health nurses with the psychoeducation program has been demonstrated through literature (Maynard, 1993). The development of the psychoeducation program for family caregivers of clients with schizophrenia was still at its infancy stage in Hong Kong. There were some educational talks for families held in mental hospitals of which the majority was organized by nurses. These programs, however, were not standardized, and outcome evaluation had not been conducted. The available literature on the psychoeducation program mainly comes from Western countries. It is unsure about the impact of the psychoeducation program on Chinese families and whether family caregivers in Hong Kong would accept the psychoeducation program.

Purpose

180 The purpose of this study was to evaluate the effectiveness of the psychoeducation program on family caregivers of clients with schizophrenia. The objective was to estimate the impact of the psychoeducation program on the burden of care, self-efficacy, and satisfaction with social support for family caregivers.

185 This was the first study in Hong Kong investigating the effectiveness of the psychoeducation program. The findings of this study could give direction for the future development of the psychoeducation program in Chinese societies.

Design

190 This was a randomized controlled study that was conducted in one of the major community mental hospitals in Hong Kong.

Sample

Family members of clients who had been diagnosed with schizophrenia by the attending psychiatrist ac-
195 cording to the criteria of the *Diagnostic and Statistical Manual of Mental Disorders* (4th ed.; American Psychiatric Association, 1994) were approached by the researchers in the admission units. Caregivers who met the criteria were recruited. One family member was
200 invited from each family as a participant in this study with priority given to spouses, parents, siblings, and other relatives. Sixty-four family members who fulfilled the following inclusion criteria and agreed to participate in this study were recruited. The inclusion
205 criteria for the participants were clients' main caregivers who cared for an adult client (age 18 or older) at least 4 hr per day, lived with a client with schizophrenia who was diagnosed within 1 year and with no more than two periods of previous hospitalization, were aged
210 18 or older, were able to understand and read Cantonese, and had not received any psychoeducation or group therapy from other health care agencies prior to the study. The exclusion criteria were caregivers who were currently providing care to another family mem-
215 ber with a chronic physical or mental illness and if the clients with schizophrenia had a history of other mental disorders.

Caregivers who agreed to participate were matched for gender and age (within 10 years of age). They were
220 randomly assigned to experimental and control groups by the researcher by drawing lots. The meta-analytic review by Cuijpers (1999) of 16 similar group intervention studies measuring the family burdens and change of social support reported large effect sizes in
225 the difference of the mean scores of relatives' burden between groups with a group size of 28 in each study group. This group size could detect an effect size of 0.70 between the experimental and control group at a 5% level of significance and a power of .80 (Cohen,

230 1992). Taking account of potential attrition at a rate of 13.8% (Monking, 1994), 64 participants per group (32 patients and 32 family caregivers per group) were recruited. Recruitment took place during a 3-month period.

235 The demographic data of the participants are shown in Table 1. Each arm had 12 (37.5%) male participants and 20 (62.5%) female participants. The majority were members of a middle-class family with a monthly income of HK$10,000 to HK$30,000 (US$1,250 to
240 US$3,750). Quite a large portion of caregivers were older: 54.7% (*n* = 35) were aged 46 to 65 and 5 participants (7.8%) were 66 or older. Parents were the main caregivers (*n* = 29, 45.31%) in this study. There was no significant difference between the groups in the
245 demographic characteristics.

Table 1
Sociodemographic Data of Participants (N = 64)

	f	%
Age		
18 to 25	1	1.6
26 to 35	10	15.6
36 to 45	13	20.3
46 to 55	25	39.1
56 to 65	10	15.6
66 or above	5	7.8
Educational Level		
Primary	31	48.4
Secondary	28	43.8
Tertiary or above	5	7.8
Relationship with client		
Spouse	14	21.9
Parent	29	45.3
Grandparent	10	15.6
Sibling	3	4.7
Friend	2	3.1
Child	6	9.4

Method

The research team developed the content of the psychoeducation program based on the framework of Atkinson and Coia (1995). It focused on knowledge and treatment of the illness, management of symptoms
250 and medication, dealing with crisis, mental health services, communication and problem-solving skills, and stress-coping skills. This framework supports that if caregivers have more knowledge of the illness and management, it will improve their confidence and their
255 perception of being supported in taking care of the clients and reducing their perception of the burden of care. In this study, the learning material was prepared by the research team to suit the local context. The psychoeducation program consisted of 10 weekly 2-hr
260 sessions. One mental health nurse conducted all the sessions to maintain consistency. Table 2 is a brief outline of each session.

The psychoeducation program was provided for the experimental group, standard levels of knowledge pro-
265 vision—that is, routine care (medical and nursing care, information giving about the mental and physical condi-

Table 2
Brief Outline of the Psychoeducation Program Content

Session 1: What does schizophrenia mean to you?
    Reminding relatives of the purpose of the group
    Letting them express their feelings and outline their problems
    Stressing confidential nature of the group
Session 2: What is schizophrenia?
    Helping relatives understand the nature, complexity, and variability of symptoms
    Exploring the need for diagnosis, its procedure, complexity, fallibility, and relationship to treatment
    Signs and symptoms, diagnosis, and positive and negative symptoms
Session 3: Why?
    Causes such as genetic, neurological, environmental, psychological, and biochemical
Session 4: Treatment of schizophrenia?
    The pros and cons of long-term medication, psychotherapy, social therapy, behavior therapy, and occupational therapy
    Rehabilitation and prognosis
Session 5: Relatives' problem
    Main points to be covered are anxiety, particularly about the future; family friction; blame and guilt; embarrassment; burden; health; and
      privacy
    Expressing that the role of caregiver is very difficult
    Teaching about problem solving and goal setting
    Mentioning the distinction between objective and subjective burden and that the latter does not depend on the former
Session 6: The family and schizophrenia
    High expressed emotion (e.g., overprotectiveness, overinvolvement, and criticism)
    Encouraging them to increase autonomy, emphasis on the positive aspects of family relationships
    Concept of stress
    Ways to reduce stress
Session 7: Creating a low-stress environment
    Main points to be covered: communication, involving the patient, privacy. Is it really a problem? Whose problem is it?
    Avoiding any sense of blaming relatives for the way they react
    Concentrating on the relatives' responses to patient's behavior
    Managing negative feelings
Session 8: Managing disturbed behavior
    Responding to delusion and hallucination
    Managing suicidal attempts
    Handling aggression and violence
    Managing withdrawal, apathy and isolation, depression
    Setting limits
    Implementing positive, practical guidelines to help relatives cope
    Managing own distress
Session 9: Using services and dealing with crisis
    Helping relatives understand the system and to make better use of services
    Comprehensive overview of services available
    List of telephone numbers
    Crisis Intervention
    Role and responsibilities of the main professionals involved, such as psychiatrist, medical social worker, community psychiatric nurse, and general practitioner
Session 10: Where do we go from here?
    Being positive about the future
    Summing up session
    Revising any points that are unclear

tions of the patient, treatment plan and effects of medications, individual counseling by nurses and social workers, and referrals to financial aid and social
270 welfare services)—was given to both experimental and control groups. There was no time limit for participants in both groups in getting information and counseling.

The researcher explained the purpose and procedure
275 of the study to the participants. All of them signed the written consent after a full explanation of the study and their rights. Demographic data of the participants were obtained. A research nurse conducted preassessment for both groups before the implementation of the
280 psychoeducation program; it was implemented after the clients were discharged. The schedule was given to the participants of the experimental group. The pro-

gram was conducted in groups with a maximum number of eight. To facilitate the attendance, four repeated
285 sessions were conducted per week (two on Saturday and two on Sunday). Participants had the freedom to choose which session they would like to attend. An experienced registered mental health nurse who worked in the acute care setting was responsible for conducting
290 the session. Postassessment was conducted immediately after the psychoeducation program by the research nurse. Three outcome measures were used: family burden, self-efficacy, and social support. These measures were chosen based on the assumption that the
295 psychoeducation program would increase caregivers' coping ability with their situations and that they would feel more confident and more supported, thus reducing their perception of burden.

Family Burden Interview Schedule (FBIS)

300
305
310

The Chinese version of the FBIS (Pai & Kapur, 1981) was used to assess the burden of care placed on families in caring for a mentally ill member. It comprised 24 self-rated items on a 3-point Likert-type scale, which assessed six domains of carer's burden: effects on family finance, routine, leisure, interaction, physical health, and mental health. Higher scores indicate greater burden of care. It has been used in studies in Hong Kong with similar populations with good reliability and validity reported (Chien & Chan, 2004). The correlation between professional raters and caregivers was 0.72 and interrater reliabilities of items were between 0.87 to 0.90 (Pai & Kapur, 1981).

General Perceived Self-Efficacy Scale (SES)

315
320
325

The SES was developed by Zhang and Schwarzer (1995) to measure one's competence in dealing with challenging and stressful encounters in various life situations. It consisted of 10 self-rated items on a 4-point Likert-type scale. The higher the total scores, the more competent the individual is in coping with a wide range of demanding situations of client care. The SES was translated into Chinese and had been used in studies related to family functioning in similar population groups to this study. It was reported to have good reliability and content validity. The Cronbach's alpha coefficients of the items were between .85 and .91 among Hong Kong Chinese (Zhang & Schwarzer, 1995; Chien & Chan, 2004).

Six-Item Social Support Questionnaire (SSQ-6)

330
335

The participants' perception of their level of social support was assessed by SSQ-6 (Chang, 1999), which measures the number of supporting persons that each family carer had and satisfaction with the support provided. The SSQ-6 has correlated highly with the original SSQ-27 with Cronbach's alpha coefficients ranging from .90 to .93 (Sarason, Sarason, Shearin, & Pierce, 1987). The items are rated on a 6-point Likert-type scale, with higher total scores indicating more satisfaction. It was translated into Chinese and has been used in Hong Kong in clients with schizophrenia and their families with satisfactory reliability and content validity. The mean Cronbach's alpha coefficient was .9 (Chien & Chan, 2004).

340
345

The control group was also monitored by regular contact to understand the condition of caregivers at that time. They were asked whether they had received any information relating to the content of the psychoeducation program from other health care agencies during the intervention period. The purpose was to rule out interfering factors that would affect the result of the study.

Analysis of Data

350

All data were analyzed by using SPSS for Windows Version 11. Demographic data were summarized by descriptive statistics such as frequencies and percent-

ages. A paired-sample *t* test was used to estimate the effects of the psychoeducation program on the mean scores between pretest and posttests of three outcome measurements in the two study groups.

Findings

355
360
365

Table 3 shows the total pretest and posttest scores of the three outcome measures: FBIS, SES, and SSQ-6 for both arms. Both arms showed improvement after the intervention period. The experimental arm showed more reduction than the control in the total score of FBIS *(t = 5.25, p < .01)*, especially in items related to family routine, family interaction, and physical and mental health of other family members. The experimental arm had more improvement in the perception of self-efficacy as measured by SES *(t = –7.16, p < .01)*, especially in the area of problem solving. The experimental arm also had more improvement than the control arm in their perception of social support *(t = –5.61, p < .01)*. There was no significant difference in results among groups with different gender and age.

Discussion

370
375

Participants in the experimental group showed significantly greater improvement when compared with the control group in their perceived family burden, self-efficacy, and social support. The results shared similarities with previous studies, such as that by Pakenham and Dadds (1987) and Mannion et al. (1994).

380
385
390
395

Participants in the experimental group learned about the causes, symptoms, and treatment of schizophrenia and behavioral management skills of difficult behaviors in the psychoeducation program. This learning experience was useful in improving the skills of caregivers in managing the mental illness. It might account for the improvement in some items of FBIS, such as there is a decrease in Item 3 "disruption of family routine due to client's irrational demands, or illness and care." Ewers, Bradshaw, McGovern, and Ewers (2002) maintained that having more understanding of the nature of schizophrenia, the common symptoms of the illness, and its effects on clients' behavior would likely lead to a change of attitude toward mental illness. The caregivers might have a new way of making sense of the problems and make different cognitive appraisals. Family caregivers would be more likely to recognize clients' behavioral deficits as possibly resulting from negative symptoms rather than attribute the behavior to "laziness." By adopting more positive appraisals of the clients' difficulties, caregivers might experience less frustration and hopelessness, thus reducing their perception of care burden.

400
405

The psychoeducation program gave knowledge to the caregivers. Schofield (1998) maintained that the knowledge could empower the caregivers so that they had more confidence in managing clients' behavior. This study showed that the experimental group showed improvement in their confidence in dealing with unexpected events, unforeseen situations, and problem solv-

Table 3
The Total Pretest and Posttest Scores of the Three Outcome Measurements

	Experimental group (*M*)		Control group (*M*)		*t* value	*p* value
	Pretest	*Posttest*	*Pretest*	*Posttest*		
Family Burden Interview Schedule	18.78	11.06	17.03	16.28	5.25	.000
General Perceived Self-Efficacy Scale	20.81	26.28	25.16	25.13	−7.16	.000
Social Support Questionnaire	23.09	27.38	25.53	25.56	−5.61	.000

ing. The experimental group had higher ratings in 7 out of 10 items in the SES when compared with the control group. Mannion et al. (1994) further supported that knowledge about mental illness helps improve caregivers' capacity to monitor symptoms or to initiate more collaborative interactions with professionals in the client's treatment, thus improving caregivers' self-efficacy.

The experimental group had more improvement than the control group in the SSQ-6. The psychoeducation program contained elements of social support, such as knowledge and skill in reducing stress and crisis intervention, and services available in the community, thus improving participants' perception of their social support. The psychoeducation program in this study was a group intervention. The participants of this study had never attended any group session of similar nature. During the sessions, the participants had a chance to interact and discuss. The interactions among family members during the sessions might have served to increase the sense of social support as demonstrated in this study. The family caregivers would know that they were not alone and find that many family caregivers shared similar problems. Solomon (1996) concurred that apart from gaining knowledge, group psychoeducation program interventions could significantly increase social support for families.

There were no dropouts in this study, which was in contrast to many previous studies that reported high dropout rates. Ensuring that caregivers attended the psychoeducation program sessions was a challenge. For example, all caregivers were reminded to attend the sessions 1 day before each session; four repeated sessions were available for caregivers, and the program was conducted on Saturdays and Sundays. As a result, all participants attended all sessions. This may be one of the factors contributing to the positive outcomes of the study.

The framework of the psychoeducation program in this study was adopted from Atkinson and Coia's (1995) framework, which provided an appropriate guide to the content. The burden of care and stress experienced by family caregivers may be similar to some extent in different cultures, and they may share similar needs and concerns. The researchers developed the content according to the local situation, for example,

information related to health care services, legal aspects, and so forth. Each topic was also specifically related to local culture. For example, when discussing the etiology of mental illness, family members often showed a lack of knowledge of the biological attribution of schizophrenia and were more concerned about stigma toward mental illness. Much effort was made to dispute the common beliefs that having a child with mental illness was punishment for the parent's sins and that mental symptoms were related to possession of the body by evil spirits. Though the family felt obliged to take care of the ill relative, the high density living environment among families in Hong Kong tended to induce more family conflicts and disharmony. The participants appreciated the input on ways to manage clients' problem behaviors and maintain harmonious interpersonal relationships. Naylor, Bowles, and Brooten (2000) maintained that it is important for nurses to understand the nature and complexity of problems experienced by the clients and their caregivers as they transition from hospital to home so that appropriate advice and support could be provided. In this study, the importance of taking into account clients' cultural background in preparing for a psychoeducation program was highlighted. Apart from the main culture, nurses should constantly be aware that subcultures may be present in society.

During the study, the researchers had an informal discussion with the participants. The participants stated that the fifth to eighth sessions were considered very useful and practical as they provided the knowledge and skills in dealing with the client's symptoms and disturbing behavior. This indicated that caregivers frequently encountered difficulties in these areas. Caregivers showed great interest in understanding the effects and side effects of the medication. They also asked a lot of questions about the negative symptoms of clients. They were not confident in dealing with the negative symptoms. Many caregivers expressed interest in the legal procedures related to admission and discharge, which was not included in the psychoeducation program.

Past studies indicated that Chinese families usually felt ashamed and were unwilling to admit to their relatives' mental illness. This study showed, however, that caregivers were willing to accept interventions and asked questions during the sessions. Although 99% of the population in Hong Kong is Chinese, Hong Kong is a very Westernized society because of its past history as a British colony. People are now becoming more open and receptive to mental illness. In recent years, the Hong Kong government has put much effort into reducing the stigma attached to mental illness. Thus, the caregivers were very receptive to the psychoeducation program.

There were 40 female caregivers and 24 male caregivers who participated in this study, which indicated that more females than males were caregivers of mentally ill persons at home. As a tradition, females were the primary caregivers of family members in Hong Kong Chinese families. This study showed that parents and grandparents constituted 60.94% of caregivers and that quite a large portion of caregivers (54.7%) were of age 46 to 65; 7.8% were of age 66 or older. One or two decades later when these caregivers die or are incapacitated, there might be no one to take up the caring role. Ways to help the clients, such as involving other family members as caregivers or support accommodation, have to be planned for the clients in the future.

This study shows that mental health nurses are in a good position to conduct a psychoeducation program. Psychoeducation programs are brief and inexpensive; they can be incorporated as a routine intervention for family caregivers. This study only involved mental health nurses in planning and implementing a psychoeducation program; this arrangement might limit the help that could be given to the caregivers on every aspect of care, for example, in financial or social welfare aspects, which showed little improvement in this study. Collaboration with other disciplines in the psychoeducation program is important. As suggested by Fung and Ma (1997), the key to help the family of mentally ill clients was a multidisciplinary approach so that holistic care could be provided.

Though the impact of the psychoeducation program on the family caregivers was mostly positive, there were some items that showed no significant difference between the groups. It could be because of the relatively short period of time between the pretest and posttest (10 weeks). Some areas might not show improvement in such a short period of time, as the caregivers take time to assimilate the knowledge. The problems that the families faced might not be able to be solved in a short period of time. A longer term support and follow-up of families and clients is necessary to ascertain the effect of psychoeducation program.

Although the results of this study are promising, it has some limitations. This study used self-reported measures that might be subject to social desirability and response bias. This study only measured the caregivers' perception of coping as Schumacher, Stewart, Archbold, Dodd, and Dibble (2000) maintained that in family caregiving research, skill is usually conceptualized in terms of coping skills rather than as skills in

providing care to the ill person. This study had not measured the caregivers' actual caring skills and their attitude; we could not assume caregivers' skills and attitude would change as a result of the psychoeducation program. Because the outcome measurements of this study were from the caregivers' perspective, it could be argued that the ultimate aim of the psychoeducation program was to reduce client's relapse and readmission rate. These were not measured in this study.

This study only included those participants who were willing to participate. Thus, this group could have already had higher motivation and were more prepared to change, leading to the positive outcome. This study was conducted in only one mental health setting in Hong Kong, so it is difficult to make any generalizations.

This study was a randomized control trial to evaluate the implementation of a psychoeducation program in Hong Kong, which adds knowledge to the impact of the psychoeducation program and the needs of Chinese family caregivers. It could help mental health professionals to develop an appropriate psychoeducation program for meeting the needs of family caregivers. Findings identified that the psychoeducation program had a positive impact on participants' perception of family burden, self-efficacy, and social support. The empirical evidence provides support for adopting the psychoeducation program as an intervention for family caregivers in Hong Kong. The psychoeducation program could be organized for the clients as well.

References

Aiken, L. H., Clarke, S. P., Cheung, R. B., Sloane, D. M., & Silber, J. H. (2003). Educational levels of hospital nurses and surgical patient mortality. *Journal of the American Medical Association, 290,* 1617–1623.

Abramowitz, I., & Coursey, R. (1989). Impact of an educational support group on family participants who take care of their schizophrenic relatives. *Journal of Consulting and Clinical Psychology, 57,* 232–236.

American Psychiatric Association. (1994). *Diagnostic and statistical manual of mental disorders* (4th ed.). Washington, DC: Author.

Anderson, C. M., Reiss, D. J., & Hogarty, G. E. (1996). *Schizophrenia and the family. A practitioner's guide to psychoeducation and management.* New York: Guilford.

Atkinson, J. M., & Coia, D. A. (1995). *Families coping with schizophrenia. A practitioner's guide to family groups.* New York: John Wiley.

Barbato, A., & D'Avanzo, B. (2000). Family interventions in schizophrenia and related disorders: A critical review of clinical trials. *Acta Psychiatrica Scandinavica, 102,* 81–97.

Barrowclough, C., Tamer, N., Watts, S., Vaughn, C., Bamrah, J. S., & Freedman, H. L. (1987). Assessing the functional value of relatives' knowledge about schizophrenia: A preliminary report. *British Journal of Psychiatry, 151,* 1–9.

Berkowitz, R., Eberlein-Fries, R., Kuipers, L., & Leff, J. (1984). Educating relatives about schizophrenia. *Schizophrenia Bulletin, 10,* 418–429.

Biegel, D. E., Song, L., & Milligan, S. E. (1995). A comparative analysis of family carers' perceived relationships with mental health professionals. *Psychiatric Services, 46,* 477–482.

Chakrabarti, S., & Kulhara, P. (1999). Family burden of caring for people with mental illness. *British Journal of Psychiatry, 174,* 463.

Chan, S., & Cheng, B. S. (2001). Creating positive attitudes: The effects of knowledge and clinical experience of psychiatry in student nurse education. *Nurse Education Today, 21,* 434–443.

Chan, S., & Iu, W. Y. (2004). The quality of life of clients with schizophrenia: Report on a study. *Journal of Advanced Nursing, 45,* 72–83.

Chan, S., Mackenzie, A., Ng, D. T. F., & Leung, J. K. Y. (2000). An evaluation of the implementation of case management in the community psychiatric nursing service. *Journal of Advanced Nursing, 31,* 144–156.

Chang, A. M. (1999). *Psychosocial nursing intervention to promote self-esteem and functional independence following stroke.* Unpublished doctoral dissertation, The Chinese University of Hong Kong.

Chien, W. T., & Chan, S. (2004). One-year follow-up of a mutual family group intervention for Chinese families of patients with schizophrenia. *Psychiatric Services, 55,* 1276–1284.

Chung, S. S., & Chau, C. F. (1997). *Psychiatric nursing (*4th ed.). Taipei, Taiwan: Farseeing.

Cohen, J. (1992). A power primer. *Psychological Bulletin, 112,* 155–159.

Cuijpers, P. (1999). The effects of family interventions on relative's burden: Meta-analysis. *Journal of Mental Health, 8,* 275–285.

Cuijpers, P., & Stam, H. (2000). Burnout among relatives of psychiatric patients attending psychoeducational support groups. *Psychiatric Services, 51,* 375–379.

Ewers, P., Bradshaw, T., McGovern, J., & Ewers, B. (2002). Does training in psychosocial interventions reduce burnout rates in forensic nurses? *Journal of Advanced Nursing, 37,* 470–476.

Fung, C., & Ma, A. (1997). Family management in schizophrenia. *Hong Kong Journal of Mental Health, 26(2),* 53–63.

Gelder, M., Gath, D., Mayou, R., & Cowen, P. (1996). *Oxford textbook of psychiatry* (3rd ed.). Oxford, UK: Oxford University Press.

Ip, G. S. H., & Mackenzie, A. E. (1998). Caring for relatives with serious mental illness at home: The experiences of family carers in Hong Kong. *Archives of Psychiatric Nursing, 12,* 288–294.

Mannion, E., Mueser, K., & Solomon, P. (1994). Designing psychoeducational services for spouses of persons with serious mental illness. *Community Mental Health Journal, 30,* 177–190.

Marsh, D. (1992). *Families and mental illness: New directions in professional practice.* New York: Praeger.

Maynard, C. (1993). Psychoeducational approach to depression in women. *Journal of Psychosocial Nursing, 31(12),* 9–14.

Meleis, A. I., Sawyer, L., Im, E. O., Hilfinger Messias, D. K., & Schumacher, K. (2000). Experiencing transitions: An emerging middle-range theory. *Advances in Nursing Science, 23,* 12–28.

Mericle, B. P. (1999). Developing the therapeutic environment. In N. Keltner, L. H. Swecke, & C. E. Bostrom (Eds.), *Psychiatric nursing* (3rd ed., pp. 320–342). St. Louis, MO: Mosby.

Monking, H. S. (1994). Self-help groups for families of schizophrenic patients: Formation, development and therapeutic impact. *Social Psychiatry & Psychiatric Epidemiology, 29,* 149–154.

Naylor, M., Bowles, K., & Brooten, D. (2000). Patient problems and advanced practice nurse interventions during transitional care. *Public Health Nursing, 17(2),* 94–102.

Pai, S., & Kapur, R. L. (1981). The burden on the family of a psychiatric patient, development of an interview schedule. *British Journal of Psychiatry, 138,* 332–335.

Pakenham, K. I., & Dadds, M. R. (1987). Family care and schizophrenia: The effects of a supportive educational program on relatives' personal and social adjustments. *Australian and New Zealand Journal of Psychiatry, 21,* 580–590.

Pekkala, E., & Merinder, L. (2002). Psychoeducation for schizophrenia (Cochrane review). In *The Cochrane library* (Issue No. 3). Oxford, UK: Update Software.

Sarason, I. G., Sarason, B. R., Shearin, E. M., & Pierce, G. R. (1987). A brief measure of social support: Practical and theoretical implications. *Journal of Social & Personal Relationships, 4,* 497–510.

Schofield, R. (1998). Empowerment education for individuals with serious mental illness. *Journal of Psychosocial Nursing, 36(11),* 35–42.

Schumacher, K. L., Stewart, B. J., Archbold, P. G., Dodd, M. J., & Dibble, S. L. (2000). Family caregiving skills: Development of the concept. *Research in Nursing & Health, 23,* 191–203.

Solomon, P. (1996). Moving from psychoeducation to family education for families of adults with serious mental illness. *Psychiatric Services, 47,* 1364–1370.

Zhang, J. X., & Schwarzer, R. (1995). Measuring optimistic self-beliefs: Chinese adaptation of the General Self-Efficacy Scale. *Psychologia, 38,* 174–181.

Note: Contributions of each author to this research are as follows: L. Y. Cheng and S. Chan were both responsible for research design and data analysis; L.Y. Cheng was responsible for data collection; and S. Chan was responsible for writing up this article.

Exercise for Article 21

Factual Questions

1. In the literature review, how is "psychoeducation program" defined?

2. Before the participants were assigned to the two groups, they were matched on what two variables?

3. For the SSQ-6, the Cronbach's alpha coefficients ranged between what two values?

4. What was the purpose of asking the control group whether they had received any information relating to the content of the program during the intervention period?

5. Were the pretest and posttest means for the control group on the Social Support Questionnaire similar to each other?

6. On the FBIS, did the experimental group have a significantly greater reduction than the control group? If yes, at what probability level?

Questions for Discussion

7. Is it important to know that the participants were assigned at random to the experimental and control groups? Explain. (See lines 219–221.)

8. In your opinion, is the program evaluated in this research described in sufficient detail? (See lines 246–298 and Table 2.)

9. For the FBIS, interrater reliabilities have been reported to be between 0.87 and 0.90. Is this an acceptable level of reliability? Explain. (See lines 309–311.)

10. In your opinion, is the use of self-reports an important limitation of this study? (See lines 548–565.)

11. In your opinion, is the use of only participants who were willing to participate an important limitation of this study? (See lines 566–572.)

12. If you were to conduct a follow-up study on the same topic, what changes, if any, would you make in the research methodology?

Quality Ratings

Directions: Indicate your level of agreement with each of the following statements by circling a number from 5 for strongly agree (SA) to 1 for strongly disagree (SD). If you believe an item is not applicable to this research article, leave it blank. Be prepared to explain your ratings. When responding to criteria A and B below, keep in mind that brief titles and abstracts are conventional in published research.

A. The title of the article is appropriate.

   SA   5   4   3   2   1   SD

B. The abstract provides an effective overview of the research article.

   SA   5   4   3   2   1   SD

C. The introduction establishes the importance of the study.

   SA   5   4   3   2   1   SD

D. The literature review establishes the context for the study.

   SA   5   4   3   2   1   SD

E. The research purpose, question, or hypothesis is clearly stated.

   SA   5   4   3   2   1   SD

F. The method of sampling is sound.

   SA   5   4   3   2   1   SD

G. Relevant demographics (for example, age, gender, and ethnicity) are described.

   SA   5   4   3   2   1   SD

H. Measurement procedures are adequate.

   SA   5   4   3   2   1   SD

I. All procedures have been described in sufficient detail to permit a replication of the study.

   SA   5   4   3   2   1   SD

J. The participants have been adequately protected from potential harm.

   SA   5   4   3   2   1   SD

K. The results are clearly described.

   SA   5   4   3   2   1   SD

L. The discussion/conclusion is appropriate.

   SA   5   4   3   2   1   SD

M. Despite any flaws, the report is worthy of publication.

   SA   5   4   3   2   1   SD

Article 22

Culturally Tailored Diabetes Education Program for Chinese Americans: A Pilot Study

Chen-Yen Wang, PhD, APRN, CDE, **Siu Ming Alain Chan**, RN, MSN[*]

ABSTRACT

Background: The prevalence of type 2 diabetes among Chinese Americans is rising, and cultural and socioeconomic factors prevent this population from achieving optimal diabetes management.

Objective: To assess the feasibility and acceptability of a culturally appropriate diabetes management program tailored to Chinese Americans with type 2 diabetes and the preliminary outcomes of the intervention.

Method: Forty eligible subjects were recruited from the community to participate in this 10-session program developed by integrating Chinese cultural values into an established Western diabetes management program. Feasibility and acceptability of the program were evaluated by the percentage of participants meeting the course objectives and satisfaction with the program. Outcome measurements included the Diabetes Quality-of-Life (DQOL) survey, body weight, blood pressure, and HbA1c levels measured before, after, and 3 months after the intervention.

Results: Thirty-three participants completed all 10 sessions and the outcome measurements. Attrition rate was 17.5%. The majority of the participants understood the course content (75%) and identified and demonstrated various diabetes management skills (70% and 82.5%, respectively). All participants who completed the program were "very satisfied" with the program. With regard to the outcome variables, 43.6% of the participants lost more than 5 pounds and most had a reduction in blood pressure at 3 months after completion of the program. Mean HbA1c decreased from 7.11 to 6.12 postintervention. Significant improvements on the DQOL also were reported.

Discussion: Culturally tailored diabetes management may be effective in Chinese Americans with type 2 diabetes. Further study, with a larger sample size and a control group, is recommended.

From *Nursing Research*, *54*, 347–353. Copyright © 2005 by Lippincott Williams & Wilkins, Inc. Reprinted with permission.

Type 2 diabetes among Chinese Americans is rising. Statistics have shown that diabetes prevalence rates in the Asia-Pacific region already exceed 8% in 12 countries and areas within the region (Cockram, 2000). A study of progression to diabetes in 657 Chinese showed that the crude annual rate of progression to diabetes in participants with impaired fasting glucose was 8.38% per year (Ko, Chan, & Cockram, 2001), whereas the conversion rate in most Western countries was 1.5–13.8% per year. The prevalence of diabetes in Chinese people in Hawaii in 1993 was four times higher than in 1989 (Centers for Disease Control and Prevention, 1993; Shim, 1995).

The literature regarding obstacles to achieving optimal diabetes management in Chinese Americans indicates that traditional American diabetes management strategies remain difficult for Chinese Americans to access, largely due to language barriers, difficulty in lifestyle transitions (Fujimoto, 1996), financial constraints (Cockram, 2000), and incomplete acculturation (Jang, Lee, & Woo, 1998).

Culturally tailored interventions have been successful for diabetes management in African American and Latino adults. In a study of 23 adult African Americans, culturally competent dietary education significantly improved fat intake, HbA1c and fasting blood glucose levels, and frequency of acute care visits (Anderson-Loftin, Barnett, Sullivan, Bunn, & Tavakoli, 2002). In a prospective study (Brown, Garcia, Kouzekanani, & Hanis, 2002) of 256 Mexican Americans, culturally tailored diet, social emphasis, family participation, and cultural health beliefs were incorporated into the intervention. The intervention consisted of 52 contact hours over 12 months provided by bilingual Mexican American nurses, dietitians, and community workers. At 6 months, participants in the experimental group had significantly lower levels of HbA1c and fasting blood glucose levels (1.4% below the control group mean).

The preferred learning style of Chinese American adults is similar to other American adults, who prefer to learn by attaching meaning to their experience (Cranton, 1994) and practice (Wlodkowski, 1985). Group classes (Jiang et al., 1999) are culturally appropriate for educating Chinese adults. Various studies

---

[*]*Chen-Yen Wang* is associate professor, and *Siu Ming Alain Chan* is a graduate student, School of Nursing and Dental Hygiene, University of Hawaii at Manoa, Honolulu.

(Arseneau, Mason, Bennett-Wood, Schwab, & Green, 1994; Gagliardino & Etchegoyen, 2001) using adult Latin Americans with type 2 diabetes have shown that participants in group classes had a significantly greater
50 reduction in HbA1c levels than the control group who received individual consultations.

However, the literature regarding diabetes mellitus management in Chinese Americans in the United States is limited. A study of diabetes knowledge and compli-
55 ance among 52 Chinese with type 2 diabetes (Chan & Molassiotis, 1999) showed no association between diabetes knowledge and compliance with treatment regimen. There was a gap between what the patients were taught and what they were doing. Strategies are
60 needed to close this "knowledge–action gap" in this population. Therefore, the purpose of this pilot study was to assess the feasibility and acceptability of a culturally appropriate diabetes management program tailored to Chinese Americans with type 2 diabetes and to
65 evaluate the preliminary efficacy of the interventions.

Methods

Theoretical Framework

The *empowerment model* guided the development of this study. The empowerment model was used to help a patient explore and develop his or her inherent ability to manage his or her life and disease (Funnell,
70 Nwankwo, Gillard, Anderson, & Tang, 2005). The empowerment model was used in this study to provide culturally tailored diabetes management information to equip patients with the knowledge to make informed decisions regarding lifestyle choices, diabetes control,
75 and consequences. Therefore, patients became responsible to manage diabetes in a way that best fit their lives (Funnell et al., 2005).

Design

A single group pretest and posttest quasiexperimental design was used to meet the objectives of this study.
80 Course content was adapted from the American Diabetes Association's Standards of Medical Care of Diabetes guidelines (American Diabetes Association, 2004).

Setting and Sample

Forty participants were recruited from Chinese American social clubs, religious organizations, clinics,
85 referrals from private physician offices, and newspaper advertisements. The participants had not received any organized diabetes education prior to this program. All of the participants were (a) previously diagnosed with type 2 diabetes and managing the diabetes with diet,
90 oral hypoglycemic agents or insulin, or both, (b) 44–87 years of age, (c) residents of Hawaii, and (d) speakers of Mandarin, Cantonese, or Taiwanese. Exclusion criteria included persons who had self-reported cardiac conditions or cancer.
95 During the 10 weeks of the program, four sessions were offered on different days of the week to accommodate participants' schedules. The investigator and a

registered nurse delivered the group sessions. A maximum of 10 persons was allowed for each session to
100 enhance the interaction between the program leader and the participants. Information presented in each session strictly adhered to a predetermined agenda and was delivered in a standardized manner to minimize variations between different sessions.

Feasibility and Acceptability Measures
105 Feasibility of this program was determined by the ability to recruit and retain participants, the ability to deliver the materials in 10 weeks, and the ability of participants to meet the in-class objectives. Ability to meet in-class objectives was assessed at the end of each
110 lesson by skills demonstration and questions and answers; each participant used the same set of evaluation criteria. An investigator-developed tool utilizing Chinese languages was used to measure acceptability. At the 3-month follow-up interview, participants were
115 asked to respond to three questions that served as single-item measures of their satisfaction with the culturally tailored intervention. Responding on a 5-point scale (1 = Very satisfied to 5 = Very dissatisfied), participants were asked the following questions: "In gen-
120 eral, how satisfied were you with the culturally tailored intervention?" and "How satisfied were you with the integration of Chinese medicine, exercise, and diet into your diabetes management?" Participants were asked to offer a yes or no answer for the following question:
125 "If you had the opportunity, would you recommend this intervention to a friend or relative?" These questions were used previously to assess patients' satisfaction with automated telephone disease management (Piette, 2000). The satisfaction scales had a Cronbach's
130 alpha of .82.

Outcome Measures

The Diabetes Quality of Life (DQOL) survey was administered before and immediately after the intervention program. The DQOL was originally created for the Diabetes Control and Complications Trial, but it
135 was culturally adapted (Cheng, Tsui, Hanley, & Zinman, 1999) for an elderly Chinese population. The Chinese version of DQOL is a 42-item, multiple-choice tool with three primary scales including satisfaction, impact, and diabetes-related worry. Test–retest reliabil-
140 ities of three subscales ranged from .94 to .99 (Cheng et al., 1999). Content validity (Cronbach's alpha = .76–.92) was performed with an expert panel (Cheng et al., 1999). Questions on the DQOL survey are related to diabetes management and how it affects an individual's
145 life. A low score on the DQOL survey is indicative of high quality of life.

Glycosylated hemoglobin levels (HbA1c) were analyzed before and 3 months after the group sessions using the Metrika A1cNow test kits. Due to budget
150 limitations, participants' HbA1c levels were not evaluated at the 10-week course completion time. The Metrika A1cNow test kit was certified by the National

Glycohemoglobin Standardization Program as a viable method in testing a client's HbA1c value (Metrika, 2003; National Glycohemoglobin Standardization Program, 2003).

Body weight was measured before, immediately after, and 3 months after the program using an upright scale in light indoor clothing to the nearest 10th of a pound. In accordance with the American Heart Association recommendations (Pickering et al., 2004), blood pressure was taken twice after sitting in a quiet room for 5 min. If the difference between two readings was larger than 2 mmHg, a third blood pressure reading was taken. Palpable obliterated pressure plus 30 mmHg was used to measure systolic blood pressure and the pressure at first heard muffling sound was used as the diastolic pressure.

Procedures

Human subject approval was received from the Internal Review Board of the university. Written permission of participation was obtained from each participant at the first session. Baseline data (e.g., questionnaires, HbA1c, weight, and blood pressure) were collected at the first session. Participants then participated in 10 educational sessions (once a week). Questionnaires (except demographics) and outcome measures were collected again at the end of program and at 3 months after the program. A certified diabetes educator taught the group sessions in Mandarin, Cantonese, or Taiwanese as required by the participants. Each group session lasted for 60 min and was held at the primary investigator's clinic in Chinatown, Hawaii. The group session agenda is shown in Table 1. A monetary incentive was given to the participants at the third month follow-up visit. Handouts of lecture notes in Chinese were given to all participants. Cultural values in dietary practice, exercise, medication, and diabetes-related self-care behavior were integrated into handouts.

To facilitate effective communications for clients with low literacy skills, the investigators included hands-on activities and presented information using videos and Microsoft PowerPoint slides. Participants with low literacy were encouraged to ask questions as needed during class; however, no additional time was offered to this group, to maintain treatment integrity across all of the participants. In addition, participants were encouraged to involve their family in the learning process outside of the classroom setting. Peer-to-peer assistance was an unexpected phenomenon during the course, as participants enthusiastically helped each other to understand the course content. This type of mutual support was another way to overcome the literacy barriers.

Dietary Education

During the first session, the investigators introduced participants to the food guide pyramid and then explained the nature of carbohydrates and their impact on blood glucose levels. A comprehensive list of carbohydrate and nutrition content of common Chinese foods was provided for the participants; this list was intended to assist them in making appropriate food selection. In addition, a placemat printed with common Chinese food nutritional values written in Chinese, a handy nutrition guide during meal times, was offered to clients. Other Chinese-oriented tools such as rice bowls, soup bowls, and Chinese-style dining utensils were used to illustrate serving sizes. Measuring cups and spoons were given to participants to assist them with food serving measurements. A knowledge empowerment and self-determination approach was used to facilitate participants' dietary changes. Throughout the program, participants engaged in hands-on activities such as packing their own lunch boxes and measuring food serving sizes.

Exercise

The second component of the program was to encourage participants to develop a regular exercise routine. The energy expenditure of various types of exercise, including Taichi and Chi-gong, was discussed with the participants, which empowered them with the knowledge to select types of exercise suitable for individual conditions and interests. Tudor-Locke, Bell, Myers, Harris, Lauzon, and Rodger (2002) demonstrated that the pedometer is a valid tool in quantifying the levels of physical activities for adults with type 2 diabetes. An activity log and pedometer were provided for each participant to record their exercise quantity.

Medication

Medication compliance was the third focus of this program, as many participants expressed concern about medication cost, efficacy, side effects, and compatibility with other Chinese medicines. Medication cost prohibited medication compliance for some participants, as many of them were retired and lived on a limited income. To lessen participants' financial burden, they were assisted in applying to medication assistance programs from various drug manufacturers or provided drug samples if it was deemed appropriate by the program's advanced practice registered nurse. However, no changes were made to participants' medication regimens until 3 months after the classes, in order to minimize variations in data. A detailed discussion on various types of insulin and oral agents was held to assist participants in understanding the purpose, actions, and potential side effects of these medications, and ways to deal with hypoglycemia induced by medications.

Self-care

Chinese values were incorporated into the diabetes self-care education program. The program offered information on how to manage diabetes during sickness; the yin and yang concept was used to illustrate types of food to consume in the event of illness. Because many participants traveled to their native countries fre-

Table 1
Objectives and Content for the Culturally Tailored Diabetes Intervention Program

Objectives	Content
1. Verbalize understanding of this program	a) Introduce the Chinese recipe books, exercise books, and some Chinese pamphlets regarding diabetes
	b) Give handout in Chinese about this program
2. Verbalize understanding of research findings	a) Translate the research findings into Chinese
	b) Application of research findings within Chinese Culture
	c) Ask participants to bring their favorite recipes to the next session
3. Demonstrate healthy food choice	a) Explain Chinese dietary patterns with detailed analysis on the starch food group in terms of rice, noodle, yam, and dumpling
	b) Analyze 5 recipes brought by the participants
4. Demonstrate self-monitoring blood glucose (SMBG) with accurate skills	a) Recognize the uneasiness doing self-monitoring in the Chinese
	b) Describe the relationship between SMBG and changes in serum glucose levels
	c) Ask participants to bring in information about their preferred exercise in the next session
5. Verbalize benefits of exercise	a) Analyze pros and cons of 5 common Chinese exercises
	b) Explain the calorie utilization of each listed exercise and their relationships with blood glucose control
	c) Ask participants to bring in medicine taken in the next session
6. Verbalize understanding of oral agents	a) Analyze pros and cons of the Chinese medicine and the Western medicine used by participants
	b) Ask participants to bring in a list of symptoms and complications they experienced in the next session
7. Develop plans for preventing/treating diabetic complications	a) Compile symptoms and complications brought by the participants on the clipboard
	b) Explain the possible methods of prevention
	c) Help participants to develop individualized plans
8. Develop plans for sick days/traveling	a) Compile the treatment plans used by the participants
	b) Explain the principle of handling sick days and traveling
9. Verbalize plans of foot and skin care	a) Show a video on the foot/skin care and its importance
	b) Ask participants to bring in preferred stress management methods in the next session
10. Demonstrate skills of stress management	a) Group sharing about the benefits of stress management
	b) Summarize the benefits of stress management

quently, information was offered on synchronizing medications or an insulin regimen for a different time zone, managing blood glucose during flight, and converting different measurement units for blood glucose.
265 Participants were also helped to explore methods of stress management; various types of Chinese-specific activities were suggested to the participants, such as meditation, Taichi, and Chi-gong. Foot and skin care activities were demonstrated to the participants.

Data Analysis
270 Descriptive statistics were used to describe and summarize central tendency and variability of demographic variables. Feasibility of this culturally tailored diabetes management program was evaluated by percentages of (a) educational sessions having more than
275 85% of participants attending, (b) participants who attended all 10 educational sessions, and (c) participants who met at least 9 of the 10 class objectives. The acceptability of the culturally tailored diabetes program was determined by program satisfaction. Percentiles
280 were used to measure the variability of satisfaction and participation rate, and mode and median were used to describe central tendency.

The DQOL was measured on an ordinal scale. Difference in total score between pretest and posttest was
285 computed with a student's t test. Differences in means between pretest and posttest for each item were computed with a t test of paired sample statistics with SPSS software. Study outcome measures were determined by the percentage of persons showing a decrease of
290 Hb1Ac levels, degree of weight loss in 3 months (if appropriate), and blood pressure reduction.

Results

The native language of most participants was Cantonese (57.6%) (Table 2). Most participants were married with a living partner (66.7%), retired (75.8%), had
295 less than $1,001 combined monthly household income (81.8%), and had an education level of high school graduate and beyond (57.6%).

Thirty-three out of the 40 recruits completed the 10-session program. The attrition rate was 17.5%. The
300 seven participants who departed cited that traveling plans were the primary reason for their inability to

complete the program. However, it was interesting to note that the seven participants who did not complete the program had all returned for the 3-month post-program evaluation appointments.

Table 2
Frequency Distribution of Demographic Data (n = 33)

Demographic Data	Frequency
Gender	
Male	48.5%
Female	51.5%
Length of time (years) in the United	16.5 (9.3)
States (*n* = 33), *M (SD)*	
1–5 years	5.0%
6–10 years	25.0%
11–20 years	40.0%
21–30 years	22.5%
31–35 years	7.5%
Native language	
Cantonese	57.6%
Mandarin	36.4%
Taiwanese	6.1%
Preferred medical treatment	
Western medicine only	66.7%
Chinese medicine only	9.1%
Western medicine plus Chinese medicine	7.5%
Home remedies and self-treatment	3.0%
Travel to home country for care	3.5%
Duration of DM (years), *M (SD)* [range]	9.03 (8.74) [1–40]
Age (years), *M (SD)* [range]	68.8 (10.1) [44–87]

Note. DM = diabetes management.

Upon the completion of this program, the 33 remaining participants were able to meet 4 to 10 (*M* = 8.22, *SD* = 2.18) course objectives. Most of the group members were able to demonstrate healthy food choices (82.5%), tell the benefits of frequent exercise (90%), identify ways to prevent or treat diabetes complications (82.5%), demonstrate stress management skills (70%), verbalize plans for foot and skin care (90%), and verbalize plans for diabetes self-management on sick days or during travel (70%). On the other hand, only 57.5% of the participants were able to demonstrate accurate self-monitoring of blood glucose levels, and only 55% of the group were able to verbalize understanding of oral hypoglycemic agents. According to the course evaluation, 100% of the participants were "very satisfied" with this culturally tailored diabetes program and would recommend this program to friends and family who have type 2 diabetes. Ninety-two percent of the group were "very satisfied" or "somewhat satisfied" with the Chinese-oriented course content and 8% remained neutral on this item.

Table 3 shows the participants' averages of HbA1c level, systolic blood pressure, diastolic blood pressure, and body weight at the start of the program, immediately after the intervention, and at 3 months after the program. Comparison of participants' weight revealed that 20.5% of the participants were able to lose 5 pounds or more during the course of the program, and

this increased to 43.6% 3 months after the completion of the program. About two-thirds of the participants weighed over 128 pounds at baseline, and 53.6% of them were able to lose 5 pounds or more 3 months after the program. The weight loss was greater among those in the upper-third weight class (weight >148 pounds); 71% of the participants who weighed more than 148 pounds at baseline were able to lose 5 pounds or more in 3 months. In contrast, only 12.6% of the participants reported weight gain during the program, of which only one participant was in the upper-third weight class at baseline. Body mass index (BMI) of the participants ranged 18.4–37.9 with a mean of 26.4 prior to the start of the program. At baseline, 18% of participants had a BMI less than 23 and 37% of participants had BMI more than 27. Forty-two percent of the participants had a reduction in BMI with the program; 24% of the participants achieved a BMI equal to or less than 23 at 3 months postintervention. The mean BMI reduced to 25.8 *(n* = 33; *SD* = 4.16) 3 months after the class. The mean HbA1c level decreased from 7.11 *(SD* = 1.1) to 6.12 *(SD* = 2.4) at 3 months after the completion of the program.

Table 3
Physiological Variables of Participants (n = 33) at Baseline, at the End of Classes, and at 3 Months Following the Intervention

	M (SD)	Range
Weight at baseline (lbs)	139.3 (26.7)	77–210
Weight after classes (lbs)	122.8 (48.9)	80–207
Weight at the third month (lbs)	121.8 (48.6)	80–202
HbA1c at baseline (%)	7.11 (1.1)	5.4–11.0
HbA1c at the third month (%)	6.12 (2.4)	5.4–8.4
Systolic BP at baseline (mmHg)	131.5 (13.6)	100–162
Systolic BP after classes (mmHg)	118.9 (42.1)	100–160
Systolic BP at 3rd month (mmHg)	113.7 (46.2)	100–190
Diastolic BP at baseline (mmHg)	69.4 (10.9)	48–90
Diastolic BP after classes (mmHg)	63.4 (23.4)	50–88
Diastolic BP at 3rd month (mmHg)	63.2 (25.9)	50–92

Note. HbA1c was not assessed at the end of class due to study design.

Discussion

This culturally tailored diabetes program was developed to address obstacles that prevent Chinese Americans from receiving optimal diabetes management. The results from this program confirmed that by approaching diabetes management from a culturally specific perspective, diabetes self-care can be effectively enhanced. It was hypothesized that by integrating Chinese cultural values into the diabetes regimen, there would be an improvement in compliance of Chinese Americans' self-care practices related to diabetes management. Findings of this culturally tailored diabetes management program were congruent with the outcomes of a structured group education mode, called Programa de Educación de Diabeticos No Insulinodependientes en América Latina (PEDNID-LA), used in several Latin American countries (Gagliardino & Etchegoyen, 2001). Similarities between our diabetes management program and PEDNID-LA include: (a)

the interactive group method was used; (b) general concepts about type 2 diabetes and physiological changes were introduced; (c) educational materials were provided in the native language; and (d) photo-
380 graphs of cultural foods were used.

An important feature of this program was the language of instruction. The classes were conducted in Cantonese, Mandarin, or Taiwanese. The use of participants' native languages helped facilitate communi-
385 cation and the learning process. Due to the mixture of participants, some of the classes were conducted with a combination of the above languages. By coincidence, all of the Taiwanese-speaking participants were able to speak and understand Mandarin fluently, so the use of
390 Taiwanese during class instruction was minimal. However, it was interesting to note that many participants were more open to discussions and interactions when the class consisted of only Cantonese speakers or Mandarin speakers. It appeared that a language divide ex-
395 isted among the participants. Some participants attended different group sessions because of a change in working hours. They still communicated openly with participants in the new group when all participants spoke the same dialect. Therefore, if resources permit,
400 it would be optimal to set up classes based on participants' dialectical preference rather than grouping participants on their cultural background alone. Also such criteria may apply to other cultures; for example, it may be feasible to group Filipino clients based on their
405 dialectical preference (e.g., Ilocano, Tagalog, or Visayan).

Appropriate diet selection is one of the keys to successful diabetes management. However, it is also one of the major obstacles for Chinese Americans. As men-
410 tioned previously, most of the diabetes education materials were developed for the Western cultures and the Chinese dietary habits varied greatly from their Western counterparts. Because the Chinese translation for diabetes is "sugar urine disease," many participants
415 took the term literally and thought that they had to avoid only sweet-tasting foods. Many participants reported that their physicians instructed them to consume less rice; subsequently, some participants avoided rice but consumed other carbohydrates (e.g., noodles or
420 buns). Hence, the dietary education component of the program emphasized the concept of carbohydrates.

In this program, participants were empowered by providing information about the nutrition content of common Chinese foods and appropriate serving sizes.
425 The pedometer was a useful tool in encouraging participants to exercise, as evidenced by participants' enthusiasm in comparing the number of steps shown on the pedometer with their peers. This type of mutual comparison created a motivation to exercise. Findings
430 supported previous studies in which understanding the determinants of exercise led to behavioral change (Plotnikoff, Brez, & Hotz, 2000).

Concurrent use of Western medicine and Chinese medicine to treat elevated serum blood glucose levels
435 may affect patients' adherence in Western medicine treatments. The percentage of participants (7.5%) using Chinese medicine was slightly lower than the 9% in the study by Wai, Lan, and Donnan (1995). In 1999, percentages of Chinese Americans living in Houston and
440 Los Angeles who used traditional Chinese clinics, used Western clinics in the United States, and traveled to the origin country for care were 25.3%, 21.3%, and 32%, respectively (Ma, 1999).

Literacy was a limitation of the study. Although in-
445 formative, the handouts provided for the participants were word-intensive, which may have created a problem for those with limited literacy skills. Some of the participants hesitated in revealing their limitations in reading comprehension skills. Various studies have
450 shown that individuals with low health literacy incur as much as four times the healthcare cost over the individuals with adequate literacy skills (AMA-MSS Community Service Committee, 2004). Hence, it was imperative for this group of participants to be able to
455 comprehend the course content.

Another obstacle that can affect health literacy is the use of different writing systems. In general, Mainland Chinese use simplified Chinese characters, whereas clients from Taiwan and Hong Kong use tradi-
460 tional Chinese characters. Because most of the participants originated from Taiwan or Hong Kong, the course handouts comprised traditional Chinese characters. Fortunately, most of the participants from Mainland China were able to comprehend the course
465 materials, as they were an older generation educated prior to the era of simplified Chinese characters. However, as Mainland China becomes the major source of Chinese immigration to the United States, it will be necessary to have simplified Chinese educational mate-
470 rials available.

The timing of the education sessions was another potential limitation to the study. The classes were held during a holiday season, and the seven participants who did not complete the classes left because of their travel
475 plans. Therefore, it would be optimal to hold classes during a period with minimal holidays. In the case of the Chinese population, program coordinators should avoid holding classes during the Chinese New Year, because it is a period of frequent travel and festivities
480 for many Chinese, which may affect the overall attendance rate and blood glucose control.

Language barriers, difficulty in lifestyle transitions (Fujimoto, 1996), financial constraints (Cockram, 2000), and incomplete acculturation (Jang, Lee, &
485 Woo, 1998) were some of the obstacles preventing Chinese Americans from accessing optimal diabetes care. This culturally tailored diabetes education program was developed to address these concerns by integrating Eastern values into Western diabetes manage-
490 ment strategies. Results indicated that most of the par-

ticipants were able to decrease their body weight, blood pressure, and HbA1c values. Course materials were delivered in participants' native languages. Most of the participants were able to gain knowledge about diabe-

495 tes, medications, prevention strategies, and self-care skills. Participants also formed a support network with some of their peers through this program. Results indicated that this culturally tailored diabetes management pilot study could be an effective tool in reducing the

500 health disparities in the Chinese American population.

References

Aiken, L. H., Clarke, S. P., Cheung, R. B., Sloane, D. M., & Silber, J. H. (2003). Educational levels of hospital nurses and surgical patient mortality. *Journal of the American Medical Association, 290,* 1617–1623.

American Diabetes Association. (2004). Standards of medical care of diabetes. *Diabetes Care, 27,* 15S–35S.

AMA-MSS Community Service Committee. (2004). *The abc's of health literacy. A proposal for the AMA-MSS 2004–2006 national service project.* Retrieved August 14, 2005, from http://www.ama-assn.org/ama1/pub/upload/mm/15/health_literacy.doc

Anderson-Loftin, W., Barnett, S., Sullivan, P., Bunn, P. S., & Tavakoli, A. (2002). Culturally competent dietary education for southern rural African Americans with diabetes. *Diabetes Educator, 28,* 245–257.

Arseneau, D. L., Mason, A. C., Bennett-Wood, O., Schwab, E., & Green, D. (1994). A comparison of learning activity packages and classroom instruction for diet management of patients with NIDDM. *Diabetes Educator, 20,* 509–514.

Brown, S. A., Garcia, A. A., Kouzekanani, K., & Hanis, C. L. (2002). Culturally competent diabetes self-management education for Mexican Americans: The Starr County border health initiative. *Diabetes Care, 25,* 259–268.

Centers for Disease Control and Prevention. (1993). *Diabetes surveillance, 1991.* Washington, DC: US Government Printing Office.

Chan, Y. M., & Molassiotis, A. (1999). The relationship between diabetes knowledge and compliance among Chinese with non-insulin dependent diabetes mellitus in Hong Kong. *Journal of Advanced Nursing, 30,* 431–438.

Cheng, A. Y., Tsui, E. Y., Hanley, A. J., & Zinman, B. (1999). Cultural adaptation of the diabetes quality-of-life measure for Chinese patients. *Diabetes Care, 22,* 1216–1217.

Cockram, C. S. (2000). Diabetes mellitus: Perspective from the Asia-Pacific region. *Diabetes Research and Clinical Practice, 50* (Suppl. 2), S3–S7.

Cranton, P. (1994). *Transformative learning: A guide for educators of adults.* San Francisco, CA: Jossey-Bass.

Fujimoto, W. Y. (1996). Overview of non-insulin-dependent diabetes mellitus (NIDDM) in different population groups. *Diabetes Medicine, 13* (9 Suppl. 6), S7–S10.

Funnell, M. M., Nwankwo, R., Gillard, M. L., Anderson, R. M., & Tang, T. S. (2005). Implementing an empowerment-based diabetes self-management education program. *Diabetes Educator, 31,* 53, 55–56, 61.

Gagliardino, J. J., & Etchegoyen, G. (2001). A model educational program for people with type 2 diabetes: A cooperative Latin American implementation study (PEDNID-LA). *Diabetes Care, 24,* 1001–1007.

Jang, M., Lee, E., & Woo, K. (1998). Income, language, and citizenship status: Factors affecting the health care access and utilization of Chinese Americans. *Health & Social Work, 23,* 136–145.

Jiang, Y. D., Chuang, L. M., Wu, H. P., Shiau, S. J., Wang, C. H., Lee, Y. J., Juang, J. H., Lin, B. J., & Tai, T. Y. (1999). Assessment of the function and effect of diabetes education programs in Taiwan. *Diabetes Research and Clinical Practice, 46,* 177–182.

Ko, G. T., Chan, J. C., & Cockram, C. S. (2001). Change of glycaemic status in Chinese subjects with impaired fasting glycaemia. *Diabetic Medicine, 18,* 745–748.

Ma, G. X. (1999). Between two worlds: The use of traditional and Western health services by Chinese immigrants. *Journal of Community Health, 24,* 421–437.

Metrika, Inc. (2003). *Clinical accuracy.* Retrieved July 20, 2003, from http://www.metrika.com/3medical/accuracy.html

National Glycohemoglobin Standardization Program. (2003). *List of NGSP certified methods.* Retrieved July 22, 2003, from http://web.missouri.edu/~diabetesingsp/index.html

Pickering, T. G., Hall, J. E., Appel, L. J., Falkner, B. E., Graves, J., Hill, M. N., Jones, D. W., Kurtz, T., Sheps, S. G., Roccela, E. J. (2004). *Recommendations for blood pressure measurement in humans and experimental animals. Part 1: Blood pressure measurement in humans: A statement for professionals from the Subcommittee of Professional and Public Education of the American Heart Association Council on High Blood Pressure Research.* Re-

trieved February 28, 2005, from http://hyper.ahajournals.org/cgi/content/full/45/1/142

Piette, J. D. (2000). Satisfaction with automated telephone disease management calls and its relationship to their use. *Diabetes Educator, 26,* 1003–1010.

Plotnikoff, R. C., Brez, S., & Hotz, S. B. (2000). Exercise behavior in a community sample with diabetes: Understanding the determinants of exercise behavior change. *Diabetes Educator, 26,* 450–459.

Shim, M. J. (1995). *Self-reported diabetes in Hawaii* (pp. 1988–1993). Manoa, HI: University of Hawaii at Manoa.

Tudor-Locke, C. E., Bell, R. C., Myers, A. M., Harris, S. B., Lauzon, N., & Rodger, N. W. (2002). Pedometer-determined ambulatory activity in individuals with type 2 diabetes. *Diabetes Research and Clinical Practice, 55,* 191–199.

Wai, W. T., Lan, W. S., & Donnan, S. P. (1995). Prevalence and determinants of the use of traditional Chinese medicine in Hong Kong. *Asian Pacific Journal of Public Health, 8,* 167–170.

Wlodkowski, R. J. (1985). *Enhancing adult motivation to learn: A guide to improving instruction and increasing learner achievement.* San Francisco, CA: Jossey-Bass.

Acknowledgments: This project was funded by the University of Washington, Center for Women's Health Research (NR04001). Authors would like to give appreciation to Margaret Heitkemper, PhD, RN, FAAN, Chairperson and Professor of University of Washington, Department of Biobehavioral Nursing and Health Systems, for mentoring and finalizing this manuscript.

Address correspondence to: Chen-Yen Wang, PhD, APRN, CDE, 1702 Kewalo Street, Apt. 1103, Honolulu, HI 96822. E-mail: chenwang@ hawaii.edu.

Exercise for Article 22

Factual Questions

1. In addition to social clubs, religious organizations, clinics, and referrals from physicians, how else were participants recruited?

2. How many questions were asked to determine participants' satisfaction with the intervention?

3. Why were the participants' HbA1c levels not evaluated at the 10-week course completion time?

4. What was the attrition rate?

5. What was the mean age of the participants?

6. Upon completion of the program, what percentage of the participants were able to demonstrate accurate self-monitoring of blood glucose skills?

7. According to the researchers, was timing of the education sessions a potential limitation of the study?

Questions for Discussion

8. The researchers characterize their research as a "pilot study." Do you agree with this characterization? Explain. (See line 61.)

9. Potential participants who had self-reported cardiac conditions or cancer were excluded. Do you think this was appropriate? Explain. (See lines 92–94.)

10. Test–retest reliabilities for the DQOL ranged from .94 to .99. What is your understanding of the meaning of "test–retest reliability"? Are .94 and .99 "high" *or* "low" values? (See lines 139–141.)

11. In your opinion, is the program described in sufficient detail? (See lines 169–269.)

12. Do you agree that "literacy" is a limitation of this study? (See lines 444–455.)

13. If you were to conduct a follow-up evaluation of this program, would you include a control group? Why? Why not?

Quality Ratings

Directions: Indicate your level of agreement with each of the following statements by circling a number from 5 for strongly agree (SA) to 1 for strongly disagree (SD). If you believe an item is not applicable to this research article, leave it blank. Be prepared to explain your ratings. When responding to criteria A and B below, keep in mind that brief titles and abstracts are conventional in published research.

A. The title of the article is appropriate.

SA   5   4   3   2   1   SD

B. The abstract provides an effective overview of the research article.

SA   5   4   3   2   1   SD

C. The introduction establishes the importance of the study.

SA   5   4   3   2   1   SD

D. The literature review establishes the context for the study.

SA   5   4   3   2   1   SD

E. The research purpose, question, or hypothesis is clearly stated.

SA   5   4   3   2   1   SD

F. The method of sampling is sound.

SA   5   4   3   2   1   SD

G. Relevant demographics (for example, age, gender, and ethnicity) are described.

SA   5   4   3   2   1   SD

H. Measurement procedures are adequate.

SA   5   4   3   2   1   SD

I. All procedures have been described in sufficient detail to permit a replication of the study.

SA   5   4   3   2   1   SD

J. The participants have been adequately protected from potential harm.

SA   5   4   3   2   1   SD

K. The results are clearly described.

SA   5   4   3   2   1   SD

L. The discussion/conclusion is appropriate.

SA   5   4   3   2   1   SD

M. Despite any flaws, the report is worthy of publication.

SA   5   4   3   2   1   SD

Article 23

HIV Medication Adherence Programs: The Importance of Social Support

Jean M. Breny Bontempi, PhD, MPH, **Laura Burleson**, MPH, **Melissa Hofilena Lopez**, MPH[*]

ABSTRACT. Since the advent of medical treatments for HIV, the promotion of adherence to these difficult treatment regimens has proven critical to disease management. Three Connecticut state-funded HIV medication adherence programs were evaluated. The purpose of this process evaluation was to explore and compare the goals and modality of each adherence program, assess client and staff satisfaction, and provide recommendations for the improvement of these programs.

Focus group interviews with clients and individual interviews with staff were conducted at each of the programs. Interviews were transcribed, coded, and analyzed with a code-and-retrieve method of theme identification. Focus group themes included the importance of social support on medication adherence and the "lifesaving" effect the program has had. The staff expressed that although complete adherence should be the long-term objective, more intermediate objectives should be considered (e.g., behavioral changes to increase clients' ability, self-esteem, and self-efficacy to take medications).

From *Journal of Community Health Nursing*, 21, 111–122. Copyright © 2004 by Lawrence Erlbaum Associates, Inc. (www.erlbaum.com). Reprinted with permission.

Along with success of prolonging life with new combination therapies for HIV comes the worry of adherence and the maintenance of a high quality of life while these medications are taken (Chesney, Morin, &
5 Sherr, 2000). This aspiration is something that challenges health care professionals, patients, and persons involved with patients who are infected with HIV. Because HIV can now be managed as a long-term and chronic disease due to advances in pharmacotherapy, it
10 is important to evaluate the effectiveness of public health interventions geared toward the control of the disease in infected persons (Chesney, 2003).

HIV therapy is complex. There are different characteristics of the treatment regimen to consider that may
15 affect medication adherence; these include the number of medications, the frequency of dosing, the complexity of the schedule, the duration of the therapy, and side effects (Chesney, 2003; Friedland & Williams, 1999). It is not uncommon for a lifelong treatment regimen to
20 include four to five different drugs at any one time (Frank & Miramontes, 1999). Scheduling complex regimens into daily activities is a problem that persons infected with HIV have discussed in relation to antiretroviral adherence (Golin, Isasi, Breny Bontempi, &
25 Eng, 2002). Because of this, it is understandable that medication adherence programs are constantly reinventing themselves to strive for interventions that will result in 100% adherence among their clients.

The evaluation of adherence programs allows planners to identify areas that need improvement to increase adherence behaviors. The types of evaluation that are used in HIV medication adherence programs are varied. Reports on the progress of the programs include participation rates; biological markers, such as
35 viral load and measurements of healthy white blood cells (or CD4 counts); patient reports; and patient satisfaction measures. Strategies for obtaining evaluation information include pill counts, patient interviews and focus groups, and, in the case of some hospital inter-
40 ventions, chart review and the number of clinic appointments kept (Chesney et al., 2000).

These strategies are in line with impact and outcome program evaluation, which shows the success (or failure) of a program by the examination of intermedi-
45 ate (impact) or long-term (outcome) measures of adherence. Although these evaluation procedures provide important information, why a given program has such outcomes is not clear. A process evaluation can answer the question of why program outcomes were (or were
50 not) realized and is recognized as a critical part of program design and evaluation (Steckler & Linnan, 2002).

This article presents the results of a process evaluation conducted of three state-funded HIV medication adherence programs in Connecticut. The evaluation
55 took place over the course of 1 year, between February 2001 and January 2002. The methods, results, and recommendations for the adherence programs are presented here.

[*] *Jean M. Breny Bontempi*, Department of Public Health, Southern Connecticut State University. *Laura Burleson*, Department of Community Health, Brown University. *Melissa Hofilena Lopez*, Connecticut Department of Public Health.

Table 1
Summary of Determinants of and Challenges to Program Success

Programs	Determinants	Challenges
Atlas	• Conducts individual assessments on all clients. • Located in a medical setting.	• Staff turnover in past year.
Crossroads	• Uses behavior change framework as an approach to increase adherence. • Conducts individual assessments on all clients. • Located in a medical setting.	• Overburdened staff because of a large number of clients.
La Familia	• Conducts individual assessments on all clients. • Covers large geographic area and serves large Hispanic population. • Community-based setting.	• Difficulty accessing medical data. • Overburdened staff because of a large number of clients spread across a large geographic area.

Description of Program Strategies

Three HIV medication adherence programs were
60 evaluated for this article; they are referred to here as
Atlas, Crossroads, and La Familia. To protect anonymity, the real names of programs, staff, and locations were changed. All three programs were located in metropolitan areas of Connecticut, and because they were
65 state funded, they were each required to follow a protocol developed by the Connecticut Department of Public Health (DPH). Although the overall goal identified by each program was identical (i.e., to improve HIV medication adherence), the methods used to
70 achieve this goal were diverse and, hence, too varied to compare across programs. Each program staff developed its intervention methods on the basis of what it thought could best achieve adherence among its own group of clients. The unique aspects of the program
75 methods are described here. Although this evaluation was not for the purpose of measuring the outcomes of these programs, we briefly highlight the diversity across the programs with regard to their stated outcomes, intervention methods, and processes of collect-
80 ing data to measure program success. A summary table of the determinants of and challenges to the programs' success is provided (see Table 1).

Atlas

The Atlas medication adherence program used a home care approach to facilitate medication adherence.
85 Strategies used included an in-depth assessment of each client, the prefilling of pill boxes for clients, and comprehensive education with regard to the HIV disease process and medications. The program visiting nurse used HIV viral load and CD4 counts to evaluate
90 the success of the program.

Crossroads

Crossroads was a hospital-based program situated within an infectious disease clinic where medications were also distributed. Unlike the other programs evaluated, the clients had the ability to meet and schedule
95 appointments with their infectious disease provider at

the same site. Staff for this adherence program included an adherence counselor (a Registered Nurse) and a treatment advocate (an Advanced Practice Registered Nurse). The Crossroads medication adherence
100 program used a behavior change model (with a focus on information, motivation, skill building, and behavioral change) as a framework for the program. This program had as its goal a decrease in viral load because of medication adherence. Strategies used within the
105 framework to foster medication adherence included education, motivational techniques, and skill building. Specific goals relative to these strategies were identified individually for each client.

La Familia

The La Familia program was an HIV treatment ad-
110 vocacy program serving Hispanic clients in the community. The program had three goals for its adherence program:

• To foster independence in each client.
• To have each client realize the importance of
115 medication adherence.
• To keep clients healthy and avoid hospitalization.

The staff included a monolingual nurse and a bilingual treatment advocate. An individualized approach was
120 used with each client, and a visit plan was set up after the initial visit. The strategies used were home visits, medication prepours, education and teaching about the importance of medication adherence, and referrals to appropriate social service agencies. Evaluation meth-
125 ods included the presence of improved viral load and CD4 counts and the checking of medicine boxes or necessary refills on individual medications.

Method

The three aims of this process evaluation were to (a) explore and compare the goals and modalities of
130 each program, (b) assess client and staff satisfaction, and (c) provide recommendations for the improvement of current programs. Through a competitive bid process, our evaluation team was hired to conduct this pro-

Table 2
Data Collection Overview

Data collection method	Data source
Focus groups	• Sample of clients from two state-funded programs.
Interviews	• Two staff persons of state-funded programs.
	• Department of Public Health staff for overall goals of programs.
Secondary data	• Client data collected at all three state-funded programs.
	• Quarterly reports from all three programs.
	• Independent evaluation of one state-funded program.

gram evaluation and met quarterly with an HIV Medi-
135 cation Advisory Committee at the Connecticut State
DPH for guidance and clarification of the evaluation
focus.

To explore and compare program modalities, data
were collected from the DPH and medication adher-
140 ence program staff with regard to the goals, methods,
and reporting mechanisms of each program. The ex-
trapolation of medical data on individual clients was
also completed through the review of medical charts.
Client and staff satisfaction were assessed through in-
145 depth qualitative research methods. Table 2 shows an
overview of the collected data.

Qualitative process evaluation methods were used
to explore the goals and modalities of each adherence
program, to assess client and staff satisfaction, and to
150 provide recommendations for improving programs.
Focus group interviews were conducted with the clients, and individual interviews were conducted with
the staff from each of these programs.

Focus Groups

The evaluation team conducted focus groups with
155 clients from two of the adherence programs. The results from an independent focus group with the third
program were used in this evaluation. The recruitment
of focus groups was done by the program staff, who
invited all their clients to attend the focus groups, in-
160 forming them of the length of time of the group, the
topics that would be covered, and that each participant
would be paid $25.00 for their participation.

Semistructured focus group guides were developed.
These guides provided a logical sequence of question-
165 ing and open-ended questions, making it possible to
obtain deeper and richer information. Focus groups
were staffed by both a moderator and a note taker. The
role of the moderator was to facilitate the discussion
around the questions on the focus group guide. The
170 note taker's role was to assist the moderator with follow-up questions and to take notes for the transcription
of the focus group tape. The identities of the focus
group participants were kept anonymous. Focus groups
lasted approximately 2 hr.

Staff Interviews

175 Staff interviews were conducted with the primary
medication adherence staff person from each program.

Interviews were tape-recorded. Staff were asked about
their satisfaction with the program, their program's
goals, and what improvements they felt could be made
180 to their program.

Data Analysis

Each focus group and interview tape was transcribed verbatim. The transcribed data were entered
into the qualitative analysis software package QSR
NVivo for an analysis of the themes. Three coders (the
185 principal investigator and two research assistants) conducted a content analysis of the transcripts with the
open-coding technique to examine conceptual patterns,
or themes, in the text. To ensure accuracy in the content analysis, the transcripts were read and coded sepa-
190 rately by the three coders, who then compared and revised the coding scheme. Specifically, concepts that
were salient and repeated in the text were identified
and used as codes to organize the text into categories.
QSR NVivo was used to organize, code, and translate
195 the data into the results for this evaluation.

Human Participants' Approval

Before data collection, all of the consent forms and
focus group and interview questions were included in
an application submitted to the Institutional Review
Board for Human Subject Research at Southern Con-
200 necticut State University. Data collection began on
approval from the Institutional Review Board.

All the focus group participants were asked to read
and sign a consent form before the start of data collection. Any member of the focus groups needing assis-
205 tance with reading the consent form had it read to
them. Each participant received a copy of the consent
form.

Results

Focus Groups

A total of 14 participants participated in the two focus groups we conducted, and 15 participants took part
210 in the independent focus group with the third program
(More, 2002). These numbers represented approximately 20% of program clients at the time of the focus
groups. Across all three of the focus groups, participants included 9 women and 20 men; 22 were His-
215 panic, 6 were African American, and 1 was White. All

the focus groups were conducted at the program's primary site.

Four themes emerged from the focus groups with regard to program satisfaction and needed improvements. They were (a) the provision of emotional and social support, (b) the provision of education on medication, (c) the need for staff to liaise between clients and medical providers, and (d) additional needs not currently being met. There was much discussion in the focus groups about adherence issues related to side effects of the medications; however, this was beyond the scope of this article.

Clients stated several ways in which their participation in the program had been helpful to them both personally and in taking their medications. Across all focus groups, clients spoke specifically about the adherence program nurses when talking about the program. There was not one comment made with regard to the program that was not specifically about the nurse. Comments about the program staff were always positive.

There was an overwhelmingly positive response to the adherence programs and staff. Clients stated that participation in the program had increased their knowledge about their HIV medications; provided them assistance with reminders to take medications; increased their social support, self-esteem, and self-confidence; and provided hope and encouragement that they would continue living. Nonadherence to medication, doctor referral, financial status, and need for support were all stated as reasons for being in the programs. Discussion around reasons for being in the adherence program initiated further dialogue on medication barriers, including side effects and forgetting to take medications.

Additionally, the La Familia evaluation included a survey with two foci: to determine the efficacy of the medication adherence program implementation and to examine variables that correlated with effective adherence to antiretroviral medication (More, 2002). With regard to client satisfaction, respondents were asked to rate the importance they gave to the kinds of support they received. Five respondents rated the medication adherence counselor to be "extremely important" to their adherence, whereas other supports included providers, family, and other professionals. "Primary care" and "respect" were noted by clients as the most critical issues influencing medication adherence (More, 2002).

Provision of social support and trust. The ways in which the adherence program nurses had been helpful to clients were many and included the provision of social support, instilling of trust, and provision of positive reinforcement. Focus group participants emphasized that the nurses were always available to them and that their contact with the nurses was among the most beneficial aspects of their participation in the program. Participants stressed that they had come to rely on the nurses' visits and phone calls and needed their continued support in living with HIV.

One participant stated, "They [the nurses] take care of me. I love the people; they go to your home, like they're my friends. Every time they say, how are you doing? Do you need anything?" Another said, "I felt so alone. It's nice to know that somebody does understand what it is all about and you can depend on that person."

Participants in the focus groups expressed many competing life issues that had previously acted as barriers in their medication adherence. These life issues included drug and alcohol abuse, insufficient housing, unhealthy interpersonal relationships, unemployment, financial constraints, poor nutrition, and the experience of stigma because of their HIV status. Either through direct support or referring support, program staff assisted clients in taking their medications by targeting each of these life issues. This attention to these other competing life issues was a significant benefit of the adherence programs according to focus group participants.

Further highlighting the importance and appreciation of social support, we asked the focus group members about their attendance in the focus group. Sentiment among focus group participants was that talking in groups about their medication adherence experiences was very helpful. Some participants were active members of support groups, whereas others were looking for groups to join.

Provision of education on medication. Education about the benefits and side effects of the medications, the provision of clear instruction and tools to assist with adherence, clarification of confusing drug regimens, and the reduction of information overload from medical providers were key elements of the adherence programs. With regard to the clarification of the adherence regimen, one client stated, "[Name of nurse] really walked me through it. Today I stand a little stronger. And I'm grateful because many things were shot to me all at once and [Name of nurse] has helped me to digest it little by little and has helped me understand."

Others expressed that the nurses keep them honest by being persistent in asking about missed doses. "[Name of nurse] snagged me one time I stopped taking the meds and I took the blood test and she goes, 'Have you been taking your meds,' and I said 'yes.' She said, 'You sure you've been taking it because we got the blood back and there is no trace of it.'" This participant went on to explain that her adherence improved because of this.

Staff as liaison. The adherence nurse serving as "a close tie to the doctor" was important to patients and helped them adhere to their medications. Adherence program nurses assisted clients by either talking to providers for them or encouraging them to ask questions of their doctors. This tie to the medical providers allowed patients to feel more empowered about their medication regimen and gave them a sense of control over their destiny.

Additional needs. Clients stressed the importance of the role of adherence program nurses to their adherence success. They expressed concern about burnout among the staff and suggested that more staff be hired to continue to provide the program services. Other improvements suggested by focus group participants included increasing staff visits to more than weekly, having programs provide more referral information, increasing the availability of protection for sexually active clients, and improving access to food and housing. Additional needs mentioned by clients included increasing access to reminder devices, such as beepers and pill boxes.

Staff Interviews

Across the two interviews, three common themes emerged. They were (a) program aspects of success, (b) the provision of social and emotional support, and (c) nurses acting as a liaison for their clients.

Program aspects of success. The staff interviewed stated that the overall program goal was total adherence to medication. This included reducing viral load, increasing CD4 counts, and decreasing missed doses and appointments. Additional patient-specific goals were described, including increasing patient knowledge about HIV medications, increasing self-empowerment to take medications, and changing individual client behavior to increase adherence. In one staff interview, the adherence program nurse stated, "The goal for me of course would be total adherence. The reality is that I don't think that's going to happen. But I would say even to achieve between 80 and 90% adherence and education, that's a large goal of this program and self-empowerment, too." Both of the program adherence nurses stated that although total medication adherence should be the long-term objective, more immediate objectives should be measured, including individual behavioral changes that would increase clients' ability, self-esteem, and self-efficacy to take their medications.

The adherence nurses stated that they felt their programs were meeting the goals, so stated by one interviewee, "If one patient has benefited, then the program is meeting its goal." Although there was not 100% adherence among all clients, other aspects of improvement showed that goals were being met.

Both of the staffs interviewed expressed feelings of satisfaction and success with their respective medication adherence programs. Quarterly adherence meetings with the state and continuing education, which was necessary for their work, were highlighted as extremely helpful ways to provide social support to program staff. Desired improvements centered on ways to better help clients adhere to their medications. Both interviewees stated that they continuously sought out ways to improve education and understanding of the importance of taking medications, found ways to help patients remember to take their medications, and provided support in other ways to make taking medications easier.

Providing social and emotional support. Time spent developing trust was a key component of the job of the medication adherence nurses. The program nurses stressed the importance of gaining client trust because of clients' competing life issues and the fact that many clients had been mistreated by the medical community. As stated by one staff member, "My place is to build relationships with [my clients]. So to me, that's the first step in compliance, trust and being able to trust what I say, being able to listen to me."

Acting as a liaison. Stated as a benefit of the adherence program by clients, the staffs also expressed the importance of staying abreast of clients' needs with their providers. As one interviewee stated,

So, I do keep in contact with all practitioners if I see any other issues, a psychological issue or I refer clients to home care if I think they need it. And I discuss everything with a social worker. I keep in touch with providers at the clinic. I mean, it's a collaborative thing.

This connection to mental health and other providers allowed the adherence program nurses to keep accurate and complete records of clients' needs.

Study Limitations

The results of this evaluation represent the views of those who participated in the client focus groups and the staff interviews. Randomization of participants was not done because of the small number of clients enrolled in the programs and the difficulty of recruiting for the focus groups. In any research study with human participants, the results are limited to those who self-select to participate, as their participation is always voluntary. This does not cause the results in this study to be any less valid than in other studies; however, it means that these results should be understood to reflect only the views of those who participated. Therefore, the recommendations discussed next should be considered preliminary and need to be adapted to the specific needs of HIV medication adherence clients in other programs.

Discussion and Recommendations for Practice

Overall, there was high staff and client satisfaction with the current state-funded HIV medication adherence programs reviewed in this process evaluation. Current and future programs should continue to employ licensed staffs (i.e., Registered, Licensed Practical, and Advanced Practice Registered Nurses) to administer the adherence intervention to clients. The adherence program nursing staff person was key, which was clearly stated in the client focus groups. These models were unique in their approach to adherence in that they had staff employed to follow up with and provide support to clients. The evaluation findings supported literature in HIV medication adherence and showed the importance of social support and how it positively affects HIV medication adherence (Holzemer et al., 1999; Power et al., 2002).

Our evaluation results highlight the importance of social support from both family and friends and, even more important, the relationship between the client and the adherence nurse. Clinician factors that contributed to increased adherence included having a consistent provider, the existence of a positive relationship between clinician and client, a knowledge of clinical regimens, and prior treatment experience (Frank & Miramontes, 1999; Friedland & Williams, 1999). Consistent with these findings, Golin et al. (2002) found that clients reported that a continuing and honest communication with their medical practitioner had a positive impact on their ability to follow their medication regimen. This was also true in our evaluation, in particular with regard to the communication between the client and the adherence nurse.

Although the client–provider relationship is critical in the adherence process, the clinician (in this case, the adherence program nurse) must be able to assess the client for readiness in starting a medication regimen, and the client should be involved in the decision-making process (Frank & Miramontes, 1999). Nurses should use effective communication techniques to establish a positive relationship with the patient, show facilitative body language, and create a clinical setting that fits the patient's needs both culturally and logistically (Chesney et al., 2000).

Use of the transtheoretical model stages of change would assist nurses in assessing the willingness of their clients to begin a medication regimen. The transtheoretical model is a model of behavior change that focuses on individual decision making and the internal and external influences that impact a decision to change a behavior and actions taken based on that decision (Prochaska, Redding, & Evers, 1997). The model conceptualizes the decision to change as a series of steps an individual must pass through including precontemplation, contemplation, preparation, action, and maintenance. The use of this theory allows practitioners to start where their clients are and help them to adopt a new behavior through a process of change.

On the basis of our results and the supporting literature, several recommendations for future and current HIV medication adherence programs were developed. They include the following:

1. Program goals should be expanded to include outcome measures beyond adherence and behavior changes, increases in knowledge, and other aspects of adherence based on adherence program methods.

2. Program impact objectives should continue to include client viral loads, CD4 counts, and missed appointments and doses. Increases in self-esteem, self-efficacy, and knowledge of medications can also be added measures. The use of behavior

change theories to inform the development of these interventions should help nurses and other staff to determine the level of commitment and readiness to change among their clients. The use of behavior change theories, such as the transtheoretical model stages of change, will also assist staff in the evaluation of program outcomes.

3. Staff must be able to promote trust with their clients and facilitate social support. As stated previously, social support is seen as a reciprocal support system that is initiated through social and interpersonal relationships and which can be given in the form of informational and emotional support. Hence, providing support that was not only effective but also instructive was clearly a strength of the visiting nurse programs and an expression of satisfaction among focus group participants.

4. The adherence nurse, and her relationship with clients, is essential in increasing adherence to HIV medications. Adherence programs should continue to include the hiring of a staff nurse to be the contact and support person for all clients.

From the review of the literature, interviews with practitioners, and firsthand experiences, it is clear that evaluation of HIV medication adherence programs is not an exact science. Through definition of the primary goals of the programs, measurable process objectives should be formulated to help planners identify how a program is successful. The objectives of the program should consider that HIV viral load and increases in CD4 counts are measures of adherence. Further, objectives should include nonbiological factors that influence patient's adherence behaviors, including skills and self-efficacy to take their medications and social support. Through the development of individualized program objectives, it is possible that more time-efficient and user-friendly reporting tools can be constructed. Most important, a considerate and caring staff is crucial to adherence through the mechanism of social support.

References

Chesney, M. A. (2003). Adherence to HAART regimens. *AIDS Patient Care and STDs, 17,* 169–177.

Chesney, M. A., Morin, M., & Sherr, L. (2000). Adherence to HIV combination therapy. *Social Science and Medicine, 50,* 1599–1605.

Frank, L., & Miramontes, H. (1999). AIDS Education and Training Center adherence curriculum. HIV InSite. Retrieved January 22, 2001, from http://hivinsite.ucsf.edu/topics/adherence/209.4504.htm

Friedland, G., & Williams, A. (1999). Attaining higher goals in HIV treatment: The central importance of adherence. *AIDS, 13*(Suppl 1), S61–S71.

Golin, C., Isasi, F., Breny Bontempi, J. M., & Eng, E. (2002). Secret pills: HIV positive patients' perceptions of the stigma and barriers associated with antiretroviral use. *AIDS Education and Prevention, 14,* 318–329.

Holzemer, W., Corless, I., Nokes, K., Turner, J., Brown, M., Powell-Cope, G., et al. (1999). Predictors of self-reported adherence in persons living with HIV disease. *AIDS Patient Care and STDs, 13,* 185–189.

More, M. E. (2002). *HIV medication adherence program: An evaluation report 2002.* New Haven, CT: Urban Policy Strategies.

Power, R., Koopman, C., Volk, J., Israelski, D. M., Stone, L., Chesney, M. A., et al. (2002). Social support, substance use, and denial in relationship to antiretroviral treatment adherence. *AIDS Patient Care and STDs, 17,* 245–252.

Prochaska, J., Redding, C., & Evers, K. (1997). The transtheoretical model and stages of change. In K. Glanz, F. M. Lewis, & B. Rimer (Eds.), *Health behavior and health education: Theory, research, and practice* (pp. 60–84). San Francisco: Jossey-Bass.

Steckler, A., & Linnan, L. (2002). *Process evaluation for public health interventions and research*. San Francisco: Jossey-Bass.

Acknowledgments: This evaluation was made possible by funding from the Connecticut Department of Public Health and the U.S. Health Resources and Services Administration.

Address correspondence to: Jean M. Breny Bontempi, Southern Connecticut State University, Department of Public Health, 144 Farnham Avenue, New Haven, CT 06515. E-mail: brenybontejl@southernct.edu

Exercise for Article 23

Factual Questions

1. According to the authors, a process evaluation can answer what question?

2. Are "Atlas," "Crossroads," and "La Familia" the real names of the programs?

3. The researchers had three aims. Two of them were to explore and compare the goals and modalities of each program, and provide recommendations for the improvement of current programs. What was the other aim?

4. What was the note taker's role in the focus groups?

5. Approximately what percentage of program clients participated in the focus groups?

6. According to the researchers, was there high overall staff and client satisfaction with the programs?

Questions for Discussion

7. The researchers state that to ensure accuracy in the content analysis, the transcripts were read and coded separately by the three coders, who then compared and revised the coding scheme. (See lines 188–191.) In your opinion, how important is it to code separately (i.e., without consulting with each other)? Explain.

8. In your opinion, are the semistructured focus group guides described in sufficient detail? (See lines 163–166.)

9. The description of the "Human Participants' Approval" in lines 196–207 is more detailed than it is in many research articles. In your opinion, is it desirable for researchers to discuss this matter in detail? Explain.

10. Do you agree with the "Study Limitations" discussed in lines 411–426? Explain.

11. This process evaluation was qualitative. In your opinion, would a quantitative process evaluation with objective instruments and statistical analyses also be desirable? Explain.

Quality Ratings

Directions: Indicate your level of agreement with each of the following statements by circling a number from 5 for strongly agree (SA) to 1 for strongly disagree (SD). If you believe an item is not applicable to this research article, leave it blank. Be prepared to explain your ratings. When responding to criteria A and B below, keep in mind that brief titles and abstracts are conventional in published research.

A. The title of the article is appropriate.

SA   5   4   3   2   1   SD

B. The abstract provides an effective overview of the research article.

SA   5   4   3   2   1   SD

C. The introduction establishes the importance of the study.

SA   5   4   3   2   1   SD

D. The literature review establishes the context for the study.

SA   5   4   3   2   1   SD

E. The research purpose, question, or hypothesis is clearly stated.

SA   5   4   3   2   1   SD

F. The method of sampling is sound.

SA   5   4   3   2   1   SD

G. Relevant demographics (for example, age, gender, and ethnicity) are described.

SA   5   4   3   2   1   SD

H. Measurement procedures are adequate.

SA   5   4   3   2   1   SD

I. All procedures have been described in sufficient detail to permit a replication of the study.

SA   5   4   3   2   1   SD

J. The participants have been adequately protected from potential harm.

SA   5   4   3   2   1   SD

K. The results are clearly described.

SA   5   4   3   2   1   SD

L. The discussion/conclusion is appropriate.

SA   5   4   3   2   1   SD

M. Despite any flaws, the report is worthy of publication.

           SA   5   4   3   2   1   SD

Article 24

Barriers in Providing Psychosocial Support for Patients with Cancer

Mari Botti, RN, RM, BN, PhD, MRCNA, Ruth Endacott, RN, DipN, MA, PhD,
Rosemary Watts, RN, RM, Crit Care Cert, BN, Grad Dip in Adv Nurs (Ed), MHSc, PhD,
Julie Cairns, RN, BN, Cert Cancer Nursing, Master of Bioethics,
Katrina Lewis, RN, Amanda Kenny, RN, RM, PhD[*]

ABSTRACT. There is sound evidence to support the notion that the provision of effective psychosocial care improves the outcomes of patients with cancer. Central to the implementation of this care is that health professionals have the necessary communication and assessment skills. This study aimed to identify key issues related to providing effective psychosocial care for adult patients admitted with hematological cancer, as perceived by registered nurses with 3 or more years of clinical experience. An exploratory qualitative design was used for this study. Two focus group interviews were conducted with 15 experienced cancer nurses. The provision of psychosocial care for patients with cancer is a dynamic process that has a professional and personal impact on the nurse. The 5 analytic themes to emerge from the data were as follows: when is it a good time to talk?; building relationships; being drawn into the emotional world; providing support throughout the patient's journey; and breakdown in communication processes. The findings from this study indicate an urgent need to develop a framework to provide nurses with both skill development and ongoing support in order to improve nurses' ability to integrate psychosocial aspects of care and optimize patient outcomes.

From *Cancer Nursing*, 29, 309–316. Copyright © 2006 by Lippincott Williams & Wilkins, Inc. Reprinted with permission.

Introduction

There is growing evidence that the provision of effective psychosocial care improves the outcomes of patients with cancer.[1,2] However, providing psychosocial care for patients with cancer can place specific
5 burdens on health professionals. The effectiveness of the care provided is dependent on the training, skills, attitudes, and beliefs of staff. The *Clinical practice guidelines for the psychosocial care of adults with cancer* have been developed by the National Breast Cancer
10 Centre and the National Cancer Control Initiative in Australia as a benchmark for the psychosocial needs of patients with cancer. These evidence-based guidelines are designed for use by all health professionals who care for people during the course of cancer diagnosis
15 and treatment. Central to the successful implementation of these guidelines is the ability for health professionals to exercise the necessary assessment and communication skills, for example, discuss prognosis and treatment options available with the patient or the move
20 from curative to palliative treatments. We know that health professionals can have low confidence in exercising these skills that can result in a failure by health professionals to provide effective psychosocial care to patients with cancer.

25 The purpose of this paper is to elicit the key issues perceived by registered nurses that arise when caring for adults with hematological cancer to enable the development of a framework to assist nurses to provide optimal evidence-based psychosocial care. In addition,
30 such a framework will assist nurses to recognize the point at which psychosocial and emotional responses to patients' needs require specialist intervention.

Background

Approximately 350,000 Australians are diagnosed with cancer each year[3] and, as a consequence, experi-
35 ence a variety of psychosocial and emotional responses. People with cancer suffer significant emotional morbidity and psychological distress and face physical issues related to their cancer and treatment, end-of-life issues, and survival issues. According to the
40 few available estimates, the prevalence of psychological distress in patients ranges from 20% to 60%,[4] and evidence suggests that 12% to 30% will experience clinically significant anxiety problems.[5] Clinical depression has been reported in up to 40% of patients in
45 palliative care[6] but is also prevalent in patients undergoing surgery for cancer[7,8] and in patients receiving chemotherapy, adjuvant therapy, or radiation ther-

[*]*Mari Botti* and *Rosemary Watts*, the Centre for Clinical Nursing Research, Epworth/Deakin Nursing Research Centre, Richmond Vic 3121, Australia. *Ruth Endacott,* La Trobe/The Alfred Clinical School, The Alfred Hospital, Prahran Vic 3121, Australia; and School of Nursing and Community Studies, University of Plymouth, Exeter EX2 6AS, England. *Julie Cairns* and *Katrina Lewis*, The Alfred, Commercial Road, Prahran Vic 3121, Australia. *Amanda Kenny*, School of Nursing, LaTrobe University, Bendigo Vic 3550, Australia.

apy.[9-11] These psychological responses can have impact on the persons and their family, affecting day-to-day functioning and capacity to cope with the burden of the disease, and may reduce adherence to recommended treatments.

The provision of optimal care for patients with cancer involves both effective physical and psychosocial care. According to the *Clinical practice guidelines for the psychosocial care of adults with cancer*,[12] the psychosocial care of a person with cancer "...begins from the time of initial diagnosis, through treatment, recovery and survival, or through the move from curative to non-curative aims of treatment, initiation of palliative care, death and bereavement" (p.37) and involves all members of the treatment team, family, friends, and carers. Health professionals can help reduce patient and family distress through interventions that strengthen the patient's own coping resources. Evidence based on meta-analyses and systematic reviews of randomized controlled trials have shown that the provision of information, psychological interventions, and emotional and social support improves patient outcomes. For example, rates of anxiety, depression, mood disturbances, nausea, vomiting, and pain[1] have been shown to decrease, and emotional adjustment and overall quality of life[2] have been shown to improve.

Nurses provide 24-hour care for patients and families and often provide psychosocial support while meeting patients' physical needs and providing symptomatic support. Providing psychosocial care for patients with cancer can place specific burdens on health professionals, and the effectiveness of the care provided is dependent on the training, skills, attitudes, and beliefs of staff. There is evidence of high stress levels among oncology nursing staff[13] and that a common source of stress is associated with the provision of emotional support for patients and their families.[14,15] Kent et al.[16] reported that a potential source of stress for health professionals is associated with caring for the dying patient and the perceived inability to relieve the patients' and/or the families' suffering. Communication in the context of cancer care includes general interactional skills to convey empathy and support and to provide medical information that is understood and retained. A failure to communicate well often seems to result from a lack of confidence or a perceived lack of knowledge.[17] Health professionals who feel insufficiently prepared in communication skills are reported to have a higher level of stress.[18]

Although it is recognized that the provision of psychosocial care is a multiprofessional process, this study uncovers psychosocial issues that arise from a nursing perspective in the context of the 24-hour management of the patient.

The Study

Aim

This study aimed to identify key issues related to providing effective psychosocial care for adult patients admitted with hematological cancer, as perceived by registered nurses with 3 or more years of clinical experience.

Methods

Design

A descriptive qualitative design was used for this study. A qualitative approach was selected because rich descriptive data, not available through quantitative methods, were desired to document the nurses' experiences. Focus groups were chosen because of their added benefits above individual interviews, in particular the synergy generated between group members,[19] their naturalistic approach in tapping into everyday social processes of communication,[20] and their "permissive" and peer support function in encouraging participants to divulge opinions and beliefs that might not emerge through an individual interview.[21] Approval for this study was granted by the Deakin University Ethics Committee and the ethics committee of the participating tertiary referral hospital.

Participants

Participants were purposively selected based on their role in providing psychosocial care. Although it is recognized that psychosocial care is a multiprofessional process, this study aimed to uncover psychosocial care in the context of the 24-hour management of the patient. The rationale for selecting experienced registered nurses was that there was an expectation they would carry the burden of providing complex psychosocial care in the ward environment. In Australia, registered nurses usually have a degree qualification. It was considered that these nurses would be role models and coaches for inexperienced nurses. Hence, the study sample was limited to experienced registered nurses. Nurses who had been working on the cancer ward at a major Melbourne tertiary level hospital, a key center in the provision of oncology services in Victoria and Australia, for 3 years or more were approached to participate in the study. A total of 15 experienced nurses participated.

The participants work on a busy hematology/oncology/radiotherapy and bone marrow transplant ward that has a complex patient acuity and associated significant morbidity. The nurses face a range of complex psychosocial issues related to patients' diagnoses and associated treatments and their personal circumstances. The 30-bed ward admits approximately 640 oncology patients, 50 bone marrow transplant patients, and more than 100 radiotherapy patients each year. At the time of the study, the ward had just commenced a Nursing Care Delivery system pilot project that was a modification of the previous Primary Nursing model utilized by the ward.

Procedure

Two focus groups, 8 participants and 7 participants,

respectively, in each group, were conducted in October 2003. One member of the research team who had experience in facilitating focus group interviews conducted the sessions. At both sessions, an observer was present to take notes pertinent to each session. Before commencing each interview, introductions were made between the participants and the researchers present. The facilitator [R.E.] gave an overview of the purpose of the interview, followed by outlining the ground rules that apply to the conduct of focus group interviews, and consent was then requested to audiotape the session. A statement was made relating to maintaining confidentiality of individual group members' perceptions at the conclusion of the session. Participants were also reminded of their right to withdraw from the study should they wish to do so. The facilitator circulated written details to participants of who to contact should they require any emotional support after the interview.

A brief biographical form was circulated to capture data such as the qualifications, experience, and role configuration of the individual participants. Before commencing the interview, the facilitator encouraged the participants to use "real life" examples to identify situations in which psychosocial support for patients and families was considered effective or could have been enhanced.

During both sessions, the facilitator used a guide consisting of open-ended questions and probes drawn from the relevant literature and existing clinical guidelines regarding the psychosocial needs of patients with life-threatening diseases. The guide was designed to allow participants to talk freely about their experiences of caring for patients with hematological cancer and their family members. The focus group sessions lasted 1 hour; both were tape-recorded and transcribed verbatim.

Ethical Considerations

Participants were invited to participate in the study based on their experience; they were informed that they did not have to take part in the study and that nonparticipation would not affect their position within the ward. Once the nurses agreed to participate in the study, they were asked to sign a consent form. Although there was no perceived inherent risk to participants, before commencing the sessions, the facilitator circulated written details of a psychologist available to them should they require emotional support at the conclusion of the session. Individual participant data have not been reported.

Data Analysis

The data were coded and analytic themes developed using content analysis. The transcripts were initially read by one member of the research team. This took some time and required the text to be understood as a whole. Notes taken by the observer during each of the focus group interviews were also read at this time to provide a context for the interview transcript. Common themes within the context of each interview were identified resulting in the identification of 5 major themes. Validation of themes occurred in 2 ways. The coding of the themes was reviewed between the project research fellow who had initially coded the data and 2 other members of the research team: one academic and one clinician. All members were in agreement with the themes. A presentation of the study findings was given to participants, further validating the findings.

Results

Demographic Characteristics

All participants were female and were registered Division 1 nurses; 20% ($n = 3$) had hospital registration with 80% ($n = 13$) having completed a Diploma of Nursing. One participant had completed an Honors degree, 2 had completed a Postgraduate Diploma in Nursing. Most participants (53%, $n = 8$) had had greater than 9 years of experience in nursing; however, the majority (53%, $n = 8$) had been in their current position for between 1 and 3 years.

Five themes were identified: when is it a good time to talk?, building relationships, being drawn into the emotional world, providing support throughout the patient's journey, and breakdown in communication processes.

When is it a good time to talk? The participants recognized that there was a need to first gain entry to the patient's environment in order to provide psychosocial care. The nurses reported that they were often able to gain such entry in a discrete and nonthreatening manner by carrying out what they termed "nursing tasks"; such tasks included meeting the patient's hygiene needs or making the patient's bed, as illustrated by the following comments:

> You know, tasks are a good excuse to get into the patient's room and talk...doing those tasks gives you permission to enter their room without them actually knowing. (focus group 1)

> ...giving them a wash and because you are doing something and not looking at them directly they'll talk because it seems safe, there's something that's happening between the two of you and they start speaking. (focus group 1)

However, the participants identified workload as a potential barrier to their ability to provide psychosocial care. Interestingly, although the participants perceived their own workload as a barrier, they also felt that patients also considered their workload as an impediment to asking for care as demonstrated by the following quotes:

> Lots of patients say you're too busy.... (focus group 1)

> Even if you are busy we like to be honest with people and just say I can't right now but I will come back because sometimes we just can't and that's a reality. (focus group 1)

The impact of workload and the provision of psychosocial care were considered to be further exaggerated when the nurse was perceived as "inexperienced" in caring for patients with cancer. This affected the ability to engage with the patient at the required level:

> ...before you feel comfortable providing social support you need to feel comfortable knowing what is going on with them medically and until you can discuss that with them at the same time, I think it's very hard to engage them. (focus group 2)

It was also acknowledged that when the nurse considered it a good time to talk to the patient, it did not always coincide with when the patient wanted to talk. A good time to talk from the patient's perspective could occur anywhere—24 hours a day, 7 days a week—and the need to provide psychosocial care during the night shift was a common scenario participants reported, as the following quote illustrates:

> So much happens at night, like people have so much time to think. (focus group 1)

To provide psychosocial care to patients admitted with hematological cancer, the participants reported that they often entered the patient's environment using the need to perform tasks to establish and engage in dialogue with patients about other issues. However, the time available to participants was related to workload issues. Workload, number of years of experience as a nurse, and the timing of the patient's need were all cited as potential barriers to the ability of the nurse to provide adequate psychosocial care.

Building relationships. To provide effective psychosocial care, there was a requirement to build a relationship with the patient. To build this relationship, there was a need to first gain the patient's trust, and it was not until this trust had been gained that psychosocial care could be provided. A key factor that participants considered assisted them to gain the trust of the patient was working as their primary nurse; this was often associated with one-to-one access to the patient discussed in terms of continuity of care. Other factors cited were the ability to demonstrate competency when carrying out routine care and the ability to demonstrate an understanding of the patient's complex medical history.

There was a general agreement among the participants that it was a quicker process to engage with patients and hence gain their trust when working in a full-time capacity as opposed to working part-time, as the following illustrations show:

> ...I only work two days a week now, so I find even though a patient tends to be long-term it takes a bit longer to build up rapport, you just can't go in there. (focus group 2)

> ...I only work one day a week.... I feel like I do my work and then I go home because they don't know me to kind of open up.... (focus group 2)

Participants, in both a positive and negative manner, discussed the relationship between primary nursing and continuity of care extensively. Although the primary nurse had the ability to deliver improved continuity of care to patients that allowed the establishment of a relationship with the patient, the primary nursing role was only available to those staff who worked full-time. This meant that relatively inexperienced nurses who worked full-time could work as primary nurses; however, it was considered by the participants that they often struggled to provide psychosocial care within this role:

> If you are full-time you get the reward of primary nursing I think but if you are not full-time...you're a bandaid fill-in basically for the shift.... (focus group 1)

> I think when you first start becoming a primary nurse after your grad year [graduate year]...and everybody thinks that you have enough experience and have your first patient and you barely cope with the complexity of their sickness...the psychosocial aspects just, you don't even think about it until much, much too late. (focus group 1)

The participants considered that an understanding of the patient's history was important in 2 significant ways in relation to building a relationship with the patient. First, this information would be relevant to any subsequent psychosocial care that the patient received, and second, it was perceived that nurses needed to be able to demonstrate such an understanding if they were to gain the patient's trust:

> ...until you gain their trust as their nurse you're not going to be able to really help them. (focus group 2)

Although the participants generally considered the care delivery modality of primary nursing facilitated continuity of care and thus enabled them to build a relationship with the patient and their significant others, they felt alone and stated that there was a void of professional dialogue with other nurses regarding the patient's plan of care. This lack of professional dialogue actually resulted in increasing the amount of stress felt by the participants. The only time nominated by participants when they considered that there was an opportunity to discuss the patient's plan of care with another nurse was at handover:

> Everybody starts to work alone in primary nursing and you only talk about that patient at handover. (focus group 1)

It was important to first gain the patient's trust in order to establish a rapport with the patient, and being the patient's primary nurse was considered an important vehicle to achieve this as was the need to demonstrate an understanding of the complexity of the patient's medical history and treatment.

Being drawn into the emotional world. For nurses working with patients diagnosed with hematological cancer, there was a recognized need to protect oneself from being taken on the emotional journey that these

375 patients travel, as the following comments demonstrate:

> …it's very easy to be drawn in emotionally…. (focus group 1)

380 > How incredibly difficult it is not to be drawn into their emotional world…. (focus group 2)

To avoid being drawn into the emotional world, it was a common scenario for participants to report that they had set personal boundaries with regard to the amount of personal information they were willing to 385 disclose. The participants reflected that they felt especially vulnerable to being drawn into the patient's emotional world when faced with the following situations: being new to the ward or lacking clinical experience in providing care to this cohort of patients:

390 > It's probably only this year that I've felt really comfortable sort of branching into that care [psychosocial care] more in depth…I set boundaries for myself…when I first started on the ward I found I gave everything and I'd come home and I'd feel completely drained and I wasn't 395 > coping and I was really upset and very involved…. (focus group 2)

Interestingly, some participants reflected that although they had boundaries in place to protect themselves against becoming too involved with patients and 400 these barriers had proved effective for a considerable period of time, occasions still arose when patients were able to get "under" these barriers and invade their personal space. Participants were undecided if this was an intentional or unintentional act by the patient; however, 405 this invasion still caught the participants by surprise:

> Participant: You care for them emotionally as well, that's the thing you…give some [information about yourself] away and then you feel like you've given too much.

> R.E.: So does it come as a bit of a shock when a particu- 410 lar patient does, as you say, get under the barrier?

> Participant: We think we are really good at it, I can go for three years and then someone will just sneak in and I get really annoyed with myself because I'm smarter than that person…. (focus group 2)

415 In summary, nurses working with patients admitted with hematological cancer recognized that they were vulnerable to being emotionally drained by being drawn into the patient's emotional world. Participants reported they had set personal boundaries for 3 key 420 reasons: to prevent becoming too involved with patients, to prevent excessive personal disclosure, and to prevent becoming emotionally drained. The unresolved question for the participants was: How can I help the patient and their family and still look after myself?

425 *Providing support throughout the patient's journey.* The analogy of describing the patient as being on a journey when admitted to hospital for treatment after the diagnosis of hematological cancer was used. Participants considered that there were key times on this 430 journey when patients needed or demanded more psy-

chosocial care and times when they needed less care. Key times nominated by the participants when more psychosocial care would be needed or demanded were times when they found it difficult to provide the appro- 435 priate care. Times nominated were when the provision of care changed from being aggressive to palliative, the end of the patient's life, and for others the interim period "…the interim period is really difficult because no-one makes a decision." Other participants nomi- 440 nated when the patient's perception of their illness changed from a state of denial to one of acceptance, and for other participants, it was simply related to the length of time the patient was hospitalized, as demonstrated by the following quotes:

445 > I find the hardest thing in nursing, the first acute [presentation] you are busy because you know that they are going to usually get better, you know they're got fevers, you can treat it…but when they come in chronic it's like throwing your hands up and saying I'm sorry there's 450 > nothing I can do. (focus group 2)

> And that's a really hard swing for us too because you push and push and give drugs and then it can be a matter of hours. We have to turn around and change the way that we provide care and that could be in a palliative nature. 455 > Perhaps you're not even ready for that and the family are not ready…I find that really challenging. (focus group 2)

The patient's journey is dynamic. At certain points of this journey, the patient requires more psychosocial care and participants recognized these times as difficult 460 times not only for the patient and their significant other but also for themselves.

Breakdown in communication processes. The communication process was considered to be ineffective by participants on 2 levels. The participants re- 465 ported that they considered ineffective communication occurred between the ward nurses and ward doctors in relation to the timing of communication. The participants cited 2 main perceived problems. First, medical staff often communicated with the patient in isolation 470 from the nursing staff, in particular when telling the patient their diagnosis and then failing to consider any of the possible ramifications of such action. Second, the nurse would be aware of sensitive information regarding the patient's diagnosis for a period of time 475 before the patient being told. This placed the nurse in a very uncomfortable position when having to care for the patient:

> …I think the doctors…shouldn't just say I'm going to tell the patient, I think you need to actually be there because 480 > the patients don't hear…. (focus group 1)

> I've known for days before a patient…that they've got terminal cancer and you just have to go in there and you just have to lie. (focus group 1)

Participants reported that they felt they received lit- 485 tle information from doctors regarding patient progress both during the period of hospitalization and after their discharge from hospital. Participants reported, for example, that if they happened to meet a patient in the hospital corridor during an outpatient's visit, they could find out how the patient was managing postdischarge. Participants reported that working solely in the ward environment was isolating, citing that this was exacerbated by not having the opportunity to rotate to the outpatients department, and as such, ongoing knowledge of patient progress was further restricted.

Ineffective communication was also reported as existing between the ward nurses themselves, and there was a general feeling among the participants that they worked in isolation from one another. As previously discussed, this feeling of isolation was partly attributed to the model of primary nursing. Handover was cited as the one time that allowed some professional dialogue to take place.

Discussion

The nurses in this study reported that they constantly faced a number of professional and personal issues when addressing the practical, emotional, and psychological demands of patients with cancer. There was a general recognition of the uniqueness of each patient's needs and that these needs could change over time whether it be the timing of the provision of information or assisting the move from curative to palliative treatment. It appeared, however, that the issues faced in constantly meeting these needs had the ability, at times, to deeply affect the nurses' level of contentment with their personal lives.

The findings from this study suggest that professional support is an area that may be improved in an effort to improve job satisfaction, particularly in responding to the expressed feeling of not working as a team member. As in Barrett and Yates' study[22] that found over one-third of nurses indicated dissatisfaction in the degree to which they felt like part of a team, nurses in this study also did not feel team members. This was voiced in 2 ways: a feeling of working in isolation, and not being included in the communication processes. The support offered to nurses working as primary nurses may need to improve to counteract the current feeling of working in isolation. However, it should be remembered that at the time of the study, the ward had just commenced the Nursing Care Delivery System pilot project. Providing feedback to nursing staff regarding the progress of patients after discharge from hospital provides not only information about patient progress but also reinforces their contribution to the interdisciplinary team, and this may be beneficial because it can then foster a sense of unity among staff members.[23]

There is a recognized deficit in the literature concerning the effects of providing care to patients with cancer on the quality of life of nursing professionals.[22,24] The findings suggested in this study support those of Ergun et al.,[24] who found that providing care to patients with cancer has a negative impact on the quality of life of oncology nurses. An Australia study, conducted by Barrett and Yates,[22] found that emotional exhaustion is a very real concern among oncology/hematology nurses with more than 70% ($n = 243$) of their sample experiencing moderate to high levels of stress.

High workload and a lack of available time were both cited by the participants as potential barriers that limited their ability to sit down and engage in conversation with patients to elicit their specific needs. These findings are supported by Barrett and Yates'[22] findings where dissatisfaction with workloads was found to be a major concern: nearly 40% of the nurses in their study perceived their workloads to be excessive. The workload issue is exacerbated by an overall reduction in nursing supply. In Australia, between 1995 and 1999, there was an overall decrease in full-time equivalent nurses per 100,000 population. This reduction in full-time equivalency is thought to be associated with an overall decrease in the level of nursing supply. Over the past 10 years, there has also been the trend for registered nurses to become part-time workers with national figures showing that the majority (53.7%) are working part-time.[25]

Findings from this study in relation to ineffective communication processes are similar to McCaughan and Parahoo's[26] findings. They found that nurses' self-perceived educational needs in caring for patients with cancer included the need for more knowledge and skills in providing psychosocial care and communication. Interestingly, the nurses in their study reported higher competence in providing physical care than in psychosocial care.

The development of effective strategies to assist clinicians to use communication skills in the provision of care is fundamental to achieving optimal psychosocial outcomes for patients. Such communication is vital to enable the provision of appropriate, accurate, and detailed information to the patient at key stages relating to the pathological process of the disease. Because this information has the potential to affect the patient's decision-making process, the provision of information must be appropriate, accurate, and detailed. Hematology is a dynamic specialty that incorporates the implementation of new and rapidly changing treatment regimens. Consideration must be given to the timing of the information. To successfully meet these demands, effective communication skills are required. Wilkinson[19] believes that in general, nurses' communication skills are inadequate and have not improved over the past 20 years. Training in communication skills can assist clinicians to improve,[27–30] and continuing training in the appropriate clinical setting may be beneficial, given that skills need to be reinforced and consolidated over time.[27,29,31]

These findings do support the development of a framework that addresses the personal and professional issues reported by experienced registered nurses as barriers to the delivery of psychosocial care. Clinical supervision is well recognized in the literature as an effective strategy for enhancing professional development, promoting self-awareness, and providing support[32-34] and has been used extensively across professional groups.[33,35-37] Clinical supervision has the potential to assist nurses with finding creative solutions to patient problems.[38] This potential can be realized through using an action learning approach to clinical supervision. Action learning uses a group process of learning and reflection, with an emphasis on getting things done.[39] A key feature of action learning is the focus on challenging assumptions but also legitimizing the reflection that is a necessary part of the process.[39] By incorporating group process into an action learning model means that nurses will find their own way to address specific issues encountered. The combination of these 2 approaches holds the potential to inform the knowledge, skills, and attitudes of nurses providing psychosocial care to patients with cancer.

A clinical supervision and action learning model is proposed by the authors. The proposed clinical supervision and action learning model is an interactive approach designed to enhance the communication skills of nurses and as such will assist nurses to manage difficult events[40] and to reduce their stress[41,42] through structured learning and reflective practice. It is proposed that individuals will learn with and from their peers by reflecting on real experiences and working on real problems. Data from this study have highlighted the need to include opportunity for nurses to discuss their own difficulties with patients; hence, such an approach was deemed preferable to a didactic teaching approach. The research team is currently giving further consideration to the implementation process of the proposed model.

Limitations

Participants were selected based on their role with patients with cancer, enhancing the trustworthiness of the data in relation to study aims. This study used a small number of participants to enable in-depth clarification and exploration. Although this limits the generalizability of the findings, the diverse patient mix to which the participants were exposed provided them with a rich source of psychosocial care opportunities and challenges. This increases the credibility of the findings and representativeness to a wider population.[43]

The participants of each focus group worked within the same setting. This serves as both a strength and a limitation as it will enhance the relevance of the findings for that particular setting but perhaps limit applicability to other settings.

Conclusion

It is clear from the findings of this study that the psychosocial needs of patients with cancer are dynamic. At present, a number of barriers are perceived to exist that impedes delivery of care to address these needs. In addition, there is clearly a professional and personal impact upon the nurse. However, for nurses to be effective in this area of care delivery and to improve patient outcomes, they must have the necessary skills and support. Therefore, a clinical supervision and action learning model with management, education, and support functions has been proposed. Such a model needs to address both the skill needs and support needs of registered nurses through the use of available evidence.

References

1. Devine EC, Westlake SK. The effects of psychoeducational care provided to adults with cancer: Meta-analysis of 116 studies. *Oncol Nurs Forum*. 1995;22:1369–1381.
2. Meyer TJ, Mark M. Effects of psychosocial interventions with adult cancer patients: A meta-analysis of randomized experiments. *Health Psychol*. 1995;14(2):101–108.
3. Australian Institute of Health and Welfare, Registries. Cancer in Australia 1998: Incidence and Mortality Data for 1998. Cancer Series; 2001 (No. 17).
4. Zabora J, Brintzenhofeszoc H, Curbow B, Hooker C, Piantadosi S. The prevalence of psychological distress by cancer site. *Psychooncology*. 2001; 10:19–28.
5. Bodurka-Bevers D, Basen-Engquist K, Carmack CL, et al. Depression, anxiety, and quality of life in patients with epithelial ovarian cancer. *Gynaecol Oncol*. 2000;78:302–308.
6. Bukberg J, Penman D, Holland JC. Depression in hospitalized cancer patients. *Psychosom Med*. 1984;46:199–212.
7. Fallowfield L, Hall A, Maguire GP, Baun M. Psychological outcomes of different treatment policies in women with early breast cancer outside a clinical trial. *BMJ*. 1990;301:575–580.
8. Royak-Schaler R. Psychological processes in breast cancer: A review of selected research. *J Psychosoc Oncol*. 1991;9(4):71–89.
9. Jenkins C, Carmody TJ, Rush AJ. Depression in radiation oncology patients: a preliminary evaluation. *J Affect Disord*. 1998;50:17–21.
10. Jacobsen PB, Bovberg DH, Redd WH. Anticipatory anxiety in women receiving chemotherapy for breast cancer. *Health Psychol*. 1998;12: 469–475.
11. Dean C. Psychiatric morbidity following mastectomy: preoperative predictors and type of illness. *J Psychosom Res*. 1987;31:385–392.
12. National Breast Cancer Centre and National Cancer Control Initiative. Clinical Practice Guidelines for the Psychological Care of Adults with Cancer. Camperdown, NSW: National Breast Cancer Centre; 2003.
13. Kelly B, Varghese F. The emotional hazards of medical practice. In: Sanders MR, Mitchell C, Byrne GJA, eds. *Medical Consultation Skills*. Melbourne: Addison-Wesley; 1997:472–488.
14. Herschbach P. Work-related stress specific to physicians and nurses working with cancer patients. *J Psychosoc Nurs*. 1992;10:79–99.
15. Catalan J, Burgess A, Pergami A, Hulme N, Gazzard B, Phillips R. The psychosocial impact on staff caring for people with serious diseases: The case of HIV infection and oncology. *J Psychosom Res*. 1996; 40:425–435.
16. Kent G, Wills G, Faulkner A, Parry G, Whipp M, Coleman R. The professional and personal needs of oncology staff: The effects of perceived success and failure in helping patients on levels of personal stress and distress. *J Cancer Nurs*. 1994;3:153–158.
17. Ley P. Communicating with patients. Improving communication, satisfaction and compliance. London: Croom Helm; 1988.
18. Ramirez AJ, Graham J, Richards MA, et al. Burnout and psychiatric disorder among cancer clinicians. *Br J Cancer*. 1995;71:1263–1269.
19. Wilkinson S. Focus groups in feminist research: power, interaction and the construction of meaning. *Womens Stud Int Forum*. 1998;21(1):111–125.
20. Wilkinson S, Bailey K, Aldridge J, Roberts A. A longitudinal evaluation of a communication skills programme. *Palliat Med*. 1999;13:341–348.
21. Kreuger RA. *Focus Groups: A Practical Guide for Applied Research*. 2nd ed. Thousand Oaks: Sage Publications; 1994.
22. Barrett L, Yates P. Oncology/haematology nurses: A study of job satisfaction, burnout, and intention to leave the specialty. *Aust Health Rev*. 2002;25(3):109–121.
23. Gullante MM, Levine NM. Recruitment and retention of oncology nurses. *Oncol Nurs Forum*. 1990;17(3):419–423.
24. Ergun FS, Oran NT, Bender CM. Quality of life of oncology nurses. *Cancer Nurs*. 2005;28(3):193–199.
25. Australian Institute of Health and Welfare. Labour forces-nurses. Australian Government; 2005. Available at: http://www.aihw.gov.au/publications/hwl/nurslfo2/nurs/fo2-col. Accessed August, 2005.

26. McCaughan E, Parahoo K. Medical and surgical nurses' perceptions of their level of competence and educational needs in caring for patients with cancer. *J Clin Nurs.* 2000;9:420–428.
27. Maguire P. Can communication skills by taught? *Br J Hosp Med.* 1990; 43:215–216.
28. Razavi D, Delvaux N, Marchal S, Bredart A, Farvaques C, Paesmans M. The effects of a 24-hour psychological training program on attitudes, communication and occupational stress in oncology: A randomised study. *Eur J Cancer.* 1993;29A:1858–1863.
29. Bird J, Hall A, Maguire P, Heavy A. Workshops for consultations on teaching of clinical communication skills. *Med Educ.* 1993;27: 181–185.
30. Baile WF, Lenzi R, Kudelka AP, et al. Improving patient–physician communication in cancer care: Outcome of a workshop for oncologists. *J Cancer Educ.* 1997;12:166–173.
31. Girgis A, Sanson-Fisher RW. How to Break Bad News. An Interaction Skills Training Manual for General Practitioners, Junior Medical Officers, Nurses and Surgeons. Woolloomooloo: NSW Cancer Council; 1997.
32. Lyth G. Clinical supervision: A concept analysis. *J Adv Nurs.* 2000;31(3): 722–729.
33. Scaife J. *Supervision in the Mental Health Professionals: A Practitioners Guide.* East Sussex: Brunner-Routledge; 2001.
34. Jones A. Possible influences on clinical supervision. *Nurs Stand.* 2001;16(1):38–42.
35. Crowe F, Wilkes C. Clinical supervision for specialist nurses. *Prof Nurse.* 1998;13(5):284–287.
36. Burke P. Risk and supervision: Social work responses to referred user problems. *Br J Soc Work.* 1997;25:115–129.
37. Gennis VM, Gennis MA. Supervision in the outpatient clinic: Effects on teaching and patient care. *J Gen Intern Med.* 1993;8(7):378–380.
38. Ayer S, Knight S, Joyce L, Nightingale V. Practice led education and development project: Developing styles in clinical supervision. *Nurse Educ Today.* 1997;17(5):347–358.
39. McGill I, Beaty L. Action Learning: A Guide for Professional, Management and Educational Development. London: Kogan Page; 1995.
40. Teasdale K, Brocklehurst N, Thom N. Clinical supervision and support for nurses: An evaluation study. *J Adv Nurs.* 2001;33:216–224.
41. Williamson GM, Dodds S. The effectiveness of a group approach to clinical supervision in reducing stress: A review of the literature. *J Clin Nurs.* 1999;8:338–344.
42. Severinsson E, Kamaker D. Clinical nursing supervision in the workplace–effects on moral stress and job satisfaction. *J Nurs Manag.* 1999;7(2): 81–90.
43. Daly J, Lumley J. Bias in qualitative research designs. *Aust N Z J Public Health.* 2002;26:299–300.

Acknowledgment: This study was supported by The Alfred Research Trusts Small Project Grant.

Address correspondence to: Mari Botti, RN, BN, PhD, MRCNA, Centre for Clinical Nursing Research, Epworth/Deakin Nursing Research Centre, 89 Bridge Road, Richmond Vic 3121, Australia. E-mail: mari.botti@deakin.edu.au

Exercise for Article 24

Factual Questions

1. The ward where this study was conducted admits approximately how many oncology patients each year?

2. There were eight participants in one focus group. How many were in the other one?

3. Were participants free to withdraw from the study?

4. Did the participants sign a consent form?

5. The researchers state that the themes were validated in two ways. What was the second way?

6. The researchers state that they used a small number of participants to enable what?

Questions for Discussion

7. Do you agree with the researchers that it was a good idea to study only experienced nurses? Explain. (See lines 127–140.)

8. While 15 nurses participated, it is not clear how many were approached. Would it be of interest to know how many were approached? Explain. (See lines 135–140.)

9. Are the focus group discussions described in sufficient detail? Explain. (See lines 175–190.)

10. Did any of the results surprise you? Were any of the results especially interesting? Explain. (See lines 219–503.)

11. Do you agree that the fact that all participants worked within the same setting is a potential limitation? Explain. (See lines 648–652.)

12. If you were planning a follow-up study to explore the topic of this research further, would you plan an additional qualitative study or a quantitative study? Explain.

Quality Ratings

Directions: Indicate your level of agreement with each of the following statements by circling a number from 5 for strongly agree (SA) to 1 for strongly disagree (SD). If you believe an item is not applicable to this research article, leave it blank. Be prepared to explain your ratings. When responding to criteria A and B below, keep in mind that brief titles and abstracts are conventional in published research.

A. The title of the article is appropriate.

   SA   5   4   3   2   1   SD

B. The abstract provides an effective overview of the research article.

   SA   5   4   3   2   1   SD

C. The introduction establishes the importance of the study.

   SA   5   4   3   2   1   SD

D. The literature review establishes the context for the study.

   SA   5   4   3   2   1   SD

E. The research purpose, question, or hypothesis is clearly stated.

    SA   5   4   3   2   1   SD

F. The method of sampling is sound.

    SA   5   4   3   2   1   SD

G. Relevant demographics (for example, age, gender, and ethnicity) are described.

    SA   5   4   3   2   1   SD

H. Measurement procedures are adequate.

    SA   5   4   3   2   1   SD

I. All procedures have been described in sufficient detail to permit a replication of the study.

    SA   5   4   3   2   1   SD

J. The participants have been adequately protected from potential harm.

    SA   5   4   3   2   1   SD

K. The results are clearly described.

    SA   5   4   3   2   1   SD

L. The discussion/conclusion is appropriate.

    SA   5   4   3   2   1   SD

M. Despite any flaws, the report is worthy of publication.

    SA   5   4   3   2   1   SD

Article 25

What Adolescents with Type I Diabetes and Their Parents Want from Testing Technology

Aaron E. Carroll, MD, MS, **Stephen M. Downs**, MD, MS, **David G. Marrero**, PhD*

ABSTRACT. The presence of diabetes in an adolescent can significantly affect his/her normal development. Mobile technology may offer the ability to lessen this negative impact. We wished to learn from adolescents with diabetes and their parents how monitoring systems that incorporated mobile communication technology could potentially help to reduce hassles associated with testing, improve compliance, and ease adolescent-parent conflict about testing behavior. We recruited adolescents between the ages of 13 and 18 years, living with type 1 diabetes mellitus, and their parents for focus groups. Qualitative analysis of the focus group data followed a set procedure. From the discussions, the following themes were identified: *issues with blood glucose monitoring* and *desired technology*. Elements of *desired technology* included *hardware requirements, software requirements, communication,* and *miscellaneous requirements*. The reported needs of this end-user group can help others to leverage maximally the capabilities of new and existing technology to care for children managing chronic disease.

From *CIN: Computers, Informatics, Nursing,* 25, 23–29. Copyright © 2007 by Lippincott Williams & Wilkins, Inc. Reprinted with permission.

Introduction

Adolescence can be a difficult time for young people and their families. In this developmental stage, a child is seeking to form a personal identity, requiring ongoing renegotiation between themselves and their
5   parents regarding norms and values. In particular, there is a redefining of what is appropriate behavior. The presence of diabetes in an adolescent can have a significant effect on this developmental process.[1-4] Parents, concerned about their child's well-being, often try
10 to dictate or enforce therapeutic behavior to their child, who is expected to "be responsible" for his/her diabetes self-care.[4-6] This is particularly evident when considering self-monitoring of blood glucose. In focus group studies conducted by our group, adolescents often re-
15 ported that they do not test as much as they were supposed to. This apparent lack of responsibility resulted in great anxiety in parents, who worry that failure to

achieve strict glycemic control will result in long-term complications associated with the disease. The result-
20 ing conflicts between parent and child created key points of stress in their relationship because many of the parents thought they were put in the position of having to constantly "nag" their children to test their blood glucose.

25 We are interested in whether mobile technology might be used to help address these issues. Specifically, we explored if a device that contained a glucose meter and was capable of transmitting glucose values to either a parent or provider could reduce adolescent-
30 parent conflict over self-management.

Mobile technology could help adolescents to work through complex information that must be processed to make good decisions. Home monitoring data can be transmitted to providers who can react to values indi-
35 cating need for therapeutic response. Because this "assistance" comes from medical professionals, it may help reduce parents' concerns, thus reducing problems associated with parental hypervigilance and manipulation of the regimen to avoid problems of hypoglyce-
40 mia. Children are usually required to check their blood sugar several times each day and make decisions about their insulin dose based upon the results and their meals. Many parents worry about giving their children the freedom to make these decisions. For this to be
45 successful, parents need to be properly informed of the technology's capabilities and convinced that their children will be more competent at managing their diabetes. In addition, using a device's ability to upload information to a provider might mitigate parental stress
50 because parents might feel that a health professional is watching out for their child. Conversely, such a device could also provide an adolescent with the means to contact the healthcare team without having to go through his or her parents. This could provide a sense
55 of empowerment by enabling an adolescent to take corrective action outside of parental awareness. Mobile technology may present an opportunity to build on past experiences and successes to give adolescents a tool

Aaron E. Carroll and *Stephen M. Downs*, Children's Health Services Research, Indiana School of Medicine, The Regenstrief Institute for Health Care; and Diabetes Prevention and Control Center, Indiana University School of Medicine, Indianapolis. Indiana. *David G. Marrero*, Diabetes Prevention and Control Center, Indiana University School of Medicine, Indianapolis.

that they can use at the point of care to improve their diabetes management, while reducing family stress and concern.

However, there is a danger in assuming that new technology will always be better. Independent consultants estimate that 25% to 50% of information technology (IT) costs are paying for redundant work processes and are therefore unnecessary.[7] Some believe that new IT is as likely to decrease efficiency as it is to increase it.[8] For instance, recent reports in the media have shown a significant backlash against previously validated physician order entry systems and electronic medical record systems in general.[9] This is not to say that the potential does not exist for the success of IT, particularly among adolescents. Adolescents as a group have been consistently more likely to accept technology as an adjunct to care. They have trusted computers to report high-risk behaviors directly to their providers more often and more accurately than they would otherwise.[10–12] Computers have also been used with some success to help with the monitoring and management of adolescent diabetes.[13–15] More novel uses of technology have also met with some success. An educational diabetes video game was used to improve some management-related skills in a relatively well-controlled population.[16] Telephonic contact and automated transmission of blood sugar data resulted in improvement in some measures of care.[17]

Unfortunately, many of the new technologies often discussed for use in patients with diabetes have been around for some time, yet have not been adopted widely. One methodology that could be used to optimize adoption and minimize later problems is that of qualitative research. Qualitative inquiry offers great potential for us to understand better the needs and desires of our end users.[18–20] Therefore, the purpose of this study was to use focus group methodology to learn from adolescents with diabetes and their parents whether mobile monitoring technology could help to reduce hassles associated with testing, improve compliance, and ease adolescent–parent conflict about testing behavior.

Methods

Sample

Adolescents with type 1 diabetes and their parents were recruited from a diabetes clinic in Indianapolis, IN. Ten focus groups were conducted with a total of 59 participants (23 males and 36 females participated); five groups consisted of adolescents with diabetes ($n = 31$) and five groups consisted of their parents ($n = 28$). The parents and the adolescents met separately, and the content of each group was not revealed to the other. This study was approved by the Institutional Review Board of Indiana University, and all subjects provided informed consent. Subjects were paid $40 to participate.

Focus Group Methodology

The purpose of these focus groups was to gather information from adolescents with type 1 diabetes and their parents related to blood glucose monitoring and the use of mobile technology to improve compliance with diabetes management. The focus group leader was a professional facilitator trained and experienced in working with healthcare populations. She used a prepared set of open-ended qualitative questions to facilitate the 2-hour sessions (e.g., "What do you like about your testing equipment and what do you not like? How can we use technology to improve the way your children manage their diabetes? Design what you think would be the ideal testing device."). Participants were then shown a prototype of a mobile technology that combines the benefits of blood glucose testing with that of a mobile phone.[21] Participants were asked to verbalize their thoughts about the device, suggest any relevant changes to it that would increase their use of this technology, and speculate how this technology might influence parent–child relations regarding self-monitoring behavior. The focus groups were all tape recorded and later transcribed. Efforts were made to elicit responses from all participants.

Qualitative Analysis

Qualitative analysis of the data was conducted using a set procedure: (1) review of the audiotapes, (2) review of the tape transcriptions, (3) discussions among investigators regarding key elements of subjects' statements, (4) determination of conceptual themes, and (5) assignment of relevant responses to appropriate thematic constructs.[22] A pediatrician, a social ecologist, and a nurse practitioner with training in medical sociology, all of whom have experience with qualitative methods, were the study team. In particular, the social ecologist (DGM) has experience with focus group methodology and has published a number of studies using the quantitative methods reported here. All of the research team members had experience with the target population through clinical work and research efforts. A group consisting of eight clinicians and two experienced qualitative researchers worked in conjunction with the research team to contribute to the development of the group questions used by the facilitator (see Acknowledgments). The pediatrician attended the focus group sessions, contributed appropriate additional questions, and took detailed notes. Transcriptions were available within a week or two of each focus group, and audiotapes were reviewed within 1 week of session completion.

Results

The five adolescent focus groups had 31 participants; the five parent focus groups had 28 participants. The numbers of males and females was about equal. Adolescents were between 13 and 18 years (mean, 14.9 years) and had been living with diabetes for between 6 months and 14 years (mean, 6.6 years). Demographic data on the focus group participants are presented in Table 1.

Table 1
Demographic Data of Focus Group Participants

	Parents (n = 28)	Adolescents (n = 31)
Gender		
Female	23	13
Male	5	18
Child's age		
13–14 y	15	14
15–16 y	8	11
17–18 y	5	6
Ethnicity		
White	26	28
African American	2	3
Parent employment status		
Working	19 (68%)	
Not working	9 (32%)	
Child's duration of diabetes (y)		
0–3	6 (21%)	
3–6	11 (39%)	
6–9	3 (11%)	
10 or more	8 (29%)	

The themes that emerged were *issues with blood glucose monitoring* and *desired technology*. Elements of *desired technology* included *hardware requirements, software requirements,* and *communication.*

Issues with Blood Glucose Monitoring

Blood glucose monitoring was a contentious issue for the focus group participants: parents struggled with controlling their adolescents' blood glucose at a time when the teenagers themselves wanted to assert more control over their lives. Discussions related to blood glucose monitoring within the adolescent groups and the parent groups clustered into the same categories: compliance with the diabetic regimen and parent–child relationships.

Compliance with the Diabetic Regimen

Self-monitoring was viewed by many of the teens as the most inconvenient, disruptive, and least favorite aspect of having diabetes. Several stated that they do not like to test and admitted that they tested less often than advised. For some, there is a social discomfort in testing in front of friends. This may explain why most participants who acknowledged skipping testing did so before lunch at school.

Parents in all groups noted that as their children hit adolescence, it became more difficult to control their children's blood glucose monitoring. Testing behavior was noted by parents and adolescents to be influenced by several forces: school, peer influences, and social stigma. Several participants stated that they frequently forgot to test at various times throughout the day or week, and some of the teens did not test if they thought their levels were high or low because they expected a negative parental reaction.

Parent–Child Relationships

Parents noted that it was difficult to determine when to step in versus when to give up control of the management of diabetes to their children. In general, as the adolescents neared adulthood, most parents felt the need to relinquish some control of managing the diabetes to their children.

Parents expressed frustration and felt they were constantly "nagging" children about testing because they were worried about irreversible damage that can occur to their children's bodies. Parents across all groups wanted to know their teenagers were testing, without being perceived negatively by their children. There was clearly tension between the desire to "let go and trust" that the adolescents would be responsible and the need to "just be sure" that they were, in fact, managing their diabetic regimen.

The adolescents stated that their parents' behaviors as a result of this concern could be overbearing or "annoying," "stressful," "controlling," "nagging," and "overprotective." Trust was discussed across the groups in that it was important for the teens to feel that their parents trusted their diabetic management. They acknowledge that it was scary for parents to let go of control and suggested keeping lines of communication open so that diabetes management could be discussed in a way that was not punitive or "blaming."

Desired Technology

Teenagers and their parents were asked to design the ultimate testing equipment (i.e., a system that would best work for their lifestyle). Although the basic technology discussed was fairly similar across groups, the suggestions of what to do with the data once the values were collected were very different between parents and adolescents.

Hardware requirements. Participants in all groups were asked to design the ideal testing device as a component of the self-management routine, without prompting from the moderator. Discussion in the adolescent focus groups initially centered on the actual method of testing. They came up with ideas for an implantable or wearable device that would test blood glucose, calculate insulin dosage, and deliver the appropriate insulin dose. This was especially popular among the teenagers because it would require no intervention by the teens themselves. Comments included:

> It would be inserted somewhere, so that every couple of hours it would just test by itself.

> I just had something that is permanently inside of you that send[s] the reading to your pump and tells you what to do.

The teenage participants then quickly moved away from the actual test into how technology could be used for all other aspects of their care. They initially focused on technology with which they were already familiar:

personal digital assistants (PDAs) and cell phones. One of the participants suggested the following:

255　It is the size of a PDA—a little smaller. It would have a calendar on it so when it tests your blood it records the level to the calendar. It would also have a thing that would automatically e-mail your doctor. Then it would have a part that would prick your finger and suck blood
260　out, so that you would not have to squeeze it out. When it was done checking the blood sugar, it would read out and spit the old tester out. It would have a number like a beeper so that you could call it from phones [in case it was misplaced]. It could be washer safe, so if it got left in
265　your clothes it could go through the washer.

Other teenagers jumped immediately to the idea of using their cell phones as a tester. They explained that their cell phone was with them at all times, looked like everyone else's cell phone, and combining the two
270　technologies would prevent them from having to carry both a phone and a tester. This idea was especially popular with the older teenagers (17–18 years old); it was moderately popular with those 15 to 16 years old and only slightly popular with those 13 to 14 years old.
275　This may be indicative of the more common use of cell phones as the participants aged.

Parents also quickly discussed the idea of using a cell phone as a tester. They felt that most adolescents had cell phones and that they almost always carried
280　them. Some of their comments included:

I think it would be cool because all kids have phones, so they would still look like a normal kid.

I'm thinking that kids don't forget cell phones. So if you can put it in there somehow, that would work.

285　However, it should be noted that parents of the younger adolescents were less excited about the idea of a cell phone. There were concerns about responsibility for having a cell phone at the age of 13 or 14 years; the parents of those 17 to 18 years old did not share those
290　concerns. Again, this seems to be an indication that the average age for cell phone use is likely somewhat older than 13 or 14 years.

After the groups discussed their designs, the facilitator focused on the cell phone/glucose meter option,
295　explaining that this type of device was available as a prototype. Reactions to this prototype were extremely positive across all groups, including participants who had not been overly enthusiastic when they thought they were discussing a concept rather than a reality.
300　Discussions about the prototype in the parent and adolescent groups clustered into the following categories: (1) software requirements, and (2) communication.

Software requirements. Participants were asked to identify what functions the tester and/or the phone
305　would need to excite them about this product. There were three primary functions that parents and adolescents identified: (1) calculations, (2) data capture/upload/storage, and (3) alarms.

Calculations. There was one primary analytic capa-
310　bility that was considered essential across all groups: calculating the amount of insulin required for a given blood glucose level, based on an individual's management plan. Insulin dose calculation was seen as a burden by the adolescents and their parents; it was compli-
315　cated by orders changing frequently so that memorization of dosages is nearly impossible.

Data capture/upload/storage. One of the most interesting features for both the parents and the adolescents was the idea of blood glucose levels being auto-
320　matically uploaded onto a Web site that parents, healthcare providers, and the teens could access at any time. Some of the teenagers saw this as a positive feature because they felt that it would decrease the "constant nagging" by their parents regarding their test re-
325　sults. Parents also liked the idea because it would be automatic, the teenagers would be unable to lie about their results, and they could not adjust or change the results to appear normal. Some of the comments about this feature included:

330　You wouldn't have to always call your parents and tell them what you got. They could just look on the computer.

I want it to go to some type of document where they can record their readings and you can hook it up to the com-
335　puter and the doctor can see all the test readings when you go. That way they won't have to write everything down.

I think that if you are going to spend all this money then my doctor should see the results at least every 2 weeks
340　because that is how often he wants to see them now.

Alarms. The idea of an alarm that would sound when it was time to test elicited a strong negative response from most of the teens but was a positive feature for the majority of the parents. The teenagers
345　stated that alarms during class or when friends were around were embarrassing and called attention to them. Others stated that they tended to ignore the alarms if they had them, so they did not see them as a helpful feature.

350　During the initial discussion, many parents saw the alarm feature as extremely important; some even felt it was a necessity. There was discussion as to whether or not it would be a "deal breaker"—that if the alarm was not an option, it would stop parents from purchasing
355　the phone. It is of importance that the parents of the younger teenagers, the 13- to 14-year-olds, felt this was a more important function than did the parents of the teenagers 15 to 18 years. However, after additional discussion among themselves, none of the parents felt
360　it was essential; they would purchase the phone even if it did not have an alarm function.

Communication

Four primary themes centered on communication: (1) parent notification of test results, (2) physician notification of test results, (3) communication between provider and adolescent, and (4) emergency assistance.

Parent notification of test results. Perhaps the most contentious issue between the parents and their teenagers was whether the self-monitoring results should be communicated directly to the parents. As the adolescents aged, they found this feature to be more offensive. The group with participants 13 to 14 years old was the most accepting of this communication; not surprisingly, the group with those 17 to 18 years old had the most negative reaction to this feature. Some of the comments from the teens regarding automatic notifications included:

> It should only tell my parents if it went really low.

> Why would you tell your parents? We are going to be adults very soon.

> If I tested and my sugar is 400 and it goes to my mom immediately, I don't want her calling and bitching me out because my sugar is high. I already know that it is high. I don't need to hear it from you, too.

> Seriously, if it sent it to my parents every time then they would just call me all the time.

During the initial discussions, this issue was a deal breaker for many of the parents. However, as discussion continued, it became apparent that the primary goal of the parents was to encourage compliance with testing; they were willing to accept anything that would increase the likelihood of testing, even if it meant that they did not get immediate feedback on test results. Some of the other parent comments concluded:

> It's not so much of us having control but giving us information so that if we need to take control we can.

> It is letting them take responsibility and letting us feel that we can oversee it.

> Text message results to the parents. See, then we wouldn't have to nag them because we would know that they are testing and we would know that they are alive.

> I would prefer to be notified just when they are out of range.

After discussion, the pediatrician told the parents that this feature was sometimes not well received by the adolescents. If the teenagers would not use the meter because of this feature, the parents were willing to omit it. They noted that they would still have access to the numbers via the Internet, or by accessing the teenagers' phone tester directly. This gave them more comfort because they would still be able to access the data and track their children's progress. One mother may have summed up the basic concern of the parents when she stated: "I don't need control. I need access."

Physician notification of test results. In contrast to the concerns raised with parental notification, the teenagers had no issue with directly providing their physicians with testing data. Indeed, they admitted that they would be more likely to test as they were supposed to and more careful with their diabetes management because they would know their clinics would be getting the whole picture. There were no negative responses to this feature of the testing device; positive comments from the teenagers included:

> I think that kids would be healthier because they will know that they couldn't cheat.

> There would be better compliance because you don't want your doctor to yell at you.

> That would be cool. It would really be convenient.

Parents also had positive reactions about this feature, and it allowed them to be somewhat more comfortable with the idea of not directly receiving the results. In fact, it was seen as a way to decrease the burden of diabetes on their children because the results would automatically flow to the clinic. This would relieve the children of the need to keep logs of their test results.

Communication between provider and adolescent. Participants were queried about how they would feel if communication regarding regimen changes occurred directly between the adolescents and their providers, with parents receiving e-mail or text messages summarizing the communication. Teenagers had an overall positive reaction to this idea. However, there was some difference regarding how communication would take place: speaking with the provider versus receiving a text message with the regimen changes.

Parents of the younger teenagers were somewhat skeptical of their children's ability to understand the changes in regimen unless the physicians were more careful about how they explained the changes. However, the parents' overall responses were positive as long as the parents were "kept in the loop." Some of their comments included:

> At this age he should start taking on the responsibility, but I would like to know what happens.

> Or just store it on a Web site where I can access it. She is my little girl, and I want to be able to keep track. I don't want to be a nag; I just want to say, "Hey, your regimen changed" or "do you need any help?"

> It would be great! It would take the monkey off our backs. Who wouldn't like that?

> I am comfortable with that because I know this is where it has to head.

Emergency assistance. One feature identified by both the teenagers and their parents as essential was some sort of emergency notification of parents, emergency personnel, or other identified individuals in the event that a blood sugar reading was dangerously high or low. Some of the recommendations included:

> It would be nice if it would contact somebody if you were really high or really low.

The phone would have to have GPS. That way if there is a situation where they are comatose, then we know where the hell they are.

475   I want it to beep me if his sugar is too high or too low. Also if it is really high or low maybe even have it contact the ER.

Can this phone have an, "I am diabetic" thing that will tell people in case they get into a car accident. Well, they

480   won't wear a bracelet.

Discussion

This study used qualitative research techniques to conduct an investigation into the needs of an end-user group to leverage maximally the capabilities of new and existing technology to care for children managing

485   chronic disease. Type 1 diabetes is a disease in which information management is imperative; there are multiple checks every day and many decisions that must be made correctly based not only on the most recent information, but also information gathered in the past. In

490   the adolescent population, this difficult task is complicated by the teens' desire to accept greater responsibility while still needing assistance from adults. Ideally, technology should help them to make this transition more easily.

495   Adolescents want their testing equipment to integrate into the social realm in which they live. They want their devices to be "cool," to mimic devices already ubiquitous in their peer groups. They don't mind such devices acting as a safety net for their excessively

500   high or low blood sugar readings, but they do not want their parents getting real-time values as they are checked. Interestingly, they are not opposed to the health system, including their physicians, receiving real-time values. They desire an interaction with the

505   healthcare system that is empowering and developmentally appropriate. Any device that seeks to capitalize on these desires and make a real difference must also account for the behavioral and relationship difficulties among adolescents, their parents, peers, and school. It

510   must help to ease the age-old conflict between developmental norms of independence and the appearance of rebellion. Furthermore, developers and users must be sensitive to developmental needs across the ages of the adolescent spectrum. Prior research has shown that the

515   safety net provided by some forms of mobile technology can have an impact on these relationships. Advances in technology have made the ability to collect and transmit data more sophisticated and synchronous.

There are several limitations to this study. Some in-

520   clude the focus group methodology itself: small convenience samples limit the generalizability of the findings; group consensus may inhibit an individual from stating his/her differing opinion; introverted individuals may be more apt to keep silent about their opinions.

525   The current study provides an opportunity to understand the potential impact of new testing technology on type 1 diabetes through the eyes of adolescents aged 13

to 18 years and their parents. Novel testing technology should set a new norm for the way adolescents interact

530   with the healthcare system. It should introduce them to the fact that it is appropriate to have a relationship with their providers without their parents' involvement. It should open lines of communication and allow for the transmission of data to parties who can make use of it.

535   Most important, it should help to reduce the burden felt by parents to enforce proper testing and management. Diabetes can be a crucible for family problems, enmeshment, and dysfunctional behavior; advances in technology should seek to lessen its impact.

540   Cell phones appear to be an excellent vehicle for meeting the needs and desires of adolescents with diabetes and their parents. Such phones already are used by a large number of adolescents and would draw no attention to their users; in fact, it might be seen as an

545   attractive addition to many users. The devices have the ability to house alarms, if desired, and transmit text messages and more detailed information. Cell phones with glucose meters embedded within them could meet most of the needs expressed by subjects in this study.

550   Such devices are under development by a number of companies. However, they must be coupled with new systems of care that leverage these abilities to change behavior and the actions of all parties involved.

References

1. Anderson BJ. Children with diabetes mellitus and family functioning: translating research into practice. *J Pediatr Endocrinol Metab.* 2001;14(Suppl 1):645–652.
2. Gowers SG, Jones JC, Kiana S, North CD, Price DA. Family functioning: a correlate of diabetic control? *J Child Psychol Psychiatry.* 1995;36(6):993–1001.
3. Daneman D, Wolfson DH, Becker DJ, Drash AL. Factors affecting glycosylated hemoglobin values in children with insulin-dependent diabetes. *J Pediatr.* 1981;99(6):847–853.
4. Anderson BJ, Brackett J, Ho J, Laffel LM. An office-based intervention to maintain parent-adolescent teamwork in diabetes management. Impact on parent involvement, family conflict, and subsequent glycemic control. *Diabetes Care.* 1999;22(5):713–721.
5. Miller-Johnson S, Emery RE, Marvin RS, Clarke W, Lovinger R, Martin M. Parent–child relationships and the management of insulin-dependent diabetes mellitus. *J Consult Clin Psychol.* 1994;62(3):603–610.
6. Coyne JC, Anderson BJ. The 'psychosomatic family' reconsidered: diabetes in context. *J Marital Fam Ther.* 1988;14:113–123.
7. Dorenfest S. The decade of the '90s: poor use of IT investment contributes to the growing healthcare crisis. *Healthc Inform.* 2000;17(8):64–67.
8. Gibbs WW. Taking computers to task. *Sci Am.* 1997;277(1):82–89.
9. Langberg ML. Challenges to implementing CPOE: a case study of a work in progress at Cedars-Sinai. *Modern Physician.* 2003; February 1; 21.
10. Turner CF, Ku L, Rogers SM, Lindberg LD, Pleck JH, Sonenstein FL. Adolescent sexual behavior, drug use, and violence: increased reporting with computer survey technology. *Science.* 1998;280(5365):867–873.
11. Millstein SG, Irwin CE Jr. Acceptability of computer-acquired sexual histories in adolescent girls. *J Pediatr.* 1983;103(5):815–819.
12. Paperny DM, Aono JY, Lehman RM, Hammar SL, Risser J. Computer-assisted detection and intervention in adolescent high-risk health behaviors. *J Pediatr.* 1990;116(3):456–462.
13. Rosenfalck AM, Bendtson I. The Diva System, a computerized diary, used in young type 1 diabetic patients. *Diabetes Metab.* 1993;19(1):25–29.
14. Horan PP, Yarborough MC, Besigel G, Carlson DR. Computer-assisted self-control of diabetes by adolescents. *Diabetes Educ.* 1990;16(3):205–211.
15. Marrero DG, Kronz KK, Golden MP, Wright JC, Orr DP, Fineberg NS. Clinical evaluation of computer-assisted self-monitoring of blood glucose system. *Diabetes Care.* 1989;12(5):345–350.
16. Brown SJ, Lieberman DA, Germeny BA, Fan YC, Wilson DM, Pasta DJ. Educational video game for juvenile diabetes: results of a controlled trial. *Med Inform (Lond).* 1997;22(1):77–89.

17. Marrero DG, Vandagriff JL, Kronz K, et al. Using telecommunication technology to manage children with diabetes: the Computer-Linked Outpatient Clinic (CLOC) Study. *Diabetes Educ.* 1995;21(4):313–319.

18. Leys M. Health technology assessment: the contribution of qualitative research. *Int J Technol Assess Health Care.* 2003;19(2):317–329.

19. Ash JS, Sittig DF, Seshadri V, Dykstra RH, Carpenter JD, Stavri PZ. Adding insight: a qualitative cross-site study of physician order entry. *Int J Med Inform.* 2005;74(7–8):623–628.

20. May C, Harrison R, Finch T, MacFarlane A, Mair F, Wallace P. Understanding the normalization of telemedicine services through qualitative evaluation. *J Am Med Inform Assoc.* 2003;10(6):596–604.

21. HealthPia America. http://www.healthpia.us

22. Morgan DL. *Focus Groups as Qualitative Research.* Beverly Hills, CA: Sage Publications; 1988.

Acknowledgments: The authors thank the adolescents, their parents, and the physician offices that referred them to our study. We are especially grateful to the adolescents who were willing to share with us their experiences of living with diabetes so that we can better understand and provide care for them. We also thank Terri Matousek of Matousek and Associates for conducting all of the focus groups, and Heather Herdman, RN, PhD, for her assistance with data analysis.

Funding: This research was funded by grants from the NIH to AEC (1 K23 DK067879-01), and from Clarian Health Partners to AEC (VFR-190).

Address correspondence to: Aaron E. Carroll MD, MS, Riley Research 330, 699 West Drive, Indianapolis, IN 46202 E-mail: aaecarro@iupui.edu

Exercise for Article 25

Factual Questions

1. What was the total number of participants?

2. How much were the participants paid for their participation?

3. Were the proceedings of the focus groups tape recorded?

4. The study team consisted of a pediatrician, a social ecologist, and who else?

5. How many of the adolescents were African American?

6. How many of the parents had children between 13 and 14 years of age?

Questions for Discussion

7. Do you think it was a good idea to have the parents and adolescents meet separately? (See lines 107–108.)

8. Do you think the method of qualitative analysis is described in sufficient detail? (See lines 136–160.)

9. To what extent do the quotations from participants interspersed throughout the Results section help you understand the results of this study? (See lines 161–480.)

10. Do you think that the use of a small convenience sample greatly limits the generalizability of the results of this study? (See lines 519–522.)

11. Do you agree that the focus group methodology may have inhibited some participants from stating differing opinions? (See lines 522–524.)

12. If you were planning a follow-up study to explore the topic of this research further, would you plan an additional qualitative study or a quantitative study? Explain.

Quality Ratings

Directions: Indicate your level of agreement with each of the following statements by circling a number from 5 for strongly agree (SA) to 1 for strongly disagree (SD). If you believe an item is not applicable to this research article, leave it blank. Be prepared to explain your ratings. When responding to criteria A and B below, keep in mind that brief titles and abstracts are conventional in published research.

A. The title of the article is appropriate.

   SA   5   4   3   2   1   SD

B. The abstract provides an effective overview of the research article.

   SA   5   4   3   2   1   SD

C. The introduction establishes the importance of the study.

   SA   5   4   3   2   1   SD

D. The literature review establishes the context for the study.

   SA   5   4   3   2   1   SD

E. The research purpose, question, or hypothesis is clearly stated.

   SA   5   4   3   2   1   SD

F. The method of sampling is sound.

   SA   5   4   3   2   1   SD

G. Relevant demographics (for example, age, gender, and ethnicity) are described.

   SA   5   4   3   2   1   SD

H. Measurement procedures are adequate.

   SA   5   4   3   2   1   SD

I. All procedures have been described in sufficient detail to permit a replication of the study.

SA   5   4   3   2   1   SD

J. The participants have been adequately protected from potential harm.

SA   5   4   3   2   1   SD

K. The results are clearly described.

SA   5   4   3   2   1   SD

L. The discussion/conclusion is appropriate.

SA   5   4   3   2   1   SD

M. Despite any flaws, the report is worthy of publication.

SA   5   4   3   2   1   SD

Article 26

One Breath at a Time:
Living with Cystic Fibrosis

Dona Rinaldi Carpenter, EdD, RN, CS, **Georgia L. Narsavage**, PhD, RN, CS[*]

ABSTRACT

The purpose of this qualitative investigation was to describe the lived experiences of families caring for a child with cystic fibrosis at the time of initial diagnosis. Phenomenological research methodology as described by Colaizzi (1978) was used to guide the investigation. A purposive sample of 9 family members voluntarily participated in the study. Data were gathered through focus groups and written narratives.

Data analysis yielded 3 essential theme clusters with subthemes: *Falling Apart, Pulling Together,* and *Moving Beyond.* Within the theme of *Falling Apart,* the subthemes of Devastation of Diagnosis, An All-Encompassing Sense of Fear and Isolation, and An Overwhelming Sense of Guilt and Powerlessness are described. The theme of *Pulling Together* included the subthemes of Perpetual Vigilance and Returning to Normalcy, and the third theme of *Moving Beyond* included the subtheme of An Optimal Unfolding of a New Kind of Consciousness. This article describes in detail the themes and subthemes identified during data analysis and the fluid nature of the relationship that exists within the essential structure of caring for a family member with cystic fibrosis.

The diagnosis of cystic fibrosis most often comes as a life-shattering experience to families. Lifestyle readjustments are made in an attempt to return to some sense of family normalcy. In order to achieve stability in their daily lives, families are vigilant in the care and monitoring of the health of a child with cystic fibrosis. Ongoing support from health care professionals that is grounded in the realities of living with cystic fibrosis is critical. This study describes how families develop their own unique way of controlling the experience of living with cystic fibrosis, one day and one breath at a time.

From *Journal of Pediatric Nursing: Nursing Care of Children and Families, 19,* 25–32. Copyright © 2004 by Elsevier, Inc. Reprinted with permission.

Until recently, cystic fibrosis (CF) was classified as a terminal childhood disease. New information and treatment protocols have changed this perception. A short lifespan is no longer the norm for individuals
5 with CF (White, Munro, & Boyle, 1996). Advances in research along with newer treatment protocols have increased life expectancy (Fiel, 1993). Many patients with CF live high-quality lives well into adulthood, often into their 40s. With increased life expectancy,
10 patients and their families are given new hope that scientists will find a cure within their lifetimes.

Despite the multitude of research studies related to CF, the nature and essence of the family caregiving experience for a child with CF is not known. The pur-
15 pose of this qualitative research study was to describe the life experience of individuals caring for a family member with cystic fibrosis. A phenomenological approach to studying the caregiver experience provides a means to describe, in depth, the lived experience of
20 providing care for a child with CF. The research question guiding the study was, *"What is the lived experience of caring for a family member with cystic fibrosis?"*

Related Literature

CF is a genetic disease caused by mutations in a
25 single gene that encodes the cystic fibrosis transmembrane conductance regulator (Hopkins, 1996). Clinical manifestations of CF vary widely and are characterized by abnormal secretions of the respiratory, gastrointestinal, and reproductive tracts and the sweat
30 glands (Wilmott & Fiedler, 1994). The severity of the disease varies considerably as well. Some patients experience mild gastrointestinal or pulmonary problems, whereas others experience severe malabsorption problems and fatal pulmonary complications. The gastroin-
35 testinal manifestations of cystic fibrosis are not as typical of the disease as are the pulmonary complications, but family members must understand the potential impact of the disease on the child's overall growth and development (Duffield, 1996). After the discovery of
40 the CF gene in 1989, treatment for cystic fibrosis changed as research related to CF gathered momentum. Although a cure is still unavailable, scientists have made progress in identification and early treatment of exacerbations, thus extending life expectancy in this
45 often devastating illness.

[*]*Dona Rinaldi Carpenter* currently teaches medical–surgical nursing as well as undergraduate and graduate research for the Department of Nursing, University of Scranton. *Georgia L. Narsavage* is associate professor of nursing; associate dean of academic programs; and director, ND program; Frances Payne Bolton School of Nursing, Case Western Reserve University.

Most patients with CF live at home and incorporate a variety of treatments into their daily lives. Family members are most often the primary caregivers, and they interact with providers from multiple disciplines as episodic care is needed (Reed, 1990; Sawyer, 1992; Tracy, 1997). Treatment generally focuses on control of symptoms using regimens of physiotherapy to loosen secretions, medications to prevent and cure infections, and enzymes as nutritional supplements for support of gastrointestinal functioning (Fiel, 1993; Hopkins, 1995). New approaches to treatment are being developed, but until a cure is achieved, pulmonary infection and inflammation that lead to respiratory failure and premature death remain the focus of therapy.

Living with CF involves changes in identities, roles, relationship abilities, and patterns of behavior for all family members (Brown & Powell-Cope, 1991). Routine therapies that are required of the CF family are rigorous, complex, and time consuming. Dealing with complex drug and therapy regimens at home can prove to be very stressful for parents and other family members. Helping families understand the purpose and effective implementation of therapies as well as what to expect when living with a family member who has a chronic disease can be effective in helping them cope with the situation.

Clearly, the medical aspects of CF and the effectiveness of medications used to manage the disease have been studied extensively using quantitative methodology (Hopkins, 1996). However, quantitative studies are, by their very nature, restricted to examining a limited number of variables. There are relatively few qualitative research studies on family care giving related to cystic fibrosis that can provide a window into the experience of living with this extremely complex multivariate disease.

What is known is that the routine stresses in caring for a child with CF can become overwhelming for everyone in the family (Eiser, Zprotch, Hiller, Havermans, & Billig, 1995). A Scottish ethnographic study of 4 families living with family members who had CF described the crisis experience and the continuing care burden. The emotional devastation felt was placed within the context of needing to share the experience with other families in an attempt to make lifestyle adjustments (Whyte, 1992). Baine, Rosenbaum, and King (1995) surveyed families living with a child with a chronic illness (diabetes or CF). The researchers identified knowing about the illness, what to expect, continuity and accessibility of care, and involvement of the family in care as being the highest priority in terms of family preparatory needs. The sense of fear and isolation expressed by the participants in a study by Baine et al. (1995) was further described in a 22-week telephone support intervention study that improved life quality for parents of children with CF (Ritchie et al., 2000). Geiss et al. (1992) described a significant relationship between perceived compliance with CF treat-

ment and the mother's decreased social contacts. Mothers of children with chronic illness experienced stressful interactions with partners and professionals as they tried to manage the child's disease and keep daily life as "normal" as possible (Stewart, Ritchie, McGrath, Thompson, & Bruce, 1994). Similarly, D'Auria, Christian, and Richardson (1997), in a grounded theory study of 20 children living with CF, found that "keeping up" or leading as normal a life as possible was a theme central to the experience of those in middle childhood. Siblings of children with CF reported being worried, jealous, and frustrated as activities were restricted for everyone in the family, and conversely, they noted "positive" outcomes of the impact of CF on the family—strengthened relationships, enhanced independence, and feelings of satisfaction as the child with CF improves (Derouin & Jessee, 1996). Coping with stress can be both positive and negative.

Interventions that can assist families in coping with the stress of CF have also been studied. Ryan and Williams (1996), describing the use of a cystic fibrosis handbook shared by parents with the children's teachers, found that this written information could enhance knowledge of the disease, support communication to overcome the sense of powerlessness that parents experience, and help the child return to a less abnormal school experience. Additionally, a pilot intervention study (Williams et al., 1997) for 22 siblings of children with CF, cancer, diabetes, and spina bifida found that an educational intervention could increase knowledge about the chronic illness, but support sessions were equally as important to the intervention. Bartholomew et al. (1997) used a CF Family Education Program intervention for 104 families and compared it with 94 "usual care" families living with CF. Knowledge and self-efficacy scores had a significant interaction effect on short-term disease management outcomes for both caregivers and children with CF.

Although the research on identified stressors and interventions is valuable in understanding coping in families who have lived with CF for extended periods of time, these studies do not explain experiences of living with a family member who has CF at the time of diagnosis. Relating the pathophysiology of the diagnosis to the coping issues, Reed (1990) has proposed possible family responses to a diagnosis of CF from a theoretical perspective. Reed (1990) described the potential for "altered family process" as families learn to live with the need to recognize problems and assist the child in a timely manner. Nevertheless, this theoretical approach to the family experience when the diagnosis is first known has not been tested or developed from a real-world perspective.

In summary, there is a large body of quantitative research related to the medical aspects surrounding the care of individuals with CF. Understanding the perspective of families caring for a child with CF at the time of diagnosis has not been studied. Qualitative research approaches are best suited to describing the phenomena of living with and adapting to CF at this critical point in time.

Method

165   The study design was descriptive and grounded in phenomenological research methodology. The anticipated outcome was to describe the essential information needed by individuals with family members who have cystic fibrosis by developing rich descriptions of
170   the life experiences of families caring for a child with cystic fibrosis. Families who are actively involved in the caring process were sought as an expert source of how to live with and care for a child with CF.

Sample

A purposive sample of 9 family members voluntar-
175   ily participated in data collection. Participants were selected based on their first-hand experience with the phenomenon of interest to allow for development of rich descriptions of the life experiences of families caring for a child with cystic fibrosis. Family members
180   involved in support groups for children with cystic fibrosis from 3 metropolitan areas participated in the study. Institutional review board (IRB) approval was obtained.

Procedures for Generation and Treatment of Data

Although the researchers intended to collect all data
185   using focus group technique, only 3 family members agreeing to participate in the study were able to attend a focus group. Parents caring for children with CF expressed great interest in participating in the research; however, family caregiving responsibilities left little
190   time for any activity that required time away from home. Therefore, the remaining 6 participants contributed to the study via written narratives. Detailed written responses to the same open-ended questions used with the focus groups were completed, providing com-
195   parable data to that collected in the focus group.

Anderson and Hatton (2000) noted that time and energy are limited in vulnerable populations, such as families living with illness. Sensitivity to issues of vulnerability is critical, and in this particular instance, data
200   collection methods required modification. Responding to the questions used for the first focus group provided an opportunity for parents to participate without leaving their family. Participants completing written narratives were asked to write in as much detail as possible
205   to ensure full and rich descriptions.

IRB approval for the study was obtained from the University of Scranton, and written informed consent for participation and audiotaping was obtained from all participants. The focus group was conducted using a
210   semi-structured interview process, and it took place in a seminar setting suitable for audiotaping. Consent forms were distributed along with a brief demographic data sheet and questionnaire. The moderator (first author) used an interview guide (see Table 1) consisting

215   of open-ended questions. Questions for the interview were generated in advance to guide and elicit rich descriptions of the experience of caring for a child with cystic fibrosis. The focus group was audiotaped and transcribed verbatim by a department assistant. De-
220   tailed field notes were kept as well by the second researcher/author. Upon conclusion of the interview, participants were encouraged to contact the researchers by phone or in writing if additional information relevant to the study became evident.

Table 1
Questions Guiding Data Collection

1. What comes to mind when you hear the words cystic fibrosis?
2. What is the meaning of caring for someone with cystic fibrosis?
3. What aspects of care have proven to be most beneficial?
4. What aspects of care have you found most manageable?
5. What do you wish you had been told when you first had to care for your child at home?
6. What additional problems have occurred that you have had to deal with at home?
7. If you were to give another person a video to help them, what information do you think it should include?

225   Participants who responded in narrative format were requested to answer the same questions used to guide the focus group, to write in as much detail as possible, and to continue writing until no new ideas came to mind. The first author contacted participants
230   by phone to clarify questions that emerged from the written narratives. Data were gathered until no new themes emerged and significant repetition of themes reflecting data saturation was established.

Data were generated and analyzed from a phe-
235   nomenological perspective using the procedures identified by Colaizzi (1978). The steps used to guide this were (1) describe the phenomenon of interest; (2) collect participants' description of the phenomena through the use of focus groups and narrative written responses;
240   (3) transcribe audiotaped interviews and written narratives; (4) return to the original transcripts and extract significant statements; (5) describe the meaning of each significant statement; (6) organize the aggregate formalized meanings into clusters of themes; (7) write an
245   exhaustive description; (8) return the exhaustive description to the subjects for validation; and (9) incorporate new data revealed during the validation into an exhaustive description.

The transcripts from the focus group and written
250   narratives were read and reread in their entirety by the first author. Significant statements related to families' experiences caring for a child with cystic fibrosis were extracted, followed by description of the formulated meaning. Clusters of themes were organized from ag-

Table 2
Selected Examples of Significant Statements and Corresponding Formulated Meanings

Significant statement	Formulated meaning
Theme cluster: "Falling Apart"	
…it's really overwhelming when you first find out your child has cystic fibrosis.	The diagnosis of CF is a life-shattering experience.
…it is easy to fall apart very quickly.	The experience is so devastating the presentation of new and un-familiar stressors can result in a very sudden sense of losing control over what one knows as normal or routine.
…when you are initially diagnosed, you think that this only hap-pened to you.	The diagnosis of CF brings with it a sense of isolation.
…we were afraid to leave the house…afraid we might go around someone that might have an infection or a cold.	Fear directs life choices immediately following diagnosis.
…to do percussions on 2 children two to three times a day is sometimes physically impossible.	Fitting everything that is required into each day is sometimes unre-alistic, yet parents feel guilty and experience a sense of power-lessness.
Theme cluster: "Pulling Together"	
…how do you put it all together to make a life that makes sense?	Living with CF means putting the requirements of care for a child with CF together with the requirements of daily living.
…we tried to get CF to be part of the fabric of our lives.	CF becomes a part of everything in the lives of the patient and family.
…your whole life changes to make living with CF manageable. It changes because it has to change.	Lifestyle adaptations are ongoing and in response to new stressors as they present themselves. Continuous adaptation is required to promote and maintain health.
Theme cluster: "Moving Beyond"	
…live for now and focus on the present.	Living with CF requires patients and families to live in the moment and hope for a cure.
…we remain conscious of everything we do.	Remain tuned in to CF at all times.

gregated formulated meanings. Table 2 depicts exam-
255 ples of significant statements and corresponding formulated meanings. Original raw data from the transcripts and narratives were examined for each theme
cluster. The researchers then integrated results, and an
260 exhaustive description was prepared describing the life
experience of families caring for a child with cystic
fibrosis.

Authenticity and Trustworthiness of Data

Techniques to enhance the rigor of this work as described by Guba and Lincoln (1994) include credibil-
265 ity, dependability, confirmability, and transferability.
These evaluative criteria for qualitative research have
been discussed at length in the literature (Beck, 1993;
Guba & Lincoln, 1985, 1994; Sandelowski, 1986;
Yonge and Stewin, 1988).

270 Participants reviewed the final exhaustive description to verify that it was representative and true to their
life experiences. Dependability and credibility do not
occur in isolation. Results are considered dependable if
they are found to be credible. Participants reported to
275 the researchers that they recognized the exhaustive
description as being true to their life experiences, thus
establishing credibility and dependability. Confirmability was achieved through the use of an audit trail and
review of raw data by the second researcher. Transfer-
280 ability or fittingness refers to the probability that the
study findings have meaning to others in similar situa-

tions (Streubert, 2003). This criterion will be evaluated
through additional research.

Results

Learning that a child has cystic fibrosis is an all-
285 encompassing, life-shattering experience that requires a
continuous series of family adjustments as unfamiliar
stressors present themselves. Data analysis revealed 3
essential theme clusters or stages related to the diagnosis of cystic fibrosis within a family. The 3 main theme
290 clusters were *Falling Apart*, *Pulling Together*, and
Moving Beyond. Subthemes were identified as being
connected to the 3 essential theme clusters. A detailed
discussion of the relationships among the essential
themes and subthemes follows. Relationships among
295 the major themes and subthemes are illustrated in Figure 1.

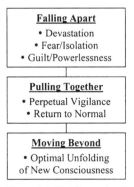

Figure 1. Initial diagnosis of cystic fibrosis.

Once a family learns that a child has cystic fibrosis, there is a sense of *Falling Apart* within the context of
300 what the family has always known to be their normal or routine lifestyle. Within this theme, there were 3 subthemes: *The Devastation of Diagnosis, An All-Encompassing Sense of Fear and Isolation*, and *An Overwhelming Sense of Guilt and Powerlessness*. The
305 initial diagnosis of CF was described as a life-shattering experience. Parents reported feeling that their life had fallen apart and that what had been routine or normal was forever changed. Parents, family members, and friends were devastated by the diagnosis,
310 setting in motion a continuous series of family adjustments in response to new and unfamiliar stressors. One parent stated, "In the beginning we were completely devastated…every single day you face the fact that this is not going to change…not tomorrow, or the next day,
315 or the next year." Further, families felt afraid. They experienced a sense of isolation and became overwhelmed with feelings of guilt and powerlessness. These emotions were reflected in one parent's comment: "When you first learn that your child has cystic
320 fibrosis, they tell you all the negative information so that even when your child is doing well, there is always a cloud." Another parent similarly noted: "The hardest part is all the negativeness. I don't think the actual physical care was ever really a concern…it was the
325 emotional aspect that seemed more important to us."

This first theme cluster or stage of *Falling Apart* is followed by a sense of *Pulling Together* as a family makes the necessary lifestyle adjustments required to care for the child with CF and to return to a routine that
330 brings with it some sense of family normalcy. Subthemes of this second theme or stage include the need for *Perpetual Vigilance* and developing *Lifestyle Adaptations That Bring a Sense of Normalcy*. Moving to the stage of pulling together requires families to be per-
335 petually vigilant in caring for the child with CF, keeping daily routines, finding ways to do things better or more efficiently, and constantly adjusting and adapting to new and different stressors as they present themselves. One participant said, "Everything with CF be-
340 comes manageable, simply because it is a requirement to getting and staying healthy. Your entire lifestyle has to change, and you make many sacrifices. You continually try to get CF to be part of the fabric of your life." Identifying lifestyle adaptations that bring a sense
345 of normalcy is also critical as families "pull together." Comments from this participant reflect the need to regain control and some sense of normalcy: "You must become really well-educated and informed. Get a basic routine…and be consistent. Being consistent helps the
350 child realize that this is going to be a way of life, for the rest of their life."

Moving Beyond is the third essential theme or stage and includes the subtheme of an *Optimal Unfolding of a New Kind of Consciousness*. Within this stage, fami-
355 lies move beyond the fear, beyond the guilt, and be-

yond the sense of powerlessness. Identification of new ways of coping facilitates achievement of a positive view and sense of control or normalcy. As one partici-pant noted, "You live for now, focus on the present,
360 and realize that missing one treatment won't kill anyone." To "move beyond," patients and families find new ways to cope and new ways to be in life that are reflective of living a life that holds an optimal level of quality. One participant vividly describes the final
365 theme cluster of moving beyond in the following comment: "All of this living helps me to believe that CF won't stop me from my dreams. I am learning to take life one breath at a time, living for today, trying not to worry about tomorrow, and looking to God for
370 strength and guidance."

Although the 3 essential themes are presented as separate entities, families describe a process where they move back and forth through the 3 stages. When and how they move among these stages of adjustment
375 seems to be directly influenced by how the child is doing in terms of health and well-being. For example, a family that has adjusted and "*Moved Beyond*" might be thrown very quickly back to the stage of "*Falling Apart*" should the child have a serious setback related
380 to his or her health. Or perhaps new treatments or medication might require a return to "*Pulling Together*" as lifestyle is once again readjusted in an attempt to achieve a state of family normalcy.

Discussion

The experience of families caring for a child with
385 cystic fibrosis involves the fluid nature of 3 essential themes or stages related to (a) *Falling Apart*, (b) *Pulling Together*, and (c) *Moving Beyond*. The themes, as well as subthemes, are consistent with Reed's theory (1990) and research in the area of chronic illness in
390 children and adults as well as family responses to living with a child with a chronic, life-threatening disease. For example, the themes can be identified in clinical case findings that examine the benefits and burdens of those living with chronic genetic diseases such as CF
395 (Geller, 1995). Geller concludes that quality of life for CF children will depend both on the severity of their disease and the ongoing care and attention they receive. Nurses in research and practice need to understand patient and families' experiences and to use their ex-
400 pert voice to assist families in providing the needed care and attention.

Published research can also be related to the theme and associated subthemes of Falling Apart. The *Devastation of the Diagnosis* has been reported in other
405 chronic childhood diseases, such as asthma (Englund, Rydstrom, & Norberg, 2001). The *Sense of Fear and Isolation* was described by participants in the telephone support intervention study (Ritchie et al., 2000). *Powerlessness* has been described by mothers of children
410 with chronic illness as stressful interactions with partners and professionals (Stewart et al., 1994).

178

The *Perpetual Vigilance* theme was identified as a component of the use of the cystic fibrosis handbook that parents shared with the children's teachers (Ryan & Williams, 1996). Adaptation that *Brings a Sense of Normalcy* was reported by D'Auria, Christian, and Richardson (1997) in their grounded theory study of 20 children living with CF, wherein leading as normal a life as possible was a theme central to the experience of those in middle childhood.

In the third theme of *Moving Beyond*, the subtheme of *An Optimal Unfolding of a New Kind of Consciousness* emerged. Tracy (1997) described similar aspects of the experience of growing up with CF in qualitative interviews with 10 adults. This study provided support for the theme of "faith" as a new consciousness of the meaning of living with chronic illness. *Moving Beyond* could also be argued as increasing self-efficacy of the family and its members seen in the CF Family Education Program comparative study (Bartholomew et al., 1997). The ability of families to move beyond the experience of devastation was seen as caregivers and children with CF worked together to optimize their lives.

Clinical implications can be derived from the descriptions of families living with CF. Detailed descriptions of their experiences provide recognition of the dynamic nature of CF and the vigilance required to attain a sense of family normalcy and to promote and maintain optimal health.

The qualitative data gathered in this study reflect the physical and emotional roller coaster that parents and families experience when caring for a child with cystic fibrosis. At the time of initial diagnosis, parents clearly need information on how to care for their child. The physical aspects of care, however, seem to be less of a concern at the time of initial diagnosis than the emotional aspects. Helping parents and patients develop a sense of control, and a belief that the ride will not always be bumpy, is a key component to care at the time of initial diagnosis.

Additional research is needed to examine how patients and families cope with cystic fibrosis over the long term. Adults living with cystic fibrosis face new challenges, such as issues surrounding marriage and childbirth. Studies addressing the transition to adulthood and the life experience of adults with cystic fibrosis can add significant information to the research literature and will be important as more and more individuals with cystic fibrosis live longer lives. Understanding the life experiences of family members caring for a child with CF will provide the empirical underpinnings for appropriate clinical interventions.

References

Anderson, D. G., & Hatton, D. C. (2000). Accessing vulnerable populations for research. *Western Journal of Nursing Research, 22*, 244–251.

Baine, S., Rosenbaum, P., & King, S. (1995). Chronic childhood illnesses: What aspects of caregiving do parents value? *Child: Care Health and Development, 21*, 291–304.

Bartholomew, L. K., Vzyzewski, D. I., Parcel, G. S., Swank, P. R., Sockrider, M. M., Mariotto, M. J., Schidlow, D. V., Fink, R. H., & Seilheimer, D. K. (1997). Self-management of cystic fibrosis: Short-term outcomes of the Cystic Fibrosis Family Education Program. *Health Education and Behavior, 24*, 652–666.

Beck, C. T. (1993). Qualitative research: The evaluation of its credibility, fittingness, and audit ability. *Western Journal of Nursing Research, 15*, 263–265.

Brown, M. A., & Powell-Cope, G. M. (1991). AIDS family caregiving: Transitions through uncertainty. *Nursing Research, 40*, 338–345.

CF Foundation. (1998). Pseudomonas Genome Project. Available at: http:///www.pseudomonas.com/cystic-fibrosis.html, Accessed.

Colaizzi, P. F. (1978). Psychological research as the phenomenologist views it. In R. Valle & M. Kings (Eds.), *Existential phenomenological alternatives for psychology*. New York: Oxford University Press.

Cystic Fibrosis. (1997). NIH Publication 97-4200. Bethesda, Maryland. Available at: http://www.esiason.org

D'Auria, J. P., Christian, B. J., & Richardson, L. F. (1997). Through the looking glass: Children's perceptions of growing up with cystic fibrosis. *Canadian Journal of Nursing Research, 29*, 99–122.

Derouin, D., & Jessee, P. O. (1996). Impact of chronic illness in childhood: Siblings' perceptions. *Issues in Comprehensive Pediatric Nursing, 19*, 135–147.

Duffield, R. A. (1996). Cystic fibrosis and the gastrointestinal tract. *Journal of Pediatric Health Care, 10*, 51–57.

Eiser, C., Zprotch, B., Hiller, J., Havermans, T., & Billig, S. (1995). Routine stresses in caring for a child with cystic fibrosis. *Journal of Psychosomatic Research, 39*, 641–646.

Englund, A. D., Rydstrom, I., & Norberg, A. (2001). Being the parent of a child with asthma. *Pediatric Nursing, 27*, 365–373.

Fiel, S. B. (1993). Clinical management of pulmonary disease in cystic fibrosis. *Lancet, 341*, 1070–1074.

Geiss, S. K., Hobbs, S. A., Hammersley-Maercklein, G., Kramer, J. C., & Henley, M. (1992). Psychosocial factors related to perceived compliance with cystic fibrosis treatment. *Journal of Clinical Psychology, 48*, 99–103.

Geller, G. (1995). Cystic fibrosis and the pediatric caregiver: Benefits and burdens of genetic technology. *Pediatric Nursing, 21*, 57–61.

Guba, E. G., & Lincoln, Y. S. (1994). Competing paradigms in qualitative research. In N. K. Denzin & Y. S. Lincoln (Eds.), *Handbook of qualitative research* (pp. 105–117). Thousand Oaks, CA: Sage.

Hopkins, S. (1995). Advances in the treatment of cystic fibrosis. *Nursing Times, 91*, 40–41.

Hopkins, K. (1996). Cystic fibrosis: Approaching treatment from multiple directions. *The Journal of NIH Research, 8*, 40–43.

Lincoln, Y. S., & Guba, E. G. (1985). *Naturalistic inquiry*. Beverly Hills, CA: Sage.

Myers, M. F., Bernhardt, B. A., Tamoor, E. S., & Holtzman, N. A. (1994). Involving consumers in the development of an educational program for cystic fibrosis carrier screening. *American Journal of Human Genetics, 54*, 719–726.

Pickler, R. H., & Munro, C. L. (1995). Gene therapy for inherited disorders. *Journal of Pediatric Nursing: Nursing Care of Children and Families, 10*, 40–47.

Reed, S. B. (1990). Potential for alterations in family process: When a family has a child with cystic fibrosis. *Issues in Comprehensive Pediatric Nursing, 13*, 15–23.

Ritchie, J., Stewart, M., Ellerton, M., Thompsons, D., Meade, D., & Viscount. P. W. (2000). Parents' perceptions of the impact of a telephone support group intervention. *Journal of Family Nursing, 6*, 25–45.

Ryan, L. L., & Williams, J. K. (1996). A cystic fibrosis handbook for teachers. *Journal of Pediatric Nursing, 7*, 304–311.

Sandelowski, M. (1986). The problem of rigor in qualitative research. *Advances in Nursing Science, 8*, 27–37.

Sawyer, E. H. (1992). Family functioning when children have cystic fibrosis. *Journal of Pediatric Nursing, 7*, 304–311.

Stewart, M. J., Ritchie, J. A., McGrath, P., Thompson, D., & Bruce, B. (1994). Mothers of children with chronic conditions: Supportive and stressful interactions with partners and professionals regarding caregiving burdens. *Canadian Journal of Nursing Research, 26*, 61–82.

Streubert, H. J. (2003). The conduct of qualitative research: Common essential themes. In Streubert H. J. Carpenter D. R. (Eds.) *Qualitative research in nursing: Advancing the humanistic imperative* (3rd ed.). Philadelphia: Lippincott Williams & Wilkins.

Tracy, J. P. (1997). Growing up with chronic illness: The experience of growing up with cystic fibrosis. *Holistic Nursing Practice, 12*, 27–35.

White, K. R., Munro, C. L., & Boyle, A. H. (1996). Nursing management of adults who have cystic fibrosis. *MedSurg Nursing, 5*, 163–167.

Whyte, D. A. (1992). A family nursing approach to the care of a child with a chronic illness. *Journal of Advanced Nursing, 17*, 317–327.

Williams, J. L. (1995). Genetics and cystic fibrosis: a focus on carrier testing. *Pediatric Nursing, 21*, 444–448.

Williams, P. D., Hanson, S., Karlin, R., Ridder, L., Liebergrn, A., Olson, J., Barnard, M. U., & Tobin-Rommerlhart, S. (1997). Outcomes of a nursing intervention for siblings of chronically ill children: A pilot study. *Journal of the Society of Pediatric Nurses, 2,* 127–137.

Wilmott, R. W., & Fiedler, M. A. (1994). Recent advances in the treatment of cystic fibrosis. *Pediatric Clinics of North America, 41,* 431–451.

Yonge, O., & Stewin, L. (1988). Reliability and validity: Misnomers for qualitative research. *The Canadian Journal of Nursing Research, 20,* 61–67.

Acknowledgments: The authors wish to thank Mary Harvey, MSW, for her assistance contacting participants, and Dr. John Sanko, University of Scranton, for his work on the project. An internal research grant from the University of Scranton, Panuska College of Professional Studies, and a grant from The Edward R. Leahy Jr. Center for Faculty Research and Development provided additional support.

Address correspondence to: Dona Rinaldi Carpenter, EdD, RN, CS, Department of Nursing, University of Scranton, Scranton, PA 18510-4595. E-mail: carpenterd1@tiger.uofs.edu

Exercise for Article 26

Factual Questions

1. What is the research question that guided this study?

2. Have any of the research studies discussed in the related literature section of this article explained experiences of living with a family member who has CF at the time of diagnosis?

3. The family members who participated in this study were drawn from how many metropolitan areas?

4. How many of the participants in this study were not able to attend a focus group?

5. How did the first author contact participants to clarify questions that emerged from the written narratives?

6. Participants reviewed the final exhaustive description to verify what?

Questions for Discussion

7. The researchers state that "Qualitative research approaches are best suited to describing the phenomena of living with and adapting to CF at this critical point in time." If you had planned to study the topic of this research, would you have planned to conduct qualitative research *or* quantitative research? Explain. (See lines 161–164.)

8. The researchers state that the study design was grounded in "phenomenological research methodology." If you have a research methods textbook, examine it to see if "phenomenological research" is covered. If so, how is it defined in the textbook? How is "phenomenology" defined in a dictionary? (See lines 165–166.)

9. The researchers state that they used a "purposive sample." What is your understanding of the meaning of this term? (See lines 174–175.)

10. Some of the data for this study were collected through focus group discussions and some were collected by having participants provide written answers to open-ended questions. In your opinion, are both methods equally good for collecting the type of data needed for this study? Explain. (See lines 184–195.)

11. How important are the "significant statements" (i.e., quotations) in Table 2 in helping you understand the results of this study?

12. The main analysis was conducted by the first author of this study. How important is it to know that the raw data were reviewed by the second author? Would it have been sufficient to have the data examined by only one researcher? Explain. (See lines 277–279.)

Quality Ratings

Directions: Indicate your level of agreement with each of the following statements by circling a number from 5 for strongly agree (SA) to 1 for strongly disagree (SD). If you believe an item is not applicable to this research article, leave it blank. Be prepared to explain your ratings. When responding to criteria A and B below, keep in mind that brief titles and abstracts are conventional in published research.

A. The title of the article is appropriate.

   SA   5   4   3   2   1   SD

B. The abstract provides an effective overview of the research article.

   SA   5   4   3   2   1   SD

C. The introduction establishes the importance of the study.

   SA   5   4   3   2   1   SD

D. The literature review establishes the context for the study.

   SA   5   4   3   2   1   SD

E. The research purpose, question, or hypothesis is clearly stated.

   SA   5   4   3   2   1   SD

F. The method of sampling is sound.

   SA   5   4   3   2   1   SD

G. Relevant demographics (for example, age, gender, and ethnicity) are described.

SA   5   4   3   2   1   SD

H. Measurement procedures are adequate.

SA   5   4   3   2   1   SD

I. All procedures have been described in sufficient detail to permit a replication of the study.

SA   5   4   3   2   1   SD

J. The participants have been adequately protected from potential harm.

SA   5   4   3   2   1   SD

K. The results are clearly described.

SA   5   4   3   2   1   SD

L. The discussion/conclusion is appropriate.

SA   5   4   3   2   1   SD

M. Despite any flaws, the report is worthy of publication.

SA   5   4   3   2   1   SD

Article 27

Nurses As Imperfect Role Models
for Health Promotion

Kathy L. Rush, RN, PhD, **Carolyn C. Kee**, RN, PhD, **Marti Rice**, RN, PhD[*]

ABSTRACT. The purpose of this qualitative study was to discover ways in which nurses describe themselves as health-promoting role models. Focus groups and individual interviews were conducted with nurses working in a variety of settings. Transcribed interviews were analyzed thematically. Nurses defined themselves as role models of health promotion according to the meaning they gave the term, their perceptions of societal expectations, and their self-constructed personal and professional domains. The term role model evoked diverse interpretations ranging from negative perceptions of the idealized image to a humanized, authentic representation. Nurses perceived that society expected them as role models to be informational resources and to practice what they preached. Nurses defined themselves independently of societal expectations according to personal and professional domains. Valuing health, accepting imperfections, and self-reflecting were aspects of the personal domain, whereas gaining trust, caring, and partnering were facets of the professional domain.

From *Western Journal of Nursing Research, 27*, 166–183. Copyright © 2004 by Sage Publications, Inc. Reprinted with permission.

With health promotion at the forefront of health care, the teaching role of the nurse is more important than ever. The credibility of nurses as health educators is linked to the expectation that they model healthy
5   behaviors, and their effectiveness as role models is judged on the basis of observable compliance with these behaviors. Using observable indicators of healthy behaviors as a gauge for determining whether nurses are adequate role models may have negative repercus-
10   sions. When nurses feel that they do not meet health-promotion role model standards, health teaching may be compromised. For example, nursing students and graduate nurses who never or only occasionally engaged in teaching patients health-promotion practices
15   were found to have low participation rates in self-breast examination, seat belt usage, and daily exercise (Valentine & Hadeka, 1986).

The concept of health promotion has shifted from a sole focus on the influence of personal lifestyle prac-
20   tices on health to encompass the effects of economic, social, and political forces on health. The notion of using personal healthy lifestyle behaviors, the primary basis for determining effectiveness as a role model of health promotion, however, persists. The degree to
25   which this expanded conception of health determinants affects the ways in which nurses regard themselves as role models for health promotion is not known. Very few studies were found that focused on nurses and role modeling activities for health promotion.

An Abbreviated History of
Health Promotion in Nursing

30   The evolution of health promotion in nursing has paralleled the historical development of the concept of health promotion. At one time, nursing was at the forefront of the public health movement with pioneers like Lillian Wald instituting major changes. Ms. Wald de-
35   veloped the Henry Street Settlement in response to the need for a healthier community and went on to influence legislation and policy to forge broad health-promotion initiatives (Baldwin, 1995). With the advent of the biomedical model, the early beginnings of nurs-
40   ing in health promotion were redirected from community determinants of health to individual lifestyle practices. More recently, nursing has begun to reincorporate the idea that healthy individual behaviors are a function of interpersonal and societal factors as well as
45   personal ones.

Conceptualizations of the
Health-Promoting Role Model

Conceptions from the Empirical Literature

The narrow *healthy lifestyle* conception has been perpetuated in the few research studies that have examined nurses as role models for health promotion (Callaghan, Kuk Fun, & Ching Yee, 1997; Connolly, Gulanick, Keough, & Holm, 1997; Haughey, Mathewson-
50   Kuhn, & Dittmar, 1992). In these studies, inferences about nurses as role models for health promotion have

[*] *Kathy L. Rush* is professor, Mary Black School of Nursing, University of South Carolina Upstate. *Carolyn C. Kee* is professor and associate dean, Byrdine F. Lewis School of Nursing, Georgia State University. *Marti Rice* is associate professor, Graduate Studies, School of Nursing, University of Alabama at Birmingham.

been based solely on whether they practice outwardly observable healthy behaviors. Nurses' views of themselves have been consistent with this conceptualization. One study reported that critical care nurses felt optimistic about being role models for patients, and 70% would recommend their lifestyle to patients "because they watch their weight, eat well enough, and think that they set a good example" (Connolly et al., 1997, p. 264). Support for an expanded conceptualization of what a role model for health promotion should be appeared in only one study. Dalton and Swenson (1986) found that in addition to practicing good health measures themselves, nurses believed role models should also teach health behaviors effectively, be knowledgeable, provide good nursing care, and be a practicing nurse.

Conceptions from the Theoretical Literature

Expanded conceptions of health-promotion role models have appeared in the theoretical literature. These alternative conceptions challenge the prevailing, narrow, healthy-lifestyle definition of the health-promotion role model. Scott (1996) commented that mandating standardized behaviors in the name of professionalism is a violation of personal freedoms and rights. Curtin (1986) rejected the position that nurses have a responsibility to be role models, because aggressive, condemning, and arrogant attitudes and approaches to patients may result. The need for health professionals to be facilitators of informed decision making and motivators of behavior change through use of their own flaws rather than being perfect role models has also been noted (Gobble & Mullen, 1983; Mitic, 1981). Clarke (1991) suggested that a subjective, personal dimension that gives attention to who the nurse is rather than what she or he does is important for role modeling health promotion. An interpersonal dimension has also been presented in the literature (Robinson & Hill, 1998). The role model for health promotion has been further defined in terms of empowerment and social-political activism (Tones, 1992; Williams, 1993).

Purpose

The purpose of this exploratory study was to discover how nurses define and describe themselves and other nurses as role models for health promotion. Understanding how nurses conceptualize themselves as role models for health promotion is a beginning step in maximizing their influence with clients in the promotion of health.

Design

To elicit nurses' views and perspectives about themselves and other nurses as role models for health promotion, a qualitative, descriptive design was chosen for the study. The use of such a design allowed for maximum-variation sampling and in-depth, semistructured interviews.

Sample

Maximum-variation sampling was used in this exploratory study so that diverse views on role modeling could be obtained (Kuzel, 1992; Maykut & Morehouse, 1994). Thus, the sample consisted of registered nurses (RNs) working in a variety of professional positions in Eastern Canada. Nurse educators and nurses working in community health clinics and traditional institutional settings such as acute and rehabilitation settings, public health regions, and the federal government were invited to participate because of their educational and practice experiences in health promotion.

To assess nurses' perceptions of the role model for health promotion, two focus-group discussions and four individual interviews were conducted. Focus-group participants were sought from (a) nurse educators involved in the professional socialization of nursing students who might be expected to be role models for health promotion and (b) nurses working in community health clinics who were actively involved in health teaching and promotion. Nurse educators from the subsidiary branch of a school of nursing affiliated with one of the province's major universities were invited to participate. The school offered a bachelor of science in nursing program, and all faculty members working in the program were invited to participate. This off-campus site was selected because the pool of faculty represented variability in terms of gender, age, clinical practice expertise, and years of experience in nursing education. Nurse educators were recruited for the focus groups directly by the researcher through electronic mail communication using an information letter explaining the purposes and procedures involved. Those interested in participating were asked to respond to the researcher by e-mail.

Nurses working in community health clinics were recruited for the focus groups through a regional clinical nurse specialist (CNS) who served as the gatekeeper for accessing this population. The regional CNS served as a liaison, manager, supporter, consultant, and coordinator for the widely dispersed, community health clinic nurses in her rural health region. The CNS distributed an information letter to potential nurse participants who were asked to e-mail or telephone the lead researcher if they were interested in participating.

Individuals participating in the individual interviews were handpicked for their direct but differing involvement in health promotion. This was done to add variability in practice experience and different insights into the concept of nurses as health-promotion role models. A total of 11 nurses participated in the two focus groups, and 4 nurses participated in the individual interviews. All were women with at least 2 years of experience in health care. A description of the sample appears in Table 1.

Table 1
Description of Sample

	Focus group (N = 11)	Individual interview (N = 4)
Gender		
Male	0	0
Female	11	4
Nursing education		
Diploma/associate's	5	1
Bachelor's	6	2
Master's	0	1
Nursing experience		
2 to 5 years	0	1
6 to 10 years	0	1
10 to 15 years	2	1
16 to 20 years	3	1
21 to 25 years	6	0
Focus groups		
Nurse educators	6	—
Nurses in community health clinics	5	—
Individual interviews		
Policy development consultant	—	1
Public health nurse educator	—	1
Rehabilitation nurse	—	1
Mental health nurse	—	1

Method

160   Approval to conduct the study was obtained from a university institutional review board. Two sessions of approximately 1 to 1.5 hours were held with the focus groups. Focus-group discussions with the nurse educa-tor group took place in a classroom at the school of

165 nursing where the nurse educators were employed. The first focus-group discussion with nurses from the community clinics took place in a conference room at a centrally located regional health office. The second group discussion took place by teleconference from

170 one of the local community clinics.

Initially, only focus-group discussions were planned to obtain a range of perspectives. However, as data collection proceeded, it became necessary to con-duct individual interviews with key informants repre-

175 senting the larger population of nurses to elicit variabil-ity in the construct. Even though the intent was not to produce consensus, the focus-group participants were so well known to one another that they brought similar perspectives to the discussion with the result that vari-

180 ability was limited to some extent. Individual inter-views also allowed for greater depth in eliciting the meaning and dimensions than was possible to achieve with focus groups alone. Individual interviews were conducted during a single session of 1 to 1.5 hours at a

185 location convenient to participants including home, work, or the researcher's office. Immediately following the sessions, the researcher made general observations of group and individual interactions and noted individ-ual participants' verbal contributions.

190   The focus-group discussions and individual inter-views were conducted using a semistructured interview guide. Participants were asked initially to respond to

195 general questions about "what health promotion meant to them" and "how they perceived nurses should role model health promotion." Next, they were asked to talk more specifically about themselves as role models of health promotion. Questions elicited the objective (ex-pectations) and subjective (meaning) dimensions

200 nurses used to define and describe themselves and other nurses as health-promoting role models. All in-terviews were tape-recorded and transcribed verbatim to ensure accuracy and allow subsequent data analysis. Confidentiality was maintained by storing tapes in a secure place accessible only to the lead researcher, hav-

205 ing only one of the researchers transcribe the tapes, and using pseudonyms for all transcriptions.

Data Analysis

Data were thematically analyzed following the processes described by Knafl and Webster (1988) and Stewart and Shamdasani (1990). Data consisting of

210 words, phrases, sentences, or paragraphs used to de-scribe a role model for health promotion were com-pared for similarities and differences and coded accord-ing to themes. Themes reflecting the range of partici-pants' responses were then compared. Similar themes

215 were grouped into preliminary categories that were refined as additional data were collected. To ensure that the themes arising from the analysis reflected the participants' descriptions of a health-promoting role model, a follow-up session was held with each focus

220 group and individual participants to discuss study find-ings.

Trustworthiness

Evidence of the trustworthiness of the data was ob-tained by peer examination and member checking (Krefting, 1990). Independent coding of focus-group

225 discussions by two of the researchers revealed remark-able similarity in the emergent themes. Differences were found only in the naming of conceptual catego-ries, and these were easily resolved through discussion by research team members. Member checking with

230 participants in both focus-group discussions and indi-vidual interviews also provided support for the credi-bility of findings. Feedback revealed that participants believed the findings reflected what was true for them.

Findings

Analysis revealed that nurse participants defined

235 themselves as role models for health promotion accord-ing to the meaning that they ascribed to the term *role model,* perceptions of societal expectations, and self-constructed personal and professional domains. A vis-ual depiction of the major themes appears in Table 2.

Theme 1: Giving Meaning to the Term "Role Model"

240   In defining themselves as role models, nurse par-ticipants first gave meaning to the term itself. For all of these participants, the words *role model* conjured up an image of the ideal accompanied by expectations for perfection. Nurse participants, however, expressed both

245 negative and positive views in response to the idealized image of the role model. They could not think about the expectations implied in the concept without thinking about how they compared with the ideal. The ideal was a mirror participants used to look at themselves, 250 and what they saw reflected related to the meaning they ascribed to *role model*.

Table 2
Conceptual Schema Describing the Nurse as a Health-Promoting Role Model

---

Theme 1: Giving Meaning to the Term Role Model
    Negative and positive meanings of the idealized role model
    Humanizing the role model of health promotion

Theme 2: Defining Self According to Society's Expectations

*Theme 3: Personal and Professional Definitions of Role
    Modeling*
    The personal domain
        Valuing health
        Accepting the self with imperfections
        Engaging in self-reflection
    The professional domain
        Gaining trust
        Caring
        Partnering

Negative and Positive Meaning of the Idealized Role Model

Those who perceived the idealized role model negatively felt threatened and uncomfortable by high and lofty expectations. Less-than-perfect self-255 comparison to the ideal left these nurse participants feeling invalidated as role models. This invalidation was expressed as, "I'm doing some of it but not all," and, "To me, the role model is supposed to be almost perfect, which we are not." Falling short of the absolute 260 rendered the ideal invalid.

The ideal as negative created an undesirable hierarchy by setting nurse participants "on a pedestal," "at a higher level," "apart," and "better than." Being positioned at this level created a sense of separation and 265 superiority, which was very uncomfortable. Participants felt that the ideal role model image imposed "expectations that maybe we're not going to live up to." The only way to be a role model was to stay on the pedestal, and yet it was so easy to fall. To fall off the 270 pedestal was to fail as a role model.

The idealized role model was additionally seen by some participants to create a lack of genuineness by cloaking the nurse in the garb of pretentiousness and insincerity. In seeking to uphold the ideal standard, 275 these nurse participants saw themselves as playing a role and projecting an image that denied the self and humanness. This view was captured by one participant who noted, "I don't like the word [role model], because to me it's like false. It's like you're playing a role, this 280 is not really you."

The idealized role model was viewed positively by other nurse participants. For them, the ideal role model represented a nonthreatening standard and an ideal for which to strive. One participant commented, "But 285 without models, we're never going to learn anything that we could possibly strive for if we're not ready to do that there and then." Other participants described the ideal as a source of inspiration and motivation: "I've been inspired by seeing people look after their 290 own health, so I'd like to be that inspiration, too, for other people."

Even though nurse participants who viewed the role model positively acknowledged that the ideal did not always represent reality, this did not invalidate the 295 ideal. These participants continued to articulate the merit found in the ideal despite perceived shortcomings. The ideal was supported even while acknowledging personal realities:

> We should role model what health is so that people can
> 300 see through us what health is or what a healthy lifestyle
> is. I say that. Part of me doesn't like it, because part of
> me says, "Why should I, I'm a person, too, and if those
> are my vices or if those are my downfalls, then so be it.
> Those are my weaknesses." But if we are health care pro-
> 305 fessionals, then I think we really need to put our money
> where our mouths are and model healthy lifestyles.

Humanizing the Role Model of Health Promotion

Countering the idealized role model were definitions of the health-promoting role model in humanistic terms. Because of their visibility and proximity to peo-310 ple who could see them as less than ideal, some nurse participants felt more comfortable with defining themselves in terms of being imperfect and sharing human struggles. One nurse participant commented,

> Everybody seems to think it is the best model, and yet a
> 315 role model is that maybe we aren't perfect and we do
> have the same struggles and frustrations as everybody
> else in the public and in the community. And how we
> cope and manage with our health and with our problems
> is as much a role model as just being totally perfect.

320 In defining the term *role model* in humanistic terms, these participants described the need to be seen "on the same level" and "equal" with patients, not better or above them. Defining the role model as more egalitarian than authoritative countered the hierarchy 325 some participants perceived as characterizing traditional conceptions of a role model. A more humanistic definition of *role model* also was seen to confer an authenticity that was problematic with the idealized role model:

> 330 If you look at Oprah Winfrey, now people love her be-
> cause she is just like them. She's getting fat again. But
> everyone is right there with her. They identify with her
> because she is a real person, and I think that's what we
> are, too.

335 Most participants struggled with giving meaning to role modeling within the context of their practice. Not only did these nurse participants use the term *health promoter* interchangeably with *role model* but wondered if being a role model influenced how they pro-

340 moted health. In their professional practice, they acknowledged that they were often health promoters despite being imperfect examples of what they were promoting. One nurse captured it in the following way: "I
mean, I can educate people and be a health promoter
345 about a lot of things, and I may not be the perfect example of any of it."

For these participants, *health promoter* rather than
role model better reflected what they did within the
context of practice with their patients:

350 I like the word *promoter* (not *role model*), because we do
promote it. We are saying this is the way we should strive
to go, again using the word *we* not *you*.

In giving meaning to the term *role model*, both
negative and positive images were found. For some,
355 the idealized role model was impossible to enact and
conveyed a false reality. For others, it represented a
goal to aspire to. Another perspective conveyed a humanistic but more acceptable reality where nurses and
patients alike struggled to achieve health-promotion
360 goals.

*Theme 2: Defining Self According to Society's
Expectations*

The second theme encompassed nurses' definitions
of themselves as role models for health promotion in
terms of societal expectations. Nurse participants per-
365 ceived two societal expectations of themselves as role
models: to be informational resources and to practice
what they preached. Participants saw themselves as
needing to have a repertoire of health information to be
a resource to patients. They also felt a need to practice
what they taught.

370 Defining themselves as informational resources was
often associated with nurse participants experiencing a
sense of being "put on the spot." These participants
spoke of being asked questions in informal situations
by neighbors, friends, or patients that "force us into
375 modeling situations" or "create my role as a role model
for positive behaviors." To be an informational resource, nurses felt the need to be knowledgeable.

Self-definitions as role models were further influenced by a belief in a societal expectation that they
380 should practice what they preached. In both formal
situations (e.g., a professional teaching situation) and
informal settings (e.g., eating out at a restaurant), some
participants felt visible and experienced a very real
pressure to meet the expectations of others. They spoke
385 of being watched and receiving clear messages of expectations for them to engage in the behaviors they
promulgated. For some, these situations were an accepted reality, but for others, they created a sense of
discomfort by drawing attention to the inconsistency
390 between what they taught and what they did:

I believe it's [being a role model] like being a preacher in
a small town, because they watch everything you do
whether you want to be watched or not. Look at me. I'm
not skinny; however, I eat properly if I possibly can and I

395 exercise everyday, because if I don't exercise, [I would
get a comment like, "I didn't see you this morning,
Jane."]

For some nurse participants, societal expectations
were demanding and uncomfortable. Others, although
400 recognizing societal expectations, did not interpret
them as behavioral imperatives.

*Theme 3: Personal and Professional Definitions of
Role Modeling*

In this theme, nurse participants defined themselves
as role models for health promotion independently of
societal expectations. This self-definition occurred to
405 varying degrees within or across two interconnected
domains: personal and professional. Personal self-
definition was expressed in terms of the individual person distinct from the professional nurse. Professional
self-definitions were related to participants' profes-
410 sional practice and were targeted toward nurturing a
health-promoting relationship with patients.

The personal domain. The personal domain encompassed three areas: valuing health, accepting the self
with imperfections, and engaging in self-reflection.
415 Participants valued health for themselves and, in turn,
cared for their own health and well-being. Visible
health-related behaviors and practices reflected participants' personal values and beliefs and were grounded
in "who I am" or "who we are." As participants cared
420 for their own health, they had the potential to be role
models in turn:

It's not because we're a nurse that we do those things. I
mean, there are lots of things we do that we probably
shouldn't do if we were truly exemplifying all health-
425 promoting activities. It's because of who we are and what
we believe to be important. I think that's it. It's not because we're nurses that we do these things, and it's not
because we have the knowledge.

Nurse participants who defined themselves in terms
430 of the personal domain were comfortable and self-
accepting of themselves as role models with imperfections. Self-acceptance seemed to come as they shifted
from being externally controlled by others' expectations to assuming internal control of themselves as role
435 models. By setting personal standards, participants
exercised control of when and how they were role
models for health promotion and constantly strove to
be the best they could be. One participant described
coming to self-acceptance as a role model with imper-
440 fections:

I feel comfortable being a health-promotion role model. I
guess now because I feel I have a choice. I feel that I can
still choose to be a role model; if I choose not to, that's
fine. If I choose to go out and have a drink one night and
445 someone chooses to say, "Karen, that's not very healthy,"
okay, [I] hear you. That's cool. I'm just not being a role
model right now. But I'm okay with that. Are you? So
I've reached that point of being okay that I'm not perfect
and I will try to be as best I can a role model, but there

450 will be times that I will not emulate good health practices. I try. I'm okay if I don't.

Nurse participants who self-defined within the personal domain possessed a degree of self-reflection and
self-awareness about where they were and what they
455 wanted to be as role models.

I'm thinking of when I'm going to Saint John and I'm
driving 140 kms an hour. Seriously, I'm thinking, "I'm a
health promoter and this is not promoting health, slow
down. This is not promoting my health, your health, or
460 anyone else's health if I ran into someone."

Another nurse participant did not define herself in
this way and was less reflective and self-aware:

If I was speeding, I wouldn't think of it in terms of being
a role model of health promotion. I'd be thinking, "I hope
465 I don't get a ticket," but I wouldn't be thinking I wasn't a
role model.

For this participant, speeding was not linked to promoting health but associated with breaking the law.

The professional domain. Self-definition as a role
470 model for health promotion within the professional
domain occurred as nurse participants situated themselves within the context of their practice. Nurse participants who defined themselves in this domain were
those who nurtured health-promoting relationships
475 through gaining trust, caring, and partnering.

Gaining trust was critical in nurturing the development of a health-promoting relationship. Participants
gained trust by being open and honest about their own
struggles with promoting personal health and by being
480 nonjudgmental about other peoples' health practices.
According to one participant, "I think it is seeing us as
human beings and not trying to hide that but admitting
to them, 'Well, yes, I have done this or I have done
that.'"

485 Nurse participants also gained trust by being accepting of patients who had had repeated failures with
incorporating health-related behaviors into their lives.
As one participant described, "Another thing, they
know they can fail and we aren't going to condemn
490 them." By not blaming the victim or conveying impa-
tience and disappointment, a health-promoting relationship based on trust was fostered.

Nurse participants exemplified caring in nurturing
health-promoting relationships. Relating and connect-
495 ing with people on a personal level was one way that
caring was demonstrated. Through use of their own
personal experiences, participants reduced professional
distance and connected with patients and their struggles. In turn, they believed this helped to engage pa-
500 tients in health-promoting efforts:

For me, it's personal, but in the last year, I've made some
changes to my lifestyle and people have noticed and have
commented and how they may try the same thing or asking if it made a difference in my health, like how I feel.
505 And some students have commented, "I think it's time
for me to do something about my lifestyle." So for me,

it's lifestyle choices. I think I've done a little role modeling that way.

Nurse participants also exemplified caring by being
510 patient and persevering with patients who had difficulty making health-promoting changes. Participants
were not always able to see visible changes or tangible
outcomes of their health-promotion work. Despite this,
they remained committed to helping patients. As one
515 participant reflected, "People come to us and they've
tried 50 times to quit smoking. We may not get there
the first time or the second time or the third time either." Nurse participants were attuned to the patient's
context and its impact on health-promoting activities
520 and made every effort to connect with patients:

First off, you have to find out who this person is and why
they are in this situation and what difficulties they had to
overcome.... Maybe their lifestyle is such because they
are so poor that all they can afford to buy is macaroni and
525 therefore their diet is not that healthy, and it has nothing
to do with the fact they don't know what they should eat
from Canada's Food Guide.

In partnering with patients, nurse participants saw
themselves as equals and on the same journey of health
530 promotion even while acknowledging that they were all
at different places in the journey. In guiding patients,
participants gently and noncritically pointed them in
the right direction to make health-promoting changes
while valuing their experiences and their capacity to
535 participate in decision making:

We need to work in partnership with patients, that we
don't know it all, nor should we be the ones that know it
all, that the patients have rich experience to share with us.
We can just be a guide for them on their journey to
540 healthy lifestyles.

Listening to the needs and priorities of individuals
and communities was an important component of partnering. As illustrated by one nurse participant,

I can't say, "If you don't breastfeed, you're the worst
545 mother in the world." You've got to let the facts fall and
let her come to the decision, and then if she does, we
have the groups to support her.

Both personal and professional domains were important components in definitions of role modeling.
550 Valuing health, accepting imperfections, and self-
reflection were aspects of the personal domain,
whereas developing trust, caring, and partnering were
facets of the professional domain.

Limitations

Maximum-variation sampling was used for this
555 study with variability sought in nursing practice settings where health promotion was a primary focus. The
lack of variability in the sample with respect to gender
and race may limit applicability of the study findings to
others. The small sample size might be seen as a limita-
560 tion of this study, although the emergence of recurring
themes in the data suggests that 15 participants ade-

quately captured the various dimensions for describing the health-promotion role model. The qualitative criterion of fittingness and transferability requires readers to assess applicability to their own personal and professional lives.

Discussion

Nurse participants in the current study articulated an expanded conception of themselves as role models for health promotion. Their views challenge long-standing conceptions of the term *role model,* reflect diverse interpretations, and reject the historical position that nurses have a duty to engage in healthy lifestyles (Haughey et al., 1992). Scott (1996) similarly rejected the traditional view by arguing that mandating standardized behaviors in the name of professionalism is a violation of personal rights and freedoms. The view that nurses need to be facilitators in decision making for health rather than role models (Mitic, 1981) was alluded to by some study participants. These participants often used the term *health promoter,* which some believed more accurately reflected their practice, interchangeably with *role model.*

Nurse participants in this study redefined the boundaries that have typically extended personal lifestyle practices into the professional domain. They created distinct and independent personal and professional domains and emphasized health-promoting practices as reflecting who they were as people, not who they were as nurses. Limiting health-promoting practices to the personal domain counters the position that nurses have a professional responsibility to model healthy behaviors and supports the idea that a nurse's credibility is based on more than simply practicing healthy lifestyles (Borchardt, 2000; Clarke, 1991; Haughey et al., 1992; O'Connor, 2002).

Nurse participants criticized the ideal standard as creating unrealistic and undesirable expectations. Instead, these nurse participants offered a more humanized, realistic, and imperfect standard to which patients could more easily relate. This view of the role model for health promotion reflects the position expressed by Gobble and Mullen (1983) that health professionals' flaws can be used to motivate behavior change. Participants also believed that relating to patients in a personal and caring way reduced professional distance and was influential in prompting patients to make health behavior changes. The importance of the relational dimension in health-promoting nursing practice has been highlighted in the literature (Clarke, 1991; Falk-Rafael, 2001; McWilliam, Spence-Laschinger, & Weston, 1999; Robinson & Hill, 1998). In the current study, nurturing the patient-nurse relationship was viewed as an essential characteristic of the role model for health promotion. Nurse participants in this study believed such a relationship models a nontraditional approach to health promotion—one that counters the traditional, authoritative, prescriptive approach. Find-

ings in a recent study, noting that an enabling nurse-patient model was used by nurse preceptors and their students, support this perspective (McWilliam et al., 1999).

If nurses perceive that they cannot be role models because of self-assessed imperfections, health-promoting efforts with patients may be adversely affected. When nurses feel invalidated as role models because of dissonance between what they practice and what they teach, information may be withheld or distorted (Dalton & Swenson, 1986; Swenson, 1991). Withholding knowledge and information fails to give patients an important resource for promoting personal health and may contribute to poor health outcomes. Poor outcomes may also result when nurses have unrealistic expectations of others. Nurses who have had personal success in achieving the ideal standard and believe others need to reach the same standard must be sensitive to the struggles of others and gauge expectations accordingly.

Conveying to patients that, for the great majority of nurses, health-promotion practices are an ideal to strive for rather than one to be fully realized offers a more realistic and balanced approach to role modeling. If nurses perceive that limitations in promoting personal health make them more believable role models, they can use this to great advantage in teaching patients. By offering personal stories about their own challenges with health-promoting practices and by sharing strategies in making health-promoting changes, nurses can be powerful in effecting behavior changes. This approach may be especially helpful when patient or societal expectations are inconsistent with nurses' self-perceptions. For example, nurses not meeting expectations for eating right, exercising, and maintaining a healthy weight have the opportunity to relate in a more humanistic way. A different perspective is posed by Borchardt (2000) who wrote that nurses who meet patient expectations for healthy behaviors place themselves in a position to advise with conviction. Such nurse exemplars must heed Curtin's (1986) concern that they not do so in an aggressive, condemning manner.

Gaining trust, caring, and partnering were integral to nurse participants' self-definitions as role models in the professional domain and formed the context within which the nurse-patient health-promoting relationship occurred. Acceptance of individual patient foibles as well as their own enhanced the effectiveness of these participants in establishing relationships that led toward better health outcomes.

Health promotion does not have to be a quest for perfection. Instead, the mutual sharing of difficulties and shortcomings enables the development of health-promoting relationships through which both nurses and patients can make healthier lifestyle changes. The reciprocity characterizing the nurse-patient relationship reflects a unique nursing approach to the health-promoting role model and captures both the human science of caring and primary health care essential to nursing practice. A vision of the ideal role model and beliefs in the necessity of perfect lifestyle behaviors can be impediments to nurses' effectiveness in health promotion. Having more realistic and humanistic expectations provides nurses with an avenue for nurturing health-promoting relationships with patients that are more likely to lead to better health outcomes.

680

References

Baldwin, J. H. (1995). Are we implementing community health promotion in nursing? *Public Health Nursing, 12,* 59–164.

Borchardt, G. L. (2000). Role models for health promotion: The challenge for nurses. *Nursing Forum, 35,* 29–32.

Callaghan, P., Kuk Fun, M., & Ching Yee, F. (1997). Hong Kong nurses' health-related behaviors: Implications for nurses' role in health promotion. *Journal of Advanced Nursing, 25,* 1276–1282.

Clarke, A. C. (1991). Nurses as role models and health educators. *Journal of Advanced Nursing, 16,*1178–1184.

Connolly, M. A., Gulanick, M., Keough, V., & Holm, K. (1997). Health practices of critical care nurses: Are these nurses good role models for patients? *American Journal of Critical Care, 6,* 261–266.

Curtin, L. L. (1986). The case of the reluctant role model: From health to heresy. *Nursing Management, 17,* 7–8.

Dalton, J. A., & Swenson, I. (1986). Nurses and smoking: Role modeling and counseling behaviors. *Oncology Nursing Forum, 13,* 45–48.

Falk-Rafael, A. R. (2001). Empowerment as a process of evolving consciousness: A model of empowered caring. *Advances in Nursing Science, 24,* 1–16.

Gobble, D., & Mullen, K. (1983). Relationships between wellness role modeling and professional training in health education. *Health Values: Achieving High Level Wellness, 7,* 19–24.

Haughey, B. P., Mathewson-Kuhn, M. A., & Dittmar, S. S. (1992). Health care of critical care nurses: Health practices of critical care nurses. *Heart and Lung: The Journal of Critical Care, 21,* 203–208.

Knafl, K. S., & Webster, D. C. (1988). Managing and analyzing qualitative data: A description of tasks, techniques, and materials. *Western Journal of Nursing Research, 10,* 195–218.

Krefting, L. (1990). Rigor in qualitative research: The assessment of trustworthiness. *The American Journal of Occupational Therapy, 45,* 214–222.

Kuzel, A. J. (1992). Sampling in qualitative inquiry. In B. F. Crabtree & W. L. Miller (Eds.), *Doing qualitative research* (pp. 31–44). Newbury Park, CA: Sage.

Maykut, P., & Morehouse, R. (1994). *Beginning qualitative research: A philosophic and practical guide.* Washington, DC: Falmer.

McWilliam, C. L., Spence-Laschinger, H. K., & Weston, W. W. (1999). Health promotion amongst nurses and physicians: What is the human experience? *American Journal of Health Behavior, 23,* 95–105.

Mitic, W. R. (1981). The health educator as a role model. *Canadian Association of Health and Physical Education Review, 48,* 12–14.

O'Connor, M. (2002). Nurse leader: Heal thyself. *Nursing Administration Quarterly, 26,* 69–79.

Robinson, S., & Hill, Y. (1998). The health promoting nurse. *Journal of Clinical Nursing, 7,* 232–238.

Scott, L. A. (1996). *Are health educators socialized to perceive role modeling as a professional responsibility?* Unpublished master's thesis, Purdue University, Lafayette, IN.

Stewart, D. W., & Shamdasani, P. N. (1990). *Focus groups: Theory and practice.* Newbury Park, CA: Sage.

Swenson, I. (1991). Nurses counseling patients about smoking cessation: Why, when, and how. *Hospital Topics, 69,* 27–29.

Tones, B. K. (1992). The theory of health promotion: Implications for nursing. In J. W. Barnett & J. M. Clark (Eds.), *Research in health promotion and nursing* (pp. 3–12). London: MacMillan.

Valentine, A. S., & Hadeka, M. A. (1986). Do nurses practice what they preach? A study of nurses' health behaviors. *Vermont Registered Nurse, 52,* 3–4.

Williams, A. (1993). Community health learning experiences and political activism: a model for baccalaureate curriculum revolution content. *Journal of Nursing Education, 32,* 352–356.

Acknowledgments: We wish to thank Georgia State University for the Katherine Suggs Chance Dissertation Award, which provided financial support for this study. We are indebted to all the nurses and nurse educators who made invaluable contributions to this study.

Exercise for Article 27

Factual Questions

1. What is the total number of nurses who participated in the focus groups?

2. Did the researchers initially plan to include individual interviews in this study?

3. Did the nurses in the focus groups know each other before participating in this study?

4. How many of the nurses who participated in the focus groups had 21 to 25 years of experience?

5. What steps did the researchers take to maintain confidentiality?

6. Did the researchers use "member checking" (i.e., having participants review the findings of the study for credibility)?

Questions for Discussion

7. The researchers refer to their study as "exploratory." Do you agree? Why? Why not? (See lines 93–95.)

8. The researchers used "maximum-variation sampling" (e.g., using a sample of nurses who are diverse in their backgrounds). Do you think this was a good idea? Explain. (See lines 106–116.)

9. How important is it to know that the researchers conducted "independent coding" of the focus-group discussions? Explain. (See lines 224–226.)

10. In the Findings section of the report, the researchers provide a number of direct quotations from participants. To what extent do the quotations help you understand the findings? Is there a sufficient number of quotations? (See lines 234–553.)

11. Do you consider the small sample size an important limitation of this study? Explain. (See lines 559–563.)

12. If you were planning a follow-up study to explore the topic of this research further, would you plan an additional qualitative study or a quantitative study? Explain.

Quality Ratings

Directions: Indicate your level of agreement with each of the following statements by circling a number from 5 for strongly agree (SA) to 1 for strongly disagree (SD). If you believe an item is not applicable to this research article, leave it blank. Be prepared to explain your ratings. When responding to criteria A and B below, keep in mind that brief titles and abstracts are conventional in published research.

A. The title of the article is appropriate.

SA   5   4   3   2   1   SD

B. The abstract provides an effective overview of the research article.

SA   5   4   3   2   1   SD

C. The introduction establishes the importance of the study.

SA   5   4   3   2   1   SD

D. The literature review establishes the context for the study.

SA   5   4   3   2   1   SD

E. The research purpose, question, or hypothesis is clearly stated.

SA   5   4   3   2   1   SD

F. The method of sampling is sound.

SA   5   4   3   2   1   SD

G. Relevant demographics (for example, age, gender, and ethnicity) are described.

SA   5   4   3   2   1   SD

H. Measurement procedures are adequate.

SA   5   4   3   2   1   SD

I. All procedures have been described in sufficient detail to permit a replication of the study.

SA   5   4   3   2   1   SD

J. The participants have been adequately protected from potential harm.

SA   5   4   3   2   1   SD

K. The results are clearly described.

SA   5   4   3   2   1   SD

L. The discussion/conclusion is appropriate.

SA   5   4   3   2   1   SD

M. Despite any flaws, the report is worthy of publication.

SA   5   4   3   2   1   SD

Article 28

The Contribution of Research Knowledge and Skills to Practice: An Exploration of the Views and Experiences of Newly Qualified Nurses

Gill Hek, MA, RGN, NDN, Cert. Ed. (FE), **Alison Shaw**, PhD, MSc[*]

ABSTRACT. The question of how best to equip nurses with research knowledge and skills has been explored in a number of studies. This paper contributes to growing evidence about how research is perceived in practice, as part of the overall preparedness of a newly qualified nurse. Taking a longitudinal qualitative approach, this study found when interviewing nurses at three months, newly qualified nurses felt that they had received too much teaching about research, were not interested in the subject and struggled to see its relevance to clinical practice. However, at 12 months, about half of the 58 newly qualified nurses who participated in this study felt that research was "embedded" in the practice of their ward/work area, and were able to give examples such as research activity on the ward, research folders, notice boards and conference feedback. In some areas, the newly qualified nurses were teaching students using evidence-based materials and said that research was often talked about. In the struggle to improve the use of research in everyday nursing practice, this study provides some evidence that newly qualified nurses feel they are engaging in relevant research activities.

From *Journal of Research in Nursing*, *11*, 473–482. Copyright ©
2006 by Sage Publications, Inc. Reprinted with permission.

Introduction

Over the last two decades, there have been major changes in the provision of pre-registration and continuing professional education for nurses in the United Kingdom, and substantial changes in healthcare policy
5   and delivery. At the centre of many debates is the fundamental questioning of the extent to which educational developments have given newly qualified nurses greater knowledge, skills and confidence to function in the modern healthcare workplace.

10   One area of debate is the expectation that newly qualified nurses need to develop research knowledge and skills during their training and to use these to provide better patient care. The research presented in this paper was designed to explore newly qualified nurses'

15   perceptions of how prepared they were for practice. Specifically, the paper focuses on newly qualified nurses' views about their research knowledge and skills at three months and 12 months post-qualifying.

Background and Literature Review

The impact of changes in the UK curricula, such as
20   Project 2000 and the subsequent outcomes of the pre-registration nursing programs, have been evaluated by many (Bedford et al., 1993; While et al., 1995; Bartlett et al., 1998, 2000; Parahoo, 1999). In particular, the relative merits of moving nursing education into higher
25   education has been rigorously debated in the United Kingdom (UK), and significant policy changes impinging on the education and practice of nurses have been seen in government proposals, such as Making a Difference (Department of Health, 1999), the NHS Plan
30   (Department of Health, 2000), and Liberating the Talents (Department of Health, 2002). The report from the then-UK nursing statutory body, Fitness for Practice (UKCC, 1999), provided a new term of reference for the education of nurses. Specifically the report empha-
35   sized the need to provide pre-registration education that enabled "fitness for practice based on health care need" (UKCC, 1999:2). This was specified through core-learning outcomes and competencies at the end of the common foundation program, and at the point of regis-
40   tration by the UK nursing statutory body as requirements for pre-registration nursing programs across the UK (UKCC, 2000). The standards for the education of pre-registration nursing programs and the standards of proficiency required for entry to the nursing register
45   are given in "Standards of proficiency for pre-registration nursing education" (NMC, 2004) and are guided by four principles: fitness for practice, fitness for purpose, fitness for award, and fitness for professional standing.

50   Across Europe, and particularly in the UK, the drive toward evidence-based nursing practice has led to greater clarity about research education in the pre-

---

[*] *Gill Hek*, reader in nursing research, Faculty of Health and Social Care, University of the West of England, Bristol. *Alison Shaw*, lecturer in primary care research, Academic Unit of Primary Health Care, Department of Community Based Medicine, University of Bristol (University of the West of England during the study).

registration nursing curriculum. Over the past 10 years,
there has been general acceptance about what newly
55   qualified nurses should know and be able to do in relation to research. The strategy for nursing Making a
Difference (Department of Health, 1999) stressed the
importance of ensuring that nursing practice is "evidence-based" and that nurses have the knowledge and
60   skills to enable them to translate research findings into
practice. This is generally accepted as being able to
read research critically, have a basic understanding of
the research process, identify areas of practice that
need researching, and to use research to improve pa-
65   tient care (Parahoo, 1999). Furthermore, the NMC
standards (NMC, 2004) identify the need and use for
research and evidence to be incorporated into practice,
and that evidence-based knowledge should be used to
individualize nursing interventions as a standard of
70   proficiency for entry to the nursing register. The recent
StLaR project (Butterworth, 2004:4) reiterates the need
for a workforce that is "educated to understand the
benefits and the pitfalls in the outcomes of the research
process" and is "research aware," while the Quality
75   Assurance Agency nursing academic and professional
standards, used to assess higher-education provision,
include for nursing awards that award holders should
be able to "use appropriate research and other evidence
to underpin nursing decisions…" (QAA, 2001).
80   A number of studies have explored how best to
equip nurses with research skills and which teaching
strategies and techniques to use (Clark & Sleep, 1991;
Harrison et al., 1991; Reed, 1995; Dyson, 1997; Mulhall et al., 2000; Blenkinsop, 2003). Some studies have
85   focused on specific groups of students (Lacey, 1996;
Burrows and Baillie, 1997; Parahoo, 1999) or qualified
staff (Veeramah, 1995; Meah et al., 1996). Many have
studied the barriers to using research (e.g., McSherry
1997; Dunn et al., 1997; Retsas & Nolan, 1999; Ka-
90   jermo et al., 2000; Parahoo & McCaughan, 2001;
French, 2005) and two large postal surveys, one in
Northern Ireland (Parahoo, 1999) and one in the southeast of England (Veeramah, 2004) both reported perceived barriers to using research following qualifica-
95   tion, and shortfalls in training. However, the researchers found generally positive attitudes toward research.
Similar findings were reported from a Swedish survey
of nursing standards (Bjorkstrom et al., 2003).
      Overall, the literature is inconclusive on the role of
100 education and how best to prepare nurses with regard
to research. There is also limited work done on how
research knowledge and skills contribute to the overall
preparedness for practice of nurses. This paper considers one aspect of "preparedness for practice"—research
105 knowledge and skills—and how newly qualified nurses
feel this contributes to their practice and their experiences.

The Study

Purpose and Aims

The Regional Workforce Development Confederation commissioned the two-year research project with
110 the aim of facilitating a greater shared understanding
between NHS service providers and nursing education
providers regarding the preparedness for practice of
newly qualified nurses.

Set against the national context and recent research,
115 the need was identified for a longitudinal qualitative
study within the region, looking in-depth at issues from
a range of perspectives (educationalists, senior practitioners, nurse managers, newly qualified nurses),
across all the branches of nursing (adult, child, mental
120 health and learning disabilities) and including a range
of clinical areas entered by newly qualified practitioners.

The data collected and analyzed in the study
yielded a substantial dataset covering a wide variety of
125 issues that have been reported elsewhere (Shaw & Hek,
2003). The findings reported here relate specifically to
the views of newly qualified nurses of their research
knowledge and skills.

Methods

A longitudinal qualitative approach was employed
130 with data collected from newly qualified nurses at three
months and 12 months post-qualification to enable
comparison over time.

Ethical Issues and Approval

The study was approved by the UK South-West
Multi-Centre Research Ethics Committee and the Uni-
135 versity Ethics Committee. The seven NHS Trusts participating in the study gave management approval.

The usual procedures for ensuring ethical research
practice were followed. Letters and information sheets
were provided to all potential participants prior to ob-
140 taining written consent. Care was taken to conduct the
research in a way that respected the views and experiences of participants and ensured the anonymity and
confidentiality of any information they provided. All
information on participants (e.g., names and addresses)
145 was stored separately from a list of identifying codes to
prevent identification. All interview tapes, transcripts
and data used in research reports were anonymized and
tapes were destroyed at the end of the study. The researchers were not directly involved in the students'
150 education and no major ethical issues emerged during
the course of the research.

Sample Selection

The sampling strategy involved several stages:
First, seven NHS Trusts employing newly qualified
nurses exiting from the university from each branch of
155 nursing were identified. Second, a maximum-variation
strategy (Patton, 2002) was used to identify nursing
students from each branch of the pre-registration nursing programs (adult, child, mental health and learning

disabilities) and each award (diploma and degree) who
were about to enter practice in one of the seven participating NHS Trusts. The sampling strategy also aimed
to include a proportional reflection of the differing
numbers of students in each branch program. Nursing
students from the degree and diploma cohorts exiting
the pre-registration nursing programs in 2001/2002
were approached and given information about the research at tutorial sessions at each campus for each
branch just prior to their qualification.

The students who were planning to take up posts in
one of the selected Trusts participating in the research
were identified. They provided contact details and indicated the Trust and ward/unit where they would take
up their first (usually D grade) post after qualifying.
Once qualified, the potential participants were approached and invited for interview. Some were not
contactable, others had not taken up their planned
posts, and others had moved away from the region. The
final sample included 43 diploma nurses and 15 degree
nurses from the two cohorts. The numbers of participants proportionally reflected the numbers of students
in each branch program/award (see Table 1).

Table 1
Newly Qualified Nurses: Participants by Award/Campus/Branch

Award/campus	Branch	Total number of students in cohort	Number of newly qualified nurses participating in study
DipHE			
Campus A	Adult	46	16
	Child	14	3
	M'Health	10	5
	L'Disabilities	6	3
Campus B	Adult	24	10
Campus C	Adult	11	6
Campus D	Adult	21	0 (not included as hospital not in study)
Total DipHE			**43**
BSc	Adult	30	15
Total BSc			**15**
Grand total		**162**	**58**

Data Collection

Two data-collection methods were used: in-depth
face-to-face interviews in the clinical setting at three
months post-qualifying, and telephone interviews at 12
months post-qualifying. For the first interviews, a topic
guide was used to ensure some comparability between
interviews through coverage of the same broad issues.
The initial topic guide was based on the literature and
on data from interviews with nursing education providers and service providers early in the study (Shaw &
Hek, 2003). However, the interviews also included
considerable flexibility in order to allow the participants to pursue their own lines of thought and introduce new topics that were of importance to them. This
approach followed the twin principles of control and

flexibility that are central to the in-depth interview
method (Burgess, 1991). The interviews explored their
early experiences as newly qualified staff nurses, examining the extent to which they felt that their nursing
education had prepared them for practice, and their
experiences of support and preceptorship provided by
the NHS Trust. Specific areas of practice where difficulties or successes had been experienced were investigated. Throughout the interviews, attention was given
to the specific area of nursing and the clinical setting
that the person had entered, exploring the role of the
particular work environment in shaping their experiences.

At the first face-to-face interview at three months,
questions focused generally on perceived knowledge
and skills and areas of practice where they felt confi-
dent/unconfident and competent/not competent. They
were also asked the extent to which they felt their education had prepared them and whether their prior expectations about working as a qualified nurse had been
met. However, following analysis of the early data
when research emerged as a theme, questions were
framed to explore the topic further at 12 months in the
telephone interviews. These tended to focus on the
extent to which research is used in practice, and
whether they would like to be able to use research in
their practice, both now and in the future.

Each face-to-face interview lasted from 45 minutes
to one hour and took place at a convenient time for the
participant—often during or shortly after the "handover" period when there were greater numbers of staff
present on the ward to free-up the newly qualified
nurse. The telephone interviews were usually shorter,
at around 30 minutes, and were arranged mostly for
when the nurse was at home or at a convenient time at
work.

Data Analysis

All the transcripts from the first interviews with the
newly qualified nurses were audiotaped and fully transcribed. This process generated a large volume of
qualitative data, which were managed and analyzed
with the assistance of the software package "AT-
LASti." Detailed notes from the follow-up semistructured telephone interviews were made for the purposes of thematic analysis.

As is common in all qualitative research, data collection and analysis were not separate stages of the
research, but were closely interwoven throughout. Insights from analysis of the data gathered earlier in the
process shaped the topics and questions covered during
later data collection. This iterative process allowed
reflection on the data and the generation of themes and
ideas for further exploration. Throughout, the aim was
to produce "thick description" (Fetterman, 1989) of the
area under investigation, using the words of the participants.

Throughout the research process, analysis of the qualitative data involved coding interview transcripts for key issues and emerging themes. Analysis drew on the principles of constant comparison (Strauss & Corbin, 1998), elements of data continually being compared with other elements to allow the development of core categories. Throughout this process, the principal researcher cross-checked the developing coding strategy and categories with the other researcher on the team, to ensure that the emerging themes were trustworthy and credible (Mays & Pope, 1995).

The data from the first interviews with newly qualified nurses were examined for key categories and themes relating to their views and experiences of the preregistration nurse training and their own preparedness for practice during the early weeks/months postqualifying. The data from the follow-up telephone interviews were examined for changes in views and experiences since the first interviews.

Findings

Research in the Curriculum

Research was a key theme within newly qualified nurses' accounts of the preregistration course. At three months, the majority of diploma nurses felt that they had received too much teaching on research during their training and struggled to see the relevance to their own nursing practice. While acknowledging that research did have its place, many were not personally interested in the subject and did not seem to have engaged with the research teaching they had received.

While recognizing the broad principle of evidence-based practice, the newly qualified nurses tended to see research as a peripheral subject within the work of a newly qualified practitioner. The majority seemed to view it as something that some people may choose to pursue at a later stage of their nursing career, but they did not necessarily see it as particularly relevant for new nurses. However, some of the degree nurses expressed a more positive view of the research teaching and reflected on the value of undertaking a research dissertation for improving their understanding of the research process—including the process of ethical review at the university and Trusts. This experience seemed to have increased their confidence to undertake research, if such an opportunity should arise in their nursing practice.

A lot of research, how to carry out your research, the different types of research, and I think yes you need to know it but at the time I was there thinking well as a D grade I won't really be involved in running that myself, I might be putting it into practice or helping put it into practice...but it's probably more something you could do maybe as a qualified if you wanted to go into that sort of field rather than actually during our training.

(NQA05 Child branch)

I think it was good to have to do [research]. I chose to come out to the hospital. I did my research here with the nurses in A & E, which was a lot more difficult with the ethics approval. I had to go through [the university] and the Trust, which was a pain, but at least I have done that so if I wanted to do it again, I would know what I was doing filling in all the forms.... It was good at least I know what I am doing now, and I understand the whole process so if I had to do something, I am sure I would be able to do it.

(NQD07 Adult branch)

...research during training didn't help...a fake trial where everyone did a bit...would be better.

(NQB09 Adult branch)

At 12 months some of the nurses perceived a greater relevance of the research component of their pre-registration education for their current and future practice. Specifically it helped them to think about research, have a basic overview of issues, and they felt they knew how to find out more about research:

...the preparation for thinking about research during the training helped me think about research now.

(NQB08 Adult branch)

...course gave me basic knowledge to do research...feel confident and competent to do it...big values of the training...didn't so much give us knowledge but taught us how to find that knowledge.

(NQB07 Child branch)

Research and Clinical Practice

At 12 months, about half the nurses felt that "research" was "embedded" in the practice of the ward. The examples they gave included conference feedback to staff, research activity on wards, such as collecting data, project work, auditing, and research folders and notice boards. In some clinical areas the nurses had got involved in teaching students and care staff using evidence-based material and they said that research was often "talked about." However, only a few of the nurses read or subscribed to nursing journals, or regularly consulted books regarding clinical issues that emerged from their practice.

Research is talked about and used on the wards.... I haven't been involved in any big projects, but if I hear about things, I like to go and find the information for myself.... I'm always on the Internet at home.

(NQC05 Adult branch)

...research on the ward is quite important, and they like staff to have the knowledge.

(NQD03 Adult branch)

I get the learning disability journal and take it into work, and the unit takes a few journals now, and people can look at these for the latest research.

(NQH01 Learning disabilities branch)

Although the majority of nurses at 12 months expressed a general awareness of research, there was little direct experience, and it was still often seen as something for certain interested nurses in the future.

Barriers to Using Research

360 Although not asked specifically, the nurses identified some "barriers" to using research in practice at 12 months. There were resource issues, such as lack of access to a computer on the ward or the library not being close to the workplace. Also, there was felt to be

365 expectations that this sort of work should take place in the nurses' own time:

> …don't have time and I'm too tired to do it in my own time.
>
> (NQA07 Adult branch)

370 It was felt by some to be quicker to ask other members of the nursing staff rather than find out through consulting research information, and there was a criticism that the link between audit and research had not been taught on their pre-registration course.

375 I haven't done any research, but lots of people are doing audits on everything…not portrayed all that well through the university…never really mentioned how audits were done…[didn't] recognize the link between research and audit.

380 (NQA05 Adult branch)

A small number of nurses were not interested in research and felt that this was made more difficult because research was never talked about within their clinical area.

385 …no formal essays to write…haven't done research.

> (NQA04 Adult branch)

…not used research at all. Research is not something that's really talked about.

> (NQA09 Adult branch)

Discussion

390 The findings in this qualitative study add to the growing amount of research in the field of research education and utilization of research findings in practice. There is some evidence that research is embedded in nursing practice in certain clinical areas, with some

395 participants in this study able to give examples of research activity in their area of practice. The findings are not generalizable, but they do provide insight from a fairly large qualitative longitudinal study, and there may be some transferability of the findings to other

400 similar settings or participants. They also make a contribution by placing research knowledge and skills within the overall context of being a newly qualified nurse, and the study does provide some understanding about how nurses feel over time about research as part

405 of their overall preparedness for practice. Similar to other studies, the barriers to using research in practice are still evident.

The diploma nurses in this study had received two discrete research modules about sources of evidence

410 and using research in practice, and the degree nurses additionally had a module to prepare them to undertake a small research project and write a dissertation. It is not possible to determine whether the degree students

415 had more positive feelings about research, nor if they had more experience of research in their clinical practice once qualified. This would be an interesting line to pursue in further studies, as would research that examined the purpose of research education and skills in the

420 curriculum, and what difference this makes to clinical practice.

There is a body of literature about the outcomes of pre-registration nursing programs, and emerging research about how best to equip nurses with research

425 skills, particularly in terms of learning strategies and teaching techniques to provide them with a general understanding of research. However, there is a need for more longitudinal research that follows students and newly qualified nurses over extended periods of time to see how research education in the formative years is

430 translated into knowledge and skills in experienced practitioners.

References

Bartlett, H., Simonite, V., Westcott, E., & Taylor, H. (2000). A comparison of the nursing competence of graduates and diplomates from UK nursing programmes. *Journal of Clinical Nursing, 9*, 369–381.

Bartlett, H., Westcott, L., Hind, P., & Taylor, H. (1998). *An evaluation of pre-registration nursing education: A literature review and comparative study of graduate outcomes*, Report no. 4, Oxford Centre for Health Care Research and Development, Oxford Brookes University.

Bedford, H., Phillips, T., Robinson, J., & Schostak, J. (1993). *Assessing competencies in nursing and midwifery education*, Final Report, English National Board for Nursing and Midwifery, London.

Bjorkstrom, M. E., Hamrin, E. K. F., & Athlin, E. E. (2003). Swedish nursing students' attitudes to aid awareness of research and development within nursing. *Journal of Advanced Nursing, 41*, 393–402.

Blenkinsop, C. (2003). Research: An essential skill of a graduate nurse. *Nurse Education Today, 23*, 83–88.

Burgess, R. G. (1991). The unstructured interview as conversation. In Burgess, R.G. (ed.) *Field research: A sourcebook and field manual*. London: Routledge.

Burrows, D. E., & Baillie, L. (1997). A strategy for teaching research to adult branch diploma students. *Nurse Education Today, 17*, 115–120.

Butterworth, T. (2004). *The StLaR HR Plan Project*. London: Department for Education and Skills, Department of Health, NHSU.

Clark, E. H., & Sleep, J. (1991). The what and how of teaching research. *Nurse Education Today, 11*, 172–178.

Department of Health (1999). *Making a Difference: Strengthening the Nursing, Midwifery and Health Visiting Contribution to Health and Healthcare*. London: Department of Health.

Department of Health (2000). *The NHS Plan: A plan for investment, a plan for reform*. London: Department of Health.

Department of Health (2002). *Liberating the talents*. London: Department of Health.

Dunn, Y., & Crighton, N., Roe, B., Seers, K., & Williams, K. (1997). Using research for practice: A UK experience of the BARRIERS scale. *Journal of Advanced Nursing, 27*, 1203–1210.

Dyson, J. (1997) Research: Promoting positive attitudes through education. *Journal of Advanced Nursing, 26*, 608–612.

Fetterman, D.M. (1989). *Ethnography: Step by step*. London: Sage.

French, B. (2005). The process of research use in nursing. *Journal of Advanced Nursing, 49*, 125–134.

Harrison, L. L., Lowery, B., & Bailey, P. (1991). Changes in nursing students' knowledge about and attitudes toward research following an undergraduate research course. *Journal of Advanced Nursing, 16*, 807–812.

Kajermo, K. N. Nordstrom, G., Krusebrant, A., & Bjorvell, H. (2000). Perceptions of research utilization: Comparisons between health care professionals, nursing students and a reference group of nurse clinicians. *Journal of Advanced Nursing, 31*, 99–109.

Lacey, A. E. (1996). Facilitating research-based practice by educational intervention. *Nurse Education Today, 16*, 96–30.

McSherry, R. (1997). What do registered nurses and midwives feel and know about research? *Journal of Advanced Nursing, 25*, 985–998.

Mays, N., & Pope, C. (1995). Rigour and qualitative research. *British Medical Journal, 311*, 109–112.

Meah, S., Luker, K. A., & Cullum, N. A. (1996). An exploration of midwives' attitudes to research and perceived barriers to research utilisation. *Midwifery, 12*, 73–84.

Mulhall, A., Le-May, A., & Alexander, C. (2000). Research-based nursing practice: An evaluation of an educational programme. *Nurse Education Today, 20,* 435–443.

Nursing and Midwifery Council (2004). *Standards of proficiency for pre-registration nursing education.* London: Nursing and Midwifery Council.

Parahoo, K. (1999). A comparison of pre-Project 2000 and Project 2000 nurses' perceptions of their research training, research needs, and of their use of research in clinical areas. *Journal of Advanced Nursing, 29,* 237–245.

Parahoo, K., & McCaughan, E. M. (2001). Research utilization among medical and surgical nurses: A comparison of their self-reports of barriers and facilitators. *Journal of Nursing Management, 9,* 21–30.

Patton, M. Q. (2002). *Qualitative research and evaluation methods. 3rd edition.* London: Sage.

Quality Assurance Agency for Higher Education (2001). *Benchmark statement: Health care programmes, nursing.* Gloucester: Quality Assurance Agency for Higher Education.

Reed, J. (1995). Using a group project to teach research methods. *Nurse Education Today, 15,* 56–60.

Retsas, A., & Nolan, M. (1999). Barriers to nurses' use of research: An Australian hospital study. *International Journal of Nursing Studies, 36,* 335–343.

Shaw, A. & Hek, G. (2003). *Preparedness for practice: A longitudinal Qualitative study of newly qualified nurses, trust stakeholders and educationalists.* Bristol: University of the West of England.

Strauss, A., & Corbin, J. (eds) (1998). *Basics of qualitative research,* second edition. London: Sage.

UKCC (1999). *Fitness for practice: the UKCC Commission for Nursing and Midwifery Education.* London: UKCC.

UKCC (2000). Requirements for pre-registration nursing programmes. London: UKCC.

Veeramah, V. (1995). A study to identify the attitudes and needs of qualified staff concerning the use of research findings in clinical practice within mental health settings. *Journal of Advanced Nursing, 22,* 855–861.

Veeramah, V. (2004). Utilization of research findings by graduate nurses and midwives. *Journal of Advanced Nursing, 47,* 183–191.

While, A., Roberts, J., & Fitzpatrick, J. (1995). *A comparative study of outcomes of pre-registration nurse education programmes.* London: English National Board for Nursing, Midwifery and Health Visiting.

Acknowledgments: The study was funded by the Avon, Gloucestershire and Wiltshire Workforce Development Confederation. We would like to acknowledge the support of nurses within the local NHS Trusts who participated and facilitated access for the research and members of the Project Steering Group who guided and supported the researchers. Some of the findings were presented at the Workgroup of European Research Nurses Conference in Lisbon 2004.

Address correspondence to: Gill Hek, University of the West of England, Faculty of Health and Social Care, Glenside, Blackberry Hill, Stapleton, Bristol, BS16 1DD. Email: Gill.Hek@uwe.ac.uk

Exercise for Article 28

Factual Questions

1. Were the researchers able to contact all of the potential participants who were qualified?

2. How many of the participants in the final sample were degree nurses?

3. Were face-to-face interviews *or* telephone interviews used at three months post-qualifying?

4. The researchers characterized what feature of their research as "common in all qualitative research"?

5. Did the researchers cross check with each other when developing coding strategy and themes?

6. At 12 months, about what percentage of the participants felt that research was embedded in the practice of the ward?

Questions for Discussion

7. Is the section on ethical issues and approval an important element of this research report? Explain. (See lines 133–151.)

8. Is the use of flexible interviews a strength of this study? Explain. (See lines 191–197.)

9. Is the use of "thick description" (i.e., using the words of participants) an important part of this study? Explain. (See lines 247–250 and the quotations interspersed in lines 295–389.)

10. How important is it to know that the principal researcher cross-checked with the other researcher? (See lines 257–261.)

11. Does this research convince you that there was a change in the perceptions of the relevance of research from 3 months to 12 months? (See lines 270–330.)

12. If you were planning a follow-up study to explore the topic of this research further, would you plan an additional qualitative study or a quantitative study? Explain.

Quality Ratings

Directions: Indicate your level of agreement with each of the following statements by circling a number from 5 for strongly agree (SA) to 1 for strongly disagree (SD). If you believe an item is not applicable to this research article, leave it blank. Be prepared to explain your ratings. When responding to criteria A and B below, keep in mind that brief titles and abstracts are conventional in published research.

A. The title of the article is appropriate.

    SA   5   4   3   2   1   SD

B. The abstract provides an effective overview of the research article.

    SA   5   4   3   2   1   SD

C. The introduction establishes the importance of the study.

    SA   5   4   3   2   1   SD

D. The literature review establishes the context for
the study.

   SA   5   4   3   2   1   SD

E. The research purpose, question, or hypothesis is
clearly stated.

   SA   5   4   3   2   1   SD

F. The method of sampling is sound.

   SA   5   4   3   2   1   SD

G. Relevant demographics (for example, age, gender,
and ethnicity) are described.

   SA   5   4   3   2   1   SD

H. Measurement procedures are adequate.

   SA   5   4   3   2   1   SD

I. All procedures have been described in sufficient
detail to permit a replication of the study.

   SA   5   4   3   2   1   SD

J. The participants have been adequately protected
from potential harm.

   SA   5   4   3   2   1   SD

K. The results are clearly described.

   SA   5   4   3   2   1   SD

L. The discussion/conclusion is appropriate.

   SA   5   4   3   2   1   SD

M. Despite any flaws, the report is worthy of publication.

   SA   5   4   3   2   1   SD

Article 29

John and Mary Q. Public's Perceptions of a Good Death and Assisted Suicide

Jill E. Winland-Brown, EdD, MSN, ARNP[*]

ABSTRACT. This phenomenological study uncovered adults' perceptions of a good death and answered a provocative question asking if assisted suicide might ever be considered. Twelve adults in fields not related to health care participated. The respondents concluded that a good death is peaceful and accepted after life goals have been met with fond memories and that it results in respect for the individual's autonomy with open communication among family members. The participants saw assisted suicide as a viable option if it allows the person to remain in control through death as his or her personal autonomy is respected and if the person's quality of life is diminished by pain or by being a burden to his or her family. Knowledge gained through this study may provide insights essential to caring for persons at the end of life. As autonomy is the hallmark of all health care providers' Codes of Ethics, providers need to be cognizant of persons' views related to end-of-life care and to honor their wishes. Some recommendations are included regarding the debate and controversy of assisted suicide.

From *Issues in Interdisciplinary Care*, *3*, 137–144. Copyright © 2001 by Sage Publications, Inc. Reprinted with permission.

The old adage about death and taxes being the only things certain in life seems true. Americans don't like talking about either one. In addition, those are the two areas where Americans seem to cheat. The expression
5 "cheating death" implies that death is to be put off as long as possible. Many physicians have an aversion to death, are taught in medical school to do all in their power to prolong life, and convey that message to patients. In fact, many physicians consider themselves
10 failures when a patient dies.

University students who take a course on death and dying sometimes have to actually write their own obituary. This makes the idea of death seem more real and inevitable. Burkhardt and Nathaniel (1998) state
15 that death is part of the life cycle in many cultures, and persons know that it will come in its own time. Although Americans intrinsically know this, they have not come to accept it, and thus attempt to cheat death.

The findings of this phenomenological study un-
20 covered persons' perceptions of a good death and an-
swered a provocative question asking if assisted suicide might ever be considered. The respondents concluded that a good death is peaceful and accepted after life goals have been met with fond memories and that it
25 results in respect for the individual's autonomy with open communication among family members. The participants saw assisted suicide as a viable option if it allows the person to remain in control through death as his or her personal autonomy is respected and if the
30 person's quality of life is diminished by pain or by being a burden to his or her family.

Sample

This purposive sample of 12 adults was accessed through word of mouth. There were 5 men and 7 women between the ages of 24 and 63, with a mean of
35 42 years. The education levels of the participants ranged from a minimum of a high school education to a PhD in engineering. The majority had several years of college. None of the participants was in a health-related field. They are referred to as John and Mary Q. Public
40 as their thoughts, ideas, and perceptions seem to be shared by many.

Process and Findings

Prior to the analysis of data using Colaizzi's (1978) phenomenological method, preunderstandings and assumptions were set aside so as not to try and read any-
45 thing into the participants' comments. The researcher reflected on what a good death meant personally and under what circumstances might assisted suicide ever be considered. A review of relevant literature was not conducted until after the themes emerged as an addi-
50 tional step to prevent possible bias during the discussions with the participants and data collection.

Informed consent was assured by having participants complete a form that discussed the confidentiality and anonymity of the responses. The study was ap-
55 proved by the Human Subjects Review Committee of the Institutional Review Board at Florida Atlantic University.

Each participant was asked to respond in writing to the following two questions: What constitutes a good
60 death?, and If you had a terminal disease and were in

[*] *Jill E. Winland-Brown* is the undergraduate program coordinator at the College of Nursing at Florida Atlantic University.

Table 1
Selected Examples of Statements and Meanings

Significant statement	Formulated meaning
Good death	
I am a firm believer that the dying cannot rest in peace if their dying wishes are not seen through.	Respecting the dying's wishes is essential for the person to rest in peace.
I have a pretty good tolerance for pain, but I am so afraid death is going to hurt, and I want to die peacefully, not in agony.	The thought that death is going to hurt precludes the thought of a peaceful death.
A good death may constitute one that ends intolerable pain or finally ends a vegetative state.	A good death is an end to intolerable pain and suffering.
Assisted suicide (AS)	
It is easy to say that AS is wrong until I am in an intolerable situation where it becomes a matter of dying with dignity.	Even if one considers AS immoral, daily intractable suffering may make it a viable option.
If there is absolutely no quality of life, I would consider AS. Perhaps it would also give me a sense of control where there is no other way.	AS is a viable alternative if it is the only way to gain control in the last few days.
If the pain is extreme, there are still small things to be happy about.	Even in extreme pain, small windows of happiness in the moment occur.

pain, would you consider assisted suicide? They were asked to share all thoughts, perceptions, and feelings until they had no more to say.

65   All the participants wrote their answers in private and were given a week to complete and return the responses. When the written responses were returned, the consent form was detached, thus preventing the identification of the participant by the signed consent form. Responses were typed on the left-hand side of the pa-
70   per for two purposes: to ensure anonymity by not recognizing handwriting and to facilitate identifying significant statements on the right-hand side.

Responses were analyzed by using the phenomenological method as described by Colaizzi (1978),
75   summarized as follows:

- Extraction of significant statements after dwelling with the data,
- formulation of meanings through the analysis of significant statements,
80   - creation of themes from the formulated meanings,
- creation of an exhaustive description of the phenomena, and
- validation of the description by participants.

85   After reading and rereading the data, significant statements were extracted that, according to Colaizzi (1978), are statements pertaining to the phenomenon. Significant statements that directly pertained to what individuals perceive a good death to be and if they
90   might ever consider assisted suicide were extracted from the data.

After repetitious statements were eliminated, 54 significant statements emerged: 35 statements about a good death and 19 statements about assisted suicide.
95   After significant statements and phrases were ex-

tracted, meanings were then formulated. Examples of significant statements and their corresponding formulated meanings relating to a good death and assisted suicide are given in Table 1.

100   Clusters of themes were organized from the formulated meanings. An example of the decision trail used for one of the cluster themes for each of the two topics is given in Table 2. The original number of the significant statement from which the formulated meaning was
105   derived is listed in parentheses in the table.

Table 2
Examples of Two Theme Clusters with Their Subsumed Formulated Meanings

To have one's final wishes honored and be treated with respect and dignity is an expectation.

Respecting the dying's wishes is essential for the person to rest in peace (A5).

Having professionals who understand and respect that elders have a body and soul is expected (J4).

There is an expectation at any age to be treated with respect and dignity (K1).

A good death is having a physician possess enough self-confidence and compassion to honor my wishes, without the fear of liability issues (L2).

Remaining in control through the dying process is essential.

Wishes in death are just as essential as wishes in life (A8).

Assisted suicide makes me in control (B9).

Knowing when and where my death will happen is the final part of what a good death is (D10).

Assisted suicide is a viable alternative if it is the only way to gain control in the last few days (J3).

Four theme clusters emerged from the data about a good death, and three theme clusters emerged from the data about assisted suicide. They will be presented separately.

What Constitutes a Good Death?

Theme 1: Coming to Peace with Oneself and Others and Accepting That Death Is a Good Death

110   Some of the participants' comments that illustrate peace and acceptance are as follows:

> A good death would be one where an individual is able to leave this life in peace, fulfillment, and comfort, without being bound by fear and regret.

115
> I believe a good death would be one that could be predicted. That way I could tell everyone my feelings for them before I died. It would also have to be a peaceful death without any pain.

> A good death is a harmonious one, surrounded by the nearest and dearest, sharing and showing love for one another. People are sad that you are leaving, and you in turn are sad to leave, but your body is worn out and there are no solutions to that.

120

> I want to die with a smile on my face, proving that life was good and happy, and I'd do it all the same way again, no regrets.

125

Although participants agreed that death may be welcome in some situations, such as conditions involving pain, collectively they felt that the ideal death would be at the end of a long life and not involve pain or suffering. With time to plan their death and the knowledge that death was imminent, individuals felt that they would come to the final stage of death—that of acceptance. Advances in medical technology are changing the way we look at death and dying (Lynch & Edwards, 1998). The respondents in this study are referring to death at the end of a good life, not as a result of a prolonged life through high-tech medical care.

130

135

Theme 2: To Have One's Final Wishes Honored and Be Treated with Respect and Dignity Is an Expectation

All the participants shared tales of horror where individual autonomy was not respected and either loved ones or health care personnel made decisions for the individual without consulting them. In addition, persons want to be treated with respect no matter what physical condition they are in, and gave examples of health care personnel treating persons with less respect than they treat animals. Some of the statements included:

140

145

> It is essential to have professionals involved in my care that understand I have a body and soul and treat me accordingly. In my opinion and experience, professionals often forget or neglect to consider they are treating a "whole person."

150

> I would hope to have arranged advance directives, and that the physician of my or my family's choosing would possess enough self-confidence and compassion to honor my wishes, without the fear of liability issues or a lawsuit.

155

Although it was hoped that the Patient Self-Determination Act (PSDA) of 1990 would make an impact in the area of advance directives by increasing the number of individuals who have them and encouraging health care professionals to honor them, health care providers still relay stories where individuals' final wishes are not honored, and they are forced to endure unwanted treatments and even life-prolonging care. The PSDA requires health care facilities receiving federal funding to create formal procedures that provide written information at admission about the person's wishes related to treatment decisions regarding their health care (Lynch & Edwards, 1998). Although the PSDA was supposed to erase many problems surrounding end-of-life decisions, it actually created as many problems as it was intended to resolve.

160

165

170

Theme 3: Saying Good-bye to Loved Ones and Leaving Them Well Prepared for Death is Essential

Communication was a theme throughout all the responses, and participants wanted to be able to make amends for past mistakes and say good-bye to loved ones. Some of their responses included:

175

> A good death would be one in which I would leave no loose ends. My family would be well prepared and we would have communicated and shared all of our hopes and dreams for each other.

180

> I would have a chance to say good-bye to family and friends, telling them how much I love them. My loved ones would be present, with my husband holding my hand, and me holding my baby, while I drift off to sleep.

185

Open communication was cited as important—not only with other family members, but with health care professionals as well. Health care providers must be prepared to assist elders in preparing for difficult choices surrounding dying (Perrin, 1997). This open communication is essential to the dying person who wants to see peace in the family. As one participant stated, "If the family cannot work through their own feelings about their loved one dying, then the dying cannot die a good death. Even if he/she is comfortable physically, they still suffer mentally and spiritually because they see the ambivalence in their family."

190

195

Theme 4: Achieving Lifelong Goals and Having Good Memories of Times Shared Is Crucial

Achieving goals implies that the individuals would have lived a long life, which was implied in all the responses. Persons want to leave a mark in the world by leaving something for others to remember them by. Some responses that reflect this include the following:

200

> With a good death, I will have achieved many of the goals I have set for myself, such as graduating college, enjoying a career, starting a family, and spending quality time with family and friends to create lasting memories.

205

> A good death also must have a reflection on my life; for example, if I can look back on my life without regrets it will make it easier to have a good death.

210   The final procedural step of data analysis in Colaizzi's (1978) method involves integrating the results of the data analysis into an exhaustive description. The first part of this study, looking at what constitutes a good death, revealed that a good death is peaceful and 215 accepted after life goals have been met with fond memories, and results in the individual's autonomy being respected with open communication among family members.

Would You Ever Consider Assisted Suicide?

As expected, when persons talk about assisted suicide, usually the first comment relates to intractable 220 pain, the inability to control the pain, and the perceived hopelessness of the situation to the individual. These participants were no different.

Theme 1: If the Quality of Life Is Diminished with Pain, Resulting in a Burden on the Family, Assisted Suicide May Be a Feasible Option

Although typically individuals mention pain as the 225 most common reason for assisted suicide, persons also refer to being a burden on family members. Responses that lead to this theme are:

If pain and suffering became synonymous with daily torture, then assisted suicide would probably be a welcome 230 relief. It is easy to say that it is wrong until I am in an intolerable situation where it becomes a matter of dying with dignity.

If I had a terminal disease and were in pain, assisted suicide would be a definite possibility. If the pain is signifi-235 cant and the quality of life for yourself is gone and the burden on your family is beyond what is acceptable, then what is the point of continuing?

Most opponents of assisted suicide state that if pain could be effectively controlled, there would be no need 240 for assisted suicide. This thought was reflected in several participants' responses. One individual stated, "If I had a terminal disease and was suffering from intolerable pain, I would seriously consider assisted suicide. But only after an exhausting search for alternative pain 245 control and treatment of my illness."

One person recognized that if there was a purpose to one's suffering, then that in itself would provide hope. He stated, "There would have to be a great reason such as helping others through one's own suffering 250 in order not to take my life. Of course, then I would have a purpose, and that would not constitute as having no quality of life."

Theme 2: One's Personal Autonomy of How to Live and How to Die Rests with the Individual

Individuals want to make decisions in life as well as in death. Responses reflecting this theme include:

255   A lot would depend on whether I know my family would make sure my wishes were carried out at the end. If I knew I was going to lose control over my body as I near death, then I would end it before that time came. I would never allow my wishes about my own destiny to be cir-260 cumvented.

I do feel that it is not for the government to say you can or cannot have the right to do this.

I strongly believe in other people's rights, and each person should be allowed to choose suicide in the case of 265 terminal illness. It should be a personal right.

Yet most persons stated that they would want to receive their family's blessing to pursue assisted suicide before they planned any further. Another individual said, "I am a firm believer that the dying cannot rest in 270 peace if their dying wishes are not seen through."

Several persons wrote that they were against assisted suicide because it was immoral, but then went on to say that it might depend on the circumstances. As one participant wrote:

275   Since I believe that assisted suicide is immoral, I would not hastily choose that as an end, rather to die naturally. If pain were unbearable, I would at least want to have that option available so I can practice autonomy by making my own decision about when and how I wish to die.

280   Yet others emphatically stated that they not only might consider assisted suicide, but they would also help family members who chose that option. One person wrote:

A good death would be one of no pain, swift, and sudden. 285   If I had to resort to some type of assisted suicide to ensure that, I would go through with it in a heartbeat. I would do the same for a friend or family member as long as that was their true wish.

Many respondents mentioned autonomy. One per-290 son wrote, "The option of assisted suicide can open a Pandora's box of issues, but I feel that ultimately it must be an allowable personal choice."

Theme 3: Remaining in Control Through the Dying Process Is Essential

Although parts of remaining in control relate to autonomy, it is more than just having one's wishes 295 honored, but also that of personally feeling the power to do something about those wishes. It is more of an active choice. Some participants' responses that implied this are as follows:

I believe that my wishes are just as important in death as 300 they were in life. I like the control that I would have over my death if I were to consider assisted suicide.

If there were absolutely no quality of life, I would consider assisted suicide a viable alternative. Perhaps it would also give me a sense of control when there is no 305 other way I, or anyone else, can control my condition.

Only one individual mentioned a method for assisted suicide and related it to having control over her life. She stated:

I like having my own "stash" so that I can have that final 310 control. I agree that I might never use the medication, but it is comforting to have the final control over my own death. I would like very much to be as controlled in my death as I am in my life. Perhaps that is the final part of what a good death would be: to know when and where it will come.

Integrating these themes into an exhaustive statement reflecting individual perceptions about assisted suicide resulted in the following description: Assisted suicide is a viable option if it allows one to remain in control through death as one's personal autonomy is respected, and if one's quality of life is diminished by pain and one is a burden to his or her family.

Colaizzi's (1978) final step involves returning to the participants with the exhaustive description to see if it accurately reflects the essence of what they were trying to communicate. Five participants (three women and two men who participated in this study) were contacted and read the themes and exhaustive description, and were asked to share whether these themes captured their feelings. Each participant was approached individually in a private setting. Not only did each participant state "absolutely true" or "yes"—they also wanted to add more information from other personal situations experienced since the study took place. Friends or relatives had been in emergency situations that could possibly result in lingering or prolonged lives, and they wanted to discuss their feelings with those friends or relatives about death and/or assisted suicide. The study seemed to open a floodgate of emotions, and had participants exploring aspects and feelings about themselves that they had never explored before. Because these themes and the exhaustive descriptions rang true with these participants, it appears that the findings resonate with the experience of what a good death means to those individuals and their perceptions of assisted suicide.

Perspectives from the Literature

Almost all persons discussed the concept of pain when referring to a good death and assisted suicide. Their view of a good death referred to not having pain, and if the pain were uncontrollable then assisted suicide might be considered.

A seminal piece sharing end-of-life choices in 1974 stated that shifts are occurring that "reflect a recognition that we have overestimated our right to kill in a military setting, and underestimated it in some medical and private settings" (Maguire, 1974). This was written more than 25 years ago and could not be truer today. When assisted suicide first became legal in Oregon, opponents thought that it would encourage widespread killing. On the contrary, the law has resulted in an improvement in end-of-life care. In 1998, although 23 people obtained lethal prescriptions of medications to end their life, only 15 actually did so. All but two of those persons had cancer. Oregon now uses much more morphine to control the pain of persons in the dying process, and the number of patients who die in a hospice setting rose by 70%, which clarifies that Oregonians do not want to kill themselves so much as to feel in control of their pain and their terminal status: "Eve-

ryone dying in Oregon has some peace of mind, because they know they will have this choice" (Smith, 1999, p. 24).

Health care providers have a responsibility to examine their own personal feelings about death, how they feel about euthanasia, about the processes available today for extending life, and whether persons have a right to choose their own fate (Davis et al., 1995, p. 174). This personal reflection is essential before health care providers can care for others. In a study of 80 health care providers, those who supported active euthanasia cited patient autonomy as the reason (76%). Of those same providers, 58% said that they could only support this if the patient's family were in agreement (Davis et al., 1995). A critical need exists for health care providers in various practice settings to become educated about the meaning of assisted suicide to their patients (Davis et al., 1995).

Physicians, as well as other health care providers, need assistance in the area of talking to patients and also in respecting and honoring their choices. In a large multisite project (the Study to Understand Prognoses and Preferences for Outcomes and Risks of Treatment [SUPPORT]), when health care providers shared with physicians the wishes of elders regarding their care, the physicians did not deter from their original treatment plan (Support Study Principal Investigators, 1995). The voices of the elders were not only not heard, but also not honored. How would these same physicians feel if a similar situation happened to them?

The American Nurses Association (ANA, 1994) has a position statement on assisted suicide that states that although nurses have an obligation to provide patients with compassionate care at the end of life, nurses should not participate in assisted suicide. It states that such an act would be a violation of the Code for Nurses. Although the ANA opposes assisted suicide, they do recognize that "respect for persons extends to all who require the services of the nurse for the promotion of health, the prevention of illness, the restoration of health, the alleviation of suffering and the provision of supportive care of the dying" (p. 3). So whereas nurses do not deliberately participate in assisted suicide, they may certainly remain with dying patients and hold their hands. The ANA also states that individual experiences are very unique: "Nurses should avoid judgment of patients or their experience and recognize that only the suffering person can define that suffering" (p. 5). This certainly relates to all health care providers.

Discussion

This study does not attempt to discuss all the end-of-life issues (e.g., hospice care, euthanasia, and assisted suicide). But knowledge gained through this study does provide insights essential to caring for persons at the end of life. The role of health care providers is to talk about death with John and Mary Q. Public and not let it be a taboo subject as if it is never going to happen. Age plays an important factor in how one views death. As one participant stated:

> It is the human character to expect to die at a ripe old age, unless we live a particularly dangerous lifestyle or have congenital or chronic health conditions. During our youth, we believe that we are immortal, that nothing can break us down; it is only with the onset of maturity we realize our vulnerability.

Although persons' perceptions about assisted suicide vary, the topic needs to be openly discussed so individual perceptions are known about the topic and individual wishes are honored.

Health care providers must be aware of their patients' views surrounding the dying process and their own views and misconceptions. Although many persons view the Hemlock Society as one that will assist with death, it is primarily a support group to assist in the dying process—whether that is how to be assertive in talking to the physician about pain control or how to receive literature on the rights of terminally ill persons. The Hemlock Society publishes newsletters and books, conducts educational seminars, and tries to influence legislators for the common purpose of raising consciousness about the rights of terminally ill persons to choose to die in a manner of their own choice (Humphry, 1991). The founder, Derek Humphry, states "people (doctors included) should only help each other to die if there is a bonding of love or friendship, and mutual respect. If the association is anything less, stand aside. This is too serious a matter to be relegated to a poor, a casual or a brief relationship" (p. 33).

One person stated that although a Hemlock Society book, *Final Exit* (Humphry, 1991), has helped many persons, it "is a shame that the book had to be written at all." She went on to say:

> I do not know how we as a society can accept this desperate measure committed by our most noblest class of citizens, the aged. We consider it humane to put our animals to sleep and conduct execution by lethal injection to criminals as it is considered the most humane option, even considering the heinous crimes of these offenders.

Autonomy is one of the ethical principles that is reflected in all health professionals' Codes of Ethics: "Americans have a constitutionally protected right (grounded in the right to privacy) that permits them to decline medical and/or surgical procedures and opt for comfort measures only. This right is present whether a person has the capacity to make decisions or not" (Lynch & Edwards, 1998, p. 31). Why, then, do health professionals hear horror stories of persons' deaths being prolonged and their wishes not being honored? The right and the practice are incongruent.

Advance directives are the mechanism by which a person's autonomy may be upheld even when that person may no longer be able to speak for himself or herself. The whole premise of advance directives is that their use recognizes persons' autonomy by using a long-held legal principle that allows individuals to determine what can and cannot be done to their bodies: informed consent (Lynch & Edwards, 1998).

End-of-life decisions require that patients discuss those choices with their health care provider. These decisions require information and reflection (Schlenk, 1997). We cannot expect that when presented with information at an emergency room or admissions department of a hospital, the patient can make such an important decision—that of life and death—at a moment's notice without reflection. Health care providers need to explore their personal feelings about death and assisted suicide before they can care for others. In addition, providers must be prepared to assist elders in preparing for difficult choices surrounding the dying (Perrin, 1997). Encouraging all persons to have advance directives is one way to accomplish this.

All the participants in this study were White Americans, with the exception of two African Americans. It must be cautioned that people from other countries and those of different cultural backgrounds may not share these views (Korpivaara, 1999). We assume that personal autonomy is the be all and end all, yet in three-fourths of the world's population, persons live in societies where the group (rather than the individual) is the primary unit, and they do not consider individual needs first, as in America (Korpivaara, 1999). Yet with 45 million people still using the emergency room as their primary health care source because they don't have an economic choice, patients do not develop a relationship with a physician in whom they may confide their end-of-life choices and hope that the physician will honor them when the time comes (Korpivaara, 1999). The bottom line is that no matter what the person's cultural background, listening to them will bring forth what is important to them (Korpivaara, 1999). Autonomy is the principle that grounds all health care professions' care today. To not respect a person's autonomy—whatever the decision may be—is not providing quality care.

Most participants felt that a good death would be a predictable death. One woman described her version of a good death as follows:

> It would be a beautiful summer day—about 78–80 degrees outside. I would wake up to the birds singing. I would then have breakfast with my husband and spend the rest of the day surrounded by those whom I love. The day would be full of joy and happiness and a lot of fun—almost as if it were a party. As the day came to an end, I would tell all my loved ones that I loved them, and I would also make peace with those that I was angry with. My husband and I would then go to bed and make love for the final time. We would both go to sleep and then I would die, never to see the sun rise again. In my little tale I believe a good death would be one which could be predicted.

Who of us would not want to die this way? Unfortunately, it is a fairy tale. Who knows what options a healthy person who has never before experienced intractable uncontrollable pain might consider if that day comes?

545   The fact that healthy persons don't expect death any time soon is exemplified by one participant, who wrote:

> I guess you could say that dying of old age would be a good death or someone who dies instantly without any pain or suffering. But in all actuality, there really is no
> 550   good death, as death is really a morbid thing and is really not looked upon as "good." People might say…he/she had a good life, or he/she went quickly, but I have never heard anyone say…he/she died a good death. It just does not sound normal.

555   Respondents questioned many ideas or issues that they stated had to be addressed before assisted suicide could be considered. For example, one individual listed:

> Who is going to oversee or regulate the assisted suicide
> 560   process? What effect would this have on the life insurance industry? Would there be any effect on research and treatment of terminal diseases? And would there be any age constraints—would assisted suicide be an option for an eight-year-old?

565   This study highlights the inadequacies of end-of-life care. Health care professionals must make a commitment to create caring environments that allow for respectful, humane care for the dying. The ANA (1994) makes the following recommendations regard-
570   ing the debate and controversy of assisted suicide:

- Advance the precepts of *Nursing's Agenda for Health Care Reform*, one of which calls for careful assessment of the appropriateness of providing high-tech curative medical care to those who
575   simply require comfort, relief from pain, supportive care or peaceful death.
- Engage in professional and public dialogue and decision making around assisted suicide. Encourage the participation of nurses in discussions
580   of this issue at the local, state, and national level.
- Collaborate with other members of the health professions and citizens to advance and ensure the availability of quality end-of-life care.
- Provide education for health professionals and
585   the community on ethical and legal rights and responsibilities surrounding health care decision making, treatment options, pain control, symptom management, and palliative care.
- Support the use of outcome measurements and
590   further research to ensure more scientifically based, responsible, and ethically sensitive end-of-life treatment.
- Advocate for the removal of barriers to the delivery of appropriate end-of-life care through
595   legislation and changes in restrictive regulatory and institutional practices.

- Promote patient and family participation in treatment decision making and the use of advance directives. (pp. 7–9)

600   All health care professionals owe it to themselves and to John and Mary Q. Public to make sure that these recommendations exist not only on paper, but that each one becomes part of a comprehensive plan to ultimately improve the quality of life at the end of life.

605   A pregnant woman usually develops a birth plan, stating who should be present during the delivery, should the process be videotaped or not, will she breast feed, and so forth. This is done because birth is a natural part of life and is expected. Why, then, do persons
610   not have a "death plan," as this event is also a natural part of life and is expected? Is there any such thing as a good death, or is death always an event to be feared? This study raised many more questions than it answered. If after reflecting on this study readers begin to
615   question issues about their own death and end-of-life care, then the researcher's goal will have been accomplished.

References

American Nurses Association. (1994). *Position statement on assisted suicide.* Washington, DC: Author.

Burkhardt, M. A., & Nathaniel, A. K. (1998). *Ethics & issues in contemporary nursing.* Albany, NY: Delmar.

Colaizzi, P. R. (1978). Psychological research as phenomenologists view it. In R. Valle and M. King (Eds.) *Existential–phenomenological alternatives for psychology* (pp. 48–79). New York: Oxford University Press.

Davis, A. J., Phillips, L., Drought, T. S., Sellin, S., Ronsman, K., & Hershberger, A. K. (1995). Nurses' attitudes toward active euthanasia. *Nursing Outlook, 43*(4), 174–179.

Humphry, D. (1991). *Final exit.* Eugene, OR: The Hemlock Society.

Korpivaara, A. (1999, December). Diversity in dying: Improving palliative care in a multicultural society. *Project on Death in America* (PDIA) *Newsletter, 6,* 3–5.

Lynch, J. J., & Edwards, S. S. (1998). Cancer care providers have an obligation to participate in advance care planning and advance directives. *Oncology Issues, 13*(2), 31–32.

Maguire, D. C. (1974, February). Death, legal and illegal. *Atlantic Monthly* [Online]. Available: http://www.theatlantic.com/politics/abortion/mag.htm

Perrin, K. O. (1997). Giving voice to the wishes of elders for end-of-life care. *Journal of Gerontological Nursing, 23*(3), 18–27.

Schlenk, J. S. (1997). Advance directives: Role of nurse practitioners. *Journal of the American Academy of Nurse Practitioners, 9*(7), 317–321.

Smith, A. (1999, July/August). Oregon's assisted suicide law scrutinized after first year. *Clinician News, 3*(7), 1–24.

Support Study Principal Investigators. (1995). A controlled trial to improve care for seriously ill hospitalized patients: The study to understand prognoses and preferences for outcomes and risks of treatments (SUPPORT). *Journal of the American Medical Association, 274*(20), 1591–1598.

Exercise for Article 29

Factual Questions

1. What was the mean age of the participants in this study?

2. Why did the researcher wait to review relevant literature until after the themes of this study emerged?

3. How long were the participants given to return their responses?

4. The researcher summarizes the phenomenological method as described by Colaizzi (1978) in a list of steps. What is the last step?

5. How many theme clusters about a good death were identified?

6. What is the third theme about assisted suicide?

7. How many of the 12 participants participated in the final step (i.e., having participants review the exhaustive description to see if it accurately reflects the essence of what they were trying to communicate during the data collection)?

Questions for Discussion

8. Do you consider this study to be "scientific" even though it does not contain statistical analyses of quantitative data? Explain.

9. The researcher states that a "purposive sample" was used. What do you think that this term means? (See lines 32–33.)

10. The participants in this study wrote their answers in private. If you had planned this study, would you have done this or would you have used some other method such as interviews? Explain. (See lines 64–66.)

11. To what extent does the information in Tables 1 and 2 help you understand the process used by the researcher to derive theme clusters from the original statements provided by the participants? Explain.

12. The researcher had some of the participants review the exhaustive descriptions to see if they accurately reflected the essence of what they were trying to communicate in their written responses. In your opinion, how important was this step? To what extent, if any, does this review strengthen the study? (See lines 323–346.)

13. In this study, ten of the participants were White and two were African American. Do you think that additional studies on this topic conducted with samples that are more diverse would be justified? Explain. (See lines 500–504.)

14. This study is an example of qualitative research. If you had planned a study on this topic, would you have planned to conduct qualitative *or* quantitative research? Explain.

Quality Ratings

Directions: Indicate your level of agreement with each of the following statements by circling a number from 5 for strongly agree (SA) to 1 for strongly disagree (SD). If you believe an item is not applicable to this research article, leave it blank. Be prepared to explain your ratings. When responding to criteria A and B below, keep in mind that brief titles and abstracts are conventional in published research.

A. The title of the article is appropriate.

    SA   5   4   3   2   1   SD

B. The abstract provides an effective overview of the research article.

    SA   5   4   3   2   1   SD

C. The introduction establishes the importance of the study.

    SA   5   4   3   2   1   SD

D. The literature review establishes the context for the study.

    SA   5   4   3   2   1   SD

E. The research purpose, question, or hypothesis is clearly stated.

    SA   5   4   3   2   1   SD

F. The method of sampling is sound.

    SA   5   4   3   2   1   SD

G. Relevant demographics (for example, age, gender, and ethnicity) are described.

    SA   5   4   3   2   1   SD

H. Measurement procedures are adequate.

    SA   5   4   3   2   1   SD

I. All procedures have been described in sufficient detail to permit a replication of the study.

    SA   5   4   3   2   1   SD

J. The participants have been adequately protected from potential harm.

    SA   5   4   3   2   1   SD

K. The results are clearly described.

    SA   5   4   3   2   1   SD

L. The discussion/conclusion is appropriate.

    SA   5   4   3   2   1   SD

M. Despite any flaws, the report is worthy of publication.

    SA   5   4   3   2   1   SD

Article 30

Hospital-Based Psychiatric Experience Before Community-Based Practice for Nurses: Imperative or Dispensable?

Derith M. Harris, RN, RPN, BEd, MEd, **Brenda Happell**, RN, RPN, BA (Hons), DipEd, PhD[*]

ABSTRACT. This article describes an Australian research project that explored the relevance of hospital-based experience in preparing psychiatric nurses for community-based practice. A qualitative design was selected to obtain in-depth information in an area in which no formal research has been undertaken. In-depth interviews were conducted with six psychiatric nurses currently engaged in community-based practice. The interviews were audiotaped, and the transcribed data were analyzed for major themes. The results indicated that the participants did not believe their hospital experience had prepared them to function effectively in the community. In some respects, hospital experience was perceived as having hindered their transition into the community environment. This exploratory study indicates the need for further research and the exploration of alternative methods to prepare psychiatric nurses for community-based practice.

From *Issues in Mental Health Nursing*, *20*, 495–503. Copyright © 1999 by Taylor & Francis. Reprinted with permission.

There has been a prevailing assumption within the psychiatric nursing profession that experience in an institutionally based psychiatric setting is a necessary prerequisite for nurses undertaking practice as commu-
5 nity psychiatric nurses. The experience they gain through this process is believed to stand them in good stead for a future role in the community. This presumption has remained strong, despite the lack of empirical testing. In view of the magnitude of the changes occur-
10 ring within psychiatric services, this is an opportune time to explore the validity of such a view.

Advances in psychiatric medicine have significantly influenced the practice of psychiatric nursing. A decrease in the number of inpatient beds and the subse-
15 quent increase in community mental health programs have increased the demand for nurses who work in community settings (Whiteford, 1993; Wilson & Dunn, 1996). The process of deinstitutionalization, however, is far from complete, and the change in the focus of
20 health care is expected to be an ongoing process. The

National Mental Health Policy of Australia (Commonwealth of Australia, 1992) outlined the philosophy of community mental health as the provision of health care in the least restrictive environment. The success of
25 this policy depends, in no small part, on the availability of staff who are suitably qualified to provide health care to mentally ill people, avoiding unnecessary hospitalization while enhancing the safety of individuals and of society. Community psychiatric nurses, as the
30 largest group of mental health professionals, must make a significant contribution to the execution of this policy. To do so, however, they must possess an adequate level of expertise for community-based practice.

The significant increase in the number of psychiatric nurses working in the community has not been ac-
35 companied by the development and implementation of specialist education in community psychiatry to meet their needs. As a consequence, "Community psychiatric nursing has remained on a casual, disorganized ba-
40 sis with no consistent pattern emerging" (Buchan & Smith, 1989, p. 5). It would appear, therefore, that the current practice of requiring institutionally based experience prior to employment within the community is not sufficiently preparing psychiatric nurses for this
45 role.

Despite the significance of this problem, no literature addressing these issues could be located. Indeed, the main themes from the literature in relation to community psychiatric nursing tend to shed doubt on the
50 degree to which institutionally based experience prepares nurses for community practice. Several writers have emphasized that a different skill base is required of community psychiatric nurses (Buchan & Smith, 1989; Savage, 1992; Simmons & Brooker, 1987; Wil-
55 son & Dunn, 1996).

The literature is less informative regarding the nature of the different skills required for community nursing practice. These skills are only alluded to in discussions of the different role of the nurse in the commu-
60 nity environment. Community-based clients often do

---

[*]*Derith M. Harris* is a PhD candidate, School of Postgraduate Nursing, University of Melbourne, Victoria, Australia. *Brenda Happell*, School of Postgraduate Nursing, University of Melbourne, Victoria, Australia.

not request a visit from the community psychiatric nurse and are often opposed to the idea. In this situation, the nurse requires a high level of engagement skills to facilitate access to the client's home. In con-
65 trast, within the hospital environment the nurse generally has automatic entree to the client's environment and can therefore apply appropriate nursing interventions even against the client's wishes, if necessary. Engagement skills, therefore, although still important
70 to the nurse in the hospital, are not as crucial to the implementation of treatment as they are in the community (Harris, 1987).

Once the community nurse has entered the client's home, subsequent interactions will differ markedly
75 from those inside the hospital. The nature of the interaction itself is distinctly different. The client is in a more powerful position, meaning that the nurse must depend more heavily on skills of persuasion and negotiation (Bowers, 1992).

80 Within the hospital environment, the psychiatric nurse is readily able to access other members of the multidisciplinary team for support and guidance. This team approach is often heavily relied on in determining and delivering the client's treatment. In the community
85 environment, the nurse is more likely to work in isolation or as part of a small team. In the community situation, the nurse must become more self-reliant on his or her knowledge base and the skills of assessment and observation (Bowers, 1992; Harris, 1987).

90 The paucity of research on the extent to which hospital-based experience prepares the psychiatric nurse for practice in the community prompted Derith Harris to pose the following research question: How useful have practicing community psychiatric nurses found
95 hospital-based experience in preparing them for their current role?

Method

Research Design

We chose a qualitative design to explore the degree to which hospital-based experience has been useful in preparing psychiatric nurses for community practice.
100 Designing a questionnaire format or attitude scale would prove problematic in the absence of existing literature and research findings to guide the process. A questionnaire format with subsequent statistical analysis would not have provided the same detailed data as
105 could be achieved through in-depth interviewing (Lincoln & Guba, 1985; Mariano, 1991).

Participants

Six community psychiatric nurses, engaged in current practice, constituted the sample for this study. They were recruited through the newsletter of the
110 Community Psychiatric Nurses Association of Victoria, Australia. Three men and three women, ages 22–45, agreed to participate. Their levels of community experience varied from three months to 12 years. All participants had been employed in psychiatric hospitals
115 for periods of between one year and six years before accepting positions in the community.

The Interviews

A semistructured interview design was used. This enabled us to obtain information that we considered important while allowing the participants to raise the
120 issues they considered most relevant to their current practice. The questions were open-ended so as to promote in-depth discussion of pertinent issues (Patton, 1987). The interviews were conducted at locations convenient to the participants.

Data Analysis

125 All interviews were audiotaped and transcribed. Data analysis commenced with the transcription and review of the tapes (Patton, 1987). The transcribed data were then further analyzed, to allow for the identification and coding of the relevant themes. Once we identi-
130 fied the themes, we cross-referenced them with the responses of other participants to detect similarities and differences. The principles of Lincoln and Guba (1985) were strictly observed to guarantee the trustworthiness of the data. Credibility was maintained through pro-
135 longed engagement, peer debriefing, and member checking. We achieved prolonged engagement by establishing rapport and creating a conversational atmosphere in which participants felt comfortable discussing their opinions. Time constraints were not imposed, and
140 follow-up interviews were agreed to if necessary. A peer debriefing process was implemented to enhance the objectivity of the study. The research was regularly discussed with a colleague, who provided a fresh and unbiased approach that kept us focused on the data, as
145 well as being a source of support and guidance.

To ensure that our interpretation of the participants' views was accurate, we implemented a twofold process of member checking. During the interviews, the interviewer would frequently rephrase the participants'
150 statements to safeguard against misinterpretation. Second, a transcript of the interview was sent to the participant for verification that his or her meanings and intentions had been fairly represented (Lincoln & Guba, 1985). Finally, an experienced qualitative re-
155 searcher conducted an external audit. The auditor randomly checked sections of the tapes to ensure the accuracy of the transcripts. The auditor confirmed the accuracy of the transcribed data.

Results

The views of the participants clearly contradicted
160 the notion that hospital-based experience is a necessary prerequisite for practice in a community setting. The differences between the two settings require that a completely different approach be adopted. Although the skills required for patient care might be also impor-
165 tant to nurses within the hospital environment, participants considered adapting to the context in which care is delivered the most crucial aspect of the role of the

community psychiatric nurse. None of the participants could identify the manner through which hospital-based experience had assisted them in the fulfillment of this distinct role.

Interpersonal skills, considered necessary for psychiatric nurses in any environment, were seen as requiring a different approach once nurses are outside of the hospital domain and attempting to enter the client's territory. As one participant stated,

> In the wards you are on your own ground and even though you perhaps do not even think about it in those terms [the clients] are displaced from their own territory. So they're careful, they are tactful…They are less sure of themselves. In their own home people react quite differently…you can lose engagement with the family and thus perhaps the client.

Adjustment to this dissimilar approach was identified as the source of some initial difficulty, as one participant suggested: "You need to learn very quickly the difference between being in charge in the ward and being a visitor in the community." This adjustment was compounded to some degree by the approach the participants had adopted within the hospital. They had become used to working in an environment they considered largely their own domain. Their right to be in the hospital ward was automatic. The participants described taking this approach with them into the community and experiencing considerable difficulty interacting with patients until they "unlearned" the methods they had used in the hospital. The degree of responsibility and autonomy inherent within community-based practice was identified as another area for which the participants' hospital experience had left them inadequately prepared:

> You are far more responsible for your own work [in the community]. In the ward you can choose to take responsibility or not. You can have your good days and your bad days, it is not as critical. In the community it is far more critical that each time you go out, you are on the ball. You have to be more experienced to be in the community. You have to be able to draw on a greater fund of knowledge in the community than in the ward.

One participant highlighted the fact that nurses practice without the same availability of information and resources they become used to in the hospital environment:

> You go out there with no information. You might have some referral letter indicating something, but you find when you get there that you get something totally different. You have to disagree. On the ward…it is more set up. The client comes in and you have a provisional diagnosis, so you are thinking along those lines. The other difference is the support staff. You have all those people around you. In the community you go out alone; you are seeing the clients in their own environment.

In adapting to this change, the participants had to alter their mindset from that of the hospital. As one participant stated: "Your whole background has been structured around the [psychiatric hospital]. You have always had support from up the line. [The community] is in a different environment."

The participants agreed that, to provide high-quality service to the public, community psychiatric nurses need to access and treat large numbers of clients according to an individualized treatment program. To achieve this goal, they need to view the client's situation more broadly than they had within the confines of the hospital. The following response demonstrates this.

> In the community there is a whole ideology of community treatment versus the hospital that is very different. I am still in the community because I still very much believe in that ethos. I think trying to keep people in a less restrictive place. Their own environment is a kinder way to go, and I think it works. I get enjoyment out of that; in the wards, sometimes I felt like a jailer. You do this now. This is the way it goes. At times, I was more rooted in the thinking of "we have always done it this way so we should do it this way." You can look a little wider and think a little differently sometimes.

Involving the family in the management and treatment of a client in the community was recognized as crucial to ensure that the family is adequately prepared to manage and support a client who is experiencing psychiatric problems. Although the importance of the family is not restricted to the community setting, it becomes magnified in this environment. It is the family who generally provides the day-to-day care of the client: "You need to be able to assess a family as much as assessing a person. You need to be able to assess their ability to deal with a situation and their knowledge to cope and also how they are reacting."

None of the participants referred to either their nursing education or their hospital-based experience as being particularly helpful in preparing them for practice in the community. One participant reinforced this view in relation to her experience on interview panels for community-based positions:

> I have a lot of interviews with nurses and I was amazed they don't know where to start with a mental state often except PAMS GOT JIMI.[1] Even some did not have that basis.

Another participant suggested that even colleagues with many years of experience, who were occupying senior positions, generally did not perform at a senior standard.

Discussion

The findings from this research confirm the major themes from the literature. The participants' views clearly demonstrate the impact of the environment on the role of the community psychiatric nurse and, subsequently, on the manner in which their nursing skills

---

[1] This is a mental status tool that is widely used in Australia by mental health care professionals. Each initial represents an important element of mental status (e.g., P = perception, A = affect, M = mood, etc.).

are used. In principle, the skills themselves might be considered applicable to psychiatric nurses regardless of the work setting. In practice, however, the approach adopted by successful nurses in the community must be completely different.

The apparent impact of the context of practice on the use of psychiatric nursing skills as expressed both in the literature and from the findings of this study should surely encourage the profession to question its existing practices. Is it valid that nurses who wish to specialize in the community field be required to gain experience in a hospital setting? Our participants not only confirmed the view that hospital-based experience was of limited benefit in preparing them for the community psychiatric nursing role, but they also, in some instances, reported it to have been a hindrance. To adapt to the community environment, the nurses had to adopt an orientation to practice that was completely different from the one they had used in the hospital environment.

A possible strategy is to offer newly graduated nurses who indicate a desire to work in the community a program of supervised practice in the community environment. Through the provision of appropriate supervision, the nursing graduate would be more likely to develop the required skills. To facilitate the success of such a program, an appropriate university course should be developed. The content of this course would ideally be designed to equip potential community psychiatric nurses with the opportunity to develop the theoretical and practical skills essential for community-based practice.

The results of a study of this size, however, cannot be generalized. Furthermore, certain aspects of the nurses' preparation and experience may be unique to Australia. The fact that the study findings do support the available literature suggests that the current practices may not be effective, and alternative strategies should be explored. A larger, quantitative study of community psychiatric nurses should be conducted to ascertain the extent to which the views of these six participants are representative of community psychiatric nurses. Should they be found to be representative, the implications would be substantial.

Conclusion

The findings of this study illustrate that the participants perceived themselves as inadequately prepared for their roles as community psychiatric nurses. Neither their nursing education nor their hospital-based experience had facilitated their transition into a new working environment. Further research is necessary to ascertain the degree to which these findings are representative of all community psychiatric nurses and to determine appropriate strategies through which the problem can be addressed.

The practice of psychiatric nursing is continuing to change dramatically. An increasing emphasis on com-munity-based care is constantly challenging the theoretical basis on which psychiatric nursing was originally established. The impact of the environment in which care is delivered on the manner in which nursing skills are implemented is strongly emphasized in the literature and is supported to some degree by the findings of this study. If this view is confirmed, it would be clear that the existing approach to the preparation of community psychiatric nurses is not functional. Alternative approaches, as suggested earlier in the article, need to be closely examined in an attempt to resolve what can only be viewed as an unsatisfactory situation—unsatisfactory not only for the nurses who find themselves unprepared for a new role but also for the recipients of their care.

References

Bowers, L. (1992). Ethnomethodology 11: A study of the community psychiatric nurse in the patient's home. *International Journal of Nursing Studies, 29*, 69–79.

Buchan, T., & Smith, R. (1989). Nursing process in community psychiatric nursing. *Australian Journal of Advanced Nursing, 6*(3), 5–11.

Commonwealth of Australia (1992). *National mental health policy.* Canberra: Australian Governmental Publishing Service.

Harris, P. (1987, April). Psychiatric assessment in the home: Applications in home care. *Quality Review Bulletin, 13*(4):131–134.

Lincoln, Y. S., & Guba, E. G. (1985). *Naturalistic inquiry.* Beverly Hills, CA: Sage.

Mariano, C. (1991). Qualitative research: Instructional strategies and curricula considerations. *Nursing and Health Care, 11*, 354–359.

Patton, M. Q. (1987). *How to use qualitative methodology in evaluation.* Newbury Park, CA: Sage.

Savage, P. (1992). Patient assessment in psychiatric nursing. *Journal of Advanced Nursing. 16*, 311–316.

Simmons, S., & Brooker, C. (1987). Making community psychiatric nurses part of the team. *Nursing Times, 83*(19):49–51.

Whiteford, H. (1993). Australia national mental health policy. *Hospital and Community Psychiatry, 44*, 963–966.

Wilson, K., & Dunn, R. (1996). Psychiatric care: Change means opportunity. *Australian Nursing Journal, 3*(9), 36–38.

Address correspondence to: Derith Harris, School of Postgraduate Nursing, University of Melbourne, Level 1, 723 Swanston St., Carlton 3053, Victoria, Australia. E-mail should be sent to: d.harris @nursing.unimelb.edu.au

Exercise for Article 30

Factual Questions

1. According to the literature review, the main themes from the literature on community psychiatric nursing tend to shed doubt on what?

2. According to the researchers, why would designing a questionnaire or attitude scale for this study be problematic?

3. Were the questions in this study open-ended *or* closed-ended?

4. How was "credibility" in the data analysis maintained?

5. Why did the interviewer frequently rephrase the participants' statements?

6. Who conducted the external audit in the data analysis stage of this study?

7. According to the researchers, can the results of this study be generalized?

Questions for Discussion

8. The participants in this study were recruited through a newsletter. In your opinion, was this a good way to recruit participants for a study of this type? Are there other ways to recruit participants? Explain. (See lines 109–111.)

9. The researchers state that they used "a semistructured interview." What is your understanding of the meaning of this term? (See line 117.)

10. In your opinion, is the data analysis in lines 125–158 described in sufficient detail? Explain.

11. How important are the quotations in the Results section of this research article? Did the quotations contribute to your understanding of the results? Explain. (See lines 159–272.)

12. The researchers suggest that further research is necessary. Do you agree? Why? Why not? (See lines 327–331.)

Quality Ratings

Directions: Indicate your level of agreement with each of the following statements by circling a number from 5 for strongly agree (SA) to 1 for strongly disagree (SD). If you believe an item is not applicable to this research article, leave it blank. Be prepared to explain your ratings. When responding to criteria A and B below, keep in mind that brief titles and abstracts are conventional in published research.

A. The title of the article is appropriate.

   SA   5   4   3   2   1   SD

B. The abstract provides an effective overview of the research article.

   SA   5   4   3   2   1   SD

C. The introduction establishes the importance of the study.

   SA   5   4   3   2   1   SD

D. The literature review establishes the context for the study.

   SA   5   4   3   2   1   SD

E. The research purpose, question, or hypothesis is clearly stated.

   SA   5   4   3   2   1   SD

F. The method of sampling is sound.

   SA   5   4   3   2   1   SD

G. Relevant demographics (for example, age, gender, and ethnicity) are described.

   SA   5   4   3   2   1   SD

H. Measurement procedures are adequate.

   SA   5   4   3   2   1   SD

I. All procedures have been described in sufficient detail to permit a replication of the study.

   SA   5   4   3   2   1   SD

J. The participants have been adequately protected from potential harm.

   SA   5   4   3   2   1   SD

K. The results are clearly described.

   SA   5   4   3   2   1   SD

L. The discussion/conclusion is appropriate.

   SA   5   4   3   2   1   SD

M. Despite any flaws, the report is worthy of publication.

   SA   5   4   3   2   1   SD

Article 31

Student Nurses' Perceptions of
Alternative and Allopathic Medicine

Ron Joudrey, MA, **Sheila McKay**, RN, MN, **Jim Gough**, PhD[*]

ABSTRACT. This exploratory study of student nurses is based on the results of the responses to one question on an open-ended questionnaire: How would you define the relationship between alternative medicine and allopathic (conventional) medicine? A specific goal of the study was to find out how the surveyed respondents conceptualized the relationship between allopathic and alternative medicine. Three themes were identified: (a) "They are not at all alike," (b) "The two can or should be used together," and (c) "Those who practice alternative medicine and those who practice allopathic do not get along very well." The discussion suggests some reasons for these perceptions and considers some implications for future health care.

From *Western Journal of Nursing Research*, 26, 356–366. Copyright © 2004 by Sage Publications, Inc. Reprinted with permission.

The long-standing hegemony of allopathic medicine has been challenged by the increasing popularity of alternative medicine. The reaction of mainstream health care providers to the growth of alternative medi-
5 cine has been given much attention in professional medical and nursing journals. Although the perceptions of those already practicing in the health care system are certainly worthy of research interest, there is also a need to investigate the views of health care practitio-
10 ners in training. The extent to which alternative and allopathic therapies become integrated will depend somewhat on how the future generation of health care workers conceptualizes the relationship between the conventional and alternative modes of health care. The
15 present study examines how student nurses perceive this relationship.

Nurses, Physicians, and the Rise of
Alternative Medicine

In recent times, health care professionals working within the dominant allopathic tradition have become aware that many of their clients are utilizing various
20 forms of alternative or complementary therapies. Research in a number of countries, including the United States (Eisenberg et al., 1998; Eisenberg et al., 1993) and Canada (McClennon-Leong & Kerr, 1999), has

clearly demonstrated such use. In response to large
25 consumer demand, a number of nursing researchers (Hayes & Alexander, 2000; McClennon-Leong & Kerr, 1999; Melland & Clayburgh, 2000; Reed, Pettigrew, & King, 2000) have called for the need to include alternative therapies in the nursing curricula. King, Pettigrew,
30 and Reed (1999) presented one practical rationale for nurses to increase their interest in such therapies: "If significantly more Americans are using some form of complementary therapy, it is imperative that nurses have a knowledge base of a variety of therapies in or-
35 der to assist clients with decision making related to therapies" (p. 250).

We contend that health care practitioners' perceptions of complementary and alternative therapies will influence the future direction of health care. Writers
40 from the sociological tradition known as symbolic interactionism have agreed that meanings held by social actors influence behavior (Stryker, 1980). Whether nurses and other health care professionals have favorable or unfavorable views of alternative therapies will
45 likely influence the extent to which these therapies are integrated into health care practice. The relationship between the two systems of health care (allopathic and alternative) has changed somewhat over time. Budrys (2001) argued that allopathic medicine had established
50 itself as the dominant form of health care by the turn of the 20th century. With this hegemony came the tendency for those working within this tradition to relegate other forms of therapy to a subordinate status. Therapies offered outside the allopathic domain were
55 viewed as quackery, unscientific, and dangerous (Budrys, 2001; Goldstein, 2000). There are, however, recent indications of increasing acceptance of some alternative and complementary therapies by physicians and nurses. For example, a Canadian study of general
60 practitioners found that 54% perceived some benefits from the use of alternative therapies and were sometimes willing to recommend their patients use these therapies (Verhoef & Sutherland, 1995). Other studies (Hayes & Alexander, 2000; King et al., 1999) found
65 evidence of favorable opinions toward alternative and

[*]*Ron Joudrey* is a sociology instructor at Red Deer College. *Sheila McKay* is nursing department chair at Red Deer College. *Jim Gough* is a philosophy instructor at Red Deer College.

complementary therapies on the part of practicing nurses. The Hayes and Alexander (2000) study of nurse practitioners found that "almost two-thirds (65%) indicated that they had recommended or referred clients for one or more alternative modalities" (p. 52). To our knowledge there have been few, if any, extant studies on how future generations of health care professionals view alternative and complementary therapies. There is a need to investigate how groups, such as student nurses, make sense of the relationship between alternative therapies and allopathic therapies because their perceptions will undoubtedly have some influence on whether the two previously hostile systems of health care will reach some sort of rapprochement in future.

Many writers, including Budrys (2001), Clarke (2000), and Goldstein (2000), have pointed out the difficulty in finding an agreed-on definition to encompass the eclectic range of therapies variously labeled as alternative, complementary, unconventional, and more recently, complementary and alternative medicine (CAM). Goldstein (2000) suggested that residual definitions of the phenomena are common. An example of a residual definition would be the following from Matcha (2000): "Alternative medicine refers to medical treatments that are not taught or offered in Western medical practice" (p. 299). This type of definition is perhaps too restrictive because there are a growing number of such therapies that are offered by allopathic practitioners (Clarke, 2000).

Finding acceptable terminology to use in this area is also problematic. Although the label "complementary and alternative medicine (CAM)" has become more common, many writers such as Budrys (2001), Clarke (2000), Goldstein (2000), and Hayes and Alexander (2000) have not used this term consistently. The tendency has often been to acknowledge the newer, more encompassing label, while also continuing to employ terms such as "complementary," "alternative," or "unconventional" in a synonymous fashion. A cover story in *Newsweek* (Cowley et al., 2002) was titled "Inside the Science of Alternative Medicine," even though the writers referred to CAM throughout the story. We decided to use the designation "alternative medicine" because this term is still employed in common parlance.

Purpose

The aim of the present study was to explore student nurses' perceptions of the relationship between allopathic and alternative medicine.

Method

Design

A qualitative, cross-sectional descriptive design was used for this exploratory survey of student nurses' perceptions.

Sample

A convenience sample was used to study student nurses at a community college in Alberta, Canada. Students in this program have the option of completing a 3-year diploma or a 4-year degree. The intent was to sample as many student nurses as possible out of the 250 enrolled in the program. A total of 81 students completed the survey for a return rate of 30.86%. A breakdown of study participants by year of program was the following: 1st year, $N = 9$; 2nd year, $N = 28$; 3rd year, $N = 11$; and 4th year, $N = 33$. No information was obtained as to whether the respondents in the first 3 years were degree or diploma students because this was not regarded by the researchers as important to the study. Among the respondents, 96.3% were women, and 3.7% were men. They ranged in age from 18 to 45 years, with a mean age of 22.7. Most participants (74%) reported being single, and 26% were married. The majority were residents of Alberta (71.6%), and the remainder resided elsewhere prior to entering the program.

Procedures

The researchers first obtained permission from the college Research Ethics Committee to carry out this study. A seven-item, open-ended questionnaire was used to survey student nurses' perceptions of alternative medicine (see the Appendix). The findings discussed in this article are the responses to one question from the larger study: How would you define the relationship between alternative medicine and allopathic medicine?

Various nursing instructors distributed the questionnaire in their classes between January and December 2000. A cover letter to potential respondents stressed that participation was voluntary and anonymous and was not a required component of their program.

Data Analysis

Responses to the study question were analyzed using schema analysis as described by Ryan and Bernard (2000). Two of the study authors compared and coded the responses in an effort to find common themes. These themes were developed inductively by carefully reading and comparing the responses, looking for repetitions of words and phrases. Responses that were judged similar and frequently mentioned formed the basis for the content of major themes. The themes discussed are illustrated with direct quotes from study participants in an effort to faithfully represent their discourse (Stryker, 1980).

The researchers initially intended to do a year-by-year comparison of student responses; however, after a careful reading of the data, no major differences were detected between those in different phases of the program. The findings presented herein are based on analysis of the collective groups of respondents.

As a means of testing the trustworthiness of the themes, the technique of member checking was used. Discussion with several study participants indicated the analysis was recognizable to them. Lincoln and Guba (1985) recommended member checking as an important technique for establishing credibility of analysis.

Results

Based on analysis of responses to the question "How do you define the relationship between alternative and allopathic medicine?" we identified three themes: (a) "They are not at all alike," (b) "The two can or should be used together," and (c) "Those who practice alternative medicine and those who practice allopathic do not get along well." The findings of the study are presented with these themes.

"They Are Not At All Alike"

A total of 15 study participants mentioned differences between the two therapeutic modes. One respondent simply stated, "They are not at all alike." Others delineated the differences more specifically. The perception of alternative medicine as being more natural, whereas allopathic is otherwise, was voiced by a few students: "Alternative medicine draws on the body's natural, innate healing forces, while conventional medicine is more synthetic, complex, and highly technological."

And, "Alternative medicine is more natural without using chemicals and invasive procedures while allopathic is the opposite."

In a few cases, the natural noninvasive nature of alternative medicine was extolled as a virtue, as illustrated by a 3rd-year student: "I don't think the two therapies are similar at all. I'd rather do the alternative first, especially if it's noninvasive, before I let someone decide that I need to be cut open. I think everything can be cured/controlled by what we eat and natural methods."

A second contrast was to perceive alternative medicine as more holistic and allopathic as more specific: "Alternative medicine deals more with the person as a whole human being, whereas conventional medicine focuses only on the physical ailment."

And in a similar vein: "Alternative medicine allows for the possibility of a mind/body connection which [sic] allopathic medicine focuses only on the physical body."

Evaluation of the two types of medicine was also noted: "I feel that it is harder to evaluate alternative medicine's effects compared to the other type"; and "Conventional therapies may be more reliable as there are more studies that prove their effectiveness but this may change as more people research alternative medicine."

"The Two Can or Should Be Used Together"

The second theme suggesting complementarity was voiced by 23 respondents. One 2nd-year student commented, "The two can or should be used together because both types of therapies can be beneficial."

One perception was that allopathic and alternative have similar goals. Consider the following statements as illustrative: "Both have the intention and purpose of improving one's health" and "They both should be working together to restore or maintain health."

Others perceived that both approaches have strengths and limitations: "Often conventional medicine can be augmented by alternative medicine or vice versa. Both therapies have strengths and limitations so a combination of the two would likely prove more effective than one used in isolation"; "I think they can complement one another. There are certainly benefits and hindrances to both types, but they each have their place in treatment of patients."

"Those Who Practice Alternative Medicine and Those Who Practice Allopathic Do Not Get Along Well"

In this theme, the focus was on the practitioners. Many spoke of the tension between allopathic and alternative practitioners using adjectives such as "shaky," "poor," "tense," "strained," and "competing" to describe the relationship. Of the respondents, 43 spoke of the opposition between allopathic and alternative practitioners, making this the most common theme. Of these student nurses, 20 attributed the conflicts to the attitudes of allopathic practitioners: "Those who practice conventional medicine are not receptive to other treatments. One reason that could be plausible is that they are defending their territory"; "There is a lot of misinformation and misunderstanding by doctors over alternative medicine"; "I think that conventional doctors and nurses do not see the positive effects that alternative medicine can have"; and "Conventional medicine is threatened by the success of alternative medicine."

Only one respondent perceived alternative practitioners as responsible for the conflict: "I think that those people who practice alternative medicine often extol the virtues of 'natural remedies' and discourage patients from seeking advice from doctors."

Several respondents (15) expressed that although present relationships are strained, the situation seems to be improving: "Alternative medicine is just beginning to be accepted by conventional health practitioners" and "I think that at this time (despite a history of conflict) that [sic] physicians and other medical practitioners like nurses are starting to insert more alternative medicine into their practices. They are still fairly focused on conventional medicine but do use alternative medicine a bit."

Some (19) hoped that the relationship would improve in the future as shown in these examples: "The time for fighting and animosity is over. They need to work more together"; "There needs to be more respect for each other between doctors, nurses, and those who practice alternative medicine. This would be in the best interest of clients."

We must note that, in most cases, particular responses could be filtered into one category. There were five responses that overlapped categories. For example, one respondent mentioned the complementarity between the therapies but also referred to conflict between the practitioners.

Discussion

This exploratory study found that although student nurses' perceptions about alternative and allopathic medicine varied, these perceptions did appear to cluster around three themes. These different conceptualizations might be a reflection of the amorphous and fluctuating relationship between the two modes of health care.

The first theme identified was "They are not at all alike." The use of the term *alternative* may have predisposed some respondents to concentrate on differences, although this was not the case with many others in the sample.

One specific difference mentioned was that alternative therapies are more holistic, whereas allopathic therapies focus only on the physical ailment. Some writers, including Clarke (2000) and Goldstein (2000), have suggested that holism is one feature that distinguishes alternative medicine from the allopathic mode. This rather common perception might have also influenced some of the study participants to notice differences. Students enrolled in this particular nursing program are also extensively exposed to the seminal work on nursing philosophy by Watson (1985) who emphasized the importance of a holistic emphasis.

Some alternative practitioners have made the claim that their therapies are superior to conventional ones because the former are more natural and noninvasive. A few of our respondents echoed this sentiment. The perception that natural is better needs more careful scrutiny because clearly some natural substances can be harmful.

The second theme was "The two can or should be used together." Those who expressed this view demonstrated a more current awareness of the efforts under way to promote more integration of the previously separate medical systems, although there was no mention of which types of therapies might be complementary. Certainly not all types of alternative medicine are likely to be integrated with conventional medical practice. We believe it is important that these students learn to make more critical distinctions between different types of alternative therapies, distinguishing those that may be harmful from those that may be beneficial. Some of these students did, however, demonstrate evidence of critical thinking by recognizing that both types of therapies have strengths and limitations.

The most common theme identified was "Those who practice alternative medicine and those who practice allopathic do not get along very well." This perception does not fit with recent evidence showing that physicians and nurses sometimes recommended their clients to alternative practitioners (Hayes & Alexander, 2000; Verhoef & Sutherland, 1995). Perhaps these students had not witnessed any examples of such crossover in their own experiences to date. As they enter practice situations, this perception may very well change, particularly if they work with physicians and nurses who are open to the use of some alternative therapies.

The tendency for several study respondents to attribute strained relationships between allopathic and alternative practitioners mostly to the nonacceptance of alternative medicine by those nurses and physicians practicing within the conventional (allopathic) tradition is worthy of comment. Clarke (2000) suggested that nurses in their efforts to achieve professional status have adopted an antitechnology ideology that rejects the medical model and advocates a model based on holistic care. If this is true, it may account for some of the accusations leveled against the allopathic practitioners by some student nurses in the present study.

In holding allopathic nurses and physicians responsible for the animosity between the two types of medicine, there seemed to be almost a carte blanche acceptance of alternative medicine and its practitioners. With a few exceptions, study participants did not hold the same critical stance toward alternative medicine as they did toward allopathic medicine. There may be some dangers in the wholesale and uncritical acceptance of alternative medicine. As the results of clinical trials investigating the safety and effectiveness of various alternative therapies become more available, this should enable nurses and other health care practitioners to discern which alternative therapies are useful and safe for clinical practice.

In a more positive vein, some of the student nurses perceived an improvement toward better relationships between allopathic and alternative practitioners, and some expressed the hope that this would continue for the best interest of clients.

The sources of these various perceptions just discussed are unclear. This particular nursing program has paid some attention to the topic of alternative medicine. Conversations with nursing instructors and students revealed there were one or two lectures devoted to this area, and the topic has been discussed in some of the scenarios the students dealt with in tutorials.

There are many other sources of information that may have influenced the respondents' perceptions: mass media, Internet, personal experiences, hearsay, testimonials, advertisements from alternative practitioners, and so on. How these other sources juxtaposed with professional socialization is an empirical question but one that should be addressed.

This small study of student nurses uncovered a variety of perceptions about how alternative medicine relates to allopathic medicine. The findings demonstrate a general receptiveness toward the integration of

alternative and conventional therapies. As new generations of nurses continue to be socialized into a more
395 holistic emphasis on health care, we believe this will
contribute to the increasing integration of two previously separate systems of health care. Medical sociolo-
gists such as Northcott (2002) argued that there is an
increasing similarity and convergence between alterna-
400 tive and conventional medicine. Such a rapprochement
is reflected in the perceptions of student nurses in the
present study. The future direction of health care will
be influenced by the perceptions of various categories
of health care practitioners. This study contributes to
405 our knowledge of these perceptions by concentrating
on a previously neglected group of study participants,
student nurses. The study is obviously limited by the
relatively small sample size, and we do not claim the
perceptions are representative of student nurses in gen-
410 eral.

APPENDIX
Survey Questions

1. How do you define alternative medicine?
2. Have you ever used any type of alternative medicine? If so, which type did you use? Were you satisfied with the results?
3. If you have never used any form of alternative
medicine, would you be willing to? Under what
conditions?
4. How would you define the relationship between alternative medicine and allopathic medicine?
5. Does your nursing program give any consideration
to alternative medicine? If yes, how is the topic
dealt with?
6. Describe your perceptions of the effectiveness of alternative medicine.
7. What factors do you feel account for the increasing
popularity of alternative medicine?

References

Budrys, G. (2001). *Our unsystematic health care system.* Lanham, MD: Row-
man & Littlefield.
Clarke, J. N. (2000). *Health, illness, and medicine in Canada* (3rd ed.). Don
Mills, ONT: Oxford University Press.
Cowley, G., Eisenberg, D., Kalb, C., Kaptchuk, T., Komaroff, A., Nonnan, D.,
et al. (2002, December 2). Health for life: Inside the science of alternative
medicine. *Newsweek,* pp. 45–75.
Eisenberg, D. M., Davis, R. B., Ettner, S. L., Appel, S., Wilkey, J., Van Rom-
pay, M., et al. (1998). Trends in alternative medicine use in the United
States, 1990–1997: Results of a follow-up national survey. *Journal of the
American Medical Association, 280,* 1569–1575.
Eisenberg, D. M., Kessler, R. C., Foster, C., Norlock, F. E., Calkins, D., &
Delbanco, L. (1993). Unconventional medicine in the United States: Prevalence, costs, and patterns of use. *New England Journal of Medicine, 328,*
246–252.
Goldstein, M. S. (2000). The growing acceptance of complementary and alternative medicine. In C. E. Bird, P. Conrad, & A. M. Fremont (Eds.), *Handbook of medical sociology* (5th ed., pp. 284–297). Upper Saddle River, NJ:
Prentice Hall.
Hayes, K. M., & Alexander, I. M. (2000). Alternative therapies and nurse
practitioners: Knowledge, professional experience, and personal use. *Holis-
tic Nurse Practitioner, 14,* 49–58.
King, M., Pettigrew, A., & Reed, F. (1999). Complementary, alternative,
integrative: Have nurses kept pace with their clients? *Medsurg Nursing, 8,*
249–256.
Lincoln, Y. S., & Guba, E. G. (1985). *Naturalistic inquiry.* Beverly Hills, CA:
Sage.
Matcha, D. A. (2000). *Medical sociology.* Boston: Allyn & Bacon.
McClennon-Leong, J., & Kerr, J. R. (1999). Alternative health care options in
Canada. *Canadian Nurse, 95,* 26–30.
Melland, H. I., & Clayburgh, T. L. (2000). Complementary therapies: Introduc-
tion into a nursing curriculum. *Nurse Educator, 25,* 247–250.
Northcott, H. C. (2002). Health care restructuring and alternative approaches to
health and medicine. In B. S. Bolaria & H. D. Dickinson (Eds.), *Health, ill-
ness, and health care in Canada* (3rd ed., pp. 460–474). Scarborough, ONT:
Nelson.
Reed, F., Pettigrew, A., & King, M. (2000). Alternative and complementary
therapies in nursing curricula. *Journal of Nursing Education, 39,* 133–139.
Ryan, G. W., & Bernard, H. R. (2000). Data management and analysis meth-
ods. In N. K. Denzin & Y. S. Lincoln (Eds.), *Handbook of qualitative re-
search* (2nd ed., pp. 769–802). Thousand Oaks, CA: Sage.
Stryker, S. (1980). *Symbolic interactionism.* Menlo Park, CA: Benjamin-
Cummings.
Verhoef, M. J., & Sutherland, L. R. (1995). Alternative medicine and general
practitioners. *Canadian Family Physician, 41,* 1004–1012.
Watson, J. (1985). *Nursing: The philosophy and science of caring.* Boulder:
Colorado Associated University Press.

Acknowledgments: We wish to express our appreciation to the
nursing students of Red Deer College who participated in this study;
to the nursing faculty who supported this project, especially nursing
instructor Sandy MacGregor; administrative assistants Ida Murray
and Patricia Couture; and Dr. Herbert C. Northcott for commenting
on the revised version of this article.

Address correspondence to: Ron Joudrey, Red Deer College, Department of Sociology, 100 College Boulevard, Alberta, Canada,
T4N 5H5.

Exercise for Article 31

Factual Questions

1. The acronym "CAM" stands for what words?

2. What percentage of the respondents were women?

3. Before conducting the study, the researchers obtained permission from whom?

4. Who distributed the questionnaire?

5. How many of the study authors compared and
coded the responses?

6. "Member checking" (i.e., discussing the findings
with the participants) was used in order to test
what?

Questions for Discussion

7. The researchers had a return rate of 30.86% (see
lines 122–123). In your opinion, how does this
return rate affect the quality of the study?

8. If you were approached to participate in a replication of this study (as a student nurse), would you
have agreed to participate? Why? Why not?

9. In your opinion, is the method of data analysis
presented in lines 152–175 described in sufficient
detail? Explain.

10. In your opinion, what are the practical implications of the results of this study?

11. Do you agree with the last sentence in the article (see lines 407–410)? Explain.

Quality Ratings

Directions: Indicate your level of agreement with each of the following statements by circling a number from 5 for strongly agree (SA) to 1 for strongly disagree (SD). If you believe an item is not applicable to this research article, leave it blank. Be prepared to explain your ratings. When responding to criteria A and B below, keep in mind that brief titles and abstracts are conventional in published research.

A. The title of the article is appropriate.

  SA   5   4   3   2   1   SD

B. The abstract provides an effective overview of the research article.

  SA   5   4   3   2   1   SD

C. The introduction establishes the importance of the study.

  SA   5   4   3   2   1   SD

D. The literature review establishes the context for the study.

  SA   5   4   3   2   1   SD

E. The research purpose, question, or hypothesis is clearly stated.

  SA   5   4   3   2   1   SD

F. The method of sampling is sound.

  SA   5   4   3   2   1   SD

G. Relevant demographics (for example, age, gender, and ethnicity) are described.

  SA   5   4   3   2   1   SD

H. Measurement procedures are adequate.

  SA   5   4   3   2   1   SD

I. All procedures have been described in sufficient detail to permit a replication of the study.

  SA   5   4   3   2   1   SD

J. The participants have been adequately protected from potential harm.

  SA   5   4   3   2   1   SD

K. The results are clearly described.

  SA   5   4   3   2   1   SD

L. The discussion/conclusion is appropriate.

  SA   5   4   3   2   1   SD

M. Despite any flaws, the report is worthy of publication.

  SA   5   4   3   2   1   SD

Article 32

Clinical Reasoning in Experienced Nurses

Barbara Simmons, PhD, RN, **Dorothy Lanuza**, PhD, RN, FAAN, **Marsha Fonteyn**, PhD, RN, **Frank Hicks**, PhD, RN, **Karyn Holm**, PhD, RN, FAAN[*]

ABSTRACT. As an essential component of nursing practice, clinical reasoning is used to assimilate information, analyze data, and make decisions regarding patient care. Little is known about the reasoning strategies of experienced nurses who are not yet experts. This qualitative descriptive study explored the cognitive strategies used by experienced nurses as they considered assessment findings of assigned patients. To date, few studies of nurses' clinical reasoning have been conducted in a practice setting during actual patient care. A small group research design was employed using the think-aloud (TA) method with protocol analysis. A total of 15 experienced nurses were asked to "think aloud" about patient assessment findings. Data were audiotaped, transcribed, and analyzed using the three steps of protocol analysis. The results suggest that experienced nurses used a conceptual language to reason about assessment findings and used heuristics to reason more quickly and efficiently.

From *Western Journal of Nursing Research*, 25, 701–719. Copyright © 2003 by Sage Publications, Inc. Reprinted with permission.

About Patient Assessments

Clinical reasoning is an essential component of professional practice and enables nurses to analyze information relevant to patient care. It can be defined as a recursive cognitive process that uses both inductive and
5 deductive cognitive skills to simultaneously gather and evaluate assessment data. The nursing shortage, increased use of technology, and high patient acuity demand complex decisions, often under conditions of uncertainty and risk. A better understanding of the rea-
10 soning processes used in actual patient care will help nurses with less experience develop additional thinking strategies.

Characteristics of Reasoning

Clinical reasoning guides the nurse in assessing, assimilating, retrieving and/or discarding components of
15 information to make decisions about patient care (Fonteyn, 1991b, 1995; Hughes & Young, 1990; Jenkins, 1985; Junnola, Eriksson, Salantera, & Lauri, 2002; Matteson & Hawkins, 1990). Sound clinical reasoning

has been identified as the "hallmark" of an expert
20 nurse. It distinguishes the professional nurse from ancillary health care workers (Branch, 2002; Coles, 2002; Cone, 2000; Fowler, 1997; Hughes & Young, 1990; Junnola et al., 2002). Benner (1984) described the following five skill categories of practice according to
25 reasoning skills and reliance on theoretical, intuitive, and experiential knowledge: novice, advanced beginner, competent, proficient, and expert nurse. Since then, several studies have investigated clinical reasoning of novice and expert nurses, but little is known
30 about the reasoning processes of nurses who are neither novice nor expert (Grobe, Drew, & Fonteyn, 1991; Hughes & Young, 1990; O'Neill, 1995). There is evidence that domain-specific knowledge, experience, and intuition are all important components of clinical rea-
35 soning (Benner, 1984; Benner & Tanner, 1987; Benner, Tanner, & Chesla, 1996; Branch, 2002; Cioffi, 1998; Claxton, Sculpher, & Drummond, 2002; Corcoran, Narayan, & Moreland, 1988; Crow, Chase, & Lamond, 1995; Hurlock-Chorostecki, 2002; Parker,
40 Minick, & Kee, 1999; Radwin, 1998; White, Nativio, Kobert, & Engberg, 1992).

In the current health care environment, nurses have more responsibility and accountability. For example, high patient acuity and complex technology once sepa-
45 rated critical care patients from those in other settings. This distinction is now blurred. In addition, graduate nurses and nurses orienting to new staff positions have limited time to learn institutional policies, procedures, and standards before assuming full responsibility for
50 patient care. As the nursing workforce ages and clinical experts retire, there are fewer mentors available. Nurses who are neither novice nor expert must use reasoning strategies rapidly and with fewer resources (Fisher & Fonteyn, 1995; Thiele, Holloway, Murphy,
55 Pendarvis, & Stucky, 1991).

Improved clinical reasoning can strengthen nursing practice by increasing the accuracy of decisions and improving patient outcomes. Most of the research on clinical reasoning to date has been done either on nov-
60 ices or on experts. Only eight published studies of

[*]*Barbara Simmons* is clinical assistant professor at the College of Nursing, Department of Medical–Surgical Nursing, University of Illinois at Chicago. *Dorothy Lanuza* is professor at Loyola University Medical Center. *Marsha Fonteyn* is professor at the School of Nursing, University of San Francisco. *Frank Hicks* is associate professor at the College of Nursing, Rush University. *Karyn Holm* is professor at the Department of Nursing, DePaul University Chicago.

clinical reasoning have used experienced nurses who were not defined as experts (dela Cruz, 1994; Edwards, 1994; Ellis, 1997; Grobe et al., 1991; Navin, 1991; Tabak, Bar-Tal, & Cohen-Mansfield, 1996; Watson, 1994; Westfall, Tanner, Putzier, & Padrick, 1986). Results of these studies indicated that decision-making styles of less experienced nurses varied according to the demands of the clinical situation, that nurses assessed and evaluated patient information concurrently, and that previous clinical experience was the most common explanation for a decision. Despite the noted benefits of identifying reasoning processes as they occur, only four studies of expert nurses have been conducted in a clinical setting during actual patient care (Fisher & Fonteyn, 1995; Fowler, 1997; Greenwood, Sullivan, Spence, & McDonald, 2000; Navin, 1991).

Benner's (1984) seminal work provided a foundation for understanding skill levels in nursing practice according to years of experience. The expert nurse was identified as having a greater understanding of clinical situations, recognizing patterns of patient responses, using intuition and informal reasoning strategies (heuristics) to make judgments, and rapidly responding to changes in patient status (Benner, 1984; Benner & Tanner, 1987; Benner, Tanner, & Chesla, 1992; Benner et al., 1996). Because the majority of practicing nurses today are neither novice nor expert, identification of the clinical reasoning strategies used by experienced nurses will provide a better understanding of the dynamic and complex nature of this process at this skill level.

Purpose

The purpose of this study was to describe the cognitive processes used by experienced nurses as they assessed patients assigned to their care. The following three research questions were posed: (a) What information do experienced nurses concentrate on while reasoning?, (b) What information do experienced nurses link together to form relationships?, and (c) What thinking strategies (heuristics) do experienced nurses use?

An experienced nurse was defined as a registered nurse with a minimum of 2 years but less than 10 years of full-time work experience on a medical–surgical unit. Based on previous research, 2 years of experience was determined to be the minimum criterion for nurses who were between novice and expert (Benner, 1984; Crow et al., 1995; Grobe et al., 1991; Navin, 1991; Tanner, Padrick, Westfall, & Putzier, 1987). It is more difficult to define the expert nurse, and controversy exists as to whether the number of years in practice should be used to determine skill level. Although 5 years of experience has been used to define the expert nurse (Benner & Tanner, 1987; Fonteyn, 1991a; Lauri, Salantera, Gilje, & Klose, 1999; Parker et al., 1999; Sims & Fought, 1989), nurses may enter and exit practice on a part-time basis to accommodate their family,

graduate education, and personal responsibilities. Simon (1989) used 10 years of work experience as the criterion for expertise. In this study, the criterion for number of years in practice was extended to less than 10 for an experienced nurse.

Patient assessment was the cognitive task chosen for measurement of clinical reasoning skills and indicated the initial encounter the nurse had with the patient. Patient assessment has been described as the first of many steps of the nursing process that requires reasoning skills (Bittner & Tobin, 1998; dela Cruz, 1994; Fisher & Fonteyn, 1995; Narayan, 1990; Narayan & Corcoran-Perry, 1997; Nissila, 1992; Tanner et al., 1987; Thiele et al., 1991; Watkins, 1998; White et al., 1992). Assessment includes gathering and organizing patient data, cues, or information into categories that are linked together through inductive reasoning to determine patient status and need for action (Byrnes & West, 2000; Carnevali & Thomas, 1993; Crow et al., 1995; Jacavone & Dostal, 1992; Lyneham, 1998; Taylor, 2000; Thompson, 1999).

Design

Information-processing theory was the conceptual framework that guided this descriptive, exploratory study. It was developed by Newell and Simon (1972) as a descriptive theory of decision-making in which a person organizes information using knowledge, experience, and cognitive processes to resolve a problem. Rather than analyzing how a decision ought to be made, this theory describes decision-making as an open system of interaction between a problem solver and a task (Ericsson & Simon, 1984; Newell & Simon, 1972; Simon, 1974, 1979, 1989). This theory is based on the assumption that there are limits to the information that can be stored in short-term memory. There also are limits to the information that can be concentrated on at one time (bounded rationality). Successful problem solving depends on adaptation to these limitations (Taylor, 2000). Miller (1956) hypothesized that the capacity of short-term memory is seven pieces of information, plus or minus two. The ability to "chunk" or organize information into familiar patterns may increase storage capacity. Experts may more easily chunk information to improve reasoning (Fonteyn, 1991b, 1995; Glaser, 1941; Greenwood, 1998a, 1998b; Lee & Ryan-Wenger, 1997; Miller, 1956). Long-term memory is infinite in its capacity to hold information for permanent storage; however, because it is more difficult to access this information, it takes longer to retrieve it. Access is gained only through association of cues with related patterns.

When applied in a health care setting, information processing can be referred to as clinical reasoning. Clinical reasoning in nursing is defined by this author as a complex, multidimensional, recursive cognitive process that uses formal and informal strategies to gather and analyze patient information, evaluate the significance of this information, and determine the value of alternative actions.

Experience, formal education, intuition, task complexity, domain-specific knowledge, and the degree of risk involved are all essential components of the reasoning process (Fonteyn, 1995; Hughes & Young, 1990; Newell & Simon, 1972; Watson, 1994). Research has shown that experts can make more efficient use of short-term memory and access stored memories by using heuristics (thinking strategies), formal education, and experience (Fisher & Fonteyn, 1995; Fonteyn, 1991b; Fonteyn & Grobe, 1993; Glaser, 1941; O'Neill, 1995).

The think-aloud method is an effective way to access the cognitive processes used in clinical reasoning. This method was described by Newell and Simon (1972) as a qualitative technique of collecting verbal data about cognitive processes during a problem task. The think-aloud method is based on several assumptions: (a) human cognition is information processing, (b) cognitive processes can be verbalized, and (c) thinking aloud indicates what information is being concentrated on at the time (Ericsson & Simon, 1984, 1996; Fonteyn & Fisher, 1995; Fonteyn, Kuipers, & Grobe, 1993; Navin, 1991; Newell & Simon, 1972; Taylor, 1997, 2000; Van Someren, Barnard, & Sandberg, 1994). Although not frequently used, this method has gained popularity in nursing studies (Corcoran et al., 1988; Fisher & Fonteyn, 1995; Fonteyn, 1991a). In one of the first studies using this method in a clinical setting, Navin (1991) determined that experienced nurses who were not experts used the following thinking strategies (heuristics) when gathering assessment data: scanning, focusing, and context building. Additional studies determined that nurses in this skill group concentrated on patient problems and interventions simultaneously (Grobe et al., 1991), used heuristics to reduce cognitive strain (Fisher & Fonteyn, 1995), and incorporated experience, formal knowledge, and heuristics in clinical reasoning (Boblin-Cummings, Baumann, & Deber, 1999; Fowler, 1997; Greenwood et al., 2000). Confusion continues to exist in the definitions of an experienced and expert nurse, and few studies have focused on nurses who were between the novice and expert skill levels (Grobe et al., 1991; Navin, 1991; Tanner et al., 1987).

Method

Sample

This study was conducted on five adult, medical–surgical units of a 250-bed teaching community hospital located outside a large Midwestern city. This hospital serves a large geriatric population, and the majority of patients that were cared for by nurses in this study were older than 65 years. Medical–surgical units were chosen because think-aloud data are best transcribed and analyzed by individuals familiar with the clinical language and domain terminology (Fonteyn et al.,

1993), and this investigator's clinical expertise is in this practice area. Voluntary participation was obtained through recruitment at unit staff meetings, but because attendance at these meetings was limited, the investigator also asked each manager to suggest potential participants who met the selection criteria. The investigator met with participants individually on a day they were working to explain the study and give them written information. If they were interested in the study, they were asked to contact the investigator personally. Inclusion criteria were (a) licensed registered nurse, (b) English speaking, and (c) employed full-time in medical–surgical nursing from 2 to 10 years. Exclusion criteria were (a) nurses working in specialty units (e.g., intensive care, emergency room), (b) nurses from outside employment agencies, (c) nurses recently transferred or hired, and (d) nurses with advanced education (e.g., certification or graduate degree). A total of 22 registered nurses in the hospital met the inclusion criteria, and 15 nurses from all three shifts agreed to participate in the study. This sample size yielded extensive verbal data and was similar to those reported by other qualitative think-aloud studies (Cioffi, 1998; Fisher & Fonteyn, 1995; Fonteyn, 1991a, 1991b, 1997; Fonteyn & Grobe, 1993; Fonteyn et al., 1993). Demographic data of the study participants are presented in Table 1.

Table 1
Demographic Data (n = 15)

Age[a]	Years of experience[a]	Education	Ethnicity
29.7 ± 3.7	4.6 ± 2.2	12 BSN 3 ADN	10 Caucasian 5 Asian

Shift	Nurses per unit	Number of patients[a]	Assessment time[a]
7–3 = 4 3–11 = 7 11–7 = 4	Neuro = 3 Ortho = 4 Rehab = 5 Cardiac = 1 Medical = 2	6.9 ± 3.4	2 hours ± 0.6

Note. BSN = Bachelor of Science in Nursing; ADN = Associate Degree in Nursing.
[a]Mean ± standard deviation.

Procedure

University and hospital Institutional Review Board approvals were obtained. All participants signed informed consents. Patients' and nurses' privacy and confidentiality were protected by using codes rather than names in the transcriptions of audiotapes. Participants determined the shift and date for data collection, and they were reminded by the investigator the day before. On the data collection day, nurses arrived for their shifts and received reports on assigned patients. They assessed all patients according to their routine, which varied from 30 minutes to 2 hours. During this time, the investigator was not present so that there would be no perceived pressure to complete assessments faster and no interference in nursing care or assessment routine. At a time determined by the participants, the investigator arrived on the unit. A quiet, private location was used for data collection. Participants were instructed to think aloud as they reasoned about the assessments of their patients. They were able to refer to written report notes as they spoke into the tape recorder. Although the investigator was present in the room during taping, there was minimal interaction between the participants and investigator except for instructions to "begin thinking aloud" or "continue thinking aloud." The investigator took written notes when drug names, diagnostic tests, or abbreviations were unfamiliar. When the participants completed thinking aloud, they were asked to clarify these terms. The length of time for data collection was approximately 20 to 30 minutes.

Data Analysis

Each audiotape was transcribed by the investigator in its entirety and categorized into segments of verbal text. The text was methodically reviewed using the following three steps of protocol analysis: referring phrase analysis, assertional analysis, and script analysis. Protocol analysis can be defined as a qualitative method of analyzing verbal data to gain insight into cognitive processes. It was initially described by Ericsson and Simon (1984) and adapted by later researchers (Fonteyn, 1991b; Fonteyn & Fisher, 1995; Fonteyn et al., 1993; Fowler, 1997; Greenwood et al., 2000; Grobe et al., 1991; Kuipers & Kassirer, 1984; Kuipers, Moskowitz, & Kassirer, 1988; Navin, 1991).

Each of the three steps of protocol analysis answered a research question proposed in this study. Referring phrase analysis isolated the information that experienced nurses concentrated on while reasoning about assessment findings. The transcript was reviewed for general meaning, and nouns and noun phrases were underlined and initially coded by the investigator according to the concept they seemed to represent. Revisions in coding and concept definitions occurred as each transcript was reviewed multiple times. Selected transcripts were then reviewed independently by another researcher familiar with protocol analysis to ensure validity of the coding system. Differences between researchers were discussed until agreement was reached. The final concepts represented the information on which the nurses concentrated during their assessment of their medical–surgical patients. Assertional analysis identified the relationships participants formed between and among the concepts identified in referring phrase analysis. Assertions were defined as positive statements or declarations made by participants about the information on which they were concentrating. These action verbs suggested several reasoning processes that participants used as they linked information together. Script analysis provided an overview of the cognitive process and thinking strategies that participants used during the reasoning task.

Results

Referring phrase analysis answered the first research question by identifying those concepts on which participants concentrated while they were reasoning about assessment findings of their patients. These concepts were consistently referred to by all participants and included the following: amount; care provider; condition; day, time, and date; device; diagnosis; event; family; frequency; location; missing clinical data; patient; plan; rationale; status; test; treatment; and value. Patient information was specific to the domain of medical–surgical nursing. An example of one participant's think-aloud data with referring phrase analysis is shown in Table 2.

Table 2
Segmented Text with Referring Phrase Analysis: Transcript 1 Through 3[a]

Text	Concept
"He gets up to a bedside commode."	Patient, status: Ambulation, device
"We've just got to keep him clean."	Care provider, plan: Hygiene, patient
"When he's up."	Status: Ambulation
"I notice his sacral perineal area is red."	Status: Skin
"And we need to put some doublegard."	Care provider, plan: Treatment
"For him—due to the diarrhea from the c diff."	Problem, rationale

a. Refers to transcript and patient number.

The second research question was answered through assertional analysis. Assertions were those statements made by participants that connected concepts together and facilitated their clinical reasoning. This step provided a final description of the reasoning processes and thinking strategies that experienced nurses used. The following four types of assertions were found: (a) anticipative (relationships of action and looking forward), (b) causal (relationships of cause and effect), (c) declarative (relationships of stating facts), and (d) evaluative (relationships of judging significance). Although assertions were not made between all concepts, several patterns emerged during analysis. Anticipative assertions were made by forming relationships among the concepts of plan, test, and treatment. Causal assertions were made by forming relationships among the concepts of problem, test, and rationale. Declarative assertions were made by forming relationships among the concepts of status, treatment, test, and problem. Evaluative assertions were made by forming relationships among the concepts of status, test, and value. The following three concepts were repeatedly used in forming these assertions: test, treatment, and problem. When connected in certain patterns, they directed thought processes forward toward understanding.

Script analysis answered the final research question and provided an explanation of how experienced nurses reasoned about assessment findings. The following five reasoning processes, which indicated the purpose of connecting concepts together, were identified in the transcripts: describe, explain, plan, evaluate, and conclude. The process was defined as, "Describe when participants related or narrated patient information." When participants interpreted information or provided a rationale, that process was defined as *explain*; and when they anticipated a nursing action, that process was defined as *plan*. When participants' reasoning resulted in forming an opinion about patient status, that process was defined as *evaluate*; and when summary statements were made about each patient, that process was defined as *conclude*. Nurses verbalized patient information (describe), clarified its meaning (explain), identified a plan of care (plan), gave an opinion about patient status (evaluate), and expressed completion of thought processes for that patient (conclude). These reasoning processes could be arranged on a continuum from simple (describe or conclude) to moderate (plan) to complex (explain or evaluate). All processes were used by each participant, but their combinations were varied.

To speed their reasoning process, nurses used thinking strategies (heuristics) that consolidated patient information and applied knowledge they had gained from work experience and education. A total of 11 heuristics were identified and defined by the researcher after reviewing the transcripts for statements that indicated a particular technique or informal mental strategy for solving problems. Heuristics were used by each of the 15 participants. The specific thinking strategy seemed to be dependent on each nurse's past experience. Heuristics and their definitions are shown in Table 3.

The most frequently used heuristics were recognizing a pattern, judging the value, providing explanations, forming relationships, and drawing conclusions. The use of these heuristics while nurses were using the complex reasoning processes *explain* or *evaluate* suggests that they employ additional mental strategies to enhance problem solving.

Recognizing a pattern was used to identify various types of patterns related to similarities in assessment findings, patient progress, choice of treatments, and test results. Sometimes, nurses used this heuristic to identify an inconsistency with what they expected from past experience (e.g., "She has very diminished lung sounds. She sounds like a lung cancer patient. She's got the lung cancer kind of crackles").

Judging the value was also used frequently as nurses quickly evaluated the meaning of assessment findings, test results, appropriateness of treatment, or patient response. There was a rich qualitative nature to the language that was used to narrate a situation, suggesting the nurses had a wide range of descriptors they used to judge the value of the information about which they were reasoning (e.g., "She is moving everything well, lungs clear…complains of generalized abdominal pain, abdomen is large, slightly distended and firm; [nasogastric tube] to low intermittent suction…she is now putting out about 200 cc's of yellowish drainage").

Table 3
Heuristics with Definitions

Heuristic	Definition
Drawing conclusions	Stating an opinion, making an inference, or reaching a decision about assessment information
Enumerating a list	Listing pieces of information consecutively; grouping information together for interpretation
Forming relationships	Connecting information together to show an association or indicate understanding of the meaning
Judging the value	Determining the significance, worth, or importance of information
Providing explanations	Stating the reason behind one's actions, beliefs, or comments
Recognizing a pattern	Identifying similarities of present information to previous situations and recalling something familiar from the past
Searching for information	Questioning the absence of information, looking for missing information, and acknowledging the importance of information that was not obtained
Setting priorities	Ranking nursing actions or patient problems according to their importance
Stating a practice rule	Verbalizing adherence to established policies and procedures and asserting what was usually followed in clinical practice
Stating a proposition	Using an if–then rule of logic to explain the relationship between pieces of information
Summing up	Reaching the end of a reasoning task and verbalizing its completion

Providing explanations helped the nurse mentally justify an interpretation of a test result, assessment finding, or patient response to a treatment. This heuristic was one of the four most frequently used and was associated with the complex reasoning process *explain* (e.g., "He was getting out of bed on his own, so I just put all side rails up times 4").

Forming relationships was used to associate the concepts data and treatment, problems and treatment, and medical history and assessment findings. This heuristic was one of the most frequently used and seemed to help nurses make sense of assessment findings (e.g., "He had a pneumothorax, and after doing the thoracentesis, they had to put a chest tube in").

Drawing conclusions was one of the four most frequently used heuristics and was associated with the complex reasoning process *evaluate*. It facilitated rapid reasoning by allowing the nurse to interpret what was held in short-term memory and then eliminate it from further concentration at a given time. Drawing conclusions was employed frequently throughout the "think-aloud" sessions as a means to group or consolidate information for interpretation into chunks before continuing. Nurses used this heuristic when they made judgments about information or expressed their opinion (e.g., "I don't think she can understand the logic behind the [patient controlled analgesia]").

455   Enumerating a list was associated with the less complex reasoning process *describe* and may have enabled nurses to spread information out for cognitive review (e.g., "She's a no [cardiopulmonary resuscitation], alert and oriented times 3…[and] failed her video
460   swallow [test]").

Searching for information was used to mentally scan for details about a doctor's order, the reason for an accucheck (blood glucose test), or a patient's plan of care. Nurses used this strategy to converse with them-
465   selves by asking for more information (e.g., "We are doing accuchecks on him every 4 hours, and actually, I'm not sure why").

Setting priorities was used when a patient situation was urgent or the patient's condition warranted quick
470   action (e.g., "My next patient is not back from surgery, so when she comes back, I'm gonna check vital signs immediately and then check her out and make sure she's got a good pulse in that foot").

Stating a practice rule was used by nurses who had
475   experience in the past with the same assessment findings, patient problems, or nursing interventions and who applied that knowledge to the present circumstance (e.g., "Usually, when you're on hospice, they're [the health team] not very aggressive and you [the pa-
480   tient] just have pain control, and you wouldn't even go for surgery let alone be on an antibiotic or receive blood").

Stating a proposition followed a rule of logic that states when particular conditions are met, certain re-
485   sults were expected to follow and vice versa (e.g., "I told her if she gets up and uses the bedside commode, she will be emptying her bladder better").

Summing up was used at the conclusion of nurses' reasoning about assessment findings, and it seemed to
490   provide the transition from one patient to another or to give closure to a line of reasoning (e.g., "That's pretty much all that's going on with her").

Discussion

Experienced nurses organized patient assessment information around specific concepts that they linked
495   together to provide greater understanding and to propel their reasoning process forward. Although 18 concepts were identified in the transcripts of the nurses' verbal reports, the six that were most frequently used were plan, rationale, status, test, treatment, and value. These
500   six concepts became the essence of the vocabulary used when reasoning about patient assessment findings. Similar concepts have been identified by Fonteyn (1991a) and Greenwood et al. (2000) in studies of nurses' clinical reasoning while assessing and planning
505   care.

According to Kuipers and Kassirer (1984) and Kuipers et al. (1988), the complete set of concepts identified through referring phrase analysis represents the language of the reasoning task and the domain being
510   investigated. In this study, the reasoning task was patient assessment and the domain being investigated was medical–surgical nursing. Domain-specific knowledge and clinical experience were evident as nurses linked information (concepts) together to interpret the value of
515   a laboratory test, determine the appropriateness of a specific treatment, anticipate a response, or evaluate progress. The ease with which nurses in this study structured and connected information indicated a familiarity with medical–surgical nursing and the patient
520   problems being examined. In addition, nurses often interpreted assessment findings while simultaneously planning interventions.

Narayan and Corcoran-Perry (1997), Grobe et al. (1991), and Corcoran (1986b) concluded that experi-
525   enced and expert nurses used knowledge, domain experience, and multiple cognitive processes to reason about a patient's readiness to wean from a ventilator, treatment for a pressure ulcer, a drug administration plan for pain control, and a plan of care for a child with
530   pharyngitis (Corcoran, 1986a; Grobe et al., 1991; Lamond & Farnell, 1998; Lee & Ryan-Wenger, 1997; Narayan & Corcoran-Perry, 1997). Lack of knowledge and oversimplification of the reasoning task were the difficulties noted in novices (Corcoran, 1986b).

535   Nurses made sense of assessment information by linking concepts together to form relationships. These relationships indicated the specific information nurses were concentrating on and determined the direction that their reasoning would take next. The six most fre-
540   quently used concepts together resulted in particular assertions: causal (cause and effect relationships), declarative (statements of facts), evaluative (judgments of significance), and anticipative (expectations of action). When linked with rationale, the concepts problem and
545   test resulted in causal assertions, whereas linking problem, test, and treatment with status resulted in declarative assertions. When linked with rationale, the concepts test and treatment resulted in anticipative assertions, whereas test and status combined with value re-
550   sulted in evaluative assertions. Rationale, status, plan, and value were the critical concepts that moved the reasoning process forward. Similar results have been documented previously (Fonteyn, 1991a; Fonteyn & Grobe, 1993; Fonteyn et al., 1993). This pattern of
555   structuring information was consistent within and between participants and may be explained by the nature of the cognitive task and/or the use of knowledge and experience.

Reasoning processes and thinking strategies (heu-
560   ristics) enabled nurses to quickly review and analyze patient information, evaluate significance, and formulate alternative actions. The nurse participants were not consciously aware of the cognitive processes they were

using or how they organized information. They emerged through the techniques of protocol analysis. The cognitive processes describe, plan, explain, evaluate, and conclude represented a continuum of thinking from simple to complex. dela Cruz (1994) and Fowler (1997) noted that expert nurses chose from a continuum of cognitive processes depending on task complexity. This study revealed similar findings in nurses who were not yet experts.

Multiple heuristics were used by experienced nurses to facilitate the reasoning process. Heuristics have been defined as rules of thumb, mental shortcuts, or methods of processing large amounts of data to reduce cognitive strain (Corcoran, 1986b; Fonteyn & Grobe, 1993; Grobe et al., 1991; Kassirer & Kopelman, 1991; Kuipers & Kassirer, 1984; Kuipers et al., 1988; Tversky, 1977; Tversky & Kahneman, 1974, 1981). A total of 11 heuristics were used by the experienced nurses in this study to reason about assessment findings. Each heuristic incorporated domain-specific (medical–surgical nursing) knowledge and experience. Only a few studies to date have identified the heuristics nurses use in clinical practice, and these studies have been conducted with expert nurses (Fisher & Fonteyn, 1995; Fonteyn, 1991a, 1997; Fonteyn & Grobe, 1993; Fowler, 1997). According to the authors' knowledge, this study is unique because it represents the first attempt to identify heuristics used by nurses with 2 to less than 10 years of experience who were not identified as experts.

The most frequently used heuristic was recognizing a pattern. This finding supports the previous work of Fonteyn (1991a, 1997), Fisher and Fonteyn (1995), Benner and Tanner (1987), and Grobe, Drew, and Fonteyn (1991). As nurses gained clinical experience through practice, they accumulated a repertoire of information they considered to be critical identifiers of certain outcomes. As later experiences began repeating earlier ones, nurses mentally skipped steps and reached conclusions that worked before. As outcomes became reinforced, fewer critical indicators were needed to reach a conclusion. Recognizing a pattern enabled the nurse to use information stored in long-term memory by matching present information with that from previous clinical experience. It is possible that inaccurate patterns or erroneous conclusions may have led to incorrect decisions.

Enumerating a list enabled nurses to mentally collect physiological and psychosocial information at the beginning of each assessment report. By organizing assessment data, nurses were able to chunk information into manageable units for further deliberation, whereas setting priorities enabled nurses to rank actions or considerations according to relative importance in acute situations.

Forming relationships allowed nurses to quickly connect information to improve understanding and speed analysis. Searching for information was a method of reflective thinking that provided time to mentally look for data that were considered necessary to proceed. Reflective thinking and asking questions determined what information was necessary in order to continue reasoning. Providing explanations was a method that nurses used often to convince themselves that a choice or seemingly logical connection was indeed correct. Judging the value enabled nurses to voice their opinions. These four heuristics provided a reflective self-check that if used often and in combination, reduced thinking biases and errors.

Stating an if–then proposition followed rules of logic, whereas stating a practice rule indicated what was typically seen or done in practice. Drawing conclusions allowed nurses to make tentative decisions, and summing up indicated that reasoning was complete for that task.

The results of this study also supported information-processing theory as the underlying conceptual framework for clinical reasoning in experienced nurses. According to this theory, a person organizes information using knowledge, experience, and cognitive processes to resolve a problem (Ericsson & Simon, 1984, 1996; Newell & Simon, 1972; Simon, 1974, 1979, 1989). Nurses in this study used knowledge and experience to group or chunk assessment information into manageable units (concepts). Experienced nurses also reviewed assessment information while concurrently planning care. This finding supports the work of Grobe et al. (1991). Although previous research has shown that expert nurses chunk information and employ thinking strategies (heuristics) to speed the reasoning process, this study indicated that experienced nurses (who were not experts) employed similar techniques. Experience may be more accurately defined according to clinical reasoning skills rather than the number of years in practice. Years in practice is only one criterion to distinguish between nursing skill levels. More research is needed to determine if the original work of Benner needs to be revisited.

The sample size for this study was relatively small, and convenience sampling was used. Representativeness and generalizability of the findings are limited. The purpose of this study was to describe the cognitive processes experienced nurses used and not to generalize the findings. The number of years worked as the criterion to select experienced nurses for this study may not have been an appropriate indicator of this skill level. Most nurses in this sample had closer to 2 years of experience (criterion of 2 to 10 years for experienced nurse). Three nurses spoke English as a second language, which may have affected understanding and thinking aloud. Hospital management changes and staffing problems at the time of data collection may also have influenced the findings. To process more information, nurses may have used techniques to speed reasoning. Whether these techniques resulted in more

accurate decisions and better patient outcomes was not
680 measured in this study.

References

Benner, P. (1984). *From novice to expert: Excellence and power in clinical nursing practice.* Reading, MA: Addison-Wesley.

Benner, P., & Tanner, C. (1987). Clinical judgment: How expert nurses use intuition. *American Journal of Nursing, 87,* 23–31.

Benner, P., Tanner, C. A., & Chesla, C. (1992). From beginner to expert: Gaining a differentiated clinical world in critical care nursing. *Advances in Nursing Science, 14,* 13–28.

Benner, P., Tanner, C. A., & Chesla, C. (1996). *Expertise in nursing practice.* New York: Springer.

Bittner, N. P., & Tobin, E. (1998). Critical thinking: Strategies for clinical practice. *Journal for Nurses in Staff Development, 14,* 267–272.

Boblin-Cummings, S., Baumann, A., & Deber, R. (1999). Critical elements in the process of decision making: A nursing perspective. *Canadian Journal of Nursing Leadership, 12,* 6–13.

Branch, B. J. (2002). *The relationship among critical thinking, clinical decision making, and clinical practice: A comparative study.* Unpublished manuscript, University of Idaho.

Byrnes, M., & West, S. (2000). Registered nurses' clinical reasoning abilities: A study of self-perception. *Australian Journal of Advanced Nursing, 17,* 18–23.

Carnevali, D. L., & Thomas, M. D. (1993). *Diagnostic reasoning and treatment decision making in nursing.* Philadelphia: J. B. Lippincott.

Cioffi, J. (1998). Decision making by emergency nurses in triage assessments. *Accident & Emergency Nursing, 6,* 184–191.

Claxton, K., Sculpher, M., & Drummond, M. (2002). Viewpoint: A rational framework for decision making by the National Institute for Clinical Excellence (NICE). *Lancet, 360,* 711–715.

Coles, C. (2002). Developing professional judgment. *Journal of Continuing Education in the Health Professions, 22,* 3–10.

Cone, K. J. (2000). *The development and testing of an instrument to measure decision making in emergency department triage nurses.* Unpublished manuscript, Saint Louis University.

Corcoran, S., Narayan, S., & Moreland, H. (1988). "Thinking aloud" as a strategy to improve clinical decision making. *Heart & Lung: Journal of Critical Care, 17,* 463–468.

Corcoran, S. A. (1986a). Planning by expert and novice nurses in cases of varying complexity: Drug administration plans to control patients' pain. *Research in Nursing & Health, 9,* 155–162.

Corcoran, S. A. (1986b). Task complexity and nursing expertise as factors in decision making processes used by nurses to plan patient care. *Nursing Research, 35,* 107–112.

Crow, R. A., Chase, J., & Lamond, D. (1995). The cognitive component of nursing assessment: An analysis. *Journal of Advanced Nursing, 22,* 206–212.

dela Cruz, F. A. (1994). Clinical decision-making styles of home healthcare nurses. *Image: The Journal of Nursing Scholarship, 26,* 222–226.

Edwards, B. (1994). Telephone triage: How experienced nurses reach decisions. *Journal of Advanced Nursing, 19,* 717–724.

Ellis, P. A. (1997). Processes used by nurses to make decisions in the clinical practice setting. *Nurse Education Today, 17,* 325–332.

Ericsson, K. A., & Simon, H. A. (1984). *Protocol analysis: Verbal reports as data.* Cambridge, MA: MIT Press.

Ericsson, K. A., & Simon, H. A. (1996). *Protocol analysis: Verbal reports as data* (Rev. ed.). Cambridge, MA: MIT Press.

Fisher, A., & Fonteyn, M. (1995). An exploration of an innovative methodological approach for examining nurses' heuristic use in clinical practice...including commentary by Graves, J. R. *Scholarly Inquiry for Nursing Practice, 9,* 263–279.

Fonteyn, M. E. (1991a). A descriptive analysis of expert critical care nurses' clinical reasoning. Unpublished doctoral dissertation, The University of Texas at Austin.

Fonteyn, M. E. (1991b). Implications of clinical reasoning studies for critical care nursing. *Focus on Critical Care, 18,* 322–327.

Fonteyn, M. E. (1995). Clinical reasoning in nursing. In J. Higgs & M. Jones (Eds.), *Clinical reasoning in the health professions* (pp. 60–71). Newton, MA: Butterworth-Heinemann.

Fonteyn, M. E. (1997). Thinking in nursing practice. In U. Gerdin, M. Tallberg, & P. Wainwright (Eds.), *Nursing informatics: The impact of nursing knowledge on health care informatics* (pp. 305–310). Amsterdam: IOS Press.

Fonteyn, M. E., & Fisher, A. (1995). Research corner. Use of think aloud method to study nurses' reasoning and decision making in clinical practice settings. *Journal of Neuroscience Nursing, 27,* 124–128.

Fonteyn, M. E., & Grobe, S. (1993). Expert nurses' clinical reasoning under uncertainty: Representation, structure, and process. *Proceedings of the Annual Symposium on Computer Applications in Medical Care,* 405–409.

Fonteyn, M. E., Kuipers, B., & Grobe, S. J. (1993). A description of think aloud method and protocol analysis. *Qualitative Health Research, 3,* 430–441.

Fowler, L. P. (1997). Clinical reasoning strategies used during care planning. *Clinical Nursing Research, 6,* 349–361.

Glaser, E. M. (1941). *An experiment in the development of critical thinking.* New York: AMS Press.

Greenwood, J. (1998a). Establishing an international network on nurses' clinical reasoning. *Journal of Advanced Nursing, 27,* 843–847.

Greenwood, J. (1998b). Theoretical approaches to the study of nurses' clinical reasoning: Getting things clear. *Contemporary Nurse, 7,* 110–116.

Greenwood, J., Sullivan, J., Spence, K., & McDonald, M. (2000). Nursing scripts and the organizational influences on critical thinking: Report of a study of neonatal nurses' clinical reasoning. *Journal of Advanced Nursing, 31,* 1106–1114.

Grobe, S. J., Drew, J. A., & Fonteyn, M. E. (1991). A descriptive analysis of experienced nurses' clinical reasoning during a planning task. *Research in Nursing & Health, 14,* 305–314.

Hughes, K. K., & Young, W. B. (1990). The relationship between task complexity and decision-making consistency. *Research in Nursing & Health, 13,* 189–197.

Hurlock-Chorostecki, C. (2002). Management of pain during weaning from mechanical ventilation: The nature of nurse decision-making. *Canadian Journal of Nursing Research, 34,* 33–47.

Jacavone, J., & Dostal, M. (1992). A descriptive study of nursing judgment in the assessment and management of cardiac pain. *Advances in Nursing Science, 15,* 54–63.

Jenkins, H. M. (1985). A research tool for measuring perceptions of clinical decision making. *Journal of Professional Nursing, 1,* 221–229.

Junnola, T., Eriksson, E., Salantera, S., & Lauri, S. (2002). Nurses' decision-making in collecting information for the assessment of patients' nursing problems. *Journal of Clinical Nursing; 11,* 186–196.

Kassirer, J. P., & Kopelman, R. I. (1991). *Learning clinical reasoning.* Baltimore: Williams & Wilkins.

Kuipers, B., & Kassirer, J. P. (1984). Causal reasoning in medicine: Analysis of a protocol. *Cognitive Science, 8,* 363–385.

Kuipers, B., Moskowitz, A. J., & Kassirer, J. P. (1988). Critical decisions under uncertainty: Representation and structure. *Cognitive Science, 12,* 177–210.

Lamond, D., & Farnell, S. (1998). The treatment of pressure sores: A comparison of novice and expert nurses' knowledge, information use and decision accuracy. *Journal of Advanced Nursing, 27,* 280–286.

Lauri, S., Salantera, S., Gilje, F. L., & Klose, P. (1999). Decision making of psychiatric nurses in Finland, Northern Ireland, and the United States. *Journal of Professional Nursing, 15,* 275–280.

Lee, J. E. M., & Ryan-Wenger, N. (1997). The "think aloud" seminar for teaching clinical reasoning: A case study of a child with pharyngitis. *Journal of Pediatric Health Care, 11,* 101–110.

Lyneham, J. (1998). The process of decision-making by emergency nurses. *Australian Journal of Advanced Nursing, 16,* 7–14.

Matteson, P., & Hawkins, J. W. (1990). Concept analysis of decision making. *Nursing Forum, 25,* 4–10.

Miller, G. A. (1956). The magical number seven, plus or minus two: Some limits on our capacity for processing information. *Psychological Reviews, 63,* 81–97.

Narayan, S. M. (1990). *Heuristic reasoning about uncertainty in a clinical nursing task.* Unpublished manuscript.

Narayan, S. M., & Corcoran-Perry, S. (1997). Line of reasoning as a representation of nurses' clinical decision making. *Research in Nursing & Health, 20,* 353–364.

Navin, P. M. (1991). *How experienced nurses gather and use data.* Unpublished manuscript.

Newell, A., & Simon, H. A. (1972). *Human problem solving.* Englewood Cliffs, NJ: Prentice Hall.

Nissila, S. E. (1992). *Lines of reasoning in clinical nursing decisions.* Unpublished manuscript.

O'Neill, E. S. (1995). Heuristics reasoning in diagnostic judgment. *Journal of Professional Nursing, 11,* 239–245.

Parker, C. B., Minick, P., & Kee, C. C. (1999). Clinical decision-making processes in perioperative nursing. *AORN Journal, 70,* 45–46.

Radwin, L. E. (1998). Empirically generated attributes of experience in nursing. *Journal of Advanced Nursing, 27,* 590–595.

Simon, H. A. (1974). How big is a chunk? *Science, 183,* 482–488.

Simon, H. A. (1979). *Models of thought* (Vol. I). New Haven, CT: Yale University Press.

Simon, H. A. (1989). *Models of thought* (Vol. II). New Haven, CT: Yale University Press.

Sims, K. A., & Fought, S. G. (1989). Clinical decision making in critical care. *Critical Care Nursing Quarterly, 12,* 79–84.

Tabak, N., Bar-Tal, Y., & Cohen-Mansfield, J. (1996). Clinical decision making of experienced and novice nurses. *Western Journal of Nursing Research, 18,* 534–547.

Tanner, C. A., Padrick, K. P., Westfall, U. E., & Putzier, D. J. (1987). Diagnostic reasoning strategies of nurses and nursing students. *Nursing Research, 36*, 358–363.

Taylor, C. (1997). Problem solving in clinical nursing practice. *Journal of Advanced Nursing, 26*, 329–336.

Taylor, C. (2000). Clinical problem-solving in nursing: Insights from the literature. *Journal of Advanced Nursing, 31*, 842–849.

Thiele, J. E., Holloway, J., Murphy, D., Pendarvis, J., & Stucky, M. (1991). Perceived and actual decision making by novice baccalaureate students. *Western Journal of Nursing Research, 13*, 616–626.

Thompson, C. (1999). Pearls, pith, and provocation—Qualitative research into nurse decision making: Factors for consideration in theoretical sampling. *Qualitative Health Research, 9*, 815–828.

Tversky, A. (1977). Features of similarity. *Psychological Reviews, 84*, 327–352.

Tversky, A., & Kahneman, D. (1974). Judgment under uncertainty: Heuristic and biases. *Science, 211*, 453–458.

Tversky, A., & Kahneman, D. (1981). The framing of decisions and the psychology of choice. *Science, 211*, 453–458.

Van Someren, M. W., Barnard, Y. F., & Sandberg, J. A. C. (1994). *The think aloud method: A practical guide to modeling cognitive processes.* San Diego, CA: Academic Press.

Watkins, M. P. (1998). Decision-making phenomena described by expert nurses working in urban community health settings. *Journal of Professional Nursing, 14*, 22–33.

Watson, S. (1994). An exploratory study into a methodology for the examination of decision making by nurses in the clinical area. *Journal of Advanced Nursing, 20*, 351–360.

Westfall, U. E., Tanner, C. A., Putzier, D., & Padrick, K. P. (1986). Activating clinical inferences: A component of diagnostic reasoning in nursing. *Research in Nursing & Health, 9*, 269–277.

White, J. E., Nativio, D. G., Kobert, S. N., & Engberg, S. J. (1992). Content and process in clinical decision-making by nurse practitioners. *Image: The Journal of Nursing Scholarship, 24*, 153–158.

Note: This research has been supported by Sigma Theta Tau International, Alpha Beta Chapter.

Address correspondence to: Barbara Simmons, UIC College of Nursing, 845 South Damen Ave. (MC 802), Chicago, IL 60612-7350.

Exercise for Article 32

Factual Questions

1. How many published studies of clinical reasoning have used experienced nurses who were not defined as experts?

2. For this study, how was "an experienced nurse" defined?

3. Were nurses with advanced education (e.g., certification or graduate degree) included in this study?

4. How were patients' and nurses' privacy and confidentiality protected?

5. Was there extensive interaction between the participants and investigator during the think-alouds?

6. Do the researchers claim that the results of this study are representative and highly generalizable?

Questions for Discussion

7. In your opinion, how important is it for researchers to identify reasoning processes as they occur in clinical settings during actual patient care? (See lines 71–76.)

8. The researchers state that controversy exists as to whether the number of years in practice should be used to determine skill level (such as using 5 years of experience to define the "expert nurse"). What is your opinion on this controversy? (See lines 108–121.)

9. In your opinion, is the think-aloud method an effective way to access the cognitive processes used in clinical reasoning? Explain. Answer this question in light of all the information in this research article. (Also, see lines 186–187.)

10. Demographic data are presented in Table 1. Are there any other demographics that would be of interest to you as a consumer of this research article? Explain.

11. Selected transcripts were reviewed independently by another researcher familiar with protocol analysis. In your opinion, was this an important aspect of the analysis? Explain. (See lines 304–309.)

12. In your opinion, what are the practical implications, if any, of this study?

Quality Ratings

Directions: Indicate your level of agreement with each of the following statements by circling a number from 5 for strongly agree (SA) to 1 for strongly disagree (SD). If you believe an item is not applicable to this research article, leave it blank. Be prepared to explain your ratings. When responding to criteria A and B below, keep in mind that brief titles and abstracts are conventional in published research.

A. The title of the article is appropriate.

SA   5   4   3   2   1   SD

B. The abstract provides an effective overview of the research article.

SA   5   4   3   2   1   SD

C. The introduction establishes the importance of the study.

SA   5   4   3   2   1   SD

D. The literature review establishes the context for the study.

SA   5   4   3   2   1   SD

E. The research purpose, question, or hypothesis is clearly stated.

SA   5   4   3   2   1   SD

F. The method of sampling is sound.

SA   5   4   3   2   1   SD

G. Relevant demographics (for example, age, gender, and ethnicity) are described.

SA   5   4   3   2   1   SD

H. Measurement procedures are adequate.

SA   5   4   3   2   1   SD

I. All procedures have been described in sufficient detail to permit a replication of the study.

SA   5   4   3   2   1   SD

J. The participants have been adequately protected from potential harm.

SA   5   4   3   2   1   SD

K. The results are clearly described.

SA   5   4   3   2   1   SD

L. The discussion/conclusion is appropriate.

SA   5   4   3   2   1   SD

M. Despite any flaws, the report is worthy of publication.

SA   5   4   3   2   1   SD

Article 33

The Use of Music to Promote
Sleep in Older Women

Julie E. Johnson, PhD, RN, FAAN[*]

ABSTRACT. Fifty-two women over the age of 70 participated in a study to investigate the use of an individualized
music protocol to promote sleep onset and maintenance.
They were recruited from the practices of physicians and
nurse practitioners and met the inclusion and exclusion
criteria of the *International Classification of Sleep Disorders* (1990), and the *Diagnostic and Statistical Manual of
Mental Disorders* (1994). Results indicated that the use of
music decreased time to sleep onset and the number of
nighttime awakenings. Consequently, it increased satisfaction with sleep. Nurses may wish to recommend the use of
music at bedtime to older women with insomnia.

From *Journal of Community Health Nursing*, 20, 27–35. Copyright © 2003 by Lawrence Erlbaum Associates, Inc.
(www.erlbaum.com). Reprinted with permission.

More than 50% of adults over the age of 65 experience some problem with sleep (National Commission
of Sleep Disorders Research, 1993). Women report
greater problems than men. Their most common com-
5 plaint is insomnia or difficulty in initiating and maintaining sleep (Tabloski, Cooke, & Thoman, 1998). As
insomnia worsens, individuals seek assistance from a
health care provider. The typical response of the provider is to prescribe a sedative hypnotic, usually a ben-
10 zodiazepine (Walsh & Engelhardt, 1992). As tolerance
to the medication develops, a parallel worsening of
insomnia occurs and medication dosage is increased.
With prolonged use of the drug, dependence and impaired psychomotor and cognitive functioning result
15 (Ashton, 1994). Consequently, these elders are at much
greater risk for car accidents (Ray, Fought, & Decker,
1992), as well as falls, hip fractures, and admission to
long-term care (Ray, Griffin, & Downey, 1989).

Music has been shown to decrease anxiety, stress,
20 and tension in a variety of populations (Davis & Thaut,
1989), including surgical patients (Moss, 1988;
Kaempf & Amodei, 1989) and individuals admitted to
the coronary care unit (Guzzetta, 1989). Other investigators have found that the use of music significantly
25 reduces pain in cancer patients (Zimmerman, Pozehl,
Duncan, & Schmitz, 1989) and agitation in elders with
Alzheimer's disease (Gerdner, 1999). Because music

can reduce muscular energy, heart and respiratory
rates, blood pressure, and alleviate psychological dis-
30 tress (Kartman, 1984), its use at bedtime to promote
relaxation and decrease insomnia may be a viable, cost-
effective, and nonaddictive alternative to sedative hyp-
notics for older women. Yet, there is little research
available to validate this assumption.

Purpose

35 The purpose of this study was to describe the impact of an individualized music protocol on the sleep of
older women experiencing chronic insomnia. The guiding research questions (RQ) were:

RQ1: Does the use of an individualized music pro-
40 tocol decrease time to sleep onset in older women
experiencing chronic insomnia?

RQ2: Do older women using an individualized music protocol report fewer nighttime awakenings following sleep onset?

45 RQ3: Does the use of an individualized music protocol influence older women's satisfaction with
their sleep experience?

The term *individualized music protocol* is defined
as "music that has been integrated into the person's life
50 and is based on personal preferences" (Gerdner, 1999).
Such an approach is preferred because individuals may
respond differently to the same piece of music. What is
enjoyable and relaxing to one person may be distasteful
and stressful to another.

Method

Sample Selection

55 The names of potential participants for this study
were obtained from three family practice physicians
and five family nurse practitioners. Inclusion and exclusion criteria for chronic insomnia were established
using the *International Classification of Sleep Disor-
60 ders* (American Sleep Disorders Association, 1990)
and the *Diagnostic and Statistical Manual of Mental
Disorders* (4th ed. [DSM-IV]; American Psychiatric
Association, 1994). Inclusion criteria included:

---

[*]*Julie E. Johnson* is a dean and professor at the College of Nursing, Kent State University.

65   1. Subjective complaints of difficulty initiating and/
      or maintaining sleep at least 3 times a week for
      more than 6 months.
     2. Seventy years of age or over.
     3. Alert and oriented.
     4. Able to read, write, and communicate verbally in
70   English.
     5. Living in their own homes.

Exclusion criteria included:

     1. Use of sedative–hypnotics within 3 months of
        the study.
75   2. Significant neurological (e.g., dementia) or med-
        ical disorders (e.g., cancer).
     3. Presence of other sleep disorders (e.g., sleep ap-
        nea, periodic limb movements).
     4. Use of medications known to disturb sleep (e.g.,
80   psychotropics, beta-blockers).
     5. A score lower than 27 on the Mini-Mental State
        Exam (MMST; Folstein, Folstein, & McHugh,
        1975).
     6. A score higher than 16 on the Center for Epide-
85   miologic Studies Depression Scale (CES-D;
        Radloff, 1977).
     7. An affirmative response to two or more questions
        on CAGE (Ewing, 1984) to determine alcohol
        abuse.

90   According to the initial screening by the primary
health care provider, 113 women met the inclusion
criteria for participation in this study. Following a telephone interview conducted by two trained research
assistants in which the study was explained and verbal
95 consent was obtained to assess potential participants
for the presence of any exclusion criteria, arrangements
were made to screen them in their health care practitioner's office. The same two research assistants questioned the potential participants for their use of pre-
100 scribed and over-the-counter medications to promote
sleep within the previous three months; reviewed their
medical records for the presence of prohibited medical
and neurological diagnoses, sleep disorders, and medications known to interfere with sleep; and administered
105 the CES-D (Radloff, 1977) to determine the presence
of depression, the MMST (Folstein, Folstein, &
McHugh, 1975) to determine cognitive function, and
the CAGE (Ewing, 1984) to assess for alcohol abuse.
Ultimately, 61 (54%) of the potential participants were
110 eliminated (see Table 1). The remaining 52 (46%) gave
informed consent to continue in the study.

Sample

The final sample consisted of 52 participants. They
ranged in age from 71 to 87 years old, with a mean of
80.5 years. Nineteen (37%) were married and 33 (63%)
115 were widowed. Thirty-seven (71%) were high school
graduates, 11 (21%) were college graduates, and 4
(8%) had a graduate degree. All lived in their own

homes and were alert, oriented, and able to read, speak,
and communicate verbally in English. They com-
120 plained of prolonged initial sleep onset at least three
times per week ($M = 49$ min, $R = 27$–69 min) for over
6 months.

Table 1
Reasons for Exclusion from Participation

Exclusion criteria	n	%
Sedative/hypnotic use	49	80
Use of medication interfering with sleep	38	63
Depression	37	61
Alcohol abuse	33	54
Prohibited medical diagnosis	31	51
Decreased cognitive function	25	41
Neurological disorders	19	31
Presence of other sleep disorders	12	20

Note. $N = 61$; may exceed 61 due to the presence of more than one exclu-
sionary criterion.

Procedure

Data were collected for 10 nights before the use of
music and for 10 nights during its use with the Stanford
125 Sleepiness Scale (Hoddes, Dement, & Zarcone, 1972)
and a sleep log. An investigator-constructed tool was
used to interview participants after they had completed
10 nights of music use.

The Stanford Sleepiness Scale is a single item
130 measure of the subjective perception of sleepiness. The
individual is asked to rate her level of sleepiness–
alertness on a scale ranging from 1 (*feeling active and
alert*) to 7 (*lost the struggle to stay awake*). It has been
used to determine sleepiness in shift workers (Paley &
135 Tepas, 1994) and in those suffering from sleep deprivation (Dinges, Whitehouse, Orne, & Orne, 1988) and
sleep fragmentation (Bonnet, 1986).

A sleep log requires that the individual write down
specific information regarding the sleep experience.
140 For this study, participants were instructed to specify
the time they got into bed. In the morning they were
asked to indicate the estimated length of time it took to
fall asleep, number of awakenings during the night, and
the time of final awakening.

145 The investigator-constructed interview tool was
used only after the use of music for 10 nights. Participants were asked to respond to questions that described
their sleep before and after the use of music and to indicate how satisfied they were with use of music to
150 help them sleep. All interviews were audio taped for
later transcription and analysis.

Participants were instructed to select their own music for bedtime use, and selections could vary nightly
providing they remained in the same category, such as
155 classical. The majority of participants ($n = 33$, 64%)
selected soothing classical music, such as Pachelbel's
Canon in D or compact discs like *Bach at Bedtime*. The
remainder selected sacred music ($n = 10$, 19%) or new
age music ($n = 9$, 17%). If a participant did not own or
160 have access to a compact disc or tape player with an
automatic shut-off, one was provided for her.

During the pretest phase of the study, participants were instructed to go to bed at night when they felt sleepy, indicate their level of sleepiness using the Stanford Sleepiness Scale, and note the time they got into bed in their sleep log. In the morning, they recorded the length of time it took to fall asleep, the number of times they awakened at night, the time they awoke in the morning, and their level of satisfaction with the night's sleep. They followed the same routine for the 10 nights they used music, with the added directive to turn the music on as soon as they got into bed.

Results

Data from the Stanford Sleepiness Scale and sleep log were analyzed by computing means and standard deviations of pre- and posttest scores. Differences between means were analyzed with t tests for correlated samples. Interview data were analyzed using conceptual coding and Strauss' (1987) constant comparative method. To validate the data, themes that emerged were discussed with the participants. From the identified and validated themes, categories were developed.

Table 2
Sleep Characteristics Before Music

Sleep characteristic	n	%
Bedtime sleepiness		
"Foggy, losing interest in staying awake"	30	58
"Sleepy, woozy"	22	42
Minutes to sleep onset		
27–31	3	5
32–36	7	14
37–41	9	17
42–46	9	17
47–51	10	19
52–56	2	4
57–61	5	10
62–66	2	4
67–69	5	10
Number of awakenings		
5	13	25
6	17	33
7	12	23
8	10	19

Note. N = 52.

Table 3
Sleep Characteristics with Music

Sleep characteristic	n	%
Bedtime sleepiness		
"No longer fighting sleep"	52	100
Minutes to sleep onset		
6–7	17	37
8–9	11	21
10–11	18	35
11–12	3	6
12–13	3	6
Number of awakenings		
1	23	44
2	19	37
3	10	19

Note. N = 52.

Results showed that there was a significant increase in level of sleepiness at bedtime ($t = 3.72$, $p < .01$) and a significant decrease in time to sleep onset ($t = 3.12$, $p < .01$) and number of nighttime awakenings ($t = 2.30$, $p < .05$) from pre- to posttest (Tables 2 and 3). Prior to the use of music, all the participants rated themselves as 5 ("foggy; losing interest in remaining awake; slowed down") or 6 ("sleepy, woozy, fighting sleep; prefer to lie down") on the Stanford Sleepiness Scale. However, they experienced prolonged sleep onsets ranging from 27 to 69 min ($M = 49$ min) and frequent nighttime awakenings ranging from five to eight ($M = 6$). With the use of music, the participants rated themselves as 7 ("no longer fighting sleep, sleep onset soon; having dream-like thoughts") on the Stanford Sleepiness Scale. Time to sleep onset ranged from 6 to 13 min ($M = 10$ min) and the number of nighttime awakenings ranged from one to three ($M = 2$). Music became more effective with each night it was used, with a peak effect reached on the fifth night and maintained thereafter. There was no significant difference for time of morning awakening from pre- to posttest.

These categories emerged from the interview data: pure frustration, restless and exhausting, a world of difference, no more dread, and very satisfied. All the women expressed a great deal of frustration with their bedtime experience before the introduction of music. These comments were representative of that feeling:

I dreaded going to bed at night. It was the most frustrating time of the day for me. I was sleepy, but just couldn't get to sleep.

It was just awful! I was SO frustrated. I was SO tired, but I didn't even really want to try to sleep 'cause I just got more frustrated and my nerves was on edge. I'd just be in that bed worryin' about sleepin'.

In addition to the frustration of being unable to fall asleep, the participants noted that their efforts to do so were exhausting. As this 73-year-old woman said,

I'd just roll 'n roll around trying to fall asleep. I did all the stuff you hear about, you know, counting sheep backwards and forwards, thinking about nice things, stuff like that. None of it worth a tinker's darn and the time would pass and I'd just roll on more. I'd just wear myself out. I was exhausted after a few hours.

This comment by an 83-year-old was also typical:

I was so darn tired when I'd go to the bed, I was just sure I could fall asleep. But, oh no! My head hit the pillow and I'd be rollin' all over the place. I was as restless as a dog without a bone. It was plum sad. I just plain wore myself out trying to get some decent sleep.

Participants noted a remarkable difference in their ability to fall and remain asleep with the use of music. These remarks were representative:

240 I can't believe the difference falling asleep to music made. I wasn't a believer when all this started, but I am now! It relaxes me and I just drift off. It's made a world of difference about how I feel about going to bed!

I don't believe the difference music has made in the way I fall asleep. It's so much better than before. I do think it could be one of those miracles.

245 The use of music also lessened the sense of dread that these women felt at bedtime. As this 71-year-old stated,

I used to hate going to bed. It was a dreadful thing to do. But now that I've tried music to help me sleep 250 better, it's not so bad to go to bed. I don't dread it now.

This 80-year-old woman agreed,

It was awful, I just dreaded getting into bed. Not now. This has really made a big difference! I actually 255 fall asleep! And if I wake up during the night, I just turn it on and go back to sleep.

Not surprisingly, the ability to fall asleep and return to sleep led to satisfaction with the use of music and the total sleep experience. These comments were repre-260 sentative:

I'm just flat out amazed at the way music helps me relax and fall asleep. It's a wonderful thing. I wish I'd known about it years ago. My sleep is just plain better with it.

265 The music is just great. I'm so satisfied with the way I fall asleep now, so when all's said and done, I'm also very satisfied with the music.

Discussion and Implications

Due to the size of the sample, the findings of this study should be interpreted with caution. However, 270 they support those of previous research (Tabloski, Cooke, & Thoman, 1998) indicating that older women experience difficulty in initiating and maintaining sleep. It was not particularly surprising that the women in this study experienced prolonged sleep onset and 275 frequent awakenings in the pretest phase of the investigation. Consequently, they were frustrated with their sleep, dreaded going to bed, and were restless sleepers. Nurses may wish to place greater emphasis on the assessment of their older, female clients' sleep patterns. 280 If problems are identified early, appropriate treatment can be provided so that such frustration and dread are minimized or avoided altogether.

The finding that the use of an individualized music protocol improved insomnia in this study's participants 285 is encouraging. As others (Davis & Thaut, 1989; Guzzeta, 1989) have noted, music decreases stress, tension, and anxiety. Insomnia may have multiple causes including age, stress, tension, and anxiety. Unfortunately, when individuals have continued difficulty 290 falling and remaining asleep, anxiety and tension may be exacerbated to the point that frustration and dread make relaxation impossible. This study shows that music is effective in decreasing the frustration and dread associated with insomnia, while increasing the ability 295 to relax. Nurses can use these findings to suggest that older women with insomnia use music to help them fall asleep. They should instruct their clients to select a piece of music that is soothing to them and/or evokes pleasant memories and feelings, get into bed, turn the 300 music on and the lights out, and close their eyes. It is important to encourage them to use music for at least five nights before assuming it does not work. They may also alter their nightly music selection if they wish.

305 Participants also noted that the use of music helped them return to sleep following nighttime awakenings. Nurses can use this information to suggest that music may promote relaxation and return to sleep in their older clients who have difficulty maintaining sleep due 310 to frequent awakenings.

A serendipitous finding of concern was the number of older women who were disqualified from participating in this study due to the habitual use of sedative-hypnotics and/or alcohol. In addition, a significant 315 number of potential participants were clinically depressed. These findings deserve further investigation, not only for their influence on sleep, but for the impact they may have on the functional and cognitive status of older women living in their own homes.

References

American Psychiatric Association. (1994). *Diagnostic and statistical manual of mental disorders* (4th ed.). Washington, DC: Author.

American Sleep Disorders Association. (1990). *International classification of sleep disorders (ICSD): Diagnostic and coding manual.* Rochester, MN: Author.

Ashton, H. (1994). Guidelines for the rational use of benzodiazepines: When and what to use. *Drugs, 48,* 25–40.

Bonnet, M. H. (1986). Performance and sleepiness following moderate sleep disruption and slow wave sleep deprivation. *Physiological Behavior, 37,* 915–918.

Davis, W. B., & Thaut, M. H. (1989). The influence of preferred relaxing music on measures of state anxiety, relaxation, and physiological responses. *Journal of Music Therapy, 26,* 168–187.

Dinges, D. F., Whitehouse, W. G., Orne, E. C., & Orne, M. T. (1988). The benefits of a nap during prolonged work and wakefulness. *Work & Stress, 2,* 139–153.

Ewing, J. A. (1984). Detecting alcoholism: The CAGE questionnaire. *Journal of the American Medical Association, 252,* 1905–1907.

Folstein, M. F., Folstein, S. E., & McHugh, M. R. (1975). "Mini-Mental State." A practical method for grading the cognitive state of patients for the clinician. *Journal of Psychiatric Research, 12,* 189–198.

Gerdner, L. A. (1999). Individualized music intervention protocol. *Journal of Gerontological Nursing, 25,* 10–16.

Guzzetta, C. (1989). Effects of relaxation and music therapy on patients in a coronary care unit with presumptive acute myocardial infarction. *Heart & Lung, 18,* 609–616.

Hoddes, E., Dement, W., & Zarcone, V. (1972). The history and use of the Stanford Sleepiness Scale. *Psychophysiology, 9,* 150–152.

Kaempf, G., & Amodei, M. E. (1989). The effect of music on anxiety. *AORN Journal, 50,* 112–118.

Kartman, L. L. (1984). Music hath charms. *Journal of Gerontological Nursing, 10,* 20–24.

Moss, V. A. (1988). Music and the surgical patient. *AORN Journal, 48,* 64–69.

National Commission of Sleep Disorders Research (1993). *Wake up America: A national sleep alert: Vol. 1. executive summary and executive report.*

Paley, M., & Tepas, D. I. (1994). Fatigue and the shiftworker: Firefighters working on a rotating shift schedule. *Human Factors, 36,* 269–284.

Radloff, L. S. (1977). The CES-D Scale: A self-report depression scale for research in the general population. *Journal of Applied Psychological Measurement, 1,* 385–401.

Ray, W. A., Fought, R. L., & Decker, M. D. (1992). Psychoactive drugs and the risk of injurious motor vehicle crashes in the elderly drivers. *American Journal of Epidemiology, 136,* 873–883.

Ray, W. A., Griffin, M. R., & Downey, W. (1989). Benzodiazepines of long and short elimination half-life and the risk of hip fracture. *Journal of the American Medical Association, 262,* 3303–3307.

Strauss, A. (1987). *Qualitative analysis for social scientists.* New York: Cambridge University Press.

Tabloski, P. A., Cooke, K. M., & Thoman, E. B. (1998). A procedure for withdrawal of sleep medication in elderly women who have been long-term users. *Journal of Gerontological Nursing, 24,* 20–28.

Walsh, J. K., & Engelhardt, C. L. (1992). Trends in the pharmacologic treatment of insomnia. *Journal of Clinical Psychiatry, 53*(Suppl.12), 10–18.

Zimmerman, L., Pozehl, B., Duncan, K., & Schmitz, R. (1989). Effects of music in patients who had chronic cancer pain. *Western Journal of Nursing Research, 11,* 298–309.

Address correspondence to: Julie E. Johnson, dean and professor, College of Nursing, Kent State University, P.O. Box 5190, Kent, OH 44242.

Exercise for Article 33

Factual Questions

1. How is the term *individualized music protocol* defined?

2. The names of potential participants for this study were obtained from how many health care professionals?

3. What was the mean age of the participants?

4. Differences between means were analyzed with what significance test?

5. Was there a significant increase in level of sleepiness at bedtime from pre- to posttest? If yes, at what probability level?

6. What was the "serendipitous finding of concern" reported by the researcher?

Questions for Discussion

7. The exclusion criteria are listed in lines 72–89 and Table 1. If you had conducted this study, would you have excluded individuals with these characteristics? Explain.

8. The researcher points out that the Stanford Sleepiness Scale has been used in three previously published studies. In your opinion, is it important to know that it has been used in other studies? Explain. (See lines 129–137.)

9. The researcher used three outcome measures (the Stanford Sleepiness Scale, a sleep log, and an investigator-constructed interview tool). Is the use of three measures instead of only one a special strength of this study? Explain. (See lines 123–128.)

10. There was no control group in this study. In your opinion, would it be desirable to use a control group in future studies on this topic? Why? Why not?

11. In your opinion, are the quantitative *or* qualitative results more important? Are they equally important? Explain.

12. Do you agree that these findings deserve further investigation? Explain. (See lines 316–319.)

Quality Ratings

Directions: Indicate your level of agreement with each of the following statements by circling a number from 5 for strongly agree (SA) to 1 for strongly disagree (SD). If you believe an item is not applicable to this research article, leave it blank. Be prepared to explain your ratings. When responding to criteria A and B below, keep in mind that brief titles and abstracts are conventional in published research.

A. The title of the article is appropriate.

SA   5   4   3   2   1   SD

B. The abstract provides an effective overview of the research article.

SA   5   4   3   2   1   SD

C. The introduction establishes the importance of the study.

SA   5   4   3   2   1   SD

D. The literature review establishes the context for the study.

SA   5   4   3   2   1   SD

E. The research purpose, question, or hypothesis is clearly stated.

SA   5   4   3   2   1   SD

F. The method of sampling is sound.

SA   5   4   3   2   1   SD

G. Relevant demographics (for example, age, gender, and ethnicity) are described.

SA   5   4   3   2   1   SD

H. Measurement procedures are adequate.

SA   5   4   3   2   1   SD

I. All procedures have been described in sufficient detail to permit a replication of the study.

    SA   5   4   3   2   1   SD

J. The participants have been adequately protected from potential harm.

    SA   5   4   3   2   1   SD

K. The results are clearly described.

    SA   5   4   3   2   1   SD

L. The discussion/conclusion is appropriate.

    SA   5   4   3   2   1   SD

M. Despite any flaws, the report is worthy of publication.

    SA   5   4   3   2   1   SD

Article 34

Factors Which Influence Latino Community Members to Self-Prescribe Antibiotics

Elaine L. Larson, RN, PhD, CIC, FAAN, **Joann Dilone**,
Magaly Garcia, MD, **Janice Smolowitz**, RN, EdD, DrNP[*]

ABSTRACT

Background: Although there is consistent evidence of a link between antibiotic use and increasing antimicrobial resistance in the community, inappropriate use of antimicrobials continues to be a global problem.

Objective: To describe knowledge, attitudes, and practices of Latino community members in upper Manhattan regarding use of antibiotics.

Methods: Written questionnaires and eight focus groups comprised of Hispanic community members (three groups), bodega employees, and healthcare providers (one group) in a Latino neighborhood in New York City.

Results: There were major knowledge deficits regarding use of antibiotics. Informants reported taking antibiotics for pain or other conditions as well as for symptoms of infection. Antibiotics were frequently obtained from bodegas without prescription, but generally only for adults, not for children.

Discussion: Interventions to improve antibiotic use that are focused on the formal healthcare system (e.g., clinicians, pharmacists, persons with health insurance) are unlikely to be effective with recently immigrated Latino community members. Successful interventions for this population should include targeted messages to bodega employees, community organizations, and children and their parents.

From *Nursing Research*, 55, 94–102. Copyright © 2006 by Lippincott Williams & Wilkins, Inc. Reprinted with permission.

There is consistent evidence of a link between antibiotic use and increasing antimicrobial resistance in the community (Diekema, Brueggemann, & Doern, 2000; Levy, 2002; Melander, Ekdahl, Jonsson, & Molstad, 2000). Nevertheless, inappropriate use of antimicrobials continues to be a global problem. Reasons for this include public expectations and demand for medication, lack of understanding about the ineffectiveness of antibiotics against viral illness, and the ease of access to antibiotics without prescription in many parts of the world (Mainous, Hueston, & Clark, 1996; McKee, Mills, & Mainous, 1999; Metlay, Shea, Crossette, & Asch, 2002).

Antibiotic misuse and resistance are more common in countries such as those in Latin America in which antibiotics are available over the counter and in which cultural patterns regarding medication use and beliefs about medication effectiveness differ (Corbett et al., 2005; Garfield, Broe, & Albano, 1995). If successful strategies to reduce misuse of antibiotics (and other medications) in the Latino population are to be developed, it is essential to understand the cultural norms regarding antibiotic use that characterize this group. The aim of this study was to describe the knowledge, attitudes, beliefs, and practices of Latino community members in northern Manhattan regarding use of antibiotics. The ultimate goal is to use this information to develop a culturally relevant and effective intervention to improve the judicious use of antibiotics among Latino community members.

Background

Antibiotic use patterns among Latinos are important because Latinos represent the fastest growing minority population in the United States (United States Census Bureau, 2001), and they have generally immigrated from countries in which antibiotics are available without prescription. In a recent survey, 39% of 631 Latino households ($n = 2,840$ individuals) in northern Manhattan reported that one or more persons had taken antibiotics in the previous 30 days, a rate even higher than that reported in a prevalence survey almost a decade ago in Mexico (Calva & Bojalil, 1996; Larson, Lin, & Gomez-Duarte, 2003). In a study of shigellosis in Oregon, Latinos had the highest prevalence of antimicrobial resistant strains (Replogle, Fleming, & Cieslak, 2000).

Multiple private and public agencies, in particular the Centers for Disease Control and Prevention (CDC) (Weissman & Besser, 2004), have undertaken public and provider campaigns and other educational and policy interventions to reduce inappropriate use of antibiotics. While many interventions have reported positive

[*]*Elaine L. Larson* is professor; *Joann Dilone* is research assistant, School of Nursing; *Magaly Garcia*, Hispanic Resource Center; and *Janice Smolowitz* is associate professor of clinical nursing, School of Nursing, Columbia University, New York, NY.

results (Gonzales, Steiner, Lum, & Barrett, 1999; Hennessy et al., 2002; Perz et al., 2002; Trepka, Belongia, Chyou, Davis, & Schwartz, 2001), they have been focused primarily on prescribing patterns in the "majority" population. Such interventions, however, have not been evaluated among recent immigrants or subgroups of the population.

Some previous research about factors which enable, predispose, or reinforce antibiotic use patterns among Latino members of the community has been conducted. Corbett et al. (2005) have reported that knowledge deficits are more common among Spanish-speaking Latinos as compared with non-Latino White people and English-language Latino people. In several studies, less knowledge has been associated with a greater demand for antibiotics (Finkelstein et al., 2003; Kuzujanakis, Kleinman, Rifas-Shiman, & Finkelstein, 2003). Braun and Fowles (2000) reported that parents who believed that antibiotics were helpful for treating colds were significantly more likely to request antibiotics from a provider. In a large survey of 543 parents from 38 managed care pediatric practices in Los Angeles, Asian and Latino parents were 17% more likely to state that antibiotics were needed than non-Latino White parents (Mangione-Smith et al., 2004). Also several studies have confirmed that many Latinos obtain antibiotics from Latin America where they are considerably cheaper and available without prescription from pharmacies and bodegas (Macias & Morales, 2001; Weinberg et al., 2003). Even in the United States, however, patients have often expressed the opinion that they can decide for themselves whether an antibiotic is needed without consulting a healthcare provider (Belongia, Naimi, Gale, & Besser, 2002).

Blanchard and Lurie (2004) have reported that significantly more Latino people when compared with non-Latino White people felt disrespected in the healthcare setting. Further, those persons who thought that they would receive better care if they were a different ethnicity or race were significantly less likely to seek care or follow the clinician's advice. Patients have indicated that even if they did not get an antibiotic prescription, they would be satisfied if they received an explanation, a contingency plan, or both (Barden, Dowell, Schwartz, & Lackey, 1998; Mangione-Smith et al., 2001). In one study, however, pamphlets regarding antibiotic use which were passively placed in waiting rooms of pediatric practices were not read (Wheeler et al., 2001).

In addition to increased direct provider–patient interactions (Mangione-Smith, Stivers, Elliott, McDonald, & Heritage, 2003), computer-based information resources have been shown to be a potentially valuable vehicle for providing high quality, accurate health information, and could be one mechanism to reinforce recommendations provided during short face-to-face visits (D'Alessandro, Kreiter, Kinzer, & Peterson, 2004). Informational messages can be tailored as appropriate to the recipient; Krueter, Farrell, Olevitch, and Brennan (2000) described a nine-step tailoring process, and Witte, Meyer, and Martell (2001) have developed a framework for developing culturally specific messages. Such information resources might be helpful within the Latino community if they have access to and use computers, but the extent to which recent immigrants from Latin America have access to computers has not been previously described.

Methods

This was an exploratory, descriptive study using focus group interviews and questionnaires.

Sample and Setting

A purposive sample of three different groups participated in this study. One group (*n* = 6) was composed of community members who were not linked into the formal healthcare system (i.e., did not have a designated primary care provider or health insurance), and a second group (*n* = 19) who had some type of health insurance. Participants in these groups were as follows: (a) women of Latino origin, born either in the United States or elsewhere, but with Spanish as their first language; (b) members of households that included at least one preschool child; and (c) residents of northern Manhattan. The rationale for including households with preschool children was that antibiotic use and resistance are more likely to occur when there are children in the household (Chiou et al., 1998; Mangione-Smith, McGlynn, Elliott, Krogstad, & Brook, 1999; McCaig, Besser, & Hughes, 2002).

The third group (*n* = 5) included two local small business employees of independent stores which sell food and toiletry items (bodegas) and three healthcare professionals with extensive experience providing services for Latino adults from the same neighborhood. This group was convened to determine whether their perspective on community use of antibiotics differed from the community members themselves.

Community participants were recruited by posting flyers in local stores, churches, day care centers, and community organizations. Bodega employees and healthcare professionals were recruited by direct contact in their place of work.

Procedures

Approval of the university institutional review board was obtained and participants signed a written Spanish-language consent form. This study was guided by the educational and environmental approach to health promotion planning espoused by Green and Kreuter (1991), the precede–proceed model, in which an educational and organizational diagnosis is the first step in planning health promotion activities. This stage of the diagnosis requires identification of factors which predispose, enable, and reinforce healthy behaviors (Figure 1), in this case antibiotic practices, as a prerequisite for planning relevant interventions to improve behavior. Focus group discussions were designed to elicit information about these three factors.

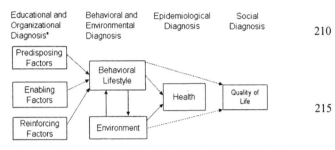

Educational and Organizational Diagnosis*   Behavioral and Environmental Diagnosis   Epidemiological Diagnosis   Social Diagnosis

*This project was undertaken to conduct the Educational and Organizational Diagnosis

Figure 1. The Green precede–proceed model (Green & Kreuter, 1991) used as conceptual underpinnings.

165   The community member focus groups were conducted in Spanish in a lounge at the study institution by a trained Latina facilitator at times convenient for participants. The facilitator (Garcia) was a native Spanish-speaking psychiatrist born in Latin America with for-
170   mal training in the conduct of focus groups. The three community member focus groups each met on two occasions—once for about 2 hr and a second time 2–3 weeks later for about 1 hr to review a summary of their previous discussion. The bodega employees and
175   healthcare professionals met in two separate groups, one conducted in Spanish and the other in English, and these two groups met only one time each. Because selling antibiotics over the counter is illegal, bodega employees were asked not to discuss whether or not they
180   sold them, but rather to respond by discussing what they thought their customers expected. These participants individually validated the summary of the focus group discussion 2–3 weeks later.

The focus groups were conducted according to the
185   methodology described by Morgan and Krueger (1998). Participants and investigators introduced themselves and the facilitator reviewed the consent form and purpose of the study. The facilitator also described the precede–proceed model and informed the group
190   that they would be discussing their use of antibiotics with regard to predisposing, enabling, and reinforcing factors. Then a short Spanish-language questionnaire (see Instruments section) was administered to introduce the topic and obtain baseline data on participants'
195   knowledge, attitudes, and practices regarding antibiotic use. The questionnaires were completed individually by participants without discussion with each other.

After the questionnaires were collected, the discussions were initiated by the facilitator, who began with
200   open-ended general statements such as "Tell us about when your family uses antibiotics" and "The last time you used an antibiotic, describe what your symptoms were." Discussions were based on a written guide that included the three concepts of predisposing, enabling,
205   and reinforcing factors associated with antibiotic use.

Scenarios were also presented to elicit specific practices. For example, "It is 4 am and your 2 year old is crying in pain and hitting her ear. You know that she has another ear infection. Let's discuss what actions
210   you would take and why." The group also discussed current sources of their health information, their computer literacy, and how health communications could be targeted to them in the most credible ways. At the end of the discussion about each of the three concepts
215   of the model, the facilitator provided a general summary and asked the group for validation and clarification.

A second 1-hr debriefing session was held after responses from the initial focus groups were summarized
220   and collated. The facilitator provided a summary of the discussion so that group members could add comments and clarifications. The themes and issues that emerged were reviewed with participants to assess credibility (i.e., that the input of the participants had been accu-
225   rately captured) and to provide an opportunity for participants to clarify, amplify, and correct the summaries. In addition, any opinions that were not expressed in the focus groups but that were raised in the written questionnaires *were* presented in this second session. Dur-
230   ing each session, a Spanish-speaking research assistant took extensive notes and all sessions were audiotaped.

Instruments

A short questionnaire provided quantitative data for comparative analysis with the qualitative data generated by the focus groups. The questionnaire was
235   adapted from that used in a community intervention study to assess knowledge and awareness of antibiotic resistance and appropriate antibiotic use (Trepka et al., 2001). It was used to gather factual information about antibiotic use in each household within the previous 3
240   months, knowledge and attitudes (i.e., predisposing factors) about appropriate use and types of antibiotics (Tables 1 and 2), and information regarding where respondents obtained antibiotics and health information (i.e., enabling and reinforcing factors). The question-
245   naire and consent forms were translated into Spanish by a professional translator in the Hispanic Research and Recruitment Center, Columbia University Medical Center, and then back-translated by the focus group facilitator to assure accuracy of the meaning of all
250   words and phrases. Lay language and, when appropriate, "street" names for medications were used. The instrument was then pilot tested with five Spanish-speaking members of the community for readability, time required to complete, and clarity. As noted above,
255   the focus group discussions were used to confirm, correct, or expand on information reported in the written questionnaire.

Data Analysis

Responses from the questionnaire were summarized using SPSS (Chicago, IL). Focus group data were ex-
260   amined using tape-based analysis as described by Mor-

gan and Kreuger (1998). About 1 week after each focus group, three of the investigators listened to the audiotape, took extensive notes, and independently identified common themes and factors related to attitudes, beliefs, and practices in the context of precede–proceed model. Each investigator categorized these factors as predisposing, reinforcing, or enabling for appropriate antibiotic use. Then the investigators compared their notes and the field notes for congruence, and agreement was reached on emerging themes by consensus. Data from the taped focus group discussions were also examined to assure that all common themes had been fully identified and explored (i.e., that saturation had been reached). The focus group facilitator then independently reviewed the audiotapes, field notes, and investigator analysis to validate the developing themes. Audiotapes were reviewed at least three times and themes were confirmed by consensus of the four investigators with feedback from participants to affirm trustworthiness of the finding.

Results

Participants

Twenty-five Latina women participated in the two community focus groups. Their mean age was 35.7 years (22–47 years); the majority of participants (92%) were born in the Dominican Republic, one in El Salvador, and two in New York City. The average family size was 4.7 members (3–8 members). All but one participant (96%) had high school or less education. The bodega employees and one of the healthcare professionals were born in the Dominican Republic; the other healthcare professionals were born in the United States. All bodega employees had a high school education.

Questionnaire

Twelve informants (44.4%) reported that they had taken an antibiotic within the past 3 months, and 13 (48.1%) reported that at least one other person in their household had taken an antibiotic. Antibiotics named included ampicillin, amoxicillin, erythromycin, amoxicillin/clavulanate potassium (Augmentin), and penicillin and were taken for a mean of 12 doses (1–28). While most reported taking an antibiotic for symptoms of infection (sore throat, ear infection, and fever), one-third (5/15) of reasons given for taking antibiotics were for other symptoms, including nausea, pain, itching, and allergies.

Predisposing factors: knowledge and attitudes. There were a number of factual misconceptions among respondents (Table 1). For example, 56% thought that antibiotics would help cure a cold and would kill both viruses and bacteria, and only 36% reported that antibiotics could be harmful to one's health. The proportion of those able to correctly identify antibiotics from a list of commonly used drugs ranged 12–92%. While the majority (56%) reported that they stopped antibiotics because the prescribed duration was complete, 48%

also reported stopping antibiotics when they felt better (Table 2).

Table 1

Predisposing Factors (Knowledge) Regarding Antibiotic Use (n = 25 community focus group respondents)

Item	Agree n (%)	
Antibiotics help cure a cold	14	(56)
Treating a cold with antibiotics will help prevent an ear infection	18	(72)
Antibiotics should be stopped as soon as the person feels better	6	(24)
Antibiotics are usually needed if there is yellow drainage in the nose	4	(16)
Some germs are becoming harder to treat with antibiotics	11	(44)
If there is excessive use of antibiotics they will not be as effective in treating infections	14	(56)
Bacteria can become resistant to antibiotics if they are taken in inadequate doses	15	(60)
Antibiotics work to kill viruses and bacteria	14	(56)
If antibiotics are taken for fewer or more than the days indicated, bacteria can become resistant	12	(48)
Antibiotics can be harmful to one's health	9	(36)

Is this an antibiotic?	Correct response n (%)		Do not know n (%)	
Amoxicillin	23	(92)	1	(4)
Aspirin	21	(84)	3	(12)
Chloramphenicol	3	(12)	13	(52)
Cough medicine	20	(80)	4	(16)
Acetaminophen (e.g., Tylenol)	18	(72)	4	(16)
Erythromycin	11	(44)	11	(44)
Albuterol	13	(52)	8	(32)
Epinephrine	8	(32)	14	(56)
Ampicillin	22	(88)	1	(4)
Theophylline	5	(20)	13	(52)
Tetracycline	18	(72)	4	(16)
Sulfa (Bactrim)	5	(20)	14	(56)
Penicillin	20	(80)	3	(12)

Enabling factors: economic and access issues. Most community informants (84%) had either no insurance or received Medicaid. While most (72%) respondents reported getting antibiotics from a pharmacy with a prescription, they also reported buying them without prescription from pharmacies (24%), bodegas (32%), or from outside the United States (20%), or obtaining them from friends or leftover from previous uses.

Reinforcing factors. When asked to name their most reliable source of information about medicines, respondents named the physician, books, and family members in rank order. Most (68%, 17/25) community participants had access to a computer, but 20% (5/25) reported never using a computer (Table 3).

Focus Group Findings for Adults

Predisposing factors. Across focus groups, participants described how knowledge toward symptom treatment and cultural attitudes about antibiotics (predisposing factors) provided the basis for self-prescribed

Table 2
Predisposing Factors (Attitudes) Regarding Antibiotic Use (n = 25 community focus group respondents)

How often do you think antibiotics should be used for the following conditions?	Always n (%)	Sometimes n (%)	Never n (%)	Do not know n (%)
Ear infection	15 (40)	15 (60)	0	0
Bronchitis	12 (48)	5 (20)	4 (16)	4 (16)
Cold	0	17 (68)	1 (4)	7 (28)
Dry cough without fever	0	3 (12)	10 (40)	11 (44)
Cold with cough and body aches	1 (4)	7 (28)	9 (36)	6 (24)
Sinusitis	5 (20)	6 (24)	5 (20)	8 (32)
Throat inflammation (tonsillitis)	16 (64)	6 (24)	1 (4)	1 (4)
Sore throat	6 (24)	14 (56)	4 (16)	0
Diarrhea	4 (16)	5 (20)	10 (40)	5 (20)
Nasal discharge or secretion	0	7 (28)	9 (36)	8 (32)
Vomiting	0	5 (20)	11 (44)	8 (32)
Conjunctivitis	3 (12)	9 (36)	8 (32)	5 (20)
Boils	2 (8)	10 (40)	6 (24)	7 (28)
Pain or burning sensation when urinating	5 (20)	15 (60)	2 (8)	2 (8)
Wounds	2 (8)	13 (52)	4 (16)	4 (16)
Tightness in chest (asthma)	2 (8)	8 (32)	8 (32)	6 (24)

Indicate reasons you have decided to stop taking an antibiotic	
I felt better	12 (48)
I had side effects	3 (12)
My prescription expired	6 (24)
It was too problematic to take	3 (12)
Cost too much	3 (12)
Did not have a prescription	3 (12)
The indicated time of treatment had expired	14 (56)

medication: "We use it there (in our country) until symptoms go away. That is the tradition." "It is a sign of friendship when you go to the pharmacist and he provides you with medicine."

Easy access to antibiotics through bodegas and other independent stores in northern Manhattan continued a tradition of care from the country of origin as did the practice of treating family and friends. Family members shared antibiotic prescriptions when they developed similar symptoms. Family members living in the country of origin routinely sent antibiotics to relatives and friends in northern Manhattan. Focus group discussions among the community members identified novel uses of antibiotics based on traditional home remedies. "In the Dominican Republic as well as here, we prepare a deodorant called Deporte. We add penicillin and oil and use it for burns, bruises or cuts on the skin."

Enabling factors. Enabling factors identified during the focus group discussions included socioeconomic and access issues. Lack of insurance, monetary constraints, and legal status had financial implications that affected treatment choice. "Some people don't have citizenship or medical insurance to go to the doctor." "Antibiotics should be more accessible to the public, the ones that are not strong. There are a lot of people who don't have any medical insurance." "My dad would tell me in my country (I suffered from my throat) that it's too much money to take me to the doc-

tor every time. It's better to keep antibiotics in the fridge, in case."

Based on contextual factors and the perception that antibiotics were necessary to treat symptoms, participants reported purchasing one or two pills of penicillin or other antibiotic at local independent pharmacies and bodegas or obtaining antibiotics from family members. "Well, I will be the first to admit it, when any person I know comes to me and tells me that they have a toothache I tell them to buy two penicillin and that will make them feel better." "If you come in with any pain they will give it to you. If you have a cold they will sell it to you. Here they become a doctor." "Antibiotics in my country you can get anywhere. They sell them to you without any prescription. When my sister-in-law came back not too long ago, she brought me back a bag full of antibiotics for different things: for the cold, in a cream for any type of burns." "It is easier and one does not have time to go to the doctor." "It's much easier with the kids, work, and business of life. We don't have time to spend the night in the hospital."

Community focus group members expressed positive, negative, and ambivalent feelings regarding sale of antibiotics in bodegas. Despite the fact that few reported in the written questionnaire that they thought antibiotics should be sold in bodegas, all informants verbally reported that they did buy them there. Because of their perception that bodegas would continue to sell antibiotics without prescription, participants recommended that bodega staff members receive education about what to sell for various symptoms.

Table 3
Enabling and Reinforcing Factors in Obtaining Antibiotics and Health Information (Written Responses Only)

Item	Affirmative Response	
	n	(%)
Where do you regularly get antibiotics?		
Pharmacy with a prescription	18	(72)
Bodega	8	(32)
Pharmacy without a prescription	6	(24)
A friend	6	(24)
Outside the United States	5	(20)
Left over from previous prescription	3	(12)
Do you generally store antibiotics at home for when they are needed?	6	(24)
Do you think antibiotics should be sold without a prescription?	9	(36)
Is it useful for bodegas to sell antibiotics?	6	(16)
When you want information on medicines, what is the most reliable source of information for you?		
Doctor	17	(68)
Books	11	(44)
Family or friends	9	(36)
Internet	2	(8)
Do you have access to a computer?	17	(68)
How often do you use the Internet?		
Never	5	(20)
1–2 times/week	7	(28)
Almost daily	13	(52)

Reinforcing factors. When symptom relief was obtained, the practice of self-prescribing was reinforced and repeated with each episode of illness: "We take the medication 2–3 times. When we feel better we stop taking it."

Participants also described experience with two types of problems associated with antibiotic use. In the first scenario, the antibiotic had secondary effects. Temporary effects included diarrhea, vomiting, and allergic reactions; permanent effects included anemia, ulcers, and liver problems. "Frequent use of antibiotics can cause anemia. Yes, my friend took antibiotics frequently and she became anemic. The doctor had to prescribe some vitamins to balance it out for her." "The antibiotics eat red blood cells." "Antibiotics can cause paleness of the skin." "Antibiotics cure one thing and destroy another."

In the second scenario, individuals perceived that resistance to the antibiotic had developed. Participants defined resistance: "It is when antibiotics have no effect on the body because of frequent use, they have to use a different antibiotic or a stronger one." "He became resistant to an antibiotic; that is why they gave him a stronger antibiotic." "The prescribed medication was not the sufficient dosage."

When symptoms were not relieved or when side effects occurred, participants reported seeking care from physicians. Despite the fact that participants reported that physicians provided a full course of treatment with an antibiotic as well as educational material, the experience in the mainstream healthcare system did not change their self-prescribing practices; that is, this reinforcing factor was not sufficient to change behavior. Cultural and contextual factors weighed heavily in the decision process and self-prescription continued with the next episode of illness.

The predisposing, enabling, and reinforcing factors that justified self-prescription by adults are summarized in Figure 2A.

Focus Group Findings for Children

Universally, participants reported that they did not self-prescribe antibiotics for their children. Initially, parents might provide common symptomatic treatments. If symptoms did not resolve, children were taken immediately to the clinician. Parents expressed concern about harming their children by purchasing over-the-counter antibiotics without consulting a physician. They were concerned also that city agencies would intervene with regard to their children's welfare. The predisposing, enabling, and reinforcing factors described in the treatment of children are summarized in Figure 2B.

Focus Group Findings from the Healthcare Community

Responses from bodega employees showed the same level of knowledge as the community members and reflected similar attitudes. Bodega employees did not voice opposition to over-the-counter sale of antibiotics but were reluctant to discuss specifics. Responses from other healthcare professionals providing services to the Latino community confirmed information obtained from the community members. Unlike bodega employees, however, healthcare professionals voiced strong opposition to the sale of antibiotics in bodegas. They also voiced concern about antibiotic resistance in the community. Discussion focused on the difficulty of enforcing the current law because of the large number of bodegas and the community's cultural expectations.

Discussion

Based on results of the questionnaire and focus group discussions, the implications of the predisposing, enabling, and reinforcing factors associated with antibiotic self-prescribing are examined below.

Predisposing Factors

Knowledge deficits about antibiotics were prevalent and of concern in this population—for example, many reported that antibiotics can be used to treat viral infections and even headaches. Of particular concern was the fact that one-third of reported reasons for taking antibiotics were for symptoms such as pain, allergy, or asthma. As has been reported by others (Belongia et al., 2002), many of our participants expressed the opinion that they could decide for themselves whether an antibiotic was needed. Clearly, effective interventions

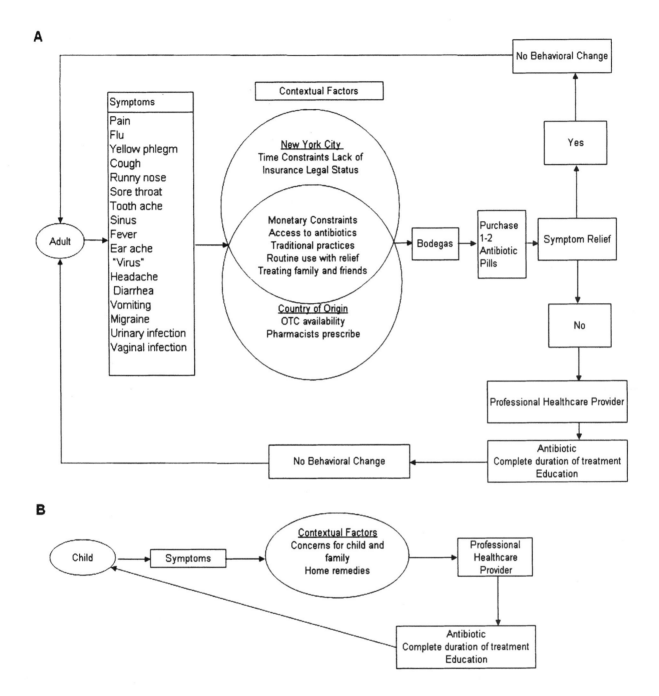

Figure 2. (A) Educational and organizational diagnosis of precede–proceed model: Latino community members' description of predisposing, enabling, and reinforcing factors associated with antibiotic use for adults. (B) Educational and organizational diagnosis of precede–proceed model. Latino community members' description of predisposing, enabling, and reinforcing factors associated with antibiotic use for children.

for this population would need to include Spanish-language educational materials, such as those available through CDC's Get Smart program (National Center for Infectious Diseases, 2005). While such materials may be necessary, however, they are certainly not sufficient unless provided in ways meaningful and relevant to this group (Wheeler et al., 2001).

Enabling Factors

One of the most important enabling factors for this population was the availability of antibiotics inexpensively from bodegas. Access was important to this group. While only about a third of participants in the written questionnaire reported buying antibiotics from a bodega, every participant then verbally confirmed during the discussion that they did indeed regularly do so. They noted that the necessity for waiting in a clinic or waiting room to see a healthcare provider was a major deterrent. Consistent with previous literature (Macias & Morales, 2001; Weinberg et al., 2003), our informants reported that they obtain antibiotics from

239

Latin America where they are cheaper and available without prescription.

495   In this culture, community participants reported that the bodega employee and the pharmacist are important and respected sources of health information. Both community members and the healthcare professionals confirmed that interventions to improve appropriate

500   antibiotic use in the Latino population would have to include bodega staff. As respected members of the community and longstanding, traditional sources of antibiotics, bodega employees could serve as important sources of information. Providing educational materials

505   to be distributed in bodegas would be consistent with their established role in the community. There have been no known attempts to include the sellers of antibiotics in educational interventions to improve their use.

Reinforcing Factors

510   Respondents named "doctors" as their major source of health information in the written survey, and yet they also reported that receiving care from a health professional did not change their self-prescribing patterns. Although this seems to be contradictory, there

515   may be great potential for a positive influence of the healthcare provider if a meaningful relationship is established. Since the participants in our study also identified that they often received their health information from family and friends and self-medicated with anti-

520   biotics obtained from bodegas, traditional interventions such as pamphlets in clinic waiting rooms are unlikely to meet with success in this population (Wheeler et al., 2001).

Of interest among our informants was that while

525   adults self-prescribed antibiotics, they stated that they would be unlikely to do so for their children. One potentially effective strategy among the Latino population would be to include the child as well as parents and Latino community organizations directly in educational

530   efforts.

Based on information provided by our participants, being told by even respected healthcare providers not to self-prescribe antibiotics was insufficient as a reinforcing factor. Such health messages must be delivered

535   in respectful and culturally sensitive ways and must be accompanied by alternative suggestions for what can or should be done (Weissman & Besser, 2004). Despite the fact that the participants in our focus groups were not highly educated, many reported using a computer

540   almost daily. Innovative and tailored Spanish-language messages delivered electronically might also be one promising component of a multifactorial, culturally relevant intervention to reduce the self-prescribing of antibiotics in this important segment of the population.

Summary and Recommendations

545   Described earlier are predisposing, enabling, and reinforcing factors that influence Latino community members to self-prescribe antibiotics. Some factors (e.g., time and money constraints, long waiting periods in clinics, and language barriers) will require long-term

550   policy and systems change. Other proximal determinants that might be promising targets as immediate intervention strategies are recommended:

1. Include small business owners who sell antibiotics in educational interventions. This would in-

555   volve (a) suggesting alternatives to antibiotics that they might offer customers so that they would not risk losing income or customers, (b) providing small business owners and employees with Spanish language, culturally appropriate

560   educational materials for dissemination to customers, and (c) working collaboratively with the Bodega Association of America (Asociacion de Bodegueros de los Estados Unidos, Inc.). Since there are about 14,000 bodegas in New York

565   alone and > 22,000 nationally (Bodega Association of the United States, 2005), such a partnership would seem an essential component of an effective and sustainable community-wide intervention.

570   2. Include lay community workers (*promotores*) and children in educational messages regarding antibiotic use and resistance through public schools or other community organizations. Community groups directed toward assisting immigrants

575   could be good partners in providing education in basic healthcare and care of minor infections.

3. Develop informational messages through the Spanish-speaking media and Internet, which are tailored to be culturally specific and relevant.

580   Clearly, interventions targeted solely to traditional, mainstream clinicians and the English-speaking population will fail to reach a large segment of the population, which may serve as one reservoir for antibiotic resistance in the community.

References

Barden, L. S., Dowell, S. F., Schwartz, B., & Lackey, C. (1998). Current attitudes regarding use of antimicrobial agents: Results from physician's and parents' focus group discussions. *Clinical Pediatrics, 37,* 665–671.

Belongia, E. A., Naimi, T. S., Gale, C. M., & Besser, R. E. (2002). Antibiotic use and upper respiratory infections: A survey of knowledge, attitudes, and experience in Wisconsin and Minnesota. *Preventive Medicine, 34,* 346–352.

Blanchard, J., & Lurie, N. (2004). R-E-S-P-E-C-T: Patient reports of disrespect in the healthcare setting and its impact on care. *Journal of Family Practice, S3,* 721–730.

Bodega Association of the United States. (2005). Retrieved August 31, 2005, from http://www.bodegaassociation.org/

Braun, B. L., & Fowles, J. B. (2000). Characteristics and experiences of parents and adults who want antibiotics for cold symptoms. *Archives of Family Medicine, 9,* 589–595.

Calva, J., & Bojalil, R. (1996). Antibiotic use in a periurban community in Mexico: A household and drugstore survey. *Social Science & Medicine, 42,* 1121–1128.

Chiou, C. C., Liu, Y. C., Huang, T. S., Hwang, T. K., Wang, J. H., Lin, H. H., et al. (1998). Extremely high prevalence of nasopharyngeal carriage of penicillin-resistant Streptococcus pneumoniae among children in Kaohsiung, Taiwan. *Journal of Clinical Microbiology, 36,* 1933–1937.

Corbett, K. K., Gonzales, R., Leeman-Castillo, B. A., Flores, E., Maselli, J., & Kafadar, K. (2005). Appropriate antibiotic use: Variation in knowledge and awareness by Hispanic ethnicity and language. *Preventive Medicine, 40,* 162–169.

D'Alessandro, D. M., Kreiter, C. D., Kinzer, S. L., & Peterson, M. W. (2004). A randomized controlled trial of an information prescription for pediatric patient education on the Internet. *Archives of Pediatric & Adolescent Medicine, 158,* 857–862.

Diekema, D. J., Brueggemann, A. B., & Doern, G. V. (2000). Antimicrobial-drug use and changes in resistance in Streptococcus pneumoniae. *Emerging Infectious Diseases, 6,* 552–556.

Finkelstein, J. A., Stille, C., Nordin, J., Davis, R., Raebel, M. A., Roblin, D., et al. (2003). Reduction in antibiotic use among US children, 1996–2000. *Pediatrics, 112,* 620–627.

Garfield, R., Broe, D., & Albano, B. (1995). The role of academic medical centers in delivery of primary care: An urban study. *Academic Medicine, 70,* 405–409.

Gonzales, R., Steiner, J. F., Lum, A., & Barrett, P. H., Jr. (1999). Decreasing antibiotic use in ambulatory practice: Impact of a multidimensional intervention on the treatment of uncomplicated acute bronchitis in adults. *Journal of the American Medical Association, 281,* 1512–1519.

Green, L., & Kreuter, M. (1991). *Health promotion planning: An educational and environmental approach* (2nd ed.). Mountain View, CA: Mayfield.

Hennessy, T. W., Petersen, K. M., Bruden, D., Parkinson, A. J., Hurlburt, D., Getty, M., et al. (2002). Changes in antibiotic-prescribing practices and carriage of penicillin-resistant Streptococcus pneumoniae: A controlled intervention trial in rural Alaska. *Clinical Infectious Diseases, 34,* 1543–1550.

Kreuter, M., Farrell, D., Olevitch, L., & Brennan, L. (2000). *Tailoring health messages: Customizing communication with computer technology.* Mahwah, NJ: Erlbaum.

Kuzujanakis, M., Kleinman, K., Rifas-Shiman, S., & Finkelstein, J. A. (2003). Correlates of parental antibiotic knowledge, demand, and reported use. *Ambulatory Pediatrics, 3,* 203–210.

Larson, E., Lin, S. X., & Gomez-Duarte, C. (2003). Antibiotic use in Hispanic households, New York city. *Emerging Infectious Diseases, 9,* 1096–1102.

Levy, S. B. (2002). The 2000 Garrod lecture. Factors impacting on the problem of antibiotic resistance. *Journal of Antimicrobial Chemotherapy, 49,* 25–30.

Macias, E. P., & Morales, L. S. (2001). Crossing the border for healthcare. *Journal of Health Care for the Poor and Under-served, 12,* 77–87.

Mainous, A. G., 3rd, Hueston, W. J., & Clark, J. R. (1996). Antibiotics and upper respiratory infection: Do some folks think there is a cure for the common cold? *Journal of Family Practice, 42,* 357–361.

Mangione-Smith, R., Elliott, M. N., Stivers, T., McDonald, L., Heritage, J., & McGlynn, E. A. (2004). Racial/ethnic variation in parent expectations for antibiotics: Implications for public health campaigns. *Pediatrics, 113,* e385–e394.

Mangione-Smith, R., McGlynn, E. A., Elliott, M. N., Krogstad, P., & Brook, R. H. (1999). The relationship between perceived parental expectations and pediatrician antimicrobial prescribing behavior. *Pediatrics, 103,* 711–718.

Mangione-Smith, R., McGlynn, E. A., Elliott, M. N., McDonald, L., Franz, C. E., & Kravitz, R. L. (2001). Parent expectations for antibiotics, physician-parent communication, and satisfaction. *Archives of Pediatric & Adolescent Medicine, 155,* 800–806.

Mangione-Smith, R., Stivers, T., Elliott, M., McDonald, L., & Heritage, J. (2003). Online commentary during the physical examination: A communication tool for avoiding inappropriate antibiotic prescribing? *Social Science & Medicine, 56,* 313–320.

McCaig, L. F., Besser, R. E., & Hughes, J. M. (2002). Trends in antimicrobial prescribing rates for children and adolescents. *Journal of the American Medical Association, 287,* 3096–3102.

McKee, M. D., Mills, L., & Mainous, A. G., 3rd. (1999). Antibiotic use for the treatment of upper respiratory infections in a diverse community. *Journal of Family Practice, 48,* 993–996.

Melander, E., Ekdahl, K., Jonsson, G., & Molstad, S. (2000). Frequency of penicillin-resistant pneumococci in children is correlated to community utilization of antibiotics. *Pediatric Infectious Disease Journal, 19,* 1172–1177.

Metlay, J. P., Shea, J. A., Crossette, L. B., & Asch, D. A. (2002). Tensions in antibiotic prescribing: Pitting social concerns against the interests of individual patients. *Journal of General Internal Medicine, 17,* 87–94.

Morgan D. L., & Krueger, R. A. (1998). *The focus group kit.* Thousand Oaks: Sage.

National Center for Infectious Diseases. (2005). Retrieved August 31, 2005, from http://www.cdc.gov/drugresistance/community/

Perz, J. F., Craig, A. S., Coffey, C. S., Jorgensen, D. M., Mitchel, E., Hall, S., et al. (2002). Changes in antibiotic prescribing for children after a community-wide campaign. *Journal of the American Medical Association, 287,* 3103–3109.

Replogle, M. L., Fleming, D. W., & Cieslak, P. R. (2000). Emergence of antimicrobial-resistant shigellosis in Oregon. *Clinical Infectious Diseases, 30,* 515–519.

Trepka, M. J., Belongia, E. A., Chyou, P. H., Davis, J. P., & Schwartz, B. (2001). The effect of a community intervention trial on parental knowledge and awareness of antibiotic resistance and appropriate antibiotic use in children. *Pediatrics, 107,* E6.

United States Census Bureau. (2001). Census 2000 Briefs and Special Reports. Retrieved August 31, 2005, from http://www.census.gov/prod/2001pubs/c2kbr01-3.pdf.

Weinberg, M., Waterman, S., Lucas, C. A., Falcon, V. C., Morales, P. K., Lopez, L. A., et al. (2003). The U.S.-Mexico Border Infectious Disease Surveillance project: Establishing bi-national border surveillance. *Emerging Infectious Diseases, 9,* 97–102.

Weissman, J., & Besser, R. E. (2004). Promoting appropriate antibiotic use for pediatric patients: A social ecological framework. *Seminars in Pediatric Infectious Diseases, 15,* 41–51.

Wheeler, J. G., Fair, M., Simpson, P. M., Rowlands, L. A., Aitken, M. E., & Jacobs, R. F. (2001). Impact of a waiting room videotape message on parent attitudes toward pediatric antibiotic use. *Pediatrics, 108,* 591–596.

Witte, K., Meyer, G., & Martell, D. (2001). *Effective health risk messages: A step-by-step guide.* Thousand Oaks, CA: Sage.

Acknowledgments: This study was funded in part by a pilot grant from Center for Evidence-based Practice in the Underserved (P20NR007799), National Institutes of Health. The authors express their gratitude to focus group participants and to Maria Cornelio, Director, Hispanic Resource Center, Columbia University Medical Center, and Mary Byrne, NP, PhD, professor of Clinical Nursing, for their support.

Address correspondence to: Elaine L. Larson, RN, PhD, CIC, FAAN, Columbia University School of Nursing, 630 West 168th Street, New York, NY 10032. E-mail: ell23@columbia.edu

Exercise for Article 34

Factual Questions

1. How were community participants recruited?

2. Why didn't the researchers ask the bodega employees to discuss whether they sold antibiotics over the counter?

3. Was the questionnaire administered "before" *or* "after" the focus group discussions?

4. The focus group discussions were based on a written guide that included what three concepts?

5. The questionnaire was pilot tested for what three characteristics?

6. Did many of the informants report buying antibiotics in bodegas?

Questions for Discussion

7. The researchers refer to the sample as a "purposive sample." Speculate on the meaning of this term. (See lines 121–122.)

8. Does the fact that the researchers conducted a debriefing session increase your confidence in the results of this study? (See lines 218–231.)

9. Is it important to know that the data analysis was initially conducted "independently"? Explain. (See lines 261–265 and 274–276.)

10. To what extent did Figure 2 help you understand the rationale and results of this study? Explain.

11. The researchers used both qualitative and quantitative methods in this study. In your opinion, did both methods contribute important information? Would this study have been as informative if only one of the methods had been used? Explain.

12. If you were to conduct a follow-up study on the same topic, what changes, if any, would you make in the research methodology?

Quality Ratings

Directions: Indicate your level of agreement with each of the following statements by circling a number from 5 for strongly agree (SA) to 1 for strongly disagree (SD). If you believe an item is not applicable to this research article, leave it blank. Be prepared to explain your ratings. When responding to criteria A and B below, keep in mind that brief titles and abstracts are conventional in published research.

A. The title of the article is appropriate.

    SA   5   4   3   2   1   SD

B. The abstract provides an effective overview of the research article.

    SA   5   4   3   2   1   SD

C. The introduction establishes the importance of the study.

    SA   5   4   3   2   1   SD

D. The literature review establishes the context for the study.

    SA   5   4   3   2   1   SD

E. The research purpose, question, or hypothesis is clearly stated.

    SA   5   4   3   2   1   SD

F. The method of sampling is sound.

    SA   5   4   3   2   1   SD

G. Relevant demographics (for example, age, gender, and ethnicity) are described.

    SA   5   4   3   2   1   SD

H. Measurement procedures are adequate.

    SA   5   4   3   2   1   SD

I. All procedures have been described in sufficient detail to permit a replication of the study.

    SA   5   4   3   2   1   SD

J. The participants have been adequately protected from potential harm.

    SA   5   4   3   2   1   SD

K. The results are clearly described.

    SA   5   4   3   2   1   SD

L. The discussion/conclusion is appropriate.

    SA   5   4   3   2   1   SD

M. Despite any flaws, the report is worthy of publication.

    SA   5   4   3   2   1   SD

Article 35

Computer-Mediated Support Group Use Among Parents of Children with Cancer: An Exploratory Study

Hae-Ra Han, PhD, RN, **Anne E. Belcher**, PhD, RN, AOCN, FAAN*

ABSTRACT. This study describes aspects of computer group use as a vehicle for self-help by parents of children with cancer. Using an electronic mail system, data were gathered from 73 parents who had participated in online support groups. Most participants were Caucasian, well educated, and reported annual incomes of more than $50,000. The perceived benefits of the computer group involvement were getting information, sharing experiences, receiving general support, venting feelings, gaining accessibility, and using writing. The disadvantages included "noise," negative emotions, large volume of mail, and lack of physical contact and proximity. The findings indicate that computer group use is more common in parents with relatively high socioeconomic status. There are certain advantages and disadvantages of computer group use that need to be recognized and addressed by health professionals and users.

From *Computers in Nursing*, 19, 27–33. Copyright © 2001 by Lippincott Williams & Wilkins, Inc. Reprinted with permission.

Background

Cancer is the second leading cause of death in children ages 5 to 15 years in the United States,[1] but approximately 70% of children diagnosed with cancer today will have a five-year or more disease-free survival.[2] The life-threatening and often chronic nature of cancer is a major stressor for children and their parents.[3-9]

Remarkable advances have been made in cancer diagnosis and treatment since the 1930s, and care for chronically ill children has shifted from the hospital to the home setting. An increasing number of children with cancer and their families cope with problems in day-to-day living at home.[10] As a result, not only are parents responsible for providing physical care, but they also must become skilled in clinical assessment, clinical decision making, and coordination of care.[11] Furthermore, the needs of the child with cancer demand constant parental vigilance. How parents cope with their child's cancer diagnosis and its treatment has been found to impact on the child's treatment-related morbidity, quality of life, and even treatment outcome.[8,12-14]

Evidence points to the central role of social support in alleviating the impact of illness so that the individual can achieve better coping outcomes.[15-17] Support groups, as a form of social support, have long been recognized as an effective intervention, producing positive psychological outcomes in cancer patients and their families.[18] Even for individuals with strong familial and interpersonal networks, support groups have been found to bridge the gap between information giving and social support.[19] According to Yalom,[20] there are 11 therapeutic factors existing in support groups: instillation of hope, universality, imparting information, altruism, the corrective recapitulation of the primary family group, development of socialization techniques, imitative behavior, interpersonal learning, group cohesiveness, catharsis, and existential factors.

Thoits[21] states that the effective provision of support is likely to arise from people who are socially similar to the support recipient and who have experienced similar stressors or situations. Self-help groups are experiential mutual-support, peer-support groups and recognized as an important part of the social support system for parents of children with cancer.[22] Self-help groups differ from counseling groups, which are structured as a formal part of the therapeutic process. The peer-support group approach has demonstrated its value in enhancing the ability of parents to cope with their child's chronic conditions.[23] However, researchers have reported that transportation, distance,[10] and time restrictions[24] are major barriers to attending face-to-face support groups.

Computers are becoming more accessible to the general public, and computer use for self-help has become a more common vehicle to connect to resources, obtain information, and gain support.[25] In a study that investigated computer-mediated support group use among six breast cancer patients, Weinberg et al.[26]

*Hae-Ra Han was a doctoral candidate at the University of Maryland School of Nursing at the time of the study. *Anne E. Belcher* is the director of the undergraduate program at the Thomas Jefferson University College of Health Professions.

60 found that the patients discussed their medical conditions, shared personal concerns, and offered support to one another. Brennan et al.[27] investigated subjects' uses of ComputerLink, a computer-mediated support group for caregivers of persons with Alzheimer's disease,

65 during a one-week period. The researchers reported that subjects used ComputerLink as an opportunity for contact with other caregivers who were experiencing similar caregiving problems and stresses. Eaglesham[25] conducted a study to examine the implications of using

70 computers as a vehicle for self-help groups. Shared experiences were often cited as a reason why people joined a computer group. Klemm et al.[28,29] reported exchange of personal experiences as one of the major categories of responses in such groups.

75 Computer-mediated self-help groups have also been reported to overcome the limitations of face-to-face support groups and to provide 24-hour availability, selective participation, anonymity, and privacy.[26,30,31] According to Finn,[30] there are more than 500,000 com-

80 puter-mediated support groups in the United States that are accessed by more than 15 million people. Computer groups are used by individuals with such diverse problems as cancer, diabetes, mental illness, alcohol or drug addiction, disability, bereavement, domestic violence,

85 and divorce.[25,30]

Despite their proliferation, little information is available about parents of children with cancer who belong to computer-mediated support groups. Furthermore, no study has examined the advantages and dis-

90 advantages of computer group use from the perspective of parent users. The exploratory nature of this study enabled researchers to collect basic information about the parent participants, as well as the perceived benefits and disadvantages of computer group use.

Methods

Settings and Sample

95 The online settings were three support groups for family members of children with cancer: N-BLASTOMA, PED-ALL, and PED-ONC. They are part of more than 70 online cancer support groups hosted by the Association of Cancer On-line Re-

100 sources, Inc. (ACOR), a nonprofit organization incorporated in New York in 1996 to create, produce, host, and manage a number of specific online resources for cancer patients, caregivers, healthcare professionals, and basic research scientists.[32] ACOR provides support

105 to more than 30,000 patients, family members, and caregivers.[32] The three online support groups for families of children with cancer post more than 100 messages per day about diagnosis, self-care skills, life stories, and encouragement as well as postings about the

110 children (i.e., how the sick children are doing). General types of messages (e.g., fund-raising activities, humor, and requests for specific medical information) are also posted to the groups. There were 222, 162, and 224

members on N-BLASTOMA, PED-ALL, and PED-

115 ONC, respectively, at the time of data collection.[33]

Seventy-three parents (55 mothers and 18 fathers) participated in the study (17 from N-BLASTOMA, 28 from PED-ALL, and 28 from PED-ONC). Selection criteria for the convenience sample were as follows: (1)

120 age 18 years or older, (2) parent of a child diagnosed with cancer, and (3) participant in a computer-mediated support group. The sample ranged in age from 25 to 55 years, with a mean age of 38. Most participants were Caucasian, well educated, and reported annual incomes

125 of more than $50,000. Diagnoses of the children included leukemia (57.5%), neuroblastoma (24.7%), and other forms of childhood cancer (17.8%). Time since diagnosis of the child's cancer varied, ranging from 2 months to 13 years (M = 29.6 months, SD = 27.8). The

130 demographic characteristics of the sample are presented in Table 1.

Table 1
*Demographics of Study Participants**

Characteristic	n	%
Gender		
Female	55	75.3
Male	18	24.7
Ethnicity		
Caucasian	65	89.0
Asian	2	2.7
Native American	1	1.4
Unknown	5	6.8
Educational level		
9–12th grade	4	5.5
Vocational and/or some college	12	16.4
College graduate	26	35.6
Graduate and/or professional school	26	35.6
Unknown	5	6.8
Annual income		
Less than $24,999	7	9.6
$25,000–$29,999	9	12.3
$30,000–$39,999	6	8.2
$40,000–$49,999	7	9.6
$50,000–$99,999	24	32.9
$100,000 or more	13	17.8
Unknown	7	9.6
Child's cancer diagnosis		
Leukemia	42	57.5
Neuroblastoma	18	24.7
Brain tumor	4	5.5
Wilms tumor	2	2.7
Non-Hodgkins lymphoma	2	2.7
Rhabdomyosarcoma	2	2.7
Germ cell tumor	1	1.4
Osteosarcoma	1	1.4
Sinonasal carcinoma	1	1.4

	M	SD
Age	38.1	6.5
Time since child's diagnosis (months)	29.6	27.8

**N* = 73.

Instrumentation

A survey was developed for the purpose of the study. The survey contained eight questions that focused on demographic data and six questions on the use of computers for support. Examples of these questions were: "Has connecting to the group been helpful to you? If so, please describe how it has been helpful to you" and "What are disadvantages of the group (if any)?"

Procedure

Using search engines on the Internet, the three data collection sites were identified. N-BLASTOMA and PED-ALL are online lists devoted to issues pertaining to neuroblastoma and acute lymphoblastic leukemia in children, respectively. PED-ONC focuses on issues that are related to various types of childhood cancer. After approval of the university's Institutional Review Board, an electronic mail message requesting approval for data collection was sent to the list of owners. Once approved, an introductory letter explaining the purpose of the study and criteria for participation was posted twice to each list within a two-week period. A consent form and the survey were then sent via electronic mail to parents who requested one from the primary investigator. Parents who participated were directed to send completed questionnaires and the consent form to the electronic mail address of the researcher. As each questionnaire was received, it was assigned a number and all identifying information was deleted as a means of maintaining anonymity and protecting confidentiality. A hard copy of each response was printed out for analysis.

Data Analysis

Frequencies and descriptive statistics were obtained for demographic characteristics of participants using the Statistical Package for the Social Sciences (SPSS) 10.0 for Windows. The subjects' descriptions of advantages and disadvantages of computer-mediated support group use were categorized by the primary investigator who is master's-prepared and has expertise in pediatric oncology nursing. The categorization of every response was reviewed by the second author who is a doctorally prepared, certified oncology nurse. Interrater reliability was 95%.

Results

Most parents (75.3%) reported that they had learned about the computer groups through an Internet search, and 12.3% replied that the group was recommended by others (e.g., relative, chat-room member, oncologist, social worker, or other parent at the hospital). Four parents read about the groups in books or newsletters. Approximately two-thirds of the participants accessed the computer groups from home. The parents reported that they had been connecting to the computer groups from two weeks to three years ($M = 13.3$ months, $SD = 11.0$). Most participants (85%) connected daily to the group, while 10.9% connected between one and three times a week. Overall, the participants spent an average of five hours a week connected to the computer groups ($SD = 6.1$), with a range from 30 minutes to 40 hours (Table 2).

Table 2

Participants' Usage of the Computer Groups

	n	%
How parent learned about the computer groups		
Internet search	55	75.3
Recommended by others	9	12.3
Books and newsletters	4	5.5
Unknown	5	6.9
Place of computer group use		
Home	46	63.0
Work	12	16.4
Home and work	10	13.7
Unknown	5	6.8
Frequency of computer group use		
Daily	62	85.0
2–3 times a week	6	8.2
Once a week	2	2.7
Unknown	3	4.1
	M	SD
Time since being connected to the computer groups (months)	13.3	11.0
Length of computer group use per week (hours)	5.0	6.1

Advantages of Computer Group Use

The participants' responses are summarized in Table 3. Benefits of the computer group use included getting information, sharing experiences, receiving general support, venting feelings, gaining accessibility, and using writing. The most frequently cited benefit of the computer group use was information giving and receiving (76.7%).

Table 3

Perceived Advantages and Disadvantages of the Computer Group Use

Category	n	%
Advantages		
Getting information	56	76.7
Sharing experiences	49	67.1
General support	21	28.8
Venting of feelings	10	13.7
Accessibility	6	8.2
Use of text	2	2.7
Disadvantages		
Noise	36	49.3
Negative emotions	19	26.0
Large volume of mail	15	20.5
Lack of physical contact	8	11.0

It is a forum to ask questions about treatment options and side effects that maybe an oncologist hasn't explained. It stops the panic in the middle of the night when you suddenly think some symptom must be abnormal. Then you ask someone in the group and you find that his or her child has had that happen and it was OK.

I joined the group to gather as much medical information as I could in a short period of time. This is a highly educated group of people who have researched much of their children's treatment protocol. I took their combined expertise.

The information obtained from the list appears to serve parents in a variety of ways, one of which includes the development of informed decision making. One mother stated "... recently we [list members] discussed the pros and cons of a new testing procedure; it helped me to make an informed decision about my daughter's participation with the test."

About two-thirds of the participants listed a number of benefits related to the issue of shared experiences. When confronted with circumstances that seem to alienate the parent from the normal world, the parent may feel that people do not understand what the family of a child with cancer is dealing with every day. The computer group gives the parent assurance that he or she is not alone.

Through this group, I have discovered that I am not alone. I have found that the fears I face are common to all cancer parents. I have found people who understand what I face emotionally every single day. There aren't words to describe how much support I receive from this group.

To find a group of people that understand the incredible pressures of trying to live with this disease, is a great relief. Most people [who have not experienced it] just don't understand. It functions like a family. I couldn't live without it.

Twenty-one (28.8%) parents described receiving general support from the computer group use. One father stated that the group had been immensely helpful by being generally supportive of each other, as they all go through what is basically a pretty rough time. Another comment about the supportive nature of the computer group was "Some of the people in the group are so inspiring that I feel I have grown spiritually and emotionally just reading their posts."

Venting feelings refers to expression of emotion.[29] Ten (13.7%) parents reported that the computer group provided an outlet for emotional disturbances. One participant described it in the following way:

The group has saved my sanity. In the area in which I live, there are no other parents of kids with cancer close by. The hospital clinic is an hour away. Plus, you have to spend a lot of time with your child, and cannot leave them for long to go to meetings. Thus, there is no one I can really talk to about this in person. Having others to talk to on-line about treatment and especially about their feelings makes me know that my feelings are normal, and therefore I feel a lot better.

Gaining accessibility to the group regardless of time and place is another unique advantage of the computer group use recognized by six parents (8.2%). The advantage of 24-hour availability and easy access from most places is seen in the following excerpts:

I can access these people any time. [It is] not like going to a physical parent support group that is time-consuming....

Getting out of the house to be involved with local support groups is just about impossible [as] I have seven children. The Internet allows me to interact with others going through similar difficulties on my own time.

Computer groups are unique because they take place solely through the medium of written text. This creates some benefits for participants, as recognized by two parents (2.7%) in this study. One parent stated:

I recognize my thoughts and put words to them. I learn more about my own thoughts [by writing them down]. Also, I believe it's easier to say what you really think in words, I'd probably chicken out in a face-to-face encounter. Plus, in-person encounters are so affected by facial and body expressions, by the way someone looks, and by the way they respond when one starts to say something. Plus you can get interrupted and lose your train of thought. Yes, I like the written word. I can go back over and read things again, posts that are too good to be read just one time, and things I wrote a few months back to recall how I was thinking then.

Disadvantages of Computer Group Use

Four disadvantages of the computer group use were identified. They included "noise," negative emotions, large volume of mail, and lack of physical contact. "Noise," which refers to posts that are not of interest, off topic, or are vapid,[25] was the most frequently (49.3%) perceived disadvantage of the computer group use.

People who send full copies of the message they are replying to within their own e-mail is a disadvantage of the computer group use.

Occasionally I get bogged down in trivia, and sometimes, too many prayers are flying around.

"Noise" sometimes leads to a rather devastating result as depicted in the following:

The group consists of people who hold a variety of opinions on many subjects. We are bound together by our children's fight with cancer. Sometimes a fringe subject will come up and some people use the list as a sounding board for something totally unrelated to cancer. Often feelings are hurt and we lose members.

Nineteen (26%) parents stated that they sometimes received a lot of news about other children losing the battle that was frightening and depressing.

You hear how each child fights the beast and yet sometimes it takes over and wins. You share your life with these people and they become friends, so it hurts and takes a piece of you when you hear the bad news.

A large volume of mail is another disadvantage of the computer group, indicated by fifteen parents (20.5%). Parents reported that they dealt with the problem by saving messages for less busy times or sorting out messages.

The lack of physical contact and physical proximity was perceived as a drawback of the computer group use by eight parents (11%): "You can't touch and hug people when you want." In this way, another participant pointed out that "... you are never sure who is listening to your conversation." Sometimes the lack of physical closeness may increase difficulties in understanding between list members: "... [It is] hard to express humor without being face to face or hearing tone of voice!"

Discussion

The findings indicate that computer group use is more common among parents with relatively high socioeconomic status. They also suggest that there are certain advantages and disadvantages of computer group use which health professionals and potential users need to recognize.

While computer users were commonly thought to be young, well-educated men with a high socioeconomic status,[34] more recent evidence indicates that the demographics of computer group users have been diversifying, with an increasing number of women [35] as well as elderly users.[36] Even though the demographic data collected may not be representative of parents participating in computer-mediated support groups, the results of this study seem to support the diversifying demographics of computer group users, especially in terms of gender. The current sample represented both genders; 55 (75.3%) of the 73 participants were women. In a study of 75 participants in computer-mediated support groups for various problems (e.g., sexual abuse, adoption, parenting, and alcoholism), Eaglesham [25] reported that approximately 60% of the sample was women, 90% of the subjects were Caucasian, 95% had some tertiary education, and the mean age was 36.7 (range of 20 to 56 years). Klemm et al.[29] content-analyzed messages posted on an online colorectal cancer support group. Of the 97 people who posted messages during the study period, 47.4% were women.

Various aspects of the computer-mediated support group for parents of children with cancer were described and appear to be of potential benefit to participants. The parents identified advantages as being able to get information, share experiences, get general support, vent feelings, access the group, and use writing. These results corroborate those of previous studies [25–29] that documented a list of advantages of computer group use, including sharing concerns and information and offering support. These results suggest that computer-mediated support groups may offer participants many of the therapeutic features of face-to-face groups in the comfort and privacy of their own homes at any time. The identified perceived benefits of the computer groups match some of Yalom's therapeutic factors [20] that exist in face-to-face support groups and indicate that a computer group can be used as a source of support and information.

The advantages of online support groups are not, however, without certain limitations. The parents identified the disadvantages of participating in the computer groups, including "noise," negative emotions, heavy volume of mail, and lack of physical contact and proximity. In Eaglesham's study,[25] participants perceived "noise," negative messages, physical distance among participants, concerns about confidentiality, financial and legal issues, and problem behaviors as disadvantages of computer group use. It is important to note that even though the parents participating in this study generally reported positive experiences, less is known about parents having negative experiences with the computer group.

Although information giving and receiving were recognized as advantages of computer group use in the study, there is a concern that members may receive misinformation and not have it corrected due to the time delay in computer communication. Information that these parents obtain from the list may significantly influence their decisions on the child's treatment. Smith [37] also points out that by sharing experiences and referring each other to print articles and Web sites, patients (and their families) have become more aware of issues and options regarding diagnosis, treatment, and recovery. Nurses and health professionals should be aware of the full range of available supportive resources, including computer groups, and be able to inform clients of the potential risks of computer group use.

The methodological implications of this study may need to be addressed. Even though it lacks the interaction of face-to-face interviews and nonverbal cues, using e-mail as a way of data collection may be less time-consuming and more cost-effective than other data collection methods. The costs of posting messages to e-mail lists may be only a few cents compared with the hundreds of dollars required to mail questionnaires to a similar number of subjects or to interview them directly. Furthermore, written e-mail may provide a rich source of communication. The electronic data obtained from the parents in this study showed how positive the parents felt about the computer group use. The respondents in this study were well-educated people who had access to a computer. The extent to which the results can be generalized to other parents of children with cancer requires further investigation. There is often a low response rate to online surveys. For example, Murray[38] posted research questions to the Nursenet discussion list, which had more than a thousand subscribers, and completed e-mail interviews with only five subscribers. Of the more than 600 users, this study included only 73 parents (12.2%). As Lakeman[39] suggested, a request for participation that is more friendly and appealing to readers may need to be prepared. The

425   calls for subjects may also need to be posted over a longer period of time to increase response rate.

Future generations of caregivers are being exposed to computers as a regular part of school curricula and thus represent a growing base of potential users.[34] For
430   caregivers who are unable or unwilling to access other support services, computer-mediated support groups may indeed represent an attractive alternative. Systematic evaluation of computer-mediated support groups is necessary. Future research should investigate users,
435   helping mechanisms, advantages, and potential disadvantages and risks related to computer-mediated support groups. The results of this study provide direction for further research in this area.

References

1. Murphy SL. *Deaths: final data for 1998.* National vital statistics reports; Vol. 48 No. 11. Hyattsville, MD: National Center for Health Statistics; 2000.
2. Moore JB, Mosher RB. Adjustment responses of children and their mothers to cancer: self-care and anxiety. *Oncol Nurs Forum.* 1997;24(3):519–525.
3. Pelcovitz D, Goldenberg B, Kaplan S, et al. Posttraumatic stress disorder in mothers of pediatric cancer survivors. *Psychosomatics.* 1996;37:116–126.
4. Roberts CS, Piper L, Denny J, Cuddeback G. A support group intervention to facilitate young adults' adjustment to cancer. *Health Soc Work.* 1997;22(2):133–141.
5. Sawyer M, Antoniou G, Toogood I, Rice M. Childhood cancer: a two-year prospective study of the psychological adjustment of children and parents. *J Am Acad Children Adolesc Psychiatry.* 1997;36(12):1736–1743.
6. Sawyer MG, Streiner DL, Antoniou G, Toogood I, Rice M. Influence of parental and family adjustment on the later psychological adjustment of children treated for cancer. *J Am Acad Children Adolesc Psychiatry.* 1998;37(8):815–822.
7. Stuber ML, Christakis DA, Houskamp B, Kazak AE. Posttrauma symptoms in childhood leukemia survivors and their parents. *Psychosomatics.* 1996;37:254–261.
8. Stuber ML, Kazak AE, Meeske K, et al. Predictors of posttraumatic stress symptoms in childhood cancer survivors. *Pediatrics.* 1997;100:958–964.
9. Suris JC, Parera N, Puig C. Chronic illness and emotional distress in adolescence. *J Adolesc Health.* 1996;19(2):153–156.
10. de Bocanegra HT. Cancer patients' interest in group support programs. *Cancer Nurs.* 1992;15(5):347–352.
11. Ray LD, Ritchie JA. Caring for chronically ill children at home: factors that influence parents' coping. *J Pediatr Nurs.* 1993;8(4):217–225.
12. Carlson-Green B, Morris RD, Krawiecki N. Family and illness predictors of outcome in pediatric brain tumors. *J Pediatr Psychol.* 1995;20(6):769–784.
13. Kupst MJ, Natta MB, Richardson CC, Schulman JL, Lavigne JV, Das L. Family coping with pediatric leukemia: ten years after treatment. *J Pediatr Psychol.* 1995;20(5):601–617.
14. Mulhern RK, Fairclough DL, Smith B, Douglas SM. Maternal depression, assessment methods, and physical symptoms affect estimates of depressive symptomatology among children with cancer. *J Pediatr Psychol.* 1992;17(3):313–326.
15. Bloom BL. Computer-assisted psychological intervention: a review and commentary. *Clin Psychol Rev.* 1992;12:169–197.
16. Grabowski VM, Jens GP. The collaborative role of the CNS in support groups. *Clin Nurse Spec.* 1993;7(2):99–101.
17. Shapiro J, Simonsen D. Educational/support group for Latino families of children with Down syndrome. *Ment Retard.* 1994;32(6):403–415.
18. Reele BL. Effect of counseling on quality of life for individuals with cancer and their families. *Cancer Nurs.* 1994;17(2):101–112.
19. Rosenberg PP. Support groups: a special therapeutic entry. *Small Group Behavior.* 1984;15:173–186.
20. Yalom ID. *The theory and practice of group psychotherapy,* 4th ed. New York: Basic Books; 1995.
21. Thoits PA. Social support as coping assistance. *J Consult Clin Psychol.* 1986;54:416–423.
22. McGee SJ, Burkett KW. Building a support group for parents of children with brain tumors. *J Neurosci Nurs.* 1998;30(6):345–349.
23. Ainbinder JG, Blanchard LW, Singer GH, et al. A qualitative study of parent-to-parent support for parents of children with special needs. *J Pediatr Psychol.* 1998;23(2):99–109.
24. Feldman JS. An alternative group approach: using multidisciplinary expertise to support patients with prostate cancer and their families. *J Psychosoc Oncol.* 1993;11(2):83–93.
25. Eaglesham SL. *On-line support groups: extending communities of concern* [dissertation]. Blacksburg, VA: Virginia Polytechnic Institute and State University; 1996.
26. Weinberg N, Schmale J, Uken J, Wessel K. On-line help: cancer patients participate in a computer-mediated support group. *Health Soc Work.* 1996;21(1):24–29.
27. Brennan PF, Moore SM, Smyth KA. Alzheimer's disease caregivers' uses of a computer network. *West J Nurs Res.* 1992;14(5):662–673.
28. Klemm P, Hurst M, Dearholt SL, Trone SR. Cyber solace: gender differences on Internet cancer support groups. *Comput Nurs.* 1999;17(2):65–72.
29. Klemm P, Reppert K, Visich L. A nontraditional cancer support group: the Internet. *Comput Nurs.* 1998;16(1):31–36.
30. Finn J. Computer-based self-help groups: on-line recovery for addictions. *Comput Human Services.* 1996;13(1):21–41.
31. Lamberg L. On-line support group helps patients live with, learn more about the rare skin cancer CTCL-MF. *JAMA.* 1997;277(18):1422–1423.
32. L-Soft. Electronic mailing lists provide support for cancer community worldwide [press release]. Washington, DC: L-Soft; 1998. Available at: http://www.lsoft.com/ACOR-press.html
33. Association of Cancer On-line Resources, Inc. List archives at LISTSERV.ACOR.ORG [On-line], 1999. Available at: http://listserv.acor.org/archives/index.html. Accessed: February 22, 1999.
34. Smyth KA, Harris PB. Using telecomputing to provide information and support to caregivers of persons with dementia. *Gerontologist.* 1993;33(1):123–127.
35. Sharf BF. Communicating breast cancer on-line: support and empowerment on the Internet. *Women Health.* 1997;26(1):65–84.
36. Noer M, Wandycz K. Senior cybernauts. *Forbes.* 1995;156(7):240–241.
37. Smith J. "Internet patients" turn to support groups to guide medical decisions. *J Natl Cancer Inst.* 1998;90(22):1695–1697.
38. Murray PJ. Nurses' computer-mediated communications on Nursenet: a case study. *Comput Nurs.* 1996;14(4):227–234.
39. Lakeman R. Using the Internet for data collection in nursing research. *Comput Nurs.* 1997;15(5):269–275.

Address correspondence to: Hae-Ra Han, Ph.D., RN, Postdoctoral Fellow, Johns Hopkins University, School of Nursing, 525 North Wolfe Street, Baltimore, MD 21205.

Exercise for Article 35

Factual Questions

1. The researchers' review of the literature led them to the conclusion that no prior study had examined the advantages and disadvantages of computer use from whose perspective?

2. What was the mean age of the participants in this study?

3. As each questionnaire was received, what was done as a means of maintaining anonymity and protecting confidentiality?

4. The researchers asked the participants how they learned about the computer groups. For what percentage was this information "unknown"?

5. How many of the participants cited lack of physical contact as a perceived disadvantage of the computer use group?

6. According to the researchers, "noise" refers to what types of posts?

7. Of the more than 600 users of the computer groups, what percentage was included in this study?

Questions for Discussion

8. What is your understanding of the meaning of the term "convenience sample"? (See lines 118–122.)

9. The researchers determined the interrater reliability of the categorization of the responses of the parents. In your opinion, how important is it to determine interrater reliability when open-ended questions are used? Explain. (See lines 165–172.)

10. The researchers present quantitative results (i.e., numbers of cases, percentages, means, and standard deviations). They also present qualitative results (i.e., discussion of findings using the participants' own words to support interpretations). In your opinion, are both types of equal importance? Explain.

11. The researchers note that collecting data using e-mail "lacks the interaction of face-to-face interviews and nonverbal cues." In your opinion, is this important? Is it offset by the cost savings? Explain. (See lines 401–410.)

12. At the end of the article, the researchers discuss possibilities for future research. Do you agree with their suggestions? Do you have additional suggestions? Explain. (See lines 434–438.)

Quality Ratings

Directions: Indicate your level of agreement with each of the following statements by circling a number from 5 for strongly agree (SA) to 1 for strongly disagree (SD). If you believe an item is not applicable to this research article, leave it blank. Be prepared to explain your ratings. When responding to criteria A and B below, keep in mind that brief titles and abstracts are conventional in published research.

A. The title of the article is appropriate.

SA   5   4   3   2   1   SD

B. The abstract provides an effective overview of the research article.

SA   5   4   3   2   1   SD

C. The introduction establishes the importance of the study.

SA   5   4   3   2   1   SD

D. The literature review establishes the context for the study.

SA   5   4   3   2   1   SD

E. The research purpose, question, or hypothesis is clearly stated.

SA   5   4   3   2   1   SD

F. The method of sampling is sound.

SA   5   4   3   2   1   SD

G. Relevant demographics (for example, age, gender, and ethnicity) are described.

SA   5   4   3   2   1   SD

H. Measurement procedures are adequate.

SA   5   4   3   2   1   SD

I. All procedures have been described in sufficient detail to permit a replication of the study.

SA   5   4   3   2   1   SD

J. The participants have been adequately protected from potential harm.

SA   5   4   3   2   1   SD

K. The results are clearly described.

SA   5   4   3   2   1   SD

L. The discussion/conclusion is appropriate.

SA   5   4   3   2   1   SD

M. Despite any flaws, the report is worthy of publication.

SA   5   4   3   2   1   SD

Article 36

Spiritual Perspectives of Nurses in the United States Relevant for Education and Practice

Roberta Cavendish, PhD, RN, CPN, **Barbara Kraynyak Luise**, EdD, RN,
Donna Russo, MA, RN, NP-P, **Claudia Mitzeliotis**, MS, RNCS, CASAC,
Maria Bauer, RN, MS, **Mary Ann McPartlan Bajo**, RN, **Carmen Calvino**, BS, RN,
Karen Horne, MS, RN, **Judith Medefindt**, BS, RN, CIC[*]

ABSTRACT. The purpose of the current study was to describe nurses' spiritual perspectives as they relate to education and practice. A multiple triangulation research design encompassing a questionnaire and a descriptive qualitative content analysis were used with the purpose of capturing a more complete, holistic, and contextual description of nurses' spiritual perspectives. Multiple triangulation included two data sources, two methodological approaches, and nine investigators. Using survey methods, Reed's Spiritual Perspective Scale (SPS) was sent to 1,000 members of Sigma Theta Tau International Nursing Honor Society (STTI). Results support Reed's premise that spirituality permeates one's life. Regardless of gender, participants with a religious affiliation had significantly higher SPS scores than those without one. Nurses having a spiritual base use it in practice. Six themes emerged from the qualitative analysis: Nurses perceive spirituality as strength, guidance, connectedness, a belief system, as promoting health, and supporting practice. The integration of spirituality in nursing curriculums can facilitate spiritual care.

From *Western Journal of Nursing Research*, 26, 196–212. Copyright © 2004 by Sage Publications, Inc. Reprinted with permission.

The unmet spiritual needs of patients and families are a cause of angst in health care settings in the United States where a majority of citizens consider themselves religious or spiritual (Gallup, 1996; Gallup & Castelli, 1989). Because of 20th-century medical advances, the focus of nursing care is more scientific and technology based. Concurrent with changing models of care is that the spiritual needs of patients are not consistently being assessed by nurses; instead, they are being delegated to the chaplain or others (Mayer, 1992; Narayanasamy, 1999b). Providing spiritual care is inherent in nursing (Chadwick, 1973; Macrae, 1995; Simson, 1986). Nursing's commitment to spiritual care, imbued in the theoretical construct of holistic care, is long standing and universal (Carson, 1989; Shelly & Fish, 1988). In clinical practice, the individual is viewed as a whole, and that which affects one dimension affects all others. Nursing scholars concur with the premise that human beings function as integrated biopsychosocial and spiritual beings, greater than the sum of their parts (Banks, 1980; Carson, 1989). With the spiritual dimension considered core (Banks, 1980), spiritual assessments are integral to nursing care plans (Shelly & Fish, 1988). Education for nurses' spiritual development, and to meet human responses in the spiritual domain, varies widely in nursing curriculums (Narayanasamy, 1999b; Van Dover & Bacon, 2001). How to provide spiritual care should be inherent in the nursing curriculum as it was in Nightingale's model for nursing education (Macrae, 1995; Nightingale, 1860/1996; O'Brien, 1999). The ability to provide spiritual care can be learned (Piles, 1990). Nurses perceive that they are ill-prepared to provide spiritual care (Cavendish et al., 2000; Dorff, 1993; Highfield, Taylor, & Amenta, 2000). Nurses' perceptions regarding spiritual care need further investigation, or the unmet spiritual needs of patients and families will continue to be a cause of angst in health care settings.

[*] *Roberta Cavendish* is a parent–child health expert, a clinical researcher, and an associate professor in the Department of Nursing at the College of Staten Island City University of New York. *Barbara Kraynyak Luise* is a specialist in community health nursing and an associate professor in the Department of Nursing at the College of Staten Island City University of New York. *Donna Russo* is the clinical educator for behavioral health at St. Vincent Catholic Medical Centers. *Claudia Mitzeliotis* is a psychiatric clinical nurse specialist at the Veterans Administration New York Harbor Healthcare System. *Maria Bauer* is a psychiatric mental health clinical nurse specialist and an adjunct lecturer in the Department of Nursing at the College of Staten Island City University of New York. *Mary Ann McPartlan Bajo* is a staff nurse on the Neurology Unit at Staten Island University Hospital North, Staten Island, New York. *Carmen Calvino* is a patient care coordinator, Staten Island University Hospital, Staten Island, New York. *Karen Horne* is the director of Health/Mental Health Services at the Edwin Gould Services for Children and Families in New York City. *Judith Medefindt* is nurse epidemiologist at Lutheran Medical Center (LMC) in Brooklyn, New York.

The Foundation of Spiritual Perspectives

40   Society's sustained interest in spirituality correlates with the numbers of individuals and families who expect that their spiritual needs will be met in health care settings (Narayanasamy, 1999b). The ability to meet human responses in the spiritual domain has re-
45 emerged as a critical concern for nursing (Barnum, 1996). Registered nurses who conduct patient assessments and hold primary responsibility for developing plans of care infrequently conduct spiritual assessments or identify spiritual needs (Narayanasamy, 1999b; Tay-
50 lor, 2002). To provide spiritual care, nurses must have spiritual self-awareness and a personal spiritual perspective (Danvers, 1998; Dossey & Keegan, 2000).

According to Clemen-Stone, Eigsti, and McGuire (1995), "Nursing began when humanity began" (p. 2),
55 and the care by a specialized group of people who are ill has existed throughout time. The importance of the spiritual dimension cannot be underestimated. This component is essential for integrating life's demands as well as transcending pain and despair. It allows patients
60 to confront, wrestle with, and reconcile crises. The way suffering is perceived then becomes essential for healing, wellness, and celebration. Nursing clearly identifies the spiritual dimension as part of holistic care, yet the intent to provide that care is often not put into prac-
65 tice. Opportunities that have the potential to enhance spirituality for the patient and the nurse are missed (Cavendish et al., 2000, 2001). Some nurses practice with an infrequent or nonexistent spiritual base (Oldnall, 1996). Nurses are often unable to differentiate
70 spiritual needs from religious needs. Patients' spiritual needs are seen as religious rituals, and spiritual care is often delegated to others (Narayanasamy, 1999a).

Clarification of the Concepts of Spirituality and Religion

A nurse might legitimately question, "In assessing this patient's holistic needs, am I identifying a 'reli-
75 gious need' or a 'spiritual need'?" The answer depends on how the community/nurses/institution use the terms. When essential care-related words are ill-defined, they can confuse caregivers (Dyson, Cobb, & Forman, 1997). When nurses have different meanings for spiri-
80 tual care, they cannot communicate clearly with each other about related care needs. For some nurses, spiritual care means helping patients with maintaining their religious practices and worship. For others, it means helping patients identify what holds the most meaning
85 in their life and then helping them to transcend the pain and suffering that usually accompanies illness. When the nurse defines spiritual needs as only religious needs (including worship and practice aspects), they may omit care for patients' transcendent and relational
90 needs. Omission of spiritual care may occur not because a nurse lacks interest but rather because the nurse defines spiritual care narrowly.

Nurses and others on the health care team must define key terms, distinguish between spirituality and
95 religion, and use them consistently in practice, research, and education. Religion and spirituality have some overlapping areas and similarities. Spirituality and religion focus on the sacred or the divine, both focus on beliefs about the sacred, and both focus on the
100 effects of those beliefs, with practices used to attain or enhance a sense of the sacred. With this knowledge, differences can be clarified.

Spirituality defined. Nursing literature defines spirituality as the essence or life principle of a person (Col-
105 liton, 1981), as a sacred journey (Mische, 1982), as the experience of the radical truth of things (Legere, 1984), as giving meaning and purpose in life (Burnard, 1990; Legere, 1984), as a life relationship or sense of connectedness with mystery, a higher power, God, or uni-
110 verse (Bradshaw, 1994; Granstrom, 1985), as a belief that relates a person to the world (Soeken & Carson, 1987), as a unique human capacity for self-transcendence that creates a fulfilling relatedness within oneself, with others, and to the unseen, God, or
115 power greater than the self, and as a unifying and healing force that centers on relationships, development, wholeness, integration, and individual empowerment (Reed, 1992). Spirituality is defined as a universal human phenomenon that recognizes the wholeness of
120 individuals and their connectedness to a higher being; it is the integrating factor in the quest for meaning and purpose in life (Cavendish et al., 2000, 2001). Savett (1997) stated, "Spirituality is humanism and then some. In the clinical setting, it is finding meaning in illness
125 and then exploring that meaning. That process can be therapeutic and healing for the patient and for the healer" (p. 17). One interesting analogy is that spirituality is a force that can be equated with no other and is as mystifying as the wind in that it cannot be seen but
130 is always felt in a spectrum of intensity from still, to tranquil or intense. Spirituality is different for each of us. Spirituality includes prayers, meditation, and the use of positive affirmations to obtain a release from fears and worries, finding a purpose and meaning in
135 life, and refocusing on the small joys of everyday life (Benson, 1997). Spirituality is broad and nondogmatic and involves learning and changing. Its energy flows from inward out in a process of subjective growth and connection.

140   *Religion defined.* Religion comes from the Latin word, *religare:* to tie together one of the organized systems of beliefs, practices, and worship of a person, group, or community (O'Conner, 2001). Its energy moves from outward in. This direction is presented
145 through a religion's belief system (e.g., in myths, doctrines, stories, dogma) and is acknowledged when one participates in other practices and observances. Religion can also offer guidance about how to live harmoniously with self, others, nature, and their perceived
150 god(s). Religion, seen "as a system of transcending

ideas" (Reed, 1992, p. 35), is complementary to spirituality. Religion provides the methods for the expression of one's spirituality (Engerbretson, 1996; Labun,
1988; Mayer, 1992; Oldnall, 1996; Reed, 1992). Relig-
155   ion can be seen as a bridge to spirituality in that it encourages ways of thinking, feeling, and behaving that
help people to experience this sense of meaningfulness.
Religious practice is also a way for individuals, often
in the context of sharing a similar orientation with oth-
160   ers, to express their spirituality. Religion includes spirituality; however, a person can be spiritual and not es-
pouse any particular religion or formal practice of religion. From these definitions, religion is a narrower
concept than spirituality.

Spirituality in Education and Practice

165   Research-based findings consistently suggest that
nurses' knowledge and skills related to spiritual care is
not adequate because of poor role preparation. A positive correlation exists between the ability of nurses
who have received spirituality education and their abil-
170   ity to provide spiritual care (Clifford & Gruca, 1987;
Harrison & Burnard, 1993; Narayanasamy, 1999b;
Piles, 1990). Clifford and Gruca (1987) stressed the
need for nurses to increase their spiritual awareness,
indicating that nurses need to start with self-reflection
175   of their own spiritual values and attitudes if they are to
help others.

Praill (1995) found that nurses who are present during times of patient distress are more likely to become
involved in a patient's spiritual care, and that nurses
180   offered spiritual care out of the center of their own
spiritual experience, suggesting that they must cultivate
personal spiritual development to provide spiritual
care.

Ross (1994) studied 685 nurses in an attempt to
185   identify factors associated with giving spiritual care.
She discovered that spiritual care could be given at
various levels of involvement with patients. Nurses
who responded at the deepest levels were aware of
their own spirituality, had experienced crises in life,
190   and were sensitive people willing to get involved at a
personal level with their patients. In addition, nurses
who belonged to a religious denomination identified
patients' spiritual needs better than nurses who had no
religious affiliation.

195   Research results indicate that the nurse's perceptions of his or her own spirituality influences the degree to which patients' spiritual needs are identified
and interventions are planned and implemented. Hall
and Lanig (1993) discovered a positive correlation be-
200   tween nurses' self-perception of Christian values and
beliefs and their degree of comfort in providing spiritual care. Chadwick (1973) found that many nurses
were aware of the presence of spiritual needs in some
of their patients but expressed that they would like fur-
205   ther education in this area. Simson (1986) concurred
with these findings and acknowledged that limited

practical guidance is available for nurses who wish to
understand a patient's spiritual needs and practices.

*Contemporary Practice Guidelines for Spiritual Care
in the United States*

The current emphasis on spirituality in society has
210   fueled the demand for nursing sensitivity regarding the
spiritual needs of individuals and families (Narayanasamy, 1999b). The inconsistency with which nurses
provide spiritual care is not congruent with the emphasis placed on spiritual care by nursing codes of conduct
215   and accreditation institutions' guides for practice. Now
that expectation for spiritual care has reached global
proportions (Taylor, 2002), the World Health Organization (WHO, 1998) redefined health. The definition
was revised to include spirituality. The four domains of
220   well-being are physical, mental, social, and spiritual.

In the United States, the Joint Commission on The
Accreditation of Healthcare Organizations (JCAHO)
must accredit all institutions seeking reimbursement for
care rendered for health care organizations. Institution
225   viability is dependent on satisfactory compliance with
JCAHO standards. The increasing demand for spiritual
and religious care prompted the addition of a spiritual
care criterion in accreditation criteria (JCAHO, 2000;
Wright, 1998). This criterion states that (a) institutions
230   must establish guidelines for the documentation of assessments of patients' spiritual beliefs and practices,
(b) pastoral care must be available for patients who
request it, and (c) hospitals must meet the spiritual
needs of dying patients and their families. The goal is
235   for the health care provider to assess the importance of
spirituality as it relates to wellness and healing.
JCAHO offers sample questions to assist nurses in their
endeavor to gather necessary information: "How does
the patient express spirituality?" "What are the pa-
240   tient's spiritual goals?" and "How would the patient
describe his or her philosophy of life?"

The International Council of Nurses (2000), a federation of national nurses' associations (NNAs), represents nurses in more than 120 countries. The ICN Code
245   for Nurses serves as the foundation for ethical nursing
practice throughout the world. The American Nurses
Association (2002) *Code for Nurses* is a guide for
nurses' ethical conduct in the United States. Both codes
contain congruent statements regarding the nurse's role
250   in promoting an environment of respect for a patient's
spirituality or religiosity during the delivery of care.
Patients have named nurses as potential spiritual resource persons (Highfield, 1992; Sodestrom &
Martinson, 1987). In the United States, the American
255   Association of Colleges of Nursing (AACN, 2002)
supports the nursing codes through association mandates to nurse educators. The "how to" of spiritual assessments, use of spiritual assessment tools, nursing
diagnoses, interventions, and outcomes are suggested
260   for inclusion in nursing curriculums. When the dialogue begins in educational programs, confidence will

be gained for articulating patients' spiritual needs thereby raising the nurses' comfort level for transferring this theory to practice settings (Altman, 1990).

A Theoretical Guide for Nursing Practice

Parse's (1981) model, which is a synthesis of Rogers's (1970, 1980) science of unitary human beings with concepts from existential-phenomenological thought, facilitates the explication of lived experiences and the significance of these experiences to those involved. Parse's model is congruent with triangulation methods. Parse's "man–environment interrelationships" facilitates the explication of emerging patterns of nurses' spiritual perspectives and participative experiences relating to spirituality in education and practice. According to Parse, while providing spiritual care, the meaning of a given health situation is guided by the nurse. Appropriate spiritual interventions to meet human responses in the spiritual domain facilitate the patient's process of transcendence. To remain a facilitator of the patient's spiritual health experience, nurses must be aware of their own personal beliefs.

Parse (1993) acknowledged the importance of the nurse's being present in the moment. The interaction between patient, family, and nurse can be a powerful experience. The goal of spiritual intervention is to enhance quality of life. One must keep in mind that only the patients can define what quality is for them: "Through true presence in living Parse's practice methodology, person and family in the presence of the nurse illuminate meaning, synchronize rhythms, and mobilize transcendence" (p. 18). As the nurse facilitates the therapeutic process, an ever-changing rhythm will develop. Through this experience, the patients will be able to share hopes and dreams as well as their personal belief system.

Purpose

This research study describes nurses' spiritual perspectives as they relate to education and practice. The study objectives were to describe the spiritual perspectives of nurses, identify the educational needs of nurses related to the spiritual domain, and discuss spiritual care practices.

Method

Design

A multiple triangulation research design encompassing a questionnaire and a descriptive qualitative content analysis were used with the purpose of capturing a more complete, holistic, and contextual description of nurses' spiritual perspectives (Knafl & Breitmayer, 1989; Thurmond, 2001). Multiple triangulation, more than one data source, methodologies, and nine investigators served to strengthen the research findings and reduce bias in all phases of the study (Polit & Hungler, 1995; Thurmond, 2001; Woods & Catanzaro, 1988). Complementary skills support the data source triangulation methodology. Survey methods (Babbie,

1990; Dillman, 1978) were used for data collection. The nurses' responses to the question, "Do you have any views about the importance or meaning of spirituality in your life that have not been addressed by the previous questions?" constituted the qualitative data.

Sample

Permission was obtained from Sigma Theta Tau International (STTI) Nursing Honor Society for a national random sample of 1,000 members. A cover letter, questionnaire, demographic form, and stamped return envelope were sent by first-class mail. Data were coded, aggregated, and analyzed as group data to maintain confidentiality. Institutional Review Board (IRB) approval was obtained.

With the N of 545, 55%, the descriptive statistics were run on the demographic variables. Data analysis indicated that age of participants ranged from 21 to 61 years. The majority of participants were women (women: $n = 533$, 97.8%; men: $n = 11$, 2%) and had completed a BS degree ($n = 442$, 81%), followed by more than a BS degree ($n = 103$, 19%). Participants reported a religious affiliation ($n = 541$, 99%) that constituted agnostic ($n = 14$, 2.6%), Buddhist ($n = 6$, 1.1%), Catholic ($n = 201$, 37%), Jewish ($n = 4$, 0.7%), Protestant ($n = 222$, 40%), and individuals who were self-described as other ($n = 94$, 17.2%). The majority of the participants were White ($n = 497$, 91%), then African American ($n = 18$, 3.3%), Asian/Pacific Islander ($n = 115$, 2.8%), Native American/Alaskan ($n = 6$, 1.1%), Hispanic ($n = 4$, 0.7%), and other ($n = 4$, 0.7%). Marital status reported married ($n = 396$, 73%), single ($n = 96$, 17.6%), living with significant other ($n = 12$, 2.2%), and ($n = 346$, 63.6%) had children. Good health status was reported by almost all ($n = 542$, 99.4%).

Data Collection

Reed's (1986) Spiritual Perspective Scale (SPS) was used. The SPS is a 10-item questionnaire that uses a 6-point Likert-type scale to measure one's spiritual perspective. The SPS tool measures an individual's spiritual perspective to the degree that spirituality permeates one's life and how one engages in spiritually related interactions, reporting a reliability of Cronbach's alpha coefficient of .90. Computing an arithmetic mean of the responses scores the SPS. Scores range from 1 (*low spiritual perspective*) to 6 (*high spiritual perspective*).

The nurses' responses to the question, "Do you have any views about the importance or meaning of spirituality in your life that have not been addressed by the previous questions?" constituted the qualitative data.

Data Analysis

A Windows 2000 computer program was used for quantitative data entry. Data were entered as an ASCII file, data cleaning was done, and data were transformed

253

Table 1
Qualitative Findings

Themes and participants' direct quotes

Spirituality is strength for acceptance

"I have been through several incidents in my life where I should have died, so I believe I am here for a reason. I believe that things happen the way they are supposed to according to God's plan."

"When a new life arrives, one knows, there must be a God! However, at times of death, disease, pain, makes me question why, usually with no answer."

Spirituality is a belief system

"To me, it's a philosophy about living and enters into my decisions and outlook on life."

"Spirituality can be very personal as well as very important and does not require a group."

Spirituality is guidance

"Spirituality is what helps me get through the difficult times in my life. It gives me hope."

"If it were not for prayer and my faith, I wouldn't have been able to cope with some of my personal challenges in life. Christ is peace."

Spirituality is connectedness

"The meaning of spirituality in my life has had a serious impact on all of my relationships."

"My spiritual connection is my personal relationship with Jesus Christ."

Spirituality promotes health

"I feel very strong about the relationship between health and spirituality. They are related."

"Spirituality provides balance and enriches my life."

Spirituality supports practice

"My spirituality affects the focus of my care."

"Spirituality is an important part of my practice and a part of my inner strength."

as indicated. The data were analyzed using the SPSS (Version 10.0 for Windows). Parametric and nonparametric statistics were conducted for data analysis. Descriptive statistics were tabulated noting frequencies, percentages, independent sample t tests, and one-way ANOVAs on demographic data. All statistical analyses were judged based on the predetermined .05 level of significance.

The qualitative data were derived from the nurses' response to the question, "Do you have any views about the importance or meaning of spirituality in your life that have not been addressed by the previous questions?" Qualitative data analysis methods included constant comparison of the conceptual linkages, theme identification, theme reduction, and theme validation (Munhall & Oiler-Boyd, 1993). Data were coded by extracting verbatim phrases used to describe spiritual perspectives, spirituality education, and spiritual practices. Data were analyzed for pattern recognition of concepts. Each researcher presented written documentation to the research committee. Themes emerged from the data as commonalities among the codes developed. Two rounds of analysis were conducted for data reduction and theme validation by nine nurse researchers who were experienced in the research method and experts on spirituality.

Results

There was no significant difference in SPS score by gender, $t(10.2) = .571$, $p = .580$, or by age looking at age 40 as a divider $t(543) = 1.551$, $p = 122$, or as age 30 as a divider $t(543) = .860$, $p = .390$. In the variable ethnicity, there was no significance in SPS score $F(5.538) = .595$, $p = .704$. Looking at White vs. non-White, there was no significant difference $t(52.6) = .288$, $p = .775$. When looking at the variable health in the questionnaire, there was a significant difference $t(2.996) = 8.419$, $p = .004$. By combining the unhealthy categories, as there are only three total participants between the two unhealthy categories, there was a significant difference in the SPS scores of healthy and unhealthy nurses, such that the healthy nurses are less spiritual $t(2.996) = 8.419$, $p = .027$. Marital status was significant. Married persons show a higher SPS score $F(5.539) = 2.558$, $p = .027$, than a single person or a person living with a significant other (the mean difference of SPS score is .8219, $p = .042$). Young (younger than 40 years) and older (older than 41 years) nurses with a religious affiliation had a higher SPS score than their counterparts without a religious affiliation, $F(5.535) = 17.689$, $p = .001$. A Tukey's post hoc comparison was conducted: The findings indicate that agnostics are significantly lower in spirituality than every other group in the questionnaire.

Older nurses are not more likely to have a religious affiliation (approximately 98% of the participants in the younger and the older categories had a religious affiliation). The existence of a religious affiliation was more influential on the SPS score than age for younger (40 years or younger) $t(308) = 5.792$, $p = .001$; and for older (41 years or older) $t(229) = 6.813$, $p = .001$. Men and women with a religious affiliation have a significantly higher SPS score than their same gender coun-

terparts without a religious affiliation. Religious affiliation was more important for women $t(5.28) = 8.102$, p
$= .001$ than for men $t(8) = 4.641$, $p = .002$. There is no
significant difference in the SPS score in the variables
nursing degree completed, degree type, length of STTI
membership, or years of experience. Findings support
Reed's work that spirituality permeates one's life. The
arithmetic mean score for participants was (4.9164);
standard deviation (.9911); range (1 to 6); and Cronbach's alpha coefficient (.9459).

Qualitative methods used to analyze the written responses included constant comparison of conceptual
linkages, theme identification, theme reduction, and
theme validation. The research question asked, "Do
you have any views about the importance or meaning
of spirituality in your life that have not been addressed
by previous questions?" A total of $n = 165$, 30.2%,
provided responses to the aforementioned question. Six
themes relating to nurses' spiritual perspectives
emerged: Spirituality is strength for acceptance; spirituality is a belief system; spirituality is guidance; spirituality is connectedness; spirituality promotes health;
spirituality supports practice. (See Table 1.)

The scientific rigor of qualitative research methods
is determined not in terms of reliability and validity but
in terms of creditability, confirmability, auditability,
and fittingness. Creditability is dependent on the researcher's ability to bracket his or her own perspective
and on the credibility of the informants (Bogdan &
Bilken, 1982). Research meeting minutes were taken to
log changes and decisions that were made during the
analysis process. Transcriptions of participants' comments were reviewed for accuracy. The criteria for confirmability and creditability were met because the nine
expert nurse researchers analyzed the participants'
statements and comments. The criterion for auditability
was met because the participants' own words have
been explicated from the transcripts to validate the
themes.

Trustworthiness was enhanced by nurse researchers
consensus for data reduction and theme development
(Guba & Lincoln, 1981). Secondary data analysis sub-
stantiated the results found on the original analysis.
The audit trail was established that consisted of the
typed and coded transcripts, research meeting minutes,
the data reduction, and data analysis notes including
the codes and themes.

Discussion

The current study demonstrated congruence between nurses who reported having a religious affiliation and their ability to meet patients' spiritual needs.
These nurses had higher SPS scores supporting Reed's
(1986) work that spirituality becomes intrinsic to one's
life. The nurse participants who acknowledged having
a spiritual base used it in practice. Because spiritual
care has re-emerged as a critical concern for nursing
(O'Neill & Kenny, 1998), the knowledge of nurses'

spiritual perspectives can provide a base to (a) develop
and support spirituality educational initiatives in the
nursing curriculum and (b) strengthen a nurse's ability
to use information related to this phenomenon within
the nursing process. As facilitator of the patient's nursing care plan, nurses are expected to provide spiritual
care. In the United States, nurses must demonstrate
compliance with the JCAHO standards for spiritual
care evaluation and provide evidence via documentation in patient records. Ethical codes for nursing conduct mandate an environment that respects diverse beliefs and practices.

The current study supports the integration of an
educational component on spirituality in the nursing
curriculum. Educators cannot assume that nurses have
a spiritual foundation for practice that is effective to
meet the spiritual needs of patients. Patients and families report that spiritual needs are poorly met in health
care settings (Carson, 1989; Narayanasamy, 1999b).
The majority of participants stated that they do not feel
comfortable dealing with spiritual aspects of care
(Granstrom, 1985; Piles, 1990). They are reluctant to
provide spiritual care even though patients may expect
spiritual interventions, and such interventions may affect the healing process (Dossey & Keegan, 2000). The
nurse's scope of practice supports spiritual care (Carson, 1989; Oldnall, 1996).

The strength of the current study is the support for
Parse's (1993) theory as relevant to guide spiritual
care. One of Parse's assumptions is that a person who
agrees to participate in a study about a particular experience can share a description of that experience with
the researcher. The nurse participants were able to describe living the experience. Parse's theory facilitates
spiritual care through the use of "presence" meaning
"to be with" (Emblen & Halstead, 1993). Presence is a
form of spiritual care as it provides the nurse with a
window of opportunity to enter the world of the patient
to give care in the form of empathy and compassion
(Gardner, 1992). There are times during nurse–patient
interactions when presence is the only therapeutic form
of intervention that the nurse can provide (Osterman &
Schwartz-Bancrott, 1996). Presence is a purposeful,
intended act. The intent to provide spiritual care was
evident in the nurses who were aware of their spiritual
beliefs.

Conclusions from this research reveal that nurses
with religious affiliations have higher SPS scores.
Nurses having a spiritual base are more likely to use it
in practice. This supports Reed's (1986) work that
spirituality permeates one's life. One cannot assume
nurses have a foundation to provide spiritual care. The
addition of an educational component to the nursing
curriculum can facilitate spiritual care for patients and
families. Teaching spiritual care concepts to practicing
nurses is key to this process. Nurses in the United
States perceive spirituality as strength, guidance, connectedness, a belief system, as promoting health, and as

supporting practice. The perspectives identified in the current study can be a catalyst for opportunities to enhance spirituality in practice settings.

References

Altman, H. B. (1990). Syllabus share: "What the teacher wants." In R. A. Neff & M. Weimer (Eds.), *Teaching college: Collected reading for the new instructor* (pp. 45–46). Madison, WI: Magna.

American Association of Colleges of Nursing. (2002). *Hallmarks of the professional nursing practice environment.* Washington, DC: Author.

American Nurses Association. (2002). *Code for nurses.* Kansas City, MO: American Nurses Publishing.

Babbie, E. (1990). *Survey research methods* (2nd ed.). Belmont, CA: Wadsworth.

Banks, R. (1980). Health and the spiritual dimension: Relationships and implications for professional preparation programs. *Journal of School Health, 50,* 195–202.

Barnum, B. S. (1996). *Spirituality in nursing: From traditional to new age.* New York: Springer.

Benson, H. (1997). *Timeless healing: The power and biology of belief.* New York: Scribner.

Bodgan, R., & Bilken, S. (1982). *Qualitative research for education: An introduction to theory and methods.* Boston: Allyn & Bacon.

Bradshaw, A. (1994). *Lighting the lamp: The spiritual dimension of nursing care.* London: Scutari.

Burnard, P. (1990). *Learning human skills: An experimental guide for nurses* (2nd ed.). Oxford, UK: Heinemann.

Carson, V. (1989). *Spiritual dimensions of nursing practice.* Philadelphia: W. B. Saunders.

Cavendish, R., Kraynyak Luise, B., Horne, K., Bauer, M., Gallo, M. A., Medefindt, J., et al. (2000). Opportunities for enhanced spirituality relevant to well adults. *Nursing Diagnosis: International Journal of Nursing Language and Classification, 11,* 151–162.

Cavendish, R., Kraynyak Luise, B., Horne, K., Bauer, M., Medefindt, J., & Russo, D., et al. (2001). Recognizing opportunities for spiritual enhancement in young adults. *Nursing Diagnosis: International Journal of Nursing Language and Classification, 12,* 77–91.

Chadwick, R. (1973). Awareness and preparedness of nurses to meet patients' spiritual needs. In J. A. Shelly & S. Fish (Eds.), *Spiritual care: The nurses' role* (pp. 177–178). Downers Grove, IL: InterVarsity Press.

Clemen-Stone, S., Eigsti, D., & McGuire, S. (1995). *Comprehensive community health nursing* (5th ed.). St. Louis, MO: Mosby Year Book.

Clifford, B., & Gruca, J. (1987). Facilitating spiritual care in rehabilitation. *Rehabilitation Nursing, 12,* 331–333.

Colliton, M. (1981). The spiritual dimensions of nursing. In E. Belland & J. Passos (Eds.), *Clinical nursing* (pp. 901–1012). New York: Macmillan.

Danvers, M. (1998). Keeping in good spirits. *Nursing Management, 5,* 35–37.

Dillman, D. (1978). *Mail and telephone surveys: The total design method.* New York: John Wiley.

Dorff, E. N. (1993). Religion at a time of crisis. *Quality of Life: A Nursing Challenge Monographs, 2,* 56–59.

Dossey, B., & Keegan, L. (2000). Self-assessment: Facilitating healing in self and others. In B. M. Dossey, L. Keegan, & C. Guzzetta (Eds.), *Holistic nursing: A handbook for practice* (3rd ed., pp. 361–374). Rockville, MD: Aspen.

Dyson, J., Cobb, M., & Forman, D. (1997). The meaning of spirituality: A literature review. *Journal of Advanced Nursing, 26,* 1183–1188.

Emblen, J., & Halstead, L. (1993). Spiritual needs and interventions: Comparing the views of patients, nurses, and chaplains. *Clinical Nurse Specialist, 1,* 175–182.

Engerbretson, J. (1996). Considerations in diagnosing in the spiritual domain. *Nursing Diagnosis: The International Journal of Nursing Language and Classification, 7,* 100–107.

Gallup, G. H. (1996). *Religion in America.* Princeton, NJ: Princeton Religious Research Center.

Gallup, G. H., & Castelli, J. (1989). *The people's religion: American faith in the 90s.* New York: Macmillan.

Gardner, D. (1992). Presence. In G. Bulchek & J. McCloskey (Eds.), *Nursing interventions: Treatments for nursing diagnoses* (2nd ed., pp. 316–324). Philadelphia: W B. Saunders.

Granstrom, S. (1985). Spiritual nursing care for oncology patients. *Topics in Clinical Nursing, 7,* 39–45.

Guba, E., & Lincoln, Y (1981). *Effective evaluation.* San Francisco: Jossey-Bass.

Hall, C., & Lanig, H. (1993). Spiritual care behaviors as reported by Christian nurses. *Western Journal of Nursing Research, 15,* 730–741.

Harrison, J., & Burnard, P. (1993). *Spirituality and nursing practice.* Aldershot, UK: Averbury.

Highfield, M. (1992). Spiritual health of oncology patients: Nurses and patient perspectives. *Cancer Nursing, 15,* 1–8.

Highfield, M., Taylor, E., & Amenta, M. (2000). Preparation to care: The spiritual care education of oncology and hospice nurses. *Journal of Palliative Nursing, 2,* 53–63.

International Council of Nurses. (2000). The ICN code of ethics for nurses. Retrieved October 19, 2003, from www.icn.ch/icncode.pdf

Joint Commission on the Accreditation of Healthcare Organizations. (2000). *Automated comprehensive accreditation manual for hospitals: The official handbook* [CD-ROM]. Available from www.JCAHO.com

Knafl, K., & Breitmayer, B. (1989). Triangulation in qualitative research: Issue of concept clarity and purpose. In J. M. Morse (Ed.), *Quantitative nursing research: A contemporary dialogue* (pp. 41–47). Rockville, MD: Aspen.

Labun, E. (1988). Spiritual care: An element in nursing care planning. *Journal of Advanced Nursing, 13,* 314–320.

Legere, T. (1984). A spirituality for today. *Studies in Formative Spirituality, 5,* 375–385.

Macrae, J. (1995). Nightingale's spiritual philosophy and its significance for modern nursing. *Image: Journal of Nursing Scholarship, 27,* 8–10.

Mayer, J. (1992). Wholly responsible for a part, or partly responsible for a whole? The concept of spiritual care in nursing. *Second Opinion, 17,* 26–55.

Mische, P. (1982). Toward a global spirituality. In P. Mische (Ed.), *Whole earth papers* (pp. 76–83). East Grange, NJ: Global Education Association.

Munhall, P., & Oiler-Boyd, C. (1993). *Nursing research: A qualitative perspective* (2nd ed.). New York: NLN.

Narayanasamy, A. (1999a). ASSET: A model for actioning spirituality and spiritual care education and training in nursing. *Nurse Education Today, 19,* 274–285.

Narayanasamy, A. (1999b). Learning spiritual dimensions of care from a historical perspective. *Nurse Education Today, 19,* 386–395.

Nightingale, F. (1996). *Notes on nursing.* New York: Dover. (Original work published 1860).

O'Brien, M. (1999). *Spirituality in nursing: Standing on holy ground.* Sudbury, MA: Jones and Bartlett.

O'Conner, S. (2001). Characteristics of spirituality, assessment, and prayer in holistic nursing. *Nursing Clinics of North America, 36,* 33–46.

Oldnall, A. (1996). A critical analysis of nursing: Meeting the spiritual needs of patients. *Journal of Advanced Nursing, 23,* 138–144.

O'Neill, D., & Kenny, E. (1998). Spirituality and chronic illness. *Image: Journal of Nursing Scholarship, 30,* 275–279.

Osterman, P., & Schwartz-Bancrott, D. (1996). Presence: Four ways of being there. *Nursing Forum, 31,* 23–30.

Parse, R. (1981). *Man-living-health: A theory of nursing.* New York: John Wiley.

Parse, R. (1993). Quality of life: Sciencing and living the art of human becoming. *Nursing Science Quarterly, 7,* 16–20.

Piles, C. (1990). Providing spiritual care. *Nurse Educator, 15,* 36–41.

Polit, D. E., & Hungler, B. P. (1995). *Nursing research: Principles and methods* (6th ed.). Philadelphia: J. B. Lippincott.

Praill, D. (1995). Approaches to spiritual care. *Nursing Times, 91,* 55–57.

Reed, P. (1986). Religiousness among terminally ill and healthy adults. *Research in Nursing and Health, 9,* 35–41.

Reed, P. (1992). An emerging paradigm for the investigation of spirituality in nursing. *Research in Nursing and Health, 15,* 349–357.

Rogers, M. (1970). *An introduction to the theoretical base of nursing.* Philadelphia: F. A. Davis.

Rogers, M. (1980). Nursing: A science of unitary man. In J. P. Riehl & C. Roy (Eds.), *Conceptual models for nursing practice* (2nd ed., pp. 329–337). New York: Appleton-Century-Crofts.

Ross, L. (1994). Spiritual care: The nurse's role. *Nursing Standard, 8,* 33–37.

Savett, L. (1997). Spirituality and practice: Stories, barriers and opportunities. *Creative Nursing, 4,* 17.

Shelly, J. A., & Fish, S. (1988). *Spiritual care: The nurses' role.* Downers Grove, IL: InterVarsity Press.

Simson, B. (1986). The spiritual dimension. *Nursing Times, 26,* 41–42.

Sodestrom, K., & Martinson, I. (1987). Patients' spiritual coping strategies: A study of nurse and patient perspectives. *Oncology Nursing Forum, 14,* 41–46.

Soeken, K., & Carson, V. (1987). Responding to the spiritual needs of the chronically ill. *Nursing Clinics of North America, 22,* 603–611.

Taylor, E. J. (2002). *Spiritual care.* Englewood Cliffs, NJ: Prentice Hall.

Thurmond, V. (2001). The point of triangulation. *Journal of Nursing Scholarship, 33,* 253–258.

Van Dover, L., & Bacon, J. (2001). Spiritual care in nursing practice: A close-up view. *Nursing Forum, 36,* 18–30.

Woods, N. F., & Catanzaro, M. (1988). *Nursing research: Theory and practice.* St. Louis MO: Mosby.

World Health Organization. (1998, January). Executive board meeting (Document 101). Geneva, Switzerland: Author.

Wright, K. (1998). Professional, ethical, and legal implications for spiritual care in nursing. *Image: Journal of Nursing Scholarship, 30,* 81–83.

Acknowledgments: The members of the Sigma Theta Tau Mu Upsilon Research Committee would like to express their appreciation to the following: the College of Staten Island Department of Nursing and the City University of New York for partial funding from a grant provided by the Professional Staff Congress.

Address correspondence to: Roberta Cavendish, Department of Nursing, College of Staten Island CUNY, 2800 Victory Boulevard, Staten Island, NY 10314.

Exercise for Article 36

Factual Questions

1. According to Cavendish et al. (2000, 2001), spirituality is defined as a universal human phenomenon that recognizes what?

2. The nurses' responses to what question constituted the qualitative data for this study?

3. A cover letter, questionnaire, demographic form, and stamped return envelope were sent by first-class mail to whom?

4. Reed's (1986) Spiritual Perspective Scale (SPS) was used to measure what?

5. Was the difference between married persons and single persons (including persons living with a significant other) statistically significant? If yes, at what probability level was it significant?

6. What are the values of the arithmetic mean and standard deviation on the Spiritual Perspective Scale?

Questions for Discussion

7. The introduction, including the literature review, in lines 1 through 295 is somewhat longer than the other introductions to the research reported in this book. In your opinion, are long introductions useful? Explain.

8. In your opinion, is the response rate of 55% adequate for this type of research? (See line 327.)

9. The Spiritual Perspective Scale is described in lines 348–358. Information is provided on internal consistency reliability (i.e., Cronbach's alpha coefficient of .90). Is the omission of validity information in this description important? Explain.

10. The data analysis methods for the qualitative data are described in lines 364–392. In your opinion, is the description sufficiently detailed? Explain.

11. To what extent do the participants' direct quotations in Table 1 help you understand the results? Do you consider them an essential part of the Results section of this research report?

12. Would this research be as informative if the researchers used only the Spiritual Perspective Scale, on which the quantitative results are based, and omitted the qualitative question? Explain.

Quality Ratings

Directions: Indicate your level of agreement with each of the following statements by circling a number from 5 for strongly agree (SA) to 1 for strongly disagree (SD). If you believe an item is not applicable to this research article, leave it blank. Be prepared to explain your ratings. When responding to criteria A and B below, keep in mind that brief titles and abstracts are conventional in published research.

A. The title of the article is appropriate.

SA   5   4   3   2   1   SD

B. The abstract provides an effective overview of the research article.

SA   5   4   3   2   1   SD

C. The introduction establishes the importance of the study.

SA   5   4   3   2   1   SD

D. The literature review establishes the context for the study.

SA   5   4   3   2   1   SD

E. The research purpose, question, or hypothesis is clearly stated.

SA   5   4   3   2   1   SD

F. The method of sampling is sound.

SA   5   4   3   2   1   SD

G. Relevant demographics (for example, age, gender, and ethnicity) are described.

SA   5   4   3   2   1   SD

H. Measurement procedures are adequate.

SA   5   4   3   2   1   SD

I. All procedures have been described in sufficient detail to permit a replication of the study.

SA   5   4   3   2   1   SD

J. The participants have been adequately protected from potential harm.

SA   5   4   3   2   1   SD

K. The results are clearly described.

SA   5   4   3   2   1   SD

L. The discussion/conclusion is appropriate.

SA 5 4 3 2 1 SD

M. Despite any flaws, the report is worthy of publication.

SA 5 4 3 2 1 SD

Article 37

The Interconnection of Childhood Poverty and Homelessness: Negative Impact/Points of Access

Cathryne L. Schmitz, PhD, RN, **Janet D. Wagner**, PhD, RN, **Edna M. Menke**, PhD, RN[*]

ABSTRACT. Child poverty negatively impacts the development of children; family homelessness compounds the issues. Both have dramatically increased over the last two decades with far-reaching, poorly understood consequences. The impact of the instability of poverty and homelessness on children is often hidden or difficult to comprehend. Few studies critically examine the impact on a child's sense of safety and security. Using mixed method inquiry, this research sought to examine the effects of poverty and homelessness on children 8 to 12 years of age. The voices of the children illuminate the underlying strengths and vulnerabilities. Results indicate that homelessness leaves children feeling a decreased sense of support and an increased sense of isolation.

From *Families in Society: The Journal of Contemporary Human Services*, *82*, 69–77. Copyright © 2001 by Families International, Inc. Reprinted with permission.

The high level of poverty among children of all ethnic groups in the United States negatively impacts their development and the nation's future. Poverty places families at risk (Belle, 1990), frequently nega-
5 tively impacting the development and emotional status of children (Committee for Economic Development, 1987; Elmer, 1977; Tuma, 1989). As a result of structural changes (Center for Hunger, Poverty and Nutrition Policy, 1995), the level of poverty facing children
10 in the U.S. is the highest in the industrial world (Children's Defense Fund [CDF], 1991). Child poverty is currently 20.5% (CDF, 1998), with children in minority and female-headed single-parent families experiencing the highest rates (CDF, 1991).
15 While the impact of homelessness cannot be separated from poverty, homelessness is a life event having traumatic effects beyond poverty. It is a systemic problem (McChesney, 1990), increasing as the shortage of affordable housing decreases and the level of poverty
20 increases (Gulati, 1992; Martin, 1991; McChesney, 1990; Shinn & Gillespie, 1994). Family homelessness

increased dramatically in the 1980s. It is still rising as "attacks on the social welfare system" continue (Gulati, 1992; Lindsey, 1998), pushing the number of children
25 (CDF, 1995) and female-headed households (Lindsey, 1997) experiencing homelessness steadily upward. The issues arising from this attack are also personal (Gulati, 1992). Homelessness is a condition that compounds the issues faced by families in poverty—frequently involv-
30 ing the loss of friends, belongings, neighborhood, school (Boxill & Beaty, 1990), and a place to "be."
Studies have shown mixed results in understanding the impact of homelessness beyond poverty. A study by Bassuk and Rosenberg (1988) suggests homeless
35 children are different from poor, domiciled children. Other studies, however, conclude children who have been homeless may not be dramatically different from other very poor children (Masten, 1992; Ziesemer, Marcoux, & Marwell, 1994). Ziesemer, Marcoux, and
40 Marwell (1994) found no significant differences between homeless and domiciled low-income children (Ziesemer et al., p. 658); and Martagon, Ramirez, and Masten (1991) found that children who are homeless "did not differ from other children in how far they are
45 expected to go in school or general hopes for the future" (p. 1). In spite of the stress of homelessness in children's lives, it may be the long-term poverty that places children at greatest risk (Ziesemer et al.).
Missing in the literature is the child's perception of
50 the situation of self and environment (Epps, 1998). Children's voices have the potential to give rise to a picture of their lives, dreams, aspirations, and needs. In listening, we may find ways to understand their experiences as a basis for designing empowering programs
55 and policies (Chalhub de Oliveira, 1997). Mixed method inquiry was used in this study to add to our understanding of the impact of poverty and homelessness on latency age children in poverty (domiciled and homeless). Both a priori and grounded theory guided

[*]*Cathryne L. Schmitz* is associate professor and director, Social Work Program, University of Southern Maine, Portland, Maine. *Janet D. Wagner* is dean, Department of Community Education and Workforce Development, Columbus State Community College, Columbus, Ohio. *Edna M. Menke* is an associate professor, College of Nursing, Department of Community, Parent–Child and Psychiatric Nursing, Ohio State University, Columbus, Ohio.

Table 1
Instruments and Interview Schedules

Instrument	Citations
Reynolds Manifest Anxiety Scale	Test description—Reynolds & Richmond, 1979, 1985
	Construct validity—Reynolds, 1980; Reynolds & Richmond, 1979
	Use with homeless populations—Bassuk & Rubin, 1987
	Reliability—Wisniewski, Mulick, Genshaft, & Coury, 1987
Achenbach Child Behavior Checklist	Description—Achenbach & Edelbrock, 1981, 1983; Kessler, 1988
	Reliability—Achenbach & Edelbrock, 1981
	Comparison mental health vs. normed populations—Achenbach, Edelbrock, & Howell, 1987
Kovacs Child Depression Inventory	Description—Kovacs, 1985
	Reliability—Kovacs, 1985
Children's Nowicki-Strickland Internal–External Locus of Control (CNSIE)	Description, reliability, construct validity, discriminative validity—Nowicki & Strickland, 1973
Child Interview Schedule	A semistructured questionnaire administered verbally; based similar instrument (Wagner & Menke, 1992). Measured child attitude including: (a) beliefs about the future, (b) attitudes toward parents, (c) beliefs about own ability to control present and future environment(s), (d) attitudes toward poverty and housing circumstances, and (e) belief in the potential for change.
Mother Interview Schedule	Minor revisions of an interview used in a previous study of homeless families by Wagner and Menke (1992) and the Homeless Survey developed by Roth, Dean, Lust, and Saveanu (1985) contained questions regarding education, demographic information, health history, obstetrical history, social history, general well-being, social network, and health care practices.

60 the design. The use of qualitative and quantitative methods increased the richness (Mitchell, 1986; Patton, 1990), adding voice to the data, clarifying the differential impact. The implications for practice are identified with a discussion of the strengths as a basis for inter-
65 vention and remediation.

Defining Home and Stability

"Every child needs a place to call home…a place of belonging and a place to keep one's things" (CDF, 1989, p. 108). Home, however, represents much more, implying "layers of meaning" (McCollum, 1990, p.
70 226). "A home provides far more than just a physical shelter against the elements" (CDF, p. 108). "It is a milieu that is safe, above all, but also strong, warm, enfolding, and reliable" (McCollum, p. 226); involving an expression of self, a place of belonging, and the
75 embodiment of personal and family history.

Home and place intertwine as a complex concept moving beyond the immediate family household. "Attachment to place is not holistic but multidimensional" (Gerson, Stueve, & Fischer, 1977, p. 156). Home "an-
80 chors a family in the community and provides children with the stability they need to develop and grow" (CDF, 1989, p. 108). The physical neighborhood, the people, and the actual dwelling all influence attachment. Families surviving amidst poverty in an inner-
85 city environment often do not live in neighborhoods

that offer the safety and security implied in "home." Further, low-income families live precariously, frequently spending up to 70% of their income on rent. They have no cushion for changes in income or hous-
90 ing costs. Therefore, all families living in poverty are at risk of homelessness at transition points (Mihaly, 1989).

Methodology

This analysis emerged from a comprehensive study of families living in poverty in Columbus, Ohio. Data
95 were gathered by an interdisciplinary team (social work and nursing) on the physical and emotional well-being of children and families living in poverty, many of whom have experienced homelessness. Data were collected on the health, mental health, support, and stabil-
100 ity issues of the families in poverty. The health and mental health of domiciled and homeless children living in poverty were analyzed and compared.

Subjects

A purposive sample was drawn of 133 families with children living in extreme poverty; families hav-
105 ing an income below the federal poverty line and receiving assistance from public services or entitlements. The female caretaker in each family (the mother or custodial grandmother) and one of the children between 8 and 12 years of age were interviewed. By de-
110 sign, half of the families involved in the study were

Table 2
Family and Child Characteristics

Variable	Frequency	Percent
Income source		
Entitlement	120	90.2
Other	13	9.8
Domicile status (*n* = 133)		
Domiciled	63	47.4
Homeless	70	52.6
Times homeless (*n* = 132)		
0	39	29.5
1	58	43.9
2	26	19.7
3–9	9	6.9
Mother's age		
22–29	47	35.4
30–39	76	57.1
40–50	10	7.7
Mother's education		
Grades 4–8	8	6.1
Some high school	56	42.1
High school graduate	49	36.8
Some college	19	14.4
College graduate	1	0.8
Mother's description		
Negative	9	6.8
Neutral	26	19.5
Positive	98	73.7
Child's gender		
Female	67	50.4
Male	66	49.6
Child's ethnicity		
African American	80	60.2
Euro American	39	29.3
Other (9 biracial, 3 Native American, 2 Latino/a)	14	10.5
Child's Age		
8	30	22.6
9	24	18.0
10	34	25.6
11	26	19.5
12	19	14.3
Child's GPA		
0–1.9	25	18.9
2–2.9	47	35.3
3–3.9	44	33.1
4	17	12.8

Note. n = 133

homeless at the time of the interview using the definition outlined by Roth, Dean, Lust, and Saveanu (1985). A family was considered homeless if it was living in: (a) a shelter or transitional housing for the homeless, (b) a residence with an actual or intended stay of less than 45 days, (c) a cheap motel, (d) a car, or (e) the street. (Children living with their mother in a shelter for battered women were not included in this study.)

The homeless families were solicited primarily from transitional housing facilities working with homeless families, cheap motels, and soup kitchens. The domiciled families living in poverty environments were solicited primarily from soup kitchens, food pantries, human service agencies, and health clinics.

Data Collection

The mother and child participated in a face-to-face interview and completed a number of standardized instruments. Standardized instruments previously used with similar populations were selected to gather data on the child's anxiety, depression, behavior, and locus of control (see Table 1). Interview schedules based on formats previously tested by Wagner and Menke (1992) were used to gather data on attitudes and beliefs. The mother provided demographic and background information about the child. The following questions guided this analysis:

Table 3
Indicators of Child Mental Health

Variable	N	Range	Mean	SD	%PastClin.Cut*
Anxiety	133	26–79	51.95	10.5	20.0
Problem behavior	132	26–93	53.05	10.5	19.7
Social competence	133	19–70	42.62	8.9	36.6
Depression	131	0–27	8.40	6.2	18.3
Locus of control	127	4–25	17.28	4.1	NA

*Percent past clinical cutoff

1. Did poverty affect child anxiety, depression, behavior, and locus of control?
2. What were the children's career goals? Did they understand the path to those goals?
3. How did the children—homeless and domiciled—view family finances?
4. Who did the children—homeless and domiciled—turn to with problems?
5. What were the major concerns of the children?

The semistructured questionnaires/interview schedules used with the mother and child were designed to be administered verbally. Content validity was addressed by using a panel of experts (faculty knowledgeable about child development and/or the conditions for poor families) and conducting a field test. The field test also addressed the face validity. Reliability/credibility was assessed by having an independent observer review the transcribed answers for confirmation of the interpretation and analysis using the methods of Kirk and Miller (1986) and Lincoln and Guba (1985).

Data Analysis

Qualitative and quantitative data provided a basis for this analysis. Themes were identified and then coded using a combination of the methods described by Bogdan and Biklen (1992), Miles and Huberman (1984), and Strauss and Corbin (1990). Statistical analysis involved primarily descriptive statistics with minimal use of inferential statistics. Relationships between this sample and large, national samples for anxiety, depression, and behavior were examined using *t* tests (see Schmitz, Wagner, & Menke [1995] for review of inferential analysis).

Results and Findings

Descriptive Data

All the families participating in the study faced multiple risk factors due to poverty and instability. The families interviewed lived in extreme poverty, with 90% relying on entitlement programs as their primary source of income (see Table 2). As a result, 53% were homeless at the time of the interview and 71% had been homeless at least once; only a quarter (26%) of the children had been homeless more than once. Many of the children had experienced instability beyond homelessness. The average family had moved 1–3 times in the previous 2.5 years, with a third (33.9%) moving 2–5 times.

The mean age of the mothers was 32 years, with 77% ranging from 27 to 37 years of age. The mother's educational level placed many of the families at risk. In line with national data, which indicates that 50% of poor single mothers have not graduated from high school, approximately half (48%) of the mothers in this study had not graduated from high school. This is more than twice the rate (17%) for nonpoor single mothers (Human Resources Division, 1991) and twice (23%) that of all adults (U.S. Bureau of the Census, 1991). A direct relationship existed between the mother's education and the child's reported academic performance, with the child's performance increasing as the mother's education increased (Schmitz, 1993).

The mothers' view of their children was assessed qualitatively. When asked to describe their children, almost three-quarters (73.4%) viewed the child positively (interrater reliability = 82%). The mothers described their children with words such as "loving," "sensitive," "concerned," "caring," "bright," "energetic," "wonderful," "understanding," "helpful," "considerate," and "affectionate." As one mother, who was homeless when interviewed, stated about her 11-year-old son, "He's charming, sweet, easy to get along with. He's inquisitive, understanding, and lovable. He's the kind of child you would like to have. The All-American boy. He's not bad 'cause he don't like to be."

The children were evenly divided in gender and dispersed across age. Children of color were overrepresented, with almost three-quarters (70%) African American, Native American, Asian American, or biracial. African American children constituted three-fifths of the sample. Life events and health problems increased the risk for many. Almost half (46%) of the children had experienced a significant life crisis involving violence, and a tenth (10.5%) had a significant health problem.

In spite of the risks, the children exhibited much strength. They were frequently performing above average academically (as reported by the mothers) and generally scored within the normal range on the standardized tests (see Table 3). In comparisons between the homeless and domiciled children on the standardized tests, the only significant difference occurred in anxiety. Children homeless at the time of the interview ex-

Table 4
Children's Goals, Concerns, and Perceptions of Support and Resources

Variable	Percent		
Career goals			
Professional	35		
Skilled	16		
Sports	16		
Artist	13		
Other	20		
Path to success			
Education	59		
Study/good grades	19		
Work hard	7		
Other	15		
Neighborhood/community concerns	% Worried		
Violence	23		
School	8		
Losing home	5		
Family has enough money	Yes	No	Unsure/DK
All children	57	23	31
Domiciled	78	14	8
Homeless	39	31	31
How can you handle your problems?	Withdraw	Tell Someone	Work it Out
Domiciled	25	57	10
Homeless	47	30	3
Who can help with child's problems?	Parents	Family	School	Friends
Domiciled	88	94	21	19
Homeless	51	64	6	13

hibited ($p < .05$) higher anxiety levels ($M = 55.06$) than domiciled children ($M = 51.37$).

Qualitative Findings

The qualitative data added depth in identifying the common struggles of the children and families, as well as the added emotional costs of homelessness. Strengths and vulnerabilities, similarities and differences (see Table 4) were uncovered. When asked if anything bothered them about their current living environment, there was little difference between the responses of the homeless and domiciled children. A quarter (25%) of the domiciled children and 23% of the homeless children said yes, while 73% of the domiciled children and 61% of the homeless children said no. They had difficulty, however, expressing what bothered them. In addition, the children viewed homelessness negatively, with only six children saying it would be okay to be without a home. Many reported they thought homelessness was "sad," "hard," "lonely," "embarrassing," "bad," or "scary" for children. When asked how children could handle being without a home, they gave responses such as "be brave," "be mad," "be sad," "be nice," "talk to someone," "don't tell anyone," and "don't give up."

Although 67% of the children said their living environment didn't bother them, a third of the children (30%) across environments were concerned about safety in their neighborhoods. Almost a third (30%) of the children—homeless and domiciled—were concerned about concrete housing and environ-

mental/neighborhood safety and crime issues. The children mentioned issues such as "gunshots," "the streets," "school," "detention," "bad people," "getting hurt," "dying," "stealing," "moving," and "not having a home."

The majority of the children interviewed had concrete goals for their future and a vision of how to reach those goals. They believed that they and/or their parents could impact that vision. More than two-thirds (64%) aspired to professional, skilled, or artistic goals. The children interested in a professional career talked about being a doctor, lawyer, teacher, judge, or nurse, while those aspiring to a skilled profession mentioned careers in law enforcement, the fire department, the armed services, computer operation, airplane piloting, or trucking. The children understood the avenues to those goals. Fifty-nine percent of the children mentioned school, college, and/or education as the vehicle to reach their goal. More than a third (36%) discussed the need to "work hard," "get good grades," "study," "get a degree," "save money," "respect the teacher," or "get a job." Only one child responded with "marriage" as her only goal.

The major differences between the homeless children and those who were domiciled occurred in perceptions of money and support. When asked if their family had enough money, more than half (57%) said yes while almost a quarter (23%) said no. The two groups diverged in perception. Twice as many domiciled children (78%) as homeless children (39%) said their families had enough money. On the other hand, twice as

263

many homeless children (32%) compared to domiciled children (14%) said their families did not have enough money.

290 The children were also asked who could help them with their problems or things that bother them. Again, differences between the homeless and domiciled children surfaced. Homeless children were less likely to view members of their family as people who could help

295 with their problems. While 94% of the domiciled children saw family members as people who could help, only 64% of the homeless children did. Half of the children mentioned parents. Parents were mentioned as people who could help them with things that bother

300 them by 88% of the domiciled and 51% of the homeless children. In addition, withdrawal and denial were reported as ways to deal with issues that bother them by 47% of the homeless children but only 25% of the domiciled children. The domiciled children were more

305 likely to tell someone about their problems while homeless children were more likely to withdraw. Finally, only 10% of the homeless children said they would try to work out their problems.

Summary of Findings

The children and families faced multiple barriers.

310 They were at risk due to income, housing instability, and mother's education. There were many similarities. Both groups were equally concerned about neighborhood safety; the levels of depression did not vary; there was no practical difference in behavior; and locus of

315 control did not differ (Schmitz, 1993). Further, in spite of the risks, many strengths emerged. The mothers were overwhelmingly positive in their description of the children, the majority of the children were performing passably in school, and most had positive goals for

320 the future.

Analysis of the relationships between the child's current domicile status and their emotional status and perceptions of safety, security, and stability revealed significant differences in anxiety and different percep-

325 tions about money, support, and safety. The children who were homeless expressed heightened awareness of financial and emotional vulnerability. They were more likely to feel like their families did not have enough money. Even though both sets of families were surviv-

330 ing on minimal income, twice as many domiciled children said their families had enough money. On the other hand, twice as many homeless children said their families did not have enough money. In addition, the homeless children were more likely to feel their parents

335 could help them with their difficulties.

Conclusion and Implications

Understanding the goals and aspirations, as well as the concerns, of children living in poverty is vital to building support programs. The findings indicate the need for both preventive and remedial programs target-

340 ing multiple levels—individuals, families, neighborhoods and communities. There were a number of fac-

tors supporting the importance of individualizing intervention. Although most of the children were functioning within the normal range on scales measuring anxi-

345 ety, depression, and behavior, a significant percentage scored in the range beyond the clinical cutoff point. Approximately a fifth of the children scored in ranges indicating the need for remedial intervention for anxiety, depression, and behavior. When we look at social

350 competence, the percent operating outside normal ranges leaps to over a third, indicating the importance of social skill training, which could be incorporated into neighborhood, school, and after-school programs. The fact that few of the children would try to work out

355 their problems underscores the importance of integrating programs teaching children surviving amid poverty to problem-solve and deal with conflict.

The needs of the children who were homeless and those who were not were similar in many respects. The

360 major differences occurred in the higher levels of anxiety, increased sense of economic instability, and decreased sense of their parents' ability to help them. These data support the conclusion of increased perception of vulnerability among homeless children. An ap-

365 parent sense of isolation also arises from the data, with the children who were homeless reporting an increased tendency to withdraw with problems and a decreased likelihood to view members of their family as people who can help with problems. These attitudes and con-

370 cerns could easily interfere with the child's ability to perform academically, form supportive relationships, and develop emotionally and behaviorally.

The outcome of this analysis supports and extends beyond previous studies in uncovering the additive

375 impact of homelessness on children and families. A review of the major findings and their implications intertwines with the conclusions and observations of related research and provides guidance in designing intervention models. Multilevel program development

380 is suggested.

Families entering homelessness (often due to a crisis) arise from those families already at risk due to poverty (Masten, 1992). Low parenting stress and fewer major life concerns have been connected to bet-

385 ter outcomes for homeless children in a study by Danseco and Holden (1998) supporting the importance of strengthening and supporting parents and families. Shelters and transitional housing are not well suited to meeting the needs of families (Huttman & Redmond,

390 1992). Both fail to address the underlying need for safe, stable housing and employment; and there is a contradiction between transitional housing rules and "the goal of self-sufficiency" (Fogel, 1997, p. 131). While these data indicate that the children need assis-

395 tance viewing their parents as people who can provide support, shelters often undermine parental authority with rigid rules and staff control. This study, however, supports the potential mediating effect of shelter (Rafferty & Shinn, 1991), which seems to buffer some

of the most negative consequences reported in many studies (Bassuk & Rosenberg, 1988; Feitel, Margetson, Chamas, & Lipman, 1992; Polakow, 1998). Giving families control for "organizing their lives in the shelter" (Thrasher & Mowbray, 1995, p. 100) supports and strengthens the mother as the "head of the family."

Frequently, children living in poverty are considered high risk and are approached from a deficit model. While the potential negative consequences of poverty and homelessness are well established (Bassuk & Rosenberg, 1988; Bassuk & Rubin, 1987; Danzig, 1997; Feitel, Margetson, Chamas, & Lipman, 1992; Polakow, 1998; Rafferty & Shinn, 1991), this study identified strengths that also exist in the families (homeless and domiciled). Supporting areas of positive functioning recognizes competencies (Thrasher & Mowbray, 1995), which can be built upon to empower children and families as they work toward the future. Supportive, family-centered services provide the opportunity and context for families to rebuild their lives (Bruder, 1997).

The strengths identified form a basis for remedial and preventive programs. Hope provides a building block for coping and positive outcomes (Farran, Herth, & Popovich, 1995). The hopes of the children framed within the context of goals for the future provide a basis for intervention. The children had strong career goals and were able to discuss the steps to their goals. These children had positive hopes and goals with a realistic understanding of the work needed to reach those goals. "Good schools and good teachers can and do make a significant difference" (Polakow, 1998, p. 17). School social workers can be pivotal in providing or facilitating the services and resources, which strengthen the children and families. They can take the lead in developing collaborative efforts that respond on institutional and community as well as the individual and family levels (Wall, 1996).

For the vast majority of the children and mothers, their overall emotional status was good. The positive attitudes of the mothers toward the child, even under frequently stressful conditions, provide a basis for engaging the mother as a part of the team to help a child experiencing difficulties. The children's career goals in combination with the fact that four-fifths of the children were receiving passing grades and half were performing above average also indicate avenues for engaging the children remedially and preventively. The grades for the oldest children did show signs of slippage, however, emphasizing the importance of intensive intervention and support for latency age children.

Neighborhood, school, and after-school programs provide ideal sites for preventive and remedial services. The preferences of the local residents provide an important source of information on program design (Goering, Durbin, Trainor, & Paduchak, 1990). Programs could build on the children's strengths while providing the services to address the needs and concerns of the children and families. The mothers' positive attitudes could be used by outreach workers to engage them in supporting their children. The children's goals could and should be nurtured and supported. Academic support and social skills training could help with long-term success. These programs could also incorporate methods designed to help the children learn to work out problems.

Staff in shelters and other social service agencies play a significant role in assisting mothers emotionally and instrumentally (Lindsey, 1996), filling a gap resulting from the inadequate social supports available to homeless families (Khanna, Singh, Nemil, Best, & Ellis, 1992). A study by Lindsey found that mothers who have restabilized from homelessness have personal strengths and resources describing "themselves as independent, persistent, strong-willed, and tough" (p. 212). Looking back at their experience of themselves while they were homeless, they "described themselves as desperate, lost, confused, and uncertain.... Many were not able to attend adequately to their children's needs" (p. 212). Shelter staff impacted the mothers' development of skills and internal resources, helping them recognize inner strengths and abilities as well as develop skills and abilities (Lindsey). Involving the mother as an "expert" who is the most knowledgeable about her child provides a significant role. She becomes a member of the team in the design of a family plan and an active participant in the implementation.

The concern of many of the children with neighborhood safety points to the need for programs enhancing both the child's sense of safety and neighborhood safety. Many of the families have experienced significant life crises and major health problems pointing to the importance of multidisciplinary neighborhood programs. Easy access is imperative since low-income families have few resources for transportation. Finally, the fact that only half the mothers completed high school is significant. This is twice the 23% national average (U.S. Bureau of the Census, 1991) and a major risk factor with changing welfare policies emphasizing parental employment. Neighborhood programs are ideal sites for adult education and training programs.

With high levels of poverty and increasing homelessness, the issues must be dealt with at multiple levels. While working at the community level to help families stabilize as they emerge from homelessness, we must also address the problems structurally (Lindsey, 1998). Both homeless and poor domiciled children are at high risk for developmental, health, and educational difficulties, which require a public-policy agenda addressing housing, services, health care, and child poverty (Danzig, 1997; Rafferty & Shinn, 1991). Long-term, the structural factors responsible for high rates of family poverty, inadequate housing, and homelessness must be addressed through major attitudinal and policy changes. Structural racism and sexism are

responsible for high rates of poverty among families of color and female-headed single-parent families, placing our children and our country at risk. Policies must attack the root causes—poverty and lack of adequate,
520 safe housing that low-income families can afford (McChesney, 1990; Shinn & Gillespie, 1994).

Social work professionals and students need to be educated in the importance of multilevel assessment and intervention. The practice and policy implications
525 are clear and interwoven. Poverty, safety/stability, and homelessness impact the level of stress facing families and neighborhoods, which in turn impacts the development of our children. Individual, family, neighborhood, and community programs can address the issues
530 remedially and preventively.

References

Achenbach, T. M., & Edelbrock, C. (1981). Behavioral problems and competencies reported by parents of normal and disturbed children. *Monograph Social Research Child Development, 46,* 188.

Achenbach, T. M., & Edelbrock, C. (1983). *Manual for the Child Behavior Checklists and Revised Child Behavior Profile.* Vermont: University of Vermont.

Achenbach, T. M., Edelbrock, C., & Howell, C. (1987). Empirically based assessment of the behavioral/emotional problems of two- and three-year-old children. *Journal of Abnormal Child Psychology, 15,* 629–640.

Bassuk, E., & Rosenberg, L. (1988). Why does family homelessness occur? A case-control study. *American Journal of Public Health, 78,* 783–788.

Bassuk, E., & Rubin, L. (1987). Homeless children: A neglected population. *American Journal of Orthopsychiatry, 57,* 279–286.

Belle, D. (1990). Poverty and women's mental health. *American Psychologist, 45,* 385–389.

Bogdan, R. C., & Biklen, S. K. (1992). *Qualitative research for education: An introduction to theory and methods.* Boston: Allyn and Bacon.

Boxill, N., & Beaty, A. (1990). An exploration of mother/child interaction among homeless women and their children in a public night shelter in Atlanta, Georgia. In N. Boxill & A. Beaty, *The waiters and the watchers: American homeless children* (pp. 49–64). New York: Hawthorne.

Bruder, M. B. (1997). Children who are homeless: A growing challenge for early care and education. *Advances in Early Education and Day Care, 9,* 223–246.

Center for Hunger, Poverty and Nutrition Policy. (1995). *Statement on key welfare reform issues: The empirical evidence.* Medford, MA: Author.

Chalhub de Oliveira, T. (1997). Homeless children in Rio de Janeiro: Exploring the meanings of street life. *Child and Youth Care Forum, 26*(3), 163–174.

Children's Defense Fund. (1991). *Child poverty in America,* Washington, DC: Author.

Children's Defense Fund. (1995). Children's hardships intensify. *CDF Reports, 16*(6), p. 1–2, 12.

Children's Defense Fund. (1998). *The state of America's children: Yearbook 1998.* DC: Author.

Committee for Economic Development. (1987). *Children in need: Investment strategies for the educationally disadvantaged.* New York: Author.

Danseco, E. R., & Holden, E. W. (1998). Are there different types of homeless families? A typology of homeless families based on cluster analysis. *Family Relations, 47,* 159–165.

Elmer, E. (1977). A follow-up of traumatized children. *Pediatrics, 59,* 273–279.

Epps, A. M. (1998). *Children living in temporary shelter: How homelessness affects their perception of home.* New York: Garland Publishing, Inc.

Farran, C. J., Herth, K. A., & Popovich, J. M. (1995). *Hope and hopelessness: Critical clinical constructs.* Thousand Oaks, CA: Sage Publications.

Feitel, B., Margetson, N., Chamas, J., & Lipman, C. (1992). Psychosocial background and behavioral and emotional disorders of homeless and runaway youth. *Hospital and Community Psychiatry, 43*(2), 155–159.

Fogel, S. J. (1997). Moving along: An exploratory study of homeless women with children using a transitional housing program. *Journal of Sociology and Social Welfare, 24*(3), 113–133.

Gerson, K., Stueve, C. A., & Fischer, C. S. (1977). Attachment to place. In C. S. Fischer, R. M. Jackson, C. A. Stueve, K. Gerson, L. M. Jones, & M. Baldessare (Eds.), *Networks and places: Social relations in the urban setting* (pp. 139–161). New York: Free Press.

Goering, P., Durbin, J., Trainor, J., & Paduchak, D. (1990). Developing housing for the homeless. *Psychosocial Rehabilitation Journal, 13*(4), 33–42.

Gulati, P. (1992). Ideology, public policy, and homeless families. *Journal of Sociology and Social Welfare, 19*(4), 113–128.

Human Resources Division. (1991). *Mother-only families: Low earnings will keep children in poverty* (GAO/HRD-91-62). Washington, DC: U.S. Government Printing Office.

Huttman, E., & Redmond, S. (1992). Women and homelessness: Evidence of need to look beyond shelters to long-term social service assistance and permanent housing. *Journal of Sociology and Social Welfare, 19*(4), 89–111.

Kessler, J., (1988). *Psychopathology of childhood.* Englewood Cliffs, NJ: Prentice-Hall, Inc.

Khanna, M., Singh, N. N., Nemil, M., Best, A., & Ellis, C. R. (1992). Homeless women and their families: Characteristics, life circumstances, and needs. *Journal of Child and Family Studies, 1*(2), 155–165.

Kirk, J., & Miller, M. L. (1986). *Reliability and validity in qualitative research.* Beverly Hills, CA: Sage Publications.

Kovacs, M. (1985). The children's depression inventory. *Psychopharmacology Bulletin, 21,* 995–999.

Lincoln, Y. S. & Guba, E. G. (1985). *Naturalistic inquiry.* Newbury Park, CA: Sage Publications.

Lindsey, E. W. (1996). Mothers' perceptions of factors influencing the restabilization of homeless families. *Families in Society, 77*(4), 203–215.

Lindsey, E. W. (1997). The process of restabilization for mother-headed homeless families: How social workers can help. *Journal of Family Social Work, 2*(3), 49–72.

Lindsey, E. W. (1998). Service providers' perception of factors that help or hinder homeless families. *Families in Society, 79,* 160–172.

Martagon, M., Ramirez, M., & Masten, A. S. (1991, April). *Future aspirations of homeless children.* Paper presented at the Society for Research in Child Development.

Masten, A. S. (1992). Homeless children in the United States: Mark of a nation at risk. *Current Directions in Psychological Science, 1*(2), 41–44.

McChesney, K. Y. (1990). Family homelessness: A systemic problem. *Journal of Social Issues, 46*(4), 191–205.

McCollum, A. T. (1990). *The trauma of moving: Psychological issues for women.* Newbury Park, CA: Sage Publications, Inc.

Mihaly, L. (1989, April). *Beyond the numbers: Homeless families with children.* Paper presented at Homeless Children and Youth: Coping with a National Tragedy. Washington, DC.

Miles, M. B., & Huberman, A. M. (1984). *Qualitative data analysis: A sourcebook of new methods.* Beverly Hills, CA: Sage Publications.

Mitchell, E. S. (1986). Multiple triangulation: A methodology for nursing science. *Advances in Nursing Science, 8,* 18–26.

Nowicki, S., & Strickland, B. R. (1973). A locus of control scale for children. *Journal of Consulting and Clinical Psychology, 40,* 148–154.

Patton, M. Q. (1990). *Qualitative evaluation and research methods* (2nd ed.). Newbury Park, CA: Sage Publications.

Polakow, V. (1998). Homeless children and their families: The discards of the postmodern 1990s. In S. Books (Ed.), *Invisible children in society and its schools* (pp. 3–22). Mahway, NY: Lawrence Erlbaum Associates.

Rafferty, Y., & Shinn, M. (1991). The impact of homelessness on children. *American Psychologist, 46,* 1170–1179.

Reynolds, C. R. (1980). Concurrent validity of What I Think and Feel: The Revised Children's Manifest Anxiety Scale. *Journal of Consulting and Clinical Psychology, 48,* 774–775.

Reynolds, C. R., & Richmond, B. O. (1979). Factor structure and construct validity of "What I Think and Feel": The revised Children's Manifest Anxiety Scale. *Journal of a Personality Assessment, 43,* 281–283.

Reynolds, C. R., & Richmond, B. O. (1985). *Revised Children's Manifest Anxiety Scale.* Los Angeles, CA: Western Psychological Services.

Roth, D., Dean, J., Lust, N., & Saveanu, T. (1985). *Homelessness in Ohio: A study of people in need.* Columbus, OH: Ohio Department of Mental Health.

Schmitz, C. L. (1993). Children at risk: Ex post facto research examining relationships among poverty, housing stability, anxiety, attitudes, locus of control, academic performance, and behavior. (Doctoral dissertation, Ohio State University, 1993). *Dissertation Abstracts International, 54,* 1097A.

Schmitz, C. L., Wagner, J. D., & Menke, E. M. (1995). Homelessness as one component of housing stability and its impact on the development of children in poverty. *Journal of Social Distress and the Homeless, 4,* 301–318.

Shinn, M., & Gillespie, C. (1994). The roles of housing and poverty in the origins of homelessness. *American Behavioral Scientist, 37*(4), 505–521.

Strauss, A., & Corbin, J. (1990). *Basics of qualitative research.* Newbury Park, CA: Sage Publications.

Thrasher, S. P., & Mowbray, C. T. (1995). A strengths perspective: An ethnographic study of homeless women with children. *Health & Social Work, 20*(2), 93–101.

Tuma, J. M. (1989). Mental health services for children: The state of the art. *American Psychologist, 44,* 188–199.

U.S. Bureau of the Census (1991). *Statistical Abstract of the United States* (111th ed.). Washington, DC: U.S. Government Printing Office.

Wagner, J. D., & Menke, E. M. (1992). Case management of homeless families. *The Journal for Professional Nursing Practice, 6*(2), 65–70.

Wagner, J., Schmitz, C. L., & Menke, E. (1995). Homelessness and depression in children: Implication for interventions. In *Directions in Child & Adolescent Therapy, 2*(3).

Wall, J. C. (1996). Homeless children and their families: Delivery of educational social services through school systems. *Social Work in Education, 18*(3), 135–144.

Wisniewski, J. J., Mulick, J. A., Genshaft, J. L., & Coury, D. L. (1987). Test-retest reliability of the Revised Children's Manifest Anxiety Scale. *Perceptual and Motor Skills, 65*, 67–70.

Ziesemer, C., Marcoux, L., & Marwell, B. E. (1994). Homeless children: Are they different from other low-income children? *Social Work, 39*, 658–668.

Note: Based on a paper presented at Public Policy Challenges for Social Work Education, the 42nd Annual Program Meeting of the Council of Social Work Education, Washington, DC, February 1996.

Acknowledgments: The authors would like to thank the Ohio Department of Mental Health for financial support of this project through grant number 92.1051, and the National Institutes of Health for their support through grant number 1R15NR02462 from the National Center for Nursing Research.

Exercise for Article 37

Factual Questions

1. In each family in this study, two people were interviewed. Who were they?

2. If a family lived in a cheap motel, was it classified as "homeless"?

3. What percentage of the children in this study were classified as African American?

4. Content validity of the semistructured questionnaires/interview schedules was addressed, in part, by a panel of experts. Who was on the panel?

5. On the standardized tests, there was only one statistically significant difference. On which variable did the homeless children have a significantly higher mean than the domiciled children?

6. Did a majority of the children have concrete goals for their future?

7. What percentage of the homeless children saw family members as people who could help?

8. According to the U.S. Bureau of the Census, what percentage of all mothers in the United States did not complete high school as of 1991?

Questions for Discussion

9. The homeless families were solicited from somewhat different sources. In your opinion, is the difference in sources important? Could it

affect the outcomes of this study? Explain. (See lines 119–124.)

10. The researchers do not report whether any of those who were solicited to participate in the study declined to do so. Would you be interested in having such information? Why? Why not?

11. The interpretation of the answers mothers gave when asked to describe their children had an "interrater reliability" of 82%. What is your understanding of the meaning of the term *interrater reliability*? In your opinion, does 82% seem sufficiently high? (See lines 195–197.)

12. Do you think that the quantitative results *or* the qualitative results are more important? Are they equally important? If you were to conduct another study on this topic, would you be inclined to use quantitative *or* qualitative methodology? Would you use both? Explain.

13. Although all three researchers hold RN degrees and one of them is an associate professor in a college of nursing, the nursing profession is not explicitly mentioned in the section of their research article titled "Conclusion and Implications." Despite this omission, do you think that the results of this study have implications for nursing professionals? Explain.

Quality Ratings

Directions: Indicate your level of agreement with each of the following statements by circling a number from 5 for strongly agree (SA) to 1 for strongly disagree (SD). If you believe an item is not applicable to this research article, leave it blank. Be prepared to explain your ratings. When responding to criteria A and B below, keep in mind that brief titles and abstracts are conventional in published research.

A. The title of the article is appropriate.

SA 5 4 3 2 1 SD

B. The abstract provides an effective overview of the research article.

SA 5 4 3 2 1 SD

C. The introduction establishes the importance of the study.

SA 5 4 3 2 1 SD

D. The literature review establishes the context for the study.

SA 5 4 3 2 1 SD

E. The research purpose, question, or hypothesis is clearly stated.

       SA   5   4   3   2   1   SD

F. The method of sampling is sound.

       SA   5   4   3   2   1   SD

G. Relevant demographics (for example, age, gender, and ethnicity) are described.

       SA   5   4   3   2   1   SD

H. Measurement procedures are adequate.

       SA   5   4   3   2   1   SD

I. All procedures have been described in sufficient detail to permit a replication of the study.

       SA   5   4   3   2   1   SD

J. The participants have been adequately protected from potential harm.

       SA   5   4   3   2   1   SD

K. The results are clearly described.

       SA   5   4   3   2   1   SD

L. The discussion/conclusion is appropriate.

       SA   5   4   3   2   1   SD

M. Despite any flaws, the report is worthy of publication.

       SA   5   4   3   2   1   SD

Article 38

Developing a Residential Care Facility Version of the Observable Indicators of Nursing Home Care Quality Instrument

Myra A. Aud, PhD, RN, **Marilyn J. Rantz**, PhD, RN, NHA, FAAN,
Mary Zwygart-Stauffacher, PhD, RN,BC–GNP/GCNS, FAAN, **Pam Manion**, MS, RN, CS, GCNS[*]

ABSTRACT. The last decade has seen a substantial growth in the development of residential care facilities (assisted living facilities). Evaluation of the quality of care in this service delivery sector has been hampered by the lack of a consensus definition of quality and the lack of reliable instruments to measure quality. Founded on extensive research on nursing home care quality, a field test of the Residential Care Facility Version of the Observable Indicators of Nursing Home Care Quality Instrument was conducted in 35 residential care facilities in Missouri. Content validity of the 34 items was rated by 4 expert raters as 3.4 on a 4-point scale of relevance. Test–retest was 0.94, interrater reliability was 0.73, and internal consistency was 0.90 for the total scale, indicating excellent results for initial field testing. A focus group confirmed the 5 dimensions of quality of care measured by the instrument as important in residential care settings.

From *Journal of Nursing Care Quality*, *19*, 48–57. Copyright © 2004 by Lippincott Williams & Wilkins, Inc. Reprinted with permission.

The rapid growth of residential care facilities, also called assisted living facilities or personal care homes, has raised quality concerns for these facilities that parallel concerns for nursing home quality. There are be-
5 tween 30,000 and 40,000 assisted living facilities in the United States caring for an estimated 1 million residents.[1] Driven in part by the increasing number of older adults, consumer demand for alternatives in long-term care, and concerns about nursing home quality, the
10 number of assisted living facilities increased rapidly in the 1990s. Because of that rapid growth, one-third of assisted living facilities have been in operation 5 years or less, and 60% of assisted living facilities have been in operation 10 years or less.[2]
15 Unlike the nursing home industry, there is no national regulatory standard for assisted living facilities; each state establishes its own definition of "assisted living facility" and its own set of regulations. Assisted

living facilities vary in size, services provided, admis-
20 sion policies, resident characteristics, and staff characteristics.[3-5] Evaluation of assisted living facilities is difficult for consumers and health care providers in the face of this variability among facilities and lack of a single definition and regulatory standard. Consumers
25 and health care providers would benefit from a tool to measure assisted living facility care quality. While the literature on quality in long-term care facilities has addressed nursing home care quality, residential care/assisted living facilities have received little atten-
30 tion. Little systematic investigation of assisted living facilities and the quality of care provided has been undertaken.[6]

To explore the feasibility of using a tool designed for measurement of nursing home care quality to
35 measure residential care facility quality, we conducted a pilot test of the Observable Indicators of Nursing Home Care Quality Instrument[7-9] in several residential care facilities in Missouri. The pilot revealed that revision of the nursing home version was necessary to ac-
40 count for differences in care, environment, and residents before it was appropriate for use in residential care facilities. This report describes the revision and subsequent validity and reliability testing of the residential care version. Further development of the resi-
45 dential care version is also described.

The Observable Indicators of Nursing Home Care Quality Instrument (Observable Indicators) was designed to measure the multidimensional concept of nursing home care quality.[10, 11] The creators of the Ob-
50 servable Indicators anticipated its use as a quality improvement tool for nursing homes and as a heuristic guide for consumers, including older adults and their family members, evaluating a facility prospectively when considering a facility for a friend or relative.[12]
55 The current version of Observable Indicators (6.0, revised July 2002) consists of 42 items. There are 5

---

[*]*Myra A. Aud*, Sinclair School of Nursing, University of Missouri at Columbia. *Marilyn J. Rantz*, Sinclair School of Nursing, University of Missouri at Columbia. *Mary Zwygart-Stauffacher*, Department of Nursing Systems, University of Wisconsin at Eau Claire. *Pam Manion*, Sinclair School of Nursing, University of Missouri at Columbia.

subscales: communication (5 items), care (9 items), staff (6 items), environment (16 items), and home/family involvement (6 items). The 16 items of
60 the environment subscale are further divided into 3 subscales: space (5 items), odor/cleanliness/condition (5 items), and lighting/noise/atmosphere (6 items). Responses to all items are selected from a 5-point Likert-type scale, with 5 as the response indicating the highest
65 quality and 1 as the response indicating the lowest quality.

The Observable Indicators was designed to be used by health care professionals, nursing home staff, lay people (such as the friends and families of residents),
70 and nursing home residents. A study funded by the National Institutes of Health/National Institute of Nursing Research is in progress for further reliability and validity testing and to determine potential use by regulators. Assessment of the quality of care with the Ob-
75 servable Indicators begins as the observer walks through the facility, its general living spaces, hallways, and other areas commonly available to the public. The walk-through takes approximately 20–30 minutes, depending on the size of the facility. Visiting the facility
80 during usual visiting hours and, if possible, close to a mealtime provides opportunities to note the features included in most of the items. Asking the staff for additional information is appropriate for some items.

Need for a Residential Care Facility Version

Quality improvement nurses from the Quality Improvement Project for Missouri (QIPMO) used the
85 Observable Indicators as a part of their consultation site visits to nursing homes. As the QIPMO project expanded to include residential care facilities, the quality improvement nurses in the St. Louis area began to
90 use the Observable Indicators to assess the quality of care in each facility. However, it was immediately apparent that some items in the tool were not appropriate for use in the residential care facility setting. The problems reflected the differences between nursing homes
95 and residential care facilities, particularly differences in resident acuity levels, staffing, special services for confused residents, and rehabilitative therapy services.

Acuity Levels and Staffing

Nursing home residents are more frail and more dependent on staff for assistance than the residents of
100 residential care facilities.[13] Direct care staffing numbers are higher in nursing homes so that personal and skilled care needs can be met. Registered nurses have a greater presence in nursing homes because health care needs of residents are greater. In the nursing home ver-
105 sion, one item refers to the more active role of direct care staff and another item asks about assistance with eating and drinking, common tasks in nursing homes. However, most residential care facility residents are independent in these tasks. Similarly, the nursing home
110 version has a question about assistance with mobility, another area where most residential care facility resi-

dents are independent, even if they use assistive devices. Two other items of the nursing home version specifically address the presence of registered nurses.
115 Registered nurses are scarce in residential care facilities, where the supervisory role is frequently filled by a licensed practical nurse.

Special Services for Confused Residents in Nursing Homes

While some residents in residential care facilities may be confused at times or may have mild cognitive
120 impairment, it is more likely that nursing home residents will have special care needs because of moderate to severe cognitive impairment.[13] Three items in the nursing home version are more appropriate to the special environments created in nursing homes for con-
125 fused residents and especially for those who wander.

Special Therapy Needs in Nursing Homes

The Observable Indicators has an item: "Were therapy staff actively working with residents to improve or restore function?" This question, while appropriate for the skilled nursing facility that frequently has an in-
130 house therapy team with services provided at least 5 days per week, is less appropriate in residential care facilities where a physical, occupational, or speech therapist may visit an individual resident as an outpatient in the same way as a therapist would visit a pri-
135 vate home. On any given day, there may be no residential care facility residents scheduled to receive therapy services. Additionally, the question, "Were staff helping some residents walk or move about the facility without assistive devices such as canes, walkers,
140 wheelchairs?" is a poor fit for some states' residential care facility regulatory requirements that residents be sufficiently independent in mobility in order to exit the facility without assistance during emergencies.

Revising the Observable Indicators Instrument

After an informal test of the Observable Indicators
145 in several residential care facilities, the instrument was revised by the authors. The outcome of that revision is the Observable Indicators of Nursing Home Care Quality: Residential Care Facility Version. The revised instrument has 34 items and retained the 5-point Likert-
150 type response format of the original 42-item nursing home version.

Revision of the nursing home version took 3 forms: deletion of items, rewording of items, and rewording of responses. Two items were reworded; 8 items were
155 deleted; and 2 items were combined into one item. One new item was added to the Residential Care Facility Version: "Were exit doors equipped with monitoring systems?" There also were minor revisions of the wording of the stem and responses of 5 items, but the
160 revisions did not alter the content of the items.

Validity

After the initial revision, 4 experts were asked to review the new Residential Care Facility Version and assess for content validity. Each of the experts was a nursing home administrator licensed to practice in Missouri who had experience with Missouri residential care facilities. Two of the experts were registered nurses and 2 had backgrounds in social work. They were evenly split from urban and nonurban areas of the state of Missouri.

Working independently, the experts were given copies of the revised instrument and a rating form with instructions to rate the relevance of each item on a 4-point rating scale. The choices on the 4-point rating scale were (1) not relevant, (2) somewhat relevant, (3) quite relevant, and (4) very relevant, following content validity measurement outlined by Waltz, Strickland, and Lenz.[14] Although it was not requested in the instructions, all of the experts wrote comments on the rating forms.

Content validity. The index of content validity for the total scale was 3.426. For the individual items, when the ratings assigned to each item by the 4 experts were averaged, only 5 of the 34 items had average ratings less than 3.00. The average ratings for those 5 items and the individual ratings by each expert are displayed in Table 1. No items had average ratings less than 2.0.

Table 1
Summary of the Experts' Average Ratings Less Than 3.0.

Item	Mean rating
Were residents out of their rooms?	2.00
Were exit doors equipped with monitoring systems?	2.00
Were residents' rooms personalized with furniture, pictures, and other things from their past?	2.25
Were homelike things, such as plants and pets, in the residents' rooms?	2.75
Were visitors visible in the facility?	2.75

All 4 experts wrote comments for the "Were residents out of their rooms?" item on the rating forms. Three of the comments refer to resident preferences. The comments were as follows:

1. Not sure that I understand this one. Out of room is equated to care?
2. Many have private rooms, consider them as apartments. Some choose to stay in and only come out for meals or activities of choice.
3. They have their apartments and it's their choice when to participate.
4. Some residents like to stay in their rooms.

While nursing home quality has been associated with seeing the residents out of their rooms, the emphasis in residential care facilities is on resident autonomy and independence, as well as on social interaction. When residential care facility residents stay in their rooms, this may reflect an institutional philosophy that

supports choice. If the residents choose to remain "at home" in their rooms, this might also attest to the quality of the arrangements of those rooms rather than absence of care or poor facility quality. However, remaining in one's room may also be a reaction to a lack of appealing recreational activities or to the failure of the staff to encourage participation.

Two of the experts wrote comments for the item about exit doors having monitoring systems. One expert explained that state regulations (Missouri) do not require monitoring systems on exit doors "unless resident's condition warrants this." The other expert wrote, "A lot of assisted living facilities do not have alarmed doors. We don't. Residents are free to come and go." Two key points emerge from their comments: (a) decisions about monitoring systems depend on assessment of resident condition, and (b) consideration of resident autonomy influences the use of monitoring systems.

The experts, as inferred from their comments, considered that the 2 items about resident rooms being personalized and the presence of plants and pets actually evaluated resident and family choices rather than the residential care facility and its quality. Comments included "This is a resident choice," and "This is not a facility function." Their ratings and choices again emphasize differences between nursing homes and residential care facilities. Nursing homes exert greater control over the environment of the residents' rooms. Residential care facilities tend to offer more choices to residents. Although individual nursing homes and residential care facilities may depart from these stereotypes of control and choice, nursing homes, in general, offer residents less scope for personalization of living spaces.[15]

The last item addressed the presence of visitors in the facility. One of the experts felt that responses to this item were dependent on time of day or day of week. Another expert asked, "How can someone unfamiliar with the resident or facility know who was present?" That expert also pointed out that visitors could be present but out of sight in the private room of a host–resident. Two experts questioned the usefulness of this item as a measure of the quality of the facility.

In comments related to other items, the experts drew attention to the variations among residential care facilities and to the independence of the residents as compared with nursing home residents as potential influences on responses. For example, comments on the items related to personal hygiene and grooming were: "If they care for their personal needs, we'll allow them to [do it their way]. We want them to stay as independent as possible" and "Some residents do their own personal care." The experts' comments for the items on staff visibility and the presence of a nurse in the facility also pointed out the differences among facilities and residents, and the impact of those differences on the number and type of staff present.

Table 2
Sample Items from the Observable Indicators of Nursing Home Care Quality: Residential Care Facility Version

Were conversations between staff and residents friendly? (Communication)				
1	2	3	4	5
Most were not	A few were	Some were	Many were	Most were

How often is a nurse present in the facility? (Staff)				
1	2	3	4	5
Monthly	Bi-weekly	Weekly	Twice a week	Daily

Were odors of urine or feces noticeable in the facility? (Environment)				
1	2	3	4	5
Pervasive throughout	Most of the time	Often	Occasionally	Hardly at all

Were a variety of activities available for residents? (look for posted schedule, calendars, group meetings, etc.) (Care)				
1	2	3	4	5
Rarely seen	A few were	Some were	Many were	Lots were

Validity of subscales. After reviewing the validity of each item, we also reviewed the validity of the subscales. As previously explained, the instrument has 5 major subscales: communication, care, staff, environment, and home/family involvement. The environment subscale is further divided into subscales for (a) odor, cleanliness, condition and (b) lighting, noise, atmosphere. The subscales had excellent validity as evidenced by the average rating for the relevance of all of the items in the subscales: communication, 3.90; care, 3.17; staff, 3.31; environment-a, 3.75; environment-b, 3.46; and home/family involvement, 3.00.

A decision was made to retain both items with a mean rating of 2.00. For the item in the care subscale, "Were residents out of their rooms?" we agreed with one expert comment that an item about residents being out of their rooms was to be equated with better care. We recognized that residents have a right to remain in their rooms, but we believe staff should facilitate engaging residents and their friends in activities and socialization with others. For the "Were exit doors equipped with monitoring systems?" item in the environment-b subscale, we agreed with an expert's comment that it appears that the use of monitoring systems on exit doors is related to specific facility choices based on resident condition or regulatory requirements. The item was retained because of the great variation among residential care facilities, and because recent regulatory changes in Missouri have required monitoring systems on exit doors for some categories of residential care facilities.

We also evaluated the remaining 3 items with ratings of less than 3.0 (see Table 1) that were in the home/family involvement subscale. The items rate the residents' rooms and the use of furnishings to create homelike dwelling places that are connected with the residents' pasts. Environmental design recommendations for residential care facilities emphasize the homelike nature of residential care as opposed to the nursing home environment with its historical links to hospital design.[16] Most residential care facilities encourage the residents and their families to bring in personal belongings to promote a homelike ambiance in resident rooms.

The last item in the home/family involvement subscale rates the visible presence of visitors. As the experts pointed out in their comments, the presence of visitors varies greatly across time of day and day of week. Furthermore, there may be unseen visitors in the residents' private rooms. Unlike the nursing home setting, where visitors are often found in lounge areas and where visitors and residents may be distinguished by cues such as clothing or functional independence, visitors and residents in residential care settings may be indistinguishable. However, we believe the presence of visitors is an indication of family and community involvement that is viewed by consumers as important to quality.[11]

After reviewing the average ratings for each subscale, each item, the distribution of individual expert ratings for the 5 items with mean ratings less than 3.0, and the comments of the experts for the 5 items with mean ratings less than 3.0, we decided to retain all 34 items for the field test of the instrument. The experts together rated no items as "not relevant" (i.e., no items had means of less than 2.0). Although there was a suspicion that these items, and possibly others in the instrument, may be highly site-specific, the instrument, in its first version, was accepted as possessing high content validity and plans were made to assess its reliability. Table 2 displays sample items from the Observable Indicators of Nursing Home Quality: Residential Care Facility Version. The complete instrument is available from the authors.

Reliability

Inter-rater reliability and test–retest reliability were measured for the Residential Care Facility Version of the Observable Indicators of Nursing Home Care Quality Instrument. Content validity assessment answers the question "Does the instrument measure what we want it to measure?" Inter-rater reliability and test–retest

Table 3
Summary of Reliability of Results

Dimension	Number of items per subscale	Test–retest correlation[*]	Inter-rater correlation[†]	Cronbach's alpha[‡]
Communication	5	.81	.76	.96
Care	6	.88	.52	.71
Staff	4	.66	.57	.38
Environment	13	.94	.79	.81
Env-OCC[§]	6	.86	.81	.81
Env-LNA[‖]	7	.93	.66	.60
Home/family	6	.86	.51	.76
Full scale	*34*	*.94*	*.73*	*.90*

[*] N equal to 140 is the total number of instruments completed.
[†] Spearman's rho. Significant at < .0001.
[‡] Cronbach's alpha. Raw alpha values rather than the standardized values are cited because all items are on the same 1–5 point scale.
[§] Env-OCC: odor/cleanliness/condition.
[‖] Env-LNA: lighting/noise/atmosphere.

reliability answer the questions "Do different assessors using the instrument at the same site and at the same time achieve similar results?" and "Does the instrument yield similar results when used again at same sites after a specified time interval?"

The Residential Care Facility Version was tested in 35 licensed residential care facilities in Missouri. A convenience sample of facilities was selected from three geographic regions in the state. Each of the 3 regional teams of quality improvement nurses from the QIPMO project recruited 10 residential care facilities in their respective regions for the reliability field test. The centers of the regions were St. Louis, Columbia, and Kansas City. Initially, 10 facilities were selected in each of the 3 regions. Later, 5 additional facilities in the southeastern quadrant of the state were added to increase the geographic diversity of the sample. The quality improvement nurses were asked to stratify the convenience sample according to facility size with 30% of the facilities licensed for 1–30 residents, 40% of the facilities licensed for 31–60 residents, and 30% of the facilities licensed for more than 61 residents. The quality improvement nurses recruited the facilities to participate in this voluntary evaluation of the instrument.

With the permission of the administrators of the facilities, pairs of QIPMO quality improvement nurses visited each facility twice during the summer and autumn of 2001. There was an interval of 7–10 days between visits. On each visit, the quality improvement nurses walked together through the facility making observations and then independently completed the instrument. Visits to the facilities were made between 8:00 A.M. and 5:00 P.M. from Monday through Friday. No visits were made in evenings or on weekends. Completed assessment tools (*n* = 140) were sent by the nurses to the QIPMO project office.

The statistical analysis included the calculation of Cronbach's alpha for the full scale and subscales and inter-rater and test–retest item correlations. To quantify the strength of agreement between raters, weighted Kappa coefficients were also calculated for each item.

Table 3 displays the reliability analyses for each subscale and the full scale. The total scale has excellent test–retest reliability, good inter-rater reliability, and excellent internal consistency. Additionally, most subscales also have excellent and good results. Therefore, preliminary psychometric studies show great promise that the instrument measures quality of residential care facilities, though further testing is needed.

Revisions of First Version of Tool

After the field test in the 35 residential care facilities, we carefully reviewed the results of the validity and reliability studies for possible revisions to items to improve item and subscale performance. As indicated earlier, the tool we tested had 34 items, some of which the content validity experts questioned. The item "Were residents out of their rooms?" that was questioned by the experts considering validity was deleted. This item had acceptable inter-rater reliability, but a nonsignificant test–retest correlation suggested a lack of stability over time. We also combined 2 items that addressed the presence and condition of plants and pets in the facility into one item "Were their pets and/or live plants in good condition?" After these changes, the subscale structure was: communication (5 items), care (5 items), staff (4 items), environment (12 items), and home/family (6 items) with the environment subscale further divided into odor/cleanliness/condition (6 items) and lighting/noise/atmosphere (6 items). The total scale was 32 items.

The statistician expressed concern that responses to several items were clustered at one end of the 5-point scale rather than distributed among the range of responses. Therefore, the anchors of these items were revised. The choice "Not Applicable" was added to 2 items.

Focus Group

Before proceeding with revisions and further testing, we decided we needed to explore additional dimensions of residential care quality and issues raised by the content experts in the comments written on their content validity forms. We recruited five additional experienced residential care administrators to participate in a focus group to discuss their perceptions of quality of residential care. Similar to the four original content experts, these participants had many years of experience as administrators or other direct care staff members in both urban and rural facilities in Missouri and surrounding states.

Using a discussion guide that was similar to the one successfully used to examine nursing home care quality,[10, 11] the focus group participants, after informed consent, were asked to recall particular facilities they had observed in the past that they thought were "excellent places, really doing a good job providing excellent resident care to their residents." Participants were debriefed on what they saw, felt, smelled, heard, and touched in those facilities. We discussed key features they thought were important for quality of care. Descriptions of facilities where they had observed poor quality care were also discussed to better understand care quality in residential care facilities.

The discussion tapes were analyzed to identify additional quality dimensions or additional items to be added to the Residential Care Facility Version. The results of the focus group interview confirmed the appropriateness of 5 dimensions of care quality as discovered in the nursing home research.[10, 11] The results also pointed out the need to add items on the topics of food choices and snack availability, access to telephone and e-mail or other computer-based communication. We added those items to the current Version 7 that is being used in a larger field test that is currently underway in 3 states.

Discussion

Measuring quality of care in residential care facilities is extremely important, given the dramatic increase in the number of these facilities nationwide. The results of this small-scale field study and follow-up focus group indicate that care quality is an important issue for facility providers, their residents, and the families and friends who visit. It is interesting that while there are many differences between residential care settings and nursing homes, the quality of care dimensions are the same. The major dimensions of communication, care, staff, environment, home, and family involvement that were discovered and confirmed in earlier work in nursing homes[7, 8, 10, 11] appear to be on-target theoretically in residential care settings. However, there are many differences that must be accounted for in the actual items measuring these dimensions.

The emphasis on autonomy and resident choice in residential care facilities is one of these differences. While nursing home staff and regulators have attempted to promote autonomy and choice, the nursing home setting is continually plagued by their reputation of regimes with which residents must comply.[16, 17] Consumers who live in residential care voice their fears of being forced from their homelike apartments to traditional institutional nursing homes.[18]

The findings of this study are limited because the relatively small sample was selected among facilities in only one state and was not randomly selected. We are currently conducting a larger scale study in which the instrument is being used in 3 states with a larger sample. With further development, we anticipate that the residential care version will be of interest to several constituencies.

An instrument to quickly evaluate quality of care in residential care is of interest to consumers. Families who are attempting to locate care for a loved one need help in judging quality of care. Decisions about moving into a residential care facility cannot be driven by only proximity, which is often the case. Given the range of quality in services that are available, consumers when making a choice need to be knowledgeable about key elements to observe in facilities. We believe that making a good choice based on quality of care is a better choice in the long run. Our research team has information posted on our Web site www.nursinghomehelp.org to help consumers as they are faced with long-term care decisions.

Regulators of residential care facilities will also benefit from having an instrument to measure residential care quality. Typically, regulators focus on compliance with established rules and regulations. The premise of the regulations is that if those minimum standards are met, then there is at least adequate quality of care. Having other ways to quickly evaluate quality of care can be of assistance to regulators who are often stretched across large numbers of facilities in varying geographic regions.

Operators of residential care facilities can also make use of an instrument to measure quality. With the current emphasis on quality improvement programs in all of long-term care,[19] quality improvement teams within facilities can objectively examine their facility and care delivery and design quality improvement projects in areas where they find that they could use improvement.

Obviously, from our point of view as researchers, other researchers interested in understanding and conducting studies in residential care settings can benefit from an instrument measuring residential care quality. Given the results of this field study, we think the Residential Care Version of the Observable Indicators holds much promise for researchers. The initial validity and reliability studies indicate that it has reasonably sound reliability and excellent validity. We anticipate that the revisions made on the basis of this field study will improve the performance of individual items, subscales, and total scale. We are confident that the dimensions of quality of care (communication, care, staffing, environment, and home/family involvement) are theoretically sound and appropriate for this setting. We encourage other researchers to contact us for the most recent version of the Observable Indicators of Nursing Home Care Quality: Residential Care Facility Version Instrument.

References

1. PriceWaterhouseCoopers. *An Overview of the Assisted Living Industry,* 1998. Fairfax, VA: Assisted Living Federation of America; 1998.
2. Hawes C, Rose M, Phillips CD. *A National Study of Assisted Living for the Frail Elderly: Results of a National Survey of Facilities.* Beachwood, OH: Meyers Research Institute; 1999.
3. Zimmerman S, Eckert JK, Wildfire JB. The process of care. In: Zimmerman S, Sloane PO, Eckert JK, eds. *Assisted Living: Needs, Practices, and Policies in Residential Care for the Elderly.* Baltimore, MD: Johns Hopkins University Press; 2001:198–223.
4. Morgan LA, Gruber-Baldini AL, Magaziner J. Resident characteristics. In: Zimmerman S, Sloane PO, Eden JK, eds. *Assisted Living: Needs, Practices, and Policies in Residential Care for the Elderly.* Baltimore, MD: Johns Hopkins University Press; 2001:144–172.
5. Hodlewsky RT. Staffing problems and strategies in assisted living. In: Zimmerman S, Sloane PO, Eckert JK, eds. *Assisted Living: Needs, Practices, and Policies in Residential Care for the Elderly.* Baltimore, MD: Johns Hopkins University Press; 2001:78–91.
6. Hawes C. Introduction. In: Zimmerman S, Sloane PO, Eckert JK, eds. *Assisted Living: Needs, Practices, and Policies in Residential Care for the Elderly.* Baltimore, MD: Johns Hopkins University Press; 2001:1–6.
7. Rantz MJ, Mehr DR, Petroski GF, et al. Initial field-testing of an instrument to measure: observable indicators of nursing home quality. *J Nurs Care Qual.* 2000;14(3):1–12.
8. Rantz MJ, Mehr DR. A quest to understand and measure nursing home quality of care. *Long-Term Care Interface.* 2001;2(7):34–38.
9. Rantz M, Jensdottir AB, Hjaltadottir I, et al. International field test results of the observable indicators of nursing home care quality instrument. *Int Nurs Rev.* 2002;49(4):234–242.
10. Rantz MJ, Mehr D, Popejoy L, et al. Nursing home care quality: A multidimensional theoretical model. *J Nurs Care Qual.* 1998;12(3):30–46.
11. Rantz MJ, Zwygart-Stauffacher M, Popejoy L, et al. Nursing home care quality: A multidimensional theoretical model integrating the views of consumers and providers. *J Nurs Care Qual.* 1999;14(1):16–37.
12. Rantz M, Popejoy L, Zwygart-Stauffacher M. *The New Nursing Homes: A 20-Minute Way to Find Great Long-Term Care.* Minneapolis, MN: Fairview Press; 2001.
13. Kane RA, Kane RL, Ladd RC. *The Heart of Long-Term Care.* New York: Oxford University Press; 1998.
14. Waltz CF; Strickland OL, Lenz ER. *Measurement in Nursing Research.* Philadelphia: FA Davis; 1984.
15. Schwarz B. Assisted living: An evolving place type. In: Schwarz B, Brent R, eds. *Aging, Autonomy, and Architecture: Advances in Assisted Living.* Baltimore, MD: Johns Hopkins University Press; 1999: 185–206.
16. Regnier VA, Scott AC. Creating a therapeutic environment: Lessons from Northern European models. In: Zimmerman S, Sloane PO, Eckert JK, eds. *Assisted Living: Needs, Practices, and Policies in Residential Care for the Elderly.* Baltimore, MD: Johns Hopkins University Press; 2001:53–77.
17. Regnier VA. The definition and evolution of assisted living within a changing system of long-term care. In: Schwarz B, Brent R, eds. *Aging, Autonomy, and Architecture: Advances in Assisted Living.* Baltimore, MD: Johns Hopkins University Press; 1999:3–19.
18. Frank J. How can I stay?: The dilemma of aging in place in assisted living. In: Schwarz B, ed. *Assisted Living: Sobering Realities.* New York: Haworth Press; 2001:15–30.
19. Kane RA. Long-term care and a good quality of life: bringing them closer together. *Gerontologist.* 2001;41(3):293–304.

Acknowledgments: The authors wish to acknowledge the contributions of the other quality improvement nurses who participated in this field study: Carol Siem, Katy Nguyen, Elizabeth Sutherland, De Minner, Amy Vogelsmeier, Clara Boland, and Dale Potter. We also wish to thank Greg Petroski for statistical support and Steve Miller for data support.

Address correspondence to: Myra A. Aud, PhD, RN, Sinclair School of Nursing (S 422), University of Missouri at Columbia, Columbia, MO 65211. E-mail: audm@health.missouri.edu

Exercise for Article 38

Factual Questions

1. Responses to all items on the Observable Indicators of Nursing Home Care Quality: Residential Care Facility Version Instrument are selected from a 5-point Likert-type scale. What does a response of 5 indicate?

2. Although it was not requested in the instructions, how many of the experts wrote comments on the rating forms?

3. How many of the 34 items had average ratings by the experts of less than 3.00?

4. The researchers point out that inter-rater reliability answers this question: "Do different assessors using the instrument at the same site and at the same time achieve similar results?" According to the researchers, what question does test–retest reliability answer?

5. Which "dimension" has the lowest test–retest reliability?

6. How many additional experienced residential care administrators participated in the focus group to discuss their perceptions of quality of residential care?

Questions for Discussion

7. The experts who examined the instrument for content validity worked independently. In your opinion, is it desirable to have them work independently *or* would it have been better if they worked in consultation with each other? (See lines 170–173.)

8. What is your opinion on the researchers' decision to retain the two items with expert ratings of 2.00? (See Table 1 and lines 275–293.)

9. Keeping in mind that the complete instrument is available from the authors (see lines 335–336 and 534–538), are the sample items in Table 2 sufficient for a research report of this type? To what extent do the items help you understand what the instrument measures?

10. The researchers discuss the content validity of the instrument in lines 180–336. Based on this information, are you convinced that the instrument has a high level of content validity? Explain.

11. The researchers state that the total scale (i.e., full scale) has "excellent" test–retest reliability. Do you agree? Explain. (See lines 385–387 and Table 3.)

12. To what extent, if any, did the focus group part of this research convince you that the instrument is valid? (See lines 418–454.)

Quality Ratings

Directions: Indicate your level of agreement with each of the following statements by circling a number from 5 for strongly agree (SA) to 1 for strongly disagree (SD). If you believe an item is not applicable to this research article, leave it blank. Be prepared to explain your ratings. When responding to criteria A and B below, keep in mind that brief titles and abstracts are conventional in published research.

A. The title of the article is appropriate.

SA   5   4   3   2   1   SD

B. The abstract provides an effective overview of the research article.

SA   5   4   3   2   1   SD

C. The introduction establishes the importance of the study.

SA   5   4   3   2   1   SD

D. The literature review establishes the context for the study.

SA   5   4   3   2   1   SD

E. The research purpose, question, or hypothesis is clearly stated.

SA   5   4   3   2   1   SD

F. The method of sampling is sound.

SA   5   4   3   2   1   SD

G. Relevant demographics (for example, age, gender, and ethnicity) are described.

SA   5   4   3   2   1   SD

H. Measurement procedures are adequate.

SA   5   4   3   2   1   SD

I. All procedures have been described in sufficient detail to permit a replication of the study.

SA   5   4   3   2   1   SD

J. The participants have been adequately protected from potential harm.

SA   5   4   3   2   1   SD

K. The results are clearly described.

SA   5   4   3   2   1   SD

L. The discussion/conclusion is appropriate.

SA   5   4   3   2   1   SD

M. Despite any flaws, the report is worthy of publication.

SA   5   4   3   2   1   SD

Article 39

Preverbal, Early Verbal Pediatric Pain Scale (PEPPS): Development and Early Psychometric Testing

Alyce A. Schultz, RN, PhD, **Ellen Murphy**, RN, MSN, **Jennifer Morton**, RN, BSN, **Audrey Stempel**, RN, MSEd, **Carole Messenger-Rioux**, RN, NNP, **Kathleen Bennett**, RN[*]

ABSTRACT. The Preverbal, Early Verbal Pediatric Pain Scale (PEPPS) is conceptualized to measure the established pain response in toddlers, a pediatric group void of pain assessment scales. It consists of seven categories, each with weighted indicators. Scores can range from 0 to 26. Using a blinded, cross-sectional design, 40 children, aged 12 to 24 months, were videotaped throughout their postoperative stay in the postanesthesia care unit. Vignettes were randomly selected and viewed by four experienced pediatric nurses. Results indicated that the PEPPS was easy to use and demonstrated acceptable interrater and intrarater reliability. Early evidence of construct validity was established by statistically significant differences in premedication and postmedication pain scores.

From *Journal of Pediatric Nursing*, 14, 19–27. Copyright © 1999 by the W.B. Saunders Company. Reprinted with permission.

Before the late 1970s, clinical and empirical work on pain and pain management focused entirely on adults. It was not until 1977 that the term "pain" even appeared in medical and nursing pediatric textbooks.
5 Twenty years later, the assessment and management of pain in children continue to challenge health professionals, with the assessment and management of pain in the nonverbal child being particularly difficult (Anand & Craig, 1996).
10 Children who have similar diagnoses and procedures receive far less pain management than their adult counterparts (Schechter, 1989; Truog & Anand, 1989). Yet, empirical evidence supports that the experience of pain impedes healing and recovery in very young children
15 just as it does in adults and older children (Eland & Coy, 1990; Fitzgerald & Anand, 1993; Marchette, Main, & Redick, 1989; Stevens & Franck, 1995). The ethical justification for this undertreatment of pain in the young has been questioned (Walco, Cassidy, &
20 Schechter, 1994).

Research-based protocols for the assessment and management of pain have been developed for adults and children who are old enough to self-report their pain (AHCPR, 1992; Schmidt, Holiday, Kleiber, Peter-
25 sen, & Phearman, 1994). It is now generally accepted that children older than 4 years of age are able to accurately self-report painful experiences. Although there is still debate, children as young as 3 years of age have been reported as reliable if they are able to count to 10
30 and understand the scales (Keck, Gerkensmeyer, Joyce, & Schade, 1996; Knott et al., 1994; Wong & Baker, 1988). Development of assessment scales for preverbal, early verbal children remains a priority (NINR, 1994).

35 Recent work has contributed assessment scales for infants (Barrier, Attia, Mayer, Amiel-Tison, & Shnider, 1989; Krechel & Bildner, 1995; Lawrence et al., 1993; Stevens, Johnston, Petryshen, & Taddio, 1996; Taddio, Nulman, Koren, Stevens, & Koren, 1995). The toddler,
40 however, continues to be included with older children who are capable of self-report (McGrath et al., 1985; Merkel, Voepel-Lewis, Shayevitz, & Malviya, 1997; Robieux, Kumar, Radhakrishman, & Koren, 1991). The purpose of this research was to develop and vali-
45 date psychometric properties of the Preverbal, Early Verbal Pediatric Pain Scale (PEPPS), designed specifically for the toddler population.

Background

This selected review of the literature addresses work in the assessment of pain in preverbal, early verbal children, defined as less than 3 years of age. No
50 studies were found that specifically addressed behaviors in the toddler population.

Behavioral Categories

A number of studies have been conducted to evaluate specific behavioral responses by infants and toddlers to painful stimuli (i.e., cry, facial expressions, and
55 body movements) (Table 1). Supporting the work of earlier research, investigators reported that although the cry response may differ across the developmental stages, from preterm to toddler, experienced practitioners were able to recognize and differentiate among
60

---

[*] All authors are at the Maine Medical Center, Portland, Maine.

cries suggestive of fussiness, hunger, and pain. They further concluded that the cry response alone is not adequate to measure the immediate pain response, particularly in preterm infants who do not always use cry
65 in response to painful stimuli (Grunau & Craig, 1987; Grunau, Johnston, & Craig, 1990; Fuller, Horii, & Conner, 1989; Porter, Miller, & Marshall, 1986).

Table 1
Pain Behaviors

Category	Descriptors	Authors
Cry/vocaliza-tion	Latency to cry, duration of cry cycle, frequency, melody, and dys-phonia	Owens & Todt, 1984; Porter, Miller, & Marshall, 1986; Fuller, Horii, & Conner, 1989; Grunau, Johnston, & Craig, 1990; Ste-vens, Johnston, & Grunau, 1995
Facial expres-sions	Brow activity, nasal root, eyes, mouth, chin, and tongue	Izard, 1982; Izard, Hembree, & Hueb-ner, 1987; Grunau & Craig, 1987; Craig, Grunau, & Aquon-Assee, 1988; Grunau et al., 1990; Fuller & Conner, 1995
Body movement	Limb movements, thrashing, jerk-ing, wiggling, withdrawing, kicking, and torso rigidity	Craig, McMahon, Morison, & Zaskow, 1984; Dole, 1986; Johnston & Strada, 1986; Mills, 1989; Bozzette, 1993

Facial expressions have also been found to differ in response to varying painful stimuli according to age
70 (Attia, Amiel-Tison, Mayer, Shnider & Barrier, 1987; Grunau & Craig, 1987; Grunau et al., 1990; McGrath et al., 1985). Composite scores, based on 10 facial actions, were found to differ with different stimuli and to differ from the cry response (Grunau & Craig, 1987;
75 Grunau et al., 1990). Body movements that also differ developmentally have been linked with the pain response. Specific movements of the body have been studied individually for their correlation with painful stimuli (Craig, McMahon, Morison, & Zaskow, 1984;
80 Attia et al., 1987; Barrier et al., 1989; McGrath et al., 1985; Gauvain-Piquard, Rodary, Rezvani, & Lemerle, 1987).

Sociability, consolability, and readiness to feed or suck have not been consistently included in behavioral
85 work assessing pain in very young children. Yet, early work on the management of pain in very young children suggests that the postoperative engagement of parents with their child is consoling to the child. Further research correlating the response of children to
90 these interventions and the subsequent reduction of pain is needed.

Assessment Scales

A recent publication by the National Institute of

Nursing Research (1994) devoted an entire chapter to the measurement of pain in the preverbal child. It was
95 noted that although valid pain assessment scales have been developed for older children and adults, no valid and reliable scales exist for the very young.

Health care providers are somewhat reticent to accept the use of behavioral characteristics as adequate in
100 the management of painful responses in very young children. Although physiological measures are viewed as more objective, they are inconclusive in determining the presence of pain (Brown, 1987; Maxwell, Yaster, Wetzel, & Niebyl, 1987; Taddio et al., 1995; Tarbell,
105 Cohen, & March, 1992). Most of the physiological indicators (e.g., taking nonmonitored heart rate or blood pressure) produce stressful stimuli in the process of their measurement, thereby negating their reliability and validity as representative of pain. Hence, emphasis
110 has focused on the observation of changes in behavior when developing scales for very young children.

Published scales for preverbal, early verbal children were reviewed for inclusion of varying behavioral categories and reported psychometric testing (Table 2).
115 The review indicated that several tools are available specifically for the infant population, from premature infants through 1 year of age. Other scales used to measure pain in early verbal children, however, also included older, verbal children. All the scales included
120 indicators for facial expression, cry, and body posture. A variety of descriptors were used within each category. In several scales, the various movements of the legs, torsos, and even arms were measured separately (Barrier et al., 1989; Lawrence et al., 1993; McGrath et
125 al., 1985; Merkel et al., 1997). This division of body responses resulted in heavier scale weights for body movements than for cry and facial expressions. No theoretical explanations were given for these decisions. The Postoperative Pain Scale (POPS), developed for
130 use with infants, included all the behavioral categories (Barrier et al., 1989) as compared with the Premature Infant Pain Profile (PIPP), which focused primarily on facial movements (Stevens et al., 1996).

All the scales reported some estimation of reliabil-
135 ity and validity (Table 2). Construct validity was addressed primarily using the known groups technique whereby premedication and postmedication pain scale scores were compared for significant differences. Convergent validity, another approach to measuring con-
140 struct validity, was examined most frequently by comparing the scale under study with the visual analogue scale as determined by nursing staff (Lawrence et al., 1993; McGrath et al., 1985; Robieux et al., 1991; Taddio et al., 1995; Tarbell et al., 1992); other investiga-
145 tors reported validity testing of their new scales with other published but nonvalidated scales (Krechel & Bildner, 1995; Merkel et al., 1997). Only one study reported that the raters or scale evaluators were blinded to the pain medication or painful procedure (Robieux et
150 al., 1991). Interestingly, the child must be awake to use

Table 2
Behavioral Categories

Scales	Age Range	Facial	Cry	Consolability & Sociability	Body Posture	Sucking/ Feeding	Reliability &Validity	Authors
PIPP	Premature Infants	✓					IRR, Construct	Stevens et al., 1996
CRIES	Neonates	✓	✓				IRR, Construct	Krechel & Bildner, 1995
POPS	1–7 months	✓	✓	✓	✓		Construct	Barrier et al., 1989
NIPS	2–6 months	✓	✓		✓	✓	IRR, Int. Consistency Construct	Lawrence et al., 1993
MBPS	4–6 months	✓	✓		✓		IRR Intrarater Int. Consistency, Construct	Taddio et al., 1995
BPS	Infant/ Toddler	✓	✓		✓		Construct	Robieux et al., 1991
FLACC	2 months–7 years	✓	✓	✓	✓		IRR, Construct	Merkel et al., 1997
TPPPS	1–5 years	✓	✓				IRR, Construct	Tarbell et al., 1992
CHEOPS	1–7 years	✓	✓		✓		IRR, Construct	McGrath et al., 1985

Abbreviations: PIPP, Premature Infant Pain Profile; CRIES, Crying, Requires oxygen, Increased vital signs, Expression, Sleeplessness; POPS, Postoperative Pain Scale; NIPS, Neonatal Infant Pain Scale; MBPS, Modified Behavioral Pain Scale; BPS, Behavioral Pain Scale; FLACC, Facial expression, Leg movement, Activity, Cry, Consolability; TPPPS, Toddler Preschooler Postoperative Pain Scale; CHEOPS, Children's Hospital of Eastern Ontario Pain Scale.

the Toddler Preschooler Postoperative Pain Scale (TPPPS) (Tarbell et al., 1992). All the scales were evaluated during needle-stick procedures or during the immediate postoperative period. The Children's Hospi-
155   tal of Eastern Ontario Pain Scale (CHEOPS) was later tested with children, aged 4 to 7 years, outside the recovery room with less than satisfactory correlations to self-reported pain (Beyer, McGrath, & Berde, 1990).

No scale specifically measured postoperative pain
160   in the toddler. Thus, the first phase of this project was to develop an assessment scale that would measure "the established pain response" or the pain stimulated by surgery in preverbal, early verbal children. This "pain response" was envisioned as a composite picture
165   characterized by physiological changes in heart rate and behavioral changes in facial expression, cry, body posture, sociability, consolability/state of restfulness, and sucking/feeding.

Development of the PEPPS

Seven pediatric nurses, each with 7 to 18 years of
170   pediatric experience, established a Pediatric Pain Committee to address the issues of pain assessment and management in preverbal, early verbal children, from premature infants to toddlers, of approximately 36 months. They were particularly concerned with pain
175   assessment of children who were unable to self-report the location and severity of their pain. In developing domains for the scale, they followed the stages suggested by Green and Lewis (1986) for establishing content validity: (1) review of relevant literature, (2) per-
180   sonal reflection of the developer's ideas about the con-

cept under study, (3) identification of components of the concept, (4) generation of multiple items that demonstrate the concept, and (5) empirical examination of the interrelationship of items and how they cluster
185   around the components of the concept.

The investigators closely observed and recorded postoperative behaviors of young children. They simultaneously completed an extensive review of the literature on pain in preverbal children. Based on consensus,
190   items that reflected the multifaceted construct of pain were generated in physiological and behavioral categories. A preliminary version of the pain assessment scale was shared with pediatric physicians, anesthesiologists, and staff nurses within the various settings where very
195   young children were provided postoperative care. Feedback from these health care providers was incorporated into the scale.

The investigators then used the scale postoperatively with a variety of preverbal, early verbal children
200   to establish face validity and utility. In preparation for further psychometric testing of the instrument, a pilot study was conducted by the investigators within their practice settings. Four investigators established interrater reliability among themselves and then with an-
205   other nurse in their same practice setting by simultaneously observing children during their postoperative period. All nurses using the scale reported that the scale was easy to use and intuitively captured the pain behaviors in this age group. Twenty-six observations
210   on 10 children were completed. Pearson's correlation revealed significantly high agreement ($r = .97$, $p \leq$

.000) among the nurses who used the scale. The results of this pilot study were reported at an international pain conference in 1994 (Murphy et al., 1994).

The strongest recommendations from the conference suggested that the scale should be targeted specifically at the toddler population, as these children are developmentally different from the infant population, but cannot use the self-report scales. The investigators returned to the bedside to focus on toddler behaviors exhibiting pain. The current version of the PEPPS contains seven categories, each containing two to four indicators of varying levels of responses to painful stimuli. Descriptors were identified that reflected behaviors ranging from the subtleties of mild pain to the demonstrative nature of severe pain (Table 3). Categorical scores can range from 0 to 4 in all categories except for the sucking/feeding category where scores range from 0 to 2. The desire to eat or suck after surgery may be more closely correlated with the feeling of nausea than pain. Total scores are determined by summing the categorical scores and can range from 0 to 26.

Methodology

The purpose of this study was to empirically examine the psychometric properties of the PEPPS. Psychometric evaluation is designed to examine the degree to which an instrument measures the same concept time after time and the extent to which it measures what it is intended to measure (Burns & Grove, 1993; Carmines & Zeller, 1979). This evaluation included examination of reliability and validity. The blinded, cross-sectional study was approved by the hospital's Institutional Review Board and conducted in the postanesthesia care unit (PACU) of a 606-bed tertiary care hospital in northern New England.

Sample

Subjects were a convenience sample of children between the ages of 12 and 24 months scheduled for urologic or general abdominal surgery. Children with known developmental delays were excluded from the study.

Procedure

Parents of children who met the study criteria were approached by the primary investigator or study coordinator for informed consent in the waiting area the morning of surgery. The study was carefully described, with particular emphasis on the option of participating and the certainty that postoperative care would not be altered by the study. Parents were assured confidentiality and the right to withdraw at any time with no adverse effects on their child's postoperative care. Parents were given a copy of the signed informed consent and an additional flyer that described the study and provided names and phone numbers of the primary investigator and study coordinator. After surgery, the children were admitted to a private treatment room within PACU. A PACU nurse was assigned to provide individual care to each child. Standard perioperative care was not altered. Parents were present in the PACU and held the children as soon as they emerged from anesthesia. The children were videotaped throughout their PACU experience, using a Panasonic AG-450 S-VHS camcorder with an Audio-Technica AT815a shotgun microphone and Maxell ST-126 BQ S-VHS videotape. The study coordinator collected demographic data, baseline pulse, and preoperative and intraoperative medication information from the chart. Heart rate and pulse oximetry were recorded every 5 minutes during the PACU period, as were the time and dose of postoperative pain medications.

Table 3

Preverbal, Early Verbal Pediatric Pain Scale (PEPPS)©

Heart Rate	Body Posture
4—40 beats/min above baseline	4—Sustained arching, flailing, thrashing and/or kicking
3—31–40 beats above baseline	3—Intermittent or sustained movement with or without periods of rigidity
2—21–30 beats above baseline	
1—10–20 beats above baseline	2—Localization with extension or flexion or stiff and nonmoving
0—baseline range	
Facial	1—Clenched fists, curled toes and/or reaching for, touching wound or area
4—Severe grimace; brows lowered, tightly drawn together; eyes tightly closed	0—Body at rest, relaxed positioning
2—Grimace; brows drawn together; eyes partially closed, squinting	**Sociability**
0—Relaxed facial expression	4—Absent eye contact, response to voice and/or touch
Cry (Audible/Visible)	2—With effort, responds to voice and/or touch, makes eye contact, difficult to obtain and maintain
4—Screaming	
3—Sustained crying	
2—Intermittent crying	
1—Whimpering, groaning, fussiness	0—Responds to voice and/or touch, makes eye contact or smiles, easy to obtain and maintain; sleeping
0—No cry	
Consolability/State of Restfulness	
4—Unable to console, restlessness, sustained movement	**Sucking/Feeding**
2—Able to console, distract with difficulty, intermittent restlessness, irritability	2—Lack of sucking, refusing food, fluids
	1—Disorganized sucking, attempting to eat or drink but discontinues
1—Distractable, easy to console, intermittent fussiness	0—Sucking, drinking and/or eating well
0—Pleasant, well integrated	0—N/A; NPO and/or does not use oral stimuli

Total score:

_____

Two to four vignettes 2 to 3 minutes long were selected for each study child for a total of 120 vignettes. Vignettes were selected to include behaviors exhibited before and after pain medication. Premedication time was defined as 10 minutes before receiving medication. Postmedication time was defined as 5 to 7 minutes after receipt of fentanyl, 7 to 10 minutes after morphine, and 20 minutes after Tylenol or B&O suppository (McEvoy, 1996). These times represent the peak periods of expected analgesic effect for each medication. Other vignettes were randomly selected from time periods that did not fit into either the premedication or the postmedication definition; these were labeled *nonmedication* vignettes. Thus, nonmedication vignettes were those time periods at least 10 minutes before any administration of pain medication or after the time of expected peak action. All vignettes were carefully selected so that no evidence of medication administration was visible. The vignettes were then randomly ordered into seven viewing tapes, each containing 15 to 20 vignettes.

Four pediatric nurses, blinded to the administration of pain medications, individually viewed each tape and scored each vignette using the PEPPS. Each viewer followed a protocol for viewing the vignettes (Table 4). Each vignette had its own scoring form. The scoring sessions were scheduled approximately 4 weeks apart. The pediatric nurses who scored the vignettes were part of the research team that developed the scale but were not involved in caring for these children preoperatively or postoperatively or in preparing the vignettes.

Table 4
Guidelines for Reviewing PEPPS Tapes

Each of you will receive a copy of the tape for review. A Master Copy of all tapes will be retained in the audiovisual department.

1. Carefully fill out the information in the upper right hand corner of the assessment form.
2. Select an area for viewing that is free from distractions.
3. View the complete vignette WITHOUT PAUSING. DO NOT REWIND THE TAPE AT ANY TIME DURING THE VIEWING. Instant replay is not allowed. YOU CAN AND PROBABLY SHOULD STOP the tape between vignettes so you can complete each scoring.
4. Record a PEPPS score for each vignette (approximately 2 to 3 minutes). If you have any additional comments, please put them on the forms.
5. When you are finished with the viewing, return the tape and all copies of the PEPPS to either Alyce Schultz or Ellen Murphy.

Reliability Measurement

Three approaches were used to examine reliability: interrater reliability, intrarater reliability, and internal consistency. Pearson's correlation was used to determine interrater and intrarater reliability. To determine interrater reliability, the four raters independently viewed and scored the behaviors captured on the 120 vignettes. To determine intrarater reliability, the raters viewed 14 vignettes a second time 2 months after the first viewing. Internal consistency of the scale was measured using Cronbach's alpha.

Validity Measurement

Empirical analysis of the content validity, as described by Green and Lewis (1986), was addressed by examining variations in the categorical scores and in the total pain scores. Representativeness of the indicators within each category was further probed by the primary investigator and study coordinator who were not involved in scoring the vignettes. All indicators within each category were examined for their frequency in scoring the varying intensities of pain response behaviors.

Construct validity was examined by testing the theoretical assumption that pain can be expected to decrease after the administration of appropriate doses of analgesic medications. Using the known groups approach, sometimes referred to as contrasting groups, premedication scores were compared with postmedication scores (Woods & Catanzaro, 1988).

Findings

Demographics

A total of 40 children, 35 boys and 5 girls, participated in the study. The children ranged in age from 12 to 24 months, with a mean age of 16.2 months. Seven children had inguinal hernia repairs, nine had hypospadius repairs, eight had an orchipexy, three had ureteral reimplantations; the other 13 children had a variety of urologic or abdominal procedures. Thirty-nine children received intraoperative pain medications.

Reliability Data

Interrater correlations ranged from .90 to .96. Intrarater correlations ranged from .96 to .98. Cronbach's coefficient alpha for the total scale was .89. Interitem correlations ranged from .15 for Sucking/Feeding and Heart Rate to .88 for Consolability and Cry (Table 5). Similarly, item to total scale correlations for Sucking/Feeding and Heart Rate were .37 and .38, respectively. Eliminating these items would only slightly improve the internal consistency.

Table 5
Item-to-Item Correlations

	Heart Rate	Facial	Cry	Body Posture	Socia-bility	Consola-bility	Sucking/Feeding
Heart Rate	–						
Facial	.2813	–					
Cry	.3803	.7789	–				
Body Posture	.2874	.6564	.7388	–			
Sociability	.3722	.6455	.7667	.7149	–		
Consolability	.4056	.7433	.8768	.7869	.8497	–	
Sucking/Feeding	.1536	.2920	.3296	.3233	.3405	.3990	–

Validity Data

Content validity was addressed during the development of the scale and by examining the utilization of items in scoring the pain response behaviors. Total pain scores covered the entire possible range of 0 to 26, with a mean score of 8.4 (*SD*, 6.57). Fifty-seven percent of the vignettes depicted pain scores of 8 or less. Only 15% of the scores were higher than 16. All items were used to score pain, with items reflecting severe pain used less frequently.

Construct validity was assessed, using the known-group method, by comparing premedication and post-medication pain scores. Twenty children received medication in PACU, with six children receiving medication twice for a total of 26 premedication vignettes. Twenty-five corresponding postmedication vignettes were available. One child was discharged from the PACU before the established time for peak performance of the analgesic (i.e., Tylenol). Using paired *t* test, there was a statistically significant difference in the premedication and postmedication scores for the 25 pairs, *t* = 14.58, *p* = .0000. There was a statistically significant difference among the pain scores for pre-medication, postmedication, and nonmedication behaviors, $F(2,477) = 145.29$, $p < .001$ (Fig. 1). Using Scheffe as the post hoc test of comparison, pain scores for postmedication-related behaviors were significantly lower than scores for nonmedication and premedication behaviors ($p < .05$), and pain scores for nonmedication-related behaviors were significantly lower than scores for premedication behaviors ($p < .05$).

Discussion

This phase of psychometric testing supports early evidence that the PEPPS is a valid and reliable scale for measuring immediate postoperative pain in the toddler, an age group void of published pain assessment scales. Two- to three-minute vignettes of the postoperative behaviors of children provided sufficient time for the viewers to assess behaviors exhibiting pain, as compared with those behaviors that exhibited a non-painful or less painful state. It is hypothesized that nurses who are taking care of the children could complete the scale in even less time because the behaviors in the PEPPS are the same behaviors reportedly used in the systematic assessment of the experienced pain response.

The sample for the study was selected from toddlers between the ages of 12 and 24 months who were scheduled for urologic or general abdominal surgery. This selection process resulted in an overrepresentation of males in the sample. However, the sample is representative of the children in this age group who are undergoing these types of surgical procedures. Future studies should address this limitation by following children after other types of surgery and equalizing representation of females. Expanding the study to include toddlers up to the age of 36 months may also

help address this gender bias. The sample in this study was Caucasian, representative of the population within the state. Future studies should be conducted in facilities where possible ethnic differences can be assessed.

Scale Score

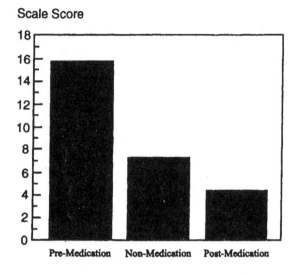

Figure 1. Comparison of mean pain scores for pre-medication, post-medication, and non-medication responses.

High interrater and intrarater reliability were evident. Generalization of these findings is limited because the raters were also members of the team that developed the scale. In the pilot study, four nurses who developed the scale and five nurses not involved in the development of the scale were able to achieve high interrater reliability ($r = .97$). The "uninvolved" nurses reported the scale as easy to use and indicative of pain response behaviors in the toddler. It will be important in future studies to use health care providers who were not intimately involved in the development of the scale to provide further estimates of reliability and utility.

Internal consistency among the categories was supported. The high item-to-total score correlations suggest that varying categories are measuring facets of the same construct, supporting the gestalt of the construct. The overall alpha of .89 suggests that the scale reflects subtle discriminations in levels of the construct (Burns & Grove, 1993). It is important to note, however, that the item-to-item correlations for the five behavioral categories (i.e., facial, cry, body posture, sociability, and consolability) ranged from .66 to .88, somewhat higher than the interitem correlations of .30 to .70 recommended by Nunnally (1978). Internal consistency should continue to be assessed in future studies. Although the categories of Heart Rate and Sucking/Feeding could be eliminated without adversely affecting internal consistency, it is too premature in the use of the instrument to support their elimination. Heart Rate as a poor indicator of pain has been reported by other investigators (Taddio et al., 1995; Tarbell et al.,

1992). Many children who are emerging from anesthesia are not yet ready to take fluids orally due to an upset stomach rather than pain. Close attention to the Sucking/Feeding category should be emphasized as the scale is tested further away from the PACU setting.

Early evidence of construct validity is supported by the significant differences in pain scores for children before receipt of pain medications as compared with their scores after analgesic administration. This analysis provided power of 1.00, with an alpha of .01, for the differences found in the premedication and postmedication scores (Borenstein & Cohen, 1988).

Almost all the children (39/40) were given pain medication intraoperatively. This anticipatory pain management appeared to work for half the children who, based on the intuitive assessment of pain by the PACU nurse caregiver, were not given pain medication during their PACU stay. From this experience, one could also extrapolate support for scores of the non-medication vignettes falling somewhere between the higher scores, when the PACU nurse determined the child needed medication, and the lowest scores, representing relief from pain after administration of an analgesic. Future examination of construct validity may provide further explanation for these findings.

The analysis provided additional validity for the domains of the scale. All the indicators within each category were used with varying frequency to capture descriptors of pain behaviors. The items suggesting greater pain were not used as often as those representing mild or moderate pain. This finding may be strongly related to the fact that all but one child received intraoperative pain medication. Further, the children in this study all had pain medication orders for their PACU stay. The children were not allowed to experience severe pain for the benefit of the study. Pain medication orders do not necessarily continue for those children after their immediate recovery period. The broad use of all the indicators should be reviewed in future studies, particularly as the scale is used by health care providers in an inpatient setting.

Using a pain assessment scale that is not specifically developed to represent the developmental stage of the toddler may leave these young children at a disadvantage for appropriate and adequate postoperative pain management. Early evidence for construct validity, reliability, and utility of the PEPPS for use in the immediate postoperative recovery period is supported by this study. Its usefulness outside this setting cannot be generalized until the scale is tested during extended postoperative experiences. Psychometric testing of newly developed scales is a continuous process and must be addressed with each study.

References

Anand, K.J.S., & Craig, K.D. (1996). Editorial. New perspectives on the definition of pain. *Pain, 67*, 3–6.

Attia, J., Amiel-Tison, A., Mayer, M.N., Shnider, S.M., & Barrier, G. (1987). Measurement of postoperative pain and narcotic administration in infants using a new clinical scoring system. *Anesthesiology, 67*(3A), 66.

Barrier, G., Attia, J., Mayer, M.N., Amiel-Tison, C., & Shnider, S.M. (1989). Measurement of post-operative pain and narcotic administration in infants using a new clinical scoring system. *Intensive Care Medicine, 15*(Suppl 1), S37–S39.

Beyer, J.E., McGrath, P.J., & Berde, C.B. (1990). Discordance between self-report and behavioral measures in 3–7-year-old children following surgery. *Journal of Pain and Symptom Management, 5*, 350–356.

Borenstein, M., & Cohen, J. (1988). *Statistical power analysis: A computer program*. Hillsdale, JH: Lawence Erlbaum Associates, Inc.

Bozzette, M. (1993). Observation of pain behavior in the NICU: An exploratory study. *Journal of Perinatology Neonatology Nursing, 7*, 76–87.

Brown, L. (1987). Physiological responses to cutaneous pain in neonates. *Neonatal Network, 6*(3), 18–22.

Burns, N., & Grove, S.K. (1993). *The practice of nursing research: Conduct, critique, & utilization*. Philadelphia: W.B. Saunders Company.

Carmines, E.G., & Zeller, R.A. (1979). *Reliability and validity assessment*. Newbury Park, CA: Sage University Paper.

Craig, K.D., Grunau, R.V.E., & Aquon-Assee, J.C. (1988). Judgement of pain in newborns: Facial activity and cry as determinants. *Canadian Journal of Behavioral Science, 20*, 442–451.

Craig, K.D., McMahon, R.J., Morison, J.D., & Zaskow, C. (1984). Development changes in infant pain expression during immunization injections. *Social Science in Medicine, 19*, 1331–1337.

Dole, J.C. (1986). A multidimensional study of infants' responses to painful stimuli. *Pediatric Nursing, 12*, 27–31.

Eland, J., & Coy, J. (1990). Assessing pain in the critically ill child. *Focus on Critical Care, 17*, 469–475.

Fitzgerald, M., & Anand, K.J.S. (1993). Developmental neuroanatomy and neurophysiology of pain. In N.L. Schechter, C.B. Berde, & M. Yaster (Eds.), *Pain in infants and children* (pp. 11–31). Philadelphia: Williams and Wilkins.

Fuller, B.F., & Conner, D.A. (1995). The effect of pain on infant behaviors. *Clinical Nursing Research, 4*, 253–273.

Fuller, B.F., Horii, Y., & Conner, D. (1989). Vocal measures of infant pain. In S.G. Funk, E.M. Tornquist, L.A. Copp, M.T. Champagne, & R.A. Weise (Eds.), *Key aspects of comfort: Management of pain, fatigue, and nausea* (pp. 46–51). New York: Springer Publishing Co.

Gauvain-Piquard, A., Rodary, C., Rezvani, A., & Lemerle, J. (1987). Pain in children aged 2–6 years: A new observational rating scale elaborated in a pediatric oncology unit—preliminary report. *Pain, 31*, 177–188.

Green, L., & Lewis, F. (1986). *Measurement evaluation in health education and health promotion*. Palo Alto, CA: Mayfield.

Grunau, R.V.E., & Craig, K.D. (1987). Pain expression in neonates: Facial action and cry. *Pain, 28*, 395–410.

Grunau, R.V.E., Johnston, C.C., & Craig, K.D. (1990). Neonatal facial and cry responses to invasive and non-invasive procedures. *Pain, 42*, 295–305.

Izard, C.E. (1982). *Measuring emotions in infants and children*. New York: Cambridge University Press.

Izard, C.E., Hembree, E.A., & Huebner, R.R. (1987). Infant's emotional expressions to acute pain: Developmental change and stability of individual differences. *Developmental Psychology, 23*, 105–113.

Johnston, C.C., & Strada, M.E. (1986). Acute pain response in infants: A multidimensional description. *Pain, 24*, 373–382.

Keck, J.F., Gerkensmeyer, J.E., Joyce, B.A., & Schade. J.G. (1996). Reliability and validity of the FACES and word descriptor scales to measure procedural pain. *Journal of Pediatric Nursing, 11*, 368–374.

Knott, C., Beyer, J., Villarruel, A., Denyes, M., Erickson, V., & Willard, G. (1994). Using the oucher: Developmental approach to pain assessment in children. *MCN, 19*, 314–320.

Krechel, S., & Bildner, J. (1995). Cries: A new neonatal post-op pain assessment score. Initial testing of validity and reliability. *Paediatric Anaesthesia, 5*, 53–61.

Lawrence, J., Alcock, D., McGrath, P., Kay, J., MacMurray, S., & Dulberg, C. (1993). The development of a tool to assess neonatal pain. *Neonatal Network, 12*, 59–67.

Marchette, L., Main, R., & Redick, E. (1989). Pain reduction during neonatal circumcision. *Pediatric Nursing, 15*, 207–210.

Maxwell, L.G., Yaster, M., Wetzel, R.C., & Niebyl, J.R. (1987). Penile nerve block for newborn circumcision. *Obstetrics and Gynecology, 70*, 415–419.

McEvoy, G.K. (1996). American Hospital Formulary Service Drug Information. Bethesda, MD: American Society of Health System Pharmacists, Inc.

McGrath, P.J., Johnson, G., Goodman, J.T., Schillinger, J., Dunn, J., & Chapman, J.A. (1985). CHEOPS: A behavioral scale for rating postoperative pain in children. In H.L. Fields (Ed.), *Advances in pain research and therapy* (Vol. 9, pp. 395–402). New York: Raven Press.

Merkel, S.I., Voepel-Lewis, T., Shayevitz, J.R., & Malviya, S. (1997). The FLACC: A behavioral scale for scoring postoperative pain in young children. *Pediatric Nursing, 23*, 293–297.

Mills, N.M. (1989). Pain behavior in infants and toddlers. *Journal of Pain and Symptom Management, 4*, 184–190.

Murphy, E., Bennett, K., Ent, S., Messenger-Rioux, C., Morton, J., Stempel, A., & Thompson, B. (1994, June). Development of a pain assessment scale for the preverbal, early-verbal child (Abstract No. 160). Presented at The

Third International Symposium on Pediatric Pain. Children and Pain: Integrating Science and Care. Philadelphia, PA.

National Institute of Nursing Research. (1994). National Nursing Research Agenda: Volume 6. *Symptom management: Acute pain.* Bethesda, MD: National Institutes of Health, U.S. Department of Health and Human Services.

Nunnally, J.C. (1978). *Psychometric theory.* New York: McGraw Hill Book Company.

Owens, M.E., & Todt, E.H. (1984). Pain in infancy: Neonatal reaction to a heel lance. *Pain, 20,* 77–86.

Porter, F.L., Miller, R.H., & Marshall, R.E. (1986). Neonatal pain cries: Effect of circumcision on acoustic features and perceived urgency. *Child Development, 57,* 790–802.

Robieux, I., Kumar, R., Radhakrishman, S., & Koren, G. (1991). Assessing pain and analgesia with a lodocaine-prilocaine emulsion in infants and toddlers during venipuncture. *Journal of Pediatrics, 118,* 971–973.

Schechter, N.L. (1989). The undertreatment of pain in children: An overview. *Pediatric Clinics of North America, 36,* 781–794.

Schmidt, K., Holiday, D., Kleiber, C., Petersen, M., & Phearman, L. (1994). Implementation of the AHCPR pain guidelines for children. *Journal of Nursing Care Quality, 8*(3), 68–74.

Stevens, B.J., & Franck, L. (1995). Special needs of preterm infants in the management of pain and discomfort. *JOGNN, 24,* 856–862.

Stevens, B.J., Johnston, C.C., & Grunau, R.V.E. (1995). Issues of assessment of pain and discomfort in neonates. *JOGNN, 24,* 849–855.

Stevens, B., Johnston, C., Petryshen, P., & Taddio, A. (1996). Premature Infant Pain Profile: Development and initial validation. *Clinical Journal of Pain, 12,* 13–22.

Taddio, A., Nulman, I., Koren, B.S., Stevens, B., & Koren, G. (1995). A revised measure of acute pain in infants. *Journal of Pain and Symptom Management, 10,* 456–463.

Tarbell, S.E., Cohen, T., & March, J.L. (1992). The toddler–preschooler postoperative pain scale: An observational scale for measuring postoperative pain in children aged 1–5. Preliminary report. *Pain, 50,* 273–280.

Truog, R., & Anand, K.J.S. (1989). Management of pain in the postoperative neonate. *Clinics in Perinatology, 16*(1), 61–78.

U.S. Department of Health and Human Services, Public Health Service, Agency for Health Care Policy and Research. (1992). *Acute pain management: Operative or medical procedures and trauma. Clinical practice guideline.* DHHS Pub. No. (AHCPR) 92-0032. Silver Spring, MD: AHCPR Clearinghouse.

Walco, G.A., Cassidy, R.C., & Schechter, N.L. (1994). Pain, hurt, and harm: The ethics of pain control in infants and children. *The New England Journal of Medicine, 331,* 541–544.

Wong, D., & Baker, C. (1988). Pain in children: Comparison of assessment scales. *Pediatric Nursing, 14,* 9–17.

Woods, N.F., & Catanzaro, M. (1988). *Nursing research. Theory and practice.* St. Louis: C.V. Mosby Company.

Note: This work was supported, in part, by a grant from the Maine Medical Center Medical Research Committee.

Address reprint requests to: Alyce A. Schultz, RN, PhD, Maine Medical Center, 22 Bramhall Street, Portland, ME 04102.

Exercise for Article 39

Factual Questions

1. "Preverbal, early verbal" children are defined as being less than how many years of age?

2. Physiological indicators (e.g., taking blood pressure) negate what?

3. In 1986, Green and Lewis suggested how many stages for establishing content validity?

4. "Premedication time" was defined as how many minutes before receiving medication?

5. In Table 5, which correlation coefficient represents the strongest relationship?

6. In this study, what percentage of the scores on the PEPPS was higher than 16?

7. Was there a statistically significant difference among the pain scores for premedication, postmedication, and nonmedication?

Questions for Discussion

8. The researchers state that they used a "convenience sample." In your opinion, is this an important issue? Explain. (See lines 245–247.)

9. This study used children undergoing surgery. In your opinion, is it safe to generalize the results to children who are not undergoing surgery? Explain.

10. The researchers state that the four pediatric nurses were "blinded" to the administration of pain medications. What do you think this means? Is it important? Explain. (See lines 299–301.)

11. Do you agree with the first sentence under the heading "Discussion"? (See lines 383–387.)

12. If you were to conduct another study on the same topic, what changes in the research methodology, if any, would you make?

Quality Ratings

Directions: Indicate your level of agreement with each of the following statements by circling a number from 5 for strongly agree (SA) to 1 for strongly disagree (SD). If you believe an item is not applicable to this research article, leave it blank. Be prepared to explain your ratings. When responding to criteria A and B below, keep in mind that brief titles and abstracts are conventional in published research.

A. The title of the article is appropriate.

SA   5   4   3   2   1   SD

B. The abstract provides an effective overview of the research article.

SA   5   4   3   2   1   SD

C. The introduction establishes the importance of the study.

SA   5   4   3   2   1   SD

D. The literature review establishes the context for the study.

SA   5   4   3   2   1   SD

E. The research purpose, question, or hypothesis is clearly stated.

SA   5   4   3   2   1   SD

F. The method of sampling is sound.

    SA   5   4   3   2   1   SD

G. Relevant demographics (for example, age, gender, and ethnicity) are described.

    SA   5   4   3   2   1   SD

H. Measurement procedures are adequate.

    SA   5   4   3   2   1   SD

I. All procedures have been described in sufficient detail to permit a replication of the study.

    SA   5   4   3   2   1   SD

J. The participants have been adequately protected from potential harm.

    SA   5   4   3   2   1   SD

K. The results are clearly described.

    SA   5   4   3   2   1   SD

L. The discussion/conclusion is appropriate.

    SA   5   4   3   2   1   SD

M. Despite any flaws, the report is worthy of publication.

    SA   5   4   3   2   1   SD

Article 40

Revised Susceptibility, Benefits, and Barriers Scale for Mammography Screening

Victoria L. Champion[*]

ABSTRACT. The purpose of this research was to revise scales measuring perceived susceptibility to breast cancer and perceived benefits and barriers to mammography utilization. A total of 618 women age 50 and over who were enrolled in a large intervention study participated in data collection. Scales were revised beginning with focus group input. Analyses included internal consistency reliability, test–retest reliability, factor analysis, confirmatory analysis, and known group techniques to test construct validity. Internal consistency ranged from .75 to .88, and test reliabilities from .59 to .72. Construct validity was confirmed with exploratory and confirmatory factor analyses, as well as known group techniques. Overall, these scales represent an improvement in those previously reported.

From *Research in Nursing & Health*, *22*, 341–348. Copyright © 1999 by John Wiley & Sons, Inc. Reprinted with permission.

Breast cancer mortality is beginning to decrease in white women across all age groups, with deaths decreasing by approximately 6% from 1989 to 1992 (Chevarley & White, 1997). This mortality decline is
5 thought to be due mainly to mammography screening. Although this trend is encouraging, statistics for overall mortality are still problematic. It is estimated that in 1999 approximately 43,300 women will die of breast cancer (Landis, Murray, Bolden & Wingo, 1999). Be-
10 cause mammography has been shown to decrease breast cancer mortality by 25%–35% in women age 50 and over when consistently used, it is extremely important to maintain screening in this age group (Andersson et al., 1988; Roberts et al., 1990; Shapiro, 1989;
15 Shapiro, Venet, Strax, Venet, & Roeser, 1982; Tabar & Dean, 1987).

Most current estimates are that between 20% and 50% of women 40 and over have the recommended yearly mammograms (Chevarley & White, 1997). In-
20 terventions based upon the Health Belief Model (HBM) variables of perceived susceptibility, benefits, and barriers (Becker, 1974) have been shown to increase breast cancer screening significantly (Champion & Huster, 1995). Previous development of susceptibil-
25 ity, benefits, and barriers scales related to mammogra-

phy has been useful in both descriptive and intervention work in general populations (Champion, 1993; 1995). The current work extends instrument development to a Health Maintenance Organization (HMO)
30 population. The purpose of the current research was to test revised scales measuring susceptibility to breast cancer and benefits and barriers related to mammography screening for validity and reliability in an HMO and general medicine clinic population.
35 Perceived susceptibility and perceived severity were together identified as a threat and initially combined in the HBM as a predictor of preventive behaviors (Becker, 1974). Theoretically, before health-promoting behaviors will occur, a threat must be rec-
40 ognized. In the case of mammography, a woman must perceive both that breast cancer is serious and that there is a possibility that she is personally at risk for breast cancer. Because little variance usually is found in breast cancer severity, perceived susceptibility alone
45 is used as the threat variable. An increase in perceived susceptibility has been linked to an increase in breast cancer screening (Stein, Fox, Murata, & Morisky, 1992; Zapka, Hosmer, Constanza, Harris, & Stoddard, 1992).
50 In addition to perceived susceptibility, perceived benefits to taking action and perceived barriers to action are central constructs of the HBM. Perceived benefits refer to the perception of positive outcomes thought to accrue from a behavior. In the case of mammogra-
55 phy screening, benefits relate to the potential to discover breast cancer early, thereby avoiding death. Perceived barriers refer to negative attributes related to the health action. For mammography screening, barriers might include fear of cancer, pain, cost, time, or fear of
60 radiation. Theoretically, a perception of more benefits to screening combined with perception of few barriers will be associated with breast cancer screening. Many investigators have verified the usefulness of perceived benefits and barriers in predicting mammography be-
65 havior. They have demonstrated that increased benefits and decreased barriers are linked to increased screening (Champion, 1992; Rakowski et al., 1992; Rakowski, Rimer, & Bryant, 1993; Slenker & Grant, 1989; Tho-

[*]*Victoria L. Champion*, Mary Margaret Walther professor of nursing and associate dean for research, Indiana University School of Nursing.

mas, Fox, Leake, & Roetzheim, 1996). In addition, in
several intervention studies investigators have demonstrated the usefulness of including these constructs in
communication messages designed to increase screening (Champion & Huster, l995; King et al., 1993;
Rimer et al., 1992). Beliefs about susceptibility, benefits, and barriers have been found to differentiate
women in various stages related to mammography
compliance (Champion & Skinner, 1999; Skinner,
Champion, Gonin, & Hanna, 1997). In order to test
theoretical relationships between revised scale scores
and stages of compliance with screening recommendations, the Transtheoretical Model was used in this study
(Rakowski et al., 1993). The conceptual definitions in
this study, which also were used for previous instrument development, are shown in Table 1.

The stages of precontemplation, contemplation, action, relapse precontemplation, and relapse contemplation were used. In the Transtheoretical Model, any behavior change or adoption is conceptualized as a continuum. Action is defined as current compliance.
Women may also relapse or become noncompliant
after initial screening. They are then staged as relapse
precontemplation or relapse contemplation.

The ability to identify the relationships between
susceptibility, benefits and barriers, and compliance
with mammography recommendations has been critical
in determining their influence on screening behavior.
The perceived susceptibility to breast cancer scale was
developed and reported initially in 1984 (Champion,
1984) and underwent subsequent revision (Champion,
1993). Benefits and barriers scales for mammography
were developed later and reported by Champion
(1995). Initial development of the perceived susceptibility scale as reported by Champion (1984) started
with extensive review of the theoretical and empirical
literature. Initially, 20–24 items were written to measure susceptibility. Content validity was established
through a panel of eight judges who were familiar with
the HBM. Items were retained if there was a 75%
agreement among judges. Approximately half of the
original items reached the 75% agreement criterion. All
items were anchored with a five-point Likert scale with
response options from "strongly agree" to "strongly
disagree." Data were collected with a general population.

The susceptibility scale as initially developed retained six items after factor analysis and item deletion
(Champion, 1984). The initial testing of the susceptibility scale demonstrated beginning validity and reliability. The susceptibility scale was revised again using a
random sample of 581 women (Champion, 1993). Content validity was judged by an expert panel consisting
of nationally known researchers and theoreticians. A
consensus of three experts was necessary for item retention. Five items were retained in this analysis for
susceptibility. Exploratory factor analysis was completed and all items loaded at .84 or above on the sus-

ceptibility factor. A Cronbach alpha of .93 was realized
with a test–retest reliability of .70. Predictive validity
was demonstrated when susceptibility was significantly
correlated with breast cancer screening behavior.

Table 1
Conceptual Definitions of Major Study Variables

Perceived suscep- tibility	Perceived beliefs of personal threat or harm related to breast cancer
Perceived benefits (mammo- graphy)	Perceived positive outcomes of obtaining a mammogram
Perceived barriers	Perceived emotional, physical or structural concerns related to mammography behaviors
Precontemplation	Never had a mammogram and not thinking about having one in the next 6 months
Contemplation	Never had a mammogram but thinking about having one in the next 6 months
Action	Had a mammogram within the last 15 months
Relapse precon- templation	Last mammogram 15 months ago or more and not thinking about having one in the next 6 months
Relapse contem- plation	Last mammogram 15 months ago or more and thinking about hav- ing one in the next 6 months

The initial benefits and barriers scales were developed in relation to the behavior of breast self-
examination and reported by Champion (1984). They
included a total of five benefits items and eight barriers
items. The two scales were found to have Cronbach's
alpha of .61 and .76, respectively. This scale was revised in 1995 (Champion, 1995) to reflect benefits and
barriers to mammography. Because benefits and barriers for mammography may be different from those for
Breast Self-Examination (BSE), a thorough examination of the literature and theory was completed again
prior to the revision. Items were developed on the basis
of literature and theoretical definitions. Eight items
initially were developed for each scale and sent to a
panel of experts for content validity. The benefits and
barriers to mammography scales were tested at the
same time the second testing for the susceptibility scale
was done. A total of 581 women participated. Confirmatory factor analysis supported construct validity.
Confirmatory factor analysis revealed factor loadings
of .44 or above for each of six benefits items and five
barriers items. Correlational analysis confirmed theoretical relationships, further supporting validity. The
Cronbach alpha was .79 for the benefit scale and .73
for the barrier scale. Test–retest correlations were
somewhat lower, as reported in the summary by
Champion (1995). This was thought to reflect actual
changes in attitudes rather than inconsistency across
measurements. The current work required scales that
were valid and reliable for an HMO population. Valid-

ity and reliability are sample specific; therefore, further testing was required.

Method

Participants

Revision of the HBM scales took place within a large intervention study to increase breast cancer screening in women age 50 and over (*N* = 804) who were members of an HMO and general medicine clinic.

The mean age of participants was 61.15 (*SD* = 9.66). Mean educational level was 12.5 years (*SD* = 2.70). Forty-six percent were married, 25% widowed, and 21% divorced. The remaining participants were never married, living with a partner, or separated. Sixty-eight percent were Caucasian and 30% African American, with the remainder being of Asian, Native American, or Hispanic descent. Eligibility criteria included being age 50 or over, not having had a mammogram in the last 15 months, not having had breast cancer, and being able to read and write English. There was a response rate of 39% from eligible women. Reasons for declining were related to hesitancy to commit to a longitudinal intervention study.

Instrument

The work of refinement began with a review of susceptibility, benefits, and barriers items from past work by the principal investigator and an advisory panel. In addition, items were presented to two focus groups of women age 50 and over to assess clarity of meaning. Women also were asked for additional items not included. Focus group comments did not contain any information suggesting needed changes in items. Prior results for the susceptibility scale indicated that all items were highly correlated; thus, two redundant items were deleted prior to testing. Three items were retained and related to perceived risk of developing breast cancer at different times in a woman's life.

Five items were retained for the benefit scale. The original item, "When I get a recommended mammogram, I feel good about myself" was deleted because it had the lowest factor loading in previous work. Other changes in benefits items were made after clarifications from a focus group. For example, a previous item, "Having a mammogram or x-ray of the breast will decrease my chances of requiring radical or disfiguring surgery for breast cancer," was changed to, "If I find a lump through a mammogram, my treatment for breast cancer may not be as bad." The items relating to decreased worry, finding breast lumps early, treatment not being as bad, best way of finding a very small lump, and decreasing chances of dying were retained.

The barriers scale also was revised. Initially, there were five items that respectively addressed worry about breast cancer, embarrassment, time, pain, and money. Items were added that related to understanding what will be done, knowing how to go about getting a mammogram, rudeness of personnel, radiation, remembering to schedule a mammogram, being too old to have a mammogram, and having other problems that are more important. The additional items were recommended as a result of the two focus group discussions. The original cost item was dropped because the current population had cost completely covered. The additional barriers are reflected in the new items. A total of 11 items were included on the revised scale. Items comprising the barrier scales do potentially represent different dimensions, raising the question of a homogeneous set of items. Past analysis has demonstrated unidimensionality of items; unidimensionality was reexamined as part of the work of revision.

Procedures

Eligible women from the HMO were identified by computer and sent an introductory letter signed by the medical director of the HMO. This letter was followed by a telephone call from a research assistant, who further described the study and asked each woman if she would be willing to participate. If agreement was obtained, the participant was sent an informed consent statement and a questionnaire that included the scales for susceptibility, benefits, and barriers. Upon return of the completed questionnaire, women were assigned to a control or intervention group. Following intervention, a second data collection occurred, via a mailed questionnaire. In this report, the second data set was used for test–retest calculations. Because the intervention may have changed actual beliefs, only control group women were used for test–retest computations.

Eligibility criteria were the same for the general medicine clinic, but the procedure was slightly different at this site. Again, a computer-generated list of eligible women was developed. These women then were approached by a research assistant when they came to the clinic for an appointment. If they agreed to be in the study, informed consent was completed, and the questionnaire data were collected at this time. After entry into the study, the same procedure was used for randomization of the intervention delivery and follow-up data collection.

Results

Construct Validity

The construct validity of the revised 19 items was examined using two types of factor analysis. First, an exploratory factor analysis using principal components extraction with a varimax rotation was completed. Varimax rotation was selected because the items were expected to factor into three independent scales. A varimax rotation provides a solution that is often more conceptually clear than oblique rotation (Kim & Mueller, 1978). Three factors were selected and accounted for 54% of the variance. The three factors also represented eigenvalues that were greater than 1. The rotated factor matrix using all 19 items with a forced three-factor solution is presented in Table 2. Factor extraction was guided by theory and eigenvalues, as well as the criterion that items greater than .4 would be retained, as suggested by Nunnally (1978). As can be seen in Table 2, all items loaded on their respective factors at .4 or above. Susceptibility items loaded on Factor 3 and all had high loadings with Factor 3 (.87 or above). Benefit items loaded on Factor 2 and again were correlated strongly, yielding loadings between .55 and .75. Barrier items loaded on Factor 1 with loadings between .48 to .79. Items did not overlap scales. That is, after loading on a primary scale, the same item did not load at above .3 on any other scale.

Table 2
Exploratory Factor Analyses for Scale Items

	Factor 1	Factor 2	Factor 3
SUS 1			.91
SUS 2			.89
SUS 3			.87
BEN 1		.55	
BEN 2		.71	
BEN 3		.73	
BEN 4		.75	
BEN 5		.75	
BAR 1	.64		
BAR 2	.72		
BAR 3	.68		
BAR 4	.79		
BAR 5	.75		
BAR 6	.64		
BAR 7	.66		
BAR 8	.64		
BAR 9	.48		
BAR 10	.67		
BAR 11	.70		

Note. SUS = susceptibility; BEN = benefits; BAR = barriers.

Items also were subjected to confirmatory factor analysis using LISREL (Joreskog & Sorbom, 1989). Exploratory factor analysis is limited in that possible relationships are not reconfirmed and data to establish a relationship are not based on theory. The measurement model of LISREL allowed exploration of how well the latent variables (susceptibility, benefits, and barriers) were measured by the items. Confirmatory factor analysis has advantages over an exploratory approach in that relationships are hypothesized between the observed variables and latent variables; thus, it tests how well items fit with theoretical concepts. A covariance matrix of the 19 items was used as input in testing the model. Fit of the model to the data was tested by the Goodness of Fit Index, which is a measure of similarity between the correlation matrix analyzed and that predicted by the estimated model. Boyd, Frye, and Aaronson (1988) suggest that a value of close to .9 is a good fit. The Goodness of Fit ratio for these data was .87 and *t* values for each item were tested for fit with each latent construct. All *t* values, shown in Table 3, were significant for each item and for the identified

latent variable. Lambda values, which are interpreted like factor loadings, ranged from .68 to .90 for the susceptibility scale, .40 to .83 for the benefit scale, and .44 to .69 for the barrier scale.

Reliability

Item analysis was completed using two criteria established by Nunnally (1978). In order to identify poorly functioning items, an increase of more than .10 in the total scale reliability when that item was deleted or correlation of less than .30 between an item and the total subscale score was identified. All items on the susceptibility score met the criteria for inclusion, and a standardized item alpha of .87 was obtained for the final scale. The three items each correlated with the scale at .72 or above. For the benefit scale, corrected item-total correlations revealed all items to be between .37 and .57. Deleting items did not increase the alpha. A final standardized item alpha of .75 was obtained. The barrier scale had 11 items, all of which correlated at .41 or above on the corrected item-total scale. Deleting any item would not have increased the standardized item alpha significantly; therefore, all items were retained. A final standardized alpha of .88 was obtained.

For women in the control group, Time 2 data collection followed Time 1 by about 6 weeks. All test–retest correlations for control group women were significant at the .01 level: perceived susceptibility ($r =$ .62), perceived benefits ($r = .61$), and perceived barriers ($r = .71$).

Predictive Validity

Theoretically, scale scores should be different for groups of women in different stages of mammography action. Questions were asked about mammography history, date of last mammogram, and whether the women intended to have one in the next 6 months at both Time 1 and Time 2. Answers to these questions were combined in computer-defined statements that characterized women as in a precontemplation, contemplation, action, relapse precontemplation, or relapse contemplation stage. To test theoretical relationships between scale scores and stage of mammography compliance, one-way analysis of variance was computed followed by Tukey's post hoc tests. Results are displayed in Table 4. Because some women became compliant 6 weeks following intervention, the action stage was relevant for women who had obtained mammograms. Both benefits and barriers had extremely significant overall *F* values, while susceptibility had a lower but significant overall *F* value. For the overall benefit score, precontemplators were significantly different from contemplators, relapse contemplators, or those in action, indicating that those who had never had a mammogram and did not intend to have one did not perceive as many benefits to the procedure as did those who had either had a mammogram in the past or were currently compliant. Relapse precontemplators were different from relapse contemplators or those in action,

Table 3
Confirmatory Factor Loadings for Scale Items

	Lambda	*t* Value
Susceptibility		
1. It is likely that I will get breast cancer.	.68	20.59
2. My chances of getting breast cancer in the next few years are great.	.90	25.92
3. I feel I will get breast cancer sometime during my life.	.77	20.93
Benefits		
1. If I get a mammogram and nothing is found, I do not worry as much about breast cancer.	.40	9.08
2. Having a mammogram will help me find breast lumps early.	.51	
3. If I find a lump through a mammogram, my treatment for breast cancer may not be as bad.	.60	15.20
4. Having a mammogram is the best way for me to find a very small lump.	.73	15.36
5. Having a mammogram will decrease my chances of dying from breast cancer.	.83	18.73
Barriers		
1. I am afraid to have a mammogram because I might find out something is wrong.	.56	14.99
2. I am afraid to have a mammogram because I don't understand what will be done.	.51	17.75
3. I don't know how to go about getting a mammogram.	.44	16.18
4. Having a mammogram is too embarrassing.	.69	21.22
5. Having a mammogram takes too much time.	.60	19.15
6. Having a mammogram is too painful.	.68	13.99
7. People doing mammograms are rude to women.	.56	15.78
8. Having a mammogram exposes me to unnecessary radiation.	.57	16.01
9. I cannot remember to schedule a mammogram.	.47	11.06
10. I have other problems more important than getting a mammogram.	.58	15.92
11. I am too old to need a routine mammogram.	.53	16.45

indicating that those who had not thought about mammograms perceived fewer benefits than those who had one in the past and were thinking about getting one or those currently compliant. Perceived barriers demonstrated even greater differences. Those who had never had a mammogram had significantly higher barrier scores than those who had either had one and relapsed or were currently in action. All other groups had significantly higher barrier scores than those currently in action.

Women were divided into compliant and noncompliant groups 6 weeks post intervention. Three independent *t* tests were computed using the dependent variables of susceptibility, benefits, and barriers respectively. For susceptibility, a significant difference between groups did not emerge. For benefits, the difference was significant ($t(2,676) = 2.88$, $p = .004$), with those who became compliant perceiving more benefits. For the barrier scale, a more significant difference emerged ($t(2,665) = 7.28$, $p \leq .001$), with compliant women having the fewest perceived barriers.

Discussion

Findings reported in this manuscript reflect the continued revision of susceptibility, benefits, and barriers scales for mammography utilization. Overall, both validity and reliability were confirmed with the revised scales.

Content validity was improved by having both expert and focus groups of women react to items. On the basis of these results, changes were made, including deleting some susceptibility items and adding some barrier items. Construct validity was tested using both exploratory and confirmatory factor analysis because they represent different conceptual processes in establishing validity. Unidimensionality of all three scales was supported by both exploratory factor analyses and confirmatory factor analyses. Even with three items, the susceptibility scale retained very high correlations among individual items, as identified both by the exploratory and confirmatory factor analyses. This was consistent with the past work on the version of the susceptibility scale that included five items (Champion, 1993).

The benefits and barriers scales also demonstrated strong construct validity, with high correlations between items and the respective scales for both exploratory and confirmatory analysis. Overall, correlations were stronger for these revised items than for previously reported scales (Champion, 1995). Correlations of benefits items with the respective scale revealed all items above .57 on factor analyses, higher than what was reported previously (Champion, 1993). In addition, using factor analysis, most of the barrier items also evidenced higher correlations than reported previously (Champion, 1995), again providing evidence of improved construct validity.

Theoretically, these scales also should be related to stage of mammography compliance. Using data from 6 weeks post intervention, all three scales did differentiate between women who were at different stages of mammography compliance. Skinner et al. (1997) demonstrated similar results for both benefits and barriers. Thus, given the short timeframe for follow-up, the scales were consistent and theoretical relationships were upheld. It is probable that these results do not reflect the full potential of these scales to predict compliance. More women might have become compliant if

Table 4
Scale Differences by Mammography Stage

	Precontemplation (a)		Contemplation (b)		Relapse Precontemplation (c)		Relapse Contemplation (d)		Action (e)	
	M	SD	M	SD	M	SD	M	SD	M	SD
Susceptibility										
	6.51	5.33	7.38	2.44	6.93	2.50	7.40	2.43	7.47	2.54
$F(4,654) = 2.46, p = .04$										
Benefits										
	17.98	4.33	20.26	2.30	19.01	3.55	20.23	2.96	20.55	3.09
$F(4,673) = 9.26, p = .001$; a diff b, d, e; c diff d, e										
Barriers										
	26.12	6.63	26.37	4.84	22.65	6.35	20.12	6.55	17.92	5.30
$F(4,662) = 26.49, p = .001$; a, b diff c, d, e; c diff d, e										

measurements had been taken 2–3 months post intervention, as it often takes 1 or 2 months to obtain a mammography appointment.

Overall, items reflected strong internal consistency reliability and test–retest reliability. The susceptibility scale showed a slight decrease in internal consistency reliability with only three items: .87 for the current data as compared to .93 reported previously (Champion, 1993). This decrease in internal consistency reliability is not considered significant. The test–retest reliability for susceptibility was somewhat decreased at .62. Because test–retest reliability may be due to inconsistency within the scale or to actual changes in attitude, however, a correlation of .62 is considered acceptable (Carmines & Zeller, 1990). Both benefits and barriers scales were relatively stable as compared to previous work. Internal consistency reliability for the barriers scale was increased (.88) as compared to .73 in the previous work. Test–retest reliabilities were higher for both benefits and barriers. For the current data, test–retest reliability was .61 for benefits and .71 for barriers as compared to previous findings (Champion, 1995) of .38 for benefits and .60 for barriers. Overall, these differences seemed to reflect changes for the better in both mammography barriers and benefits scales.

All three scales have potential use for nursing practice and research. The constructs of susceptibility, benefits, and barriers have been shown in past work to be related to mammography behavior (Aiken, West, Woodward, & Reno, 1994; Champion & Huster, 1995; Hyman, Baker, Ephraim, Moadel, & Philip, 1994; Rakowski et al., 1992; Rakowski, Fulton, & Feldman, 1993). Results of this past research, along with current results, indicate that the scales are valid and reliable. The susceptibility scale was refined to include only three items, which maintained good validity and reliability. The benefit scale was clarified, with five items retained. The barrier scale was enlarged somewhat to reflect additional barriers identified by women currently considering mammography utilization. Validity and reliability should be reassessed with each new population. Research interventions to promote change could include modification of risk perceptions, benefits

perceptions, or barriers perceptions. For example, if a woman did not believe she was susceptible to breast cancer, she could be counseled on her individual risk profile. The benefits of mammography could be discussed. Finally, individual barriers could be identified and joint solutions to overcome these barriers developed. Because scales have been thoroughly tested, research using these constructs is supported. The scales also are useful in that they may be quickly administered in a clinical situation, and they allow for immediate assessments and interventions based upon the results.

The current study has several limitations. First, there was a short timeframe for assessment of mammography compliance following the intervention, which may not have allowed all women who were so disposed to obtain mammography. Second, mammography behavior was based on self-reports. Finally, although the constructs were related to mammography, the variance accounted for is not complete. Additional predictors need to be identified.

References

Aiken, L. S., West, S. G., Woodward, C. K., & Reno, R. R. (1994). Health beliefs and compliance with mammography-screening recommendations in asymptomatic women. *Health Psychology, 13*, 122–129.

Andersson, I., Aspegren, K., Janzon, L., Landberg, T., Lindholm, K., Linell, F., Ljunberg, O., Ranstam, J., & Sigfusson, B. (1988). Mammographic screening and mortality from breast cancer: The Malmo Mammographic Screening Trial. *British Journal of Medicine, 297*, 943–948.

Becker, M. H. (Ed.). (1974). The Health Belief Model and personal health behavior. Thorofare, NJ: Charles B. Slack.

Boyd, C. J., Frye, M. A., & Aaronson, L. S. (1988). Structural equation models and nursing research. Part I. *Nursing Research, 37*, 249–252.

Carmines, E., & Zeller, R. (1990). Reliability and validity assessment. Newbury Park, CA: Sage.

Champion, V. L. (1984). Instrument development for Health Belief Model constructs. *ANS: Advances in Nursing Science, 6*, 73–85.

Champion, V. L. (1992). The relationship of age to factors influencing breast self-examination practice. *Health Care for Women International, 13*, 1–9.

Champion, V. L. (1993). Instrument refinement for breast cancer screening behaviors. *Nursing Research, 42*, 139–143.

Champion, V. L. (1995). Development of a benefits and barriers scale for mammography utilization. *Cancer Nursing, 18*, 53–59.

Champion, V. L., & Huster, G. (1995). Effect of interventions on stage of mammography adoption. *Journal of Behavioral Medicine, 18*, 169–187.

Champion, V. L., & Skinner, C. S. (1999). Differences in perceptions of risk, benefits, and barriers by stage of mammography adoption. Manuscript submitted for publication.

Chevarley, F., & White, E. (1997). Recent trends in breast cancer mortality among white and black U.S. women. *American Journal of Public Health, 87*, 775–781.

Hyman, R. B., Baker, S., Ephraim, R., Moadel, A., & Philip, J. (1994). Health belief model variables as predictors of screening mammography utilization. *Journal of Behavioral Medicine, 17,* 391–406.

Joreskog, K. G., & Sorbom, D. (1989). LISREL VII: A guide to the program and applications. (2nd ed.) Chicago: Scientific Software, Inc.

Kim, J., & Mueller, C. W. (1978). Factor analyses: Statistical methods and practical solutions. Beverly Hills, CA: Sage.

King, E. S., Resch, N., Rimer, B., Lerman, C., Boyce, A., & McGovern-Gorchov, P. (1993). Breast cancer screening practices among retirement community women. *Preventive Medicine, 22,* 1–19.

Landis, S., Murray, T., Bolden, S., & Wingo, P. (1999). *Cancer statistics. CA: A Cancer Journal for Clinicians, 49,* 8–32.

Nunnally, J. C. Psychometric theory (2nd Ed.). McGraw-Hill Publishing Co.: New York, 1978.

Rakowski, W., Dube, C. E., Marcus, B. H., Prochaska, J. O., Velicer, W., & Abrams, D. B. (1992). Assessing elements of women's decisions about mammography. *Health Psychology, 11,* 111–118.

Rakowski, W., Fulton, J. P., & Feldman, J. (1993). Women's decision making about mammography: A replication of the relationship between stages of adoption and decisional balance. *Health Psychology, 12,* 209–214.

Rakowski, W., Rimer, B. K., & Bryant, S. A. (1993). Integrating behavior and intention regarding mammography by respondents in the 1990 National Health Interview Survey of health promotion and disease prevention. *Public Health Reports, 108,* 605–624.

Rimer, B. K., Resch, N., King, E., Ross, E., Lerman, C., Boyce, A., Kessler, H., & Engstrom, P. F. (1992). Multistrategy health education program to increase mammography use among women ages 65 and older. *Public Health Reports, 107,* 369–380.

Roberts, M. M., Alexander, F. E., Anderson, T. J., Chetty, U., Donnan, P. T., Forrest, P., Hepburn, W., Huggins, A., Kirkpatrick, A. E., Lamb, J., Muir, B. B., & Prescott, R. J. (1990). Edinburgh trial of screening for breast cancer: Mortality at seven years. *The Lancet, 335,* 241–246.

Shapiro, S. (1989). Determining the efficacy of breast cancer screening. *Cancer, 63,* 1873–1880.

Shapiro, S., Venet, W., Strax, P., Venet, L., & Roeser, R. (1982). Prospects for eliminating racial differences in breast cancer survival rates. *American Journal of Public Health, 72,* 1142–1145.

Skinner, C. S., Champion, V. L., Gonin, R., & Hanna, M. (1997). Do perceived barriers and benefits vary by mammography stage? *Psychology, Health and Medicine, 2,* 65–75.

Slenker, S. E., & Grant, M. C. (1989). Attitudes, beliefs, and knowledge about mammography among women over forty years of age. *Journal of Cancer Education, 4,* 61–65.

Stein, J. A., Fox, S. A., Murata, P. J., & Morisky, D. E. (1992). Mammography usage and the Health Belief Model. *Health Education Quarterly, 19,* 447–462.

Tabar, L., & Dean, P. B. (1987). The control of breast cancer through mammography screening. What is the evidence? *Radiologic Clinics of North America, 25,* 993–1005.

Thomas, L., Fox, S., Leake, B., & Roetzheim, R. (1996). The effects of health beliefs on screening mammography utilization among a diverse sample of older women. *Women and Health, 24,* 77–91.

Zapka, J. G., Hosmer, D., Constanza, M. E., Harris, D. R., & Stoddard, A. (1992). Changes in mammography use: Economic, need, and service factors. *American Journal of Public Health, 82,* 1345–1351.

Note: Grant sponsor: National Center for Nursing Research (NIH). Grant sponsor: National Cancer Institute (NCI); grant number: R01 CA 58606.

Address correspondence to: Victoria L. Champion, Indiana University School of Nursing, 1111 Middle Drive, Indianapolis, IN 46202.

Exercise for Article 40

Factual Questions

1. The acronym HBM stands for what words?

2. In the initial development of the perceived susceptibility scale by Champion (1984), how was content validity established?

3. Why were only control group women used for test–retest computations?

4. As a result of the exploratory factor analyses, the researcher states, "Items did not overlap." What does this statement mean?

5. What is the value of *r* for the test–retest reliability of the perceived benefits scale determined using the control group women?

6. According to Table 4, which group had the highest mean benefits score? What was their mean score?

7. According to Table 4, which group had the lowest mean benefits score? What was their mean score?

Questions for Discussion

8. In lines 160–162, the researcher states, "Validity and reliability are sample specific; therefore, further testing was required." In your own words, explain what you think the researcher means by this statement.

9. In lines 199–204, the researcher describes how the wording of one item was changed. Do you think that the change improved the item? Explain.

10. In lines 227–253, the researcher describes how participants were recruited for the study. However, the researcher does not specify the percentage who declined to participate. Would you be interested in having this information? Why? Why not?

11. The items for the three scales are presented in Table 3. What is your opinion of the items?

12. The researcher states that mammography behavior was based on self-reports, which is a limitation of the study. In your opinion, how important is this limitation? (See lines 481–482.)

13. Has this study convinced you that the three scales are reasonably reliable and valid for the participants who were tested? Explain.

Quality Ratings

Directions: Indicate your level of agreement with each of the following statements by circling a number from 5 for strongly agree (SA) to 1 for strongly disagree (SD). If you believe an item is not applicable to this research article, leave it blank. Be prepared to explain your ratings. When responding to criteria A and B below, keep in mind that brief titles and abstracts are conventional in published research.

A. The title of the article is appropriate.

      SA   5   4   3   2   1   SD

B. The abstract provides an effective overview of the research article.

      SA   5   4   3   2   1   SD

C. The introduction establishes the importance of the study.

      SA   5   4   3   2   1   SD

D. The literature review establishes the context for the study.

      SA   5   4   3   2   1   SD

E. The research purpose, question, or hypothesis is clearly stated.

      SA   5   4   3   2   1   SD

F. The method of sampling is sound.

      SA   5   4   3   2   1   SD

G. Relevant demographics (for example, age, gender, and ethnicity) are described.

      SA   5   4   3   2   1   SD

H. Measurement procedures are adequate.

      SA   5   4   3   2   1   SD

I. All procedures have been described in sufficient detail to permit a replication of the study.

      SA   5   4   3   2   1   SD

J. The participants have been adequately protected from potential harm.

      SA   5   4   3   2   1   SD

K. The results are clearly described.

      SA   5   4   3   2   1   SD

L. The discussion/conclusion is appropriate.

      SA   5   4   3   2   1   SD

M. Despite any flaws, the report is worthy of publication.

      SA   5   4   3   2   1   SD

Article 41

Nurse Entrance Test Scores:
A Predictor of Success

Sherri Orso Ellis, MSN, RN[*]

ABSTRACT. A program evaluation was conducted to determine if requiring higher scores on critical thinking components of the Nurse Entrance Test would have a positive effect on the percentage of students that could be retained in a diploma nursing program. The program evaluation revealed that using the Nurse Entrance Test as a tool for admissions screening, specifically portions of the examination that predict critical thinking, was effective in helping to predict success through level 1 nursing courses.

From *Nurse Educator*, *31*, 259–263. Copyright © 2006 by Lippincott Williams & Wilkins, Inc. Reprinted with permission.

According to the U.S. Department of Health and Human Services,[1] anticipated shortages in numbers of nurses available to meet healthcare needs in the United States will reach 29% by the year 2020 if current trends
5 remain unchanged. A dwindling supply of qualified faculty in nursing schools throughout the country further compounds the problem by limiting the number of applicants who can be accepted into nursing programs. Student attrition becomes a major focus as nursing
10 programs attempt to discover and implement effective interventions aimed at increasing retention rates.[2]

Statistics reported by the National Council of State Boards of Nursing reveal that the number of first time applicants sitting for the NCLEX-RN, the national li-
15 censure examination for registered nurses, decreased by 20% from 1995 to 2003.[2] Additional data from the U.S. Department of Health and Human Services indicate declining numbers of graduates from diploma, associate degree (AD), and baccalaureate programs.
20 Only 4% of graduates in 1999 were from diploma programs compared with 9% in 1992. This is partially due to the fact that over the past few decades, many hospital-based diploma programs have closed.[1] The latest data compiled and reported by the National League for
25 Nursing (NLN) reveal that as of the year 2000, only 78 diploma nursing programs remained in operation.[3] The need exists to make the most efficient use of available resources, faculty, and allocated dollars by implement-

ing measures to effectively lower attrition rates in
30 schools of nursing.[2]

The only diploma program offered in the state of Louisiana is the Baton Rouge General Medical Center School of Nursing (BRGMC SON), located in the capital city of Baton Rouge. The school's mission is to
35 prepare registered nurses for entry-level practice. The program is designed for completion over a 3-year period. Major components include 25 hours of prerequisite college credit in specific core courses, 3 levels of intense coursework, and a substantial number of hours
40 focused on clinical experiences.

Background

As with most nursing programs, the director and faculty of BRGMC SON were concerned about high attrition rates. Since 1998, the school has used the Nurse Entrance Test (NET) as a tool for the identifica-
45 tion of qualified applicants. Informal trending of NET scores and student performance data compiled by the director of the school of nursing revealed that after admission to the program, approximately one-third of the students were not successfully passing level 1
50 courses. Trended data of NET scores suggested that candidates with lower scores on areas of the test that predicted critical thinking ability were more likely to be unsuccessful. This initial observation prompted the admissions committee to adopt a change in admission
55 criteria.[4]

Change in Admission Criteria

Prior to 2005, candidates for admission were required to complete 8 specific college credit courses with a grade of "C" or better, maintain a grade point average of at least 2.7, and provide evidence that they
60 had completed a computer literacy course and either a high school or college chemistry course with a grade of "C" or better. Candidates were required to take the NET, achieve a composite percentile of 50 or better, and score an average of 50 or better on the "critical
65 thinking appraisal" section of the test. With the change in admission criteria, applicants accepted into the program in the spring of 2005 were required to meet higher standards for admission with regard to NET

[*]*Sherri Orso Ellis* is instructor, School of Nursing, Baton Rouge General Medical Center, Baton Rouge, LA.

scores. The required composite percentile remained 50 or above. However, in addition to this requirement, applicants for 2005 were required to score 50% or better on each component of the critical thinking appraisal portion of the NET. Components in this section include inferential reading, main idea of passage, and predicting of outcomes.

Need for Program Evaluation

To address the impact of this change, a committee was formed to compare retention in the program between before and after the change in admission criteria. To date, those admitted under the new criteria have completed level 1 nursing courses. These courses include pharmacology, fundamentals of nursing, and a course introducing medical–surgical nursing. The medical–surgical course incorporates basic medical–surgical topics, with an increased emphasis on pathophysiology.

A program evaluation project was initiated to determine if increasing the admissions criteria to require higher NET scores on portions of the examination that predict critical thinking ability would result in a higher percentage of students being retained in the program. A secondary purpose of this evaluation was to determine if increased NET scores on the critical thinking analysis portion of the examination significantly increased the proportion of students retained at the end of level 1 nursing courses.

Review of Literature

The NET, developed by Educational Resources, Inc. (ERI), is a diagnostic instrument used by diploma, AD, and baccalaureate nursing programs as part of admissions criteria and as a tool for identifying "at-risk" student populations. The NET provides diagnostic scores for essential skills areas, including math, reading comprehension, reading rate, critical thinking appraisal, test-taking skills, and learning styles. The test also scores certain nonacademic indicators, such as stress level and social interaction in addition to providing composite percentages and percentile scores. All or some of these scores may be used as diagnostic tools or for screening purposes, depending on individual institution needs.[5]

Although use of the NET varies, several researchers have published studies on the use of the NET as a predictor of student success. One study conducted by Sayles et al.[6] sought to determine if there was a positive correlation between NET and PreRN scores, successful completion of an AD program, and subsequent success on NCLEX-RN. Sayles et al. documented that maintaining a higher grade point average (numerical value not assigned) for nursing-related courses, math, reading, and NET composite scores, the PreRN composite score, and the grade earned on the highest level nursing course, which teaches concepts related to circulation and oxygenation, were all found to have statistical significance. The results of this study indicated

that standardized tests such as the NET could be successfully used as tools to screen applicants for admission, predict success in nursing programs, and to identify at-risk students.

Various studies[6–8] have helped to validate the premise that early identification and intervention for students categorized as at risk can help improve retention and increase the likelihood of academic success. The NET is often used as a tool to identify at-risk student populations. Students entering the AD nursing program at Texas Woman's University (TWU), many of whom speak English as a second language, are required to take the NET test. Data collected at this institution revealed that students who scored less than 55% on reading comprehension were more likely to be unsuccessful in the program. Based on these data, TWU developed the Student Success Program with the goal of improving retention. Students who fall into this at-risk group are required to enter the Student Success Program. Within this program, they participate in regular nursing courses along with additional courses specially designed to help them become expert learners, improve language and communication skills, and overcome cultural barriers. Although it is in its early stages, the program has shown to be successful in helping to retain students throughout the program.[7]

Symes et al.[9] reported a follow-up evaluation of the Nursing Success Program established at TWU in the fall of 2000. This program was established to identify at-risk nursing students and to provide early intervention, with the goal of increasing retention rates throughout the program. According to this report, the decision to use reading comprehension as a tool for the identification and advisement of this student population originated from earlier data showing a relationship between low reading comprehension scores on the NET and high attrition rates. Results of this study indicate that reading comprehension scores on the NET test have a significant relationship to retention in the nursing program.

Numerous studies to help validate the use of the NET as a predictor of success in nursing programs have been conducted by ERI. Simmons et al.[8] collected data from nursing programs in 12 states that used the NET as a part of admissions criteria or for screening at-risk student populations. The sample was representative of each of the 3 program types. Overall findings indicated that NET composite scores and reading comprehension scores were most significant in predicting student success. Higher NET scores on inferential reading were correlated with better critical thinking skills. It was determined that early identification of at-risk students may positively affect attrition rates by helping nursing programs to initiate early interventions aimed at retention.

In some instances, use of the NET as a predictor of success has been shown to have no significance. Gallagher et al.[10] studied a random sample of 121 students from William Rainey Harper College who took both the Registered Nurse Entrance Exam before admission and the NET before entering nursing courses in the fall 1995 term. Both the Registered Nurse Entrance Exam and the NET were examined for their ability to predict success in the first nursing course, and to determine if the NET would be a better predictor of success for use in their nursing program. The study revealed that with the exception of mathematics, NET scores had no significant relationship to success for students who scored a "C" or better compared with those who scored less than a "C" in the first nursing course.

Conceptual Framework

According to the NET Technical and Developmental Report published by ERI,[5(p32)] "the critical thinking appraisal of the NET has been reported to predict success in certain types of professions or instructional programs in which critical thinking is known to play an important role." The NET evaluates critical thinking ability by the participant's success on three sections of the test that include inferential reading, predicting outcomes, and main idea of passage. Developers of the NET propose that the mental activities required to execute the nursing process are analogous to the mental processes required to critically think and that the two processes are "closely related cognitive skills."[5(p33)]

Although there is an abundance of research that recognizes critical thinking as an essential core component of nursing, the concept can be hard to define. Hynes and Bennett[11(p26)] wrote that critical thinking, as defined by Fowler, is making informed and purposeful decisions by looking beyond the obvious and, as defined by Bittner and Tobin, as "a process influenced by knowledge and experience using strategies such as reflective thinking as a part of learning to identify the issues and opportunities and holistically synthesize the information in nursing practice." In a recent article, Turner[12] documented that critical thinking, although widely discussed and examined, has multiple definitions and lacks clarity. She cites the usage of overlapping terms such as *decision making*, *problem solving*, and *clinical reasoning* in the literature devoted to the concept of critical thinking. No matter how critical thinking is defined, most agree that it is required by nurses to practice in a safe and competent manner, with the ability to make sound judgments that will positively affect patient outcomes.

The Critical Thinking Model for Nursing Judgment, developed by Kataoka-Yahiro and Saylor,[13] provides insight into the process of critical thinking. This model dictates that critical thinking is not simply the nursing process. It is a process affected by five factors: experience, knowledge base, attitude, standards, and competencies. The authors make reference to the fact that the NLN includes criteria specific to critical thinking in its standards for accreditation. With this emphasis on critical thinking as a necessary component of nursing

curriculum, nurse educators are challenged to discover methods of measuring and evaluating students' ability to think critically.[13]

Methods

Sample

The population for this program evaluation consisted of students admitted into the nursing program in the spring of 2003, 2004, and 2005. The total sample size included 137 students. For the purpose of analysis, the groups were divided into those students admitted before changes in admission criteria ($n = 82$) and those admitted after changes in admission criteria ($n = 55$).

Protection of Rights

This evaluation process required no active subject participation. Approval to use data from school records was granted by the director of the school. All data were obtained from records on file with the school. Institutional Review Board approval was obtained from Southeastern Louisiana University prior to data collection.

Variables

The dependent variables in this evaluation were retention in the program, specifically retention at the end of level 1 nursing courses, and the status at the end of level 1 nursing courses. Independent variables included inferential reading, predicting outcomes, and main idea of passage scores on the NET exam. Other variables considered were age, gender, marital status, NET composite percentile, math and reading comprehension percentages, and semester of enrollment.

Design and Procedure

Descriptive statistics were examined to summarize the sample characteristics. A percentage was calculated for those students retained in the program at level 1 before and after changes in admissions criteria. A χ^2 analysis was performed to determine if a significant difference existed in the proportion of students retained in the program before and after the admissions criteria changes. Table 1 contains demographic data and represents percentages scored on the NET for the two groups.

Results

Data were analyzed using the SPSS program. The first group represents students who entered the program in 2003 and 2004, before the requirement of higher NET scores on the critical thinking analysis portion of the exam. According to percentages calculated between the two groups, 89.1% of the students in group 2 were retained at the end of level 1 nursing courses compared with 70.7% in group 1. At the end of level 1 nursing courses, 24 students (29.3%) were no longer in the program. Fifty-eight students (70.7%) were retained. Group 2 consisted of 55 students admitted in the spring of 2005, after the implementation of higher NET scores for admission. At the end of level 1 nursing courses,

Table 1
Demographic Characteristics of Students in Old and New Criteria

Variables	Old criteria (n = 82)		New criteria (n = 55)	
	n	%	n	%
Gender				
Male	13	15.9	4	7.3
Female	69	84.1	51	92.7
Marital status				
Married	38	46.3	18	32.7
Single	44	53.7	37	67.3
# of NET attempts				
1	61	74.4	34	61.8
> 1	21	25.6	21	38.2
NET composite percentile				
< 50	1	1.2	–	–
50–70	22	26.8	9	16.4
71–80	19	23.2	12	21.8
81–100	40	48.8	34	61.8
Math %				
< 50	1	1.2	–	–
50–70	20	24.4	16	29.1
71–80	43	52.4	20	36.4
81–100	18	22.0	19	34.5
Reading %				
< 50	–	–	–	–
26–50	2	2.4	–	–
51–75	54	65.9	32	58.2
> 75	26	31.7	23	41.8
Inferential reading %				
< 50	–	–	–	–
26–50	14	17.1	4	7.3
51–75	45	54.9	31	56.4
> 75	23	28.0	20	36.4
Main idea of passage %				
< 50	–	–	–	–
26–50	3	3.7	–	–
51–75	32	39.0	19	34.5
> 75	47	57.3	36	65.5
Predicting outcomes %				
< 50	–	–	–	–
26–50	13	15.9	2	3.6
51–75	61	74.4	50	90.9
> 75	8	9.8	3	5.5
Level 1 status				
Out of program	24	29.3	6	10.9
Retained	58	70.7	49	89.1

6 students (10.9%) were no longer in the program and 49 students (89.1%) were retained.

To determine statistical significance, a χ^2 analysis was performed; χ^2 is a nonparametric statistic that compares the actual number in a group with the expected number. The question answered by a χ^2 is if the expected number and the actual number within the groups that are being compared differ significantly. The χ^2 analysis of the 2 groups showed that a significantly higher proportion of students within group 2 were retained in the program at the end of level 1 nursing courses. With a sample size of 137 and 1 degree of freedom, χ^2 was equal to 6.488 ($\chi^2 = 6.488$, $df = 1$, $N = 137$). Statistical significance was established at the .05 level ($p = .011$).

Discussion

The program evaluation was conducted to determine if raising admission requirements to include higher expected scores on critical thinking portions of the NET would have a positive effect on the numbers of students that could be retained in the program. Research related to student success in diploma nursing programs is limited, and there is currently no research available on the use of NET scores as a predictor of success or as a screening tool for admissions in diploma nursing programs. However, the results of this evaluation are consistent with findings from research studies conducted with associate and baccalaureate nursing programs where NET scores were used to predict student success. Math and reading comprehension NET scores have shown to be useful in identifying at-risk students and providing direction when counseling and advising students and have been shown to have a positive correlation with success on NCLEX-RN.[6]

Although there are no research studies specific to diploma programs, research conducted with AD and baccalaureate programs showed that students who scored higher on the math and reading comprehension sections of the test were more likely to be successful in nursing programs.[5,6]

The results of the program evaluation indicate that a significantly higher proportion of students that were required to have higher critical thinking scores on the NET prior to admission were retained in the program through level 1 nursing courses. Although there is currently no research specific to the use of critical thinking portions of the NET as an admissions tool, there is a large segment of literature depicting critical thinking as a necessary component of nursing. A concept analysis conducted by Turner[12] on the subject of critical thinking found over 646 literary sources since 1981. The model of Kataoka-Yahiro and Saylor[13(p351)] was created to promote critical thinking as "an essential part of autonomous, excellent nursing practice." Nurses are routinely called upon to accurately assess the health needs of acutely ill patients and to respond with appropriate interventions. Because we know that knowledge alone is not enough to ensure safe actions and sound clinical judgment, nurse educators are challenged to incorporate the critical thinking component in their programs. The BRGMC SON places emphasis on clinical performance. Students are required to synthesize the knowledge attained in the classroom and demonstrate the ability to apply that knowledge in the clinical setting. This program evaluation indicates that using critical thinking NET scores may prove to be one effective method of identifying prospective students who possess critical thinking skills that can be further developed to foster success in the program.

The process of using higher critical thinking scores on the NET as an admissions tool for the BRGMC SON diploma program will require further evaluation. A follow-up study will be conducted after those students admitted to the spring 2005 class have completed the program and have had an opportunity to take the NCLEX-RN exam. Further analysis of data at that time will help determine if NET critical thinking scores can help predict success beyond level 1 nursing courses. Proportions of students retained throughout the program to graduation and eventual success on the NCLEX-RN examination will be evaluated to determine the effectiveness of critical thinking NET scores as an early predictor of success.

Limitations

There are several limitations that must be considered when reviewing the results of this program evaluation. First, this evaluation was conducted with data from a diploma nursing program. There are limited numbers of diploma programs still in operation throughout the United States. The results of this evaluation may not be applicable to other types of nursing programs. Second, changes in admissions criteria at this school of nursing became effective in the spring semester of 2005. At the time of this evaluation, students admitted for the year 2005 had completed only level 1 courses. Therefore, a determination of the effect of increased critical thinking NET scores throughout the program cannot yet be determined. Finally, the author recognizes that other extraneous variables, such as age, gender, marital status, and grade point average, exist and could possibly affect success or nonsuccess in the program.

Implications

Because of the growing shortage of nurses, the need exists for educators to find ways to identify the most qualified applicants and those who will most likely be successful in nursing programs. The results of this program evaluation have helped establish that using the NET critical thinking analysis as a screening tool for admissions may be one way to achieve this goal. A follow-up study is recommended to determine if critical thinking analysis NET scores will affect success beyond level 1 nursing courses.

Conclusion

Critical thinking is a necessary component of nursing practice. The use of purposeful, goal-directed thinking helps guide nurses as they use their experience, knowledge, and intuitiveness to make decisions that impact patient care.[14] Nursing faculty are being challenged to find ways to identify applicants with critical thinking skills and to foster those skills throughout their nursing programs to produce competent, skilled, novice nurses who have the ability to make sound clinical nursing judgments. Rote memorization and retention of knowledge are not enough.

Nursing faculty are charged with the task of identifying those nursing students with good critical thinking skills and helping to further develop the skills that will be necessary to synthesize information using the critical thinking process. Also, they have a responsibility to identify those students who are weak in the area of critical thinking and to use teaching methods that will help develop the ability to make sound decisions. This program evaluation indicates that using the critical thinking analysis portion of the NET in conjunction with other interventions can be an effective method of screening applicants for admission and helping identify those potential candidates that have a higher probability of success in early nursing courses.

References

1. Health Resources and Services Administration. Projected supply, demand, and shortages of registered nurses: 2000–2020. 2002. Available at: http://bhpr.gov/healthworkforce/reports/rnproject/default.htmAmerican. Accessed October 24, 2005.
2. Association of Colleges of Nursing. Nursing shortage fact sheet. Available at: http://www.aacn.nche.edu/Media/Backgrounders/shortagefacts.htm. October 24, 2005.
3. National League for Nursing. Table 407. Number of diploma nursing programs, students and graduates, academic years: 1975–76 to 1999–2000. Available at: http://bhpr.hrsa.gov/healthworkforce/reports/factbook02/FB407.htm. Accessed October 24, 2005.
4. Baton Rouge General School of Nursing. *A Diploma Program in Nursing [Brochure]*. Baton Rouge, LA: Baton Rouge General; 2004.
5. Educational Resources, Inc. *Nurse Entrance Test: Technical & Developmental Report*. Shawnee Mission, Kan: Educational Resources, Inc; 2004.
6. Sayles S, Shelton D, Powell H. Predictors of success in nursing education. *Assoc Black Nurs Faculty*. 2003;14(6):116–120.
7. Symes L, Tart K, Travis L, Toombs MS. Developing and retaining expert learners. *Nurse Educ*. 2002;27(5):227–231.
8. Simmons LE, Haupt GA, Davis L. *The Usefulness of the Nurse Entrance Test (NET) for Prediction of Successful Completion in a Nursing Program*. Shawnee Mission, Kan: Educational Resources, Inc; 2004.
9. Symes L, Tart K, Travis L. An evaluation of the Nursing Success Program. *Nurse Educ*. 2005;30(5):217–220.
10. Gallagher PA, Bomba C, Crane LR. Using an admissions exam to predict student success in an ADN program. *Nurse Educ*. 2001;26(3):132–135.
11. Hynes P, Bennett J. About critical thinking. *Can Assoc Crit Care Nurs*. 2004;15(3):26–29.
12. Turner P. Critical thinking in nursing education and practice as defined in the literature. *Nurs Educ Perspect*. 2005;26(5):272–277.
13. Kataoka-Yahiro M, Saylor C. A critical thinking model for nursing judgment. *J Nurs Educ*. 1994;33(8):351–356.
14. L'Eplattenier N. Tracing the development of critical thinking in baccalaureate nursing students. *J N Y State Nurses Assoc*. 2001;32(2);27–32.

Address correspondence to: Sherri Orso Ellis, School of Nursing, Baton Rouge General Medical Center, Baton Rouge, LA 70806, USA. E-mail: sherri.ellis@brgeneral.org

Exercise for Article 41

Factual Questions

1. The critical thinking portion of the NET contains what three components?

2. This study included how many participants who were admitted after changes in admission criteria?

3. Under the old criteria, what percentage of the participants were retained?

4. Under the new criteria, what percentage of the participants were retained?

5. Is the difference between the answers to Questions 3 and 4 statistically significant? If yes, at what probability level?

6. What percentage of participants under the new criteria had a NET composite percentile of 81 to 100?

Questions for Discussion

7. How helpful was the Conceptual Framework in helping you understand this study? (See lines 194–240.)

8. How important is the issue of protecting participants' rights? (See lines 248–254.)

9. Is the demographic information on gender and marital status in Table 1 important for understanding this study? Explain. (See Table 1.)

10. Do you think that the planned follow-up is important? Explain. (See lines 358–368 and 393–396.)

11. Do you agree with the second limitation discussed by the researcher? (See lines 376–382.)

12. In the Contents of this book, this article is classified as an example of Test Reliability and Validity Research. In your opinion, would it also be appropriate to classify it as an example of Program Evaluation/Process Evaluation? Explain.

Quality Ratings

Directions: Indicate your level of agreement with each of the following statements by circling a number from 5 for strongly agree (SA) to 1 for strongly disagree (SD). If you believe an item is not applicable to this research article, leave it blank. Be prepared to explain your ratings. When responding to criteria A and B below, keep in mind that brief titles and abstracts are conventional in published research.

A. The title of the article is appropriate.

   SA   5   4   3   2   1   SD

B. The abstract provides an effective overview of the research article.

   SA   5   4   3   2   1   SD

C. The introduction establishes the importance of the study.

   SA   5   4   3   2   1   SD

D. The literature review establishes the context for the study.

   SA   5   4   3   2   1   SD

E. The research purpose, question, or hypothesis is clearly stated.

   SA   5   4   3   2   1   SD

F. The method of sampling is sound.

   SA   5   4   3   2   1   SD

G. Relevant demographics (for example, age, gender, and ethnicity) are described.

SA   5   4   3   2   1   SD

H. Measurement procedures are adequate.

SA   5   4   3   2   1   SD

I. All procedures have been described in sufficient detail to permit a replication of the study.

SA   5   4   3   2   1   SD

J. The participants have been adequately protected from potential harm.

SA   5   4   3   2   1   SD

K. The results are clearly described.

SA   5   4   3   2   1   SD

L. The discussion/conclusion is appropriate.

SA   5   4   3   2   1   SD

M. Despite any flaws, the report is worthy of publication.

SA   5   4   3   2   1   SD

Article 42

Effects of Distraction on Children's Pain and Distress During Medical Procedures: A Meta-Analysis

Charmaine Kleiber, RN, MS, PhD(c), and **Dennis C. Harper**, PhD, ABPP[*]

ABSTRACT

Background: It is difficult to determine the usefulness of distraction to decrease children's distress behavior and pain during medical procedures because many studies use very small samples and report inconsistent findings.

Objectives: To investigate the mean effect sizes across studies for the effects of distraction on young children's distress behavior and self-reported pain during medical procedures.

Method: Hunter and Schmidt's (1990) procedures were used to analyze 16 studies (total $n = 491$) on children's distress behavior and 10 studies (total $n = 535$) on children's pain.

Results: For distress behavior, the mean effect size was 0.33 (±0.17), with 74% of the variance accounted for by sampling and measurement error. For pain, the mean effect size was 0.62 (±0.42) with 35% of the variance accounted for. Analysis of studies on pain that limited the sample to children 7 years of age or younger (total $n = 286$) increased the amount of explained variance to 60%.

Conclusions: Distraction had a positive effect on children's distress behavior across the populations represented in this study. The effect of distraction on children's self-reported pain is influenced by moderator variables. Controlling for age and type of painful procedure significantly increased the amount of explained variance, but there are other unidentified moderators at work.

From *Nursing Research*, 48(1), 44–49. Copyright © 1999 by Lippincott Williams & Wilkins, Inc. Reprinted with permission.

Children consistently name invasive medical procedures as the cause of the most painful experiences (Hester, 1993). Younger children are particularly in need of intervention because they report more pain (Lander & Fowler-Kerry, 1991; Vessey, Carlson, & McGill, 1994) and display more behavioral distress during medical procedures (Dahlquist, Power, Cox, & Fernbach, 1994; Humphrey, Boon, van Linden, van den Heuvell, & van de Wiel, 1992; Jay, Ozolins, Elli-

ott, & Caldwell, 1983; Katz, Kellerman, & Siegel, 1980). One of the most frequently used nonpharmacological interventions for acute pain management is distracting the child's attention away from the medical procedure (McCarthy, Cool, Petersen, & Bruene, 1996). However, the results of research on the effects of distraction are mixed. In a review of the literature completed by these authors, 33% of the studies on distraction and distress behavior reported statistically insignificant results, and 75% of the studies on distraction and pain reported insignificant results. It is unknown whether the statistical insignificance was due to small sample sizes, small effect sizes, or the variability in the effectiveness of distraction. This study investigates the effect of distraction on children's distress behavior and self-reported pain across study populations, using meta-analysis methodology to control for sample size.

Relevant Literature

Distraction is a class of cognitive coping strategies that divert attention from a noxious stimulus through passively redirecting the subject's attention or by actively involving the subject in the performance of a distractor task (Fernandez, 1986). Thus, distraction involves the *cognition*, expectancies, or appraisals of an individual, and results in a modification of the individual's behavior. According to McCaul and Malott (1984), distraction affects pain perception because: (a) pain perception is partially a cognitively controlled process; and (b) distraction consumes part of an individual's finite attentional capabilities, leaving less attention or focus available to perceive pain.

McGrath (1991) suggests that distraction affects the perception of pain because it directly interferes with neuronal activity associated with pain. The *gate control* theory of pain (Melzack & Wall, 1965; Wall, 1978) suggests that pain is modulated by a gating mechanism that opens and closes nerve impulses to the brain. The gating mechanism is influenced by cognitive processes, such as attention to the noxious stimuli. The relation-

[*]*Charmaine Kleiber* is a doctoral student, College of Nursing, University of Iowa, and an advanced practice nurse, University of Iowa Hospitals and Clinics, Iowa City, Iowa. *Dennis C. Harper* is a professor at the Department of Pediatrics, College of Medicine, University of Iowa, Iowa City, Iowa.

ship between cognitive processes and the perception of
50 pain has been questioned by others, however. Willis
and Coggeshall (1991) suggest that there may be dual
neuronal pathways for the sensation of pain and the
reaction to pain, and cite studies reporting that patients
who have had frontal lobotomy feel pain but are not
55 "concerned" by it, and that patients who have had spinal transection do not feel pain but continue to have a
vigorous flexor response to painful stimuli. In a descriptive study of pain after major surgery, Beyer,
McGrath, and Berde (1990) found discordance between
60 the intensity of children's perceived pain and behavioral reactions to pain. The relationships between pain
stimulation, pain-related behavior, and perceived pain
are probably more complex than previously thought.

Some researchers use distress behaviors (e.g., cry-
65 ing, moaning, fighting, and verbal resistance) as a
proxy for pain. However, behavior can be influenced
by many things other than pain (e.g., fear, anxiety, and
temperament). Therefore, the research on the use of
distraction with children during medical procedures
70 should be explored and judged for its separate effects
on pain and on behavioral distress, as put forth in this
analysis.

The purpose of this analysis is to quantitatively estimate the effect of distraction interventions on young
75 children's perceived pain and observed distress behavior during medical procedures. The research questions
are: (a) What are the average effect sizes for pain and
distress behavior among the studies included in the
analysis?; (b) What is the variability among the effect
80 sizes?; and (c) How much of the observed variance is
due to sampling and measurement error?

Method

Sample

Standard search procedures were used to locate
published and unpublished studies. Electronic databases searched were Cancerlit (1992–August 1996),
85 Healthstar (1994–September 1996), Medline (1966–
October 1996), and CINAHL (1982–August 1996),
using the key terms *pain*, *distraction*, *imagery*, and
attention, and was limited to the age group *infant to 12
years* and to the *English* language. A hand search of the
90 CINAHL database from 1970 to 1982 was conducted
using the key terms *pain* and *children*. Additional
sources included the Psychology Database at the University of Iowa libraries (containing journal articles
from 1967 to October 1996 and book chapters from
95 1967 to 1980 and 1987 to 1996); the Periodical Abstracts Database (indexing articles from 1,600 common
journals from 1986 to 1996); ERIC (an index of educa-
tion-related literature); and Wilson Database (WLS).
The search strategy for those databases included the
100 keywords *imagery* or *imagination*, *attention*, *distraction*, *pain*, and *child age* group. Unpublished studies
were discovered by searching the Dissertation Abstracts database for 1961 to 1996 using an intentionally

broad search strategy with the keywords *child* and *pain*
105 or *distraction* or *distress*. Although this strategy captured a large number of studies, very few of them dealt
with medical procedures. Reference lists accompanying research and review articles on children and pain
were scanned for any studies missed through the data-
110 base searches. The searches resulted in a large number
of citations for initial screening: 192 from Medline;
784 from Dissertation Abstracts; and 136 from the psychological databases.

Study Selection

The inclusion criteria were: (a) mean age of sub-
115 jects was under 12 years; (b) study designs were randomized clinical trials (RCT) or repeated measures
(RM) designs; (c) means and standard deviations (*SDs*)
for both control and experimental conditions were
available for the outcome variables *self-reported pain*
120 or *observed behavioral distress*; and (d) distraction was
the intervention. For the purposes of this analysis, distraction was defined as *any intervention intended to
focus the subject's attention away from pain or discomfort*.

125 Nineteen studies (see Table 1) met all of the inclusion criteria. Seventeen studies included published
means and *SDs*, and two authors (S. Arts, personal
communication, May 12, 1997; R. Blount, personal
communication, June 2, 1997) provided the unpub-
130 lished statistics. An additional eight authors, whose
published works were missing group means and *SDs*,
either did not have the information available or did not
respond to inquiries.

Hunter and Schmidt's (1990) method for meta-
135 analysis differs from some other methods in that the
individual results of studies are not weighted according
to the methodological strength of the research. This
method argues that all relevant studies should be retained to provide the largest possible database. Meth-
140 odological inadequacies should be considered if theoretically plausible moderator variables fail to account
for unexplained variance.

Study Descriptions

The studies used in the meta-analyses are summarized in Table 1. The mean age for subjects was 6.6
145 years, with a range of 3 to 15 years. The medical procedures varied in complexity and painfulness. The rationale for accepting studies with varying procedures
was that this was an effort to sample the universe of
painful experiences that children encounter. Therefore,
150 the intensity of the medical procedure experience was
not restricted through the choice of studies included in
the analysis.

The distraction interventions (independent variable)
varied in complexity, from simple things that could be
155 manipulated, such as a kaleidoscope, to a package of
distraction techniques that included concentrating on
breathing, imagery, and nonprocedural talk. The

302

Table 1
Effects of Distraction on Children's Self-reported Pain and Observed Distress Behavior

Author	Year	Design	Total N	Mean Age (years)	Age Range	Procedure	Control Condition	Experimental Treatment Condition	Pain Scale	Pain Effect Size	Distress Scale	Distress Effect Size
Arts, et al.	1994	RCT	80	9.7	4–12	Intravenous (IV) before surgery	Placebo cream at IV site	Music via earphones	FACES	+.04347	Global Distress Scale	+.06666
Blount, et al.	1992	RCT	60	5	3–7	Injection (well child)	Usual treatment	Distraction with party blower	FACES	+.12121	OSBD	–.20905
Broome, et al.	1992	RM	14	6.6	3–15	Bone marrow aspiration or lumbar puncture (BMA/LP)	Usual treatment	Imagery, breathing, rehearsal	FACES	–.90275	OSBD	–.214285
Gonzalez, et al.	1993	RCT	28	4.7	3–7	Injection (well child)	Usual treatment	Nonprocedural talk by parent	OUCHER	–.86890	OSBD	–.87363
Manne, et al.	1990	RCT	23	4.7	3–9	Venipuncture (oncology)	Usual treatment	Distraction with party blower	FACES	–1.50710	PBRS	–.72607
Smith, et al.	1996	RM	27	4.5	3–8	Venipuncture (hematology or oncology)	Usual treatment	Distraction using a toy	Child's Global Rating Scale	–.31679	OSBD	+.07117
Vessey, et al.	1994	RCT	100	7.4	3–12	Venipuncture (well child)	Usual treatment	Distraction with kaleidoscope	FACES	–.65404	CHEOPS	–.44490
Fowler-Kerry, et al.	1987	RCT	160	5.5	4–7	Injection (well child)	Usual treatment	Music via earphones	VAS	–.51333	NA	NA
McGrath, et al.	1986	RM	15	7.6	3–11	BMA/LP	Usual treatment	Imagery, breathing, nonprocedural talk, and concentrating	VAS	–1.35980	NA	NA
Smith, et al.	1989	RCT	28	10.75	6–18	BMA/LP	Sensory information	Nonprocedural talk by a professional	VAS	+.07710	NA	NA
Elliot, et al.	1983	RM	4	8.2	5–12	Burn treatment	Usual treatment	Distraction, relaxing images, reinforcement	NA	NA	Burn Treatment Distress Scale	–.81554
Foertsch[a]	1993	RM	13	5.8	3–12	Burn treatment	Usual treatment	Imagery	NA	NA	OSBD	–.21318
Jay, et al.	1985	RM	5	4.5	3–7	BMA/LP	Usual treatment	Imagery, reinforcement	NA	NA	OSBD	–1.07331
Olsen[a]	1991	Sequential	60	6.9	4–9	Venipuncture (general pediatrics)	Usual treatment	Story via headphones	NA	NA	Child Behavior Observation Code	–.72607
Powers, et al.	1993	RM	4	4	3–5	Venipuncture (hematology, oncology)	Usual treatment	Distraction and breathing	NA	NA	OSBD	–.660
Schur[a]	1986	RM	17		4–9	BMA/LP	Usual treatment	Music with headphones	NA	NA	OSBD	–.67270
Stark, et al.	1989	RM	4	5.4	4–7	Dentistry procedure	Usual treatment	Distraction with story and poster	NA	NA	Anxiety and Disruptive Behavior Code	–.3123
Winborn[a]	1987	RCT	20	6.9	4–9	Dental procedure	Usual treatment	Distraction with music	NA	NA	BRPS	–.25721
Zabin[a]	1982	RCT	32	7.8	6–11	Venipuncture or finger stick (general pediatrics)	Cartoon before procedure	Cartoon during procedure	NA	NA	Total Disruptive Behavior	+.18202

[a] Unpublished dissertation
NA = not applicable; RCT = randomized clinical trial, independent control and experimental groups; RM = repeated measures, one group measured at baseline and in experimental condition; OSBD = Observation Scale of Behavioral Distress; CHEOPS = Children's Hospital of Eastern Ontario Pain Scale; PBRS = Procedural Behavior Rating Scale; BRPS = Behavioral Rating Profile Scale

consistent intent of the distraction interventions was to
divert the child's attention away from the medical procedure.

The self-reported pain measures used in these studies are generally visual one-item scales. Most of the
behavioral distress scales used in these studies are adaptations of the Behavior Rating Profile Scale created
by Melamed (Melamed, Hawes, Heiby, & Glick,
1975). Behaviors such as crying, whining, grimacing,
and thrashing were coded as either present or absent at
varying intervals throughout the procedure and a final
total score was given for behavioral distress.

Meta-Analysis Procedure

An effect size statistic (*d*) for each study was computed directly from means and *SD*s. Cohen's (1977)
formula for *d* ([mean of experimental condition − mean
of control condition]/pooled group *SD*) was used for
RCT design studies. For RM studies, the denominator
of the equation was the control condition *SD* (Hunter &
Schmidt, 1990, p. 352). Reported means and *SD*s were
always used for calculating *d* when available, which
was the case for 14 studies. One study reported results
in logged form; the numbers were anti-logged for use
in this analysis. Four studies reported results in graphic
form. The authors of this review independently transformed graphed data into numeric data. One hundred
percent agreement was reached on the transformed
numbers. Means and *SD*s were then calculated for each
study.

Hunter and Schmidt's (1990) meta-analytic technique was used to calculate the mean effect size
weighted by sample size

$$\left(\bar{d} = \frac{\Sigma[(ni)(di)]}{\Sigma\, ni} \right);$$

the observed variance of the *d* values

$$\left(S^2_d = \frac{\Sigma[ni(di - \bar{d})^2]}{\Sigma\, ni} \right);$$

and sampling error.

$$\left(S^2_{ed} = \left\{ \frac{n-1}{n-3} \right\} \frac{4[1 + \frac{\bar{d}^2}{8}]}{n} \right.$$

For studies with RM dependent group designs, a different formula

$$\left(S^2_{ed} = \frac{2(1-r)}{n} + \frac{\bar{d}^2}{2n} \right)$$

was used to calculate sampling error because it is affected by the correlation between pretest and posttest
scores (Becker, 1988). When the size of the correlation
between the scores is unknown, the relationship can be
estimated from data given in the studies (Dunlap,
Cortina, Vaslow, & Burke, 1996). Seventeen sets of
baseline and control condition scores for 17 children
reported in the studies by Elliott and Olson (1983); Jay,

Elliott, Ozolins, Olson, and Pruitt (1985); Powers,
Blount, Bachanas, Cotter, and Swan (1993); and Stark
et al. (1989) were used to calculate a correlation coefficient (*r* = .55).

Correction for measurement error was accomplished through procedures described by Hunter and
Schmidt (1990, pp. 313–316). Because none of the
studies in this analysis reported reliability for self-
reported pain, previous studies of parallel forms reliability for self-report of pain in children 3–7 years old
were used to estimate measurement error. Beyer,
McGrath, and Berde (1990) reported correlations ranging from .87 to .98 between the Oucher Scale and a
chromatic visual analogue scale. Keck, Gerkensmeyer,
Joyce, and Schade (1996) reported a correlation of .63
for children's ratings on the FACES and a word
graphic visual analogue scale. Reliabilities for behavioral scales are usually determined with interrater
agreement percentages, using number of agreements
divided by total number of observations, or Cohen's
kappa statistic. Jay, Elliott, Katz, and Siegel (1987)
reported an interrater reliability of .98 for the Observed
Scale of Behavioral Distress (OSBD). Manne et al.
(1990) reported a mean kappa coefficient of .86 for the
items in the Procedure Behavior Rating Scale (PBRS).

Results

The results are reported in Table 2. The effect sizes
for both pain and behavioral distress had negative
signs, meaning that distraction decreased self-reported
pain and observed distress behavior. Because readers
are used to thinking of beneficial effects as positive,
the absolute values of the effect sizes are used in this
report.

Pain

The average effect size (absolute value) for the 535
children who reported on perceived pain was 0.62
(±0.42), indicating that the mean pain score for children who received distraction was more than half of
one standard deviation below the mean pain score for
the control group. The large *SD* of $\bar{d}$ and the wide
credibility interval indicate that there is some variability in children's responses to the distraction intervention. The percent of variance accounted for by sampling error alone is calculated as 30.58%. Measurement
error accounted for another 4.3% of the variance.

As stated previously, younger children tend to report more pain with medical procedures. Therefore, a
subanalysis was conducted on the three studies with
subjects exclusively between the ages of 3 and 7 years
(Blount et al., 1992; Fowler-Kerry & Lander, 1987;
Gonzales, Routh, & Armstrong, 1993). Because all of
the subjects had injections as part of well-child care,
this subanalysis also controlled for the type of medical
procedure. For the 268 children in these three randomized clinical trials, the average effect size was .47
(±0.26). Sampling and measurement error accounted

Table 2
Meta-Analysis Results of the Effects of Distraction on Pain and Observed Distress

	Self-report of Pain, All Subjects	Self-report of Pain, Subjects ≤7 Years Old	Observed Behavioral Distress, All Subjects
Total no. of studies (subjects)	10 (535)	3 (268)	16 (491)
No. of subjects in RCT designs; RM designs	479; 56	268; 0	403; 88
Absolute value of mean effect size $\pm$ *SD*	.62 $\pm$ .42	.47 $\pm$ .26	.33 $\pm$ .17
Observed variance of the effect size	.18818	.09212	.09613
Sampling error variance	.05751	.05026	.07060
Measurement error variance	.00813	.0046	.00038
Variance accounted for by sampling error and measurement error	35%	60%	74%
90% credibility intervals	−.07 to +1.31	−.01 to +.91	+.05 to +.61

for 60% of the variance in the effect size. Thus, it appears that moderator variables other than age and procedure type influence the effectiveness of distraction.

Distress

The analysis for behavioral distress shows an average effect size (absolute value) of 0.33 (±0.17) for the 491 children in the sample studies. The credibility interval for $\bar{d}$ does not include zero, indicating that distraction has a positive effect on children's distress behavior. Sampling error and measurement error accounted for 73.44% and .4% of the observed variance, respectively. Hunter and Schmidt (1990) suggest that when approximately 75% of the observed variance is accounted for, the remaining variance is likely to be caused by a combination of other statistical artifacts, namely reliability of the independent variables, study differences in range restriction, and instrument validity.

Discussion

This meta-analysis found a moderate effect size for the influence of distraction on observed distress behavior in children. Sampling and measurement error accounted for almost 74% of the observed variance among the studies, indicating that the positive effect of distraction on distress behavior is seen across the populations sampled by the studies.

For the effect of distraction on self-reported pain, the 90% credibility interval was wide and encompassed zero. Credibility intervals are calculated with the corrected standard deviation of the mean effect size and are used in meta-analyses to determine whether or not moderator variables are operating (Whitener, 1990). When the interval includes zero, variability in the effect size might be due to remaining statistical artifacts or to moderator variables. Because only about 35% of the observed variance was accounted for by sampling error and measurement error, a subanalysis that controlled for age and type of medical procedure was completed. Although substantially more of the observed variance was accounted for in this subanalysis,

there is still some variability left to explain. Possible moderator variables that come to mind are inconsistencies in the distraction interventions and variations in the characteristics of the children.

Research has shown that the child's innate temperament influences distress behavior during painful procedures (Corbo-Richert, 1994; Lee & White-Traut, 1996; Schechter, Bernstein, Beck, Hart, & Scherzer, 1991; Young & Fu, 1988). However, the relationships between child temperament and perceived pain have not been explored. The child's history of bad experiences with procedures is another possible moderator. In a study of preparation methods for medical procedures, Dahlquist et al. (1986) found a significant main effect for quality of previous medical experience on the behavioral distress of children during throat culture. The amount of past exposure to medical procedures was not related to behavioral distress. Thus, it appears that it is the *quality* of the child's experiences and not the quantity that matters. Systematic inquiry is needed to explore the influences of temperament and prior experience on children's responses during medical procedures, and to search for additional moderator variables.

Using distraction with children during medical procedures will reduce the amount of observed distress behavior for most children. The magnitude of the benefit will vary from child to child. Distraction is a low-cost intervention that has no risk to the patient and has a measurable benefit.

References

References marked with an asterisk (*) indicate studies included in the meta-analysis.

*Arts, S. E., Abu-Saad, H. H., Champion, G. D., Crawford, M. R., Fisher, R. J., Juniper, K. H., & Ziegler, J. B. (1994). Age-related response to lidocaine-prilocaine (EMLA) emulsion and effect of music distraction on the pain of intravenous cannulation. *Pediatrics, 93*(5), 797–801.

Becker, B. J. (1988). Synthesizing standardized mean-change measures. *British Journal of Mathematical and Statistical Psychology, 41*, 257–278.

Beyer, J. E., McGrath, P. J., & Berde, C. B. (1990). Discordance between self-report and behavioral pain measures in children aged 3–7 years after surgery. *Journal of Pain and Symptom Management, 5*, 350–356.

*Blount, R. L., Bachanas, P. J., Powers, S. W., Cotter, M. C., Franklin, A., Chaplin, W., Mayfield, J., Henderson, M., & Blount, S. D. (1992). Training children to cope and parents to coach them during routine immunizations:

Effects on child, parent, and staff behaviors. *Behavior Therapy, 23,* 689–705.

*Broome, M. E., Lillis, P. P., McGahee, T. W., & Bates, T. (1992). The use of distraction and imagery with children during painful procedures. *Oncology Nursing Forum, 19,* 499–502.

Cohen, J. (1977). *Statistical power analysis for the behavioral sciences* (revised ed.). New York: Academic Press.

Corbo-Richert, B. H. (1994). Coping behaviors of young children during a chest tube procedure in the pediatric intensive care unit. *Maternal-Child Nursing Journal, 22,* 134–146.

Dahlquist, L. M., Gil, K. M., Armstrong, F. D., DeLawyer, D. D., Greene, P., & Wuori, D. (1986). Preparing children for medical examinations: The importance of previous medical experience. *Health Psychology, 5,* 249–259.

Dahlquist, L. M., Power, T., Cox, C., & Fernbach, D. (1994). Parenting and child distress during cancer procedures: A multi-dimensional assessment. *Children's Health Care, 23,* 149–166.

Dunlap, W. P., Cortina, J. M., Vaslow, J. B., & Burke, M. J. (1996). Meta-analysis of experiments with matched groups or repeated measures designs. *Psychological Methods, 1,* 170–177.

*Elliott, C. H., & Olson, R. A. (1983). The management of children's distress in response to painful medical treatment for burn injuries. *Behaviour Research and Therapy, 21*(6), 675–683.

Fernandez, E. (1986). A classification system of cognitive coping strategies for pain. *Pain, 26,* 141–151.

*Foertsch, C. E. (1993). *Investigation of an imagery-based treatment for the control of children's behavioral distress during burn dressing changes.* Unpublished doctoral dissertation, University of Iowa.

*Fowler-Kerry, S., & Lander, J. R. (1987). Management of injection pain on children. *Pain, 30,* 169–175.

*Gonzalez, J. C., Routh, D. K., & Armstrong, F. D. (1993). Effects of maternal distraction versus reassurance on children's reactions to injections. *Journal of Pediatric Psychology, 18*(5), 593–604.

Hester, N. O. (1993). Pain in children. In J. Fitzpatrick & J. Stevenson (Eds.) *Annual review of nursing research: Vol. 11* (pp. 105–142). New York: Springer.

Humphrey, G. B., Boon, C. M., van Linden van den Heuvell, G. E, & van de Wiel, H. B. (1992). The occurrence of high levels of acute behavioral distress in children and adolescents undergoing routine venipunctures. *Pediatrics, 90,* 8–91.

Hunter, J. E., & Schmidt, F. L. (1990). *Methods of meta-analysis: Correcting error and bias in research findings.* Newbury Park, CA: Sage.

Jay, S. M., Elliott, C. H., Katz, E., & Siegel, S. E. (1987). Cognitive-behavioral and pharmacologic interventions for children's distress during painful medical procedures. *Journal of Consulting and Clinical Psychology, 55*(6), 860–865.

*Jay, S. M., Elliott, C. H., Ozolins, M., Olson, R. A., & Pruitt, S. D. (1985). Behavioral management of children's distress during painful medical procedures. *Behaviour Research and Therapy, 23,* 513–520.

Jay, S. M., Ozolins, M., Elliott, C. H., & Caldwell, S. (1983). Assessment of children's distress during painful medical procedures. *Health Psychology, 2,* 133–147.

Katz, E. R., Kellerman, J., & Siegel, S. (1980). Behavioral distress in children with cancer undergoing medical procedures: Developmental considerations. *Journal of Consulting and Clinical Psychology, 48,* 356–365.

Keck, J. F., Gerkensmeyer, J. E., Joyce, B. A., & Schade, J. G. (1996). Reliability and validity of the Faces and Word Descriptor Scales to measure procedural pain. *Journal of Pediatric Nursing, 11,* 368–374.

Lander, J., & Fowler-Kerry, S. (1991). Age differences in children's pain. *Perceptual and Motor Skills, 73,* 415–418.

Lee, L. W., & White-Traut, R. C. (1996). The role of temperament in pediatric pain response. *Issues in Comprehensive Pediatric Nursing, 19,* 49–63.

*Manne, S. L., Redd, W. H., Jacobsen, P. B., Gorfinkle, K., Schorr, O., & Rapkin, B. (1990). Behavioral intervention to reduce child and parent distress during venipuncture. *Journal of Consulting and Clinical Psychology, 58,* 565–572.

McCarthy, A. M., Cool, V. A., Petersen, M., & Bruene, D. A. (1996). Cognitive behavioral pain and anxiety interventions in pediatric oncology centers and bone marrow transplant units. *Journal of Pediatric Oncology Nursing, 13,* 3–12.

McCaul, K. D., & Malott, J. M. (1984). Distraction and coping with pain. *Psychological Bulletin, 95,* 516–533.

McGrath, P. A. (1991). Intervention and management. In J. P. Bush & S. W. Harkins (Eds.), *Children in pain.* New York: Springer-Verlag.

*McGrath, P. A., & deVeber, L. L. (1986). The management of acute pain evoked by medical procedures in children with cancer. *Journal of Pain and Symptom Management, 1*(3), 145–150.

Melamed, B., Hawes, R., Heiby, E., & Glick, J. (1975). The use of film modeling to reduce uncooperative behavior of children during dental treatment. *Journal of Dental Research, 54,* 797–801.

Melzack, R., & Wall, P. D. (1965). Pain mechanisms: A new theory. *Science, 150,* 971–979.

*Olsen, B. R. (1991). *Brief interventions for routine use with children in a phlebotomy laboratory.* Unpublished doctoral dissertation, West Virginia University.

*Powers, S. W., Blount, R. L., Bachanas, P. J., Cotter, M. W., & Swan, S. C. (1993). Helping preschool leukemia patients and their parents cope during injections. *Journal of Pediatric Psychology, 18*(6), 681–695.

Schechter, N. L., Bernstein, B. A., Beck A., Hart, L., & Scherzer, L. (1991). Individual differences in children's response to pain: Role of temperament and parental characteristics. *Pediatrics, 87,* 171–177.

*Schur, J. M. (1986). *Alleviating behavioral distress with music or Lamaze pant-blow breathing in children undergoing bone marrow aspirations and lumbar punctures.* Unpublished doctoral dissertation, University of Texas Southwestern Medical Center at Dallas.

*Smith, K. E., Ackerson, J. D., & Blotcky, A. D. (1989). Reducing distress during invasive medical procedures: Relating behavioral interventions to preferred coping style in pediatric cancer patients. *Journal of Pediatric Psychology, 14*(3), 405–419.

*Smith, J. T., Barabasz, A., & Barabasz, M. (1996). Comparison of hypnosis and distraction in severely ill children undergoing painful medical procedures. *Journal of Counseling Psychology, 43*(2), 187–195.

*Stark, L. J., Allen, K. D., Hurst, M., Nash, D. A., Rigney, B., & Stokes, T. F. (1989). Distraction: Its utilization and efficacy with children undergoing dental treatment. *Journal of Applied Behavior Analysis, 22*(3), 297–307.

*Vessey, J. A., Carlson, K. L., & McGill, J. (1994). Use of distraction with children during an acute pain experience. *Nursing Research, 43,* 369–372.

Wall, P. D. (1978). The gate control theory of pain mechanisms. A re-examination and re-statement. *Brain, 101,* 1–18.

Whitener, E. (1990). Confusion of confidence intervals and credibility intervals in meta-analysis. *Journal of Applied Psychology, 75,* 315–321.

Willis, W. E., & Coggeshall, R. E. (Eds.) (1991). *Sensory mechanisms of the spinal cord* (2nd ed.). New York: Plenum Press.

*Winborn, M. D. (1987). *Associative and dissociative preparatory strategies for children undergoing dental treatment.* Unpublished doctoral dissertation, Memphis State University.

Young, M. R., & Fu, V. R. (1988). Influence of play and temperament on the young child's response to pain. *Children's Health Care, 18,* 209–217.

*Zabin, M. A. (1982). *The modification of children's behavior during blood work procedures.* Unpublished doctoral dissertation, West Virginia University.

Acknowledgments: The authors thank Sue Gardner, RN, PhD(c), and Barbara Rakel, RN, PhD, for their assistance with this analysis. This research was supported by National Institute of Nursing Research, National Institutes of Health, Individual Predoctoral Fellowship # NR07170-02.

Address reprint requests to: Charmaine Kleiber, RN, MS, PhD, 1819 Flanigan Street, Iowa City, IA 52246; e-mail: charmaine-kleiber@uiowa.edu

Exercise for Article 42

Factual Questions

1. According to the researchers, are behaviors such as crying and moaning always good proxies for pain?

2. How did the researchers "discover" unpublished studies?

3. All studies selected for this meta-analysis had what as the "intervention"?

4. For the purposes of this study, how was "distraction" defined?

5. When distraction with a party blower was used in Manne et al.'s (1990) study, what was the Pain Effect Size?

6. When Zabin (1982) used the cartoon during the procedure, what was the Distress Effect Size?

7. What was the average effect size (absolute value) for the 535 children who reported on perceived pain?

Questions for Discussion

8. Do you believe that the search procedure described in lines 82–113 is described in sufficient detail?

9. In lines 114–133, the researchers describe their inclusion criteria (i.e., the criteria used to determine whether a study would be included in this meta-analysis). The criteria specifically did not include "methodological strength of the research." (See lines 134–142.) Do you believe that methodological strength should have been included? Explain.

10. Examination of Table 1 reveals a large number of different experimental treatment conditions. Do you believe that this is a strength or weakness of this meta-analysis? If you had been conducting this meta-analysis, would you have restricted it to studies that involved similar experimental treatment conditions? Explain.

11. Given the overall average effect size for perceived pain, do you think that this study makes a strong case for using distraction with children? (See lines 238–243.)

12. Overall, how well did this meta-analysis help you understand the effects of distraction on children's pain and distress during medical procedures?

Quality Ratings

Directions: Indicate your level of agreement with each of the following statements by circling a number from 5 for strongly agree (SA) to 1 for strongly disagree (SD). If you believe an item is not applicable to this research article, leave it blank. Be prepared to explain your ratings. When responding to criteria A and B below, keep in mind that brief titles and abstracts are conventional in published research.

A. The title of the article is appropriate.

SA   5   4   3   2   1   SD

B. The abstract provides an effective overview of the research article.

SA   5   4   3   2   1   SD

C. The introduction establishes the importance of the study.

SA   5   4   3   2   1   SD

D. The literature review establishes the context for the study.

SA   5   4   3   2   1   SD

E. The research purpose, question, or hypothesis is clearly stated.

SA   5   4   3   2   1   SD

F. The method of sampling is sound.

SA   5   4   3   2   1   SD

G. Relevant demographics (for example, age, gender, and ethnicity) are described.

SA   5   4   3   2   1   SD

H. Measurement procedures are adequate.

SA   5   4   3   2   1   SD

I. All procedures have been described in sufficient detail to permit a replication of the study.

SA   5   4   3   2   1   SD

J. The participants have been adequately protected from potential harm.

SA   5   4   3   2   1   SD

K. The results are clearly described.

SA   5   4   3   2   1   SD

L. The discussion/conclusion is appropriate.

SA   5   4   3   2   1   SD

M. Despite any flaws, the report is worthy of publication.

SA   5   4   3   2   1   SD

Notes:

Notes:

Notes:

Notes:

Notes:

Answer Key

A Cross Section of Nursing Research

Journal Articles for Discussion and Evaluation

FOURTH EDITION

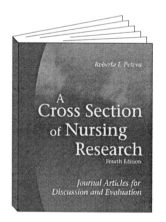

Pyrczak Publishing
P.O. Box 250430
Glendale, CA 91225

Visit us at **www.Pyrczak.com** to learn more about all our titles
and request *free* examination copies for your consideration.

Answers to Factual Questions

Article 1: Reasons Registered Nurses Leave or Change Employment Status

1. Yes. Hospitals with the lowest employee satisfaction had the lowest patient satisfaction, and hospitals with the highest employee satisfaction had the highest patient satisfaction. (See lines 32–36.) **2.** Job satisfaction, supervision, work environment, and personal factors. (See lines 59–62.) **3.** The first year. (See lines 156–157.) **4.** Hours worked. (See lines 233–236 and Table 2.) **5.** Nurses gave more than one reason. (See the footnote to Table 2.) **6.** The sample size in this study ($n = 84$) is relatively small in proportion to the magnitude of the nursing turnover problem. (See lines 304–307.)

Article 2: Post-Anesthesia Care Unit Nurses' Knowledge of Pulse Oximetry

1. No. (See lines 48–49.) **2.** 20. (See lines 69–72.) **3.** By having a panel of three critical care and PACU nurse educators review the questionnaire. (See lines 72–75.) **4.** 62 ± 9.09. (See lines 119–120.) **5.** The absorption of light by hemoglobin. (See lines 122–124.) **6.** $r = .25$. (See lines 187–188.)

Article 3: Ethical Issues Faced by Nursing Editors

1. 13. (See lines 123–125.) **2.** 90. (See lines 127–129 and 191–192.) **3.** 66%. (See lines 127–128.) **4.** 3. (See lines 164–181.) **5.** 42%. (See Table 1 and lines 248–250.)

Article 4: Physical Activity Barriers and Program Preferences Among Indigent Internal Medicine Patients with Arthritis

1. Non-English speaking, acutely ill, demented, or psychotic patients. (See lines 27–29.) **2.** 75%. (See Table 1.) **3.** Fewer than 10%. (See lines 64–65.) **4.** –0.24. (See lines 74–75.) **5.** Women. The probability is $p = 0.01$. (See lines 92–93.) **6.** An adequate sample size for evaluating age, gender, and ethnic differences. (See lines 158–160.)

Article 5: Ethics Content in Community Health Nursing Textbooks

1. The biomedical perspective. (See lines 70–73.) **2.** *Public health nursing* and *community health nursing*. (See lines 120–123 and Table 1.) **3.** The text index. (See lines 142–144.) **4.** No. (See lines 187–189.) **5.** Stanhope and Lancaster. (See lines 197–199. Note that the answer can also be derived by careful inspection of Table 2.) **6.** Six. (See lines 314–316.) **7.** A number of case studies with discussion questions. (See lines 419–422.)

Article 6: Buried Alive: The Presence of Nursing on Hospital Web Sites

1. 25%. (See lines 121–123.) **2.** Four. (See lines 137–139.) **3.** It was defined according to the site depth of nurse-related content and was based on the number of pages the user had to click through to get to that content. (See lines 165–168.) **4.** Pictures, graphics, or text that related to nurses, nursing care, or nursing practice. (See lines 222–224.) **5.** Providing information on nurse employment opportunities. (See lines 406–409.) **6.** Involvement of nurses on hospital committees charged with Web site development. (See lines 441–443.)

Article 7: Relationships of Assertiveness, Depression, and Social Support Among Older Nursing Home Residents

1. No. (See lines 57–58 and 174–182.) **2.** No, because the mean score was 9.0, while the highest possible score is 30. (See lines 67–71 and 83–85.) **3.** $r = -.33$. (See lines 85–86.) **4.** No. (See lines 88–91.) **5.** No. (See lines 88–89.) **6.** Inverse. (See lines 98–101.)

Article 8: Extending Work Environment Research into Home Health Settings

1. A score on the Organizational Support for Nursing subscale of the Nursing Work Index–Revised. (See lines 133–137.) **2.** 38. (See lines 169–171.) **3.** Two weeks after the initial survey mailing. (See lines 201–202.) **4.** .31; it is significant. (See Table 2.) **5.** Care quality with a correlation coefficient of .49. (See Table 2.) **6.** No. (See lines 297–299 and Table 2.)

Article 9: Parent Behavior and Child Distress During Urethral Catheterization

1. Because these children typically do not have life-threatening conditions, yet they must undergo procedures that are frightening, uncomfortable, and take more than a minute or two to complete. (See lines 37–42.) **2.** Because it has been shown that young children are most likely to display distress behavior during medical procedures. (See lines 227–230.) **3.** The faces of the child and parent. (See lines 292–294.) **4.** 100%. (See lines 322–323.) **5.** Eight. (See lines 368–371.) **6.** No. (See lines 416–418.) **7.** Possible differences between male and female catheterizations. This study included two boys and eight girls. (See lines 493–496.)

Article 10: Survey Return Rates As a Function of Priority versus First Class Mailing

1. 40. (See lines 43–47.) **2.** Yes, $50. (See lines 89–91.) **3.** A replacement addressee was chosen, and a new packet was mailed. (See lines 117–122.) **4.** 35.4%. (See lines 142–143 and the bottom row in Table 1.) **5.** 35. (See Table 1.) **6.** .52. (See lines 147–148 and Table 1.)

Article 11: Life Review Therapy As an Intervention to Manage Depression and Enhance Life Satisfaction in Individuals with Right Hemisphere Cerebral Vascular Accidents

1. To determine if life review therapy could produce lower levels of depression and higher levels of life satisfaction among individuals with CVA. (See lines 34–37.) **2.** Using a table of computer-generated random numbers, the researcher randomly assigned subjects. (See lines 171–173.) **3.** Their physician or designated staff members at the rehabilitation center where the study was conducted. (See lines 177–179.) **4.** One hour. (See lines 230–233.) **5.** Yes. (See lines 257–265.) **6.** 14. (See lines 373–374.) **7.** Yes. (See lines 340–355.)

Article 12: Preop Fluid Bolus Reduces Risk of Postop Nausea and Vomiting: A Pilot Study

1. 71%. (See lines 14–18.) **2.** Broad generalizations. (See lines 43–53, especially lines 52–53.) **3.** One-liter fluid bolus preoperatively. (See lines 83–86.) **4.** 90. (See lines 91–92.) **5.** They were equal in age but significantly different in weight. (See lines 134–139.) **6.** Yes, there was a significant difference at the probability level: $p = .001$. (See lines 142–144.) **7.** Nausea and vomiting in each group. (See lines 193–195.)

Article 13: An Intervention Study to Enhance Medication Compliance in Community-Dwelling Elderly Individuals

1. Stimulant strategies. (See lines 94–95.) **2.** A large urban home health care agency and a large urban ambulatory care clinic of a major teaching hospital. (See lines 213–215.) **3.** Four. (See lines

255–258.) **4.** The cost of the caps. (See lines 296–297.) **5.** The telephone group, with a mean of 11.5. (See Table 1.) **6.** Yes. (See lines 389–391 and the footnote to Table 2.) **7.** The absence of a significant difference between the two intervention groups. (See lines 472–474.)

Article 14: The Impact of an HIV/AIDS Training Course for Baccalaureate Nursing Students

1. 20. (See lines 47–48.) **2.** Etiology, transmission, prevalence, and symptomatology. (See lines 63–65.) **3.** .96. (See lines 74–75.) **4.** Returning a noncompleted form in the envelope provided. (See lines 84–88.) **5.** No. (See lines 94–97. Note that the chi-square test yielded a probability of $p > .05$.) **6.** 21.83. (See lines 115–116.) **7.** 65.68. (See lines 123–125.)

Article 15: Effects of Two Educational Methods on the Knowledge, Attitude, and Practice of Women High School Teachers in Prevention of Cervical Cancer

1. 24. (See lines 157–160.) **2.** By a lecture and flash cards. (See footnotes to all tables.) **3.** 10.49 on the pretest and 18.76 on the posttest. (See Table 2.) **4.** Yes. It went up from 49.84 to 58.21 on the posttest. (See Table 3.) **5.** The control group. (See Table 4, which shows that 53.5% of the control group said "no.") **6.** Yes, at the $p = .0001$ level. (See lines 199–201.)

Article 16: Physical Restraint Reduction in the Acute Rehabilitation Setting: A Quality Improvement Study

1. 18. (See lines 51–54.) **2.** Any witnessed or unwitnessed event in which the patient was found on the ground secondary to an unplanned event. (See lines 146–149.) **3.** One year, from March 2003 through February 2004. (See lines 159–162.) **4.** 29.2%. (See lines 174–177.) **5.** 64.2%. (See lines 184–186.)

Article 17: An Intervention to Enhance Nursing Staff Teamwork and Engagement

1. 15. (See lines 82–84.) **2.** Yes, at the $p < .001$ or $p = .00$ level. (See lines 287–291 where $p < .001$ and Figure 2, where $p = .00$.) **3.** Yes, at the $p < .033$ level. (See lines 315–318 and Figure 5.) **4.** Measurement of patient satisfaction. (See lines 321–322.) **5.** Yes. (See lines 328–329.)

Article 18: Vaccine Risk/Benefit Communication: Effect of an Educational Package for Public Health Nurses

1. 3. (See lines 241–243.) **2.** Fewer than 5%. (See lines 270–271.) **3.** 50%. (See Table 1.) **4.** Yes, at the $p < .0001$ level. (See Table 2.) **5.** 74%. (See lines 440–441.) **6.** By trained research assistants (RAs) using silent stopwatches. (See lines 648–651.)

Article 19: The Pain Management Knowledge of Nurses Practicing in a Rural Midwest Retirement Community

1. Convenience sample. (See lines 61–63.) **2.** Four weeks after a pain education intervention. (See lines 72–74.) **3.** Yes, at the $p < .0001$ level. (See lines 103–105.) **4.** Five. (See lines 129–130, 156–157, and Table 1.) **5.** 89.1%. (See the fourth item in Table 3.)

Article 20: A Comparison Pilot Study of Public Health Field Nursing Home Visitation Program Interventions for Pregnant Hispanic Adolescents

1. Choice A: Adolescent mothers. (See lines 106–108.) **2.** Previous performance accomplishments, modeling, verbal persuasion, and emotional arousal. (See lines 208–211.) **3.** 121 in the control group and 104 in the intervention group. (See lines 289–290.) **4.** The intervention group. (See lines 345–

348 and Table 2.) **5.** 49. (See lines 327–328.) **6.** First-time pregnant adolescents in Orange County, California. (See lines 435–437.)

Article 21: Psychoeducation Program for Chinese Family Caregivers of Members with Schizophrenia

1. A strategy of teaching patients and families about disorders, treatments, coping techniques, and resources. (See lines 105–108.) **2.** Gender and age. (See lines 218–219.) **3.** .90 to .93. (See lines 330–332.) **4.** To rule out interfering factors that would affect the result of the study. (See lines 345–347.) **5.** Yes, they were 25.53 and 25.56. (See Table 3.) **6.** Yes, at the $p < .01$ level and/or the $p = .000$ level. (See lines 357–360 and Table 3.)

Article 22: Culturally Tailored Diabetes Education Program for Chinese Americans: A Pilot Study

1. Newspaper advertisements. (See lines 83–86.) **2.** Three. (See lines 113–129.) **3.** Because of budget limitations. (See lines 149–151.) **4.** 17.5%. (See line 299.) **5.** 68.8. (See the last row in Table 2.) **6.** 57.5%. (See lines 315–319.) **7.** Yes. (See lines 471–472.)

Article 23: HIV Medication Adherence Programs: The Importance of Social Support

1. Why program outcomes were (or were not) realized. (See lines 48–51.) **2.** No. (See lines 61–63.) **3.** To assess client and staff satisfaction. (See lines 128–132.) **4.** To assist the moderator with follow-up questions and to take notes for the transcription of the focus group tape. (See lines 169–172.) **5.** 20%. (See lines 211–213.) **6.** Yes. (See lines 427–429.)

Article 24: Barriers in Providing Psychosocial Support for Patients with Cancer

1. 640. (See lines 147–149.) **2.** Seven. (See lines 154–155.) **3.** Yes. (See lines 168–170.) **4.** Yes. (See lines 195–196.) **5.** A presentation of the study findings was given to participants, further validating the findings. (See lines 217–218.) **6.** In-depth clarification and exploration. (See lines 640–642.)

Article 25: What Adolescents with Type I Diabetes and Their Parents Want from Testing Technology

1. 59. (See lines 103–104.) **2.** $40. (See lines 111–112.) **3.** Yes. (See lines 133–134.) **4.** A nurse practitioner. (See lines 142–145.) **5.** 3. (See Table 1.) **6.** 15. (See Table 1.)

Article 26: One Breath at a Time: Living with Cystic Fibrosis

1. "What is the lived experience of caring for a family member with cystic fibrosis?" (See lines 20–23.) **2.** No. (See lines 145–147 and 159–161.) **3.** Three. (See lines 179–182.) **4.** Six. (See lines 191–195.) **5.** By phone. (See lines 229–231.) **6.** That it was representative and true to their life experiences. (See lines 270–272.)

Article 27: Nurses As Imperfect Role Models for Health Promotion

1. 11. (See lines 155–156.) **2.** No. (See lines 171–176.) **3.** Yes. (See lines 176–180.) **4.** 6. (See Table 1.) **5.** Storing tapes in a secure place accessible only to the lead researcher, having only one of the researchers transcribe the tapes, and using pseudonyms for all transcriptions. (See lines 203–206.) **6.** Yes. (See lines 229–232.)

Article 28: The Contribution of Research Knowledge and Skills to Practice: An Exploration of the Views and Experiences of Newly Qualified Nurses

1. No. (See lines 175–177.) **2.** 15. (See lines 178–179.) **3.** Face-to-face interviews. (See lines 182–185 and 209.) **4.** Data collection and analysis were not separate stages of the research, but were closely interwoven throughout. Insights from analysis of the data gathered earlier in the process shaped the topics and questions covered during later data collection. (See lines 240–245.) **5.** Yes. (See lines 257–261.) **6.** About half; 50%. (See lines 332–333.)

Article 29: John and Mary Q. Public's Perceptions of a Good Death and Assisted Suicide

1. 42 years. (See lines 33–35.) **2.** To prevent possible bias during the discussions with the participants and during data collection. (See lines 48–51.) **3.** A week. (See lines 64–66.) **4.** Validation of the description by participants. (See lines 73–84.) **5.** Four. (See lines 106–109. Also, the four themes are listed in italics under the heading "What Constitutes a Good Death?") **6.** Remaining in control through the dying process is essential. (See Theme 3 under the heading "Would You Ever Consider Assisted Suicide? and see lines 293–294.") **7.** Five. (See lines 326–330.)

Article 30: Hospital-Based Psychiatric Experience Before Community-Based Practice for Nurses: Imperative or Dispensable?

1. The degree to which institutionally based experience prepares nurses for community practice. (See lines 47–51.) **2.** Because of the absence of existing literature and research findings to guide the process. (See lines 100–102.) **3.** Open-ended. (See lines 121–123.) **4.** Through prolonged engagement, peer debriefing, and member checking. (See lines 134–136.) **5.** To safeguard against misinterpretation. (See lines 148–150.) **6.** An experienced qualitative researcher. (See lines 154–155.) **7.** No. (See lines 310–311.)

Article 31: Student Nurses' Perceptions of Alternative and Allopathic Medicine

1. Complementary and alternative medicine. (See lines 80–86 and lines 96–97.) **2.** 96.3%. (See line 130.) **3.** The college Research Ethics Committee. (See lines 137–139.) **4.** Various nursing instructors. (See lines 146–148.) **5.** Two. (See lines 154–155.) **6.** The trustworthiness of the themes. (See lines 170–171.)

Article 32: Clinical Reasoning in Experienced Nurses

1. Eight. (See lines 60–62.) **2.** A registered nurse with a minimum of 2 years but less than 10 years of full-time work experience on a medical–surgical unit. (See lines 101–104.) **3.** No. (See lines 240–245.) **4.** By using codes rather than names in the transcriptions of audiotapes. (See lines 256–258.) **5.** No. (See lines 274–278.) **6.** No. (See lines 662–664.)

Article 33: The Use of Music to Promote Sleep in Older Women

1. Music that has been integrated into the person's life and is based on personal preferences. (See lines 48–50.) **2.** Eight: three family practice physicians and five family nurse practitioners. (See lines 55–57.) **3.** 80.5 years. (See lines 112–114.) **4.** *t* tests for correlated samples. *Note*: This is also known in the statistical literature as *t* tests for dependent data. (See lines 175–177.) **5.** Yes, at the *p* < .01 level. (See lines 182–186.) **6.** The number of older women who were disqualified from participating in this study due to the habitual use of sedative-hypnotics and/or alcohol. (See lines 311–314.)

Article 34: Factors Which Influence Latino Community Members to Self-Prescribe Antibiotics

1. By posting flyers in local stores, churches, day care centers, and community organizations. (See lines 146–148.) **2.** Because selling antibiotics over the counter is illegal. (See lines 177–181.) **3.** Before. (See lines 184–197.) **4.** Predisposing, enabling, and reinforcing factors associated with antibiotic use. (See lines 203–205.) **5.** Readability, time required to complete, and clarity. (See lines 251–254.) **6.** Yes; all reported doing so. (See lines 387–390 and 484–488.)

Article 35: Computer-Mediated Support Group Use Among Parents of Children with Cancer: An Exploratory Study

1. Parent users. (See lines 88–91.) **2.** 38.1 or 38. (See lines 122–123, where it is reported as 38, and Table 1, where it is reported as 38.1.) **3.** It was assigned a number, and all identifying information was deleted. (See lines 156–159.) **4.** 6.9%. (See Table 2.) **5.** 8. (See Table 3 and lines 313–315.) **6.** Posts that are not of interest, off topic, or are vapid. (See lines 285–286.) **7.** 12.2%. (See lines 421–422.)

Article 36: Spiritual Perspectives of Nurses in the United States Relevant for Education and Practice

1. The wholeness of individuals and their connectedness to a higher being; it is the integrating factor in the quest for meaning and purpose in life. (See lines 118–122.) **2.** Do you have any views about the importance or meaning of spirituality in your life that have not been addressed by the previous questions? (See lines 315–318, 359–362, 375–379, and 441–444.) **3.** A national random sample of 1,000 members of the Sigma Theta Tau International (STTI) Nursing Honor Society. (See lines 319–321.) **4.** An individual's spiritual perspective. (See lines 349–351.) **5.** Yes, at the $p = .042$ level. (See lines 408–411.) **6.** Mean equals 4.9164; standard deviation equals .9911. (See lines 434–436.)

Article 37: The Interconnection of Childhood Poverty and Homelessness: Negative Impact/Points of Access

1. The female caretaker in each family (the mother or custodial grandmother) and one of the children between 8 and 12 years of age. (See lines 107–109.) **2.** Yes. (See lines 113–117.) **3.** 60.2%. (See Table 2.) **4.** Faculty knowledgeable about child development and/or the conditions for poor families. (See lines 147–150.) **5.** Anxiety. (See lines 222–225.) **6.** Yes. (See lines 261–263.) **7.** 64%. (See lines 295–297 and Table 4.) **8.** 23%. (See lines 495–500.)

Article 38: Developing a Residential Care Facility Version of the Observable Indicators of Nursing Home Care Quality Instrument

1. The highest quality. (See lines 62–66.) **2.** All four. (See lines 177–179.) **3.** 5. (See Table 1 and lines 181–184.) **4.** Does the instrument yield similar results when used again at same sites after a specified time interval? (See lines 342–347.) **5.** Staff. (See Table 3.) **6.** Five. (See lines 422–425.)

Article 39: Preverbal, Early Verbal Pediatric Pain Scale (PEPPS): Development and Early Psychometric Testing

1. 3. (See lines 48–50.) **2.** Their reliability and validity as representative of pain. (See lines 105–109.) **3.** Five. (See lines 176–185.) **4.** Ten. (See lines 281–282.) **5.** The value of .8768 for the relationship between Cry and Consolability. (See Table 5.) **6.** 15%. (See lines 358–359.) **7.** Yes. (See lines 373–376 and 448–454.)

Article 40: Revised Susceptibility, Benefits, and Barriers Scale for Mammography Screening

1. Health Belief Model. (See lines 19–21.) **2.** Through a panel of eight judges who were familiar with the HBM. Items were retained if there was a 75% agreement among judges. (See lines 106–109.) **3.** Because the intervention may have changed actual beliefs. (See lines 240–242.) **4.** That after loading on a primary scale, the same item did not load at above .3 on any other scale. (See lines 276–278.) **5.** $r = .61$. (See lines 324–328.) **6.** The action group. It had a mean of 20.55. (See Table 4.) **7.** The precontemplation group. It had a mean of 17.98. (See Table 4.)

Article 41: Nurse Entrance Test Scores: A Predictor of Success

1. Inferential reading, main idea of passage, and predicting of outcomes. (See lines 73–75 and 199–202.) **2.** 55. (See lines 244–247.) **3.** 70.7. (See the last row in Table 1.) **4.** 89.1. (See the last row in Table 1.) **5.** Yes, at the .05 level, with $p < .011$, which is lower than .05 but higher than .01. (See lines 295–301.) **6.** 61.8%. (See Table 1.)

Article 42: Effects of Distraction on Children's Pain and Distress During Medical Procedures: A Meta-Analysis

1. No. (See lines 64–72.) **2.** By searching the Dissertation Abstracts database for 1961 through 1996 using an intentionally broad search strategy with the keywords *child* and *pain* or *distraction* or *distress*. (See lines 101–105.) **3.** Distraction. (See lines 114–121.) **4.** Any intervention intended to focus the subject's attention away from pain or discomfort. (See lines 121–124.) **5.** –1.50710. (See Table 1.) **6.** +.18202. (See Table 1.) **7.** 0.62. (See lines 238–239.)